West Front of United States Capitol 1826

The Congressional Club

Cook Book

The Congressional Club

2001 New Hampshire Avenue, N.W., Washington, D. C. 20009

The Congressional Club
Cook Book

A Collection of
National and International Recipes

Ninth Edition
in Honor of the Bicentennial

Compiled and Published by

The Congressional Club

Washington, D. C.

1976

Foreword

Through representing the favorite recipes from states within our country as well as nations around the world, *The Congressional Club Cook Book* offers the opportunity to experience the specialties of an impressive scope of experts.

This Bicentennial Edition is a particularly meaningful volume, for it reflects the culture and heritage at this unique time in history.

May this collection be the source of special pleasure to you and all who have the good fortune of enjoying the culinary arts of those who have shared their knowledge.

Betty Ford

The White House
March 1976

Acknowledgments

For encouragement and help in preparing this Bicentennial Edition, the committee is grateful to Dr. Leonard Beck, curator of special collections in the Rare Book Division, Library of Congress; the Capitol Historical Society; the Kiplinger Washington Collection for the inside cover pictures of the United States Capitol and to Mr. Reeves Tilley, United States Bureau of Standards, for the Metric Guide.

The Congressional Club wishes to express its sincere thanks and appreciation for the support of all the companies whose advertisements appear in the advertising section.

Recipes from the earliest American cook books may be found at the beginning of each food section.

Preface

MRS. RICHARDSON PREYER, NORTH CAROLINA
President

We are delighted that you have a copy of the ninth edition of our cook book published in celebration of the two hundredth birthday of our country.

Thousands of volunteer hours by Congressional Club members have made possible this publication. Our entire membership thank Mrs. John R. Foley of Maryland and Mrs. Herman Schneebeli of Pennsylvania and their wonderful committee members for the magnificent job they have done.

You may have seen an old recipe for baking ham that says to "soak ham overnight, rub in brown sugar, and dot with cloves. Before putting ham in roaster, cut three inches off of hock." When asked about this last instruction, the donor of the recipe said, "Well, that's what my grandmother said to do; so I always do this." As it turned out, when the grandmother was questioned about this part of the recipe, she said that's what her grandmother said to do. Finally, the mystery was solved.

Granny's roaster was small; so everytime she baked a ham, she had to cut three inches off the hock.

Well, we hope that you folks will enjoy some of our grandmothers' recipes; just don't "saw off" the hock.

Whether you're trying out Byrddie Byrd's scrumptious souffle or Jezebel's zippy sauce, we hope you will have fun and pleasure putting our recipes to use. In behalf of our Bicentennial Cook Book Committee and all other Congressional Club Members, here's wishing you more and more joyful mealtimes.

Emily Preyer

Identification of
Early American Cooking Equipment

Art work by Lydia de La Viña

Table of Contents

GRAND STAIRCASE

The Congressional Club

The Congressional Club

Yesterday and Today

The American novelist Henry James, revisiting Washington on his last tour of this country in 1904, found the city and its social world inhabitants unchanged from twenty years before. The Washington world, he noted, was extraordinarily easy and pleasant and distinguished by the fact that one could single out "not more than half-a-dozen members of the Lower House and not more than a dozen of the Upper." Even less recognized were the wives of Members of Congress although these ladies actually brightened the Washington scene as they rode their carriages through the dirt streets of the Capital dutifully "dropping" their cards on the wives of top government officials. Few Congressional wives were accepted in the social life of the city. Most led solitary lives while away from their home states.

Recognizing this situation, Congressman Frank O. Lowden of Illinois remarked casually that "Congressional women should have a club for Congressional women in Washington". The suggestion was taken seriously and twenty-five Congressional wives soon met at the home of Mrs. James B. Perkins of New York to form the nucleus of a club exclusively for wives of Members of Congress. Mrs. Perkins was elected President. The first order of business thereafter was preparation of a plan for club members to lobby their husbands for an official Congressional Act of Incorporation.

A Bill of Incorporation was introduced on May 20, 1908 by Congressman Julius Kahn of California. Mrs. John Sharp Williams, a Vice President of the Club and wife of the Minority Leader of the House, learned that her husband was using parliamentary maneuvers for the purpose of defeating the measure. She decided to employ some diversionary tactics of her own. At noon on the day for final decision, Congressman Williams was approached by a House page who presented Mrs. Williams' card, stating she was waiting in the lobby, hoping he could take her to lunch. The Congressman responded immediately to the invitation and happily escorted his attractive wife into the dining room. While they were lunching, the Resolution of Incorporation was passed by the House unanimously. On May 30, 1908, the Congressional Club, with 195 members, became the official organization for Congressional wives.

In December 1908 President and Mrs. Howard Taft attended the opening reception at the first Congressional Club House, the former residence of Maryland Senator Arthur P. Gorman, at 1432 K street, Northwest. Club members brought their own silver, rugs, china, glassware and art objects to decorate the Club House for the party.

A few years later Mrs. John Henderson, wife of a Missouri Senator, donated the land and signed notes for $30,000 for the construction and furnishing of the present Club house. President Woodrow Wilson was the guest of honor at its dedication and formal opening in 1914.

YESTERYEARS . . .

1927

FOREWORD

By Mrs. Herbert C. Hoover

As truly as food is, first and last, our most important concern in life—so perhaps governing, in one of its forms or another, is the second in importance.

And so it seems peculiarly appropriate that the other half (on the general average) of our great governing body should be concerning itself with food—not only with the food of its own individual lawmaker, but with the cooked food for the nation. For our cooking, like our governing is for the people by the people. It is astonishing how closely each of the great majority of us keeps to the food and cooking habits of her own line of ancestors, and how little given to experimenting to see if her neighbors and compatriots near and far have better ways

. . .

. . . The housewife everywhere may through this effort of the Congressional Club have pleasant and helpful contact with the whole cross-section of American homes. For her own table, for her own family, she may prepare, knowingly, the very dishes which are the favorites in these representative homes, which she would have served her if she visited them in Washington, in Florida or in Oregon. Or she may even fancy that she is going to dine in an embassy or legation in the Capital or abroad, or in some representative home in a foreign country, and prepare some of the dishes described by members of the diplomatic corps.

. . .

Lou Henry Hoover

1933

FOREWORD

Cooking should be considered as an art, and the arts should certainly be of assistance in the government; therefore it seems particularly appropriate that the wives of our lawmakers should get out a cook book, for good cooking means good health and good health is the basis of all good work. I am grateful for the opportunity to share in this enterprise, and I hope that the recipes which I have contributed may prove as popular with all those who use the book as they have proved in our own family.

Eleanor Roosevelt

ELEANOR ROOSEVELT
(MRS. FRANKLIN D. ROOSEVELT)

Over the years the eligibility requirements for membership were broadened to include women Members of Congress, wives of Supreme Court Justices and wives of members of the President's Cabinet. Associate membership was opened to the daughters and daughters-in-law of Club members. Lifetime honorary membership is conferred upon the wife of the President, the wife of the Vice President and the wife of the Speaker of the House. Seven First Ladies have come from the club's membership. They are: Mrs. Harding, Mrs. Hoover, Mrs. Truman, Mrs. Kennedy, Mrs. Johnson, Mrs. Nixon and Mrs. Ford.

The Congressional Club has been the recipient of many beautiful gifts. One of the most impressive is a collection of mannequins, four feet tall, dressed in faithful

YESTERYEARS . . .

reproductions of the inaugural gowns of First Ladies beginning with Mrs. Lincoln. These are displayed in individual cabinets in the Congressional Club Museum and Foundation Room. The Doll Room houses a collection of dolls from around the world, costumed in national, provincial or native dress. These have been contributed by wives of Ambassadors in Washington's diplomatic community. It also includes dolls representative of the numerous ethnic and cultural backgrounds of the American people.

Although the Club continues its basic purpose of promoting friendship among Congressional wives, it has widened its scope to include Red Cross work, community service activity and classes in creative writing, painting, public speaking, languages,

YESTERYEARS . . .

physical exercise and flower arranging. Program teas, coffees or luncheons, featuring well known speakers, musicians, singers or personalities, are scheduled weekly. The annual breakfast each spring honoring the First Lady is the highlight of the Club's busy schedule.

Since 1927 publishing the Congressional Club Cook Book has been one of the Club's most important projects. Through its sales, the Club has been a self-sustaining organization. The success of the cook book has increased with each subsequent edition. The Club is proud to present its newest cook book in honor of the nation's Bicentennial.

Cook Book Committee

Editors

MRS. JOHN R. FOLEY, Maryland
MRS. HERMAN T. SCHNEEBELI, Pennsylvania

MRS. JAMES A. BURKE .... Massachusetts
MRS. CHARLES CHAMBERLIN .... Michigan
MRS. ROBERT N. GIAIMO .... Connecticut
MRS. WILLIAM L. HUNGATE .... Missouri
MRS. JOHN Y. MCCOLLISTER .... Nebraska
MRS. SPARK MATSUNAGA .... Hawaii
MRS. JACK R. MILLER .... Iowa
MRS. WALTER MOELLER .... Ohio
MRS. WILLIAM J. RANDALL .... Missouri
MRS. KENNETH J. ROBINSON .... Virginia
MRS. FRED SCHWENGEL .... Iowa
MRS. ALFRED D. SIEMINSKI .... New Jersey
MRS. HENRY P. SMITH III .... New York
MRS. NEAL SMITH .... Iowa
MRS. ANITA W. ULLMAN .... Oregon

Advertising

MRS. WINSTON PROUTY, Chairman .... Vermont
MRS. HAROLD RUNNELS, Co-chairman .... New Mexico
MRS. JOHN W. BYRNES .... Wisconsin
MRS. RICHARD ICHORD .... Missouri
MRS. ROBERT J. LAGOMARSINO .... California
MRS. MELVIN PRICE .... Illinois

Entertaining and Protocol
in
The Nation's Capital

At the beginning of the nation, when social etiquette reflected British court manners, President and Mrs. Washington planned their official functions with a simplicity and practicality distinctly American. Lavish, expensive banquets were ruled out as extravagant. At Washington's official dinners, usually boiled leg of mutton and a glass of wine were served. On very special occasions soup, fish, fowl and dessert would also be offered. President Washington received gentlemen visitors in very limited groups in small drawing rooms from which chairs had been removed so that the guests would have to stand. The President would bow and say a few words to each visitor in turn; he made a point never to shake hands. The emphasis was on dignity and formality without ostentation. Evening *levees,* always stiff and very formal, ended promptly as the First Lady rose to announce: "General Washington retires at ten o'clock and I usually precede him. Good Night."[1]

Concern for ceremony and protocol grew with the administration of President and Mrs. John Adams, only to be overthrown in the name of democracy by President Jefferson. The now traditional *levees* were abruptly abolished and receptions were held only on New Year's Day and the Fourth of July. A staunch believer in equality, Jefferson tried to eliminate all rules of precedence. He made himself available to anyone at any time.[2]

Succeeding administrations restored ceremony to the White House. The style of entertaining and the degree of formality at official state functions has depended a great deal on the personalities and wishes of the President and his wife. Social and economic conditions in this country and around the world have also been a great influence.

President and Mrs. Ford have created an informal, relaxed home atmosphere in their entertaining without detracting from the protocol and precedence neces-

[1] *Life and Scenes,* Mary Clemmer Ames, 1873
[2] *Social Usages at Washington,* Florence H. Hall, 1906

sary for official White House functions. They enjoy being hosts and enjoy their own parties. After the honored guests leave, the Fords start the dancing and remain for the entire evening so that their other guests will feel free to remain. The decorations and entertainment on these occasions are varied and innovative. They are tailored to the tastes and interests of the honored guests. Stars of country music and musical comedy as well as of opera and ballet have entertained at these parties. Round tables are used for seating guests at state dinners. On only two occasions to date has the rigidly formal format of a head table with an E seating arrangement been used by the Fords.

Uncertainty in matters of protocol in the early years of this country was not unique to America. At this same time, European diplomats, in the hopes of solving their problems regarding precedence while they were meeting at the Congress of Vienna to draw a new political map, agreed to the rules of precedence set forth in *The Regulation of Vienna* in March, 1815. This regulation established that there are three classes of diplomatic representatives: Ambassadors, Ministers and Chargé d'Affaires. Within each classification the rank of each diplomatic representative is determined by the date he presented official notification of his arrival.[3] These rules still prevail. Because they were so practical, they had a profound influence in determining matters of domestic protocol in the United States.

Since protocol determines social procedure in official Washington, a set of rules governing precedence in the ranking of official guests at formal affairs was established. (See Table of Precedence on following page.)

Ambassadors and Ministers are ranked, in their respective classes, according to their length of service in Washington. The Ambassador with the longest, continuous service in Washington is the Dean of the Diplomatic Corps.

Associate Justices of the Supreme Court rank according to their length of service on the court. Cabinet members, with the exception of the Secretary of State, rank in the order in which the departments were created. Senators rank according to their length of service in the Senate with the President Pro Tem of the Senate ranking first. Representatives also rank according to length of service in the Congress. If two or more Senators or Representatives have the same length of service, rank is determined by the dates on which their respective states were admitted to the Union.

[3] *The Map of Europe by Treaty,* Volume 1, Edward Hertslet, 1875

Unofficial Table of Precedence

The President of The United States
The Vice President of The United States
The Speaker of The House of Representatives
The Chief Justice of The United States
Former Presidents of The United States
The Secretary of State
The Secretary General of The United Nations
Ambassadors of Foreign Powers
Widows of Former Presidents of The United States
Ministers of Foreign Powers (Chiefs of Diplomatic Missions)
Associate Justices of The Supreme Court of The United States
The Cabinet
    The Secretary of The Treasury
    The Secretary of Defense
    The Attorney General
    The Secretary of The Interior
    The Secretary of Agriculture
    The Secretary of Commerce
    The Secretary of Labor
    The Secretary of Health, Education, and Welfare
    The Secretary of Housing and Urban Development
    The Secretary of Transportation
Director, Office of Management and Budget
The United States Representative to The United Nations
Members of The United States Senate
Governors of States
Former Vice Presidents of The United States
Members of The United States House of Representatives

States in Order of Admission to the Union

Delaware	December 7, 1787	Michigan	January 26, 1837
Pennsylvania	December 12, 1787	Florida	March 3, 1845
New Jersey	December 18, 1787	Texas	December 29, 1845
Georgia	January 2, 1788	Iowa	December 28, 1846
Connecticut	January 9, 1788	Wisconsin	May 29, 1848
Massachusetts	February 6, 1788	California	September 9, 1850
Maryland	April 28, 1788	Minnesota	May 11, 1858
South Carolina	May 23, 1788	Oregon	February 14, 1859
New Hampshire	June 21, 1788	Kansas	January 29, 1861
Virginia	June 26, 1788	West Virginia	June 20, 1863
New York	July 26, 1788	Nevada	October 31, 1864
North Carolina	November 21, 1789	Nebraska	March 1, 1867
Rhode Island	May 29, 1790	Colorado	August 1, 1876
Vermont	March 4, 1791	North Dakota	November 2, 1889
Kentucky	June 1, 1792	South Dakota	November 2, 1889
Tennessee	June 1, 1796	Montana	November 8, 1889
Ohio	March 1, 1803	Washington	November 11, 1889
Louisiana	April 30, 1812	Idaho	July 3, 1890
Indiana	December 11, 1816	Wyoming	July 10, 1890
Mississippi	December 10, 1817	Utah	January 4, 1896
Illinois	December 3, 1818	Oklahoma	November 16, 1907
Alabama	December 14, 1819	New Mexico	January 6, 1912
Maine	March 15, 1820	Arizona	February 14, 1912
Missouri	August 10, 1821	Alaska	January 3, 1959
Arkansas	June 15, 1836	Hawaii	August 21, 1959

Basic Nutrition

Nutrition scientists have translated knowledge of the nutrient needs of people and nutritive values of foods into an easy to use guide for food selection.

Since essential nutrients are widely dispersed in nature, they can be obtained from many combinations of foods with varying ease.

The following food guide divides foods into four groups on the basis of their similarity in nutrient content. Each of the broad food groups has a special contribution to make towards an adequate diet.

Daily Food Guide

MEATS

Daily amount recommended: at least 2 servings. The total amount may be any combination of the foods in this group. One serving equals 2 to 3 ounces.

| *Foods included:* | beef | lamb | liver | fish | eggs |
| | veal | pork | poultry | shellfish | cheese |

Alternate choices:	dried beans	nuts
	dried peas	peanut butter
	lentils	

FRUITS AND VEGETABLES

Daily amount recommended: at least 4 servings. One serving equals ½ cup.
Foods included: all fruits and vegetables. The following fruits and vegetables, especially rich in vitamins A and C, should be included every day.

Sources of Vitamin A	*Sources of Vitamin C*
apricots	broccoli
broccoli	brussel sprouts
cantaloupes	cantaloupes
carrots	citrus fruit or juice
leafy greens	guavas
mangoes	papayas
persimmons	green peppers
pumpkin	sweet red peppers
sweet potatoes	fresh strawberries
winter squash	tomatoes or tomato juice
other deep yellow vegetables	

POTATOES, BREADS, CEREALS

Daily amount recommended: at least 4 servings. One serving equals 1 slice of
bread, 1 medium potato or ¾ cup cereal or rice.

Foods included: potatoes and whole grain or enriched products such as:

breads	rice
crackers	cooked cereals
flour	ready-to-eat cereals
macaroni	grits
spaghetti	corn meal
noodles	rolled oats

Valuable amounts of B vitamins, iron, protein and food energy are provided
by these foods.

MILK

Daily amount recommended: children .... 2 or 3 glasses
teenagers .... 4 glasses
adults .... 2 glasses
1 glass equals 8 ounces.

Foods included: whole, skim or evaporated milk, buttermilk or plain yogurt.

A portion of the daily calcium requirement can be supplied by hard cheeses,
American cheese, cottage cheese and other foods prepared with milk.

Cooking With Wine

Inasmuch as the final flavor in any dish prepared with wine is not the flavor of the wine itself, it is a needless expense to use a high priced wine. A good, inexpensive wine or even wine left over from the dinner table is not only thriftier, it is also most satisfactory. A rather dry wine is best. Since wine may intensify the saltiness in food, a regular table wine is usually preferred to a cooking wine which is saltier.

The acid content in wine is important in cooking because it is the acid that acts as a tenderizer of tough cuts of meat in the marinating or simmering processes of food preparation. It also joins with the natural elements in the meat to produce new flavors, not necessarily the flavor of the wine used.

The alcoholic content in wine evaporates when the wine is heated. Therefore, foods cooked with wine can be included in an alcohol restricted diet.

Wine may be substituted for other liquids in casseroles. It serves to blend the flavors of the other ingredients. It is best to use sherry if the amount of liquid is small.

During cooking, wine may lose its flavor and aroma. If so, add a little more after the dish is fully cooked.

If the recipe does not specify the amount of wine to use, the following proportions generally may be followed.

¼ cup burgundy per pound of roast or stew meat
¼ cup dry white wine per pound of boiled, sauteed or fricasseed chicken
1 tablespoon per cup in sauces
1 teaspoon per serving in soup
1 tablespoon per serving with fruit

Guide for Baking Cakes at High Altitudes

Altitude	3000–5000 feet	5000–7000 feet	Over 8000 feet
Shortening decrease by	1 tablespoon	2 tablespoons	3 tablespoons
Sugar decrease by	1½ tablespoons	3 tablespoons	4 tablespoons
Baking powder decrease by	. . . . .	¼ of specified amount	½ of specified amount
Oven temperature increase by	. . . . .	. . . . .	25°F

APPETIZERS & BEVERAGES

Syllabubs:

To make a fine Syllabub from the Cow.

Sweeten a quart of cyder with double refined sugar, grate nutmeg into it, then milk your cow into your liquor, when you have thus added what quantity of milk you think proper, pour half a pint or more, in proportion to the quantity of syllabub you make, of the sweetest cream you can get all over it.

The American Cookery
Amelia Simmons, 1796

CHEESE WAFERS

½ pound butter or margarine, softened
2 cups flour
8 ounces sharp cheddar cheese, grated

1 teaspoon cayenne pepper
½ teaspoon salt
2 cups Rice Krispies

Cut butter into flour, add cheese and seasonings and fold in cereal. Drop in small rounds on ungreased cookie sheet and flatten with spoon. Bake at 350° for about 15 minutes. Do not allow them to get too brown.

Mrs. Lyndon B. Johnson

MRS. LYNDON B. JOHNSON, Wife of former President of the United States (Texas)

CHEDDAR CHEESE WAFERS

1 pound sharp cheddar cheese, grated
¼ pound butter
1 teaspoon salt

2 teaspoons Worcestershire sauce
½ teaspoon cayenne pepper
1 cup flour

Combine all ingredients in a mixing bowl and knead well. Shape in a roll about 2 inches in diameter and wrap in waxed paper. Refrigerate for several hours or freeze.

Slice the roll in thin rounds, place on greased baking sheet and bake in preheated 450° oven for 7 minutes. Serve hot. May be frozen. Makes about 4 dozen wafers.

Mrs. Arthur L. Miller

MRS. ARTHUR L. MILLER, Wife of former Representative (Nebraska)

3

NIPPY CHEESE STRAWS

2½ cups flour
½ teaspoon salt
¾ teaspoon cayenne pepper
1 pound extra sharp cheddar cheese,
  finely grated

½ pound margarine
2 tablespoons water

Sift together dry ingredients 3 times. With large fork blend cheese with flour mixture. Melt margarine, add water, then slowly blend with the above mixture. Knead dough lightly and divide into 2 parts. Roll out on slightly floured paper toweling into a rectangle about ⅓ inch thick. Cut into strips ½ inch wide and about 2½ inches long. Place on slightly greased cookie sheets. Preheat oven to 300°. Turn down to 225°. Bake 1 hour to 1¼ hours until golden brown. Makes about 100 cheese straws. May be frozen.

Mrs. John C. Stennis

MRS. JOHN C. STENNIS, Wife of Senator (Mississippi)

CHEESE STRAWS

¼ pound butter
½ pound sharp cheddar cheese, grated
1½ cups flour
½ teaspoon red pepper

1 teaspoon salt
1 egg, beaten
36 pecan halves
olives

Let butter and cheese soften to room temperature. Combine first 5 ingredients and mix well. Shape into a log about the diameter of a half dollar. Refrigerate. Cut in ¼ inch slices. Paint each slice with egg and decorate with a pecan half. The dough may be put through a cookie press to make straws or shaped over stuffed olives and rolled into balls. Bake at 325° for 10 to 15 minutes. May be frozen before baking. Makes 3 dozen.

Mrs. Wendell Ford

MRS. WENDELL H. FORD, Wife of Senator (Kentucky)

4

EASY CHEESE STRAWS

½ cup grated sharp cheddar cheese
1 egg yolk

½ package prepared piecrust mix
paprika

Add cheese and egg yolk to piecrust mix. Blend well. Roll ⅛ inch thick. Sprinkle with paprika. Cut into 3 x ½ inch strips. Bake in preheated 425° oven for 8 to 10 minutes.

Mrs. Clifford Davis

MRS. CLIFFORD DAVIS, Wife of former Representative (Tennessee)

FRANCES' CHEESE BISCUITS

¼ pound sharp cheese, grated
¼ pound butter, softened
1 cup flour

½ teaspoon salt
⅛ teaspoon cayenne pepper
confectioners sugar

Mix cheese with butter. Add flour, salt, and pepper. Roll out ¼ inch thick and cut with very small biscuit cutter to make bite size biscuits. Bake in 300° oven 30 minutes or until slightly brown. While hot, roll in confectioners sugar.

Mrs. Charles G. Rose, III

MRS. CHARLES G. ROSE, III, Wife of Representative (North Carolina)

GOUGERE

1 cup water
1/4 pound butter
1 teaspoon salt
1/8 teaspoon pepper
dash of nutmeg
1 cup sifted flour
4 eggs

2 cups grated gruyere cheese,
loosely packed

Glaze:
1 egg, beaten
1 teaspoon water

Bring water to a boil with the butter and seasonings and boil slowly until the butter has melted. Remove from heat and immediately pour in all the flour at once. Beat vigorously with an electric hand mixer until blended thoroughly. Then beat over moderately high heat for 1 to 2 minutes or until mixture leaves the sides of the pan and forms a mass.

Remove saucepan from heat and add eggs, 1 at a time, beating after each addition until the egg has been absorbed into the mixture. After the last egg, beat for a minute more to make sure all is well blended. Add the cheese to the warm choux mixture. Place mounds the size of 1 heaping teaspoon an inch or 2 apart on a buttered baking sheet. Make a glaze of egg beaten with water. Brush the top of each mound. Bake at 425° for about 20 minutes or until golden. Cool on rack. May be frozen.

MRS. MARK O. HATFIELD, Wife of Senator (Oregon)

OLIVE CHEESE NUGGETS

1/2 stick butter
1/4 pound cheddar cheese, grated
3/4 cup sifted flour

1/8 teaspoon salt
1/2 teaspoon paprika
36 to 40 medium size stuffed olives

Blend butter and cheese. Add flour, salt and paprika. Blend and mix to form a pastry type dough. Flatten a teaspoonful of dough in floured palm of hand and wrap around an olive. Bake on ungreased baking sheet at 400° for 12 to 15 minutes until golden brown. May be served hot or cold. Makes 3 dozen canapes.

MRS. ROBERT T. STAFFORD, Wife of Senator (Vermont)

6

ARTICHOKE APPETIZER

½ cup chopped onion
½ cup water
½ teaspoon salt
⅛ teaspoon pepper
⅛ teaspoon oregano
2 to 3 drops bottled hot sauce

4 eggs, well beaten
¼ cup fine dry bread crumbs
8 ounces grated cheddar cheese
2 6 ounce jars marinated artichoke
   hearts, drained, finely chopped
pimiento strips

Cook onion 5 minutes in water. Drain. Add salt, pepper, oregano, onion and hot sauce to eggs. Stir in bread crumbs, cheese and artichoke hearts. Spread on 11 x 7½ x 1½ inch pan. Bake at 350° for 17 to 18 minutes. Cut into 1 inch squares and garnish with pimiento strips. Makes 6½ dozen.

Mrs. Jamie L. Whitten

MRS. JAMIE L. WHITTEN, Wife of Representative (Mississippi)

SESAME COCKTAIL MUNCHERS

1 loaf melba thin sliced white bread
1½ sticks butter, softened

soft sesame seeds

Leaving crusts on bread, spread one side of each slice with butter. Cut each slice into 4 triangles and arrange on large cookie sheet in single layer. Sprinkle each triangle with sesame seeds. Bake in preheated 325° oven until golden brown, about 20 minutes. Cool. Store in a tightly covered tin box. Will keep indefinitely. Makes 116 triangles.

Mrs. Willard S. Curtin

MRS. WILLARD S. CURTIN, Wife of former Representative (Pennsylvania)

CHEESE AND BACON APPETIZERS

1 cup shredded cheddar cheese
1 egg yolk
1 tablespoon mayonnaise

24 toast rounds
3 slices bacon, cut in 2 inch pieces

Combine cheese, egg yolk and mayonnaise, mixing to a paste. Spread thickly on toast rounds. Top with a bacon piece. Place under broiler set at 350° for 5 minutes. Serve hot.

Mrs Homer Ferguson

MRS. HOMER FERGUSON, Wife of former Senator (Michigan)

PIZZA APPETIZERS

1 2¼ ounce can ripe olives, chopped
1½ cups drained, cooked tomatoes,
   chopped
1 cup grated sharp cheese
1 teaspoon grated parmesan cheese

1 teaspoon grated onion
1½ teaspoons oregano
⅛ teaspoon garlic salt
7 slices buttered toast

Mix all ingredients except toast. Spread mixture on toast. Cut each slice into 4 pieces and bake 10 minutes at 400°. Serve immediately. Makes 28 appetizers.

Mrs. Fred E. Busbey

MRS. FRED E. BUSBEY, Wife of former Representative (Illinois)

COTTAGE CHEESE AND HORSE RADISH CANAPES

½ pound creamed cottage cheese
4 tablespoons prepared horse radish
2 teaspoons Worcestershire sauce
salt

pepper
9 to 12 slices white bread,
   crusts removed
paprika

Mix cottage cheese, horse radish and Worcestershire sauce, draining liquid from the horse radish. Add salt and pepper to taste. With small, round cutter, cut 18 circles out of bread slices. Toast bread on one side under broiler. Heap cottage cheese mixture in mound on untoasted side of each circle. Toast under broiler at 450° for about 4 minutes or until cottage cheese just begins to brown. Remove from oven, sprinkle with paprika and serve immediately.

Mrs. Clarence D. Long

MRS. CLARENCE D. LONG, Wife of Representative (Maryland)

MUSHROOM AND CREAM CHEESE CANAPES

1 large package cream cheese
2 egg yolks
¼ teaspoon salt
2 tablespoons butter or margarine

1 tablespoon minced onion
1 small can mushrooms, chopped
10 slices bread, cut in squares

Mix first 6 ingredients and spread on bread. Bake 10 minutes at 350°. May be frozen.

Mrs. Harold C. Hagen

MRS. HAROLD C. HAGEN, Wife of former Representative (Minnesota)

8

MUSHROOM SANDWICHES

2 tablespoons flour
¼ to ⅓ cup sherry
1 can mushroom soup
4 3 ounce cans chopped mushrooms

salt, pepper, onion salt, garlic salt,
    Worcestershire sauce and Tabasco
    to taste
butter
bread

Combine flour and sherry and stir until smooth. Add to mushroom soup mixed with mushrooms. Add seasonings. Simmer slowly for about 10 minutes, stirring constantly. Refrigerate until mixture is thick enough to spread. Butter top and bottom of each sandwich and cut into halves or quarters. Heat until golden brown. Serve hot. May be frozen before heating. Makes 8 to 10 sandwiches.

Mrs. Kenneth Allison Roberts

MRS. KENNETH ALLISON ROBERTS, Wife of former Representative (Alabama)

CHEESE LOG

1 pound longhorn cheese, finely grated
1 8 ounce package cream cheese,
    softened
1 cup finely chopped nuts

1 teaspoon garlic powder
½ teaspoon chili powder
½ teaspoon paprika
½ cup mayonnaise
mixture of chili powder and paprika

Combine grated cheese, cream cheese, nuts, garlic powder, chili powder, paprika and mayonnaise and mix well. Form into either a ball or a log. Put on wax paper. Sprinkle with a mixture of equal parts of chili powder and paprika. Refrigerate. Serve at

Mrs. Glenn English

MRS. GLENN ENGLISH, Wife of Representative (Oklahoma)

9

INDIAN CHEESE BALL

1 10 ounce package grated sharp
   cheddar cheese
1 3 ounce package cream cheese,
   softened
¼ cup shredded coconut

2 tablespoons cream sherry
1 tablespoon chopped chutney
1 teaspoon curry powder
¼ teaspoon salt
¼ cup finely chopped pecans

Blend together all ingredients except nuts. Chill 20 minutes and form into ball.
Roll cheese ball in pecans. May be frozen.

Mrs. Thomas G. Morris

MRS. THOMAS G. MORRIS, Wife of former Representative (New Mexico)

PECAN CHEESE BALL

1 pound sharp cheddar cheese, grated
1 large package cream cheese
½ medium onion, finely chopped
1 2 ounce jar stuffed olives,
   finely chopped
1 teaspoon Worcestershire sauce
1 cup finely chopped pecans

cayenne pepper to taste
1 tablespoon finely chopped parsley
chopped nuts and parsley
paprika and chili powder (optional)

Mix cheeses together thoroughly and add onion, olives, Worcestershire sauce, pecans
and pepper. Mix until smooth, add parsley and let stand 15 minutes. Shape into
a ball and roll in a mixture of equal parts of chopped nuts and parsley or paprika
and chili powder. May be frozen.

Mrs. Dan Daniel

MRS. DAN DANIEL, Wife of Representative (Virginia)

TASTY CHEESE BALL

1 jar VeraSharp cheese
½ jar Roca blue cheese
1 large package cream cheese
1 tablespoon Worcestershire sauce

1 tablespoon vinegar
garlic salt to taste
1 cup chopped walnuts

Mix cheeses, Worcestershire sauce, vinegar and garlic salt together. Shape into a
ball and roll in the nuts.

Mrs. David E. Bradley

MRS. DAVID E. BRADLEY, Daughter of former Representative James Harvey (Michigan)

10

HERB CHEESE BALL

1 large package cream cheese, softened
1 teaspoon mixed dry herbs
1/8 teaspoon paprika
1/8 teaspoon seasoned salt
1/2 teaspoon dried parsley flakes

2 tablespoons Miracle Whip salad dressing
1 teaspoon Worcestershire sauce
10 drops Tabasco sauce
2 teaspoons finely chopped pimientos
parsley for garnish

Combine all ingredients in electric mixer. Shape into a ball. Chill. Sprinkle with parsley before serving. May be frozen.

Mrs. Robert M. Lemke

MRS. ROBERT M. LEMKE, Daughter-in-law of former Representative William Lemke (North Dakota)

CHEESE BALL

2 3 ounce packages cream cheese
1 10 ounce package sharp cheese, grated
1/2 teaspoon Worcestershire sauce
1/4 teaspoon salt

1/4 teaspoon seasoning salt
1 tablespoon grated onion
1/2 cup finely chopped pecans
4 teaspoons dry sherry
paprika

Have cheese at room temperature. Combine all ingredients except paprika and mix thoroughly. Shape into ball, sprinkle with paprika and refrigerate 4 hours before serving. May be frozen. Makes 8 servings.

Mrs. George M. Grant, Jr.

MRS. GEORGE GRANT, JR., Daughter-in-law of former Representative George Grant (Alabama)

CHILI CON QUESO

1/2 pound velveeta cheese
1/2 pound longhorn cheese
1/2 pound jack or white cheese
1/2 cup Half and Half

1 cup beer
2 small cans green chilies, diced
garlic salt and onion salt to taste

Melt cheese in double boiler with Half and Half. Add beer, garlic salt, onion salt and green chilies.

Mrs. Raúl H. Castro

MRS. RAÚL H. CASTRO, Wife of Governor (Arizona)

11

SALLY'S CHILI CON QUESO

1 medium onion, finely chopped
butter
1 small can green jalapeno peppers
   (hot or mild according to taste)
1 10½ ounce can stewed tomatoes,
   drained

8 ounces sharp cheddar cheese, cubed
8 ounces Monterey jack or mozzarella
   cheese, cubed
tortilla chips

Heat onion in electric or heavy frying pan in a small amount of butter until transparent. Add peppers and tomatoes and stir until heated through. Add cheese and continue stirring over low heat until cheese is melted.

Serve hot in a chafing dish or fondue pot as a dip with tortilla chips. This is also delicious as a sauce for scrambled eggs or an omelet.

Mrs. Thomas L. Judge

MRS. THOMAS L. JUDGE, Wife of Governor (Montana)

CHILI CON QUESO (CHEESE DIP)

1 large onion, diced
3 tablespoons butter (or bacon
   drippings)
1 10 ounce can tomatoes with
   green chilies
1 cup canned tomatoes

1 teaspoon comino seed, mashed or
   ground
3 cloves garlic, mashed
1½ pounds Kraft's Old English
   Cheese, grated

Saute onion in buter until soft. Add remaining ingredients, except cheese, and cook slowly for 30 minutes. Add grated cheese and stir until melted. Serve in a chafing dish as a dip.

Mrs. Robert J. Huber

MRS. ROBERT J. HUBER, Wife of former Representative (Michigan)

BLUE CHEESE DIP OR SPREAD

1 cup sour cream
1 cup mayonnaise
4 ounces blue cheese, crumbled

¼ teaspoon garlic powder
⅛ teaspoon paprika

Combine all of the ingredients, mixing by hand. Chill 2 hours before serving to allow flavors to blend. Makes 2½ cups.

Mrs. Albert H. Quie

MRS. ALBERT H. QUIE, Wife of Representative (Minnesota)

DEE'S DIP WITH BELGIAN ENDIVE

1 cup mayonnaise
¾ cup blue (or roquefort) cheese
½ cup dairy sour cream
½ teaspoon vinegar

1 teaspoon lemon juice
dash garlic salt
Belgian endive
raw vegetables

Mix together all ingredients, except vegetables, and chill. Serve with Belgian endive or other fresh vegetables. Makes 2½ cups.

Mrs. Jack Edwards

MRS. JACK EDWARDS, Wife of Representative (Alabama)

PARTY CAULIFLOWER DIP

2 heads cauliflower
2 8 ounce packages cream cheese
2 3 ounce packages blue cheese
mayonnaise
garlic powder
onion powder

oregano
Tabasco
Worcestershire sauce
crushed red pepper
soy sauce (optional)

Wash cauliflower, cut apart the flowers and cut each lengthwise into 2 or 3 slices. Put in ice water to stay crisp. Beat together both kinds of cheese, adding mayonnaise, a spoonful at a time, until the mixture is stiff like a meringue. Add seasonings to taste, mixing very well. Refrigerate until ready to serve.

Mrs. James B. Allen

MRS. JAMES B. ALLEN, Wife of Senator (Alabama)

VEGETABLE DIP

1 tablespoon unflavored gelatin
1 tablespoon lemon juice
1 cup dairy sour cream
1 3 ounce package cream cheese
½ cup mayonnaise
1 rounded tablespoon sugar
1½ teaspoons salt
½ cup minced onion

½ cup minced radishes
½ cup finely chopped cucumber
½ cup finely chopped bell pepper
pepper
garlic salt
onion salt
dash of Tabasco sauce

Dissolve gelatin in lemon juice and set aside. Mix other ingredients together, using seasonings to taste. Add gelatin to thicken. Chill until serving time.

Mrs. Wm. Jennings Bryan Dorn

MRS. WM. JENNINGS BRYAN DORN, Wife of former Representative (South Carolina)

DILLWEED DIP

1 cup dairy sour cream
1 cup Hellmann's mayonnaise
1 tablespoon dillweed
1 tablespoon seasoned salt

1 tablespoon dry minced onions
1 tablespoon parsley flakes
raw vegetables

Mix first 6 ingredients together and refrigerate 2 to 3 hours before serving. Serve as a dip with raw vegetables.

Mrs. Jim Santini

MRS. JIM SANTINI, Wife of Representative (Nevada)

MUSHROOM DIP

1 medium onion, finely chopped
margarine
½ pound fresh mushrooms,
    finely chopped

2 tablespoons lemon juice
1 teaspoon Worcestershire sauce
salt and cracked pepper to taste
mayonnaise

Simmer onions in margarine 3 to 4 minutes. Add mushrooms and simmer an additional 5 minutes, stirring constantly. Add remaining ingredients, mixing in enough mayonnaise to bind. Keeps well in refrigerator.

Mrs. William Henry Harrison

MRS. WILLIAM HENRY HARRISON, Wife of former Representative (Wyoming)

TARAMASALATA (FISH ROE DIP)

⅓ 8 ounce jar tarama (Greek product)
1 small onion, finely grated
2 cups olive oil

5 slices white bread, trimmed
juice of 3 lemons
crackers or toast

Mash tarama and add onion. Add a little olive oil and beat thoroughly to a smooth paste. Moisten bread and squeeze out excess water. Continue beating tarama mixture, alternately adding small bits of moistened bread, olive oil and lemon juice. Beat until cream colored. Serve as a dip with crackers or spread on toast. May be frozen. Makes 2 cups.

Mrs. Jim Wright

MRS. JIM WRIGHT, Wife of Representative (Texas)

CHILI PEPPER CHEESE HORS D'OEUVRES

1 small can green chili peppers
longhorn cheese slices
2 eggs, beaten

2 tablespoons milk
2 or 3 tablespoons flour
oil

Open the peppers lengthwise and stuff each with a thin slice of cheese. Beat eggs and milk in a bowl and add flour to make a thin batter. Close peppers and dip in the batter. Fry in oil until golden. Cut each in half crosswise and serve hot. Makes 4 servings.

Mrs. Henry Bellmon

MRS. HENRY BELLMON, Wife of Senator (Oklahoma)

CAVIAR PIE

4 hard cooked eggs, chopped
1 small onion, chopped
4 tablespoons butter, softened
2 cans flat anchovies
2 tablespoons chopped parsley

1 tablespoon mayonnaise
1 8 ounce jar black caviar
few drops of lemon juice
1 pint dairy sour cream

Mix eggs, ½ of onion and butter and spread on bottom of 9 inch pie plate. Refrigerate for 30 minutes. Mash anchovies, parsley and mayonnaise and spread over egg mixture. Mix caviar and remaining onions and spread over anchovies. Chill. Before serving, sprinkle with lemon juice and spread sour cream on top. Makes 12 to 14 servings.

Mrs. John W. Byrnes

MRS. JOHN W. BYRNES, Wife of former Representative (Wisconsin)

QUICHE LORRAINE

Crust:
3 tablespoons butter
1¼ cups sifted flour
pinch of salt
3 tablespoons shortening
3 to 4 tablespoons cold water

Filling:
4 eggs
¾ cup light cream
¾ cup heavy cream
2 tablespoons butter, melted
1 tablespoon flour
pinch of salt
pinch of cayenne pepper
pinch of nutmeg
½ pound fried, crisp bacon, crumbled
1 cup grated Swiss cheese
1 bunch scallions, chopped

Melt butter and shortening together and combine with flour and salt. Add water and blend well. Shape in a ball, wrap in wax paper and refrigerate for 1 hour. Then knead into a circle, roll out and fit into a quiche pan. Fit buttered aluminum foil over bottom and sides of crust and cover bottom with uncooked rice to hold the pastry in place while baking. Bake crust for 7 minutes in preheated 400° oven. Remove rice and aluminum foil and bake an additional 5 minutes. Cool.

Filling: With a wire whisk beat together the eggs, cream, butter, flour and seasonings. Sprinkle the bacon, cheese and scallions over crust and pour on the egg mixture. Bake 40 minutes at 375°.

FLEUR M. FEIGHAN, Daughter of former Representative Michael A. Feighan (Ohio)

PUPUS

1 3 ounce package cream cheese,
    softened
¾ tablespoon Worcestershire sauce

2 tablespoons diced glazed ginger
1 small can lychee nuts, drained

Mix cream cheese, Worcestershire sauce and ginger together. Stuff lychee nuts with mixture.

MRS. WILLIAM F. NORRELL, former Representative (Arkansas)

16

DEVILED EGGS

10 hard cooked egg whites, halved
Hellmann's mayonnaise
1 cup lobster meat (or ½ pound
   cooked, cleaned shrimp, diced)
white wine

¼ cup minced celery
salt to taste
Tabasco sauce
caviar

Spread egg whites with mayonnaise. Wash lobster meat with a little white wine and drain. Mix lobster meat with celery and a little mayonnaise. Season with salt and Tabasco. Fill egg whites with salad mixture and top with a dot of mayonnaise and a smaller dot of caviar. Serve chilled. Makes 10 servings.

Mrs. Lucien N. Nedzi

MRS. LUCIEN N. NEDZI, Wife of Representative (Michigan)

HOT CRAB DIP

1 8 ounce package cream cheese
1 6 ounce can crabmeat
1½ teaspoons chopped onion

½ tablespoon horse radish
¼ teaspoon salt
dash pepper

Mix all ingredients. Bake at 375° for 15 minutes or until bubbly.

Mrs. Sherman W. Tribbitt

MRS. SHERMAN W. TRIBBITT, Wife of Governor (Delaware)

MARY LIB'S HOT CRAB DIP

1 7 ounce can crabmeat
1 8 ounce package cream cheese,
   softened
1 tablespoon milk

2 teaspoons Worcestershire sauce
2 tablespoons chopped green onions
crackers or toast rounds

Combine all ingredients except crackers and mix well. Pour into shallow buttered casserole and bake at 350° for 15 minutes. Serve with toast rounds or crackers.

Mrs. Thomas S. Kleppe

MRS. THOMAS S. KLEPPE, Wife of former Representative (North Dakota) , presently Secretary of the Interior

17

HOT CHEESE CRAB DIP

2 8 ounce packages cream cheese
1 7½ ounce can crabmeat, undrained
2 tablespoons lemon juice
½ teaspoon seasoned salt

½ teaspoon Accent
dash of Tabasco
wheat thins

Mix together dip ingredients and heat in shallow casserole in 300° oven about 10 minutes until bubbly. May also be heated in chafing dish. Serve with wheat thins.

Mrs. Benjamin F. James

MRS. BENJAMIN F. JAMES, Wife of former Representative (Pennsylvania)

CRABMEAT FOR CHAFING DISH

1 pound crabmeat
3 small jars Kraft cream cheese
   with chives
¼ pound butter

1 teaspoon Worcestershire sauce
3 drops Tabasco
crackers or melba toast

Heat all dip ingredients together in double boiler until blended. Place in chafing dish and serve with crackers or melba toast.

Mrs. Mark Andrews

MRS. MARK ANDREWS, Wife of Representative (North Dakota)

CRABMEAT HORS D'OEUVRES

¼ pound butter
1 small package Velveeta cheese

2 small cans crabmeat
crackers

Melt butter and cheese together and add crabmeat. Mix well. Serve hot as a dip with crackers.

Mrs. Otis G. Pike

MRS. OTIS G. PIKE, Wife of Representative (New York)

CHILLED CRAB DIP

1 3 ounce package cream cheese
½ cup mayonnaise
1 teaspoon grated onion
½ teaspoon curry powder

2 tablespoons condensed milk
½ teaspoon Worcestershire sauce
1 can crabmeat
crackers

Blend first 6 ingredients together. Fold in crab meat. Chill and serve with small crackers.

Mrs. Paul J. Kilday

MRS. PAUL KILDAY, Wife of former Representative (Texas)

CRAB SPREAD

1 8 ounce package cream cheese,
   softened
1 can crabmeat
1 can water chestnuts, chopped
¼ cup dairy sour cream

¼ cup mayonnaise
1 tablespoon soy sauce
1 tablespoon lemon juice
2 tablespoons chopped green onion
Worcestershire sauce, to taste
melba toast or crackers

Beat cream cheese. Add remaining ingredients, except toast, and mix until blended. Serve with melba toast or crackers.

Mrs. Walter Norblad

MRS. WALTER NORBLAD, Wife of former Representative (Oregon)

CLAM ENTREE

2 tablespoons butter
1 tablespoon dried onion
1 medium green pepper, diced
⅔ cup chopped celery
1 8 ounce can clams, reserve liquid
8 to 10 saltines, crumbled

½ teaspoon Worcestershire sauce
¼ teaspoon salt
⅛ teaspoon pepper
dash of Tabasco
dash of paprika

Melt butter and saute the onion, green pepper and celery until softened. Remove from heat, add clams and saltine crumbs. If dry, add clam juice. Add Worcestershire, salt and pepper and heat together. Serve on shells. Sprinkle with Tabasco and paprika. Makes 4 servings.

Mrs. J. James Exon

MRS. J. JAMES EXON, Wife of Governor (Nebraska)

19

SHRIMP STUFFED MUSHROOMS

40 small mushrooms
butter
½ pound shrimp, finely chopped
1 tablespoon shredded green onion
½ cup finely chopped parsley
1 egg

1 tablespoon mayonnaise
½ teaspoon celery salt
½ teaspoon white pepper
dash of Tabasco
1 tablespoon brandy

Remove stems from mushrooms. Lightly saute mushroom caps in butter. Cut off and throw away tougher parts of stems. Chop remainder and combine with remaining ingredients. Stuff mixture into hollow mushroom caps. Place on cookie sheet and bake in a 350° oven until they are bubbling hot, about 15 minutes. Filling only may be frozen.

Mrs. Edward J. Derwinski

MRS. EDWARD J. DERWINSKI, Wife of Representative (Illinois)

TOMATO SHRIMP MOUSSE

1½ tablespoons gelatin
½ cup water
1 can tomato soup
2 3 ounce packages cream cheese

2 4½ ounce cans shrimp, mashed
1½ cups onion and celery, chopped
1 cup mayonnaise
salt to taste

Soften gelatin in water. Bring soup to boil, add cheese and beat until smooth and melted. Add gelatin. Cool until slightly thickened. Add shrimp with onions, celery and mayonnaise. Chill. Remove from refrigerator and unmold ½ hour before serving.

Mrs. Harrison A. Williams Jr.

MRS. HARRISON A. WILLIAMS, JR., Wife of Senator (New Jersey)

20

SHRIMP MOUSSE

1 envelope unflavored gelatin
2 tablespoons lemon juice
½ cup boiling chicken broth
½ cup Hellmann's mayonnaise
¼ cup milk
1 tablespoon chopped parsley
1 tablespoon minced onion

1 teaspoon prepared mustard
1 teaspoon dried dillweed
¼ teaspoon pepper
1 7 ounce can shrimp
½ cup shredded cucumber, drained
olive slice
crackers

Soften gelatin in lemon juice. Add broth and stir until gelatin is dissolved. Add next 7 ingredients and beat well. Chill 30 minutes. Beat until frothy. Fold in shrimp and cucumber and pour into 2 cup fish mold. Chill until firm. Unmold and use olive slice to resemble an eye. Serve with crackers. Makes 25 servings.

Mrs. John M. Ashbrook

MRS. JOHN M. ASHBROOK, Wife of Representative (Ohio)

FRESH SHRIMP MOLD

1 pound fresh shrimp, cooked
3 packages unflavored gelatin
1 small can minced clams, drain
  and reserve juice
1 8 ounce package cream cheese
1 cup mayonnaise

2 medium onions, grated
1 cup chopped celery
1 tablespoon Worcestershire sauce
salt and pepper to taste
parsley
paprika

Reserve a few whole shrimp for garnish and cut the remainder in small pieces. Soften gelatin in clam juice. Mash cream cheese and mix with mayonnaise. Add cut up shrimp, onions, celery, clams and seasonings. Mix well and adjust seasoning. Stir in the gelatin mixture and pour into a 6 cup mold. Chill until firm. Turn out onto a large platter and garnish with parsley, paprika and the whole shrimp.

Mrs. Charles Raper Jonas

MRS. CHARLES RAPER JONAS, Wife of former Representative (North Carolina)

SHRIMP MOLD HORS D'OEUVRES

3 3 ounce packages cream cheese
1 can tomato soup, heated
2 tablespoons unflavored gelatin
3 tablespoons cold water
1 cup mayonnaise
2 cups canned shrimp, drained

garlic salt to taste
juice of 1 lemon
1 small onion, grated
½ cup finely cut celery
½ cup finely cut green pepper
fresh dill

Dissolve cream cheese in hot soup, stirring until it is well blended. Soften gelatin in cold water and dissolve in the soup. Let cool. Add mayonnaise to the soup mixture. Then add shrimp, mashing it as it is added. Season with garlic salt and add lemon juice. Add onion, celery and pepper, mixing well. Pour into a large fish mold and refrigerate. It takes less than 2 hours to set. After unmolding, sprinkle fresh dill over the top.

Mrs Melvin R Laird

MRS. MELVIN LAIRD, Wife of former Representative (Wisconsin)

SHRIMP MOLD DIP

¼ pound margarine
11 ounces cream cheese
3 tablespoons lemon juice
1 small onion, finely minced
½ teaspoon salt
pepper to taste

2 tablespoons mayonnaise
1 teaspoon Worcestershire sauce
3 4 ounce cans shrimp, rinsed and
  drained
¾ cup finely chopped celery

Mix all ingredients together, putting in shrimp and celery last. Put into mold and refrigerate at least 1 day. May be frozen.

Mrs Elford A. Cederberg

MRS. ELFORD A. CEDERBERG, Wife of Representative (Michigan)

22

SHRIMP DIP

1 8 ounce package cream cheese,
  softened
1 cup sour cream
1 tablespoon lemon juice
3 tablespoons thinly sliced green onion
¼ to ½ teaspoon crushed red pepper
  (or hot sauce)

1 tablespoon milk
1 7 ounce can small shrimp, chopped
salt to taste
crisp raw vegetables (such as
  cauliflowerets, sliced zucchini, carrot
  or celery sticks, red or green pepper
  strips or cherry tomatoes)

Beat together cream cheese and sour cream until smooth and fluffy. Stir in lemon juice, green onion, red pepper, milk and shrimp. Season with salt. Cover and chill 2 to 4 hours to blend flavors. To serve, surround with a variety of crisp vegetables.

Mrs. Steven D. Symms

MRS. STEVEN D. SYMMS, Wife of Representative (Idaho)

ELSIE'S SHRIMP AND CRAB FILLING

1 3 ounce can small shrimp
1 3 ounce can crabmeat
4 hard cooked eggs, finely chopped

salt, celery salt, pepper, onion juice
  to taste
1 teaspoon lemon juice
½ cup mayonnaise

Drain and rinse shrimp and crab. Mash shrimp with fork and chop crabmeat. Combine ingredients with seasonings and mix well with mayonnaise.

Mrs. Thomas L. Judge

MRS. THOMAS L. JUDGE, Wife of Governor (Montana)

HOT SHRIMP AND LOBSTER DIP

2 packages Stouffer's frozen lobster
  newburg
2 cans Campbell's frozen shrimp soup

1 tablespoon Worcestershire sauce
melba toast

Combine lobster and 1 can of soup in blender. Blend until pieces of lobster and shrimp are fine. Put in top of double boiler with Worcestershire and remaining can of soup and heat. Serve in chafing dish with melba toast.

Mrs. J. Kenneth Robinson

MRS. J. KENNETH ROBINSON, Wife of Representative (Virginia)

23

SEAFOOD MOLD

4 3 ounce packages cream cheese, softened
2 packages unflavored gelatin
1/3 cup cold water
1 can cream of tomato soup, heated
3 cups lobster (or crab)
1/2 cup finely chopped celery
1 onion, grated
2 cups mayonnaise
1 tablespoon Worcestershire sauce
1 teaspoon seasoned salt
Tabasco to taste
crackers

Beat cream cheese until fluffy. Soften gelatin in cold water and dissolve in hot soup. Combine with the cream cheese and beat with electric beater until smooth. Fold in remaining ingredients except crackers. Pack lightly in oiled mold and chill. Unmold and serve with crackers.

Mrs. V. Ayres Mount

MRS. VIRGINIA AYRES MOUNT, Daughter of former Representative William H. Ayres (Ohio)

OYSTER PATTIES

4 dozen small oysters, with liquor
2 tablespoons butter
1 medium onion, grated
1 tablespoon flour
1/2 cup chopped canned mushrooms, with liquid
salt and pepper to taste
dash of cayenne pepper
2 tablespoons chopped parsley
1/4 teaspoon lemon juice
12 large patty shells (or 48 miniature shells)

Bring oysters and liquor to a boil and simmer for 10 minutes. Melt butter and add onion. Blend in flour until smooth. Add mushrooms, salt, pepper, cayenne pepper, parsley, lemon juice and oysters. Cook for 5 minutes. Pour into patty shells. Bake in 425° oven for 15 minutes.

Mrs. Richard C. White

MRS. RICHARD C. WHITE, Wife of Representative (Texas)

OYSTER ROLL

1 8 ounce package cream cheese
2 tablespoons mayonnaise
2 tablespoons milk
½ teaspoon powdered garlic
salt and white pepper to taste

1 can smoked oysters, chopped
½ cup toasted pecans, chopped
parsley and paprika
assorted crackers

Soften cheese and add next 4 ingredients. Place on plastic wrap and chill in refrigerator until hardened. Remove from refrigerator and spread with oysters and pecans. Roll into a log and decorate with parsley and paprika. Chill. Serve with assorted crackers.

Mrs Glenard P. Lipscomb

MRS. GLENARD P. LIPSCOMB, Wife of former Representative (California)

SMOKED OYSTER DIP

1 4 ounce can smoked oysters
1 8 ounce package cream cheese, softened
½ cup chopped black olives

juice of 1 lemon
2 tablespoons Worcestershire sauce
½ cup mayonnaise

Blend ingredients well in blender. May be stored in refrigerator several days but remove 1 hour before serving.

Mrs. LaMar Baker

MRS. LAMAR BAKER, Wife of former Representative (Tennessee)

CHICKEN KELAGUEN

1 medium size chicken, washed,
  cut in half
½ cup lemon juice
½ cup grated coconut
4 hot chili peppers, mashed

½ cup onions (or green onions),
  chopped
salt and pepper to taste
dash of monosodium glutamate
  (optional)
corn tortillas

Broil chicken in the oven or barbecue over charcoal until medium done. Bone and chop the meat coarsely in a bowl. Add lemon juice and mix thoroughly. The acid in the lemon juice will make the chicken more tender. Add the remaining ingredients, mix well and chill. Serve with warm or crisply fried corn tortillas. Makes 6 servings.

Mrs. Ricardo J. Bordallo

MRS. RICARDO J. BORDALLO, Wife of Governor (Guam)

SMOKED TURKEY SPREAD

¾ cup finely chopped smoked turkey
½ cup chopped almonds
¼ cup chopped celery

1 teaspoon chopped capers
mayonnaise
toasted, buttered bread rounds (or
  crackers)

Combine turkey, almonds, celery and capers. Add enough mayonnaise to bind the mixture. Serve with toasted, lightly buttered rounds of bread or assorted crackers. Chopped ingredients may be frozen and then blended with mayonnaise after thawing.

Mrs. Frank H. Miller

MRS. FRANK H. MILLER, Daughter of former Senator Edward V. Long (Missouri)

COCKTAIL BUFFET TURKEY BREAST

1 5 or 6 pound turkey breast
1 tablespoon fine herbs
1 tablespoon salt
½ teaspoon pepper
1 tablespoon curry powder
1 teaspoon paprika

1 onion
1 carrot
1 stalk celery
½ orange, sliced
1 cup gin
1 cup water
mayonnaise

Rub both sides of turkey breast with a mixture of herbs, salt, pepper, curry powder and paprika. Place in pan with vegetables and orange slices and roast, uncovered, at 350° until tender, about 3 hours. Baste frequently with gin and water. Cool in juices. Remove from pan, wrap in foil and refrigerate until cold. To serve, carefully remove meat in 1 piece from each side of bone. Slice paper thin across the grain, then form slices into original shape and return to breast bone. Serve with mayonnaise. May be frozen.

mrs. J. Kenneth Robinson

MRS. J. KENNETH ROBINSON, Wife of Representative (Virginia)

CHOPPED CHICKEN LIVERS

½ cup chicken fat (or margarine)
2 medium onions, sliced
1 pound chicken livers, washed and
   drained

2 hard cooked egg yolks
1½ teaspoons salt
¼ teaspoon freshly ground pepper

Melt ¼ cup fat in a skillet. Add onions and saute 10 minutes, stirring frequently. Remove onions and set aside. Melt remaining fat in same skillet. Saute the livers 10 minutes, stirring occasionally. Grind the onions, livers and egg yolks together or chop very fine in a wooden bowl. Add salt and pepper and mix well. Chill. May be frozen. Makes 1½ to 2 cups.

Mrs. Walter E. Powell

MRS. WALTER E. POWELL, Wife of former Representative (Ohio)

MOLDED CHOPPED CHICKEN LIVERS

1 pound chicken livers
butter
8 hard cooked eggs
2 large onions, chopped
vegetable oil

3 slices white bread, crusts removed
½ teaspoon sugar
2 teaspoons salad dressing
salt to taste
crackers or toast rounds

Cook livers in butter until lightly browned but pink inside. Grind with eggs using fine blade. Saute onions in oil until tender and grind with liver and egg mixture. Wet the bread with cold water, squeeze out some of the water and put through grinder. Add with sugar, salad dressing and salt to first mixture and blend thoroughly. Spoon into mold and chill. Serve with crackers or toast rounds.

MRS. MARVIN L. ESCH, Wife of Representative (Michigan)

RUTH'S LIVER PATE

1 8 ounce package liverwurst
1 3 ounce package cream cheese
1 small onion, grated
2 tablespoons bourbon
1 envelope gelatin

½ cup cold water
2 cans consomme
3 tablespoons sherry
Ritz crackers (or triscuits)

Mix first 4 ingredients together. Soften gelatin in cold water and dissolve in the consomme. Add sherry and mix well. Pour consomme mixture into a greased loaf pan or mold to about a ¼ inch thickness and allow to set. Over this spread a layer of the liverwurst mixture. Continue layering these mixtures until all is used. Chill. Unmold and serve with crackers.

MRS. DONALD G. BROTZMAN, Wife of former Representative (Colorado)

CHIPPED BEEF SPREAD

3 large packages cream cheese
½ onion, chopped
4 tablespoons mayonnaise
3 teaspoons Dijon mustard

5 tablespoons chopped parsley
2 packages chipped beef
triscuits or crackers

Mix together the cream cheese, onion, mayonnaise, mustard and 3 tablespoons parsley. Cut the chipped beef into small bits with scissors. Add ¾ of the beef to cheese mixture. Roll into a ball and roll it in remaining chipped beef and parsley. Serve with triscuits or crackers. Makes 12 servings.

Mrs Goodloe E. Byron

MRS. GOODLOE BYRON, Wife of Representative (Maryland)

PECAN SPREAD

1 8 ounce package cream cheese
2 tablespoons milk
1 2½ ounce jar dried beef
¼ cup chopped bell pepper
2 tablespoons dried onion flakes
½ teaspoon garlic salt
½ cup sour cream

2 tablespoons mayonnaise
¼ teaspoon pepper
½ teaspoon salt
½ cup chopped pecans
butter
crackers

Let cream cheese soften and mix with milk. Add coarsely chopped beef and next 7 ingredients. Blend and pour in greased 8 inch pie pan. Top with pecans that have been heated in melted butter. Bake at 350° for 20 minutes. Serve with assorted crackers. May be frozen.

Mrs. Robert E. Jones

MRS. ROBERT E. JONES, Wife of Representative (Alabama)

PECAN GALLA DIP

1 2½ ounce jar dried beef, finely cut
2 tablespoons onion flakes
1 8 ounce package cream cheese, softened
2 tablespoons milk
½ teaspoon garlic flakes
¼ teaspoon pepper
¼ cup finely chopped green pepper
½ cup dairy sour cream
½ cup coarsely chopped pecans
2 tablespoons butter or margarine
crackers

Combine first 8 ingredients and mix thoroughly. Saute pecans lightly in butter and stir into first mixture. Pour into shallow casserole and bake 20 minutes at 350°. Serve hot with crackers.

Mrs. Bob Wilson

MRS. BOB WILSON, Wife of Representative (California)

HOT CHIPPED BEEF DIP

8 ounces cream cheese
1 16 ounce container dairy sour cream
4 ounces dried beef, chopped
1 onion, chopped
1 green pepper, chopped
fritos

Mash cheese and mix thoroughly with remaining ingredients. Pour into shallow casserole and bake at 350° for 20 minutes. Serve with fritos. May be frozen.

Mrs. Pierre S. du Pont IV

MRS. PIERRE S. DU PONT IV, Wife of Representative (Delaware)

TENNESSEE STEAK POT

2 pounds beef tenderloin, cut in bite size cubes
½ stick butter
⅔ cup white wine
¼ cup catsup
2 teaspoons corn starch
1½ teaspoons seasoned salt
¼ teaspoon dried dill
freshly ground black pepper to taste
cocktail sauce (optional)

Brown steak quickly in butter just to rare or medium rare stage. Remove steak cubes to heated chafing dish over a candle warmer. Blend wine, catsup, corn starch, salt, dill and pepper and stir into rich pan drippings from meat. Cook, stirring constantly, until mixture boils and thickens. Pour over steak cubes, stirring to combine meat and sauce. Serve with fondue forks or cocktail picks for spearing meat. May be served with cocktail sauces for dipping.

Mrs. Ray Blanton

MRS. RAY BLANTON, Wife of Governor (Tennessee)

30

CHINESE SPARERIBS

1 10 ounce jar damson plum jelly
⅓ cup dark corn syrup
⅓ cup soy sauce
¼ cup chopped scallions

2 cloves garlic, minced
2 teaspoons ground ginger
2 pounds spareribs, cut by butcher
  into bite size pieces

Combine first 6 ingredients and heat in saucepan until jelly melts. Pour over ribs, cover and marinate for 24 hours. Place on rack in a foil lined pan. Bake in a 350° oven for 1 hour, turning and basting with marinade. Serve in a chafing dish.

Mrs. Stephen L. Neal

Mrs. STEPHEN L. NEAL, Wife of Representative (North Carolina)

MYSTERY SAUCE WITH FRANKFURTERS

6 ounces mustard
1 10 ounce jar currant jelly

2 pounds cooked frankfurters, in
  bite size pieces

Stir mustard with jelly until well mixed. Cook slowly over low heat, stirring until smooth. Place in chafing dish, add frankfurters and keep hot. Serve with toothpicks. May be frozen.

Mrs. George Marvin Wallhauser

Mrs. GEORGE MARVIN WALLHAUSER, Wife of former Representative (New Jersey)

BOURBON HOT DOGS

1 pound cocktail hot dogs (or large
  ones, cut up)
¾ cup bourbon

1½ cups catsup
1½ cups brown sugar
1 tablespoon grated onion

Place all ingredients in double boiler. Cook 1 hour or more. If too thick, add more bourbon. Serve in chafing dish. Sauce may be refrigerated and reused.

Mrs. Ralph Harvey

Mrs. RALPH HARVEY, Wife of former Representative (Indiana)

HOT APPETIZERS

1 small can Vienna sausages

1 can Pillsbury plain Weiner Wrap dough

Cut each weiner wrap dough into 3 pieces and each sausage into 2 pieces. Wrap the sausage pieces in the dough and put cut side down on an oiled cookie sheet. Bake 13 to 16 minutes at 375°. Makes 14 servings.

Mrs. William Henry Harrison

MRS. WILLIAM HENRY HARRISON, Wife of former Representative (Wyoming)

SAUSAGE WRAP UPS

8 ounces shredded cheddar cheese, softened
1½ sticks butter or margarine, softened

20 skinless sausage links
20 slices fresh white bread, crusts removed

Blend cheese and butter to spreading consistency. Cook sausage links according to package directions, drain well and cool. Roll bread slices flat with a rolling pin and spread each slice with cheese mixture. Place 1 sausage link on each slice and roll up. Fasten each roll with 3 toothpicks, then cut into 3 pieces. Bake at 400° for 8 to 12 minutes or until lightly browned. May be frozen before baking. Makes 60 appetizers.

Mrs. Walter E. Powell

MRS. WALTER E. POWELL, Wife of former Representative (Ohio)

SAUSAGE BALLS

2 cups Bisquick
1 pound hot sausage (mild if preferred)

1 cup grated sharp cheese

Mix all ingredients together and shape in nickel size balls. Bake in 350° oven until brown. These may be frozen and reheated before serving. Makes 110 balls.

Mrs. John J. Duncan

MRS. JOHN J. DUNCAN, Wife of Representative (Tennessee)

SAUERKRAUT BALLS

1 onion, finely chopped
3 tablespoons butter
1 cup ground cooked ham
1 cup ground cooked corned beef
1 clove garlic, minced
6 tablespoons flour

2 cups sauerkraut, drained and ground
¾ cup beef stock
1 tablespoon chopped parsley
1 egg, beaten
dry bread crumbs

Saute onion in butter. Add ham, corned beef and garlic. Stir over low heat until very hot. Sprinkle with flour and continue to cook, stirring until well blended. Add sauerkraut, beef stock and parsley. Cook, stirring constantly, until mixture forms a thick paste. Spread paste on a platter and chill. Form into 1 inch balls. Dip in egg and then roll in bread crumbs. Fry in 350° deep fat until browned. May be frozen after dipping in egg and bread crumbs. Makes 2 dozen.

MRS. FRANK H. MILLER, Daughter of former Senator Edward V. Long (Missouri)

COCKTAIL MEAT BALLS

Sauce:
¾ cup chili sauce (or hot catsup)
½ cup water
¼ cup vinegar
2 tablespoons brown sugar
3 or 4 drops Tabasco
few grains cayenne pepper
2 tablespoons minced onion
2 teaspoons Worcestershire sauce
1½ teaspoons salt
1 teaspoon mustard
¼ teaspoon pepper

Meat balls:
2 pounds ground beef
1¼ cups bread crumbs
3 tablespoons minced onion
1½ teaspoons horse radish
4 drops Tabasco
3 eggs, beaten
1½ teaspoons salt
1 teaspoon pepper
flour

Combine all sauce ingredients and simmer over low heat for 5 minutes. Turn off heat.
Mix all meat ball ingredients except flour, form into small balls, roll in flour and brown. Drain well. Place in sauce and serve in fondue dish with toothpicks. May be frozen or prepared and refrigerated and then reheated in a 350° oven.

MRS. DAVID JACK DIXON, Daughter of Representative Wilbur D. Mills (Arkansas)

APPETIZER MEAT BALLS

Meat Balls:
¾ pound ground lean beef
¼ pound ground lean pork
¾ cup rolled oats
½ cup milk
¼ cup finely chopped water chestnuts
1 tablespoon Worcestershire sauce
½ teaspoon onion salt
½ teaspoon garlic salt
few drops hot pepper sauce
2 tablespoons butter or margarine

Sweet Sour Sauce:
1 cup sugar
¾ cup vinegar
¾ cup water
1 teaspoon paprika
½ teaspoon salt
2 teaspoons corn starch
1 tablespoon cold water

Combine all meat ball ingredients except butter and mix thoroughly. Shape into small balls and brown well in butter. Drain on absorbent paper. Add to hot sweet sour sauce and simmer 30 minutes. Insert toothpicks into meat balls. Serve hot. May be frozen. Makes 4 dozen.

Sweet Sour Sauce: Combine sugar, vinegar, water, paprika and salt in large skillet. Cook 5 minutes, stirring occasionally. Blend corn starch and water; add to hot mixture. Cook, stirring until mixture thickens slightly.

Mrs. Robert J. Huber

MRS. ROBERT J. HUBER, Wife of former Representative (Michigan)

MEXICAN APPETIZERS

2 pounds ground beef
1 onion, finely chopped
butter or margarine
2 1 pound cans red kidney beans
1 small bottle taco sauce
1 tablespoon Worcestershire sauce

hot chili powder to taste
4 ounces grated cheddar cheese
1 small bottle green stuffed olives
   sliced
corn chips

Brown ground beef and onion in butter. Mix kidney beans with liquid in blender until soupy. Add to browned beef. Add taco sauce and season with Worcestershire sauce and chili powder. Pour into chafing dish and sprinkle with cheese and olives. Serve with corn chips.

Mrs. John Myers

MRS. JOHN MYERS, Wife of Representative (Indiana)

34

STEAK TARTARE

1 pound twice ground first rate beef
1 egg yolk
6 capers, rinsed and mashed
3 teaspoons Dijon mustard
3 tablespoons finely chopped onion
(or shallots)

1½ teaspoons sea salt
1 teaspoon fresh lemon juice
½ teaspoon Worcestershire sauce
freshly ground pepper
½ cup finely chopped parsley

Mix ground beef lightly with all ingredients except parsley. Form into small balls about the size of a large marble and roll each one in parsley. Place on flat tray, cover with plastic wrap and refrigerate. When ready to serve, add toothpick to each. May be frozen.

Mrs. Dean P. Taylor

MRS. DEAN P. TAYLOR, Wife of former Representative (New York)

ICED TEA

4 rounded tablespoons loose black tea
6 sprigs mint, 8 inches long
3 cups boiling water

1 cup reconstituted lemon juice
1 cup granulated sugar
cold water

Combine tea, mint and boiling water in pot and steep 30 minutes. Strain into gallon jar. Add lemon juice and sugar and stir until sugar is dissolved. Add cold water to fill jar. Chill thoroughly before serving over ice. Makes 4 quarts.

Mrs John Currie Mackie

MRS. JOHN CURRIE MACKIE, Wife of former Representative (Michigan)

GOURMET ICED TEA

⅓ cup loose tea
1 quart boiling water
¼ cup sugar

1 quart cold water
1 6 ounce can frozen limeade, defrosted

Steep the tea in boiling water for 3 to 5 minutes, depending on strength desired. Strain and pour in large pitcher. Add sugar and cold water to limeade. Mix well and combine with tea. Keeps in refrigerator for a week and gets better. Makes 8 glasses.

Mrs. Robert McClory

MRS. ROBERT McCLORY, Wife of Representative (Illinois)

MINT TEA

1¼ cups sugar
juice of 3 lemons
4 cups boiling water

3 tablespoons tea
6 sprigs mint, bruised
2 cups cold water

Mix sugar, lemon juice and 2 cups boiling water. Set aside to cool. In a second bowl, mix tea, mint and remaining boiling water. Let steep and then strain. Combine both liquid mixtures and add the cold water. Will keep in the refrigerator indefinitely. Makes 1½ quarts.

Mrs. John Y. McCollister

MRS. JOHN Y. MCCOLLISTER, Wife of Representative (Nebraska)

RUSSIAN TEA

¾ cup instant tea
1 3 ounce package lemonade mix
1 cup sugar
1 teaspoon ground cloves

2 cups orange flavored instant powdered breakfast drink
2 teaspoons ground cinnamon
¼ teaspoon salt
boiling water

Combine all dry ingredients. Store in tightly covered container. Stir in 2 heaping teaspoons of mix per cup of boiling water and let steep approximately 5 minutes. Makes 4⅓ cups dry mix.

Rebecca Dial

REBECCA DIAL, Daughter of former Senator Nathaniel Barksdale Dial (South Carolina)

CRANBERRY TEA

1 cup sugar
1 quart water
2 sticks cinnamon
12 to 15 whole cloves

5 tea bags
1 1 quart can apple juice
1 pint cranberry juice cocktail

Boil sugar, water, cinnamon and cloves for 5 minutes. Add tea bags and steep for 5 minutes. Remove tea bags and spices. Add juices. Serve hot or cold. Makes 2½ quarts.

Mrs. B. Everett Jordan

MRS. B. EVERETT JORDAN, Wife of former Senator (North Carolina)

SPICED TEA

3 tablespoons tea
6 cups boiling water
6 whole cloves
3 1 inch sticks cinnamon

½ cup fresh orange juice
3 tablespoons lemon juice
1 cup sugar

Steep tea 5 minutes in 3 cups boiling water with cloves and cinnamon. Strain. Add juices and sugar. When ready to serve, add remaining boiling water. Makes 12 cups.

Mrs Hubert H. Humphrey

MRS. HUBERT H. HUMPHREY, Wife of former Vice President of the United States, presently Senator (Minnesota)

CRANBERRY WASSAIL

1 quart apple cider
1 pint cranberry juice
1 cup orange juice
¾ cup lemon juice

1 teaspoon allspice
1 teaspoon whole cloves
3 cinnamon sticks
¾ cup sugar

Combine liquids and put in bottom of automatic percolator. Put other ingredients in percolator basket. Allow pot to go through full cycle. Makes 16 cups.

Mrs. Robert G. Stephens, Jr.

MRS. ROBERT G. STEPHENS, JR., Wife of Representative (Georgia)

WASSAIL

2¼ cups sugar
4 cups water
2 2½ inch sticks of cinnamon
8 whole allspice berries
10 whole cloves

1 whole piece ginger root
   (or 1 teaspoon powdered ginger)
4 cups orange juice
2 cups lemon juice
2 quarts apple cider

Combine sugar and water and boil 5 minutes. Remove from heat; add spices. Let stand, covered, 1 hour. Strain. Just before serving, combine syrup, fruit juices and cider and bring quickly to a boil. Remove from heat and serve at once. Makes 4½ quarts.

Mrs. Steven D. Symms

MRS. STEVEN D. SYMMS, Wife of Representative (Idaho)

WARM CRANBERRY PUNCH

1 quart apple cider
1 quart cranberry juice
6 whole cloves
4 whole allspice

1 stick cinnamon
½ cup brown sugar
¼ teaspoon salt

Combine cider and cranberry juice in automatic percolator. Place spices, brown sugar and salt in percolator basket. Allow to go through percolator cycle. Serve warm. Makes 8 servings.

Mrs. John C. Brophy

MRS. JOHN C. BROPHY, Wife of former Representative (Wisconsin)

COFFEE PUNCH

7 tablespoons instant coffee
1 teaspoon cinnamon
1⅔ cups chocolate syrup
1 cup confectioners sugar

3½ cups hot water
5 quarts milk
½ gallon vanilla ice cream

Dissolve coffee, cinnamon, syrup and sugar in hot water. Chill. Combine half of syrup mixture with 2½ quarts of milk. Add 1 quart of ice cream in individual scoops. Pour into punch bowl and serve. Combine remaining syrup with remaining milk and ice cream when needed. Syrup may be frozen. Makes 40 servings.

Mrs. D. R. Matthews

MRS. D. R. MATTHEWS, Wife of former Representative (Florida)

LIME PUNCH

2 packages lime Jello
3 cups boiling water
1½ cups lemon juice
grated rind of 4 lemons
3½ quarts orange and pineapple juice

2 quarts water
sugar to taste
green coloring
1 quart ginger ale

Dissolve lime Jello in boiling water. Add the lemon juice, grated rind, orange and pineapple juice and remaining water. Sweeten to taste. Add green coloring. Freeze this mixture. When ready to serve, let thaw to mushy consistency. Add ginger ale. Makes 2 gallons of punch.

Mrs. L. H. Fountain

MRS. L. H. FOUNTAIN, Wife of Representative (North Carolina)

IRISH COFFEE

1 heaping teaspoon sugar
1 cup strong black hot coffee

2 tablespoons Irish whiskey
 (approximately)
1 tablespoon heavy cream

Put the sugar in a warmed, stemmed whiskey glass, add the hot coffee to dissolve the sugar and stir well. Add whiskey to within an inch of the brim of the glass. Hold a teaspoon, curved side up, across the glass and pour the cold cream slowly over the spoon. Do not stir. The cream should float on top so that the hot coffee and whiskey are sipped through the cream. Makes 1 serving.

Mrs. James A. Burke

MRS. JAMES A. BURKE, Wife of Representative (Massachusetts)

ZOMBIE

2 ounces Bacardi rum, light
1 ounce Bacardi rum, dark
1 ounce Bacardi rum, 151
1 ounce pineapple juice
1 ounce orange juice
juice of 1 lemon (or lime)

Garnish:
¼ shot Bacardi, 151
1 tablespoon confectioners sugar
pineapple chunk or cherry

Pour all but garnish ingredients into a large shaker. Mix well. Pour into glass. Float Bacardi, 151 and confectioners sugar on top. Decorate with pineapple or cherry. Makes an individual serving.

Maureen Ellen Foley

MAUREEN ELLEN FOLEY, Daughter of former Representative John R. Foley (Maryland)

SAN JUAN FREEZE

2 ounces orange juice
1½ ounces light Puerto Rican rum

1 ounce Coco Lopez
¼ cup ripe banana

Combine ingredients and place in electric blender. Add a few ice cubes and blend until smooth. Serve immediately. Makes 1 serving.

Jaynie K. Miller

JAYNIE K. MILLER, Daughter of former Senator Jack R. Miller (Iowa)

YANKEE MINT JULEP

1 cup mint leaves
6 teaspoons sugar
12 teaspoons water
large quantity of finely crushed ice
6 ounces apricot (or peach) brandy
12 ounces cognac
6 ounces dark rum

Garnish:
mint sprigs
confectioners sugar

Crush mint leaves in a shallow cup. Add sugar and water. Stir, discard leaves and chill mint syrup. Spoon syrup equally into chilled 16 ounce goblets. Fill ¼ full with crushed ice. Into each goblet pour 1 ounce of brandy. Stir. Add more ice. Add 2 ounces cognac to each one. Stir. Add more ice. Add 1 ounce rum to each. Wipe goblet dry. Blend each drink with a spoon until goblet is glistening with frost. Top with sprigs of mint, coated with confectioners sugar. Makes 6 servings.

Mrs. Emilio Q. Daddario

MRS. EMILIO Q. DADDARIO, Wife of former Representative (Connecticut)

VODKA DELIGHT

18 ounces orange juice
6 ounces vodka

½ box frozen strawberries

Mix ingredients together and serve at once. Makes 1½ pints.

Mrs. Charles H. Leavy

MRS. CHARLES H. LEAVY, Wife of former Representative (Washington)

CRANBERRY PUNCH

3 cans frozen lemonade concentrate
1 pint cranberry juice
2 quarts cold ginger ale

1 quart vodka
ice

Mix lemonade and cranberry juice together and let stand overnight. Add ginger ale and vodka to juice mixture and pour over ice when ready to serve. Makes 40 servings.

Mrs. John Y. McCollister

MRS. JOHN Y. McCOLLISTER, Wife of Representative (Nebraska)

PEACH BRANDY

fresh peaches (or plums, apricots or bing cherries)	4 cups sugar inexpensive vodka

Fill a wide mouthed gallon jar with as many peaches as possible, skins, pits and all. Add the sugar and fill to the top with vodka, covering the fruit. Put jar lid on and seal tightly. Every day for 2 weeks turn the jar, alternating it from an upright to an upside down position. Open jar, drain off liquid and discard fruit. Strain the brandy through cheesecloth for a clearer appearance. Serve in liqueur glasses or substitute it for bourbon in a whisky sour for a delicious cocktail.

Mrs. John R. Foley

MRS. JOHN R. FOLEY, Wife of former Representative (Maryland)

KAHLUA

2 cups instant coffee	⅕ gallon cheap brandy
8 cups sugar	1 long vanilla bean
4 cups boiling water	

Mix coffee and sugar in water until completely dissolved. Add brandy and stir. Pour into a 1 gallon brown jug and add vanilla bean. Store in dark place for 4 to 6 weeks. Makes 1 gallon.

Mrs. Fred J. DeMeritte

MRS. FRED J. DEMERITTE, Daughter-in-law of former Associate Justice Hugo L. Black, Supreme Court

SOUTHERN EGG NOG

12 eggs, separated	1 quart Half and Half
1 cup sugar	4 tablespoons confectioners sugar
1 cup bourbon	1 pint whipping cream
¼ cup rum	1 teaspoon vanilla
¼ cup brandy	nutmeg (optional)

Beat egg yolks until lemon yellow. Gradually add sugar. Add bourbon, brandy and rum very slowly. Add Half and Half. Let stand at least overnight in refrigerator. To serve, whip egg whites until stiff, gradually adding confectioners sugar. Fold into bourbon mixture. Whip cream, add vanilla and fold into bourbon mixture. Serve in punch bowl and sprinkle with nutmeg if desired. Makes 12 servings.

Mrs. George M. Grant

MRS. GEORGE M. GRANT, Wife of former Representative (Alabama)

NOTES

SOUPS & SANDWICHES

Scotch Barley Broth

Get a sheep's head and feet with the skin and wool on, and singe the wool off with red hot irons (the best way is to send them to a smith's shop to be done) when singed, take a clean brush and some warm water, and brush them well till they are quite clean; put them into a soup-pot with six quarts of water, and when the scum rises skim it clean, put in half a pound of Scotch barley, six onions whole, six turnips whole, six leeks, and six of the white heads of cellery split in two, two carrots cut in quarters, a Savoy or white cabbage cut small, and half a pint of oatmeal, stew it for four hours, and season it with salt; chop a handful of parsley fine, and a few mary golds, put them in, let it boil up five minutes, then put the head and feet into a soup-dish, and the soup and ingredients over all, with crispt bread in a plate.

The New Art of Cookery
Richard Briggs, 1792

Capitol Bean Soup

Whether or not bean soup is the most popular item on the menu in the Capitol restaurants, it is certainly the best known. As the speciality of the house, it is usually recommended by Members of Congress when entertaining guests there for the first time.

Bean Soup, a favorite of Speaker of the House, Joseph G. Cannon of Illinois, was omitted from the menu one hot and humid day in 1904. When Speaker Cannon arrived for lunch and learned he could not order it, he was more than a little upset.

"Thunderation", roared the Speaker, "I had my mouth set for bean soup. From now on, hot or cold, rain, snow or shine, I want it on the menu every day."

From that time on, Bean Soup has appeared on the menu of the Capitol dining rooms every single day regardless of the weather.

If you cannot foresee a visit to the Senate or House dining room, but would like to try this soup, the recipe is given below.

BEAN SOUP

2 pounds number 1 white Michigan   1 smoked ham hock
  beans   salt and pepper to taste

Cover beans with cold water and soak overnight. Drain and recover with water. Add the ham hock and simmer slowly for about 4 hours until the beans are cooked tender. Season with salt and pepper as desired. Just before serving, bruise beans with a large spoon or ladle to cloud the soup. Makes 6 servings.

OLD FASHIONED VEGETABLE SOUP

1½ quarts warm water
2 pounds ground beef (or 1 big
   soup bone and 3 pieces soup meat)
1 large can tomatoes
1 large potato, diced
2 medium onions, chopped
3 stalks celery with leaves, chopped
3 carrots, chopped
1 small package frozen chopped okra
1 small can English peas

left over vegetables
salt to taste
coarse ground pepper
oregano
garlic powder
Worcestershire sauce
Tabasco
parsley flakes
thin spaghetti, broken up (or alphabet
   macaroni) (optional)

Place water over medium heat, add meat and boil until meat juices mix with water. Add vegetables. Season well with salt and add other flavorings to taste. When soup begins to boil, turn heat to low and let it simmer for several hours. Stir often during cooking so vegetables will not burn. Carefully skim off any grease as it accumulates on the top of the soup. A small amount of spaghetti may be added for the last 45 minutes of cooking time. Soup is ready when the vegetables sink to the bottom of the kettle and the soup no longer foams on top. Makes 20 servings.

MRS. JAMES B. ALLEN, Wife of Senator (Alabama)

VEGETABLE SOUP

1 large soup bone
water
1 onion, chopped
1 carrot
1 stalk celery
1 bay leaf
salt and pepper
3 medium onions, whole or halved
½ medium head cabbage, shredded

3 stalks celery, chopped
3 carrots, chopped
4 medium potatoes, diced
1 turnip, cut up
1 bay leaf
meat from soup bone
salt and pepper
1 cup tomatoes (or ½ to ⅔ cup
   tomato paste)

To make beef stock, cover soup bone with enough water to yield 8 cups of stock and add next 5 ingredients. Simmer for 1½ hours. Refrigerate overnight. Remove fat and strain. Add remaining ingredients to beef stock and cook until vegetables are tender. May be frozen. Makes 10 to 12 servings.

MRS. ROBERT H. MOLLOHAN, Wife of Representative (West Virginia)

HIGH HAMPTON VEGETABLE SOUP

2½ quarts liquid (½ water,
    ½ chicken broth)
1 soup bone
2 pounds cubed chuck beef
1 beef bouillon cube
1 chicken bouillon cube

1 tablespoon coarsely ground pepper
2 20 ounce cans tomatoes
2 or 3 stalks celery, coarsely cut
1 small package frozen cut okra
1 or 2 onions, cut up
1 2 pound package frozen vegetables

Combine first 6 ingredients and boil gently for 1 hour. Add all the vegetables and simmer for 5 or 6 hours. Remove soup bone and scrape off all meat. Return meat to soup. May be frozen indefinitely. Makes 12 servings.

Mrs. Charles G. Rose, III

MRS. CHARLES G. ROSE, III, Wife of Representative (North Carolina)

RED RIDING HOOD SOUP

½ pound ground beef
2 cups fresh or canned tomatoes
2 cups water
1 package frozen mixed vegetables

1 package dry onion soup mix
2 tablespoons sugar
1 small can tomato paste

Saute ground beef. Add remaining ingredients and simmer about ½ hour. May be frozen. Makes 4 servings.

Mrs. Albert L. Vreeland

MRS. ALBERT L. VREELAND, Wife of former Representative (New Jersey)

CARROT SOUP

4 medium carrots, ground or grated
2 tablespoons butter

4 cups beef consomme
cream (or milk) as desired

Cook carrots in butter until soft. Put in blender and add consomme and cream. Heat in top of double boiler.

Frances P. Bolton

FRANCIS P. BOLTON, former Representative (Ohio)

TURKEY CORN CHOWDER

4 tablespoons margarine
4 medium onions, sliced
5 medium potatoes, peeled, sliced
3 stalks celery, sliced
4 teaspoons salt
½ teaspoon pepper
2 cups water
1 chicken bouillon cube

5 cups milk (or turkey stock
  and dry milk powder)
2 cans whole kernel corn, drained
1 can cream style corn
¼ teaspoon dried thyme
1 cup light cream
1½ teaspoons paprika
3 cups diced, cooked turkey
parsley

Melt margarine in large kettle and saute onions until golden, stirring often. Add potatoes, celery, salt, pepper, water and bouillon cube. Cook, covered, 15 minutes or until vegetables are tender but not overdone. Add remaining ingredients. Heat. May be frozen. Makes 10 to 12 servings.

Mrs. Mike McCormack

MRS. MIKE McCORMACK, Wife of Representative (Washington)

TURKEY SOUP

turkey carcass, disjointed
2 to 3 quarts water
2 bay leaves
2 teaspoons salt
2 teaspoons poultry seasoning
1 onion, sliced

1 cup leftover bread stuffing
1 cup turkey gravy
½ bunch celery, chopped
½ bunch carrots, sliced
1 cup uncooked noodles
water as needed

Cover carcass with water and add first 4 ingredients. Simmer slowly for 45 minutes until meat comes off bones easily. Cool, remove meat from carcass and discard bones.

Replace meat in stock. Add stuffing and gravy and bring to a slow boil, stirring occasionally. Add celery, carrots and noodles and cook until tender. Soup will be thick. Add water if desired. May be frozen. Makes 12 servings.

Mrs. John W. Byrnes

MRS. JOHN W. BYRNES, Wife of former Representative (Wisconsin)

CHICKEN CORN SOUP

1 4 pound chicken, cut up
3 quarts water
1 cup chopped celery
2 tablespoons chopped parsley
¼ teaspoon saffron
1 teaspoon salt
¼ teaspoon pepper

6 cups chicken broth (with water added as needed)
2 cups corn, cut off cob
1 cup fine uncooked noodles
2 hard cooked eggs, chopped (optional)

Cook chicken in water with celery, parsley, saffron, salt and pepper. Skin and debone chicken and cut into bite sized pieces. Bring broth to a boil and add corn and noodles. Boil 5 minutes or until noodles are tender and then add chicken. If desired, add the chopped eggs.

Mrs. Edwin D. Eshleman

MRS. EDWIN D. ESHLEMAN, Wife of Representative (Pennsylvania)

MANHATTAN CLAM CHOWDER

¼ cup finely cut bacon
¼ cup minced onion
1 pint shucked fresh clams with liquor (or 2 7 ounce cans clams)
2 cups finely diced raw potatoes
1 cup water
⅓ cup diced celery

1 1 pound can cooked tomatoes
1 teaspoon salt
⅛ teaspoon pepper
¼ teaspoon thyme
2 teaspoons minced parsley

Saute bacon and onion in large kettle. Drain clams. Add clam liquor, potatoes, water and celery to onion and bacon. Cook until potatoes are tender, about 10 minutes. Just before serving, add clams, tomatoes and seasonings. Heat. Serve at once. Makes 6 servings.

Mrs. Donald J. Mitchell

MRS. DONALD J. MITCHELL, Wife of Representative (New York)

WHITE FISH CHOWDER

1 cup chopped celery
¼ cup chopped onion
½ stick butter
½ package frozen vegetables
1 pound white fish filets
   (grouper, flounder or cod)

1½ cups water
2 cans cream of mushroom soup
1 can mushrooms, stems and pieces
1 12 ounce can evaporated milk
1 cup sherry
salt

Saute onion and celery in butter until onion is clear. Add frozen vegetables, cover and steam about 4 minutes. Poach fish filets in water until tender. Drain, set fish aside and add liquid to the vegetables. Add soup, mushrooms with juice and milk. Heat slowly to a boil, add flaked fish and sherry. Salt sparingly. Makes 6 servings.

Mrs. Durward G. Hall

MRS. DURWARD G. HALL, Wife of former Representative (Missouri)

SEAFOOD GUMBO

⅔ cup plus 2 tablespoons flour
⅔ cup oil
1½ to 2 pounds okra, sliced
10 sprigs parsley, chopped
2 stalks celery, chopped
½ green pepper, chopped
1 large onion (or 1 bunch green
   onions), chopped
1 clove garlic, minced

¼ pound ham, small cubes (optional)
1 1 pound can tomatoes, cut up
2 quarts hot water
1 pound raw shrimp, peeled and
   deveined
1 pound can fresh crabmeat
oysters (optional)
cooked rice

Brown flour in oil. Add okra and parsley and simmer stirring often for about 1 hour. Add celery, green pepper, onion, garlic and ham, cooking until vegetables are transparent. Add tomatoes and simmer about 5 minutes. Slowly add hot water and simmer covered for 1 hour. Add shrimp last half hour. Add crabmeat and oysters last 15 minutes. Skim if necessary. Flavor is improved if it is made the day before it is to be served and then reheated. Serve in soup bowl over mound of cooked rice. Makes 10 servings.

Mrs. David C. Treen

MRS. DAVID C. TREEN, Wife of Representative (Louisiana)

CRAB SOUP

2 cans cream of celery soup
2 soup cans whole milk
1 pound crabmeat

salt and pepper
dash of mace
sherry to taste

Combine ingredients, adding sherry as desired. Heat and serve. Makes 6 to 8 servings.

Mrs David E. Satterfield III

MRS. DAVID E. SATTERFIELD III, Wife of Representative (Virginia)

CRAB BISQUE

1 can cream of tomato soup
1 can bouillon (or consomme)
1 can split pea soup
½ cup thick cream

½ cup sherry
1 pound crabmeat
toasted English muffins

Combine soups in saucepan on stove over moderate heat. Do not boil. Stir in cream, sherry and crabmeat. Heat gently. Serve with muffins. May be frozen. Makes 6 servings.

Mrs. Rufus C. Holman

MRS. RUFUS C. HOLMAN, Wife of former Senator (Oregon)

CRAB AND CORN SOUP

6 tomatoes
2 green peppers, chopped
2 carrots, chopped
1 large onion, chopped
2 tablespoons parsley
3 cups water

2 pounds crabmeat
12 ears corn, grated
2 quarts milk
salt and pepper
1 tablespoon Worcestershire sauce

Cook tomatoes, green peppers, carrots, onion and parsley in water until tender. Add remaining ingredients and heat through. May be frozen. Makes 6 servings.

Mrs. Goodloe E. Byron

MRS. GOODLOE BYRON, Wife of Representative (Maryland)

OYSTER STEW

2 dozen oysters (whole or chopped), reserve liquor
2 tablespoons butter
2 tablespoons flour
½ teaspoon salt
few grains cayenne pepper
4 cups milk
seasoning
whipped cream
minced parsley

Inspect the oysters and remove any bits of shell. Melt butter in a heavy bottomed saucepan; add flour, salt and cayenne gradually and stir until quite free of lumps. Add milk and oyster liquor a little at a time and stir until mixture boils. Add oysters; simmer for 5 minutes. If too thick, add more milk. Season to taste and serve in a heated tureen. When serving, top with whipped cream and parsley. Makes 4 to 5 servings.

Mrs. Marvin Mandel

MRS. MARVIN MANDEL, Wife of Governor (Maryland)

PINTO BEAN SOUP

6 slices bacon, diced
1 cup chopped onions
3 cups parboiled pinto beans
½ cup Minute rice
1 8 ounce can stewed tomatoes
4 cups water
salt and pepper to taste

Fry bacon. Remove bacon and fry onion in bacon fat. Mix bacon and onion with remaining ingredients and cook over slow heat at least 1 hour. May be frozen. Makes 6 servings.

Jaynie K. Miller

JAYNIE K. MILLER, Daughter of former Senator Jack R. Miller (Iowa)

52

CARROT SOUP WITH CORIANDER

¼ pound butter
1½ cups finely chopped onion
½ cup dry white wine (or dry sherry)
6 cups finely diced carrots
2 teaspoons ground coriander
2 cups chicken broth

2 cups milk (or cream)
salt to taste
freshly ground pepper to taste
1 cup toasted croutons
freshly chopped parsley

Melt butter in heavy saucepan and add onion. Cook, stirring often, until onion is golden brown. Add wine and carrots. Sprinkle with coriander and stir. Cover closely with a round of wax paper. Cook over very low heat about 1 hour, taking care that carrots do not stick or burn.

Add chicken broth and simmer 20 minutes. Add milk, salt and pepper. Bring to a boil and serve garnished with croutons and parsley. May be frozen. Makes 6 servings.

Alicia Grant

ALICIA GRANT, Daughter of former Representative George M. Grant (Alabama)

ONION SOUP

3 large onions, thinly sliced
3 tablespoons butter, melted
1 tablespoon flour
½ teaspoon salt
freshly ground black pepper to taste

5 cups beef broth (or canned consomme)
4 thick slices French bread
4 tablespoons grated parmesan cheese
4 tablespoons Swiss cheese (or gruyere)

Cook onions in butter until golden, cooking slowly and stirring occasionally. Sprinkle the flour over onions and stir for a few minutes. Add salt and pepper. Add broth, stirring constantly. Bring to a boil, lower heat and simmer, partially covered, for 30 minutes.

Toast bread in oven until brown and place in large ovenproof soup tureen. Sprinkle with parmesan cheese. Pour soup over toast and top with Swiss cheese. Brown cheese under the preheated broiler and serve immediately. Makes 4 servings.

Mrs. Richard White

MRS. RICHARD C. WHITE, Wife of Representative (Texas)

CELERY ROOT PUREE

1 pound celery root, peeled and diced	2 tablespoons butter
2 cups hot water	1 large Idaho potato, freshly boiled
juice of 1 lemon	1/4 teaspoon white pepper
	1 teaspoon salt

Cover celery root with hot water, add lemon juice and boil, covered, for 20 minutes. Drain. On high speed blend butter, gradually adding celery root, pieces of potato, white pepper and salt. Pour celery puree into top of double boiler and keep warm until serving time. Serve with Stuffed Duck Bordelaise. Makes 6 servings.

Mrs. Gerald R. Ford

MRS. GERALD R. FORD, Wife of President of the United States (Michigan)

MUSHROOM SOUP

2 pounds beef marrow bones	1 tablespoon salt
1 stalk celery, chopped	1/4 pound butter
1 medium onion, chopped	2 large yellow onions, sliced
2 bay leaves	1 pound mushrooms, sliced
3 quarts water	1/4 cup flour

In a large, heavy kettle, brown marrow bones slowly. When well browned, add celery, onion, bay leaves, water and salt. Bring to a boil, stir, reduce heat and simmer, uncovered, for 2 hours. Remove from heat and let cool. Remove bones and bay leaves. If marrow has not cooked out of bones, push it through gently into stock.

In another kettle melt butter and add yellow onions. Cook onions slowly until they are transparent. Add mushrooms and cook until tender. Add flour and stir with whisk until flour is blended with other ingredients and has colored slightly. Add beef stock, stirring until mixture comes to a boil. Reduce heat and simmer for 1 hour, uncovered. May be frozen. Makes 8 servings.

Mrs. Hamilton Fish, Jr.

MRS. HAMILTON FISH, JR., Wife of Representative (New York)

54

FRESH MUSHROOM SOUP

¾ pound fresh mushrooms
3 tablespoons butter
½ teaspoon caraway seeds
½ teaspoon paprika
1 tablespoon flour

4 cups chicken stock
1 egg yolk
1 cup sour cream
1 tablespoon chopped fresh dill

Wipe mushrooms with a damp cloth. (Do not immerse in water.) Slice and saute in butter with caraway seeds and paprika for 3 minutes over low heat. Sprinkle with flour, blend well, and gradually add chicken stock. Simmer, covered, for 30 minutes. Just before serving, whip egg yolk until creamy. Add sour cream and dill, mixing well. Spoon into a soup tureen and slowly pour hot soup over it, stirring with a whisk to mix thoroughly. Makes 6 servings.

Mrs. John H. Ware

MRS. JOHN H. WARE, Wife of former Representative (Pennsylvania)

HEARTY LENTIL SOUP

5 slices bacon, diced
1 cup chopped onion
1 cup diced carrots
1½ cups lentils
2 cups diced potatoes
1 small clove garlic
½ cup tomato paste
2 whole cloves

2 bay leaves
1 tablespoon salt
2 teaspoons Accent
pepper
6 cups water
4 cups beef broth
2 tablespoons red wine vinegar
2 cups sliced Smokey Links sausages

Cook bacon until browned; remove to soup kettle. Saute onions and carrots in bacon fat. Place all ingredients except vinegar and meat in kettle and simmer, stirring occasionally, for 1½ hours. Add vinegar and sausage and simmer an additional ½ hour. May be frozen. Makes 10 to 12 servings.

Mrs. Albert H. Quie

MRS. ALBERT H. QUIE, Wife of Representative (Minnesota)

LENTIL SOUP

1 package lentils
¼ pound bacon
2 medium onions, sliced
2 medium carrots, diced
2 quarts water
1 cup sliced celery
2½ to 3 teaspoons salt

½ teaspoon pepper
½ teaspoon dried thyme
2 bay leaves
1 large potato, pared and grated
1 ham bone (or 2 ham hocks)
2 tablespoons lemon juice

Wash lentils and soak overnight in cold water to cover. Next day, drain thoroughly. In a Dutch oven saute bacon until golden. Add onions and carrots and saute until onions are golden. Add lentils, water and remaining ingredients, except lemon juice. Cover and simmer 3 hours, stirring occasionally. Remove bay leaves and ham bone, cutting all bits of meat from the bone into the soup. Add lemon juice just before serving. If soup is to be refrigerated before serving, do not add lemon juice until soup is reheated. Makes 9½ cups.

Mrs. John F. Baldwin

MRS. JOHN F. BALDWIN, Wife of former Representative (California)

CHEDDAR CHEESE SOUP

4 tablespoons butter
1 medium size onion, finely chopped
1 medium carrot, finely chopped
1 medium stalk celery, finely chopped
1 small green pepper, finely chopped
4 tablespoons flour

4 cups chicken stock
1 pound aged cheddar cheese, grated
1 teaspoon dry mustard
⅛ teaspoon cayenne pepper
⅓ cup heavy cream
salt

Melt butter over moderate heat, being careful not to brown it, and add chopped vegetables. Stir frequently and cook until they are quite soft but not brown, about 10 minutes. Add flour and stir until completely absorbed. Pour in chicken stock. Bring soup to a boil over high heat, stirring constantly with a wire whisk. When it has thickened somewhat, reduce heat and simmer with the pan partially covered for about 30 minutes.

Strain the entire mixture through a fine sieve, pressing down hard on the vegetables with the back of a spoon before discarding them. Return strained soup to the pan and bring to a simmer over moderate heat. Add cheese gradually, stirring constantly until cheese has completely melted. Add mustard and cayenne. Stir in cream. If you prefer the soup thinner, add a little more cream. Taste for seasoning and, if desired, add additional mustard or cayenne. Serve at once. Makes 4 to 6 servings.

Alicia Grant

ALICIA GRANT, Daughter of former Representative George M. Grant (Alabama)

FAVORITE PEANUT SOUP

½ stick butter
1 tablespoon diced onion
1 stalk celery with leaves, diced
2 tablespoons flour
1 quart hot chicken broth

1 cup peanut butter
dash celery salt
½ teaspoon salt
2 teaspoons lemon juice
¼ cup ground peanuts

Melt butter in cooking vessel and add onion and celery. Saute for 5 minutes but do not brown. Add flour and mix well. Add chicken broth and cook for 30 minutes over very low heat. Remove from heat, strain and add peanut butter, celery salt, salt and lemon juice, mixing well. Blend thoroughly and reheat but do not boil. Sprinkle ground peanuts on soup just before serving. Makes 4 servings.

Mrs. David E. Satterfield III

MRS. DAVID E. SATTERFIELD III, Wife of Representative (Virginia)

PEANUT SOUP

¼ pound butter
1 cup chopped peanuts
1 cup chopped carrots
½ cup chopped celery
¼ cup chopped green onion

1 clove garlic, crushed
¼ cup flour
2 13 ounce cans chicken broth
1 cup milk
chopped parsley

Melt butter in saucepan over medium heat. Add peanuts, carrots, celery, onion and garlic and saute until vegetables are tender. Blend in flour. Gradually stir in broth and simmer 15 minutes. Stir in milk and heat to serving temperature. Garnish with parsley. Makes 6 servings.

Mrs. Carroll D. Kearns

MRS. CARROLL D. KEARNS, Wife of former Representative (Pennsylvania)

BROCCOLI OR SPINACH SOUP

½ pint milk
¾ pint light cream
2 tablespoons flour
2 tablespoons butter
1 teaspoon salt

¾ cup cooked broccoli or spinach
1 pinch pepper
4 sprays of parsley
1 cup celery leaves
1 thin slice of onion

Place the above in a blender in the order given. When well blended, heat in a double boiler, stirring occasionally. May be served iced or heated. May be frozen. Makes 3 cups.

Mrs. William E. Simon

MRS. WILLIAM E. SIMON, Wife of Secretary of the Treasury (Virginia)

CREAM OF CUCUMBER SOUP (HOT OR COLD)

1 pint milk
2 cups raw, sliced cucumbers
  (unpeeled)
1½ tablespoons flour
2 tablespoons butter

1 teaspoon salt
$\frac{1}{16}$ teaspoon pepper
1 thin slice of onion
1 dash savory (optional)
2 sprigs parsley

Place all ingredients except parsley in blender and run until well blended, 1 to 3 minutes. Heat on stove until starting to boil. Strain and serve. If served iced in hot weather, add sprigs of parsley and piece of ice to soup bowl. Makes 6 to 8 servings.

Mrs. Edwin Fuller Parham

MRS. EDWIN FULLER PARHAM, Daughter of former Representative Edward William Pou (North Carolina)

ASPARAGUS CHILLER

1 10½ ounce can cream of asparagus
  soup
½ cup yogurt

1 soup can water
½ cup chopped cucumber
1 tablespoon chopped red onion

Blend soup and yogurt; gradually stir in water. Add cucumber and onion. Chill 4 hours or more. Makes 2 to 3 servings.

Mrs. Robert N. Giaimo

MRS. ROBERT N. GIAIMO, Wife of Representative (Connecticut)

CURRY AVOCADO SOUP

1 tablespoon butter or margarine
¼ to ½ teaspoon curry
2 cups water
1 package chicken noodle soup mix

1 avocado, peeled and halved
½ cup milk
1 cup light cream

Melt butter, stir in curry powder and cook over low heat for 3 minutes. Stir in water and soup mix and after bringing to a boil, cook, covered, for 7 minutes.

Into glass container of blender pour just enough hot soup to conceal blades. Blend briefly. Add remainder of soup and blend until smooth. Add ½ avocado and blend ½ minute. Stir in milk and cream. Slice remaining avocado and add to soup. Refrigerate. Makes 6 servings.

Mrs. Henry P. Smith

MRS. HENRY P. SMITH III, Wife of former Representative (New York)

COLD AVOCADO SOUP

1 can frozen potato soup, thawed
1 cup Half and Half
1 avocado, peeled and halved
1 teaspoon chopped onion

1 tablespoon Spice Island chicken stock
1 teaspoon lemon juice
salt and pepper to taste

Place all ingredients in blender and blend well. May be frozen. Makes 4 servings.

Mrs. James M. Collins

MRS. JAMES M. COLLINS, Wife of Representative (Texas)

AVOCADO SOUP

3 large avocados, peeled and seeded
1 can clear chicken broth
1 tablespoon lemon juice
1½ cups water

pepper
¾ teaspoon salt
½ cup light cream
3 bacon slices, cooked and crumbled

Place first six ingredients in blender, blend until smooth. Chill about 2 hours. Just before serving, stir in cream. Top each serving with crumbled bacon. Makes 6 servings.

Mrs. Tazewell Shepard, Jr.

MRS. TAZEWELL SHEPARD, JR., Daughter of Senator John Sparkman (Alabama)

AVOCADO AND COLD CONSOMME

2 avocados, peeled
lettuce
1 can jellied beef consomme

4 tablespoons dairy sour cream
1 4 ounce jar red caviar

Cut avocados in half, remove seed and place on bed of crisp lettuce. Fill with jellied consomme. Put sour cream on top of consomme and top with caviar. Makes

Mrs. Dean P. Taylor

MRS. DEAN P. TAYLOR, Wife of former Representative (New York)

BORSCH

1 can consomme or bouillon
1 48 ounce can V8 juice
1 20 ounce can sliced beets and juice

½ pint sour cream (cottage cheese or yogurt)
1 hard cooked egg, grated (optional)

Mix first 4 ingredients in an electric blender. Serve very cold. Some of the cream may be reserved for garnish or the grated egg may be used. This recipe is best made with sour cream but for the diet conscious, cottage cheese or yogurt may be used. Makes 10 servings.

Mrs. Wallace F. Bennett

MRS. WALLACE F. BENNETT, Wife of former Senator (Utah)

CUCUMBER SUMMER SOUP

1 10 ounce can tomato soup
1 soup can evaporated milk
1 cup beet juice
1 peeled cucumber, chopped
1 green pepper, chopped
few drops of Tabasco
1 tablespoon sugar

salt and pepper to taste
4 tablespoons tarragon vinegar
1 teaspoon Accent

Garnish:
sour cream
chives (or dill sprig)

Using half of each ingredient listed, blend tomato soup, milk and beet juice for 1 minute. Add cucumber and green pepper gradually. Add seasonings and blend until liquid. Repeat with remaining ingredients. Chill in refrigerator for a few hours or overnight. Serve in chilled soup dishes, garnished with sour cream and chives. Makes 6 servings.

Mrs. Hugo L. Black

MRS. HUGO L. BLACK, Wife of former Associate Justice, Supreme Court (Alabama)

GAZPACHO (COLD SPANISH VEGETABLE SOUP)

1 clove garlic
1 tablespoon sugar
½ teaspoon salt
1 46 ounce can tomato juice
½ cup oil
¼ cup vinegar
2 tablespoons lemon juice

1 tablespoon Worcestershire sauce
2 cups diced tomatoes
1 cucumber, chopped
1 green pepper, diced
1 cup chopped celery
½ cup sliced onions
croutons

Mash garlic; combine with the sugar and salt. Add the tomato juice, oil, vinegar, lemon juice and Worcestershire sauce. Put part of this in blender. Add some of the chopped vegetables gradually and pulverize. Remove from blender and repeat with remaining ingredients until all the chopped vegetables have been blended. Chill soup at least 1 hour before serving. Serve with croutons on top. This soup will keep at least a week in the refrigerator. Makes 12 servings.

Mrs. Robert McClory

MRS. ROBERT MCCLORY, Wife of Representative (Illinois)

ARIZONA GAZPACHO

2 green peppers
2 sweet red peppers
2 medium size onions
3¼ pounds ripe tomatoes, quartered
(or 2 14 ounce cans pear shaped
tomatoes)

2 cucumbers, cut in chunks
⅔ cup red wine vinegar
⅛ teaspoon Tabasco
garlic powder to taste
1 48 ounce can tomato juice
salt to taste

Finely dice 1 green pepper, 1 red pepper, 1 onion. Set aside. Cut remaining peppers and onion in chunks, combine with remaining ingredients in blender and blend only until top ingredients have reached blades. Chill well before serving. Garnish individual servings with reserved diced peppers and onions. Makes 10 servings.

Mrs. John B. Conlan

MRS. JOHN B. CONLAN, Wife of Representative (Arizona)

CHILLED GARDEN SOUP

1 teaspoon salt
1 pint chicken broth (or bouillon)
1 medium potato, peeled and diced
1 medium cucumber, chopped
1 medium onion, chopped
1 large stalk celery with leaves,
chopped

1 tart apple, peeled and diced
1 cup light cream
1 tablespoon butter
1 teaspoon curry powder
freshly ground pepper
chives (or parsley), chopped

Add salt to boiling broth and add vegetables and apple. Simmer until tender. Put through food mill or mix in blender until smooth. Stir in cream, butter, curry powder and pepper. Chill thoroughly. Garnish with chives. Makes 6 servings.

Mrs. Herman T. Schneebeli

MRS. HERMAN T. SCHNEEBELI, Wife of Representative (Pennsylvania)

62

VICHYSSOISE

2½ cups diced potatoes
3 medium onions, diced
2 stalks celery with leaves
1½ cups chicken stock
1½ cups milk

1½ cups light cream
⅛ teaspoon white pepper
salt to taste
chopped chives

Boil potatoes, onions and celery until tender. Drain. Put through coarse strainer or mix in blender. Heat stock, milk, cream and seasonings in top of double boiler. Add potato mixture and heat 10 to 15 minutes to blend flavors, but do not boil. Chill thoroughly. Garnish with chopped chives. Makes 8 servings.

Mrs. Wiley Mayne

MRS. WILEY MAYNE, Wife of former Representative (Iowa)

CARROT VICHYSSOISE

2 cups peeled, diced potatoes
1¼ cups peeled, sliced carrots
1 tablespoon chopped onion
3 cups canned chicken broth

white pepper and salt to taste
1 cup dairy sour cream
1 heaping teaspoon chopped chives
parsley

Simmer potatoes and carrots with onion in chicken broth until tender. Season with salt and pepper. Cool, puree in blender and chill thoroughly in refrigerator. Approximately 1 hour before serving, add chives to sour cream and fold into chilled puree. Serve with parsely topping. Makes 4 to 6 servings.

Mrs George M. O'Brien

MRS. GEORGE M. O'BRIEN, Wife of Representative (Illinois)

SENEGALESE

2 medium onions, chopped	2 apples, chopped
3 stalks celery, chopped	8 cups chicken stock, strained
4 tablespoons butter (or chicken fat)	1 bay leaf, ground
1 tablespoon curry	1 cup light cream
2 tablespoons flour	1 cup chopped cooked chicken

Saute onions and celery in butter until wilted. Add curry directly to fat and cook 5 minutes. Add flour, then apples, stock and bay leaf and simmer ½ hour. Cool. Add cream. Garnish with chicken. May be frozen. Makes 10 servings.

Mrs. Robert H. Mollohan

MRS. ROBERT H. MOLLOHAN, Wife of Representative (West Virginia)

MARCIA'S SENEGALESE SOUP

1 can cream of celery soup	2 cups chicken broth
2 cans cream of chicken soup	3 teaspoons curry powder
1 cup light cream	apples, cubed

Combine all ingredients, except apples, in blender. Blend at moderate speed until smooth. Taste for seasoning and add additional curry if desired. Chill in refrigerator. At serving time, garnish each soup bowl with unpeeled apple cubes. Makes 8 servings.

Mrs. Thomas E. Cole

MRS. THOMAS E. COLE, Daughter-in-law of former Representative W. Sterling Cole (New York)

TOMATO CLAM SOUP

1 can condensed tomato soup	¼ teaspoon salt
1 cup buttermilk	1 8 ounce can minced clams
1 teaspoon Worcestershire sauce	sprigs of parsley

Beat tomato soup with buttermilk, Worcestershire sauce and salt until smooth. Stir in clams and liquid; cover. Chill several hours or overnight. Garnish with parsley. Makes 4 servings.

Mrs. Robert N. Giaimo

MRS. ROBERT N. GIAIMO, Wife of Representative (Connecticut)

VEGETABLE SANDWICH

2 ripe tomatoes, chopped
1 cucumber, finely chopped
1 cup celery, finely chopped
1 green pepper, finely chopped
1 onion, finely chopped

1 envelope plain gelatin
¼ cup vegetable juice
salt to taste
2 cups mayonnaise
bread

Drain vegetables. Soak gelatin in vegetable juice and dissolve over warm water. Add this to vegetables. Add salt and fold in mayonnaise. Refrigerate overnight. Spread on bread when ready to serve. Makes 25 sandwiches.

Mrs. David N. Henderson

MRS. DAVID N. HENDERSON, Wife of Representative (North Carolina)

REUBEN SANDWICH

1 12 ounce can corned beef, shredded
⅓ cup chopped green pepper
2 tablespoons catsup
1 teaspoon horse radish
1 8 ounce can sauerkraut, well drained

½ teaspoon caraway seeds
4 slices Swiss cheese (or 1 cup shredded)
4 large hard rolls, split (or 8 slices pumpernickel bread)

Combine corned beef, green pepper, catsup and horse radish and mix thoroughly. Spoon onto 1 side of each roll. Cover with sauerkraut and sprinkle with caraway seeds. Top with cheese and place top half of roll on each sandwich. Makes 4 sandwiches.

Mrs. Jack R. Miller

MRS. JACK R. MILLER, Wife of former Senator (Iowa)

OPEN HAMBURGER SANDWICHES

1 pound hamburger (or ground round)
salt
pepper

5 slices of bread
butter or margarine
prepared mustard

Mix chopped meat with salt and pepper. Toast one side of bread under broiler. When brown, spread untoasted side with butter and mustard. Then spread with the chopped beef. Broil for 5 minutes or until done. Serve immediately. Makes 5 servings.

Mrs. Clarence D. Long

MRS. CLARENCE D. LONG, Wife of Representative (Maryland)

HOT PORK SANDWICHES

4 pounds pork tenderloin, baked
2 cups cracker crumbs
4 eggs, beaten
½ cup prepared mustard

1 cup diced celery
salt and pepper
buns

Grind or shred the pork. Add crumbs, eggs, mustard, celery, salt and pepper, mixing well. Bake at 300° for 1½ hours. Serve on buns. May be frozen. Makes 50 servings.

Mrs. John E. Henderson

MRS. JOHN E. HENDERSON, Wife of former Representative (Ohio)

SOUFFLES, EGG & CHEESE DISHES

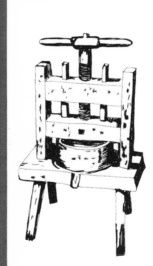

Eggs in Ragou

Boil twelve eggs hard, take off the shells, and with a little knife very carfully cut the whites across longways, so that the whites may be in two and the yolks whole, and be careful neither to break the whites nor the yolks; chop a gill of pickled mushrooms very fine, half an ounce of truffles and morels boiled in three or four spoonfuls of water, save the water, wash the truffles and morels, chop them fine, boil a little parsley and chop it fine, mix all these together with the truffle water you saved, grate in a little nutmeg, beaten mace, pepper and salt, put it into a stew pan, with a gill of water or gravy, a gill of red wine, a spoonful of ketchup, a little butter mixed with flour, stir altogether, and it boil up; fry a good quantity of crumbs of bread, lay the eggs in order in the dish, the hollow side of the whites uppermost, that they may be filled; then fill them with the fried crumbs of bread as high as they will lay, pour the sauce all over them, and garnish with fried crumbs of bread.

The New Art of Cookery
Richard Briggs, 1792

CHEESE SOUFFLE WITH MUSHROOM SAUCE

8 slices bread
butter
½ pound sharp cheese, grated
3 eggs, beaten
1¼ cups milk

Mushroom sauce:
1 bouillon cube
½ cup hot water
1 can mushroom soup
1 can whole mushrooms
1 cup dairy sour cream
¼ cup cream

Remove crusts from bread. Butter both sides and cut into cubes. Arrange bread and cheese in layers in a casserole. Mix egg and milk together and pour over all. Refrigerate overnight. Remove from refrigerator 1 hour before baking and then bake at 325° for 1 hour or until firm.

Dissolve bouillon cube in hot water and combine with other sauce ingredients. Heat. Serve sauce with the souffle. Makes 8 servings.

MRS. CHALMERS P. WYLIE, Wife of Representative (Ohio)

BREAKFAST CASSEROLE

very thin bread slices
½ pound mushrooms
butter
¾ pound shaved ham
8 ounces mild cheddar cheese, shredded

6 eggs
3 cups milk
½ teaspoon salt
½ teaspoon dry mustard
bread crumbs

Put single layer of bread slices on bottom of buttered 13 x 9 inch pan. Saute mushrooms in butter and alternate layers of ham, mushrooms and cheese. Cover with bread slices. Beat eggs, milk, salt and mustard. Pour egg mixture over casserole, sprinkle with bread crumbs and dot with butter. Refrigerate overnight. Bake in 350° oven 1 hour and 20 minutes. Makes 12 servings.

MRS. ROBERT A. GRANT, Wife of former Representative (Indiana)

EGG STRATA

6 thin slices bread, crusts removed
butter
3 slices American cheese
(or Old English)

4 eggs, beaten
3 cups milk
1 teaspoon dry mustard
salt to taste

Place 3 bread slices in single layer in well buttered shallow casserole. Cover with cheese slices. Top with remaining bread buttered on top. Combine eggs, milk, mustard and salt and pour over sandwiches. Refrigerate overnight. Place casserole in pan of water and bake at 350° for 1 hour. Makes 3 servings.

Mrs. Alvin E. O'Konski

MRS. ALVIN E. O'KONSKI, Wife of former Representative (Wisconsin)

CHEESE FONDUE SOUFFLE

8 slices stale bread
1½ pounds cheddar cheese, grated
1 rounded teaspoon brown sugar
¼ teaspoon paprika
½ teaspoon dry mustard
½ teaspoon Beau Monde seasoning
½ teaspoon salt

⅛ teaspoon Java cracked pepper
⅛ teaspoon cayenne pepper
2½ cups milk (more or less)
6 eggs, slightly beaten
½ teaspoon Worcestershire sauce
1 green onion (or shallot), finely minced

Use bread of medium thickness, cut off crusts and dice into ¼ inch cubes. Arrange ½ the bread cubes on the bottom of a buttered, flat casserole. Cover with a generous layer of grated cheese. Repeat both layers. Mix the next 7 ingredients, moisten with a little milk and combine with eggs, remaining milk, Worcestershire and onion. Pour over cheese dish. Add a little more milk if more liquid is necessary to just barely cover the edges. Cover and chill 24 hours. Remove from refrigerator 3 hours before serving time. Let stand a little over 1 hour at room temperature. Set in a pan of cold water and bake at 325° for 1¼ to 1½ hours or longer for a brown and crusty surface. Serve at once. Makes 8 servings.

Mrs. Byron R. White

MRS. BYRON R. WHITE, Wife of Associate Justice, Supreme Court (Colorado)

70

FOOL PROOF SWISS CHEESE SOUFFLE

4 tablespoons butter	½ teaspoon mustard
6 slices white bread	1 teaspoon salt
½ pound grated Swiss cheese	½ teaspoon paprika
6 eggs	½ cup grated sharp cheese
2 cups milk	

Trim crust from edges of bread. Butter the bread and cut into cubes. Layer the bread cubes and Swiss cheese alternately in baking dish. This may be prepared and refrigerated until it is to be baked. Beat eggs, add milk, mustard, salt and paprika. Pour over bread and cheese. Sprinkle grated sharp cheese over the top. Bake 1 hour at 325°. Makes 6 to 8 servings.

Mrs. Edwin Fuller Parham

MRS. EDWIN FULLER PARHAM, Daughter of former Representative Edward William Pou (North Carolina)

HIGH HAT CHEESE SOUFFLE

¼ cup butter or margarine	½ pound sharp American cheese,
¼ cup flour	thinly sliced
½ teaspoon salt	4 egg yolks
dash cayenne	4 egg whites, stiffly beaten
1 cup milk	

Melt butter and blend in flour, salt and cayenne. Add milk and cook quickly, stirring constantly, until mixture thickens and bubbles. Add cheese and stir until cheese melts. Remove from heat. Beat egg yolks until thick and lemon colored. Slowly add cheese mixture to egg yolks, stirring constantly. Cool slightly and then pour slowly into egg whites, folding together thoroughly.

Pour mixture into an ungreased 1½ quart souffle dish or casserole. For a top hat, which will puff up in the oven, trace a circle through mixture 1 inch from the edge and 1 inch deep. Bake at 300° for 1¼ hours or until knife comes out clean.

Mrs. Ralph S. Regula

MRS. RALPH REGULA, Wife of Representative (Ohio)

FABULOUS CHEESE SOUFFLE

1 tablespoon parmesan cheese	1¼ cups milk
5 tablespoons butter or margarine	6 eggs, separated
6 tablespoons flour	½ cup parmesan cheese
1½ teaspoons salt	½ cup coarsely grated Swiss cheese
dash of cayenne	¼ teaspoon cream of tartar

Butter a 1½ quart souffle dish and dust lightly with the tablespoon of parmesan cheese. Fold a sheet of waxed paper, 26 inches long, lengthwise into thirds. Lightly butter one side of paper. Wrap it around souffle dish, buttered side against dish and a 2 inch rim extending above the top edge of dish. Tie with a string.

Melt butter in saucepan and remove from heat. Stir in flour, 1 teaspoon salt and cayenne until smooth. Gradually stir in milk. Stir over heat until it boils. Reduce heat and simmer, stirring constantly, until mixture becomes very thick and begins to leave bottom and sides of pan. Beat yolks with wire whisk and gradually beat into cooked mixture. Add parmesan and Swiss cheeses, beating until well blended.

With egg whites at room temperature, add remaining salt and cream of tartar. Beat at high speed until stiff peaks form. Fold ⅓ of egg whites into warm cheese mixture until well blended. Carefully fold in remaining egg whites until just blended. Turn into prepared dish. At this point, the souffle may be kept in refrigerator for up to 4 hours.

Bake in a preheated 350° oven for 40 minutes or until souffle is puffed and golden brown. Increase baking time 12 to 15 minutes if it was refrigerated. Remove collar from souffle and serve immediately. Makes 4 to 6 servings.

Mrs. Bill Burlison

MRS. BILL BURLISON, Wife of Representative (Missouri)

CHEESE SOUFFLE

2 teaspoons butter, melted	1 cup grated cheddar cheese
3 teaspoons flour	5 eggs, separated
2 cups milk	1 teaspoon salt

Combine melted butter with flour over medium heat. Add milk gradually, stirring constantly. Add cheese and cook until creamy. Cool. Add beaten egg yolks and mix well. Beat egg whites on high speed for 5 minutes and fold into cooled mixture. Pour into buttered casserole, set in a pan of water and bake in a 350° oven for 1 hour. Makes 8 servings.

Mrs Homer Ferguson

MRS. HOMER FERGUSON, Wife of former Senator (Michigan)

SUNDAY MORNING SOUFFLE

10 slices white bread
butter
½ pound medium sharp cheddar
cheese, grated

3 eggs, beaten until light
2 cups milk
1 teaspoon salt

Cut crusts off bread and spread slices of bread with butter. Cut in cubes. Alternate layers of buttered bread cubes and grated cheese in pyrex or souffle dish. Mix together eggs, milk and salt. Pour mixture over bread and cheese. Cover and refrigerate 12 hours. Remove from refrigerator and let stand until room temperature is reached. Bake at 275° for 45 minutes. Serve at once. Makes 8 servings.

Mrs. James R. Mann

MRS. JAMES R. MANN, Wife of Representative (South Carolina)

IMITATION OMELETTE DISH

10 slices bread, crusts removed and
cut in fourths
butter
1 pound extra sharp cheddar cheese,
grated
3 eggs, beaten

2½ cups milk, scalded
1 teaspoon salt
1 teaspoon dry mustard
1 teaspoon Worcestershire sauce
paprika
parsley

Dot bread with butter. Line bottom of large, greased baking dish with half the bread. Add layer of half the cheese. Repeat. Add eggs to milk. Stir in salt, mustard and Worcestershire sauce. Pour mixture over bread and cheese. Let stand 6 hours or overnight. Bake at 325° for 1 hour. Top with paprika and garnish with parsley. Makes 10 servings.

Mrs. John C. Stennis

MRS. JOHN C. STENNIS, Wife of Senator (Mississippi)

EGG CASSEROLE

½ cup chopped onion
2 tablespoons butter
2 tablespoons flour
1¼ cups sweet milk
salt
pepper

cayenne
Worcestershire sauce
1 cup shredded sharp cheese
6 hard cooked eggs, halved lengthwise
1½ cups crushed potato chips
10 to 12 slices fried bacon, crumbled

Cook onion in butter until tender, not brown. Blend in flour. Add milk and seasonings, stirring well. Add cheese and stir until blended. Layer egg slices in pan, cut side up. Cover with cheese sauce and top with potato chips and bacon crumbs. Bake in 350° oven 30 minutes. Makes 4 servings.

Mrs. Tim Lee Carter

MRS. TIM LEE CARTER, Wife of Representative (Kentucky)

CURRIED EGG CASSEROLE

1½ small onions, chopped
butter
18 hard cooked eggs, sliced
2 cans mushroom soup

¾ teaspoon curry powder
1½ teaspoons Worcestershire sauce
1 can sliced mushrooms, drained

Saute onions in butter until tender. Combine with remaining ingredients and mix well. Bake in greased casserole at 350° for 30 minutes. Makes 12 servings.

Mrs. John L. McMillan, Jr.

MRS. JOHN L. MCMILLAN, Wife of former Representative (South Carolina)

74

EGGS FLAMENCO

3 large potatoes, peeled
3 tablespoons butter
small ring Kielbasa (or smoked
    sausage), thinly sliced
salt
1 large tomato, thinly sliced

6 eggs
salt and pepper to taste
4 tablespoons light cream
chopped parsley
chopped chives

Cover potatoes with cold water and bring to a boil. Drain, cool and cube. Place in iron skillet with butter and sliced sausage. Add salt and cook, stirring occasionally, over moderate heat about 10 minutes. Transfer to a shallow earthernware casserole. Top with tomato slices and break eggs in spaces between slices. Season and pour cream over top. Sprinkle with parsley and chives and bake at 350° until eggs are set. Serve immediately. Makes 6 servings.

Mrs. Frank E. Evans

Mrs. Frank E. Evans, Wife of Representative (Colorado)

SUNDAY BRUNCH

6 slices Canadian bacon
1 pound grated cheddar cheese
6 eggs

1 pint sour cream
milk

Put Canadian bacon in bottom of baking pan. Build a nest around each piece of bacon with cheese. Crack eggs into nests. Dilute sour cream with a small amount of milk. Pour over eggs. Bake slowly at 350° until set, about 50 minutes. Makes 6 servings.

Mrs. Marvin Esch

Mrs. Marvin L. Esch, Wife of Representative (Michigan)

EGGS CECILE

6 slices Virginia ham
12 thin slices Swiss cheese
6 eggs

salt and pepper to taste
1 8 ounce carton sour cream
paprika

Place Virginia ham over bottom of a lightly buttered shallow baking dish or in 6 individual dishes. Top each ham slice with 2 slices of the cheese. Break whole eggs into the dish so that each one covers a ham cheese layer. Lightly salt and pepper the eggs. Spread sour cream completely over top, taking care not to break egg yolks. Sprinkle with paprika. Bake in preheated 400° oven for approximately 20 minutes. Serve immediately.

Mrs. Paul J. Kilday

MRS. PAUL KILDAY, Wife of former Representative (Texas)

SCALLOPED BACON AND EGGS

¼ cup chopped onion
2 tablespoons butter
2 tablespoons flour
1½ cups milk
1 cup shredded sharp American cheese

6 hard cooked eggs, sliced
1½ cups potato chips, crumbled
10 to 12 slices crisp bacon,
   crumbled

Cook onion in butter, blend in flour. Add milk and stir until thickened. Add cheese; stir until melted. In a 10 x 6 x 1½ inch baking dish, make two layers of egg slices, cheese sauce, potato chips and bacon in that order. Bake at 350° for 20 to 30 minutes. Do not overbake. May be prepared and refrigerated prior to baking.

Mrs Walt Horan

MRS. WALT HORAN, Wife of former Representative (Washington)

76

EGGS WITH ZUCCHINI

1 medium zucchini, unpeeled
2 tablespoons butter
2 tablespoons chopped onion
2 tablespoons chopped green pepper
(optional)

1 peeled tomato, sliced
6 eggs
6 scant tablespoons water
salt and pepper

Chop zucchini and saute in butter with onion, green pepper and tomatoes. Beat eggs, add water, salt and pepper and pour over vegetable mixture. Scramble as usual. The water makes the eggs lighter and fluffier.

Mrs. Milton R. Young

Mrs. Milton R. Young, Wife of Senator (North Dakota)

DANDY DEVILED EGGS

hard cooked eggs
croutons, crushed
butter
mayonnaise

prepared mustard
salt and pepper to taste
dill or chives

Cut eggs lengthwise and gently remove yolks. Saute crouton crumbs in butter. Add to a mixture of egg yolks, mayonnaise, mustard, salt and pepper. Stuff egg whites. Do not prepare too far in advance of serving so that the croutons will remain crunchy. Garnish with dill or chives.

Mrs. E. Ross Adair

Mrs. E. Ross Adair, Wife of former Representative (Indiana)

BAKED DEVILED EGGS

12 hard cooked eggs
1½ tablespoons lemon juice
    (or vinegar)
2 teaspoons prepared mustard
1 teaspoon Worcestershire sauce
1 teaspoon salt
¼ teaspoon pepper

½ cup mayonnaise
1 pound crabmeat
1 8 ounce can button mushrooms, drained
2 cups rich cream sauce
curry to taste

Cut eggs in half lengthwise. Press yolks through sieve and combine with lemon juice, mustard, Worcestershire, salt, pepper and mayonnaise. Beat until smooth. Adjust seasonings and refill egg whites. Place in flat baking dish. Spread crab and mushrooms over all the eggs. Flavor cream sauce with curry, pour over casserole and bake at 350° for 30 minutes or until hot and bubbly. Makes 6 to 8 servings.

Mrs. Omar Burleson

MRS. OMAR BURLESON, Wife of Representative (Texas)

CHEESE DISH

4 slices bread, buttered and cubed
1 cup cheese, cubed (or grated)
2 cups milk

2 eggs, beaten
½ teaspoon salt
1 teaspoon mustard

Combine all ingredients, put in casserole and let stand for ½ hour. Bake at 400° for 45 minutes. Makes 2 servings.

Mrs. David E. Satterfield III

MRS. DAVID E. SATTERFIELD III, Wife of Representative (Virginia)

CHEESE CASSEROLE

18 to 20 single saltine crackers, crumbled
1 cup grated cheese

3 eggs
1 stick butter or margarine, melted
2 cups milk

Put cracker crumbs in bottom of a well greased 2 quart casserole and cover with cheese. Mix eggs, butter and milk and pour over cracker cheese mixture. Let stand in refrigerator at least 30 minutes. Bake at 400° until set, approximately 20 to 30 minutes. This is good rewarmed. Makes 6 to 8 servings.

Mrs. Roy A. Taylor

MRS. ROY A. TAYLOR, Wife of Representative (North Carolina)

CHEESE AND GRITS CASSEROLE

2 cups quick cooking grits
1 tablespoon salt
8 cups boiling water
½ pound margarine
1 roll snappy cheese

garlic powder to taste
1 teaspoon Tabasco sauce
2 teaspoons Worcestershire sauce
2 eggs

Add grits and salt to boiling water. Cook 5 minutes. Add margarine and cheese and stir until melted. Add a little garlic powder, Tabasco and Worcestershire to unbeaten eggs, mix well. Combine all ingredients and put in buttered casserole. Bake in preheated 350° oven for 1 hour. This may be prepared and refrigerated or frozen and then baked when desired. Makes 16 servings.

Mrs John Currie Mackie

MRS. JOHN CURRIE MACKIE, Wife of former Representative (Michigan)

MAUD'S MACARONI

8 ounces spaghetti (Maud's
   "macaroni")
salt and pepper
2 cups diced sharp cheese

butter
1 egg, beaten
2 cups milk

Cook spaghetti according to package directions. Drain. Put half in buttered baking dish. Sprinkle with salt and pepper and 1 cup of cheese. Dot with butter. Repeat with remaining spaghetti and cheese. Add egg to milk and pour over ingredients. Additional milk may be needed to cover completely. Bake at 325° about 1 hour or until slightly browned. Do not overcook or cheese will toughen. May be frozen. Makes 8 servings.

Mrs. Tom S. Gettys

MRS. TOM S. GETTYS, Wife of former Representative (South Carolina)

BAKED CHILIES RELLENOS

2 small cans green chilies
2 eggs, beaten
½ cup flour

¼ teaspoon baking powder
1 cup grated sharp cheddar cheese
½ cup milk

Line bottom of greased 8 inch pan with chilies. In bowl mix eggs, flour, baking powder, cheese and milk. Spread mixture over chilies. Bake at 325° for 25 minutes. Makes 6 to 8 servings.

Mrs. Robert Lagomarsino

MRS. ROBERT J. LAGOMARSINO, Wife of Representative (California)

QUICK MEXICAN CASSEROLE

1 6 ounce package Fritos
1 15 ounce can chili and beans
1 15 ounce can enchilada sauce
1 8 ounce can tomato sauce

1 tablespoon instant onion
½ pound grated cheese
1 8 ounce carton sour cream

Mix all ingredients together except sour cream and a little of the cheese. Bake 30 minutes at 350°. Remove from oven and spread sour cream over top. Sprinkle with remaining cheese and return to oven for 10 minutes. Makes 6 to 8 servings.

Elizabeth C. Rhodes

ELIZABETH C. RHODES, Daughter of Representative John J. Rhodes (Arizona)

COTTAGE CHEESE DUMPLINGS

1 pound dry cottage cheese	1 teaspoon salt
4 eggs, beaten	½ cup bread crumbs
8 heaping tablespoons flour	4 tablespoons melted butter

Force cheese through ricer or strainer. Add eggs, flour and salt and mix well until smooth. Form into balls. Drop into 2 quarts boiling water and cook for 15 minutes. Drain. Roll cheese balls in bread crumbs which have been slightly browned in butter. Makes 6 servings.

Mrs. Joe Skubitz

MRS. JOE SKUBITZ, Wife of Representative (Kansas)

NOTES

VEGETABLES

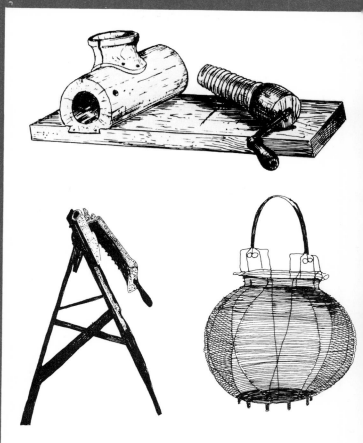

To boil all Kinds of GARDEN STUFF

In dressing all sorts of kitchen garden herbs, take care that they are clean washed: that there be no small snails, or caterpillars between the leaves; and that all the coarse outer leaves, and those that have received any injury by the weather, be taken off. Next wash them in a good deal of water, and put them into a culendar to drain. Care must likewise be taken, that your pot or sauce-pan be clean, well tinned, and free from sand or grease.

The Frugal Housewife or Complete Woman Cook
Susannah Carter, 1795

SUNDAY ARTICHOKES

½ cup butter or margarine
2 cups sliced fresh mushrooms
1 teaspoon salt
1 teaspoon crushed sweet basil
½ teaspoon crushed oregano
¼ teaspoon garlic powder

1 tablespoon fine dry bread crumbs
2 tablespoons fresh lemon juice
2 8 ounce packages frozen artichoke
    hearts, thawed (or 2 cans artichoke
    hearts)
½ cup parmesan cheese

Melt butter in a large, heavy skillet. Saute mushrooms until golden. Sprinkle with salt, basil, oregano and garlic powder during cooking. Stir in bread crumbs and lemon juice, mixing well. Arrange artichoke hearts in a lightly buttered shallow glass baking pan. Spoon mushroom mixture over artichokes. Sprinkle cheese over all. Bake at 350° for 25 to 30 minutes until juices bubble and cheese is browned. Makes 8 servings.

Mrs. Ralph S. Regula

MRS. RALPH S. REGULA, Wife of Representative (Ohio)

ARTICHOKES AU VIN BLANC

6 small artichokes
1 tablespoon olive oil
1 clove garlic, minced
1 small onion, minced

pinch savory
2 teaspoons salt
1 cup dry white wine
additional olive oil and wine if needed

Trim tops, stems and a few of the outer leaves from artichokes. In a pot or deep casserole put olive oil, garlic, onion, savory and salt. Place artichokes upright in the pot and pour wine over them. Cover tightly and simmer slowly for 45 minutes, adding a little more wine and touch more of olive oil if necessary. When the hearts are tender, remove from heat. Serve the artichokes with the sauce either poured over them or on the side as a dip. Makes 6 servings.

Mrs. Jim Wright

MRS. JIM WRIGHT, Wife of Representative (Texas)

FRESH ASPARAGUS WITH HOLLANDAISE SAUCE

fresh asparagus
salt

Hollandaise sauce:
4 egg yolks
¼ pound butter cut in thirds
2 to 3 teaspoons lemon juice
dash of salt and white pepper

Wash stalks thoroughly and scrub gently with vegetable brush. To remove woody base break stalks instead of cutting. Stalk will snap at point where the tender part starts. Cut a strip of aluminum foil to place across bottom and up both sides of saucepan extending over the edges. Fold lengthwise making strip 4 to 5 inches wide. Lay asparagus on foil. Add boiling salted water to cover. Cook covered until just tender 10 to 15 minutes. Remove asparagus by lifting ends of foil strip. Serve with Hollandaise sauce.

Hollandaise sauce: place egg yolks and ⅓ of butter in top of double boiler. Stir rapidly over hot water with wooden spoon until butter melts. Add second piece of butter, stirring constantly. As mixture thickens and butter melts, stir in third piece of butter. (Water in bottom of double boiler should never boil.) When all butter has melted remove pan from hot water and stir rapidly 2 minutes. Stir in lemon juice slowly. Add salt and pepper and place again over hot water. Stir until thickened, 2 or 3 minutes, and remove from heat.

If sauce should curdle, beat in 1 or 2 tablespoons boiling water. Makes 1 cup sauce.

Mrs. Daniel J. Flood

MRS. DANIEL J. FLOOD, Wife of Representative (Pennsylvania)

ASPARAGUS SOUR CREAM CASSEROLE

10 cans asparagus spears, drain and reserve liquid
2 pints sour cream
4 cans cream of celery soup

Worcestershire sauce
2 packages onion soup mix
bread crumbs
parmesan cheese

Place asparagus in two, 2 quart casseroles. Combine sour cream with celery soup and sprinkle with Worcestershire. Remove as many onions as possible from dry soup mix and discard. Add remaining brown mixture to sour cream mixture. Thin to pouring consistency with reserved asparagus liquid. Pour over asparagus spears covering them completely. Sprinkle with bread crumbs and parmesan cheese. Bake at 350° for 30 minutes or until bubbly. May be frozen. Makes 20 servings.

Mrs. Charles Raper Jonas

MRS. CHARLES RAPER JONAS, Wife of former Representative (North Carolina)

ASPARAGUS CASSEROLE

4 tablespoons butter
4 tablespoons flour
2 cups milk (or 1 cup milk and
  1 cup asparagus liquid)

1 tall can asparagus, drained
5 hard cooked eggs, finely chopped
HiClub crackers, crumbled
grated cheese

Combine and cook butter, flour and milk over medium heat until thick. Cut asparagus into 1 inch pieces. Layer asparagus, eggs and cracker crumbs in the order given and cover with part of sauce mixture. Repeat layers. Bake at 375° until it bubbles and then sprinkle cheese over top. May be frozen. Makes 8 to 10 servings.

Mrs. Wendell Ford

MRS. WENDELL H. FORD, Wife of Senator (Kentucky)

CRUMB TOPPED ASPARAGUS

½ cup shredded Swiss cheese
¼ cup crumbled blue cheese
1½ cups medium white sauce
½ cup sliced almonds

2 10 ounce packages frozen asparagus
  spears, cooked
¼ cup buttered bread crumbs

Stir cheese into hot white sauce until melted. Add almonds. Place asparagus in buttered casserole and cover with cheese sauce. Sprinkle bread crumbs on top. Bake at 350° for 30 to 40 minutes or until bubbly and lightly browned on top. Makes 6 servings.

Mrs. Wiley Mayne

MRS. WILEY MAYNE, Wife of former Representative (Iowa)

ASPARAGUS AND EGG CASSEROLE

2 cans cream of mushroom soup
½ pound Velveeta cheese, grated
1 3 ounce can deviled ham

2 cans asparagus, well drained
6 hard cooked eggs, sliced
seasoned stuffing mix for crumb topping

Combine soup, cheese and ham in a double boiler and heat until cheese is melted. Layer asparagus and eggs in a casserole. Pour sauce over all. Top with stuffing mix. Bake 30 minutes at 350°. Makes 8 servings.

Mrs. John Y. McCollister

MRS. JOHN Y. McCOLLISTER, Wife of Representative (Nebraska)

ASPARAGUS ALMOND CASSEROLE

1 can cut asparagus, drained
1 can cream of mushroom soup
2 hard cooked eggs, chopped

2 tablespoons slivered almonds
red pepper and paprika to taste
½ cup grated Cheddar cheese

Combine asparagus with soup, eggs and almonds. Season with a little red pepper and paprika. Mix well. Place in buttered casserole. Spread cheese over top. Bake about 30 minutes at 350°.

Mrs. E. C. Gathings

MRS. E. C. GATHINGS, Wife of former Representative (Arkansas)

ASPARAGUS PARMESAN CASSEROLE

2 packages frozen asparagus
6 hard cooked eggs, sliced
1 can mushroom soup

½ cup milk
parmesan cheese

Let asparagus thaw enough to separate. Place half of it in casserole dish and cover with a layer of sliced eggs. Layer the remaining asparagus and top with remaining eggs. Dilute soup with milk. Pour over asparagus and eggs. Sprinkle cheese over top. Bake 30 minutes in 350° oven. Makes 6 servings.

Mrs. Garner E. Shriver

MRS. GARNER E. SHRIVER, Wife of Representative (Kansas)

88

ASPARAGUS SOUFFLE

¼ pound butter
3 heaping tablespoons flour
1½ cups milk
1 can cream of mushroom soup
salt and pepper to taste

2 cans asparagus, drained
1 pound sharp cheese, grated
sliced almonds
paprika

Melt butter, stir in flour until well blended, add milk and mushroom soup. Cook until thick and creamy. Season with salt and pepper. Place a layer of asparagus in a greased casserole. Add a layer of cheese, sprinkle with almonds and then add a layer of the sauce. Repeat layers until all ingredients are used. Top with cheese and almonds. Sprinkle with paprika. Bake at 350° about 30 minutes until cheese is light brown and almonds are toasted. May be frozen. Makes 12 servings.

MRS. WM. JENNINGS BRYAN DORN, Wife of former Representative (South Carolina)

BAKED ASPARAGUS

1 20 ounce can asparagus, drained
sharp cheese, grated
12 crackers, coarsely crushed
butter

1 cup light cream
liquid from asparagus
1 can cream of mushroom soup

Place a layer of asparagus in baking dish. Cover generously with cheese and cracker crumbs. Dot with butter. Mix cream, asparagus juice and soup. Pour over asparagus in dish. Bake in 350° oven for 30 to 40 minutes. Makes 6 servings.

MRS. HENRY AMISS HORNTHAL, Daughter of former Representative Thomas Hall (North Dakota)

ASPARAGUS CHEESE CASSEROLE

1 large can asparagus spears, drained
1 large can English peas, drained
1 can cream of mushroom soup

¾ cup grated sharp cheese
⅔ cup cracker crumbs
½ stick butter

Place both vegetables in a greased casserole dish. Add soup and top with grated cheese and cracker crumbs. Dot with butter. Bake at 350° for 25 or 30 minutes until browned. Makes 10 servings.

MRS. DAVID JACK DIXON, Daughter of Representative Wilbur D. Mills (Arkansas)

HEARTY ASPARAGUS

saltine crackers
2 cans asparagus spears, reserve juice
4 hard cooked eggs
salt and pepper to taste

2 cups medium white sauce
1 cup grated sharp cheese
butter or margarine

Crumble several saltine crackers into a buttered baking dish. In layers, add 1 can asparagus spears, 2 eggs sliced, salt, pepper and a little of the asparagus juice, cracker crumbs, a little more juice, 1 cup of white sauce and ½ cup cheese. Repeat layers ending with cheese. Dot with margarine or butter and bake at 325° until cheese is melted and sauce is bubbling. May be frozen. Makes 8 servings.

Mrs. Tom S. Gettys

MRS. TOM S. GETTYS, Wife of former Representative (South Carolina)

BAKED ASPARAGUS AND DEVILED EGGS

10 hard cooked eggs
2 small cans deviled ham
½ teaspoon Worcestershire sauce
1 teaspoon grated onion
½ teaspoon salt
¾ teaspoon dry mustard
dash of pepper
1 tablespoon milk (or cream)
3 packages frozen asparagus (or 3 cans asparagus spears, drained)

Sauce:
6 tablespoons flour
¼ pound margarine, melted
3 cups milk
2 cups grated New York sharp cheese
¼ teaspoon dry mustard
1½ teaspoons salt
pepper

Topping:
2 to 3 cups buttered bread crumbs

Slice eggs in half lengthwise. Remove and mash yolks. Add ham, Worcestershire, onion, salt, mustard, pepper and milk. Mix well. Fill egg whites and set aside. Cook asparagus according to package directions, drain and set aside. To make sauce, stir flour into margarine, add milk and cook over low heat, stirring until thick. Stir in cheese, mustard, salt and pepper, mixing well. Cook until cheese is melted.

In a well greased, 2 quart shallow rectangular casserole, place asparagus and top with eggs. Pour cheese sauce evenly over all. Top with buttered bread crumbs. Bake at 350° for 25 to 30 minutes. May be prepared and refrigerated for 1 or 2 days before baking. Makes 12 to 14 servings.

Mrs. Andrew G. Pattillo, Jr.

MRS. ANDREW G. PATTILLO, JR., Daughter of former Representative A. Sydney Herlong Jr. (Florida)

BAKED BARLEY

1¼ cups barley
4 cups chicken broth (or meat broth)
2 eggs, beaten
½ cup grated sharp cheese
1 green pepper, diced

1 4 ounce can mushrooms, chopped
1 small onion, diced (or 1 2 ounce can
   pimiento)
butter or margarine

Cook barley in broth slowly until thick and tender. Add eggs and cheese. Saute green pepper, mushrooms and onion in butter. Add to barley. Put in greased 1 quart mold. Bake about 30 minutes at 350° until center is firm. Makes 6 to 8 servings.

Mrs. Edward H. Jenison

MRS. EDWARD H. JENISON, Wife of former Representative (Illinois)

FRENCH BEAN CASSEROLE

1½ sticks margarine or butter
½ cup onions, chopped
2 4 ounce cans sliced mushrooms
1 5 ounce can water chestnuts,
   thinly sliced
⅓ cup flour
1 teaspoon salt
½ teaspoon pepper

1 cup milk
½ cup mushroom liquid
1 cup shredded cheddar cheese
2 teaspoons soy sauce
⅛ teaspoon Tabasco sauce
2 packages frozen French cut
   green beans, thawed
1 can French fried onions, crumbled

Saute onions, mushrooms and water chestnuts in ½ cup margarine until tender. Set aside. Melt remaining margarine and blend in flour, salt and pepper. Gradually add milk, mushroom liquid and cheese, stirring until cheese melts. Add soy sauce and Tabasco, blending well. In the bottom of a buttered 8 x 11 inch pan, layer half the sauteed vegetables, half the green beans and cover with half the cheese sauce. Repeat layers, ending with remaining sauce. Bake in a preheated 350° oven for 15 minutes. Remove from oven, sprinkle French fried onion crumbs on top and return to oven to bake an additional 10 minutes. Makes 8 servings.

Mrs. Spark Matsunaga

MRS. SPARK MATSUNAGA, Wife of Representative (Hawaii)

GREEN BEANS SMITANE

3 packages frozen French style
   green beans
1 cup finely chopped onion
4 tablespoons butter
4 tablespoons flour

1 cup mayonnaise
¾ cup dairy sour cream
¼ cup dry white wine
salt and pepper to taste

Cook beans according to package directions. Drain and set aside. Saute onion in butter until onions are limp. Stir in flour and blend well. Add mayonnaise, sour cream, wine, salt and pepper, stirring constantly until it is creamy. Add the beans to the sauce, heat through and serve. Sauce will keep in refrigerator for about 2 days. Just reheat slowly while beans are cooking. Makes 8 servings.

MRS. LUCIEN N. NEDZI, Wife of Representative (Michigan)

EASY GREEN BEAN CASSEROLE

1 can French style green beans, drained
1 can cream of mushroom soup

1 can French fried onions

Pour green beans in casserole. Mix cream of mushroom soup with beans. Bake 30 minutes at 350°, then cover top with French fried onions. Return to oven for 5 minutes. Serve hot.

MRS. L. H. FOUNTAIN, Wife of Representative (North Carolina)

ORIENTAL GREEN BEANS

1 4 ounce can sliced mushrooms, well drained
1 small onion, chopped
¼ pound butter
2 tablespoons flour
1 cup milk
1 cup Half and Half
½ pound sharp cheese, grated

⅛ teaspoon Tabasco sauce
1½ teaspoons soy sauce
½ teaspoon salt
½ teaspoon Accent
½ teaspoon pepper
2 cans French cut green beans
1 can water chestnuts, sliced
½ cup slivered almonds

Saute mushrooms and onion in butter. Add flour and stir until smooth. Add milk and Half and Half. Add cheese, Tabasco sauce, soy sauce, salt, Accent and pepper. Stir until thickened and cheese is melted. Add green beans and water chestnuts and mix. Put into greased casserole, and top with slivered almonds. Bake at 375° about 20 minutes or until bubbly. Makes 6 servings.

Mrs. Jackson E. Betts

MRS. JACKSON E. BETTS, Wife of former Representative (Ohio)

GREEN BEANS IN LEMON CREAM SAUCE

1½ pounds fresh small green beans (or 1 20 ounce bag frozen French style beans)
4 tablespoons butter
¾ cup heavy cream
1 egg

salt and freshly ground pepper to taste
2 tablespoons freshly grated parmesan cheese
¼ teaspoon freshly grated nutmeg
juice of 1 lemon

Cook fresh beans in salted water, uncovered, until they are just barely cooked, still bright green and slightly crisp. Drain beans thoroughly, add butter and stir in all but 2 tablespoons of cream. Cook over medium heat for 1 minute.

Break egg in small bowl and add salt, pepper, remaining cream, parmesan cheese and nutmeg. Stir well. Add lemon juice. Beat well with a fork until all ingredients are well blended. Pour over beans. Continue cooking for 2 or 3 minutes, mixing with a wooden spoon until the sauce has thickened and coated all the beans. Makes 6 servings.

Alicia Grant

ALICIA GRANT, Daughter of former Representative George M. Grant (Alabama)

SOUTHERN GREEN BEANS

2 cups water
¼ pound salt pork or bacon
6 cups green beans, preferably
   pole beans
1 teaspoon salt
1 onion, chopped (optional)
small new potatoes (optional)

Place water and salt pork in heavy saucepan. Bring to boil, reduce heat and simmer 20 minutes. Add beans, salt, and onion, if desired. Add more water, if necessary, to cover top of beans. Bring to boil again, reduce heat and cook another hour until done. If desired, small new potatoes may be placed on top of beans the last 30 minutes of cooking. May be frozen. Makes 6 to 8 servings.

Mrs. Tom Bevill

MRS. TOM BEVILL, Wife of Representative (Alabama)

FRENCH CUT BEANS WITH CHESTNUTS

5 packages frozen French style beans
1 8 ounce can mushrooms
1 or 2 medium onions, chopped
¼ pound butter
3 cans cream of mushroom soup
1 cup light cream
¾ pound sharp cheddar cheese, grated
⅛ teaspoon Tabasco
2 teaspoons soy sauce
1 teaspoon salt
1 tablespoon Accent (optional)
1 clove garlic
1 teaspoon paprika
½ teaspoon chili powder
1 5 ounce can water chestnuts,
   drained and sliced
¾ cup almonds, sliced

Cook beans according to directions on package. Saute mushrooms and onions in butter. Combine with all other ingredients except beans, water chestnuts and almonds. Put half of mixture into each of 2 average sized casserole dishes. Add a layer of beans, a layer of chestnuts and another layer of beans. Top mixture with almonds. Bake at 375° for 20 minutes. Makes 12 to 15 servings.

Mrs. Tolise G. Norwood

MRS. TOLISE G. NORWOOD, Daughter of former Representative E. C. Gathings (Arkansas)

HOT BEAN SALAD CASSEROLE

1 1 pound can kidney beans
1 cup sliced celery
⅓ cup chopped sweet pickles
¼ cup chopped onion
1 cup grated cheese
few drops hot sauce

½ teaspoon salt
½ teaspoon chili powder
½ teaspoon Worcestershire sauce
½ cup mayonnaise
1 cup crushed corn chips
pepper rings

Drain beans and combine with celery, pickles, onion, cheese. Blend seasonings with mayonnaise, add to bean mixture and toss lightly. Spoon into a 1 quart shallow baking dish. Sprinkle with corn chips. Bake at least 10 minutes in 450° oven. Garnish with pepper rings. May be frozen. Makes 8 servings.

Mrs. Harold Runnels

MRS. HAROLD L. RUNNELS, Wife of Representative (New Mexico)

BAKED BEANS

2 pounds pea beans
1 medium onion, quartered
½ pound salt pork
½ to ⅔ cup molasses
2 teaspoons dry mustard

¼ teaspoon red pepper
1 teaspoon ginger
1½ tablespoons salt
1 pint boiling water (or more as needed)

Pick over the beans and soak in cold water overnight. In the morning, parboil beans until the skins split. Put onion in bottom of bean pot and add beans. Cut through rind of the salt pork to a depth of ½ inch and place on top of beans. Mix molasses, mustard, red pepper, ginger and salt with boiling water. Pour this over the beans and pork. If necessary, add more boiling water to cover. Bake at 300° for at least 6 hours, adding more boiling water as the beans cook. Makes 8 to 10 servings.

Margaret Chase Smith

MARGARET CHASE SMITH, former Senator (Maine)

RANCH STYLE FRIJOLES

2 pounds pinto beans
salt
2 large onions, diced
4 cloves garlic, diced
1 can roasted green chilies, chopped
1 can taco sauce

1 can tomatoes
2 teaspoons salt
½ teaspoon black pepper
1 teaspoon cumino seed
1 to 2 teaspoons red chili powder
(optional)

Soak pinto beans in cold water overnight. Drain, wash and cover with about 2 inches water. Add salt and boil over moderate heat for about 1 hour, adding water as needed. Mix onion, garlic and chili with the taco sauce and tomatoes. Stir this into the beans. Add seasonings. Cook over reduced heat for 1½ hours or until beans are tender. If spicier beans are desired, add red chili powder. May be frozen.

Mrs. Barry Goldwater

MRS. BARRY M. GOLDWATER, Wife of Senator (Arizona)

SOUR CREAM BEETS

1 cup dairy sour cream
¼ cup mayonnaise
¼ teaspoon dry mustard

½ teaspoon sugar
1 green onion, chopped
1 can cooked beets

Combine all ingredients except beets. Blend well and pour sauce over hot beets. Makes 4 or 5 servings.

Mrs Fred Schwengel

MRS. FRED SCHWENGEL, Wife of former Representative (Iowa)

BROCCOLI WITH CAPERED BUTTER

1½ to 2 pounds fresh broccoli
6 tablespoons butter

2 tablespoons crushed capers with
some liquid

Cut broccoli to desired size pieces. Carefully steam in lightly salted water and place in a hot serving dish. Melt butter and brown very lightly. Draw capers through hot butter and remove. Pour butter over broccoli and serve immediately. Makes 5 to 6 servings.

Mrs Warren G. Magnuson

MRS. WARREN G. MAGNUSON, Wife of Senator (Washington)

BEA'S ROQUEFORT BROCCOLI

1 package frozen chopped broccoli
1 small package Philadelphia cream
cheese

1 small package roquefort or blue
cheese
1 cup cream sauce
Cheezits, crumbled

Cook broccoli until tender and drain well. Dice cheeses into warm cream sauce and let melt. Mix with broccoli and pour into medium casserole. Top with cheese cracker crumbs. May be prepared and refrigerated until baking time. Bake in 350° oven until bubbly. May be frozen. Makes 4 to 5 servings.

Mrs. Clifford Davis

MRS. CLIFFORD DAVIS, Wife of former Representative (Tennessee)

BROCCOLI CASSEROLE

2 10 ounce packages chopped broccoli
1 can mushroom soup
3 eggs, well beaten
2 cups grated sharp cheese

1 cup mayonnaise
4 tablespoons chopped onion
¼ teaspoon pepper
cracker crumbs

Cook broccoli according to directions on package. Drain and mash. Mix all ingredients except crumbs together, pour into casserole. Sprinkle with cracker crumbs and bake for 45 minutes at 350°. May be frozen. Makes 8 servings.

Mrs. Dan Daniel

MRS. DAN DANIEL, Wife of Representative (Virginia)

CURRIED BROCCOLI CASSEROLE

2 packages frozen broccoli
2 cans cream of chicken soup
2 to 4 tablespoons mayonnaise
1 tablespoon lemon juice

½ teaspoon curry powder
½ cup bread crumbs
2 tablespoons margarine, melted
parmesan cheese

Cook broccoli according to package directions, drain and arrange in baking dish. Heat the soup, mayonnaise, juice and curry powder together and pour over broccoli. Toss bread crumbs with margarine and put on top of casserole. Sprinkle a little parmesan cheese over crumbs if desired. Bake in a 350° oven for 30 minutes until bubbly. Makes 6 servings.

Mrs. Joseph L. Carrigg

MRS. JOSEPH L. CARRIGG, Wife of former Representative (Pennsylvania)

BROCCOLI MOLD

2 packages frozen broccoli
3 eggs, beaten
½ teaspoon salt

1 tablespoon melted butter
1 cup mayonnaise
1 cup milk

Cook broccoli as directed on package, drain and chop into small pieces. Beat eggs, add salt, butter, mayonnaise and milk and mix gently. Combine this mixture with the broccoli. Pour into a casserole. Place casserole in pan of water and bake 30 to 45 minutes at 375° until knife inserted in the middle comes out clean. Makes 6 servings.

MRS. SAM GIBBONS, Wife of Representative (Florida)

BROCCOLI CHEESE CASSEROLE

2 packages frozen broccoli
1 cup grated cheddar cheese
2½ teaspoons dry Good Seasons
  French dressing mix

1 can French fried onions, reserve
  some for topping
1 can cream of mushroom soup
⅔ cup evaporated milk, heated

Cook and drain broccoli, and put in greased 1½ quart casserole. Sprinkle with cheese and dressing mix. Stir, and add onions. Mix soup and milk and pour over casserole mixture. Top with reserved onions. Bake at 325° for 25 or 30 minutes. Makes 6 servings.

MRS. JACKSON E. BETTS, Wife of former Representative (Ohio)

BROCCOLI WITH SHRIMP SAUCE

2 10 ounce packages frozen broccoli
¼ cup cream cheese with chives
¼ cup milk

1 can cream of shrimp soup
2 tablespoons lemon juice
2 tablespoons toasted slivered almonds

Cook broccoli according to package directions, drain and set aside. Blend cream cheese and milk in a small saucepan; add soup and mix well. Cook, stirring constantly, until mixture is hot. Add lemon juice and mix well. Arrange broccoli in an 11 x 8 inch shallow casserole dish. Pour sauce over broccoli and sprinkle with almonds. Bake at 350° about 10 minutes or until mixture is bubbly. May be frozen. Makes 6 to 8 servings.

Mrs. Richard H. Ichord

MRS. RICHARD H. ICHORD, Wife of Representative (Missouri)

EASY BROCCOLI AND RICE CASSEROLE

1 cup cooked rice
1 can cream of mushroom soup
⅓ large jar Cheez Whiz

1 package frozen chopped broccoli, thawed
½ onion, chopped

Mix all ingredients, put in casserole and bake in 350° oven for 45 minutes.

Mrs John C. Kunkel

MRS. JOHN C. KUNKEL, Wife of former Representative (Pennsylvania)

BROCCOLI RICE CASSEROLE

1 package frozen chopped broccoli
¼ cup chopped onion
½ cup chopped celery
3 tablespoons butter or margarine
½ cup milk

1 8 ounce jar Cheese Whiz
2 cups cooked rice
1 can water chestnuts, thinly sliced
1 can cream chicken soup

Cook broccoli as package directs. Drain. Saute onion and celery in butter until tender. Add milk and ½ jar of cheese. Combine with broccoli and remaining ingredients, place in greased casserole and top with remaining cheese. Bake at 350° until heated thoroughly, about 30 minutes. May be prepared and refrigerated until time to bake. Makes 4 servings.

Mrs. Bob Casey

MRS. BOB CASEY, Wife of Representative (Texas)

QUICK BROCCOLI CASSEROLE

1 or 2 packages frozen chopped
broccoli
1 cup cooked rice

1 cup evaporated milk
1 medium size jar Cheese Whiz
buttered bread crumbs

Thaw and drain broccoli. Add rice, milk and cheese and mix well. Pour in casserole and cover generously with bread crumbs. Bake at 350° for 40 minutes. May be frozen. Makes 6 servings.

Mrs J Edgar Chenoweth

MRS. J. EDGAR CHENOWETH, Wife of former Representative (Colorado)

CREAMED RED CABBAGE

1 medium head red cabbage, sliced
water
1 large onion, sliced
¼ pound butter, melted
¼ cup flour

2 cups milk
salt and pepper to taste
½ cup grated gruyere (or parmesan
cheese)

Cook red cabbage in water just to cover until tender. Drain and spoon cabbage into a 2 quart casserole. Slowly cook onion in butter until onion is transparent. Stir in flour with whisk and add milk, stirring continually over medium heat until sauce thickens. Stir in salt and pepper and pour sauce over cabbage. Sprinkle cheese over top and bake, uncovered, in 325° oven 30 minutes or until sauce is bubbling. May be frozen. Makes 4 servings.

Mrs Hamilton Fish, Jr.

MRS. HAMILTON FISH, JR., Wife of Representative (New York)

GERMAN CABBAGE

1 head red cabbage, chopped coarsely
1 large apple, chopped
1 medium onion, chopped

½ cup vinegar
2 or 3 tablespoons of brown sugar
water

Combine cabbage, apple and onion. Add vinegar and water to cover. Add sugar to taste. Cover pan and simmer 1½ hours. Makes 6 servings.

Mrs. Wiley Mayne

MRS. WILEY MAYNE, Wife of former Representative (Iowa)

KRAUT FLECKERL (NOODLES AND CABBAGE)

1 3 pound head cabbage, cored and
   shredded
1½ teaspoons salt
½ pound butter

2 teaspoons sugar
½ teaspoon freshly ground black pepper
1 pound broad noodles, broken in half,
   cooked and drained

Place shredded cabbage in a bowl and add salt, mixing well. Allow to stand for at least 1 hour. Rinse and drain well, squeezing out all liquid.

Melt half the butter in a saucepan and add cabbage, sugar and pepper. Cook over low heat for 1½ hours or until browned, stirring frequently. Add remaining butter at intervals until all has been used. Season to taste.

Add noodles to cabbage and stir until well mixed. Heat for a few minutes, stirring frequently.

Rebecca Dial

REBECCA DIAL, Daughter of former Senator Nathaniel Barksdale Dial (South Carolina)

PARTY CARROTS

5 tablespoons sweet butter
2 tablespoons orange flavored honey
4 7 ounce cans Belgian baby carrots

3 tablespoons Grand Marnier
   (or Cointreau)

In a casserole melt butter and stir in honey. Add the carrots and coat them thoroughly with the sauce. Pour the Grand Marnier over them. Bake in a 350° oven for 15 minutes, basting occasionally. Makes 8 servings.

Mrs. Emilio Q. Daddario

MRS. EMILIO Q. DADDARIO, Wife of former Representative (Connecticut)

101

CARROT RING

2 cups mashed cooked carrots
3 eggs, separated
2 tablespoons melted butter
¾ cup milk
1 cup dried bread crumbs
2 tablespoons chopped onion

2 tablespoons chopped parsley
1 teaspoon salt
¼ teaspoon paprika
creamed peas (optional)
cooked lima beans (optional)

Mix together all ingredients except egg whites and peas and beans. Beat egg whites until stiff and carefully fold into first mixture. Pour into 2 quart buttered ring mold. Set in pan of hot water and bake 40 minutes in 350° oven. Unmold carefully and fill center with creamed peas or cooked fresh lima beans. Makes 8 servings.

Mrs. Craig Hosmer

MRS. CRAIG HOSMER, Wife of former Representative (California)

PINEAPPLE COATED CARROTS

8 whole, scraped carrots, cut into
   julienne strips
½ teaspoon salt
1 cup drained crushed pineapple

1 tablespoon grated orange rind
½ cup brown sugar
¼ teaspoon cinnamon
4 tablespoons butter

Place carrots in pot with water to cover. Add salt. Cover and cook until tender. Drain. Return to pot. Add pineapple, orange rind, sugar, cinnamon and butter. Cook slowly for 10 minutes, stirring occasionally. Serve immediately. Makes 6 servings.

Mrs. Thomas G. Morris

MRS. THOMAS G. MORRIS, Wife of former Representative (New Mexico)

MILLIE'S CAULIFLOWER CASSEROLE

1 medium head cauliflower (or 2 packages frozen)
½ pound fresh mushrooms (or 2 8 ounce cans)
¼ cup diced green pepper
⅓ cup butter

¼ cup flour
2 cups milk
salt to taste
8 slices pimiento cheese
paprika

Separate cauliflower into small pieces and cook until tender. Drain. Brown mushrooms and pepper in butter. Blend in flour. Gradually stir in milk and cook until thickened. Add salt.

In 1½ quart casserole layer half the cauliflower, half the cheese and half the cream sauce mixture. Repeat layers. Sprinkle top with paprika. Bake at 350° until thoroughly hot. May be frozen. Makes 6 servings.

Mrs. John H. Terry

MRS. JOHN H. TERRY, Wife of former Representative (New York)

KENTUCKY CORN PUDDING

2 cups cream style corn
4 tablespoons flour
1 tablespoon sugar
1 teaspoon salt

1 tablespoon butter, melted
2 eggs, well beaten
2 cups milk

Mix corn, flour, sugar and salt together. Combine butter, eggs and milk with corn mixture. Pour in greased baking dish and bake at 350° for 1 hour. Stir from bottom 2 or 3 times during first 30 minutes of baking time. Makes 5 to 6 servings.

Mrs. Walter D. Huddleston

MRS. WALTER D. HUDDLESTON, Wife of Senator (Kentucky)

103

CORN PUDDING

1½ cups cream style corn
1 cup whole kernel corn
2 tablespoons flour
½ stick butter
1 cup milk

1 tablespoon sugar
2 teaspoons salt
⅛ teaspoon white pepper
3 eggs, lightly beaten

Mix corn and flour together and set aside. With a portion of the butter, grease a 1½ quart casserole. Melt remaining butter in a small saucepan and add the milk, sugar, salt and pepper. Heat but do not boil. Add the milk and butter mixture gradually to eggs. Fold in corn mixture. Pour pudding into the casserole, set on a rack in a pan of hot water and bake at 350° for about 1½ hours or until firm. Stir occasionally during first 45 minutes of baking time. Makes 6 servings.

Mrs. Hugh Q. Alexander

Mrs. HUGH Q. ALEXANDER, Wife of former Representative (North Carolina)

JEAN'S CORN PUDDING

1 1 pound can cream style yellow corn
1 1 pound whole kernel yellow corn, drained
1 egg, slightly beaten

⅓ cup packaged dry bread crumbs
½ cup dairy sour cream
salt and pepper to taste
parsley to taste

Mix all ingredients and turn into a buttered 1½ quart casserole. Bake at 350° for 40 minutes. Makes 4 to 6 servings.

Mrs Frank A. Stubblefield

Mrs. FRANK A. STUBBLEFIELD, Wife of former Representative (Kentucky)

BAKED CORN PUDDING

2 eggs
1 small can evaporated milk plus cream
  to make 1 cup
1 teaspoon salt
pepper to taste

½ teaspoon dry mustard
¼ cup grated onion
2 cups canned cream style corn
¼ cup cracker crumbs

Beat eggs and milk together. Add remaining ingredients and mix well. Put in a buttered casserole, set in a pan of water and bake at 350° for about 1 hour. Makes 4 servings.

Mrs. Olin E. Teague

MRS. OLIN E. TEAGUE, Wife of Representative (Texas)

CORN CUSTARD

1 can whole kernel corn, drained
3 eggs, beaten

4 cups reconstituted milk
1½ teaspoons salt

Combine ingredients in an 8½ x 13 inch glass baking dish. Bake at 350° for 35 to 45 minutes. Makes 8 servings.

Mrs. Helen H. Dingell

MRS. HELEN H. DINGELL, Member of Congressional Club (Michigan)

CORN CASSEROLE

½ green pepper, chopped
½ onion, chopped
2 tablespoons butter
2 tablespoons flour
1 teaspoon salt
¼ teaspoon paprika

¼ teaspoon mustard
1 cup milk
2 cups whole kernel corn
1 egg, beaten
1½ cups dry bread crumbs
1 tablespoon melted butter

Saute green pepper and onion in butter. Add flour, salt, paprika, mustard and milk. Cook until it becomes thick. Add corn, egg and 1 cup of dry bread crumbs and put in greased casserole. Toss remaining bread crumbs with melted butter and sprinkle over top of casserole. Bake 30 minutes at 400°. Makes 8 servings.

Mrs. Charles H. Leavy

MRS. CHARLES H. LEAVY, Wife of former Representative (Washington)

BAKED EGGPLANT PARMESAN

1 large eggplant	3/4 cup chopped mozzarella cheese
1 1/4 teaspoons salt	2 cups tomato sauce
1 cup olive oil	3/4 cup grated parmesan cheese
1 clove garlic	

Stem and peel eggplant and cut it into 1/4 inch slices. Sprinkle with salt. Heat oil in a large skillet. Add garlic, cook for 1 minute and remove. Pat eggplant dry on absorbent paper and fry, a few slices at a time, until golden on both sides. Drain on absorbent paper. Arrange one layer of eggplant in a deep casserole dish. Sprinkle with some of the mozzarella, tomato sauce and parmesan. Repeat this procedure until all eggplant is used, ending with a layer of tomato sauce and a sprinkling of parmesan cheese. Bake in a preheated 400° oven uncovered for 20 minutes. May be frozen. Makes 4 to 6 servings.

Mrs. Jane J. Howard

MRS. JAMES J. HOWARD, Wife of Representative (New Jersey)

BREADED EGGPLANT CASSEROLE

1 large eggplant, peeled	1/2 cup grated parmesan cheese
3 eggs, beaten	1 1/2 teaspoons dried oregano
1 cup packaged dried bread crumbs	1/2 pound sliced mozzarella cheese
2/3 cup salad oil	3 8 ounce cans tomato sauce

Cut eggplant into 1/4 inch slices. Dip each slice first into eggs, then into crumbs. Saute in hot oil until golden brown on both sides. Place a layer of eggplant in a 2 quart casserole, sprinkle with some parmesan and oregano and over that layer some mozzarella. Cover well with some tomato sauce. Repeat layers until all eggplant is used, topping last layer of sauce with several slices of mozzarella. Bake in preheated 350° oven 1/2 hour or until sauce is bubbly and cheese is melted. May be frozen. Makes 4 to 6 servings.

Mrs Fred Bradley

MRS. FRED BRADLEY, Wife of former Representative (Michigan)

106

AUNT LIZZ'S EGGPLANT CASSEROLE

1 pint cooked eggplant
2 tablespoons margarine
1 cube beef bouillon
1 cup boiling water
2 eggs
3 crackers, crushed
1 cup seasoned croutons

¼ pound sharp cheese, cubed
½ cup milk
1 teaspoon sugar
¼ cup chopped onion
salt and pepper to taste
½ cup crushed potato chips (or
   buttered crumbs)

Squeeze water from eggplant. Drain well. Dissolve margarine and bouillon cube in boiling water. Add this and all other ingredients except potato chips to eggplant. Mix very well. Put in greased casserole. Let stand at least 1 hour. Preheat oven to 400°. Place covered casserole in oven and turn oven temperature back to 350°. Bake 45 minutes. Remove cover and sprinkle crushed potato chips over top. Bake uncovered another 15 minutes. Serve piping hot. May be prepared and refrigerated or frozen until it is to be baked. Makes 8 servings.

Mrs. Earl L. Butz

MRS. EARL LAUER BUTZ, Wife of Secretary of Agriculture (Indiana)

EGGPLANT SOUFFLE

1 large eggplant, peeled and cubed
8 saltine crackers, finely crushed
1 large egg, slightly beaten
¼ teaspoon freshly ground pepper
   (or lemon pepper)

few drops of Tabasco sauce
¼ cup dry sherry (optional)
½ cup grated Swiss cheese

Cook eggplant in boiling salted water for 5 minutes. Drain and puree in blender. Combine puree, crumbs, egg, pepper and Tabasco, mixing well. Add sherry if desired.

Spread ⅓ of mixture in buttered 1 quart casserole. Spread ⅓ of cheese over eggplant. Repeat layers, ending with cheese on top. Bake in preheated 350° oven until souffle is firm and brown on top. Makes 4 servings.

Mrs. Dean P. Taylor

MRS. DEAN P. TAYLOR, Wife of former Representative (New York)

EGGPLANT CASSEROLE

4 cups peeled and diced eggplant
1 egg, slightly beaten
1/3 cup milk
1/2 cup chopped onion
1 can cream of mushroom soup

3/4 cup herb stuffing
1 cup grated sharp cheddar cheese
1/2 cup crushed herb stuffing
2 tablespoons butter

Cook eggplant in salted water 6 to 7 minutes until tender and drain. Mix egg, milk, onion, soup and herb stuffing. Alternate this mixture and eggplant in layers in a casserole and top with cheese, crushed stuffing and butter. Bake in 375° oven for 45 minutes. May be frozen. Makes 4 servings.

Mrs. Otis G. Pike

MRS. OTIS G. PIKE, Wife of Representative (New York)

CHEESE STUFFED EGGPLANT

1 medium size eggplant
2 cups water
4 tablespoons lemon juice
1/2 teaspoon salt
8 ounces tomato sauce
1/2 teaspoon crushed oregano leaves

1/2 cup chopped onion
1 tablespoon butter, melted
1 cup cubed, cooked ham
1/3 cup coarsely grated carrot
1/2 cup chopped celery
2 cups shredded cheddar cheese

Cut eggplant in half lengthwise. Scoop out center leaving an edge 1/2 inch thick. Combine water, 2 tablespoons lemon juice and salt and heat to the boiling point. Add eggplant shells, cover and parboil 5 minutes. Drain and set aside.

Chop eggplant pulp, combine with tomato sauce, remaining lemon juice and oregano and heat to boiling. Remove from heat. Meanwhile, saute onion in butter until tender. Remove from heat and stir in ham, carrots, celery and cheese.

Put 2/3 of eggplant mixture in a buttered baking dish and arrange the eggplant shells on top. Fill shells with ham and cheese mixture and cover with remaining tomato sauce. Bake at 375° for 25 to 30 minutes. May be frozen. Makes 4 servings.

Mrs. Evan Howell

MRS. EVAN HOWELL, Wife of former Representative (Illinois)

108

ENDIVE MORNAY

8 Belgian endive
boiling water
8 slices cooked ham

Mornay sauce:
2 tablespoons butter
3 tablespoons flour
2 cups milk

¼ teaspoon salt
dash of white pepper
½ cup whipping cream
2 egg yolks
¼ cup grated Swiss cheese
pinch of nutmeg
¼ cup grated parmesan cheese

Put endive in large pan and cover with boiling water. Boil for 10 minutes. Drain. Repeat procedure 2 more times. Drain carefully. Roll in paper toweling to dry. Roll each endive in a slice of ham and lay in a casserole in a single layer.

Melt butter, add flour and cook for 5 to 8 minutes. This roux should have a pale golden color and must not be allowed to brown. Remove from heat. Combine milk, salt and white pepper, heat to just under the boiling point and add to the roux when it has stopped bubbling. Beat with wire whip until completely blended. Return to heat and stir constantly until it comes to a boil. Lower heat and cook uncovered for 30 minutes. Strain through a fine sieve. Beat cream and egg yolks together and add to the hot mixture. Stir in Swiss cheese and nutmeg. Return to heat and bring to a boil. Boil 1 minute.

Pour sauce over the endive. Sprinkle with parmesan cheese. At serving time, bake in 400° oven for 15 minutes until top is lightly browned. Makes 8 servings.

Mrs. Edward J. Derwinski

MRS. EDWARD J. DERWINSKI, Wife of Representative (Illinois)

GRIT CASSEROLE

1 cup uncooked grits
¼ pound butter or margarine
1 roll garlic cheese, diced

milk
2 eggs, beaten
cheddar cheese, grated

Cook grits according to directions on package. Stir in butter and garlic cheese until melted. Add enough milk to eggs to make a cup. Add to grit mixture. Put in casserole and top with grated cheese. Bake about 45 minutes at 350°.

Mrs. Carroll Hubbard

MRS. CARROLL HUBBARD, Wife of Representative (Kentucky)

JOHN'S SOPHISTICATED GRITS

1 quart milk
¼ pound butter
1 cup regular grits
1 teaspoon salt

⅛ teaspoon pepper
1 cup grated gruyere cheese
⅓ cup grated American cheese

Bring milk to a boil, taking care not to scorch it. Cut butter into pieces and add to milk. When butter melts, add grits and cook, stirring constantly, until mixture is the consistency of cream of wheat. Remove from heat. Season with salt and pepper. Beat at high speed with an electric beater for 5 minutes until it is creamy. Pour half of grits into a slightly greased casserole. Mix cheeses and put half the cheese over top of grits. Add remaining grits and top with remaining cheese. Bake uncovered at 300° until brown on top, 40 minutes to 1 hour. May be frozen. Makes 8 to 10 servings.

Mrs. John Sanders

MRS. JOHN SANDERS, Daughter of former Representative John E. Rankin (Mississippi)

BLUE GRASS GRITS CASSEROLE

2 cups quick cooking grits
1 tablespoon salt
8 cups boiling water
½ pound margarine
1 roll nippy cheese

¼ teaspoon garlic powder (or
    garlic salt)
1 teaspoon Tabasco sauce
2 teaspoons Worcestershire sauce
2 eggs, unbeaten

Add grits to salted, boiling water. Add margarine, stir and cook 5 minutes. Mix cheese, garlic powder, Tabasco sauce, Worcestershire sauce and eggs and combine with cooked grits mixture. Put in buttered casserole and bake in preheated 350° oven for 1½ hours. May be kept in refrigerator 24 hours or may be frozen before baking. Makes 16 servings.

Mrs. Tim Lee Carter

MRS. TIM LEE CARTER, Wife of Representative (Kentucky)

110

GRITS AND CHEESE CASSEROLE

1 cup grits	1 egg, beaten
¼ pound butter	milk, added to egg to make 1 cup
¾ pound grated American cheese	⅛ teaspoon garlic powder

Cook grits and stir butter and cheese into hot mixture. When melted and mixed well, pour in egg, milk and garlic. Bake in buttered casserole at 350° or 375° about 45 minutes or until done. May be frozen. Makes 10 servings.

Mrs. E. C. Gathings

MRS. E. C. GATHINGS, Wife of former Representative (Arkansas)

BAKED HOMINY

1 large can yellow hominy, drained	8 tablespoons flour
2 tablespoons butter	2 cups milk
1 green pepper, diced	½ pound diced American cheese
1 onion, diced	1 small can diced pimiento
1 small can sliced mushrooms	1 egg, beaten
4 tablespoons butter	buttered bread crumbs

Saute hominy in butter. Add green pepper, onion and mushrooms. Make white sauce of butter, flour and milk. Cook until thick and add cheese, pimiento and egg. Mix sauce with hominy and put in greased 8 inch casserole. Cover with buttered bread crumbs. Bake at 325° for 1 hour. Makes 6 servings.

Mrs. Robert Lagomarsino

MRS. ROBERT J. LAGOMARSINO, Wife of Representative (California)

HOMINY GRITS CASSEROLE

4 cups water
1 teaspoon salt
1 cup hominy grits
¼ pound butter

1 roll Kraft garlic cheese
2 eggs
milk
grated cheese

Bring water to a boil. Add salt and hominy grits. Boil 5 minutes. Melt the butter and garlic cheese in double boiler and add to grits. Break 2 eggs into measuring cup. Finish filling cup with milk. Stir to mix. Pour slowly into grits. Pour mixture into buttered casserole. Bake at 325° for 30 minutes. Remove from oven and sprinkle cheese over top. Let set until 15 minutes before serving time. Then put in 325° oven until cheese melts. May be frozen. Makes 8 to 10 servings.

Mrs. g. Floyd Breeding

MRS. J. FLOYD BREEDING, Wife of former Representative (Kansas)

ROSE'S GOURMET LEEKS

1 bunch leeks
1 medium carrot, peeled
1 medium onion, chopped
1½ tablespoons corn oil

2 tablespoons long grain rice
1 tablespoon chopped parsley
salt and paprika to taste
½ cup boiling water

Remove tough outer leaves of leeks and cut off stringy root area. Under running water, wash off sand carefully and thoroughly from all leaves. Chop leeks into approximately 1 inch chunks and carrot into ½ inch slices. Saute onions lightly in corn oil. Add carrot slices; sprinkle with the rice. Add chopped leeks, parsley, salt and then sprinkle generously with paprika. Add boiling water, bring quickly to boil, lower heat and cook for 20 to 25 minutes. May be frozen. Makes 2 to 3 servings.

Mrs. George E. Danielson

MRS. GEORGE E. DANIELSON, Wife of Representative (California)

BRAISED LETTUCE

6 heads lettuce, washed and quartered
½ cup beef stock

1 tablespoon butter
½ teaspoon salt

Boil lettuce with beef stock and butter in a covered saucepan for 15 minutes. Remove lettuce from saucepan. Boil juice remaining in pan until it is reduced to about ¼ cup and pour over lettuce. Keep lettuce warm until serving time. Serve with Stuffed Duck Bordelaise. Makes 6 servings.

Mrs Gerald R. Ford

Mrs. Gerald R. Ford, Wife of President of the United States (Michigan)

RESTUFFED MUSHROOMS

1 pound large mushrooms
4 tablespoons cracker crumbs
2 tablespoons minced parsley
3 tablespoons minced shallots

salt
paprika
¼ pound butter, melted
1 teaspoon lemon juice

Chop mushroom stems and mix with remaining ingredients. Fill mushroom caps with mixture and broil five minutes. Makes 4 servings.

Mrs. Howard Baker Jr

Mrs. Howard H. Baker, Jr., Wife of Senator (Tennessee)

STUFFED MUSHROOMS

1 pound medium sized fresh
   mushrooms
1 cup finely chopped pecans
3 tablespoons chopped parsley
½ stick butter, softened

1 clove garlic, crushed
¼ teaspoon thyme
½ teaspoon salt
¼ teaspoon black pepper
½ cup heavy cream

Wipe mushrooms with damp paper towel. Break off stems. Arrange mushroom caps in shallow baking dish, hollow side up. Chop stems and combine with pecans, parsley, butter, garlic, thyme, salt and pepper. Mix together and heap in mushroom caps. Pour cream over all. Bake, uncovered, in 350° oven for 20 minutes. Baste once or twice with cream in the dish. Makes 6 servings.

Mrs. A. Sydney Herlong, Jr.

Mrs. A. Sydney Herlong, Jr., Wife of former Representative (Florida)

113

MUSHROOMS WITH CAMEMBERT AND ALMONDS

10 to 12 medium, whole, fresh
   mushrooms
2 ounces camembert cheese
½ stick butter
2 tablespoons minced parsley

2 tablespoons minced chives
dash Tabasco
1 2 ounce package slivered almonds,
   crushed
2 tablespoons dry sherry

Wipe mushrooms, remove stems and save for sauces. Place whole caps in baking dish, hollow side up. Cream together cheese, butter, parsley and chives. Add Tabasco and almonds to cheese mixture. Stir in sherry. Fill caps with mixture and broil about 3 inches from flame until hot and bubbly. May be frozen. Makes 4 to 6 servings.

Mrs. Sterling Cole

MRS. STERLING COLE, Wife of former Representative (New York)

MUSHROOMS FLORENTINE

1 pound fresh mushrooms, washed
   and dried
butter
2 packages frozen spinach, thawed
1 teaspoon salt

¼ cup chopped onion
½ stick melted butter
1 cup freshly grated Cheddar cheese
garlic salt

Saute mushroom stems and caps in butter until brown, browning cap side of mushrooms first. Line a 10 inch casserole with spinach which has been seasoned with salt, onion and butter. Sprinkle with ½ cup grated cheese. Arrange sauteed mushrooms over the spinach. Season with garlic salt. Cover with remaining cheese. Bake for 20 minutes at 350° or until cheese is melted and browned. This casserole may be prepared and refrigerated until it is to be baked. Makes 6 to 8 servings.

Mrs. Guy Vander Jagt

MRS. GUY VANDER JAGT, Wife of Representative (Michigan)

114

SKIP'S SCALLOPED MUSHROOMS

1 pound fresh mushrooms, sliced
2 cups soft French bread crumbs
¼ pound butter, melted

salt and pepper
⅓ cup dry white wine

In a 1½ quart buttered baking dish arrange in layers, ⅓ of the mushrooms, ⅓ of the crumbs and ⅓ of the butter. Sprinkle with salt and pepper. Repeat another layer of each ingredient. Cover with remaining mushrooms. Pour wine over all. Cover and bake at 325° for 25 minutes. Top with remaining crumbs and butter. Bake uncovered for 10 minutes or until bread crumbs are toasted. Makes 6 servings.

Mrs John W Byrnes

MRS. JOHN W. BYRNES, Wife of former Representative (Wisconsin)

FRIED OKRA

1 pound okra
½ cup milk
½ cup corn meal

2 tablespoons flour
½ teaspoon salt
vegetable oil

Cut stem ends and tips off okra pods. Cut each pod into ½ inch pieces. Place in bowl; sprinkle with milk. Drain and toss with corn meal, flour and salt mixed together. Heat ½ inch of oil in heavy skillet over medium high heat. Fry okra pods until brown and crisp. Makes 4 servings.

Mrs. Tom Bevill

MRS. TOM BEVILL, Wife of Representative (Alabama)

BLACKEYE PEAS (WITH MEAT)

1 pound ground meat (veal, pork, beef or wild meat)
1 tablespoon finely chopped onion
½ teaspoon crushed bay leaves
1 pound can blackeye peas, drained

¼ cup tomato sauce
2 tablespoons molasses (or brown sugar)
1 teaspoon dry mustard

Shape meat into balls and saute with onion and bay leaves until done. Drain free of grease. Then combine in casserole with all other ingredients. Cover and bake in 350° oven for 30 minutes. Makes 4 servings.

Mrs. James H. Quillen

MRS. JAMES H. QUILLEN, Wife of Representative (Tennessee)

SCHWENKFELDER POTATO FILLING

2 quarts diced dried bread
1 pint mashed potatoes
¼ cup potato water
¼ cup turkey broth (from cooking giblets and neck)
½ cup turkey giblets, ground
¼ cup chopped celery
¼ cup chopped onion
1 teaspoon salt
⅛ teaspoon pepper
1 cup milk
2 eggs, well beaten

All ingredients must be level. Blend in the order given. Bake in a large roasting pan for about 1 hour at 400°. Makes 10 to 12 servings.

Mrs Richard Schultz Schweiker
MRS. RICHARD SCHULTZ SCHWEIKER, Wife of Senator (Pennsylvania)

POTATO FILLING

¾ cup chopped celery and leaves
½ cup boiling water
½ teaspoon salt
¼ teaspoon pepper
1 tablespoon chopped parsley
pinch of saffron
2 cups mashed potatoes
2 eggs, beaten
2 cups bread cubes
1 cup milk
butter

Cook celery in water with salt, pepper, parsley and saffron until soft, about 10 minutes. Lightly mix with the potatoes, eggs, bread cubes and milk. Spoon into a well buttered casserole, dot top with butter and bake in a 350° oven for 40 minutes. Makes 6 servings.

Mrs. Edwin D. Eshleman
MRS. EDWIN D. ESHLEMAN, Wife of Representative (Pennsylvania)

TOLL HOUSE POTATOES

6 medium to large potatoes, boiled
bottled French dressing
½ cup cream sauce
½ cup mayonnaise

1 onion, finely chopped
butter
bread crumbs
cheese (optional)

Cool and dice potatoes and then marinate them in French dressing for at least 3 hours. Combine cream sauce and mayonnaise. Saute onion in butter and add to sauce. Mix sauce with potatoes and place in casserole dish. Cover with bread crumbs and cheese and bake at 400° for about 20 minutes or until bubbly. May be prepared and refrigerated 24 hours before baking. Makes 6 to 8 servings.

MRS. JOHN H. TERRY, Wife of former Representative (New York)

SPRINGTIME POTATOES

4½ pounds small new potatoes
4½ tablespoons chopped green onions
1 cup chopped cucumber
3 teaspoons salt

dash pepper
1½ cups dairy sour cream
6 tablespoons chopped green pepper

Scrape potatoes and boil until tender. Drain. Heat remaining ingredients but do not boil. Pour mixture over hot potatoes. May be frozen. Makes 12 servings.

MRS. OMAR BURLESON, Wife of Representative (Texas)

HOT GERMAN POTATO SALAD

4 medium potatoes
6 slices bacon
2/3 cup chopped onion
2 teaspoons flour
4 to 6 teaspoons sugar

1½ teaspoons salt
½ teaspoon celery seed
dash pepper
2/3 cup water
6 tablespoons vinegar

Boil potatoes in their jackets, peel and cut into thin slices. Fry bacon slowly in skillet; drain on absorbent paper; crumble. Saute onion in bacon fat until golden brown. Blend in flour, sugar and seasonings. Cook over low heat, stirring until smooth and bubbly. Remove from heat. Stir in water and vinegar. Bring to a boil, stirring constantly. Boil 1 minute. Stir potatoes and crumbled bits of bacon in carefully. Remove from heat; cover and let stand until ready to serve. Makes 4 servings.

Mrs. Douglas R. Smith

MRS. DOUGLAS R. SMITH, Daughter-in-law of Representative Neal Smith (Iowa)

POTATO CASSEROLE

6 medium potatoes
1 can cream of chicken soup
1 pint sour cream
¼ cup green onions, chopped

1 cup grated longhorn or cheddar
  cheese
salt and pepper to taste

Boil potatoes with skins on. Peel and dice. Add other ingredients and bake at 325° for 45 minutes. Makes 4 servings.

Elizabeth C. Rhodes

ELIZABETH C. RHODES, Daughter of Representative John J. Rhodes (Arizona)

PARTY POTATOES

1 3 ounce package cream cheese
½ cup dairy sour cream
5 boiled potatoes, mashed
1 tablespoon chopped chives

salt and pepper to taste
milk (optional)
paprika

Beat cream cheese and sour cream together and slowly add potatoes. Beat in chives and seasonings. Add a little milk if it is too stiff. Put in a buttered 9 x 9 inch pan. Sprinkle with paprika. Bake in a 350° oven for 30 minutes. This casserole may be prepared, covered lightly and refrigerated until it is to be baked. If this is done, increase baking time to 1 hour. Makes 7 to 8 servings.

Mrs. Bert Bandstra

MRS. BERT BANDSTRA, Wife of former Representative (Iowa)

RUSSIAN POTATOES

4 to 6 medium potatoes, peeled
2 to 3 medium yellow onions, peeled
salt and pepper to taste

½ stick butter
¾ cup dairy sour cream
parsley sprigs

Cut potatoes and onions into large cubes and place in a greased casserole. Add salt and pepper, mix well, cover and bake at 400° for about 40 minutes, checking after 30 minutes. Before serving add butter and, when butter is melted, add sour cream, stirring in gently. Garnish with parsley. Makes 5 to 6 servings.

Mrs. Warren G. Magnuson

MRS. WARREN G. MAGNUSON, Wife of Senator (Washington)

NEWT'S SCALLOPED HASHED BROWNS

2 pounds frozen hashed brown
  potatoes
1 can cream of chicken soup
1 pint sour cream (or Smetina)
1 teaspoon butter, melted
½ teaspoon black pepper

½ cup chopped onion
1 cup grated sharp cheddar cheese
1 cup grated American cheese
2 cups corn flakes
1 stick butter, melted

Spread potatoes evenly in a large flat, buttered baking dish. Combine soup, sour cream, 1 teaspoon of butter, pepper, onion and cheeses and pour over the potatoes. Stir corn flakes in remaining butter and spread over top of soup mixture. Bake in 350° oven for 45 minutes. May be prepared and refrigerated until it is to be baked. May be frozen. Makes 12 servings.

Mrs. William H. Bates

MRS. WILLIAM H. BATES, Wife of former Representative (Massachusetts)

POTATOBURGERS

6 medium potatoes
4 eggs, beaten
⅔ cup grated sharp cheese
1 teaspoon salt

⅛ teaspoon pepper
¼ cup flour
butter

Peel, boil and mash potatoes. Add eggs, cheese, salt and pepper. Mix well. Form into round patties and roll in flour. Fry in butter slowly until browned. Makes 6 servings.

Mrs. William F. Norrell

MRS. WILLIAM F. NORRELL, former Representative (Arkansas)

120

SWEET POTATO PONE

5 cups grated yams
4½ cups sugar
1 teaspoon vanilla
1 cup cooking oil
4 eggs, separated
½ teaspoon cinnamon
2½ teaspoons nutmeg

3½ cups sifted flour
2 teaspoons baking soda
⅔ cup water
1 teaspoon salt
2 cups chopped nuts
½ cup raisins
½ cup grated coconut

Cook potatoes with 1½ cups sugar for about 3 minutes. Cool. Add vanilla and set aside. Cream remaining sugar with oil; add egg yolks and spices. Sift some of the flour into this and mix. Continue to add flour, a little at a time, until all has been blended. Mix baking soda with water and add to batter along with salt, nuts, raisins and coconut. Stir in potato mixture. Beat egg whites until stiff and fold into batter. Pour into a greased and floured 14 x 10 x 2 inch cake pan but do not fill more than ⅔ full as it rises during baking. Bake for 1 hour at 350°. For slicing, cook a little longer and remove from pan while still quite warm. May be frozen. Makes 12 servings.

Lindy (Mrs. Hale) Boggs

LINDY (MRS. HALE) BOGGS, Representative (Louisiana)

HAWAIIAN SWEET POTATO BALLS

4 large cooked sweet potatoes, mashed
3 tablespoons butter
1 teaspoon salt
⅛ teaspoon pepper
pinch of nutmeg

pinch of cinnamon
3 tablespoons brown sugar, packed
1½ cups crushed cereal flakes
8 pineapple slices
8 maraschino cherries

Combine sweet potatoes, butter, seasonings and brown sugar. Drop ⅓ to ½ cup sweet potato mixture onto waxed paper containing crushed cereal flakes and roll into ball. Place ball on pineapple slice in buttered pan. Top with cherry. Bake at 350° for 20 minutes. Makes 8 servings.

Mrs. Melvin Price

MRS. MELVIN PRICE, Wife of Representative (Illinois)

121

ORANGE SWEET POTATOES

6 large sweet potatoes
½ pound butter
1½ cups sugar
¾ cup orange juice
2 eggs

1 teaspoon vanilla
dash nutmeg
8 orange shells
marshmallows

Boil potatoes until tender. Drain, peel and mash. Beat in mixer until light and fluffy. Add other ingredients, except orange shells and marshmallows and mix well. Scoop out orange shells and fill with potato mixture. Heat at 350° and add a marshmallow to top of each. Do not freeze. Makes 8 servings.

Mrs. George Corley Wallace

MRS. GEORGE CORLEY WALLACE, Wife of Governor (Alabama)

BOURBON PECAN SWEET POTATOES

4 pounds sweet potatoes
¼ pound butter
½ cup bourbon
⅓ cup orange juice

¼ cup firmly packed brown sugar
1 teaspoon salt
½ teaspoon apple pie spice
⅓ cup chopped pecans

Boil potatoes until tender. Peel and mash. Add remaining ingredients except pecans and mix well. Pour into casserole and ring top with pecans. Bake at 350° for 45 minutes. May be frozen. Makes 8 to 10 servings.

Mrs. Robert H. Michel

MRS. ROBERT H. MICHEL, Wife of Representative (Illinois)

SWEET POTATOES WITH BOURBON

2½ cups cooked, mashed sweet
  potatoes
½ teaspoon salt
pepper to taste
1 tablespoon brown sugar

2 tablespoons bourbon
2 tablespoons butter
6 tablespoons cream (approximately)
pineapple slices (or orange shells)
marshmallows

Add salt, pepper, brown sugar and bourbon to the mashed sweet potatoes and beat. Add butter and then add cream as needed to make mixture moist but not runny. Bake on pineapple slices with marshmallows on top in a 350° oven for 20 minutes. Makes 8 servings.

Mrs. Walter D. Huddleston

MRS. WALTER D. HUDDLESTON, Wife of Senator (Kentucky)

122

BRANDIED SWEET POTATOES

⅔ cup brown sugar
½ cup chopped pecans
½ cup melted butter
½ teaspoon cinnamon
4 cups cooked sweet potatoes
⅓ cup orange juice
2 to 3 tablespoons brandy

1 teaspoon salt
dash of pepper
⅛ to 1 teaspoon orange peel
   (optional)
1 teaspoon ginger
¼ teaspoon allspice

Combine ⅓ cup brown sugar, pecans, ¼ cup melted butter and cinnamon. Mix and set aside for topping. Combine cooked sweet potatoes, remaining butter, remaining brown sugar, orange juice, brandy, salt, pepper, orange peel, ginger and allspice. Mix well. Put in shallow buttered baking dish. Spread nutmeat topping over sweet potatoes. Bake at 350° for 30 minutes. May be frozen. Makes 8 servings.

Mrs Lionel Van Deerlin

MRS. LIONEL VAN DEERLIN, Wife of Representative (California)

SWEET POTATO CASSEROLE

3 pounds sweet potatoes
¾ cup light brown sugar
3 tablespoons butter
½ teaspoon cinnamon

½ teaspoon nutmeg
¼ teaspoon salt
1 cup milk

Cook sweet potatoes in boiling salted water until tender, peel and mash. Stir in all of remaining ingredients except 2 tablespoons sugar. Turn into a greased 1½ quart casserole and sprinkle remaining sugar on top. Bake in a preheated 400° oven for 30 minutes. Makes 8 to 10 servings.

Margaret Mackie Sanders MD

MARGARET MACKIE SANDERS, M.D., Daughter of former Representative John C. Mackie (Michigan)

ALMOND SWEET POTATO PUFF

2 cups mashed, cooked sweet potatoes
2/3 cup orange juice
1/2 teaspoon grated orange rind
1/4 cup brown sugar, packed

3 tablespoons melted butter
2 eggs, separated
1/4 cup chopped, blanched almonds
salt

Combine sweet potatoes, orange juice, rind, brown sugar and butter. Whip until light. Beat egg yolks and blend into potato mixture along with half of the almonds. Beat egg whites until stiff but not dry and then fold into potato mixture. Salt to taste. Turn into greased 2 quart casserole and sprinkle remaining nuts over the top. Bake at 375° for 30 to 35 minutes. Makes 6 servings.

Mrs. Jerry L. Pettis

MRS. JERRY L. PETTIS, Representative (California)

SWEET POTATO SOUFFLE

6 medium size sweet potatoes
1 cup sugar
1/2 stick butter
juice of 1 lemon

1/2 cup raisins
1/2 cup crushed pineapple
marshmallows

Boil, peel and mash sweet potatoes. Place in blender with sugar, butter and lemon juice and mix at high speed until thoroughly blended. Fold in raisins and pineapple. Bake in buttered casserole at 275° for 35 to 40 minutes. Cover top with marshmallows, return to the oven and bake until golden brown. Makes 10 to 12 servings.

Mrs. John L. Mc Millan, Jr.

MRS. JOHN L. MCMILLAN, JR., Daughter-in-law of former Representative John L. McMillan (South Carolina)

124

WILD RICE AMANDINE CASSEROLE

2 cups wild rice
¼ pound butter or margarine
2 tablespoons chopped onions and chives
1 tablespoon chopped shallots (or onions with tops)

3 tablespoons chopped green pepper
4½ cups hot chicken bouillon (or broth)
salt and pepper to taste
¾ cup slivered almonds

Wash and drain wild rice. Heat butter in a large skillet and add rice and chopped ingredients. Cook over low heat until the rice begins to turn yellow or translucent. Stir in broth, seasonings, and almonds. Pour into a greased casserole and bake, covered, in 325° oven for 1¼ hours or until rice is tender and liquid is absorbed. May be frozen. Makes 8 to 10 servings.

Mrs. Harry A. Blackmun

MRS. HARRY A. BLACKMUN, Wife of Associate Justice, Supreme Court (Minnesota)

WILD RICE CASSEROLE

1 cup wild rice, uncooked
1 onion, chopped
3 stalks celery, chopped
1 teaspoon seasoned salt

½ cup white wine (optional)
2 tablespoons butter
salt and pepper to taste
1 quart chicken broth

Combine all ingredients and bake at 325° for 2 hours. May be frozen. Makes 8 servings.

Mrs. Hamer H. Budge

MRS. HAMER H. BUDGE, Wife of former Representative (Idaho)

125

ALICE'S RICE CASSEROLE

1 cup Uncle Ben's converted rice
1 pint sour cream
1 cup cheddar cheese cubes
1 4 ounce can green chili peppers,
  drained and chopped

1 cup gruyere cheese cubes
parmesan cheese
paprika (optional)

Cook rice according to package directions and mix with cream. Put half of rice in a buttered 2 quart casserole and cover with the cheddar cubes. Add a layer of green chilies and a layer of gruyere cheese. Add remainder of rice and sprinkle with parmesan. Paprika may be used for color. Heat in 350° oven about 30 minutes, uncovered. Top will brown. May be prepared early in day and heated later. Makes 8 servings.

Mrs. Tom Steed

MRS. TOM STEED, Wife of Representative (Oklahoma)

MONTEREY RICE

1 cup raw rice
salt to taste
2 cups dairy sour cream
1 6 ounce can green Ortega chilies,
  chopped

½ pound jack cheese, grated
½ pound cheddar cheese, grated
1 tablespoon butter

Reserve ¼ cup jack and ¼ cup cheddar cheese. Cook rice according to package directions. Drain and salt. In buttered casserole, layer rice, sour cream, chilies and cheese. Dot with butter and sprinkle reserved mixed cheeses over the top. Bake at 350° for 30 to 40 minutes. May be frozen.

Mrs. Burt L. Talcott

MRS. BURT L. TALCOTT, Wife of Representative (California)

126

CONSOMME RICE

1 cup raw long grain white rice	2 tablespoons butter
1 medium onion, grated	1 can beef consomme
1 can sliced mushrooms	6 ounces water

Put rice in buttered casserole. Saute onions and mushrooms in butter over low heat. Combine consomme with water and add it with the mushrooms, onion and butter to the rice. Cover tightly. Bake 1 hour in 375° oven. May be stirred half way through baking time. Cover again and continue to bake. Makes 6 servings.

Mrs. A. Sydney Herlong, Jr.

Mrs. A. Sydney Herlong, Jr., Wife of former Representative (Florida)

TEXAS GREEN RICE

2 cups raw rice	1 cup chopped green onions with tops
1½ to 2 cups milk	1 or 2 cloves garlic, minced
½ cup salad oil	1 pound sharp cheese, grated
1 cup chopped green pepper	salt and pepper to taste
1 cup chopped parsley	

Cook rice as package directs. Combine all ingredients, reserving some of the cheese. Put in a casserole and top with remaining cheese. Bake in a 350° oven for 1 hour. May be frozen. Makes 12 servings.

Mrs. Jack Brooks

Mrs. Jack Brooks, Wife of Representative (Texas)

RICE CASSEROLE DRESSING (WITH SAUSAGE)

1 pound pork sausage links
2 tablespoons sausage drippings
½ cup chopped onions
1 cup sliced fresh mushrooms
2 tablespoons minced parsley
1 cup uncooked rice

2¾ cups chicken broth
1 teaspoon salt
1 cup walnuts, chopped
¼ teaspoon nutmeg
dash of pepper

Cook sausage until done. Remove from skillet, drain and cut into ½ inch pieces. Add onions, mushrooms and parsley to 2 tablespoons of sausage drippings and saute until onions are tender but not brown. Cook rice in chicken broth with salt. Toss sauteed ingredients lightly with hot rice, sausage, walnuts, nutmeg and pepper, moistening with remaining chicken broth if dressing seems dry. Makes 6 to 8 servings.

Mrs. Edward J. Derwinski

MRS. EDWARD J. DERWINSKI, Wife of Representative (Illinois)

RICE PILAF

2 tablespoons butter or oil
1 cup long grain rice
1 onion, finely chopped
½ green pepper, diced
2 cups stock, any kind (or combined with tomato juice)

salt
pepper
½ teaspoon Accent

Melt fat in a heavy pan and add rice. Toss with a wooden spoon and cook over fairly low heat until rice is just coated with fat and translucent. Do not allow rice to brown. Stir until fat begins to bubble. Add onion and green pepper. Cook until soft. In the meantime bring liquid to a boil and add salt, pepper and Accent. Pour the boiling liquid over rice mixture. Cover tightly and allow to simmer over very low heat until rice is tender and has absorbed all the liquid, about 25 or 30 minutes. Makes 4 servings.

Mrs Fred Bradley

MRS. FRED BRADLEY, Wife of former Representative (Michigan)

RICE CASSEROLE

1 can beef bouillon soup	1 teaspoon salt
1 can water	3 tablespoons corn oil
1 cup long grain rice	1/4 teaspoon pepper
1/4 teaspoon garlic salt	

Combine all ingredients in saucepan. Heat but do not boil. Pour in casserole; bake covered in a preheated 375° oven for 30 minutes. Makes 6 to 8 servings.

Mrs. Horace R. Kornegay

MRS. HORACE R. KORNEGAY, Wife of former Representative (North Carolina)

SPINACH SUPREME

2 packages frozen chopped spinach	2 1/2 tablespoons sherry
1 1/2 tablespoons butter	1 teaspoon salt
1 tablespoon flour	pinch of nutmeg
2 1/2 tablespoons shredded parmesan	1/2 cup dairy sour cream

Cook spinach according to package directions. Drain well. Melt butter in pan and stir in flour. Return spinach to pan. Stir in cheese, sherry, salt, nutmeg and sour cream. Heat thoroughly in pan or put in casserole and reheat in oven at 350°. Makes 6 to 8 servings.

Mrs. Winston L. Prouty

MRS. WINSTON L. PROUTY, Wife of former Senator (Vermont)

SPINACH RICE CASSEROLE

1 package frozen chopped spinach, cooked	2 tablespoons butter
1 cup grated sharp cheese	1/4 teaspoon nutmeg
3 cups cooked rice	1/3 cup milk
2 eggs, beaten	1/2 teaspoon Worcestershire sauce
2 tablespoons finely chopped onion	1 teaspoon salt
	1 cup buttered bread crumbs

Mix all ingredients except bread crumbs. Place in greased casserole. Top with buttered crumbs. Bake at 350° for 35 minutes until golden brown. Makes 6 servings.

Mrs. James Harvey

MRS. JAMES HARVEY, Wife of former Representative (Michigan)

JANEY'S SPINACH CASSEROLE

2 packages frozen chopped spinach
½ cup chopped onion
1 stick butter
1 10 ounce can artichoke hearts

1 pint sour cream
1 4 ounce jar shredded parmesan
  cheese

Cook spinach as directed on package. Drain well. Cook onion in butter until clear. Drain artichokes, squeezing water out of each quarter. Add sour cream. Mix all ingredients together. Put in greased casserole. Sprinkle cheese over top and bake in 350° oven for 30 minutes. Makes 8 servings.

Mrs. Clifford McIntire

MRS. CLIFFORD MCINTIRE, Wife of former Representative (Maine)

SAVORY CHOPPED SPINACH

2 packages frozen chopped spinach
2 3 ounce packages cream cheese,
  softened
5 slices bacon

1 cup sour cream
2 tablespoons dried minced green onion
2 tablespoons horse radish
salt to taste

Cook spinach according to package directions. Drain thoroughly. Add cream cheese and stir until blended. Fry bacon until crisp. Drain and crumble. In a greased casserole combine spinach mixture with bacon and remaining ingredients. Bake in 350° oven for 45 minutes or until thoroughly heated. Makes 6 servings.

Mrs. Thomas E. Cole

MRS. THOMAS E. COLE, Daughter-in-law of former Representative W. Sterling Cole (New York)

130

ACORN SQUASH

2 acorn squash
4 strips bacon
bacon fat
1 cup minced onion
3 stalks celery, chopped

1 green pepper, chopped
½ cup tomato sauce (or catsup)
salt and pepper
butter
bread or cracker crumbs

Cut squash in half, remove seeds and membrane and arrange on buttered baking sheet. Fry the bacon until crisp, crumble and reserve. In bacon fat saute onion, celery and green pepper until tender. Stir in tomato sauce. Sprinkle squash with salt and pepper and dot with butter. Fill squash with vegetable mixture and sprinkle with crumbs. Bake in 350° oven for 30 minutes or until tender. Sprinkle bacon over top of each one. Makes 4 servings.

MRS. WILLIAM J. RANDALL, Wife of Representative (Missouri)

JENNYE'S BAKED SQUASH

3 pounds small yellow squash, sliced
¼ cup butter
salt and pepper to taste
¼ cup sugar

½ cup chopped onion
½ cup milk
2 large eggs
buttered cracker crumbs

Cook squash in salted water until tender. Do not overcook. Drain and put squash into a baking dish. Add butter immediately and then the salt, pepper, sugar and onions. Beat milk and eggs together and pour over squash. Mix well. Top with buttered crumbs. Bake in 450° oven for 20 minutes. May be frozen. Makes 8 servings.

MRS. FRANK A. STUBBLEFIELD, Wife of former Representative (Kentucky)

SQUASH CRISP

2 12 ounce packages frozen squash,
   thawed
1 tablespoon butter
1 tablespoon flour
1 egg, beaten
1 tablespoon prepared mustard
1 tablespoon brown sugar

1 teaspoon salt
⅛ teaspoon pepper

Topping:
2 tablespoons butter
1 tablespoon brown sugar
1 cup crushed corn flakes (or Special K)

Mix all ingredients together and place in buttered casserole. Combine topping ingredients and sprinkle over top. Bake in 350° oven for 30 minutes. Makes 6 to 8 servings.

MRS. BERKLEY BEDELL, Wife of Representative (Iowa)

SQUASH SWISS CHEESE CASSEROLE

3 to 4 pounds yellow squash
2 medium onions, minced
2 bay leaves
6 sprigs parsley
½ teaspoon leaf thyme
boiling salted water
6 tablespoons butter
6 tablespoons flour
3 cups milk

dash of salt
1 teaspoon seasoned salt
several dashes ground nutmeg
dash of Worcestershire sauce
4 egg yolks, beaten
1⅓ cups shredded Swiss cheese
cayenne pepper
buttered bread crumbs

Cut squash into ⅓ inch slices; place in large saucepan with onions, bay leaves, parsley and thyme. Cover with boiling water and cook until squash is barely tender. Drain, remove parsley and bay leaves and set aside.

Heat butter in saucepan, blend in flour and gradually add milk and salt. Cook, stirring constantly until thickened. Add seasoned salt, nutmeg and Worcestershire sauce. Remove from heat. Gradually blend in egg yolks by first adding a small amount of the hot mixture to the beaten yolks in a small bowl. Repeat this procedure several times and then return it all back to the saucepan. Stir in 1 cup of cheese and add cayenne pepper. Combine squash and sauce, stirring gently, and turn into a large buttered baking dish about 2 inches deep. Mix remaining cheese with an equal amount of bread crumbs. Sprinkle over squash and bake at 350° for 35 minutes or until top is brown and bubbly. May be frozen. Makes 12 servings.

Mrs. Kenneth Allison Roberts
MRS. KENNETH ALLISON ROBERTS, Wife of former Representative (Alabama)

SQUASH CRUMB CASSEROLE

2 pounds yellow summer squash
salt and pepper
1 can cream of chicken soup
½ pint dairy sour cream

¼ pound margarine, melted
1 package Pepperidge Farm stuffing
crumbs

Cook squash in boiling salted water. Drain and season lightly with salt and pepper. Add soup and sour cream. Toss crumbs in the margarine and add half of them to the squash. Put in a casserole, top with remaining crumbs and bake at 350° for 30 minutes. Makes 8 servings.

Mrs. Maurice G. Burnside
MRS. MAURICE G. BURNSIDE, Wife of former Representative (West Virginia)

SUMMER SQUASH CASSEROLE

3 pounds yellow squash
1 tablespoon salt
1½ cups cheddar cheese, grated
1 cup cottage cheese
5 eggs, beaten

1 cup bread crumbs
2 tablespoons parsley
½ teaspoon pepper
4 tablespoons melted butter

Peel and grate or finely chop squash. Mix with salt and let stand 30 minutes. Press all the liquid from the squash. Mix together squash, cheeses, eggs, crumbs, parsley and pepper in a 3 quart casserole. Spread butter over the top. Bake ½ hour at 350°. Makes 6 to 8 servings.

Mrs. Robert T. Stafford

MRS. ROBERT T. STAFFORD, Wife of Senator (Vermont)

SQUASH CASSEROLE

3 pounds yellow squash, sliced
3 medium onions, chopped
4 tablespoons butter (or bacon drippings)
salt and pepper to taste

2 eggs, beaten
½ pound sharp cheese, grated
Ritz crackers, crumbled
melted butter

Boil squash and onions in small amount of salted water until tender. Drain and mash. Add butter, salt and pepper. When cool, add eggs and cheese. Mix thoroughly. Put in a greased, shallow 8 inch casserole and top with the crumbs and butter. Bake at 350° for 30 to 40 minutes.

Mrs. John J. Flynt, Jr.

MRS. JOHN J. FLYNT, JR., Wife of Representative (Georgia)

133

YELLOW SQUASH SOUFFLE

10 to 12 medium size yellow squash
1 tablespoon chopped onion
½ stick butter or margarine
1 cup toasted bread crumbs
   (or soda cracker crumbs)
1 teaspoon salt

1 teaspoon sugar
½ cup milk
1 egg
2 teaspoons baking powder
bread crumbs
butter

Cook squash and onion in small amount of water until tender. Drain. Add butter and bread crumbs to hot mixture and beat until well mixed. Add salt, sugar, milk, whole egg and baking powder and mix thoroughly. Pour into well buttered casserole, top with bread crumbs and dot generously with butter. Bake uncovered at 400° for 30 to 40 minutes. Serve immediately. Makes 6 to 8 servings.

Mrs. G. Elliott Hagan

MRS. G. ELLIOTT HAGAN, Wife of former Representative (Georgia)

SQUASH SOUFFLE

2 pounds yellow squash
2 eggs, beaten
½ pound New York State cheese, grated
2 cups thick white sauce

1 onion, grated (optional)
salt and pepper
bread crumbs

Cook squash until tender, drain and mash into a fine pulp. Add beaten eggs, grated cheese, white sauce and onion. Season to taste. Cook in covered double boiler for 1 hour. Put in casserole, top with bread crumbs and bake at 375° until bottom of casserole bubbles, about 20 minutes. Makes 8 servings.

Mrs. Horace R. Kornegay

MRS. HORACE R. KORNEGAY, Wife of former Representative (North Carolina)

134

TOMATOES AMERICANA

3 medium large ripe tomatoes
¾ cup dried bread crumbs
½ teaspoon minced chives
2 tablespoons finely chopped onion
2 tablespoons butter

½ teaspoon basil flakes
½ teaspoon sugar
2 teaspoons parsley flakes
¼ cup crumbled blue cheese
salt and pepper to taste

Cut off tops of tomatoes and hollow out inside. Invert and drain on paper toweling. Saute bread crumbs, chives and onion in butter. Stir in remaining ingredients. Fill tomato cavities with the cheese stuffing. Place in a casserole and bake at 375° for about 15 minutes. Serve hot. Makes 3 servings.

Mrs. Otis G. Pike

MRS. OTIS G. PIKE, Wife of Representative (New York)

CHEESE TOMATOES

3 large tomatoes
salt and pepper to taste
4 ounces shredded cheddar cheese

2 tablespoons butter
¼ cup soft bread crumbs

Cut tomatoes in half and place in shallow pan. Season with salt and pepper. Mix cheese, butter and bread crumbs. Broil tomatoes 5 minutes. Top each half with cheese mixture. Broil 2 to 3 minutes longer.

Mrs. Willard S. Curtin

MRS. WILLARD S. CURTIN, Wife of former Representative (Pennsylvania)

RISSOTTO

½ cup uncooked rice
2 cups canned tomatoes
3 or 4 small onions, sliced
1 teaspoon salt
butter, size of egg

2 teaspoons sugar
pinch of baking soda
1 cup sweet cream
12 ripe olives (optional)

Combine rice, tomatoes, onions, salt, butter and sugar. Add baking soda to the cream and then add to other ingredients. Bake covered, in a 300° oven until liquid is absorbed, about 2 hours. Olive slices may be used as garnish when ready to serve. May be frozen. Makes 6 to 8 servings.

Mrs. Charles A. Mosher

MRS. CHARLES A. MOSHER, Wife of Representative (Ohio)

SCALLOPED TURNIPS

3 medium size turnips, peeled
2 tablespoons butter
2 tablespoons flour
1½ cups milk

1 teaspoon salt
⅛ teaspoon pepper
½ cup grated cheese

Cut turnips in slices and boil in salted water about 15 minutes. Make a white sauce with butter, flour, milk, salt and pepper. Pour this over the turnips and sprinkle cheese on top. Bake for about 10 minutes at 350° and serve very hot. Makes 4 servings.

Mrs. Carl Albert

MRS. CARL ALBERT, Wife of Speaker, House of Representatives (Oklahoma)

ZUCCHINI FRITTATA

3 tablespoons olive oil
1 medium onion, minced
1 clove garlic
5 small zucchini, thinly sliced
1 large tomato, peeled and diced
salt and pepper to taste

1 teaspoon herbs (parsley, sweet marjoram, thyme, sweet basil or summer savory)
9 eggs
2 tablespoons grated parmesan cheese

Heat oil in skillet and cook onion and garlic until golden brown. Add zucchini, tomato and seasonings. Cover and cook until zucchini is tender. Remove from heat. Beat eggs lightly, add cheese and mix with the cooled vegetables. Pour this mixture back into the skillet, cover and cook over low heat. Occasionally pull the mixture away from the sides of the pan and cook until the frittata is solid. Brown lightly in the broiler. Cut into wedges and serve immediately. Makes 6 servings.

Mrs. Bob Straub

MRS. ROBERT W. STRAUB, Wife of Governor (Oregon)

136

ZUCCHINI CHEESE CASSEROLE

5 medium zucchini, sliced
3 eggs, beaten
½ pound grated cheddar cheese
½ jar pimientos

butter
garlic salt
corn flake or cracker crumbs

Cook zucchini squash until tender, drain and mash. Add the next 5 ingredients, mix well and put in casserole. Sprinkle with crumbs. Bake at 325° for 40 minutes or until set and slightly brown. May be frozen. Makes 8 servings.

Mrs. John Dellenback

MRS. JOHN DELLENBACK, Wife of former Representative (Oregon)

ZUCCHINI CREOLE

6 medium zucchini, sliced
3 tablespoons butter
3 tablespoons flour
2 8 ounce cans tomatoes, chopped
1 green pepper, chopped
1 onion, chopped

1 teaspoon salt
1 tablespoon brown sugar
1 bay leaf
4 whole cloves
bread crumbs
grated cheese

Boil zucchini in salted water for 3 minutes and then drain. Stir butter and flour together in pan until blended. Add tomatoes, green pepper, onion and the zucchini, mixing well. Add salt, brown sugar, bay leaf and cloves and pour into a baking dish. Cover with bread crumbs and grated cheese. Bake uncovered in a 350° oven for 30 minutes. Makes 6 servings.

Mrs. Clair W. Burgener

MRS. CLAIR W. BURGENER, Wife of Representative (California)

ZUCCHINI CASSEROLE

4 medium zucchini, sliced ½ inch thick
¾ cup shredded carrot
½ cup chopped onion
6 teaspoons butter or margarine

2½ cups Pepperidge Farm stuffing mix
1 can cream of chicken soup
½ cup sour cream

Cook zucchini until tender, drain and set aside. Cook carrot and onion in 4 teaspoons of butter. Stir in 1½ cups of stuffing mix, soup and sour cream. Stir in zucchini and put in casserole. Melt remaining butter, add remaining stuffing mix and toss. Sprinkle over casserole. Bake at 350° for 30 to 40 minutes. Makes 8 servings.

Mrs. David E. Bradley

MRS. DAVID E. BRADLEY, Daughter of former Representative James Harvey (Michigan)

SOUTH AMERICAN ZUCCHINI

2 pounds small fresh zucchini (or
    2 pints frozen), cubed
2 slices bacon
⅓ cup chopped green pepper
½ teaspoon steak sauce

1 8 ounce can tomato sauce
3 tablespoons minced onion
1 teaspoon sugar
¼ teaspoon pepper

Cook zucchini in small amount of boiling water until tender. While it cooks, fry bacon until crisp; remove to paper towel to drain. Saute green pepper; add steak sauce, tomato sauce and onion. Add sugar and pepper. Crumble in the bacon and simmer uncovered for about 10 minutes. Drain zucchini well and add to sauce mix. Makes 4 servings.

Mrs. Fred E. Busbey

MRS. FRED E. BUSBEY, Wife of former Representative (Illinois)

138

ZUCCHINI SQUASH

6 zucchini squash, parboiled
6 eggs, beaten
6 tablespoons scraped onion
parmesan cheese

3 cups bread crumbs
salt and pepper to taste
paprika
butter

Cut zucchini squash lengthwise and scoop out pulp. Mix pulp with eggs, onion, parmesan cheese, bread crumbs, salt and pepper to make a dry, dressing type filling. Stuff the squash hulls with this mixture, mounding slightly. Sprinkle with paprika and dot with butter. Put in 400° oven until butter melts and squash is heated through.

Mrs. Tazewell Shepard, Jr.

MRS. TAZEWELL SHEPARD, JR., Daughter of Senator John Sparkman (Alabama)

FRESH CORN ZUCCHINI CASSEROLE

6 ears fresh corn
6 small zucchini, sliced ¼ inch thick
4 medium tomatoes, quartered
1 green pepper, thinly sliced
1 Bermuda onion, thinly sliced,
  separated into rings

¼ cup butter, melted (or vegetable oil)
1 tablespoon flour
1½ teaspoons salt
1 teaspoon sugar
white pepper
1 teaspoon chili powder

Cut corn off the cob with a heavy sharp knife. Use a tablespoon to scrape cob. Combine all vegetables in a large mixing bowl. In a small pan heat butter and stir in flour until smooth. Add salt, sugar, pepper and chili powder. Mix thoroughly with the vegetables and pour into a 2 quart baking casserole and bake in a preheated 325° oven for 1½ hours. May be prepared and refrigerated until time to bake. May be frozen. Makes 8 servings.

Mrs. Stephen M. Young

MRS. STEPHEN M. YOUNG, Wife of former Senator (Ohio)

OMY'S RATATOUILLE

2 garlic cloves, chopped
1 onion, sliced
½ cup olive oil
1 large eggplant, unpeeled, diced
3 zucchini squash, sliced

1 green pepper, sliced
1 28 ounce can Italian tomatoes
1 teaspoon fresh basil (or dried oregano)
salt and pepper to taste

Saute garlic and onion in oil. Add eggplant and mix. Add zucchini and green pepper and cook 10 minutes. Add remaining ingredients and cook, covered, for 30 minutes. Uncover and simmer 30 more minutes. Makes 6 servings.

Mrs. Frank E. Evans

MRS. FRANK E. EVANS, Wife of Representative (Colorado)

RATATOUILLE

2 tablespoons olive oil
1 garlic clove
2 large onions, cut in ½ inch slices
2 large green peppers, seeded, cut in ½ inch slices

1 medium eggplant, cut in 1 inch cubes
6 medium zucchini, cut in 1 inch slices
4 large tomatoes, quartered
2 teaspoons salt
1 teaspoon basil

Rub a large casserole with oil and garlic. Discard garlic. Layer the vegetables in casserole, sprinkling each layer with a mixture of the salt and basil. Cover and bake in a 325° oven for 3 hours. Serve either hot or cold. Makes 8 servings.

Mrs. Hamer H. Budge

MRS. HAMER H. BUDGE, Wife of former Representative (Idaho)

SIMPLIFIED RATATOUILLE

2 large onions, sliced
2 tablespoons butter or margarine
1 large eggplant (or 2 medium)
2 large zucchini

2 large yellow squash
salt to taste
6 fresh tomatoes, peeled and cut in pieces

In a skillet cook onions in butter until tender but not brown. Transfer to a large ovenproof casserole. Wash and cut into 2 inch pieces the eggplant, zucchini and yellow squash. Toss, in the casserole, with onions and salt. Cover and bake in a preheated 400° oven for 30 minutes. Add the tomato pieces, cover and bake for an additional 15 minutes. May be frozen. Makes 6 to 8 servings.

Mrs. Alfred D. Sieminski

MRS. ALFRED D. SIEMINSKI, Wife of former Representative (New Jersey)

ONION CAULIFLOWER BAKE

1 10 ounce package frozen cauliflower,
thawed
2 10 ounce packages frozen onions in
cream sauce
¾ cup shredded sharp American
cheese

¼ cup toasted slivered almonds
1 tablespoon snipped parsley
½ cup canned French fried onions,
crumbled
French fried onion rings (optional)

Cut cauliflower into bite size pieces. Prepare creamed onions according to package directions. Add cauliflower, cheese, almonds and parsley to onions. Turn into a 1½ quart casserole. Bake uncovered in 350° oven for 35 minutes or until bubbly and heated through. Top with crumbled French fried onions and bake 5 minutes longer. Garnish with onion rings at serving time if desired. Makes 8 servings.

Mrs. Richard Kelly

Mrs. RICHARD KELLY, Wife of Representative (Florida)

CREAM POTATO PLUS

5 cups diced cooked potatoes
salt
1 10 ounce package frozen peas,
defrosted
1 8 ounce can baby onions, drained

3 slices American cheese, cut in
¼ inch strips
1 can cream of celery soup
1 3 ounce package cream cheese
⅓ cup milk
pinch of savory

Sprinkle cooked potatoes with salt. Combine with peas, onions and ½ the cheese strips in buttered 2 quart casserole. Combine soup, cream cheese, milk and savory and heat slowly over low heat. Stir constantly until well blended. Pour soup mixture over vegetables in casserole and toss gently. Top with remaining cheese strips. Cover and refrigerate. To serve, uncover and bake in 350° oven for 45 minutes. Makes 6 servings.

Mrs. Clair W. Burgener

Mrs. CLAIR W. BURGENER, Wife of Representative (California)

SPINACH AND ARTICHOKE CASSEROLE

4 packages frozen chopped spinach
salt
2 jars marinated artichokes, slightly
  drained

3 3 ounce packages cream cheese
6 tablespoons milk
4 tablespoons margarine
⅓ cup parmesan cheese

Cook spinach with salt according to package directions and drain. Place artichokes in casserole and cover with spinach. Mix cheese, milk and margarine and spread over spinach. Sprinkle with parmesan cheese. Refrigerate 6 to 24 hours. Bake at 375° until bubbly, about 25 minutes. Makes 8 servings.

MRS. JOHN J. RHODES, Wife of Representative (Arizona)

PATRICIA'S SPINACH CASSEROLE

3 tablespoons butter
3 tablespoons flour
1½ cups milk
salt to taste
white pepper
1 8 ounce package cream cheese
4 packages frozen chopped spinach,
  thawed and drained

1 teaspoon salt
1 teaspoon nutmeg
½ teaspoon garlic salt
2 small jars artichokes, drained
parmesan cheese

Blend butter and flour over low heat until frothy. Stirring constantly, add milk and continue cooking until sauce thickens. Remove from heat and add salt and pepper. Break up cream cheese, add to white sauce and blend well. Cook spinach until tender. Drain and mix with cheese sauce and seasonings. Line greased casserole with artichokes and cover with spinach mixture. Top generously with parmesan. Bake at 375° for 20 to 25 minutes. Makes 8 to 10 servings.

MRS. ROBERT E. JONES, Wife of Representative (Alabama)

SPINACH BONNIE

4 10 ounce packages frozen chopped spinach
5 tablespoons butter or margarine
11 ounces cream cheese, softened
juice of 1 lemon
salt, pepper and seasoned salt to taste
dash of nutmeg
2 1 pound cans artichoke hearts, drained

Cook spinach only until thawed. Drain and set aside. Blend butter and cream cheese. Add lemon juice. Combine with spinach and seasonings. Place artichokes, pointed ends up, in a 16 x 8 inch, ungreased casserole dish. Arrange so that each serving will contain artichokes. Spread spinach mixture over and around artichokes. Cover with aluminum foil which has been lightly pierced. Bake at 350° for 30 minutes. If prepared early and refrigerated, take from refrigerator an hour before baking time. Makes 8 servings.

Mrs. Bob Casey

MRS. BOB CASEY, Wife of Representative (Texas)

SPINACH STUFFED TOMATOES

2 packages frozen chopped spinach
salt and pepper to taste
½ stick butter
1 3 ounce package cream cheese
6 to 8 fresh tomatoes

Cook spinach according to package directions. Drain well in colander. Season with salt and pepper. Melt butter and cheese and mix thoroughly with spinach. Remove pulp from inside of tomatoes and stuff with spinach mixture. Bake in 350° oven for short time. Makes 6 to 8 servings.

Mrs. Kenneth Allison Roberts

MRS. KENNETH ALLISON ROBERTS, Wife of former Representative (Alabama)

143

TOMATOES STUFFED WITH CORN

6 large firm tomatoes
sugar and salt
1 cup minced onion
1 cup minced green pepper
6 tablespoons butter
1 cup minced, cooked ham
1½ teaspoons ground cumin seed

3 cups scraped fresh corn
½ cup heavy cream
1 teaspoon salt
½ teaspoon sugar
freshly ground pepper to taste
6 tablespoons minced fresh parsley
6 teaspoons butter, softened

Cut off and discard top half of tomatoes and remove seeds. Scoop out the pulp, chop it and put in a sieve to drain. Sprinkle the pulp and the insides of the shells lightly with sugar and salt, and invert the shells on paper towels to drain for at least 30 minutes.

In large skillet, saute onion and green pepper in butter until softened. Add ham and cumin seed and stir the mixture over high heat for 1 minute. Add tomato pulp and cook mixture over moderate heat for 4 minutes. Stir in corn, cream, salt, sugar and pepper. Cook mixture, covered, for 3 minutes. Remove cover and stir mixture over high heat for 1 minute. Sprinkle the inside of each tomato shell with 1 tablespoon of parsley. Fill shells with corn mixture, dot each with 1 teaspoon butter and place in a lightly buttered baking pan. Bake at 350° for 10 to 15 minutes or until tomatoes are soft.

Mrs. Stephen L. Neal

MRS. STEPHEN L. NEAL, Wife of Representative (North Carolina)

TOMATO FLORENTINE

6 medium tomatoes
salt
1 tablespoon flour
½ teaspoon salt
½ cup milk

1 egg yolk, slightly beaten
3 tablespoons butter or margarine, melted
1 10 ounce package frozen chopped spinach, cooked and well drained

Cut ½ inch slice off top of each tomato and scoop out pulp, leaving a shell ¼ inch thick. Sprinkle inside of each with salt. Combine flour and ½ teaspoon salt; blend in milk. Stir in egg yolk and 1 tablespoon of butter and add to spinach. Cook and stir over medium heat until mixture simmers. Fill tomatoes with the creamed spinach. Place in shallow baking dish. Top each with 1 teaspoon butter. Bake in 375° oven for 20 minutes. Serve hot. Makes 6 servings.

Mrs. John Kyl

MRS. JOHN KYL, Wife of former Representative (Iowa)

VEGETABLE CASSEROLE

1 cup chopped green pepper (large
   pieces)
1 clove garlic, minced
¼ cup butter
¼ cup flour
⅔ cup milk
¾ teaspoon salt
⅛ teaspoon pepper

⅛ teaspoon basil
⅛ teaspoon oregano
¼ teaspoon sugar
½ cup shredded cheddar cheese
1 28 ounce can tomatoes, drained
2 9 ounce packages frozen corn
1 16 ounce can onions, drained
grated cheese

Cook green pepper and garlic briefly in butter. Add flour and milk to make a white sauce. Then add salt, pepper, basil, oregano and sugar. Cook and stir until it thickens. Add shredded cheese, tomatoes, corn and onions, stirring all together. Pour into casserole and top with grated cheese. Cover and bake at 350° for 45 minutes. Makes 8 to 10 servings.

Mrs. James P. Johnson

MRS. JAMES P. JOHNSON, Wife of Representative (Colorado)

MIXED VEGETABLE CASSEROLE

2 10 ounce packages frozen mixed
   vegetables
1 cup chopped celery
1 cup chopped onion

1 cup mayonnaise
1 cup grated sharp cheese
1 cup crumbled Ritz crackers
¼ pound butter or margarine, melted

Cook mixed vegetables according to package directions and drain. Add the celery, onion, mayonnaise and cheese, mixing well. Place in a lightly greased casserole, sprinkle with crumbs and pour butter over top. Bake at 350° for 30 minutes. May be frozen. Makes 8 to 10 servings.

Mrs. Armistead I. Selden

MRS. ARMISTEAD I. SELDEN, Wife of former Representative (Alabama) presently Ambassador to New Zealand

145

VEGETABLES WITH DRESSING

Dressing:
4 tablespoons salad oil
2 tablespoons Worcestershire sauce
3 drops Tabasco
1 onion, grated
4 hard cooked eggs, grated
1 teaspoon dry mustard
1 pint mayonnaise

Vegetables:
1 can small butter beans, drained
1 can French style green beans, drained
1 can small peas, drained
6 tablespoons butter or margarine

Mix dressing ingredients. Refrigerate overnight to blend flavors. Remove from refrigerator 2 hours before it is to be served to allow it to come to room temperature. Do not heat. Heat vegetables in butter but do not stir. Pour dressing over hot vegetables to serve. Makes 12 servings.

Mrs. John Y. McCollister

MRS. JOHN Y. MCCOLLISTER, Wife of Representative (Nebraska)

VEGETABLES MORNAY

2 packages frozen mixed vegetables
1 teaspoon salt
1/4 teaspoon garlic salt
2 tablespoons butter

Mornay Sauce:
1/4 cup butter
1/3 cup flour
1 cup vegetable liquid

1 cup light cream
1/4 cup grated parmesan cheese
pinch of nutmeg
pinch of thyme
garlic salt to taste
1 teaspoon salt
2 tablespoons white wine

soft bread crumbs
butter

Prepare frozen vegetables according to package directions. Drain and reserve liquid for sauce. Season vegetables with salt, garlic salt and butter and mix gently. Spread in greased 10 x 10 inch baking dish. Cover with mornay sauce. Sprinkle with bread crumbs and dot generously with butter. Bake uncovered at 350° for 30 to 40 minutes. May be frozen. Makes 6 servings.

Mornay Sauce: Blend butter and flour over low heat. Add vegetable liquid gradually, stirring constantly, and cook until thick. Add remaining ingredients, except crumbs and butter, and simmer about 5 minutes. Taste and add additional seasonings if desired.

Mrs. James E. Van Zandt

MRS. JAMES E. VAN ZANDT, Wife of former Representative (Pennsylvania)

146

MACARONI DELIGHT

1½ pound package elbow or shell
    macaroni
1 large onion, chopped
1 spear celery, chopped
1 green pepper, seeded and chopped
2 tablespoons bacon drippings (or
    other shortening)

1 28 ounce can stewed tomatoes
salt and pepper to taste
⅓ cup grated sharp cheddar cheese
paprika
1 6 ounce can tomato juice (optional)

Cook macaroni according to package directions. Rinse and drain. Meanwhile, saute onion, celery and green pepper in bacon drippings until tender. Add tomatoes and season with salt and pepper. Put cooked macaroni in casserole and add vegetable mixture. Combine thoroughly. Top with cheese and paprika. Place in 350° oven for 20 to 30 minutes or until thoroughly heated. If macaroni does not have enough liquid, add tomato juice.

Mrs. Thurgood Marshall

MRS. THURGOOD MARSHALL, Wife of Associate Justice, Supreme Court (Virginia)

APRICOT NOODLE PUDDING

½ pound fine noodles, cooked
3 eggs
¼ cup sugar
2 tablespoons sour cream
2 teaspoons vanilla
pinch of salt

1 tablespoon lemon juice
3 or 4 tablespoons butter or margarine
scant ½ cup sugar
¼ cup water
½ box dried apricots

Mix together the first 8 ingredients. Cook sugar, water and apricots for 10 minutes and add to noodle mixture. Tuck apricots under noodles. Bake in a well greased pan for 1¼ hours at 350°. May be frozen. Makes 8 servings.

Mrs Milton J Shapp

MRS. MILTON J. SHAPP, Wife of Governor (Pennsylvania)

JIFFY HOLLANDAISE

½ cup salad dressing or mayonnaise   **1 teaspoon lemon juice**
2 teaspoons prepared mustard

Whip all ingredients together. Heat and stir over low heat to just below boiling. Makes ½ cup sauce.

Mrs. Daniel J. Flood

Mrs. Daniel J. Flood, Wife of Representative (Pennsylvania)

148

SALADS &
SALAD DRESSING

Gold Fish in Jelly

Fill two or three small fish-moulds with very strong blanc' mange, when cold turn them out, and gild the fish with leaf-gold, let them stand for one hour, that the gold may dry on; have a mould, put a little mould jelly at the bottom, when it is cold lay the gold fish in back downwards, put in some jelly blood-warm to fasten them to their places; when it is cold fill the moulds up with blood-warm jelly, and let them stand all night; the next day turn them out into a dish, and garnish with flowers, or anything you fancy.

The New Art of Cookery
Richard Briggs, 1792

CHICKEN TUJAGUE

8 chicken breast halves
2 cans chicken broth
1 teaspoon salt
¼ teaspoon black pepper
¼ teaspoon paprika
1 chicken bouillon cube
1 vegetable bouillon cube
¼ cup vinegar

¾ cup olive oil
2 packages French salad dressing mix
1 cup finely chopped celery
1 shallot, finely chopped
2 hard cooked eggs, chopped
½ cup mayonnaise
¼ teaspoon Dijon mustard
salt and pepper to taste

Simmer together first 7 ingredients for 25 minutes. Reserve stock. Remove skin of chicken and chop chicken into cubes. Combine vinegar, oil and dressing mix. Pour this, along with 1 pint of chicken stock, over chicken and marinate at least 6 hours, preferably overnight. Mix together the celery, shallot, eggs, mayonnaise and mustard. Fold in the well drained chicken. Add salt and pepper. Chill. If to be served hot, heat in 300° oven. Makes 6 to 8 servings.

Lindy (Mrs. Hale) Boggs

LINDY (MRS. HALE) BOGGS, Representative (Louisiana)

DELUXE TOMATO WITH CHICKEN SALAD

6 medium tomatoes
½ cup chopped, cooked chicken
¾ cup diced cucumber
¼ cup chopped nuts
¼ cup mayonnaise

salt to taste
lettuce
parsley
cauliflower buds

Scald, peel and chill tomatoes. Carefully scoop out the inside of each tomato and remove seeds from the pulp. Chill all ingredients. When ready to serve, mix chicken, cucumber, tomato pulp and nuts with mayonnaise. Add salt if needed. Fill tomatoes. Arrange on lettuce leaves. Garnish with mayonnaise and decorate each tomato top with parsley and cauliflower buds.

Mrs. Russell V. Mack

MRS. RUSSELL V. MACK, Wife of former Representative (Washington)

151

CHICKEN ARTICHOKE SALAD

1 package chicken flavored Ricearoni
6 green onions, sliced
½ cup chopped green pepper
¼ cup sliced stuffed green olives
marinade from artichokes

⅓ cup mayonnaise
¼ teaspoon curry powder
2 6 ounce jars marinated artichoke
  hearts, diced
2 cups diced cooked chicken

Prepare Ricearoni as directed on package, omitting butter. Combine Ricearoni, onions, green pepper and olives. Mix marinade, mayonnaise and curry together and add to rice mixture. Add artichokes and chicken. Toss lightly. Makes 16 to 20 servings.

Mrs. Robert D. Ray

Mrs. Robert D. Ray, Wife of Governor (Iowa)

CHICKEN PECAN SALAD ON PINEAPPLE RINGS

2 cups cubed cooked chicken
1 cup sliced celery
2 tablespoons chopped pimiento
½ cup roasted pecans
½ cup mayonnaise

2 teaspoons lemon juice
salt and pepper to taste
4 fresh (or canned, drained) pineapple
  rings
crisp salad greens

Combine chicken, celery, pimiento, all but 2 tablespoons of the pecans, mayonnaise and lemon juice. Sprinkle with salt and pepper. Place pineapple on salad greens, top with chicken salad and sprinkle with remaining pecans. Makes 4 servings.

Mrs. Phil Landrum

Mrs. Phil M. Landrum, Wife of Representative (Georgia)

152

CHINESE CHICKEN SALAD

1 cup thinly sliced celery
1 cup thinly sliced bell peppers
2 cups shredded lettuce
1 cup shredded, cooked chicken
3 tablespoons shoyu sauce

1 tablespoon sesame seed oil
2 tablespoons vegetable oil
1 tablespoon sugar
pinch of monosodium glutamate
(optional)

Combine in a salad bowl ready for serving: celery, sliced bell peppers, shredded lettuce and shredded chicken. Combine shoyu sauce, sesame seed oil, vegetable oil, sugar and monosodium glutamate. Place in bottle and shake well. Pour over salad and toss gently.

Mrs. Hiram L. Fong

MRS. HIRAM L. FONG, Wife of Senator (Hawaii)

ANN'S CHARLESTON SHRIMP SALAD

3 pounds cooked shrimp, chopped
6 hard cooked eggs, chopped
chopped olives
1 cup diced celery

juice of 3 lemons
salt and pepper to taste
Hellmann's mayonnaise

Combine shrimp with other ingredients. Chill. Makes 6 to 9 servings.

Mrs. James Burrows Edwards

MRS. JAMES BURROWS EDWARDS, Wife of Governor (South Carolina)

SHRIMP SALAD

1 pound shrimp, boiled, deveined and
   diced
½ cup minced celery
¼ cup minced olives
2 hard cooked eggs, chopped
¼ cup dairy sour cream

¼ cup mayonnaise
1 tablespoon lemon juice
pinch of cayenne
salt and pepper to taste
lettuce

Mix shrimp, celery, olives and eggs. Blend sour cream with mayonnaise and lemon juice and season with cayenne, salt and pepper. Combine with shrimp mixture and toss until completely mixed. Chill. Serve on crisp lettuce. Makes 8 servings.

Mrs. Olin E. Teague

MRS. OLIN E. TEAGUE, Wife of Representative (Texas)

SHRIMP REMOULADE

2 hard cooked egg yolks
1 raw egg yolk
¼ teaspoon salt
1 teaspoon horse radish
1 teaspoon prepared mustard
3 tablespoons tarragon vinegar
¼ cup cider vinegar
½ cup salad oil

1 tablespoon chopped parsley
1 tablespoon minced onion
1 pound boiled shrimp, peeled and
   deveined
shredded lettuce
lemon wedge
parsley sprig

Blend egg yolks, salt, horse radish and mustard and beat thoroughly with a fork. Add 2 teaspoons vinegar and beat a few minutes. Add 1 teaspoon oil and beat 2 or 3 minutes. Continue to add vinegar and oil alternately until all is used. Add parsley and onion; stir until blended. Pour over shrimp. Refrigerate in covered dish several hours. To serve, pour over shredded lettuce and garnish with lemon and parsley. Makes 4 servings.

Mrs. Richard C. White

MRS. RICHARD C. WHITE, Wife of Representative (Texas)

154

TANGY SHRIMP REMOULADE

3 tablespoons hot prepared mustard
1 tablespoon horse radish
½ cup tarragon vinegar
1 teaspoon salt
½ teaspoon cayenne pepper
1 tablespoon paprika
½ cup finely minced green onions

½ cup finely minced celery
1 clove garlic, finely minced
2 tablespoons catsup
1 cup salad oil
2 pounds cooked, cleaned shrimp
shredded lettuce

Combine all ingredients except shrimp and lettuce, blending well. Pour over shrimp and chill. Serve on shredded lettuce. Makes 8 servings.

Mrs Henry Amiss Hornthal

MRS. HENRY AMISS HORNTHAL, Daughter of former Representative Thomas Hall (North Dakota)

FRESH APPLE SALAD

4 cups cored and diced apples
1 cup diced oranges (or canned oranges)
1 cup diced pineapple (fresh or canned)
½ cup green seedless grape halves
½ cup currants, raisins or dates
1 cup diced celery

lemon juice
½ cup chopped pecans

Dressing:
1 3 ounce package cream cheese
2 to 3 tablespoons pineapple juice
½ pint whipping cream
2 tablespoons confectioners sugar

Mix fruits and celery together and sprinkle with a little lemon juice. Add nuts. To make dressing beat softened cream cheese, add pineapple juice and beat in the whipping cream until stiff. Sweeten with confectioners sugar. Before serving, toss fruits with enough dressing to moisten. Remaining dressing keeps for several days in the refrigerator. Makes 12 servings.

Mrs. Steven D. Symms

MRS. STEVEN D. SYMMS, Wife of Representative (Idaho)

155

AVOCADO SALAD

2 avocados
1 cup pineapple cubes, drained
1 cup seedless grape halves

2 navel oranges, peeled and sectioned
1 bottle French dressing
lettuce

Cut avocados in half lengthwise and scoop out pulp. Save the shells. Combine avocado pulp with other fruits and marinate in the French dressing about 20 minutes. Fill avocado shells with the fruit and serve on a bed of lettuce.

Mrs. Willard S. Curtin

MRS. WILLARD S. CURTIN, Wife of former Representative (Pennsylvania)

GRAPEFRUIT AVOCADO SALAD

6 pink grapefruit, peeled
1 3 ounce package cream cheese
8 ounces grated cheddar cheese
hearts of lettuce

endive
4 avocados, peeled and sliced
1 bottle cole slaw dressing

Section grapefruit and carefully remove all membrane. Roll cream cheese into 12 individual cheese balls. Do the same with the grated cheese. Place lettuce and endive on salad plates. Arrange grapefruit sections and avocado slices alternately on top of the greens. Top with cheese balls and add dressing sparingly. Makes 12 servings.

Mrs Homer Ferguson

MRS. HOMER FERGUSON, Wife of former Senator (Michigan)

156

JANE'S BANANA SALAD

½ cup vinegar
⅓ cup sugar
1 egg, beaten
¼ teaspoon salt
¼ teaspoon cayenne
¼ teaspoon paprika
½ teaspoon dry mustard

1 tablespoon flour
1 tablespoon butter
½ teaspoon celery seed
roasted peanuts, crushed
4 bananas, sliced
lettuce

Heat the vinegar. Beat sugar into the egg and add salt, cayenne, paprika, mustard and flour. Mix into hot vinegar, return to heat and stir constantly until thick. Remove from heat and beat in the butter. Add celery seed and a few crushed peanuts. When cold, mix with banana slices and serve on lettuce leaves. Makes 6 servings.

Mrs. Thomas G. Morris

MRS. THOMAS G. MORRIS, Wife of former Representative (New Mexico)

MANDARIN ORANGE AND LETTUCE SALAD

1 cup chopped celery
1 tablespoon minced parsley
2 green onions with tops, sliced
½ head shredded lettuce, chilled
1 11 ounce can mandarin oranges,
   drained

Dressing:
½ teaspoon salt

dash of pepper
2 tablespoons sugar
1 tablespoon vinegar
¼ cup salad oil
dash of Tabasco

Garnish:
¼ cup slivered almonds
2 tablespoons sugar

Mix celery, parsley and onions together and refrigerate. Just before serving, add them to the lettuce and oranges and toss lightly with the dressing. Sprinkle with caramelized almonds. Makes 6 servings.

Dressing: Mix dressing ingredients and refrigerate. Keeps for several days. Shake well just before adding to salad.

Garnish: Put almonds and sugar in heavy skillet over medium heat and stir until sugar melts and turns light brown, coating the almonds. Remove from heat and keep stirring until nuts look chalky and do not stick together. Place on waxed paper to dry. May be prepared in advance and kept in a tightly covered jar.

Mrs. Harry A. Blackmun

MRS. HARRY A. BLACKMUN, Wife of Associate Justice, Supreme Court (Minnesota)

157

PRINCESS SALAD

2⅓ cups small marshmallows
1 7 ounce bottle 7 Up
1 3 ounce package lime gelatin
2 3 ounce packages cream cheese,
　　softened
¾ cup chopped pecans
1 cup drained crushed pineapple

⅔ cup mayonnaise
½ pint whipping cream, whipped

Garnish:
glazed grapes
fresh fruit

Cook marshmallows in 7 Up over medium heat until melted. Add gelatin to hot mixture and stir until dissolved. Cream the cream cheese with a fork and stir into gelatin mixture. Beat until smooth. Add nuts and pineapple. Chill until slightly thickened. Add mayonnaise to whipped cream and fold into mixture. Garnish with glazed grapes and fresh fruit. May be frozen. Makes 8 servings.

[signature]

MRS. CHALMERS P. WYLIE, Wife of Representative (Ohio)

24 HOUR SALAD

1 20 ounce can pineapple tidbits
3 egg yolks
2 tablespoons sugar
2 tablespoons vinegar
1 tablespoon butter
dash of salt

1 16 ounce can pitted light sweet
　　cherries, drained
1 can pears, drained
2 cups miniature marshmallows
1 cup whipping cream, whipped
orange sections
mint leaves

Drain pineapple, reserving 2 tablespoons syrup. In top of double boiler, beat egg yolks slightly; add the reserved pineapple syrup, sugar, vinegar, butter and salt. Place over hot water; cook, stirring constantly, until mixture thickens slightly and barely coats a spoon, about 12 minutes. Cool to room temperature. Combine fruits and marshmallows, pour custard over them and mix gently. Fold whipped cream into fruit mixture. Turn into serving bowl, cover and chill 24 hours. Garnish with orange sections and mint leaves. Makes 6 to 8 servings.

[signature]

MRS. HOWARD W. CANNON, Wife of Senator (Nevada)

158

FRUIT FLUFF SALAD

1 6 ounce package lime Jello
1 large carton Cool Whip
1 large can crushed pineapple, well
   drained
1 can seedless grapes, drained

1 can mandarin oranges, drained
1 large carton creamed small curd
   cottage cheese
lettuce

Thoroughly mix dry Jello with Cool Whip. Add fruits and cottage cheese. Chill and serve on lettuce leaf. Makes 8 servings.

Mrs. Harold T. Johnson

MRS. HAROLD T. JOHNSON, Wife of Representative (California)

TROPICAL SALAD AND DRESSING

4 cups hearts of palms
1 cup pineapple, cubed, drained
¼ cup chopped dates
¼ cup chopped candied or preserved
   ginger

Dressing:
4 tablespoons vanilla ice cream
2 tablespoons mayonnaise
2 tablespoons crunchy peanut butter
pineapple juice (or preserved ginger
   juice)
few drops green cake coloring

Toss salad ingredients together lightly. For dressing, mix ice cream, mayonnaise and peanut butter thoroughly. Thin with pineapple or ginger juice. Add coloring and pour over salad and serve. Makes 4 to 5 servings.

Mrs. Claude Pepper

MRS. CLAUDE PEPPER, Wife of Representative (Florida)

LIZ'S FIVE CUP SALAD

1 cup small marshmallows
1 cup pineapple chunks
1 cup orange sections

1 cup pecans
1 cup grated coconut
sour cream (optional)

Toss marshmallows, fruit, nuts and coconut together. Top with sour cream, if desired. Makes 6 servings.

Mrs. James Lee Fisk

MRS. JAMES L. FISK, Daughter of former Representative Jed Johnson, Sr. (Oklahoma)

159

FOUR BEAN SALAD

¾ cup vinegar
¼ cup vegetable oil
1 cup sugar
2 cans cut green beans, drained
1 can yellow wax beans, drained
1 can garbanzo beans (chick peas), drained
1 can dark red kidney beans, drained
¼ cup chopped green onions
1 cup chopped celery

Mix together the first 3 ingredients and stir until sugar is dissolved. Combine with vegetables. This should marinate overnight to blend flavors. Makes 15 servings.

Mrs. Mike McCormack

MRS. MIKE MCCORMACK, Wife of Representative (Washington)

GOURMET SALAD

1 box frozen broccoli
1 box frozen French style green beans
1 box frozen cut asparagus
1 can artichoke hearts
1 cucumber, peeled and thinly sliced
¼ cup chopped onion
2 tablespoons lemon juice
2 tablespoons garlic vinegar
2 teaspoons anchovy paste
1 cup mayonnaise
½ cup Half and Half

Cook broccoli, green beans and asparagus until almost done. Cut broccoli into pieces. Add remaining ingredients to vegetables, mix together and refrigerate 24 hours. Makes 8 servings.

Mrs. Christopher Bond

MRS. CHRISTOPHER S. BOND, Wife of Governor (Missouri)

TANGY COLE SLAW

4 cups shredded cabbage
½ cup finely chopped green pepper

Dressing:
½ cup mayonnaise
2 tablespoons lemon juice

1 tablespoon grated onion
½ teaspoon celery seed
1 teaspoon sugar
½ teaspoon salt
⅛ teaspoon pepper

paprika

Toss cabbage and green pepper. Mix dressing ingredients until smooth. Stir into vegetables. Garnish with paprika. Makes 6 servings.

Mrs. Jack Brooks

MRS. JACK BROOKS, Wife of Representative (Texas)

160

CABBAGE SLAW

¼ cup vinegar
¼ cup oil
½ cup sugar
1 medium head cabbage, thinly sliced

Optional:
chopped onion
chopped green pepper
chopped red pepper

Boil vinegar, oil and sugar 4 to 5 minutes. Pour hot dressing over cabbage. The onion and peppers may be added. Dressing will keep in refrigerator at least 2 weeks.

MRS. ARTHUR L. MILLER, Wife of former Representative (Nebraska)

HOLIDAY CARROT SALAD

10 carrots, peeled and grated
1 onion, finely chopped
1 16 ounce can pitted olives, sliced
1 small jar sweet pickles, chopped

¾ cup mayonnaise
½ teaspoon salt
lettuce

Combine all ingredients except lettuce. Chill and serve on lettuce leaf. Makes 8 servings.

MRS. ROBERT J. LAGOMARSINO, Wife of Representative (California)

AUDREY'S CARROT SALAD

2 cans sliced carrots, drained
1 green pepper, finely chopped
1 onion, very finely sliced (or dehydrated onion)
½ teaspoon salt
1 can tomato soup

½ cup salad oil
1 cup sugar
1 teaspoon mustard
1 teaspoon Worcestershire sauce
⅓ cup vinegar

Mix all ingredients together and marinate for at least 12 hours. This salad will keep for a week or longer.

MRS. WILLIAM G. MILLIKEN, Wife of Governor (Michigan)

161

SCANDINAVIAN CUCUMBER SALAD

2 medium size cucumbers, peeled,
   thinly sliced

Dressing:
½ cup white wine vinegar
2 tablespoons water

½ teaspoon salt
3 tablespoons sugar
⅛ teaspoon ground black pepper
1 tablespoon dried dill
3 tablespoons chopped parsley

Make dressing by combining all ingredients, blending thoroughly. Pour over the cucumbers, cover with plastic wrap and let stand 3 hours before serving.

Mrs. Walter Norblad

MRS. WALTER NORBLAD, Wife of former Representative (Oregon)

CUCUMBER YOGURT SALAD

¼ clove garlic, mashed
⅓ cup olive oil (or vegetable oil)

2 cups unflavored yogurt
2 cucumbers, diced

Combine garlic with olive oil and yogurt and mix well. Combine with cucumbers. Makes 4 to 6 servings.

Mrs. William F. Norrell

MRS. WILLIAM F. NORRELL, former Representative (Arkansas)

EVER READY SALAD

2 medium onions
3 peeled tomatoes
2 stalks celery
1 green pepper
1 carrot

2 cucumbers, peeled
1 clove garlic, minced
Good Seasons Italian salad dressing
lettuce (optional)

Chop vegetables coarsely. Mix with garlic and pour Good Seasons Italian salad dressing over all. This will keep nicely for several days in the refrigerator and can be served alone or tossed with lettuce. Makes 6 servings.

Mrs. Milton R. Young

MRS. MILTON R. YOUNG, Wife of Senator (North Dakota)

162

SUMMER SALAD

2 pounds cottage cheese
½ large cucumber, sliced
1 package radishes, sliced

12 green onions, chopped
1 small container dairy sour cream
salt and pepper

Mix ingredients together and chill several hours in refrigerator to blend flavors. Makes 8 to 10 servings.

Mrs. William Broomfield

MRS. WILLIAM S. BROOMFIELD, Wife of Representative (Michigan)

HEARTY MUSHROOM SUPPER SALAD

½ cup chopped onion
½ cup chopped celery
½ cup dairy sour cream
¼ cup mayonnaise
2 tablespoons fresh lemon juice
1 tablespoon snipped parsley
1 tablespoon horse radish
1 teaspoon salt

¼ teaspoon dried oregano leaves
½ teaspoon pepper
1 pound fresh mushrooms, thinly sliced
1 pound cooked turkey (or lamb or roast beef), cut in julienne strips
salad greens
cherry tomatoes

Mix all ingredients, except the last 4, to make the dressing. Toss mushrooms and meat with dressing in bowl. Refrigerate at least 1 hour but no longer than 3 hours for flavors to blend. To serve, mound mixture on fresh greens and garnish with tomatoes. Makes 4 to 6 servings.

Mrs. Burt L. Talcott

MRS. BURT L. TALCOTT, Wife of Representative (California)

RAW MUSHROOM SALAD

1 pound mushrooms
2 center celery stalks
2 hard cooked eggs, each cut into
   8 pieces
2 tablespoons minced green onion
2 pimientos, minced

salt
freshly ground pepper
1 cup salad or olive oil
¼ cup wine vinegar
romaine or head lettuce

Wash, drain and dry mushrooms. Cut from rounded side through stems to make good size bites. Cut up celery and add to mushrooms. Add eggs, onion, pimientos and season all with salt and pepper. Combine oil and vinegar. Pour over mixture in bowl and toss lightly. Serve on romaine or head lettuce. Makes 8 servings.

Mrs. Henry P. Smith III

MRS. HENRY P. SMITH III, Wife of former Representative (New York)

LOW CALORIE MUSHROOM SALAD

¼ pound fresh mushrooms (or 1
   small can mushrooms, drained)
¼ pound fresh spinach
¼ head iceberg lettuce
8 cherry tomatoes, sliced

Dressing:
6 tablespoons unflavored yogurt
2 tablespoons low calorie French
   dressing
¼ teaspoon crumbled basil leaves
1/16 teaspoon garlic powder

Rinse, pat dry and slice mushrooms. Tear spinach and lettuce into bite size pieces and toss with mushrooms and tomatoes. For dressing, combine all ingredients and blend thoroughly. Spoon dressing on individual salad servings. Makes 6 servings, 29 calories each.

Mrs. John H. Ware

MRS. JOHN H. WARE, Wife of former Representative (Pennsylvania)

POTATO SALAD

4 large potatoes
1 onion, chopped
4 stalks celery, chopped
3 hard cooked eggs
3 to 4 sweet pickles, diced
salt

pepper
mayonnaise
pickle juice
mustard
paprika

Boil potatoes in skins. Cool and peel. Cut in cubes. Add onion, celery, 2 chopped eggs, pickles, salt and pepper. Thin mayonnaise with pickle juice to desired consistency. Add mustard to taste. Combine with potatoes. Garnish with remaining egg, sliced or sieved, and paprika. Makes 6 to 8 servings.

Mrs. Robert H. Mollohan

MRS. ROBERT H. MOLLOHAN, Wife of Representative (West Virginia)

GERMAN POTATO SALAD

2 pounds potatoes, boiled and peeled
¼ cup minced onion (or shallot)
1 cup hot beef or chicken broth
¼ cup white wine vinegar
salt and freshly ground pepper to taste
⅓ cup mayonnaise

2 tablespoons Dusseldorf or Dijon
    mustard
½ cup julienne strips of ham (or
    smoked tongue)
½ cup julienne strips of dill pickle
1 tablespoon chopped parsley
1 tablespoon chopped chives

Cut potatoes into thin slices and while still warm, combine with the onion. Mix together the broth, vinegar, salt and pepper and pour over potatoes. Let them marinate for 30 minutes. Drain off any liquid not absorbed. Put potatoes in serving bowl and fold in mayonnaise that has been combined with mustard. Garnish with ham, pickle, parsley and chives. Makes 6 servings.

Mrs. Stephen L. Neal

MRS. STEPHEN L. NEAL, Wife of Representative (North Carolina)

HERB GARDEN SALAD

2/3 cup dry white wine
1/2 cup white tarragon vinegar
1 3/4 quarts cubed boiled new potatoes
1/4 cup snipped parsley
1/4 cup snipped chives
1/4 cup snipped fresh dill
3 teaspoons salt

1 teaspoon seasoned salt
1 teaspoon freshly ground pepper (or lemon pepper)
1/4 cup salad oil
3 medium tomatoes
lettuce

Combine wine and vinegar in a saucepan and bring to a boil. Pour over potatoes. Add parsley, chives, dill, 2 teaspoons of salt, seasoned salt, 3/4 teaspoon of pepper and salad oil. Toss well together and refrigerate.

Cut tomatoes in wedges and sprinkle with remaining salt and pepper. Refrigerate. Just before serving, drain tomatoes and toss with potato mixture. Arrange on crisp lettuce. Makes 6 to 8 servings.

Mrs. Dean P. Taylor

MRS. DEAN P. TAYLOR, Wife of former Representative (New York)

GREEK PEPPER SALAD

mixed salad greens for 6 servings
6 radishes, thinly sliced
2 stalks celery, chopped
2 green onions, chopped
12 Greek peppers (pepperoncini)
1/4 cup Kraft's oil and vinegar dressing

2 tablespoons Marie's dressing with bacon
1/2 cup seasoned croutons
6 ripe olives
6 small chunks feta cheese
lemon pepper

Wash and tear salad greens. Add radishes, celery, onion and 6 Greek peppers, chopped crosswise. Toss with oil and vinegar dressing. Add Marie's dressing and croutons and toss again lightly. Garnish with ripe olives, remaining Greek peppers and the cheese. Dust with lemon pepper.

Mrs. Robert M. Lemke

MRS. ROBERT M. LEMKE, Daughter-in-law of former Representative William Lemke (North Dakota)

166

CANDY'S ROAST PEPPER SALAD

2 large bell peppers
1 large tender cucumber
2 large tomatoes, sliced
2 tablespoons chopped parsley
1 small red onion, sliced

Dressing:
¼ cup corn oil
⅛ cup apple cider vinegar
splash or two of any good drinking wine
1 tablespoon cold water (optional)
½ teaspoon sweet basil
sea salt and paprika to taste

Wash and dry peppers. Roast over flame on top of stove, turning frequently until pepper skin is roasted all over. Turn off flame and let them sit 8 to 10 minutes on grid. Peel pepper skin, remove seeds, chop into bite size pieces and cool in refrigerator at least ½ hour. Peel and slice cucumber, add tomatoes, parsley and onion. Combine ingredients for dressing and mix well. Chill. Add chilled pepper to other salad vegetables and toss with chilled salad dressing. Makes 4 servings.

Mrs. George E. Danielson

Mrs. George E. Danielson, Wife of Representative (California)

VERMONT SPINACH SALAD

1 pound spinach, ice cold
5 slices bacon
1 onion, chopped
¼ cup water
3 tablespoons lemon juice

3 tablespoons cider vinegar
1 teaspoon salt
1 teaspoon sugar
½ teaspoon dry mustard

Clean spinach and remove heavy stems. Fry bacon until crisp, remove from pan and crumble. In bacon drippings, saute onion until clear. Add remaining ingredients and bring to a boil. Pour over cold spinach, toss well and add bacon pieces. The dressing may be prepared and refrigerated and then reheated to boiling just before serving. Makes 6 servings.

Mrs. Winston L. Prouty

Mrs. Winston L. Prouty, Wife of former Senator (Vermont)

SPINACH SALAD

1 package fresh spinach
1 can water chestnuts, thinly sliced
1 can bean sprouts, drained
2 hard cooked eggs, chopped
¼ pound bacon, fried and crumbled

Salad Dressing:
½ cup salad oil
½ cup vinegar
½ cup sugar
⅔ cup catsup
2 teaspoons salt
2 teaspoons Worcestershire sauce
1 medium onion, chopped
1 clove garlic

Toss spinach with chestnuts, bean sprouts, eggs and bacon. For dressing, combine all ingredients in blender and beat until thoroughly blended. Pour over salad ingredients and toss lightly. Makes 6 servings.

Mrs. John M. Ashbrook

Mrs. JOHN M. ASHBROOK, Wife of Representative (Ohio)

HEARTY SPINACH SALAD

1 pound fresh spinach, cleaned and dried
salt and pepper
2 tablespoons sugar
1 pound bacon, cooked and crumbled
4 hard cooked eggs, sliced
1 small head iceberg lettuce, cleaned, dried and broken in bite size pieces

1 package frozen peas, thawed
1 sweet red onion, sliced

Dressing:
1 cup Hellmann's mayonnaise
1 cup Miracle Whip
½ pound Swiss cheese, grated

Arrange spinach in the bottom of a large salad bowl. Combine salt, pepper and sugar and sprinkle half of mixture over spinach. Layer remaining ingredients over spinach in the order given. Sprinkle with remaining seasoning mixture. Combine mayonnaise and Miracle Whip and spread over top of salad. Top with grated cheese. Cover bowl and refrigerate for 24 hours. Toss and serve. Makes 8 servings.

Mrs. Carroll D. Kearns

Mrs. CARROLL D. KEARNS, Wife of former Representative (Pennsylvania)

168

SPINACH TOMATO SALAD

1 package raw spinach
2 or 3 hard cooked eggs
1 small onion
tomato wedges
1 small can water chestnuts
bacon, cooked and crumbled

Dressing:
1 cup oil
¼ cup sugar
½ cup vinegar
⅓ cup catsup
½ teaspoon Worcestershire sauce
1 teaspoon salt

Mix salad ingredients, setting aside bacon. Combine dressing ingredients and pour over salad. Crumble bacon on top. Makes 10 servings.

Mrs. Laurie C. Battle

MRS. LAURIE C. BATTLE, Wife of former Representative (Alabama)

SPINACH SALAD FLAMBE

2 bunches fresh tender spinach
white vinegar
watercress
8 strips bacon, cubed
4 tablespoons raw sugar

4 tablespoons wine vinegar
1 teaspoon Worcestershire sauce
juice of 1 lemon
1 jigger cognac

Remove stems from spinach leaves. Wash in cold water to which a little vinegar has been added and dry well. Place leaves in salad bowl with some watercress. Fry bacon until cooked. Add sugar, wine vinegar and Worcestershire sauce. Heat to a boil, remove bacon and pour over spinach leaves. Squeeze lemon juice over leaves and toss until wilted. Drain dressing off salad and place spinach leaves on plate. Add cognac to bacon, ignite and spoon over spinach. Serve at once.

Mrs. Reinhold Puetz

MRS. REINHOLD PUETZ, Daughter of former Representative Courtland C. Gillen (Indiana)

169

CUCUMBER AND SHELL SALAD

1 8 ounce package shell macaroni
1 cucumber, chopped
1 can black olives, pitted
1 cup sour cream
1 tablespoon vinegar

2 tablespoons mayonnaise
½ cup French dressing
¼ pound blue cheese
salt
pepper

Cook macaroni until tender and drain. Add cucumber and olives. Mix remaining ingredients together and add to macaroni. Chill thoroughly. Makes 6 servings.

Mrs. Goodloe E. Byron

MRS. GOODLOE BYRON, Wife of Representative (Maryland)

PASTA SALAD

8 ounces thin spaghetti
½ cup spring onions, thinly sliced
½ cup green pepper, diced

parsley (optional)
½ cup Italian salad dressing
½ cup mayonnaise

Cook spaghetti according to directions. Do not overcook. Drain and let cool. Add other ingredients. Refrigerate. Makes 6 to 8 servings.

Mrs Glenard P. Lipscomb

MRS. GLENARD P. LIPSCOMB, Wife of former Representative (California)

COLD SPAGHETTI SALAD

1 pound thin spaghetti
½ green pepper, chopped
1 package radishes, thinly sliced
1 small bunch celery, chopped
1 cucumber, peeled and diced
1 small bunch chopped green onions
   with a few tops

Dressing:
1 8 ounce carton dairy sour cream
½ cup Durkee's sauce
⅓ cup vinegar
1 cup mayonnaise
⅓ cup sugar

Cook spaghetti according to package directions. Rinse and drain. Combine salad ingredients. Mix dressing ingredients well and pour over salad. Mix thoroughly and chill well before serving.

Mrs. Larry Winn, Jr.

MRS. LARRY WINN, JR., Wife of Representative (Kansas)

COLD RICE SALAD

1 cup raw rice
2 cups water
1 package frozen peas, cooked
4 tablespoons chopped green onions
  and tops
½ cup drained mushrooms

½ cup chopped unpeeled cucumber
1 cup mayonnaise
½ cup Italian salad dressing

Optional:
chicken or shrimp

Cook rice in water. Drain. Combine with vegetables. Mix mayonnaise and salad dressing and add to other ingredients. Refrigerate at least 12 hours or overnight. To make a luncheon salad, add chicken or shrimp 1 hour before serving. Makes 6 to 8 servings.

Mrs. Larry Winn, Jr.

MRS. LARRY WINN, JR., Wife of Representative (Kansas)

DIG DEEP SALAD

1 medium head lettuce, shredded
2 red onions, sliced
2 green peppers, diced
1½ cups chopped celery
1 can water chestnuts, sliced
1 package frozen green peas,
  thawed and drained

1 pint Hellmann's mayonnaise
Romano cheese, grated
2 hard cooked eggs, sliced
2 fresh tomatoes, sliced
½ pound bacon, cooked and crumbled

In a large salad bowl, layer the following ingredients in the order given: lettuce, onion slices, green pepper, celery, water chestnuts and peas. Cover layer of peas with mayonnaise, spreading liberally. Sprinkle cheese over mayonnaise. Cover with plastic wrap and refrigerate 24 hours. About 45 minutes before serving, remove from refrigerator and garnish with egg slices, tomato slices and bacon bits. Makes 10 servings.

Mrs. Lucien N. Nedzi

MRS. LUCIEN N. NEDZI, Wife of Representative (Michigan)

SEVEN LAYER SALAD

1 small head crisp lettuce, shredded
½ cup chopped celery
½ cup chopped green pepper
½ cup chopped onion
1 package frozen peas, cooked, cooled and thoroughly drained

½ cup mayonnaise
1½ cups dairy sour cream
2 tablespoons sugar
6 ounces cheddar cheese, shredded
8 strips bacon, crisply fried, drained and crumbled

Arrange lettuce evenly in bottom of 8 x 9 inch pan. Sprinkle celery on top of lettuce, then green pepper, onion and peas. Mix mayonnaise with sour cream and spoon over vegetable mixture. Sprinkle sugar over sour cream mixture. Sprinkle top with the cheese and bacon. Cover tightly with foil, leaving air space between foil and salad. Refrigerate for at least 8 hours. Makes 9 servings.

Mrs J Edgar Chenoweth

MRS. J. EDGAR CHENOWETH, Wife of former Representative (Colorado)

LAYER SALAD

1 head lettuce
1 cup mayonnaise
1 tablespoon cream
1 onion, thinly sliced
¼ cup sugar

1 package frozen peas, cooked and chilled
½ pound Swiss cheese, cut in julienne strips
½ pound bacon, cut in 1 inch pieces

Tear lettuce into bite size chunks and place half of it in bowl. Blend mayonnaise and cream and drizzle half of it over lettuce. Top with half the onion slices. Sprinkle half the sugar over onion and top with half of peas and cheese. Repeat layers, cover and chill at least 2 hours before serving. Fry bacon, drain off fat and sprinkle over salad. Do not toss.

Mrs Bert Bandstra

MRS. BERT BANDSTRA, Wife of former Representative (Iowa)

172

TOMATO CUCUMBER MARINADE SALAD

2 medium tomatoes, sliced
2 cups peeled and thinly sliced
  cucumber
1 cup thinly sliced onion, separated
  into rings
½ cup salad oil

¼ cup white wine vinegar
1 teaspoon salt
1 teaspoon basil
1 teaspoon tarragon
⅛ teaspoon pepper
shredded lettuce

Alternate layers of tomato, cucumber and onion in shallow glass dish. Combine salad oil, vinegar, salt, basil, tarragon and pepper; beat well with electric beater. Pour over layered vegetables. Chill, covered, 5 to 6 hours. Drain, reserving marinade. Arrange marinated vegetables on shredded lettuce. Reserved marinade may be served as additional dressing. Makes 6 servings.

Mrs. John Kyl

MRS. JOHN KYL, Wife of former Representative (Iowa)

TOMATO ASPIC SALAD WITH CRABMEAT

2 packages unflavored gelatin
½ cup cold water
2 cups tomato juice
2 tablespoons vinegar
1 tablespoon Worcestershire sauce

1 teaspoon salt
red pepper to taste
1 small onion, finely grated
½ pound crabmeat

Soften gelatin in cold water and dissolve over hot water until clear. Mix thoroughly with remaining ingredients. Pour into lightly oiled mold and refrigerate overnight. Makes 8 servings.

Mrs. Charles Raper Jonas

MRS. CHARLES RAPER JONAS, Wife of former Representative (North Carolina)

CRABMEAT MOUSSE

1 tablespoon gelatin
3 tablespoons cold water
¼ cup mayonnaise
3 tablespoons lime juice
2 tablespoons lemon juice
1 tablespoon chopped parsley

1 tablespoon chopped chives
1 tablespoon prepared mustard
salt and pepper to taste
2 cups flaked cooked crabmeat
¾ cup heavy cream, whipped
1 avocado, peeled and mashed

Soften gelatin in cold water and dissolve over hot water. Mix with mayonnaise, 2 tablespoons lime juice, lemon juice, parsley, chives, mustard, salt and pepper. Fold in crabmeat and whipped cream. Pour into a buttered ring mold and chill. To serve, unmold and fill center with avocado mixed with remaining lime juice. Makes 6 servings.

Mrs David E Bradley

MRS. DAVID E. BRADLEY, Daughter of former Representative James Harvey (Michigan)

LOBSTER MOLD

1 tablespoon gelatin
¼ cup cold water
1 can tomato soup
1 8 ounce package cream cheese
⅓ cup finely chopped celery

2 teaspoons onion juice (or 1 teaspoon onion salt)
1 teaspoon Worcestershire sauce
2 cans lobster, drained
1 cup mayonnaise

Soak gelatin in cold water. Heat tomato soup until warm. Stir in softened gelatin until dissolved. Beat in cheese with electric or rotary beater. Cool. Add celery, seasonings and lobster that has been broken in small pieces. Fold in mayonnaise. Place in wet mold and chill until set. Makes 20 servings.

Elizabeth G. Van Exem

ELIZABETH GASQUE VAN EXEM, former Representative (South Carolina)

SHRIMP SALAD MOLD

1 package lemon Jello
1 cup hot water
2 3 ounce packages cream cheese
1 can tomato soup
1 tablespoon chopped onion

¾ cup mayonnaise
2 cups cooked shrimp
1 cup chopped celery
½ cup chopped green pepper
½ cup grated cucumber

Dissolve Jello in hot water. Beat cheese into tomato soup. Combine all ingredients. Put into greased fish mold. Chill and serve. Makes 12 servings.

Mrs. Arch A. Moore, Jr.

Mrs. Arch A. Moore, Jr., Wife of Governor (West Virginia)

MOLDED SALMON

2 envelopes unflavored gelatin
½ cup cold water
1 chicken bouillon cube
1 cup boiling water
1 cup mayonnaise
3 tablespoons chili sauce
2 tablespoons lemon juice
½ teaspoon monosodium glutamate
  (Accent)

1 tablespoon grated onion
¼ teaspoon Worcestershire sauce
dash of cayenne
salt to taste
1 cup salmon
½ cup sliced stuffed olives
1 cup finely diced celery
lettuce

Soften gelatin in cold water. Dissolve bouillon cube in boiling water, stir in gelatin until dissolved and combine with next 8 ingredients. Mix thoroughly and chill until the consistency of egg white. Add salmon, olives and celery. Pour into lightly greased mold and chill until firm. Serve on lettuce leaves. Makes 8 servings.

Mrs. Benjamin F. James

Mrs. Benjamin F. James, Wife of former Representative (Pennsylvania)

SALMON MOLD

½ teaspoon sugar
1 heaping tablespoon flour
1 teaspoon salt
1 teaspoon dry mustard
4 tablespoons water
2 egg yolks, lightly beaten
2 tablespoons melted butter
1 cup milk
¼ cup vinegar
1 envelope gelatin

4 tablespoons cold water
2 cups flaked salmon

Cucumber Sauce:
½ cup heavy cream, stiffly beaten
salt and pepper to taste
2 tablespoons vinegar
1 medium cucumber, pared and
  finely ground

Combine sugar, flour, salt, mustard and water in top of double boiler. Add yolks, butter, milk and vinegar. Cook, stirring constantly, until thick. Dissolve gelatin in cold water and add to cooked mixture. Add salmon, mix well and pour into mold. Refrigerate overnight.

For sauce, combine whipped cream, seasonings and vinegar and fold in cucumber. Unmold the salmon salad and serve with the cucumber sauce. Makes 6 servings.

Jill J. Cochran

JILL TEAGUE COCHRAN, Daughter of Representative Olin E. Teague (Texas)

DOTTIE'S ROYAL TUNA CRAN SALAD

2 7 ounce cans tuna, flaked
2 hard cooked eggs, chopped
½ cup stuffed olives, chopped
1 cup finely diced celery
1 tablespoon finely diced onion
1 cup Hellmann's mayonnaise
1 envelope unflavored gelatin
½ cup cold water
½ cup hot water

Topping:
1 3 ounce package lemon Jello
¾ cup hot water
½ cup orange juice
1 1 pound can cranberry sauce
lettuce

Combine first 6 ingredients and mix thoroughly. Soften gelatin in cold water, dissolve in hot water and stir into tuna mixture. Spread evenly in greased 9 x 9 x 2 inch pan. Refrigerate until firm. To make topping, dissolve Jello in water and orange juice and beat with cranberry sauce. Cool, then pour over the cold tuna mixture. Chill overnight or until firm. Cut in squares and serve on lettuce with red side up.

Mrs. Thomas S. Kleppe

MRS. THOMAS S. KLEPPE, Wife of former Representative (North Dakota), presently Secretary of the Interior

MAMIE'S CHICKEN MAYONNAISE

1 4 to 5 pound hen
2 cups chopped celery
3 tablespoons India relish
2 tablespoons whole capers
½ to 1 cup blanched chopped almonds
4 hard cooked eggs, chopped

½ teaspoon finely chopped garlic
4 envelopes gelatin
½ cup cold water
1 cup hot chicken broth
1 pint mayonnaise
salt to taste

Boil hen until tender. Cool, bone and dice meat. Mix with celery, relish, capers, almonds, eggs and garlic. Soak gelatin in water and dissolve in hot broth. Cool and add the mayonnaise. Pour over chicken mixture and mix well, adding salt. Pour into mold and chill in refrigerator until firm. May be prepared and refrigerated overnight. Slice to make 24 servings.

Mrs. Richardson Preyer

MRS. RICHARDSON PREYER, Wife of Representative (North Carolina)

PRESSED CHICKEN

2 cups cooked, cubed chicken
6 hard cooked eggs, chopped (or
   sliced lengthwise)
2 cups chopped celery
½ green pepper, chopped
2 teaspoons salt
juice ½ lemon

1 teaspoon onion juice
15 blanched almonds, split
4 tablespoons mayonnaise
1 tablespoon gelatin
2 tablespoons cold water
½ cup chicken stock
½ pint cream, whipped

Combine first 9 ingredients. Soften gelatin in cold water 5 minutes; then dissolve in heated stock. Cool and add to chicken mixture. Add whipped cream and pour into mold. Makes 6 servings.

Elizabeth G. Van Exem

ELIZABETH GASQUE VAN EXEM, former Representative (South Carolina)

177

APPLEBERRY SALAD

1 3 ounce package red Jello
1 cup boiling water
1 10 ounce package frozen strawberries

1 cup applesauce
lettuce
½ cup sour cream

Dissolve Jello in boiling water and add strawberries. Stir until berries are thawed. Add applesauce and chill until firm. Serve on lettuce with sour cream. Makes 7 servings.

Mrs. Tom Steed

Mrs. Tom Steed, Wife of Representative (Oklahoma)

JELLIED WALDORF SALAD

1 3 ounce package lemon Jello
1 cup hot water
½ cup mayonnaise
1½ cups diced apples

1 cup diced celery
½ cup nuts
½ cup whipping cream

Dissolve gelatin in hot water; chill until syrupy. Blend in mayonnaise until smooth. Add apples, celery and nuts. Whip cream and fold into mixture. Turn into a quart mold which has been rinsed in cold water. Chill. Makes 8 servings.

Mrs Fred Schwengel

Mrs. Fred Schwengel, Wife of former Representative (Iowa)

APRICOT SALAD

1 20 ounce can crushed pineapple
2 packages apricot Jello
2 envelopes Dream Whip

2 3 ounce packages cream cheese
1 cup diced celery

Bring the pineapple to a boil and add Jello. Set aside to cool. Whip Dream Whip, add cream cheese and whip well. Fold into Jello mixture and add celery. Refrigerate. Makes 16 servings.

Mrs Clarence Miller

Mrs. Clarence Miller, Wife of Representative (Ohio)

APRICOT BLENDER SALAD

1 3 ounce package apricot Jello
1 cup boiling water

1 8 ounce package Philadelphia
  cream cheese
1 large can apricots, with juice

Put Jello in blender. Add boiling water and stir until dissolved. Add other ingredients and blend. Pour into a 1 quart mold and chill until set. Makes 8 servings.

Mrs. Jamie L. Whitten

MRS. JAMIE L. WHITTEN, Wife of Representative (Mississippi)

BLUEBERRY CONGEALED SALAD

2 3 ounce packages raspberry Jello
3 cups hot water
1 cup Half and Half
1 cup sugar
2 envelopes unflavored gelatin
½ cup cold water
1 teaspoon vanilla

1 8 ounce package cream cheese,
  softened
1 cup chopped pecans
1 tablespoon lemon juice
1 20 ounce can blueberries, drain
  and reserve juice
water as needed

Dissolve 1 package of Jello in 2 cups hot water. Cool. Pour into mold and set in refrigerator to congeal.

Heat Half and Half, add sugar and stir until sugar is dissolved. Soak gelatin in cold water and dissolve in hot Half and Half. Add vanilla, cream cheese and nuts. Spread this over first layer and return to refrigerator to congeal.

Dissolve remaining package of Jello in remaining hot water and add lemon juice. To the blueberry juice add enough water to make 1 cup and add to Jello. Mix in blueberries. Cool and pour over second layer. Chill until congealed. Unmold. Makes 12 servings.

Mrs. Bill Nichols

MRS. BILL NICHOLS, Wife of Representative (Alabama)

SWEET CHERRY MOLD

1 6 ounce package cherry gelatin
1 cup hot water
1 cup cold water
1 29 ounce can pitted bing cherries

1 14 ounce can crushed pineapple
1 3 ounce package cream cheese, softened
1 cup heavy cream, whipped

Put gelatin in bowl, add hot water and stir until gelatin dissolves. Add cold water. Drain cherries and pineapple and add both juices to gelatin. Arrange fruits in bottom of a 1½ quart ring mold. When gelatin is slightly jelled, pour half of it over fruit in the mold. Chill. Add cream cheese to whipped cream and whip until well blended and fluffy. Gently stir remaining gelatin into this mixture and pour it over the chilled gelatin in the mold. Chill several hours until firm. Makes 8 servings.

Mrs Walter D. Huddleston

Mrs. WALTER D. HUDDLESTON, Wife of Senator (Kentucky)

BING CHERRY SALAD

1 package cherry Jello
1 cup boiling cherry juice
1 3 ounce package cream cheese
1 cup pineapple juice

1 cup chopped pecans
1 cup drained, crushed pineapple
1 cup pitted, canned bing cherries

Dissolve gelatin in hot liquid. Add cream cheese softened with a little of the hot gelatin mixture. Pour in pineapple juice. Stir until smooth. Chill until sirupy. Beat until fluffy. Fold in nuts, pineapple and cherries. Pour into a 1½ quart mold, rinsed in cold water. Chill until firm.

Mrs. E. C. Gathings

Mrs. E. C. GATHINGS, Wife of former Representative (Arkansas)

FRESH CRANBERRY SALAD

1 package fresh cranberries, ground
1 whole orange, ground
2 cups sugar
1 large package lemon Jello
2 cups hot water

1 cup ice cubes
1 cup diced celery
1 cup chopped pecans
lettuce
mayonnaise

Combine berries, orange and sugar. Dissolve Jello in hot water; then add ice cubes. Add fruit, celery and nuts. Pour into 1 large or 14 individual molds. Chill until firm. Serve on lettuce. Mayonnaise is good on this salad.

Mrs. Mills Godwin

MRS. MILLS E. GODWIN, JR., Wife of Governor (Virginia)

CRANBERRY DELIGHT

1 package black cherry Jello
1 cup hot water
1 cup canned whole cranberry sauce
¾ cup cold water

1 cup drained, crushed pineapple
¼ cup chopped pecans
mayonnaise (optional)
lettuce

Dissolve Jello in hot water. Blend in cranberry sauce. Add cold water, stirring until well mixed. Chill until slightly thickened. Fold in crushed pineapple and pecans. Spoon into 8 individual molds or one 4 cup mold. Chill until firm. Unmold and serve on crisp lettuce leaves with mayonnaise if desired. Makes 6 to 8 servings.

Mrs. David C. Treen

MRS. DAVID C. TREEN, Wife of Representative (Louisiana)

CRANBERRY MOLDED SALAD

1 6 ounce package red Jello
2 cups boiling water
1 can whole cranberry sauce
1 cup drained, crushed pineapple

½ cup broken nuts
lettuce
sour cream

Dissolve Jello in boiling water. Add cranberry sauce, pineapple and nuts. Chill until firm, stirring several times. Unmold on lettuce and serve with sour cream.

Mrs. Meldrim Thomson, Jr.

MRS. MELDRIM THOMSON, JR., Wife of Governor (New Hampshire)

ANNIE'S CRANBERRY SALAD

1 3 ounce package cherry Jello
¾ cup hot water
¼ cup cold water
1 small can crushed pineapple, drained

¼ cup chopped pecans
⅓ cup finely chopped celery
1 can whole cranberries
1 teaspoon almond flavoring

Dissolve Jello in hot water. Add cold water. Add pineapple, pecans, celery, cranberries and almond flavoring. Stir and pour in greased mold and refrigerate. Makes 8 servings.

Mrs. David N. Henderson

MRS. DAVID N. HENDERSON, Wife of Representative (North Carolina)

CRANBERRY NUT MOLD

1 package unflavored gelatin
¼ cup cold water
1 can jellied cranberry sauce

½ cup chopped walnuts
2 firm bananas, sliced

Dissolve gelatin in cold water and heat in double boiler until gelatin is thick. Use fork to stir cranberry sauce. Add softened gelatin; stir in bananas and nuts. Pour into a 1 quart mold to set. Unmold to serve.

Mrs. Daniel Walker

MRS. DANIEL WALKER, Wife of Governor (Illinois)

CRANBERRY SALAD

1 3 ounce package lemon Jello
1 cup hot water
1 16 ounce can cranberry jelly
1 cup chopped celery
1 cup chopped apples
¾ cup chopped nuts

1 orange, sectioned
lettuce
salad dressing
whipped topping (optional)
orange slices (optional)
whole nuts (optional)

Dissolve Jello in hot water. Cool slightly and stir in cranberry jelly. When mixture is quite smooth, place in refrigerator until it begins to jell. Fold celery, apples, nuts and orange sections into Jello mixture. Place in mold to congeal. Serve on bed of lettuce. Top with salad dressing or dressing mixed with whipped topping. Garnish with orange slices, whole nuts or both. Makes 6 to 8 servings.

Mrs. Joe L. Evins

MRS. JOE L. EVINS, Wife of Representative (Tennessee)

GOLDEN SALAD IN GRAPE MOLDS

1 3 ounce package lemon Jello
1 3 ounce package orange Jello
1 cup boiling water
1 tablespoon unflavored gelatin
½ cup cold water
1 cup fresh orange juice
juice and rind of 1 lemon

1 cup drained white seedless grape
halves
2 cups crushed pineapple
1 cup mandarin oranges, drained and
diced
salad greens
fresh grapes

Dissolve Jello in boiling water. Soften gelatin in cold water and add to Jello. Place mixture in top of double boiler over hot water and stir until thoroughly dissolved. Add fruit juices and rind. Cool slightly. Place a small amount of gelatin mixture in 2 grape molds, 4 quart size, and chill until thickened. Arrange grape halves, cut side up, in molds to resemble a cluster of grapes. Chill until firm.

Mix together all the other fruit with the remaining gelatin mixture. After grape design is firmly set, add the fruit mixture, putting equal amounts into each mold. Chill until set. Serve on a bed of salad greens and garnish with fresh grapes. Makes 16 servings.

Mrs. Hugh Q. Alexander

MRS. HUGH Q. ALEXANDER, Wife of former Representative (North Carolina)

RASPBERRY SALAD

1 3 ounce package raspberry Jello
1 cup boiling water
1 box frozen raspberries, partially
thawed
½ cup applesauce
1 teaspoon lemon juice

Salad dressing:
8 large marshmallows, cut up
1 cup dairy sour cream

Dissolve Jello in boiling water. Add raspberries, applesauce and lemon juice. Mix well and pour into oblong casserole and refrigerate to jell. To make dressing, combine marshmallows and sour cream. Refrigerate overnight. Beat until thoroughly blended. Serve over salad. Makes 6 servings.

Mrs. Wiley Mayne

MRS. WILEY MAYNE, Wife of former Representative (Iowa)

STRAWBERRY FOAM SALAD

1 large can peaches, drained
½ pound Philadelphia cream cheese
1 cup peach juice
1 package strawberry Jello

½ pint whipping cream
1 teaspoon vanilla
1 tablespoon sugar
maraschino cherries (optional)

Mash peaches and cream cheese together. Bring peach juice to a boil and pour over Jello. Add cheese mixture and cool. When almost set, fold in the cream, whipped with the vanilla and sugar. Chill. Maraschino cherries may be added on the top. Makes 6 servings.

Mrs. James A. Rhodes

MRS. JAMES A. RHODES, Wife of Governor (Ohio)

STRAWBERRY CRANBERRY SALAD

2 3 ounce packages strawberry Jello
2 cups boiling water
1 tablespoon unflavored gelatin
¼ cup cold water

1 10 ounce package frozen
  strawberries
1 can whole berry cranberry sauce
1 20½ ounce can crushed pineapple

Dissolve Jello in hot water. Soften gelatin in cold water and dissolve in hot Jello. Stir strawberries into hot liquid. Add cranberry sauce and pineapple. Pour into oblong pan and chill until set. Makes 8 to 10 servings.

Mrs. R. Walter Riehlman

MRS. R. WALTER RIEHLMAN, Wife of former Representative (New York)

STRAWBERRY SALAD

2 3 ounce packages strawberry Jello
1 cup boiling water
2 10 ounce packages frozen sliced
  strawberries, thawed

1 large can crushed pineapple, drained
3 bananas, mashed
1 cup chopped pecans
2 cartons sour cream

Dissolve Jello in boiling water. Add next 4 ingredients. Put ½ of mixture in a 9 x 13 inch pan and refrigerate until firm. Spread with sour cream and top with remaining Jello mixture. Refrigerate.

Mrs. Carroll Hubbard

MRS. CARROLL HUBBARD, Wife of Representative (Kentucky)

STRAWBERRY JELLO SALAD

1 large package strawberry Jello
1 15 ounce can crushed pineapple,
  with juice
1½ cups orange juice

1 can evaporated milk, chilled
1 8 ounce package cream cheese

Combine the Jello, pineapple and orange juice. Heat until Jello is dissolved. Chill until partially jelled. Whip milk with chilled beaters in a chilled bowl until it forms peaks. Add cream cheese and mix thoroughly. Add Jello mixture and again mix thoroughly. Place in mold or pan and chill until firm. Makes 4 to 6 servings.

Mrs. Tolise G. Norwood

MRS. TOLISE G. NORWOOD, Daughter of former Representative E. C. Gathings (Arkansas)

GRAPEFRUIT ASPIC

2 envelopes plain gelatin
1 cup cold grapefruit juice
1 cup boiling grapefruit juice
3 tablespoons lemon juice
¾ cup sugar

¾ cup diced celery
½ cup slivered almonds
4 large Florida grapefruit, sectioned
2 large Florida avocados, peeled and
  sliced

Soak gelatin in cold grapefruit juice. Dissolve in boiling grapefruit juice. Add lemon juice, sugar, celery and almonds. Remove white membrane from grapefruit sections and add them with avocado slices to gelatin mixture. Congeal in large ring mold. Makes 12 servings.

Mrs. A. Sydney Herlong, Jr.

MRS. A. SYDNEY HERLONG, JR., Wife of former Representative (Florida)

CITRUS SALAD

1 medium grapefruit
1 3 ounce package lemon gelatin
¾ cup hot water
⅓ cup lime juice
¼ cup dry sauterne (or other white
 table wine)

2 11 ounce cans mandarin oranges,
 drain, reserve juice
lettuce
mayonnaise or yogurt topping (optional)

Cut all the white membrane from the grapefruit, lift out the grapefruit sections and cut in half. Set aside. Combine gelatin and hot water and stir until gelatin is completely dissolved. Stir in lime juice, wine and ¾ cup reserved orange juice. Chill until mixture begins to thicken. Stir in orange and grapefruit sections. Pour into a 1 quart mold and chill until firm. Serve plain on lettuce leaves or with a mayonnaise or yogurt topping. Makes 4 to 6 servings.

Mrs. William H. Rehnquist

MRS. WILLIAM H. REHNQUIST, Wife of Associate Justice, Supreme Court (Arizona)

ORANGE JELLO SALAD

1 3 ounce package orange Jello
1 cup boiling water
1 can frozen orange juice

1 can mandarin oranges, drained
1 small can crushed pineapple

Dissolve Jello in boiling water. Cool. Add remaining ingredients, mix, pour into a 1 quart mold and refrigerate until set. Makes 6 servings.

Mrs. Olin E. Teague

MRS. OLIN E. TEAGUE, Wife of Representative (Texas)

ORANGE SALAD

1½ cups small curd cottage cheese
1 large carton Cool Whip
1 small package orange Jello

1 20 ounce can pineapple tidbits, well
 drained
1 large can mandarin oranges, well
 drained

Mix cottage cheese and Cool Whip. Add the dry Jello and stir. Fold in the pineapple and oranges. Chill. Makes 6 servings.

Mrs. Maurice G. Burnside

MRS. MAURICE G. BURNSIDE, Wife of former Representative (West Virginia)

186

ORANGE SHERBET SALAD

1 6 ounce package orange Jello
2¾ cups boiling water
1 6 ounce can frozen orange juice

1 pint orange sherbet
1 11 ounce can mandarin oranges, drained

Dissolve Jello in boiling water. Cool. Add juice and sherbet. Stir until dissolved. Add oranges. Chill. Makes 8 individual molds.

Mrs. Walter Moeller

MRS. WALTER MOELLER, Wife of former Representative (Ohio)

ORANGE GELATIN RING WITH AMBROSIA FRUIT SALAD

2 3 ounce packages orange gelatin
2 cups boiling liquid (fruit juice and water)
1 pint orange sherbet
2 11 ounce cans mandarin oranges, well drained

1 13 ounce can pineapple chunks, well drained
1 cup miniature marshmallows
1 cup flaked coconut
1 cup dairy sour cream
½ cup whipping cream, whipped
lettuce

Dissolve gelatin in boiling liquid. Immediately add sherbet and stir until melted. Add 1 can orange slices. Pour into a 1½ quart ring mold and chill until firm. Toss together remaining oranges, pineapple, marshmallows and coconut. Fold in sour cream and whipped cream. Unmold gelatin on lettuce leaves and fill center with the ambrosia fruit salad. Makes 6 to 8 servings.

Mrs. James R. Mann

MRS. JAMES R. MANN, Wife of Representative (South Carolina)

LIME MOLD SALAD

2 packages lime Jello
1 cup boiling water
1 20 ounce can crushed pineapple

½ cup finely chopped maraschino cherries, green, red and black
½ cup chopped black walnuts
1 pint dairy sour cream

Dissolve Jello in hot water. Cool and add fruit and nuts. Fold in sour cream last. Put in mold and chill several hours before serving. Makes 8 servings.

Mrs. George Arthur Weaver

MRS. GEORGE ARTHUR WEAVER, Daughter of former Representative M. G. Burnside (West Virginia)

187

LIME JELLO MOLD

1 can crushed pineapple, drained, reserve juice
water
1 large package lime Jello

1 large package lemon Jello
1 cup cottage cheese
½ cup mayonnaise
½ cup black walnuts

Combine pineapple juice with enough water to make 2 cups and bring to a boil. Pour over Jello and stir to dissolve. Cool. Add remaining ingredients and pour into mold. Makes 6 servings.

Mrs. Sherman W. Tribbitt

MRS. SHERMAN W. TRIBBITT, Wife of Governor (Delaware)

MOLDED FRUIT SALAD

2 packages lemon Jello
1⅔ cups boiling water
2 3 ounce packages cream cheese
1 20 ounce can crushed pineapple

1 small bottle maraschino cherries, drained
1 cup pecans

Dissolve Jello in boiling water. Mash cheese and mix thoroughly with Jello. Add remaining ingredients and pour into lightly oiled mold or oblong casserole. Chill until firm. Makes 12 servings.

Mrs. John L. McMillan, Jr.

MRS. JOHN L. McMILLAN, JR., Daughter-in-law of former Representative John L. McMillan (South Carolina)

QUICK AND EASY FRUIT SALAD

1 3 ounce package orange Jello
1 large carton Cool Whip
1 8 ounce carton cottage cheese

1 large can chunk pineapple, drained
1 large can fruit cocktail, drained
¼ cup chopped nuts (optional)

Mix Jello with Cool Whip until Jello is thoroughly blended. Mix in cottage cheese. Add drained fruit. Add nuts if desired and pour into mold. Unmold and sprinkle tops of individual servings with nuts. Makes 12 servings.

Mrs. Richard Kelly

MRS. RICHARD KELLY, Wife of Representative (Florida)

CONGEALED PINEAPPLE AND CHEESE SALAD

2 cups crushed pineapple with juice
juice of 1 lemon
1 cup sugar
2 tablespoons gelatin

½ cup cold water
1 cup grated American cheese
½ pint whipping cream, whipped

Heat pineapple. Add lemon juice and sugar. Stir until sugar is dissolved. Soak gelatin in cold water. Add to hot mixture. When mixture begins to set, add cheese and whipped cream. Mix thoroughly and put in mold to congeal. Makes 10 to 12 servings.

MRS. JAMIE L. WHITTEN, Wife of Representative (Mississippi)

PINEAPPLE DELIGHT SALAD

1 3 ounce package lemon Jello
1 3 ounce package lime Jello
4 cups boiling water

1 3 ounce package cream cheese
15 large marshmallows
1 8 ounce can crushed pineapple
½ pint whipping cream, whipped

Dissolve Jello in 2 cups water and set aside. Melt cream cheese and marshmallows in remaining water and beat by hand until completely melted. Do not boil. Combine the 2 mixtures and chill until almost firm. Fold in pineapple and whipped cream and chill until set. Makes 8 servings.

MRS. HENRY BELLMON, Wife of Senator (Oklahoma)

WHITE SALAD

1 small can crushed pineapple
⅓ cup sugar
1 envelope unflavored gelatin
¼ cup cold water

1 3 ounce package Philadelphia cream cheese
½ pint whipping cream, whipped

Combine pineapple and sugar in a saucepan and bring to a boil. Remove from heat and cool slightly. Soften gelatin in cold water and add to boiled mixture. Let cool. Mash cream cheese, adding a little of the gelatin mixture to help soften it. Fold into gelatin mixture. Then fold in whipped cream. Refrigerate.

MRS. EUGENE SILER, Wife of former Representative (Kentucky)

MINCEMEAT SALAD

1 6 ounce package lemon Jello
1½ cups hot water
2 cups orange juice

2 cups mincemeat
½ cup chopped nuts
pinch of sugar

Dissolve Jello in hot water. Cool. Add remaining ingredients, stirring occasionally. When it starts to set, pour into a large, oiled mold. Chill until set; unmold and serve. Makes 10 to 12 servings.

Mrs. D. R. Matthews

MRS. D. R. MATTHEWS, Wife of former Representative (Florida)

MARIE'S HORSE RADISH SALAD

1 3 ounce package lime Jello
1 3 ounce package lemon Jello
2 cups boiling water
1 cup Hellmann's mayonnaise
1 can Eagle Brand condensed milk

1 small carton small curd cottage cheese
1 20 ounce can crushed pineapple
3 tablespoons horse radish
1 cup chopped nuts
maraschino cherries (optional)

Dissolve Jello in boiling water. Cool. Combine remaining ingredients, except cherries, add to Jello and mix thoroughly. Refrigerate until firm in a 9 x 13 inch pan. To serve, garnish with maraschino cherries. Makes 18 to 20 servings.

Mrs. Carroll D. Kearns

MRS. CARROLL D. KEARNS, Wife of former Representative (Pennsylvania)

COTTAGE CHEESE SALAD

1 package lime Jello
1 package lemon Jello
2 cups hot water
1 20 ounce can crushed pineapple, drained
1 large can evaporated milk

1 cup chopped nuts
2 apples, chopped
2 cups small curd cottage cheese
1 cup mayonnaise
lettuce

Mix together all ingredients except lettuce; chill until set. Serve on lettuce leaf. Makes 8 servings.

Mrs. Harold T. Johnson

MRS. HAROLD T. JOHNSON, Wife of Representative (California)

CHEESE AND FRUIT SALAD

1 tablespoon unflavored gelatin
¼ cup cold water
½ cup roquefort cheese, softened
2 3 ounce packages cream cheese
¼ teaspoon salt

¼ teaspoon paprika
1 teaspoon onion juice
1 cup whipped cream
fresh or canned fruit
French dressing

Soften gelatin in cold water. Dissolve over hot water. Blend cheeses, salt, paprika and onion juice until smooth with no lumps of roquefort remaining. Mix thoroughly with gelatin and fold in whipped cream. Pour into mold and chill. Serve with fruit which has been marinated in French dressing at least 24 hours. Makes 4 to 6 servings.

Mrs. Alvin E. O'Konski

Mrs. Alvin E. O'Konski, Wife of former Representative (Wisconsin)

ARTICHOKE SALAD

2 envelopes unflavored gelatin
½ cup cold water
2 cans beef consomme, heated
juice of 2 lemons
few drops Tabasco
½ teaspoon grated onion
½ cup chopped stuffed olives

1 15 ounce can artichoke hearts,
   drained and finely chopped
½ cup chopped celery (optional)
salt and pepper to taste
salad greens
curry mayonnaise (or roquefort
   dressing)

Soften gelatin in cold water. Add to hot consomme and stir until dissolved. Add juice, Tabasco, onion, olives, artichokes, celery if desired and seasoning. Chill until syrupy. Spoon into oiled 1½ quart mold. Chill until firm. Serve on salad greens topped with curry mayonnaise. Makes 8 servings.

Mrs. Ralph W. Yarborough

Mrs. Ralph W. Yarborough, Wife of former Senator (Texas)

MOLDED ASPARAGUS SALAD

2 envelopes unflavored gelatin
½ cup cold water
1 large can chopped asparagus, drain
   and reserve liquid
water
¾ cup sugar
½ teaspoon salt
½ cup vinegar

juice of 1 lemon
1 teaspoon grated onion
1 cup chopped water chestnuts
1 cup chopped celery
¼ cup chopped pimiento
salad greens
mayonnaise

Soak gelatin in cold water. To the liquid from the asparagus, add enough water to make 1½ cups and add the sugar, salt, vinegar and lemon juice. Heat together until it boils. Dissolve gelatin in hot liquid. Cool. Add vegetables except greens. Pour into individual molds or pan. Chill until set. Serve on salad greens with mayonnaise. Makes 8 servings.

Mrs Thomas B. Abernethy

MRS. THOMAS G. ABERNETHY, Wife of former Representative (Mississippi)

ROSY BEET MOLD

1 3 ounce package raspberry gelatin
1 cup boiling water
3 tablespoons vinegar
1 tablespoon horse radish

1 8 ounce can diced beets, drain
   and reserve juice
1 7 ounce can crushed pineapple, drain
   and reserve juice

Dissolve gelatin in hot water. Add vinegar, horse radish, beet juice and pineapple juice. Cool until consistency of egg whites. Stir in beets and pineapple. Pour into mold. Chill until set. Makes 6 servings.

Mrs. Rufus C. Holman

MRS. RUFUS C. HOLMAN, Wife of former Senator (Oregon)

BEET SALAD

1 cup diced canned beets, drain and
  reserve liquid
water
1 package lemon Jello
3 tablespoons vinegar
¾ tablespoon grated onion

1 cup chopped celery
1 teaspoon horse radish
1 teaspoon salt
lettuce
mayonnaise

Heat beet liquid with enough water added to make 1½ cups. Dissolve Jello in
it. Grate, finely chop or put beets through blender. Add beets to Jello. Add next
5 ingredients and put into individual molds or pan. Chill. Serve on lettuce leaves
with mayonnaise. Makes 8 servings.

Mrs. Thomas G. Abernethy

MRS. THOMAS G. ABERNETHY, Wife of former Representative (Mississippi)

BROCCOLI SALAD MOLD

2 packages frozen chopped broccoli
1 package unflavored gelatin
¼ cup cold water
¾ can boiling consomme
2 hard cooked eggs, chopped
½ cup mayonnaise
¼ teaspoon salt
2 teaspoons lemon juice

2 dashes Tabasco
1 heaping tablespoon grated onion
lettuce leaves

Sauce:
½ pint dairy sour cream
2 or 3 teaspoons horse radish

Cook broccoli until almost tender. Drain. Soften gelatin in cold water and dissolve
in hot consomme. Mix the broccoli with remaining ingredients, except lettuce, and
combine with consomme. Pour into oiled ring mold and chill until firm. Unmold
on lettuce and serve with horse radish sauce made by whipping sour cream and
horse radish together. Makes 8 servings.

Mrs. William H. Ayres

MRS. WILLIAM H. AYRES, Wife of former Representative (Ohio)

COLESLAW PARFAIT SALAD

1 package lemon gelatin
1 cup hot water
½ cup mayonnaise
½ cup cold water
2 tablespoons vinegar
¼ teaspoon salt
1½ cups finely shredded cabbage

½ cup radish slices
½ cup diced celery
2 to 4 tablespoons diced green pepper
1 tablespoon diced onion
lettuce
thin radish slices
mint leaves

Dissolve gelatin in hot water. Blend in mayonnaise, cold water, vinegar and salt. Chill mixture until partially set. Then beat until fluffy. Add cabbage, radish slices, celery, green pepper and onion. Pour into individual molds or a 1 quart mold. Chill until set. Unmold on ruffles of lettuce and garnish with thin slices of radish and leaves of mint. Makes 6 to 8 servings.

Mrs. James E. Holshouser, Jr.

Mrs. James E. Holshouser, Jr., Wife of Governor (North Carolina)

PATRICIA'S CUCUMBER SALAD

1 package lime Jello
1 cup hot water
1 tablespoon plain gelatin
cold water
¾ cup shredded cucumber

3 tablespoons grated onion
½ cup chopped almonds
1 cup cottage cheese
1 cup mayonnaise

Dissolve Jello in hot water. Add plain gelatin which has been softened in a bit of cold water. Combine all other ingredients and then add to the Jello mixture. Pour into molds and place in refrigerator until congealed. Makes 8 servings.

Mrs. Robert E. Jones

Mrs. Robert E. Jones, Wife of Representative (Alabama)

194

LIME SOUFFLE

1 package lime Jello
1 cup hot water
1 cup dairy sour cream
½ cup mayonnaise
2 tablespoons lemon juice

½ teaspoon salt
few drops red pepper seasoning
1 large cucumber, finely chopped
12 thin cucumber slices
romaine or endive (optional)

Dissolve Jello in hot water; stir in sour cream, mayonnaise, lemon juice, salt and red pepper seasoning. Chill 30 minutes. Fold cucumber into thickened gelatin mixture. It may be mixed in a blender to make it fluffy. Pour into mold and chill. Unmold when set. Trim a sliver from each cucumber slice and stand them flat around mold. If a ring mold is used, fill center with crisp romaine or curly endive.

Mrs. Paul J. Kilday

MRS. PAUL KILDAY, Wife of former Representative (Texas)

EMERALD SALAD

2 packages lime Jello
1½ cups boiling water
1½ cups shredded cucumber
2 tablespoons chopped green onions

2 cups cream style cottage cheese
2 cups mayonnaise
⅔ cup slivered blanched almonds

Dissolve Jello in boiling water and cool until slightly set. Combine drained cucumber and onions. To this mixture add cottage cheese, mayonnaise and almonds and fold into Jello. Pour into mold and chill. Makes 12 servings.

Mrs. Richard G. Scott

MRS. RICHARD G. SCOTT, Daughter of former Senator Arthur Vivian Watkins (Utah)

CUCUMBER LIME SALAD

1 3 ounce package lime Jello
¾ cup hot water
¼ cup lemon juice
1 teaspoon onion juice

½ cup dairy sour cream, whipped
½ cup mayonnaise
1 cup chopped unpeeled cucumber

Dissolve Jello in hot water and add lemon juice. Cool and add other ingredients. Pour into molds and chill. Makes 10 servings.

Mrs. Patrick H. Mathews

MRS. PATRICK H. MATHEWS, Daughter of former Representative C. A. Fuller (Arkansas)

PEAS AND PEANUT SALAD

4 eggs, whipped
⅔ cup vinegar
½ cup water
⅔ cup sugar
½ teaspoon salt
3 rounded teaspoons dry mustard
1 tablespoon gelatin

1½ cups whipping cream, whipped
2 packages frozen peas
1 teaspoon sugar
salt to taste
½ cup Spanish peanuts
mayonnaise

Combine the eggs, vinegar, ¼ cup water, sugar, salt and mustard. Whip together and cook in a double boiler until thick. Soak gelatin in remaining water and add to hot mixture, mixing well. Cool. Add whipped cream to the cooked mixture and pour into a slightly greased 9 inch ring mold. Refrigerate.

Boil peas, adding sugar and salt, for just 2 minutes. Drain well and chill. Add peanuts and enough mayonnaise to bind them together. Unmold gelatin salad and fill center with the peas and peanuts mixture. Makes 12 to 14 servings.

Mrs. James A. McClure

MRS. JAMES A. MCCLURE, Wife of Senator (Idaho)

TOMATO CHIFFON SALAD

2 envelopes unflavored gelatin
2¼ cups tomato juice
3 tablespoons finely chopped onion
3 tablespoons finely chopped green
  pepper
1 bay leaf

½ teaspoon celery salt
½ cup instant nonfat dry milk
½ cup water
2 tablespoons lemon juice
salad greens
cottage cheese (optional)

Sprinkle gelatin on ½ cup tomato juice to soften. In saucepan simmer together remaining tomato juice, onion, green pepper, bay leaf and celery salt about 10 minutes; remove bay leaf. Stir in gelatin until dissolved. Cool to a jelly consistency. Sprinkle nonfat dry milk over water and beat until stiff. Blend in lemon juice and fold in tomato mixture. Turn into a mold that has been rinsed in cold water. Chill until firm. To serve, unmold on salad greens and fill center with cottage cheese if desired. Makes 6 to 8 servings.

Amy Gronna Cowing

MRS. AMY GRONNA COWING, Daughter of former Senator A. J. Gronna (North Dakota)

196

TOMATO ASPIC

2 cups V8 juice
1 envelope unflavored gelatin
1 tablespoon vinegar
1 tablespoon grated onion
½ teaspoon salt

pepper to taste
celery, finely cut
olives, chopped
green peppers, chopped (optional)

Pour ¼ cup of the V8 juice in a bowl and sprinkle with gelatin. Heat remaining juice until it reaches the boiling point. Pour over softened gelatin and mix to dissolve. Add vinegar, onion, salt, pepper, celery, olives and green pepper. Pour into greased mold and chill until set. Makes 8 servings.

Mrs. Roy A. Taylor

Mrs. Roy A. Taylor, Wife of Representative (North Carolina)

TOMATO LEMON ASPIC

1 small onion, finely chopped
2 cups V8 juice (or tomato juice)
1 package lemon Jello

3 tablespoons lemon juice
1 cup chopped olives and celery

Boil onion in 1 cup of juice and pour over Jello. Add remaining juice and lemon juice. Refrigerate until it thickens. Add olives and celery. Pour into mold and chill until firm. Makes 8 servings.

Mrs. Robert Thomas Ashmore

Mrs. Robert Thomas Ashmore, Wife of former Representative (South Carolina)

FROZEN FRUIT SALAD

1 3 ounce package cream cheese
2 tablespoons cream
2 tablespoons lemon juice
⅓ cup mayonnaise
dash of salt
2 tablespoons sugar

1 cup drained, crushed pineapple
1 cup diced orange sections
½ cup chopped cherries
½ cup chopped pecans
1 cup whipping cream, whipped

Mash cream cheese and soften with 2 tablespoons cream. Add lemon juice, mayonnaise, salt and sugar. Blend in fruits and nuts. Fold in whipped cream and freeze in mold or shallow pan. Makes 8 servings.

Mrs. James O. Eastland

Mrs. James O. Eastland, Wife of Senator (Mississippi)

FROZEN COLESLAW

1 teaspoon salt
1 large head cabbage, shredded
1 cup vinegar
¼ cup water
2 cups sugar

1 teaspoon celery seed
1 teaspoon mustard seed
1 carrot, grated
1 medium red onion, grated

Add salt to cabbage and let stand 1 hour. Mix vinegar, water, sugar, celery seed and mustard seed and bring to a boil. Boil 1 minute. Cool. Add cabbage, carrot and onion and mix well. May be frozen before serving but allow ample time to defrost. Makes 10 to 12 servings.

Mrs. Lon M. Buzick

MRS. LON M. BUZICK, Member of Congressional Club (Kansas)

COOKED SALAD DRESSING

1 tablespoon flour
2 tablespoons sugar
1 teaspoon salt
1 teaspoon dry mustard

⅔ cup milk
1 egg, beaten
1 tablespoon butter or margarine
¼ cup cider vinegar

Combine flour, sugar, salt and mustard in top of double boiler. Add milk gradually. Cook over hot water until thickened, stirring constantly. Stir part of hot mixture into beaten egg. Return egg mixture to double boiler and cook 5 minutes, stirring constantly. Add butter and blend. Remove from heat and cool slightly. Add vinegar and beat until smooth. Store covered in refrigerator. Makes 1 cup.

Amy Gronna Cowing

MRS. AMY GRONNA COWING, Daughter of former Senator A. J. Gronna (North Dakota)

198

TANGY MAYONNAISE DRESSING

1 cup mayonnaise	1 teaspoon mixed herb seasoning
½ tablespoon lemon juice	1 tablespoon grated onion
¼ teaspoon salt	1 clove minced garlic
¼ teaspoon paprika	½ teaspoon Worcestershire sauce
⅛ teaspoon curry powder (optional)	½ pint dairy sour cream

Mix together all ingredients and beat until thoroughly blended. Flavor is improved if dressing is made the day before serving. Makes about 1 pint.

Mrs. Craig Hosmer

MRS. CRAIG HOSMER, Wife of former Representative (California)

FRUIT SALAD DRESSING

1 tablespoon grated onion	2 rounded teaspoons celery seed
¾ cup sugar	2 teaspoons vinegar
1 egg	1 pint Mazola oil
1 teaspoon salt	juice of 1 large lemon
1 rounded teaspoon paprika	

Mix onion and sugar and let stand 1 hour. Beat egg, dry ingredients and vinegar together. Add sugar and onion mixture. Very slowly beat in oil, alternating with lemon juice. Blend thoroughly.

Mrs. Everett McKinley Dirksen

MRS. EVERETT M. DIRKSEN, Wife of former Senator (Illinois)

POPPY SEED DRESSING

½ cup sugar	1 teaspoon poppy seed
½ teaspoon salt	4 tablespoons vinegar
1 tablespoon dry mustard	2 teaspoons grated onion
1 tablespoon paprika	1 cup salad oil

Blend with mixer all ingredients except oil. Add salad oil in thirds, beating after each addition. This dressing is delicious on fresh fruits and will keep for several weeks in refrigerator.

Mrs. Tazewell Shepard, Jr.

MRS. TAZEWELL SHEPARD, JR., Daughter of Senator John Sparkman (Alabama)

CELERY SEED DRESSING

1 pound confectioners sugar
3 teaspoons dry mustard
3 teaspoons salt
3 teaspoons grated onion

1 cup vinegar
2 cups corn oil
3 tablespoons celery seed

Beat first 4 ingredients in electric blender. Gradually add vinegar, oil and celery seed and beat until thoroughly blended. Makes 1 quart.

Mrs. Robert A. Grant

MRS. ROBERT A. GRANT, Wife of former Representative (Indiana)

BUTTERMILK DRESSING

1 pint Hellmann's mayonnaise
1 pint buttermilk
2 teaspoons salt
½ teaspoon black pepper

1 teaspoon onion powder
½ teaspoon garlic powder
½ teaspoon monosodium glutamate
2½ tablespoons dried parsley

Mix all ingredients together and place in refrigerator uncovered for 24 hours. Place in covered jars. Keeps indefinitely in refrigerator. This is also delicious used as a dip with carrot sticks and celery or on a baked potato. Makes 2 pints.

Mrs. Clifford Davis

MRS. CLIFFORD DAVIS, Wife of former Representative (Tennessee)

FRENCH DRESSING

1 cup corn oil
½ cup vinegar
½ cup catsup
1 teaspoon salt

3 tablespoons sugar
1 tablespoon minced onion
1 clove garlic

Mix all ingredients together and store in refrigerator for use as needed. Makes 1 pint.

Mrs. Mark Andrews

MRS. MARK ANDREWS, Wife of Representative (North Dakota)

LEMON DRESSING

¾ cup olive oil
⅓ cup lemon juice
1 teaspoon salt

¼ teaspoon pepper
1 teaspoon mustard

Combine all ingredients in blender. Blend well. Pour into jar and store in refrigerator. Makes 1 cup.

Mrs. E. C. Gathings

MRS. E. C. GATHINGS, Wife of former Representative (Arkansas)

DRESSING FOR LETTUCE SALAD

1 hard cooked egg
½ teaspoon salt
½ teaspoon sugar
½ teaspoon pepper
1 teaspoon prepared mustard

3 tablespoons oil
1 tablespoon vinegar (or juice of ½ lemon)
1 leek, finely chopped (or spring onion)
1 head lettuce

Using a fork, finely mash egg. Add salt, sugar, pepper and mustard. Stir in oil, vinegar and leek. Thoroughly dry lettuce and tear into small pieces. Pour dressing over lettuce and serve. Makes 4 to 5 servings.

Mrs. D. R. Matthews

MRS. D. R. MATTHEWS, Wife of former Representative (Florida)

SPRING SALAD DRESSING

2 teaspoons Dijon mustard
2 teaspoons red wine vinegar
2 teaspoons egg yolk
  (break yolk and measure)
¼ teaspoon Worcestershire sauce
Tabasco sauce to taste
6 tablespoons olive oil

salt to taste
freshly ground pepper to taste
2 teaspoons heavy cream
½ teaspoon lemon juice
1 teaspoon chopped parsley (or chives)

Combine mustard, vinegar, egg yolk, Worcestershire and Tabasco in salad bowl. Beat rapidly with wire whisk. Slowly add the oil, beating constantly, until slightly thickened. Blend in remaining ingredients. Serve over any salad greens. Makes about ½ cup.

Mrs. Herman T. Schneebeli

MRS. HERMAN T. SCHNEEBELI, Wife of Representative (Pennsylvania)

ORIENTAL SALAD DRESSING

2 hard cooked eggs
½ cup ripe olives, slivered
3 tablespoons sugar

3 tablespoons wine vinegar
3 tablespoons mayonnaise

Sliver egg whites and mix with other ingredients. Pour over salad greens and top with sieved egg yolks. Makes 6 servings.

Mrs. Durward G. Hall

MRS. DURWARD G. HALL, Wife of former Representative (Missouri)

PARMESAN DRESSING

¼ cup salad oil
¼ teaspoon pepper
2 buds garlic, minced
½ teaspoon salt
1 tablespoon lemon juice

1 pinch dry mustard
2 rounded tablespoons parmesan cheese
2 quarts torn salad greens

Combine all ingredients, except salad greens, in a glass jar and shake vigorously until thoroughly blended. Pour dressing over salad greens and toss gently until each piece is coated.

Mrs. Thomas E. Cole

MRS. THOMAS E. COLE, Daughter-in-law of former Representative W. Sterling Cole (New York)

BLUE CHEESE DRESSING

4 ounces blue cheese
1 quart mayonnaise
½ pint buttermilk
2 teaspoons Worcestershire sauce
2 tablespoons onion juice

1 teaspoon garlic powder
1 teaspoon Tabasco
1 teaspoon A.1. sauce
½ teaspoon salt

Break up blue cheese by hand. Gently combine with remaining ingredients. Refrigerate. Makes 1½ quarts.

Mrs. David Jack Dixon

MRS. DAVID JACK DIXON, Daughter of Representative Wilbur D. Mills (Arkansas)

ROQUEFORT SALAD DRESSING

2 wedges roquefort cheese
1 pint mayonnaise
½ pint dairy sour cream
juice of 1 lemon

chopped green onion tops
ground pepper
milk (optional)

With an electric beater mix until creamy all ingredients except milk. If it becomes too thick later on, thin with a little milk. Keeps well for several weeks in the refrigerator. Makes 1 quart.

Mrs. John Dellenback

MRS. JOHN DELLENBACK, Wife of former Representative (Oregon)

ROQUEFORT DRESSING

1 6 ounce package roquefort cheese
   (or blue cheese)
¼ cup lemon juice (or white vinegar)
¾ cup olive oil
1 medium onion, finely chopped
6 hard cooked eggs, chopped

Tabasco
Worcestershire sauce
garlic powder
pepper
pinch of salt

Crumble cheese with a fork and slowly add lemon juice. Then add olive oil, stirring constantly with fork. Add onion and eggs. Season to taste with Tabasco, Worcestershire, garlic powder, pepper and salt. Mix well and chill thoroughly. Shake well before using.

Mrs. James B. Allen

MRS. JAMES B. ALLEN, Wife of Senator (Alabama)

ROQUEFORT SOUR CREAM DRESSING

2 cups mayonnaise
3 teaspoons chopped chives
1 teaspoon garlic powder
2 to 3 teaspoons freshly ground pepper

½ teaspoon Worcestershire sauce
1 cup dairy sour cream
½ cup buttermilk
3 ounces roquefort cheese, crumbled

Mix all ingredients together and refrigerate a few hours before using. Makes 1 quart.

Mrs. James A. McClure

MRS. JAMES A. McCLURE, Wife of Senator (Idaho)

NOTES

FISH & SEAFOOD

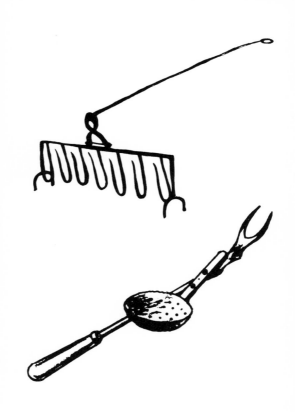

To stew Mussels

Take one hundred mussels, put them in a pail of water, and wash them with a birch broom, then put them in a pail of spring water and salt for two hours, wash them out, put them into a saucepan and cover them close; stew them gently till they open, strain the liquor from them through a sieve, pick them out of the shells, and take out the beard (if there is a crab under the tongue throw that mussel away) put them into a stew-pan, drain the liquor from the settlings and put half of it in, with a gill of white wine, a little grated nutmeg, and a piece of butter mixed with flour, stew them gently and keep them stirring till they are thick and smooth; put them in a hot dish, with toasted sippets for garnish.

The New Art of Cookery
Richard Briggs, 1792

LING COD A LA FRIEDERIKE

4 large pieces ling cod (or other tender   1 cup dairy sour cream
   white fish)   parmesan cheese

Place fish on a flat greased baking dish. Over all the pieces spread sour cream about ½ inch thick. Sprinkle generously with parmesan cheese. Do not season. Bake at 400° for exactly 20 minutes. Serve immediately on preheated plates.

Mrs. Warren G. Magnuson

MRS. WARREN G. MAGNUSON, Wife of Senator (Washington)

FILET OF FLOUNDER WITH CREAMY LEMON SAUCE

2 pounds filets of flounder   boiling water
salt   2 or 3 tablespoons lemon juice
pepper   2 eggs
butter or margarine   parsley flakes

Sprinkle filets of fish with salt and pepper and lay them flat in buttered large pyrex baking dish. Dot tops with butter. Add boiling water to almost cover fish. Add lemon juice to water. Bake in covered baking dish in preheated 350° oven for about 15 minutes. Remove filets from baking dish and reserve liquid.

Beat eggs until evenly blended. Add hot fish liquid and stir. Pour liquid into heavy enamel sauce pan and stir constantly over low heat until mixture thickens. Add salt and pepper to taste and more lemon juice if necessary. As soon as sauce has thickened pour over fish. Sprinkle with parsley flakes and serve. Makes 6 servings.

Mrs. Clarence D. Long

MRS. CLARENCE D. LONG, Wife of Representative (Maryland)

FESTIVE FLOUNDER

salt
12 flounder filets
milk
flour
butter for browning
6 large scallops, diced
6 raw shrimp, diced
2 tablespoons butter
½ pound mushrooms, minced
¼ teaspoon chopped parsley
¼ teaspoon chopped tarragon
¼ teaspoon chopped chives

1 garlic clove, crushed
1 medium onion, finely chopped
salt and pepper to taste

Sauce:
4 tablespoons butter
2 tablespoons flour
1 cup milk
½ pint heavy cream
4 ounces grated Swiss cheese
4 ounces grated parmesan cheese

Salt filets lightly. Dip in milk, then in flour and brown lightly on both sides in butter. Place in long shallow baking dish.

Combine scallops and shrimp with 2 tablespoons butter, mushrooms, parsley, tarragon, chives, garlic, onion, salt and pepper. Cook on medium high burner for 5 minutes, then slowly for 10 to 15 minutes, stirring often. Cover filets with this mixture.

To make sauce, heat 2 tablespoons of butter and blend in flour. Slowly add milk, blending until smooth and thickened. Slowly add the cream and half of each cheese. Pour sauce over casserole. Dot with remaining butter. Sprinkle with remaining cheese. Bake in a 350° oven until cheese browns. Makes 6 to 8 servings.

Mrs. Emilio Q. Daddario

MRS. EMILIO Q. DADDARIO, Wife of former Representative (Connecticut)

FLOUNDER STUFFED WITH SHRIMP

¼ cup finely chopped green onion
3 tablespoons margarine
1 4 ounce can sliced mushrooms,
    drained
¾ pound small shrimp, shelled and
    deveined
½ cup fine bread crumbs
2 tablespoons chopped fresh parsley
dash of salt and pepper
6 flounder filets

Sauce:
2 tablespoons margarine
2 tablespoons flour
1 tablespoon lemon juice
1 cup milk
1 egg, beaten
paprika

Cook onion in margarine until tender. Add mushrooms and shrimp, stirring until shrimp turn pink. Add bread crumbs, parsley, salt and pepper. Put 1 tablespoon of shrimp stuffing at one end of each filet and roll up. Place, seam side down, in a buttered baking dish.

Heat margarine, stir in flour and cook 1 minute. Add lemon juice and milk, stirring after each addition. Pour sauce slowly into egg so as to prevent curdling. Add remaining stuffing to sauce and pour over filets. Sprinkle with paprika. Bake 25 minutes in preheated 375° oven.

Mrs John J. Williams

Mrs. JOHN J. WILLIAMS, Wife of former Senator (Delaware)

FLOUNDER CASSEROLE

2 pounds flounder filet
2 cans cream of shrimp soup
45 Ritz crackers, crushed
1 tablespoon Worcestershire sauce

1 teaspoon garlic juice (optional)
1 teaspoon onion juice (optional)
¼ pound margarine, melted

Place flounder and shrimp soup in buttered casserole and bake 25 minutes at 350°. Mix remaining ingredients and sprinkle over top of flounder. Bake 10 minutes more. May be frozen. Makes 8 servings.

Elizabeth G. Van Exem

ELIZABETH GASQUE VAN EXEM, former Representative (South Carolina)

209

FISH FILETS

6 filets of sole or flounder
salt and pepper
¼ pound butter, melted
¼ teaspoon thyme
1 bay leaf
¼ teaspoon salt

⅛ teaspoon pepper
1 tablespoon minced onion
¾ teaspoon dill weed
1 cup sour cream
1 teaspoon sugar

Cut filets in half and season lightly with salt and pepper. Arrange in buttered flat pan. Combine remaining ingredients to make a sauce and spread over filets. Bake at 375° for 15 minutes after sauce starts to bubble. Makes 10 to 12 small servings.

Mrs. Robert T. Stafford

Mrs. Robert T. Stafford, Wife of Senator (Vermont)

FILETS FLORIDIAN

2 pounds any fish filets
3 tablespoons oil
1 orange, juice and grated rind

1 teaspoon salt
nutmeg
pepper to taste

Thaw filets if frozen. Divide into serving portions and place side by side in a well greased shallow baking dish, skin side down. Combine remaining ingredients and pour over fish. Bake in a 350° oven for 25 to 30 minutes. Test with a fork and if the fish flakes easily, it is ready to be served. Makes 6 servings.

Mrs. Robert L. F. Sikes

Mrs. Robert L. F. Sikes, Wife of Representative (Florida)

BARBECUED SALMON

1 large fresh salmon
¾ cup butter flavored Wesson oil
1 teaspoon Lawry's seasoning salt
½ teaspoon garlic powder
½ teaspoon onion powder

2 tablespoons lemon juice
1 teaspoon Accent
paprika
parsley flakes
additional lemon juice

Filet fish, keeping skin on outside. Combine oil with seasonings; brush on salmon. Barbecue flesh side down for about 5 to 8 minutes to brown. Turn over. Squeeze more lemon juice over flesh side and continue to barbecue for about 15 minutes. Test with a knife to see if it flakes. It is then ready. Makes 6 servings.

Mrs. Don Bonker

Mrs. Don Bonker, Wife of Representative (Washington)

BAKED SALMON FILETS

4 fresh salmon filets
salt

lemon pepper
butter

Place each salmon filet in a square of aluminum foil. Sprinkle each with salt and lemon pepper, top with a teaspoon of butter. Gently cover with the foil and place on baking sheet. Bake in a 450° oven for 15 minutes. Makes 4 servings.

Mrs. Calvin L. Rampton

Mrs. Calvin L. Rampton, Wife of Governor (Utah)

GLAZED SALMON HILDEBRAND

1 whole salmon

Stock:
bouillon, cubes or canned
3 quarts water
2 lemons, sliced
4 large onions, quartered
16 whole cloves
2½ bay leaves
3 stalks celery with leaves
24 whole peppercorns
handful of parsley sprigs
3 tablespoons salt

½ cup lemon juice
1 cup white wine vinegar (or white wine)

Glaze:
2 envelopes unflavored gelatin
1 quart salmon stock, strained

Garnish:
cucumbers, thinly sliced
pimiento
green olives
hard cooked eggs, sliced
parsley

Tie salmon in cheesecloth. Combine stock ingredients, piercing the onion sections with the cloves, and heat. After it has started to simmer, add salmon and poach until it flakes easily. Remove skin while still warm. Cool. Place in refrigerator to chill before glazing.

For glaze, stir gelatin into stock and heat until dissolved. Set aside to cool. Chill about 1 cup of glaze until thick and syrupy. Pour over fish, covering well, and chill until set. Decorate fish with garnishes. Chill another cup of glaze and pour over fish to seal decoration. Refrigerate. Pour remaining glaze in pan to depth of 1 inch. When set, cut in cubes and serve on platter with fish.

Mrs. James Day Hodgson

MRS. JAMES DAY HODGSON, Wife of former Secretary of Labor, presently Ambassador to Japan (California)

POACHED SALMON, SAUCE VERTE

fresh whole salmon (8 to 8½ pounds)

Court bouillon:
5 quarts water
1 cup French tarragon vinegar
¼ cup salt
4 carrots, sliced
2 large onions, sliced
1 bay leaf
1 teaspoon thyme, crumbled
½ cup chopped parsley
1 tablespoon peppercorns

Garnish:
1 14 ounce can French petit pois
2 15 ounce cans artichoke bottoms

oil and vinegar dressing
3 hard cooked eggs, sliced
4 gherkins, sliced
black olives, cut in strips
lemon slices
parsley

Sauce:
1 tablespoon each chopped capers,
  parsley, chives and watercress
¼ cup water
1½ cups mayonnaise
1 tablespoon tarragon vinegar
3 drops Tabasco sauce

Combine all court bouillon ingredients except peppercorns, bring to a boil and simmer for 1 hour. Add peppercorns and simmer another 10 minutes. Strain into a shallow pan large enough to hold the fish flat. Remove the head and tail from the salmon and wrap in cheesecloth 20 inches longer than the fish. Put fish into bouillon, allowing long ends of cheesecloth to hang out of the pan. Cover tightly, bring to a boil and simmer for 30 minutes or until fish flakes easily. Use long ends of cheesecloth to lift fish from the pan to a platter. Carefully pull out cheesecloth, remove skin and remove white fatty layer and dark meat in center of fish. Decorate with garnishes and chill. Serve with sauce. Makes 10 to 12 servings.

Garnish: Marinate peas and artichoke bottoms in oil and vinegar dressing. Drain and put peas in artichokes. Place these around platter and garnish with eggs, gherkins, olives, lemon slices and parsley.

Sauce: Simmer herbs in water 5 minutes; press through sieve; let cool. Stir into mayonnaise mixed with vinegar and Tabasco sauce.

Mrs. Sidney R. Yates

MRS. SIDNEY R. YATES, Wife of Representative (Illinois)

213

PIROK (RUSSIAN PIE)

pastry for double crust pie
2/3 cup uncooked rice
1 onion, chopped
1 tall can salmon (or 1 pound fresh, boned salmon)

salt and pepper to taste
3 hard cooked eggs, quartered

Line pie plate with pastry. Steam rice with the onion. Combine with salmon and its juice. Mix well. Season with salt and pepper. Put half the rice and fish mixture in unbaked pie shell. Press egg quarters into mixture. Top off with balance of rice and fish. Cover with pie crust, seal edges well and cut steam vents. Bake ½ hour at 350° or until well browned. (Bake fresh salmon 1 hour.) Serve as a main dish. Makes 6 servings. This dish was brought to Alaska by the early Russian colonists and was first made with salt salmon.

Mrs. Jay S. Hammond

MRS. JAY S. HAMMOND, Wife of Governor (Alaska)

BONE FREE BAKED SHAD

1 tablespoon butter (or vegetable oil)
1 shad, cleaned and scaled
1 teaspoon chopped mixed parsley and chives

salt and pepper to taste
lemon juice

Rub butter over surface of fish. Season with parsley, chives, salt and pepper. Encase in aluminum foil, closing securely. Bake at 250° for 5 hours. Bones will dissolve. To serve, sprinkle generously with lemon juice.

Margaret Chase Smith

MARGARET CHASE SMITH, former Senator (Maine)

214

MOUSSE OF SOLE

5 fresh filets of sole, cut in pieces
2 cups light cream
5 eggs

4 egg whites
2 tablespoons melted butter
salt and pepper
hollandaise sauce

Put sole, 1 cup of cream, eggs, egg whites, butter, salt and pepper in blender and blend 3 minutes or until smooth. Combine with remaining cream and pour mixture in souffle dish. Set in pan of hot water and bake at 350° for 30 minutes or until a knife inserted in center comes out dry. Serve hot with hollandaise sauce. (Frozen fish filets are not suitable.) Makes 6 servings.

Mrs. Pierre S. du Pont. IV

MRS. PIERRE S. du PONT IV, Wife of Representative (Delaware)

FRESH TROUT IN IDAHO

trout
flour (or Shake and Bake)
salt and pepper
Lawry's seasoning salt (optional)

lemon slices
paprika
tartar sauce (or dairy sour cream and
   horse radish combination)

Wash trout, scale gently with a knife and dry. Dust lightly with flour and season with salt and pepper or Lawry's seasoning to taste. Put on foil or Teflon sheet and bake at 400° for 20 minutes until lightly browned. Serve with lemon slices dusted with paprika and tartar sauce.

Mrs. Frank Church

MRS. FRANK CHURCH, Wife of Senator (Idaho)

BAKED TROUT AND CHEESE

1 pound trout filets
6 ounces American cheese, sliced
1/4 cup chopped parsley
1 teaspoon ground oregano (or thyme)
1/4 cup corn oil

2 medium onions, chopped
2 tablespoons flour
1/8 teaspoon salt
1/8 teaspoon pepper
1 1/2 cups milk

Alternate layers of fish and cheese in lightly greased oblong baking dish, ending with cheese. Sprinkle with parsley and oregano. Heat oil in skillet; add onions and cook until tender, stirring frequently. Mix flour, salt and pepper into skillet. Pour in milk; cook, stirring constantly until thickened. Pour over fish. Bake at 400° until fish flakes easily with a fork, about 20 to 30 minutes. Makes 4 servings.

Mrs. Richard H. Ichord

MRS. RICHARD H. ICHORD, Wife of Representative (Missouri)

SWISS CHEESE AND TUNA PIE

3 eggs
½ teaspoon salt
½ teaspoon dry mustard
few grains cayenne pepper
1 cup heavy cream
½ cup apple cider

1 tablespoon cider vinegar
1 9 inch unbaked pastry shell, chilled
2 6½ ounce cans tuna, drained and flaked
2 cups grated Swiss cheese
1 tablespoon flour

Beat eggs and the next three ingredients together until foamy. Beat in cream and the combined cider and vinegar. Cover bottom of pie shell with a layer of tuna. Sprinkle half the cheese over the tuna. Repeat layering. Sprinkle flour over cheese. Pour egg mixture over all. Bake at 425° for 15 minutes and then at 300° for 25 minutes or until knife comes out clean when inserted midway between center and edge of filling. Serve hot. Makes 6 servings.

Mrs. Steven D. Symms

MRS. STEVEN D. SYMMS, Wife of Representative (Idaho)

TUNA BROCCOLI CASSEROLE

2 10 ounce packages frozen broccoli spears
1 12 ounce can tuna
1 can cream of mushroom soup

¼ cup cooking sherry
8 slices cheddar cheese
paprika

Cook broccoli according to package directions. Do not overcook. Drain and arrange in buttered 8 x 11 x 1½ inch baking dish. Cover with a layer of tuna. Dilute soup with sherry and pour over tuna. Top with cheese slices. Sprinkle with paprika and bake at 325° for 20 to 25 minutes. Makes 6 servings.

Mrs. Richard M. Simpson

MRS. RICHARD M. SIMPSON, Wife of former Representative (Pennsylvania)

CLAM SOUFFLE

2 cans Snow's minced clams,
  undrained
2 cups coarsely crumbled saltine
  cracker crumbs

2 cups milk
2 eggs
minced onion
butter

Combine ingredients. Put into well buttered baking dish. Bake in 350° oven about 40 minutes or until set. Makes 6 to 8 servings.

Margaret Chase Smith

MARGARET CHASE SMITH, Former Senator (Maine)

STUFFED CHINESE CLAMS

2 dozen cherry stone clams
½ onion, chopped
1 soup spoon chopped garlic
2 pounds lean chopped beef

2 teaspoons ground ginger
salt and pepper to taste
¼ pound bread crumbs
melted butter

Remove clams from shells and chop. Saute the onion and garlic with the meat. Add ginger, salt and pepper to the clams and add to meat mixture. Mix well and cook in pan on top of stove for 5 minutes. Fill clam shells with this mixture and top with bread crumbs tossed in melted butter. Bake in a 350° oven for 5 minutes. Makes 6 servings of 8 filled shells each.

Mrs. George Marvin Wallhauser

MRS. GEORGE MARVIN WALLHAUSER, Wife of former Representative (New Jersey)

LINGUINI WITH CLAM SAUCE

2 cloves garlic, mashed or minced
3 tablespoons unsaturated oil
1 7 ounce can minced clams
1 small hot red pepper, crumbled

½ cup finely chopped parsley
½ pound linguini or tagliarini
2 tablespoons grated parmesan
  cheese (optional)

Saute garlic in oil until golden. Add the clams, including the liquid, the red pepper and parsley. Cook just long enough to heat through. Cook the linguini in lightly salted water, according to directions, and mound on a warm platter. Spoon the clam sauce over all and sprinkle with grated cheese. Makes 6 servings.

Mrs. Frank Annunzio

MRS. FRANK ANNUNZIO, Wife of Representative (Illinois)

LINGUINI WITH WHITE CLAM SAUCE

olive oil
2 large onions, chopped
4 large cloves garlic, mashed
2 cans flat anchovies, with oil

4 8 ounce cans minced clams (or
  4 cups fresh minced clams), drained,
  reserve juice
½ cup chopped parsley
1 pound linguini

Cover bottom of 2 quart saucepan with ¼ inch olive oil. Heat oil slowly and add onions. Cook onions until transparent but not brown. Add garlic and anchovies. Cook and stir until anchovies disintegrate. Pour in clam juice and sprinkle parsley over top. Simmer 15 minutes. This may be prepared and set aside to be reheated before adding clams. Just before serving, add clams and simmer 5 minutes. Do not boil once clams have been added. Serve in warm soup plates over linguini which has been cooked according to directions on package. Makes 4 servings.

Mrs. Hamilton Fish, Jr.

MRS. HAMILTON FISH, JR., Wife of Representative (New York)

FRIED CHESAPEAKE BAY SOFT SHELL CLAMS

4 cups dry pancake mix
1 quart fresh, shucked, soft shell clams,
  drained

fat or oil
salt
cocktail or tartar sauce

Put pancake mix in large shallow bowl. Add clams, a few at a time and toss lightly until well coated. Shake off excess breading. Fry 1½ to 2 minutes in deep fat at 375° until golden brown or in 1 to 2 inches of hot fat in large frying pan, turning until browned. Drain on paper towel. Repeat process until all clams are cooked. Salt lightly and serve at once with cocktail or tartar sauce. Makes 6 servings of 12 clams each.

Mrs. Fred E. Busbey

MRS. FRED E. BUSBEY, Wife of former Representative (Illinois)

BAKED CRAB SALAD

2 large potatoes, boiled and diced
¼ pound fresh shrimp, cleaned, boiled and diced
1 can crabmeat
1 to 1½ cups mayonnaise
1 tablespoon Worcestershire sauce

1 tablespoon grated onion
salt and pepper to taste
monosodium glutamate as desired
¼ cup cracker meal
1 tablespoon melted butter

Mix first 6 ingredients and seasonings together and place in baking dish. Combine cracker meal and butter and sprinkle over top of salad and bake for 15 to 20 minutes. Serve hot.

Mrs. George Ariyoshi

MRS. GEORGE R. ARIYOSHI, Wife of Governor (Hawaii)

CRAB SUPREME

1 cup chopped celery
8 slices bread, crusts removed, cubed
3 cups fresh crab (or Alaskan frozen)
1 onion, chopped
½ cup chopped green pepper
½ cup mayonnaise

4 eggs, beaten
2½ cups milk
1 can mushroom soup
grated cheese
paprika

Cook celery slowly 10 minutes in a little water. Drain. Put half of bread cubes in greased shallow casserole. Mix crab, onion, green pepper, celery and mayonnaise. Layer over bread. Cover mixture with remaining bread cubes. Mix eggs and milk and pour over casserole. Cover and refrigerate overnight. Bake 15 minutes at 350°. Then spoon soup over top and sprinkle with a generous amount of grated cheese and paprika. Return to oven for 1 hour or until golden brown. May be frozen. Makes 8 servings.

Mrs Wright Patman

MRS. WRIGHT PATMAN, Wife of Representative (Texas)

219

BAKED CRAB CASSEROLE

1 pound crabmeat
1 cup Pepperidge Farm herb stuffing
milk
4 hard cooked eggs, cut in chunks
1 teaspoon cayenne pepper

1 cup Hellmann's mayonnaise
1 teaspoon Worcestershire sauce
1 teaspoon lemon juice
bread crumbs
butter

Pick over crabmeat to remove any membrane. Place stuffing in a cup and add milk until it reaches the 1 cup mark. Mix with eggs, pepper, mayonnaise, Worcestershire and lemon juice. Add crabmeat and mix gently. Pour into buttered casserole. Top with bread crumbs and dot with butter. Bake at 350° for 20 to 30 minutes. Makes 8 servings.

Mrs. John L. McMillan, Jr.

MRS. JOHN L. McMILLAN, Wife of former Representative (South Carolina)

CRAB LASAGNE

½ pound uncooked lasagne noodles
2 cans frozen shrimp soup, thawed
1 pound fresh Dungeness crabmeat
  (or 2 cans crabmeat)
2 cups small curd cottage cheese
6 ounces cream cheese

1 egg
2 teaspoons basil
1 medium onion, chopped
salt and pepper to taste
tomatoes, thinly sliced
cheddar cheese, shredded

Cook noodles 15 minutes. Combine soup with crabmeat and heat. Mix cottage cheese, cream cheese, egg, basil, onion, salt and pepper. In a baking dish, place a layer of noodles and cover with half of cheese mixture. Over this spread all of the mixed shrimp and crabmeat. Cover with remaining noodles and remaining cream cheese mixture. Top with tomato slices. Bake 15 minutes in a 350° oven. Sprinkle top with cheddar cheese and continue baking for ½ hour. Let set for 10 to 15 minutes after it is baked to make serving easier. May be frozen. Makes 8 to 10 servings.

Mrs. Daniel J. Evans

MRS. DANIEL J. EVANS, Wife of Governor (Washington)

PHYL'S CRAB MORNAY

2 tablespoons butter
2 tablespoons flour
1 cup milk
2 cups grated American cheese

2 eggs, beaten
¼ pound mushrooms, sauteed
1 pound backfin crabmeat

Melt butter, stir in flour, add milk and cook until smooth. Add cheese and stir until melted. Mix 2 tablespoons of the sauce with the eggs and return to cheese sauce. Stir constantly over low heat for 2 minutes and add mushrooms and crabmeat. Spoon into ramekins and put under broiler until brown. Makes 4 servings.

Mrs J. Glenn Beall, Jr.

Mrs. J. Glenn Beall, Jr., Wife of Senator (Maryland)

CRAB MORNAY

4 tablespoons margarine, melted
4 tablespoons flour
2 garlic cloves, minced
2 cups milk
salt to taste

½ pound Swiss cheese, cut up
1 pound crabmeat
dash of Tabasco
parmesan cheese

Cook margarine, flour and garlic over low heat. Slowly add milk. Cook and stir until thick. Add salt, Swiss cheese, crabmeat and Tabasco. Mix thoroughly. Pour into ramekins and sprinkle with parmesan cheese. Bake 30 minutes at 350°. Makes 8 servings.

Mrs. Jack Edwards

Mrs. Jack Edwards, Wife of Representative (Alabama)

CRUISE INN CRAB IMPERIAL

1 teaspoon salt
¼ teaspoon pepper
⅛ teaspoon cayenne pepper
2 tablespoons Dijon mustard
¼ cup parsley flakes
½ cup mayonnaise

12 ounces backfin crabmeat

Garnish:
mayonnaise
paprika

Mix together the salt, pepper, cayenne pepper, mustard, parsley and mayonnaise. Add crabmeat. If needed, add more mayonnaise to hold mixture together. Fill hard seafood shells with mixture. Frost with mayonnaise and sprinkle with paprika. Place in 425° oven for 10 minutes until bubbly. Makes 4 servings.

Mrs Charles A. Vanik

MRS. CHARLES A. VANIK, Wife of Representative (Ohio)

CRAB EASTERN SHORE

1 egg, beaten
3 tablespoons mayonnaise
1½ teaspoons mustard
½ teaspoon dried herbs

1 teaspoon parsley
pinch of salt
1 pound backfin crabmeat

Combine egg, mayonnaise, mustard, herbs, parsley and salt. Pour over crabmeat and mix well. Put in ramekins and bake at 400° for 12 to 15 minutes. Makes 4 servings.

Mrs J. Glenn Beall, Jr.

MRS. J. GLENN BEALL, JR., Wife of Senator (Maryland)

222

CRAB QUICHE

½ cup mayonnaise
2 tablespoons flour
2 eggs, beaten
½ cup milk
7½ ounce can crabmeat (or 6 ounce package frozen)

8 ounces shredded Swiss cheese
⅓ cup sliced green onions, using some tops
1 9 inch unbaked pastry shell

Combine mayonnaise, flour, eggs and milk and mix until blended. Stir in the crabmeat, cheese and onions. Pour into pastry shell and bake at 350° for 45 minutes. May be frozen after baking.

Mrs. James E. Van Zandt

MRS. JAMES E. VAN ZANDT, Wife of former Representative (Pennsylvania)

LOBSTER CASSEROLE

2 cups boiling water
6 tablespoons butter
1 teaspoon salt
1 cup uncooked Uncle Ben's long grain rice
½ onion, finely chopped
½ green pepper, finely chopped
4 tablespoons flour
2 cups milk

1 cup heavy cream
1 to 2 red pimientos, finely chopped
¼ cup diced American cheese
2 tablespoons sherry cooking wine
salt to taste
dash of Tabasco
1 pound lobster meat
1 cup buttered bread crumbs

In boiling water, melt 2 tablespoons butter and add salt. Pour over rice in a buttered casserole, cover and bake for 45 minutes at 350°. Cool.

Saute onion and green pepper in 2 tablespoons of butter. Melt remaining butter and add flour to make a sauce. Blend in milk and stir until thickened. Add cream and then the onion and green pepper. Add pimientos and cheese. Add sherry. Season with salt and Tabasco. Combine sauce with lobster. Add the cooked rice. Stir well. Pour in greased casserole and top with buttered bread crumbs. Bake covered at 350° for 30 minutes. May be frozen. Makes 8 servings.

Mrs. James B. Longley

MRS. JAMES B. LONGLEY, Wife of Governor (Maine)

223

KNUCKLEMEAT LOBSTER STEW

2 pounds lobster claw meat	salt and pepper to taste
2 tablespoons butter	cream to taste
1 quart milk	

Braise lobster meat in butter. Add milk and bring to the boiling point. Remove from heat, season with salt, pepper and cream. Serve piping hot. Makes 6 servings.

Mrs. James A. Burke

MRS. JAMES A. BURKE, Wife of Representative (Massachusetts)

LOBSTER RAGOUT

1 pound lobster meat, canned chunk (or crabmeat)	½ teaspoon Worcestershire sauce
1 can cream of chicken soup	1 teaspoon curry powder
1 can chicken gumbo soup	butter or warm water (optional)
¾ cup light cream	½ cup dry sherry
	toast points or rice

Put lobster meat, soups, cream, Worcestershire sauce, curry powder and sherry into top of double boiler or chafing dish. For easier blending, blend curry powder with a little butter or warm water before adding to other ingredients. Mix ingredients thoroughly but gently so as not to break lobster chunks. Cook over water until the curry is cooked and hot. Serve over toast points or rice. If you do not use toast points, do serve crisp French bread. Makes 4 servings.

Mrs. Brendan T. Byrne

MRS. BRENDAN T. BYRNE, Wife of Governor (New Jersey)

LOBSTER AND SHRIMP A LA PARISIENNE

4 to 5 cooked lobster tails
2 medium onions, chopped
½ pound butter
2 cups sliced fresh mushrooms
1 cup chopped chives
2 cups shrimp, cooked, peeled
    and deveined
salt
pepper

cayenne pepper
1 jigger pernod
1 jigger cognac
½ cup white wine
2 13 ounce cans shrimp bisque
2 cups hollandaise sauce
1 pint whipping cream, whipped
cooked rice

Remove meat from lobster tails and cut into thick slices. Saute onions in butter until clear, add mushrooms and chives and cook for a few more minutes. Add lobster and shrimp with salt, pepper and cayenne to taste. Add the pernod and cognac and ignite. Stir in the wine and cook briefly. Carefully blend in the bisque and hollandaise sauce. Fold in whipped cream just before serving. Serve over rice. Makes 8 servings.

Mrs. Frank M. Karsten

MRS. FRANK M. KARSTEN, Wife of former Representative (Missouri)

OYSTERS A LA OLIVIER

24 large oysters
flour
1½ sticks butter
1 tablespoon chopped green onions
½ teaspoon minced garlic
1 8 ounce can mushrooms, chopped

½ teaspoon salt
½ teaspoon black pepper
1 wine glass dry sherry
1 tablespoon Worcestershire sauce
4 slices buttered toast
2 tablespoons chopped parsley

Dry oysters and dust with flour. In heavy frying pan, heat ½ stick butter until bubbly. Quickly brown oysters in the butter until edges curl. Remove from heat. In another pan, saute onions, garlic and mushrooms in remaining butter. Add salt, pepper, sherry and Worchestershire sauce. Stir until blended. Place oysters on buttered toast and pour sauce over them. Garnish with chopped parsley. Makes 4 servings.

Lindy (Mrs. Hale) Boggs

LINDY (MRS. HALE) BOGGS, Representative (Louisiana)

OYSTERS LOUISIANA

1 cup chopped green onions, tops and
  bottoms
1 cup chopped celery
¼ cup chopped bell pepper
¼ cup minced parsley
¼ pound butter

2 pints oysters, drained and chopped
salt
Worcestershire sauce
Tabasco
⅔ cup crushed Waverly crackers
8 patty shells

Cook onions, celery, bell pepper and parsley in butter. Add oysters and season with salt, Worcestershire and Tabasco to taste. Add cracker crumbs. Serve hot in patty shells. Makes 8 servings.

MRS. RUSSELL B. LONG, Wife of Senator (Louisiana)

OYSTER ROCKEFELLER CASSEROLE

2 pints oysters, with liquor
¾ cup bread crumbs
¾ cup cracker crumbs
1 teaspoon salt
¼ teaspoon freshly ground pepper

2 10 ounce packages frozen spinach,
  thawed and drained
¼ pound American cheese, grated
1 small can parmesan cheese

Combine oysters, bread crumbs, cracker crumbs, salt and pepper and set aside. In a baking dish arrange layers of half the spinach, half the oyster mixture and half the cheeses. Repeat layers, in the same order, with the remaining half of each ingredient. Never make more than 2 layers of each one. Bake at 325° for 35 minutes. May be frozen. Makes 6 servings.

MRS. FRANK WILLIAM BOYKIN, Wife of former Representative (Alabama)

226

OYSTER AND EGGPLANT CASSEROLE

1 medium eggplant
¾ cup chopped onion
¼ cup butter, melted
½ cup bread crumbs

salt and pepper
1½ pints shucked oysters, in liquor
½ cup light cream
¼ cup grated sharp cheddar cheese

Bake eggplant in a preheated 350° oven for 50 minutes. Peel and cut into 1 inch cubes and set aside. Saute onion in butter until golden. Add bread crumbs, salt and pepper and mix well. Remove from heat. In a heavy saucepan, heat oysters in their liquor until edges curl, about 4 or 5 minutes. Sprinkle a fourth of the onion and bread crumb mixture over the bottom of a buttered 2½ quart casserole. Over this layer half of the oysters, half of the eggplant and some of the onion mixture. Repeat layers in the same order. Sprinkle cream over the top and cover with grated cheese. Bake uncovered in a 350° oven for 15 minutes or until brown on top. Makes 4 servings.

Mrs. Robert L. F. Sikes

Mrs. ROBERT L. F. SIKES, Wife of Representative (Florida)

SCALLOPED OYSTERS PAPRIKA

1 pint oysters
¼ cup oyster liquor
2 tablespoons light cream
½ cup day old bread crumbs
1 cup rusk crumbs

1 stick butter, melted
salt
freshly ground pepper
paprika

Drain oysters. Combine oyster liquor and cream and set aside. Mix both kinds of crumbs together with the butter and sprinkle a thin layer of them on bottom of a buttered 1 quart casserole. Cover with half the oysters, half the liquor and cream mixture and a light sprinkling of salt and pepper. Cover with a second layer of each of the remaining ingredients and in the same order, reserving some of the crumbs to top off the dish. Sprinkle with paprika. Never make more than two layers of oysters in a scallop because the middle layer will remain uncooked. Bake in a preheated 425° oven for 30 minutes. Makes 4 servings.

Mrs. Lee Metcalf

Mrs. LEE METCALF, Wife of Senator (Montana)

OYSTERS IN CASSEROLE

1 quart select oysters, drained, reserve liquor
½ cup melted butter
3 cups crushed oyster crackers
1 cup light cream

½ teaspoon salt
¼ teaspoon seasoned pepper
½ teaspoon Worcestershire sauce
3 drops Tabasco sauce
paprika

Cut oysters into bite size pieces and divide into 2 equal portions. Mix butter with cracker crumbs. Spread a third of the crumbs on the bottom of a buttered casserole. Cover the crumbs with half the oysters. Over them spread another third of the crumbs and cover with remaining oysters. Mix together the cream, oyster liquor and seasonings. Pour over the oysters. Top with remaining crumbs and sprinkle with paprika. Bake at 350° for about 40 minutes. Do not overcook. Serve immediately. Makes 8 servings.

Mrs. Hugh Q. Alexander

Mrs. Hugh Q. Alexander, Wife of former Representative (North Carolina)

SCALLOPED OYSTERS

1½ cups cracker crumbs
½ cup melted butter
1 pint oysters, drained
½ teaspoon salt
¼ teaspoon pepper

¼ cup diced celery
2 tablespoons minced parsley
⅓ cup oyster liquor
⅓ cup milk

Mix cracker crumbs with butter. Spread ⅓ of the crumbs in a greased baking dish, 10 x 16 x 1½ inches. Layer over them half the oysters, salt, pepper, celery, parsley, liquor, mixed with milk and crumbs. Repeat layer using remaining half of each ingredient, ending with crumbs. Bake at 450° about 30 minutes. Makes 4 to 6 servings.

Mrs. Donald J. Mitchell

Mrs. Donald J. Mitchell, Wife of Representative (New York)

STIR SHRIMP AND PEAS

2 pounds fresh shrimp, shelled and
   deveined
1 tablespoon corn starch
2 teaspoons salt
2 tablespoons sherry

2 or 3 scallions, chopped
3 or 4 slices fresh ginger root
3 tablespoons shortening
1 10 ounce package frozen peas
cooked rice

Mix shrimp, corn starch, 1½ teaspoons salt, sherry, scallions and ginger root. Let stand. Heat shortening in skillet until very hot. Add seasoned shrimp and stir vigorously for 2 minutes. Add peas and remaining salt. Stir and cook together for 2 or 3 mintues more. Serve with rice. Makes 4 servings.

Mrs. Berkley Bedell

MRS. BERKLEY BEDELL, Wife of Representative (Iowa)

JIFFY SHRIMP SKILLET

2 cans cream of shrimp soup
1½ cups boiling water
1⅓ cups Minute rice
2 8 ounce packages frozen cleaned
   shrimp
1 cup diced celery
1 cup diced green pepper

2 teaspoons curry
1 teaspoon salt
dash pepper
1 cup sliced ripe olives (optional)
½ cup toasted slivered almonds
sprig of parsley

Place shrimp soup in skillet and add water. Cover and bring to a boil. Stir in rice, shrimp, celery, green pepper, curry, salt and pepper. Cover; bring to a boil and cook 10 minutes, or until rice and shrimp are done. Stir occasionally. Just before serving add olives and sprinkle with toasted almonds. Garnish with parsley. Makes 8 servings.

Mrs Fred Bradley

MRS. FRED BRADLEY, Wife of former Representative (Michigan)

229

SHRIMP 'N SHERRY

1 pound shrimp, peeled and deveined
flour
salt and pepper
2 tablespoons butter or margarine,
  melted

2 teaspoons mustard
4 tablespoons Worcestershire sauce
juice of 1 lemon
1½ cups dry sherry
toast

Roll shrimp in flour seasoned with salt and pepper and brown on both sides in butter. Mix mustard, Worcestershire sauce, lemon juice and sherry together to make a sauce. Add to shrimp after turning them. Cook for a few minutes and serve on toast with sauce spooned over them as a topping. Makes 4 servings.

Mrs. Frank W. Boykin

MRS. FRANK WILLIAM BOYKIN, Wife of former Representative (Alabama)

SHRIMP SAUTE WITH HERBED RICE

2 pounds fresh or frozen shrimp
6 tablespoons butter or margarine
¼ teaspoon powdered garlic
⅛ teaspoon thyme
⅛ teaspoon pepper
¼ cup lemon juice
1 tablespoon dried parsley flakes

Optional:
2 cups hot boiled rice
¼ cup butter or margarine, melted
3 tablespoons chopped chives
¼ teaspoon each basil, thyme, savory
  and pepper·
½ teaspoon garlic salt
1 teaspoon dried parsley flakes

Shell and devein shrimp. Wash and drain. Melt butter in skillet. Add garlic, thyme and pepper. Add shrimp and saute 4 to 5 minutes. Do not overcook as it will toughen shrimp. Remove shrimp to hot platter and keep warm. Add lemon juice to pan drippings, heat and stir until just before mixture simmers. Add parsley flakes and pour over shrimp. May be served alone or with rice thoroughly mixed with butter and seasonings. Serve hot. Makes 4 servings.

Mrs. Bob Casey

MRS. BOB CASEY, Wife of Representative (Texas)

JAMBALAYA

1 tablespoon flour
1 tablespoon lard, melted
2 medium onions, chopped
2 buds garlic, chopped
1 green pepper, chopped
1 6 ounce can tomato paste
1 pound shrimp, peeled and deveined
1 pound cooked ham, chopped

1 10 ounce can tomatoes
4 cups water
salt and pepper
dash of Tabasco
thyme
Worcestershire sauce
1 cup raw rice
chopped parsley

Make a roux by stirring flour into lard and browning lightly. Add onions, garlic, green pepper and tomato paste and cook for a few minutes. Add shrimp, ham, tomatoes, water and seasonings to taste. Let simmer, covered, about 10 minutes. Add rice, replace cover and boil until rice is done, about 20 minutes. Do not stir or rice will be gummy. To serve, sprinkle with parsley. This may be prepared early in the day, put in a casserole and refrigerated. Reheat for about 30 minutes in a 350° oven just before serving. Makes 6 to 8 servings.

Mrs. Russell Long

MRS. RUSSELL B. LONG, Wife of Senator (Louisiana)

CREOLE JAMBALAYA

1 tablespoon oil (or bacon grease)
2 tablespoons flour
1 pound cooked ham, cubed (or combined with sliced, cooked smoked sausage)
1 medium green pepper, chopped
3 cups cooked, cleaned shrimp

5 cups diced canned tomatoes
2 large onions, chopped
1 clove garlic, minced
1 sprig parsley, chopped
2½ cups water
pepper to taste
2 cups raw, long grain rice

Put oil in 5 quart saucepan, add flour, ham and green pepper. Cook, stirring constantly, 5 minutes. If mixture appears dry, add more oil. Add shrimp, tomatoes, onions, garlic, parsley, water and pepper. Bring to boil, add rice, pressing into liquid. Cover and simmer 30 minutes or until liquid is absorbed. Makes 10 servings.

Mrs. David C. Treen

MRS. DAVID C. TREEN, Wife of Representative (Louisiana)

SHRIMP CREOLE

2 cups medium white sauce
1 garlic clove, cut
½ bottle chili sauce
1 dash Tabasco

1⅓ pounds shrimp, cooked, peeled, deveined
cooked rice

Make white sauce in top of double boiler which has been rubbed with garlic clove. Add chili sauce, Tabasco and bite size pieces of shrimp. Heat over boiling water until ready to serve. Serve over rice. Makes 4 to 6 servings.

MRS. EVERETT M. DIRKSEN, Wife of former Senator (Illinois)

BTT SHRIMP CREOLE

2 tablespoons butter
1 onion, chopped
1 cup chopped celery
1 green pepper, chopped
1½ tablespoons flour
1 can tomatoes

1 bay leaf
1 teaspoon salt
1 teaspoon vinegar
1 16 ounce can green peas, drained
2 pounds boiled shrimp, cleaned
cooked rice

Melt butter and add onion, celery and green pepper. Cook about 2 minutes and stir in flour. Add tomatoes and simmer 30 minutes. Add bay leaf, salt, vinegar and green peas. Stir thoroughly. Add shrimp and heat through. Serve over rice. Makes 6 servings.

MAUREEN ELLEN FOLEY, Daughter of former Representative John R. Foley (Maryland)

SHRIMP MUSHROOM SUPREME

1 pound fresh mushrooms
3 tablespoons butter
1 tablespoon flour
3 ounces dry marsala wine
2 cups cream
1 teaspoon grated lemon rind
1 teaspoon onion juice
1 tablespoon chopped parsley
2 pounds freshly boiled shrimp, shelled and deveined
fine bread crumbs, buttered
grated parmesan cheese

Saute mushrooms 8 to 10 minutes in butter. Sprinkle in flour, blending it with butter in pan. Blend in wine, cream, lemon rind, onion juice and parsley. Stir over low flame until thickened. To this sauce add shrimp and transfer to baking dish. Top with bread crumbs and cheese. Bake for 15 minutes in a 400° oven. Makes 6 servings.

Mrs. Byron R. White

MRS. BYRON R. WHITE, Wife of Associate Justice, Supreme Court (Colorado)

SHRIMP AND ARTICHOKE SUPREME

2 pounds shrimp, shelled and deveined
1 9 ounce package frozen artichoke hearts
½ pound fresh mushrooms
4 tablespoons butter
1 clove garlic, crushed
2 tablespoons finely chopped shallots
¼ cup flour
½ teaspoon pepper
¾ cup milk
1 8 ounce package grated cheddar cheese
⅔ to 1 cup dry white wine
1 7½ ounce can King crabmeat, drained and flaked
seasoned corn flake crumbs
½ tablespoon melted butter

Cook shrimp in salted boiling water 3 minutes. Drain. Cook artichoke hearts according to package directions. Drain. Saute mushrooms in 2 tablespoons butter for 5 minutes. Remove from pan and set aside. Saute garlic and shallots in remaining butter for 5 minutes. Remove from heat and stir in flour and pepper. Add milk. Bring to a boil stirring. Remove from heat and add half of cheese. Stir until melted. Add wine and stir well. In a 2 quart casserole, combine sauce, crabmeat, shrimp, artichoke hearts, mushrooms and remaining cheese. Mix lightly. Sprinkle with crumbs tossed with melted butter. Bake in preheated 375° oven for 30 minutes or until mixture bubbles and crumbs are browned. May be frozen after baking. Makes 6 to 8 servings.

Mrs. Lon M. Buzick

MRS. LON M. BUZICK, Member of Congressional Club (Kansas)

233

SHRIMP SQUASH CASSEROLE

1½ pounds yellow squash
¾ cup raw shrimp, shelled, deveined
2 tablespoons butter
2 tablespoons flour
½ teaspoon salt
⅛ teaspoon black pepper

1 cup chicken bouillon
½ cup whipping cream
1 tablespoon instant minced onion
½ cup coarse bread crumbs
¼ cup grated parmesan cheese
1 tablespoon butter, melted

Wash and dry squash and cut crosswise into ¼ inch slices. Thoroughly rinse shrimp under cold water. Drain. Heat butter in sauce pan and blend in flour, salt and pepper. Cook until it bubbles. Remove from heat and add bouillon gradually, stirring constantly. Bring to a boil and continue cooking for 1 to 2 minutes. Blend in cream and onion. Mix in raw shrimp.

Layer half the squash in bottom of a 1½ quart casserole and spoon half the shrimp sauce over it. Repeat with remaining squash and shrimp sauce. Cover tightly and bake in a 400° oven for 30 minutes. Remove casserole from oven. Toss crumbs and cheese with butter and sprinkle them on top of uncovered casserole. Reduce heat to 350°. Return uncovered casserole to oven for 15 minutes or until crumbs are golden brown.

Mrs. Lyndon B. Johnson

MRS. LYNDON B. JOHNSON, Wife of former President of the United States (Texas)

BAKED SHRIMP

1 medium clove garlic, peeled
¾ cup butter or margarine, softened
dash of paprika
2 tablespoons minced parsley
1 tablespoon finely chopped onion
¼ cup dry sherry

2 pounds cooked shrimp, peeled and
  deveined
salt to taste
1 cup dry, fine bread crumbs
melted butter

Crush garlic clove to a pulp and combine with butter. Place over low heat until butter is melted. Remove from heat and add paprika, parsley, onion and sherry. Add shrimp and toss to coat thoroughly. Add salt. Arrange shrimp in shallow baking dish and sprinkle with crumbs. Pour melted butter over top and bake at 350° for 20 to 25 minutes. May be frozen. Makes 8 to 10 servings.

Mrs Winston L Prouty

MRS. WINSTON L. PROUTY, Wife of former Senator (Vermont)

REPUFFABLE SHRIMP SOUFFLE

3 tablespoons butter or margarine
2 tablespoons corn starch
½ teaspoon salt
¼ teaspoon pepper
1 cup milk

1 cup finely chopped cooked shrimp
(or turkey or chicken)
4 egg yolks, well beaten
5 egg whites, stiffly beaten

Melt butter, remove from heat and blend in corn starch and seasonings. Slowly stir in milk, stirring until mixture is smooth. Cook and stir over medium heat until sauce boils and thickens, 5 to 6 minutes. Add shrimp, remove from heat and cool for 5 minutes. Slowly stir a little of cooled mixture into yolks and beat vigorously. Return yolk mixture to shrimp mixture and mix well. Fold egg whites into shrimp base. Pour into 2 quart souffle dish and set in shallow pan containing an inch of water. Bake at 350° for 1¼ hours.

To repuff, leave in souffle dish, place dish in shallow pan with an inch of water and reheat at 350° until puffed, about 25 to 30 minutes. Makes 5 to 6 servings.

Mrs Elford A. Cederberg

MRS. ELFORD A. CEDERBERG, Wife of Representative (Michigan)

SHRIMP SUPREME

1 pound large raw shrimp
1 tablespoon chicken seasoned
stock base
1 cup hot water
½ cup rice
4 tablespoons butter
1 tablespoon arrowroot (or 3
tablespoons flour)

1½ cups milk
½ teaspoon dillweed
1 tablespoon Eschalot wine vinegar
1 teaspoon seasoned salt
½ teaspoon salt
1½ cups shredded cheddar cheese
paprika

Shell and devein shrimp. Dissolve stock base in hot water; bring to a boil; add rice. Lower heat, cover and steam until rice is cooked. Melt butter, remove from heat and stir in arrowroot. Add milk, return to heat and cook, stirring constantly until thickened and smooth. Stir in dillweed, vinegar and salts. Add shrimp and simmer gently for about 10 minutes or until shrimp turn red. Spoon rice into a buttered 1½ quart baking dish. Pour shrimp mixture over rice, top with shredded cheese and sprinkle with paprika. Bake at 350° for 25 to 30 minutes or until cheese is melted and shrimp are hot. May be frozen but do not add cheese until it is to be baked. Makes 6 servings.

Mrs. Edward H. Jenison

MRS. EDWARD H. JENISON, Wife of former Representative (Illinois)

SHRIMP CASSEROLE SUPERB

2 cups cooked rice
1 large can shrimp (or 2 small cans)
1 pint cream
6 tablespoons tomato catsup
1 teaspoon Worcestershire sauce
¼ teaspoon Tabasco

Mix all ingredients and place in buttered casserole. Bake 1 hour at 250°. Makes 6 to 8 servings.

Mrs. Edwin Fuller Parham

MRS. EDWIN FULLER PARHAM, Daughter of former Representative Edward William Pou (North Carolina)

SHRIMP AND RICE CASSEROLE

1¼ pounds cooked shrimp
¾ cup uncooked rice
½ large onion, chopped
1 tablespoon butter or margarine
1 can mushroom soup
1 teaspoon lemon juice
dash of garlic salt
salt and pepper to taste
½ cup sour cream
¾ cup grated sharp cheddar cheese
½ bell pepper, cut in rings

Clean shrimp. Cook rice according to directions on package. Saute onion in butter until tender. Combine with soup, lemon juice and seasonings to make sauce. Fold rice and shrimp into sauce. Fold in sour cream. Pour into buttered baking dish. Sprinkle cheese on top. Parboil bell pepper rings for 2 minutes and use them to decorate top of casserole. Place in preheated 325° oven for 30 minutes or until hot and cheese has melted. Makes 6 servings.

Mrs. Bob Casey

MRS. BOB CASEY, Wife of Representative (Texas)

236

SEAFOOD CASSEROLE

3 to 4 pounds peeled shrimp	3 cups chopped celery
1 pound crabmeat	1 large bell pepper, chopped
6 cups cooked rice	6 tablespoons Worcestershire sauce
1 quart mayonnaise	2 tablespoons salt
3 cups chopped onion	1 tablespoon black pepper

Mix all ingredients together. Place in large buttered casserole and cover with foil. Bake at 350° for 35 minutes. Remove foil the last 5 minutes. May be frozen. Makes 20 servings.

Mrs. William Lowe Waller

MRS. WILLIAM LOWE WALLER, Wife of Governor (Mississippi)

MIMI'S HOLIDAY SEAFOOD THERMIDOR

2 1 pound packages frozen haddock (or cod)	2 cans frozen shrimp soup
	½ cup light cream
1 pound frozen cleaned shrimp	⅓ cup dry sherry
1 pound frozen scallops	2 tablespoons brandy (optional)
2 10½ ounce cans cream of mushroom soup	2 tablespoon dried chopped parsley
	grated parmesan cheese (optional)

Let fish thaw in refrigerator. Put haddock in shallow baking dish. Wrap shrimp loosely in aluminum foil. Wrap scallops in like manner. Bake all of them in 350° oven for 15 minutes or until fish flakes. Shrimp may take a little longer. Combine soups and cream. Heat, stirring until hot and smooth. Add sherry and brandy. Break haddock into large pieces and add to soup mixture with the shrimp and scallops. Add parsley. Put into chafing dish and heat or put in shallow baking dish, sprinkle with cheese and bake in 350° oven until hot and bubbly. May be frozen. Makes 12 servings.

Mrs. Clifford Davis

MRS. CLIFFORD DAVIS, Wife of former Representative (Tennessee)

VERMONT SEAFOOD CASSEROLE

½ cup butter
½ cup chopped green pepper
½ cup chopped onion
½ cup sliced celery
⅔ cup flour
½ teaspoon garlic salt
½ teaspoon salt
¼ teaspoon paprika
¹⁄₁₆ teaspoon cayenne
2 cups milk

1 can frozen shrimp soup, thawed
1 3¾ ounce can crabmeat, drained
1 4½ ounce can tiny shrimp, drained
1 4 ounce can mushroom pieces,
   drained
1 5 ounce can water chestnuts,
   drained, halved
½ cup grated cheddar cheese
½ cup fine bread crumbs
2 tablespoons butter for topping

Melt butter in a 2 quart pan. Add green pepper, onion and celery and saute until tender. Stir in flour, garlic salt, salt, paprika, and cayenne. Add milk; stir constantly until smooth. Add soup, crabmeat, shrimp, mushrooms and water chestnuts. Put in a 2 quart casserole, top with cheese, crumbs and butter. Bake at 350° for 15 to 25 minutes. Cream of celery soup may be substituted for the cream sauce with almost as good results. Makes 8 to 10 servings.

Mrs. Robert T. Stafford

MRS. ROBERT T. STAFFORD, Wife of Senator (Vermont)

BAKED SEAFOOD SALAD CASSEROLE

1 pound crabmeat, flaked
1 cup cooked shrimp, shelled and
   deveined
1 green pepper, finely chopped
1 small onion, finely chopped
1 cup chopped celery

½ teaspoon salt
¹⁄₁₆ teaspoon pepper
dash of Worcestershire sauce
1 cup mayonnaise
1 cup buttered bread crumbs

Remove any bits of shell from crabmeat. Cut shrimp in half. Mix crabmeat and shrimp with vegetables and seasonings. Then add mayonnaise. Put into shells, top with bread crumbs and bake at 350° for 30 minutes. Makes 8 servings.

Mrs. Lyle H. Boren

MRS. LYLE H. BOREN, Wife of former Representative (Oklahoma)

SEAFOOD CHEESE CASSEROLE

1 green pepper, chopped
2 stalks celery, chopped
1 medium onion, chopped
4 tablespoons flour
4 tablespoons butter
2 cups light cream
1 cup grated sharp cheese
½ teaspoon salt

⅛ teaspoon pepper
1 small can pimientos
3 pounds cooked shrimp, shelled and deveined
1 can crabmeat
4 hard cooked eggs, sliced
¾ cup buttered cracker crumbs

Cook green pepper, celery and onion in small amount of water until tender. Make white sauce of flour, butter, cream, cheese, salt and pepper. Combine all ingredients except crumbs. Put in a 3 quart casserole, top with crumbs and bake 15 minutes at 400°. May be frozen. Makes 10 to 12 servings.

Mrs. Robert G. Stephens, Jr.

MRS. ROBERT G. STEPHENS, JR., Wife of Representative (Georgia)

SEAFOOD MUSHROOM CASSEROLE

2 pounds cooked shrimp
1 can backfin crabmeat
2 slices bread, cubed
1 cup Carnation milk
1 cup mayonnaise
2 hard cooked eggs, diced
1 tablespoon parsley

1 teaspoon chopped onion
⅛ teaspoon pepper
1 teaspoon Accent
1 can sliced mushrooms, drained
2 tablespoons sherry
Pepperidge Farm dressing
butter

Mix together all ingredients except dressing and butter. Put in casserole, sprinkle with Pepperidge Farm dressing and dot with butter. Bake in a preheated 350° oven for 20 minutes or until brown. Makes 8 servings.

Mrs. Harold C. Hagen

MRS. HAROLD C. HAGEN, Wife of former Representative (Minnesota)

BAKED SCALLOPS

2 pounds scallops
¼ cup butter or margarine, melted
¼ cup sherry (or catsup)
½ teaspoon salt
dash pepper

¼ teaspoon sugar
2 cups cracker crumbs
¼ cup chopped green onion
1 tablespoon melted butter or margarine

Combine scallops, butter, sherry, salt, pepper, sugar and crumbs. Place in casserole or 6 well greased shells. Combine onion and 1 tablespoon of butter; place on top of scallop mixture. Bake in 350° oven for 25 to 30 minutes or until brown. May be frozen. Makes 6 servings.

Mrs Winston L. Prouty

MRS. WINSTON L. PROUTY, Wife of former Senator (Vermont)

COQUILLES ST. JACQUES

½ cup white wine
½ cup water
2 sprigs parsley
2 green onions, chopped
1 bay leaf
7 tablespoons butter
1½ pounds scallops
½ pound mushrooms, chopped
⅓ cup water

juice of 1 lemon
½ teaspoon salt
½ teaspoon pepper
2 tablespoons flour
4 egg yolks
1 cup whipping cream
parmesan cheese
buttered crumbs

Bring to a boil the wine and ½ cup water with parsley, onion, bay leaf and 2 tablespoons butter. Add scallops, lower heat and simmer until tender, 4 to 5 minutes. Strain scallops and save broth. Add mushrooms to 2 tablespoons melted butter and brown. Add ¼ cup water, lemon juice, salt and pepper and cook for 5 minutes. Drain and combine liquid with wine broth. Blend remaining butter and flour, add it to the broth liquid, stirring to avoid lumps. Cook until thick. Add chopped scallops and let mixture cool. Beat egg yolks with cream and stir into cooled sauce. Cook sauce again over hot water, stirring until thickened. Add mushrooms. Heap into individual ramekins or shells, top with cheese and crumbs and brown under broiler. Makes 4 servings.

Mrs. Lee Metcalf

MRS. LEE METCALF, Wife of Senator (Montana)

240

BETTY'S PAELLA VALENCIANA

12 chicken thighs, boned and cut up
12 pork sausages, cut bite size
2 pounds lean pork, cubed
2 cups diced ham (optional)
1 cup olive oil
1 large onion, finely chopped
4 medium tomatoes, chopped
1½ teaspoons paprika
2 garlic cloves, minced
2 teaspoons salt
¼ teaspoon pepper
2 green peppers, seeded and sliced
3⅔ cups converted rice
1 pound any white fish, cut in small pieces

8 cups boiling water
2 cups clam juice
large pinch saffron threads, soaked in 1 tablespoon warm water
1 cup green beans
1 pound shrimp, cooked, peeled and deveined
2½ dozen steamed clams (or mussels)
10 canned artichokes
2 lemons, thinly sliced
pimiento strips
chopped parsley

In a paella dish, fry chicken, sausage and pork in hot oil until lightly browned. Remove from pan and keep warm. In the same oil, saute onions until golden. Add tomatoes and boil until most of the liquid is reduced. Lower heat, add paprika, garlic, salt, pepper and green peppers. Mix well and return chicken, sausage, and pork to pan. Stir in the rice and brown lightly about 5 minutes. Add fish, boiling water, clam juice, saffron and green beans. Mix thoroughly. Insert shrimp, clams and artichokes in rice mixture but do not stir. Cook at high temperature until liquid is absorbed and rice is soft, approximately 20 minutes. Garnish with lemon slices, pimiento and parsley. Serve directly from cooking dish.

Mrs. John Myers

MRS. JOHN MYERS, Wife of Representative (Indiana)

NOTES

POULTRY & GAME, SAUCES & STUFFINGS

Turkey a la Braise

Pick and draw a turkey, bone it, and make the following force-meat: take the flesh of a fowl, a pound of lean veal, and a few crumbs of bread, season it with beaten mace, nutmeg, pepper and salt, mix it up with the yolks of eggs, and stuff the turkey with it, skewer up the breast, dip the breast into boiling water, and lard it; lay a layer of fat bacon at the bottom of a stew-pan, and a layer of veal on the bacon, put the turkey on the larded side uppermost, put in a quart of gravy, a gill of white wine, some cloves and mace, and a bundle of sweet herbs, put a layer of veal and bacon over it, cover it close, and stew it gently for two hours (put fire over as well as under it) then take out the turkey, strain off the gravy, and skim off the fat; put a little butter into the stew pan, melt it, put in a spoonful of flour, and stir till it is smooth, and put in some mushrooms, truffles and morels, artichoke bottoms, force-meat and egg-balls, put in the turkey, season it with Cayan pepper and salt, squeeze in the juice of a lemon and boil it up for a ten minutes; put the turkey in a dish, pour the sauce over it, and garnish with lemon and beet-root.

The New Art of Cookery
Richard Briggs, 1792

KOTTA RIGANATI (GREEK CHICKEN)

2 3 pound chickens
½ cup olive oil
¼ cup lemon juice
2 teaspoons salt
¼ pound butter

2 cups canned tomatoes
1 teaspoon pepper
1 tablespoon oregano
salt
cooked rice

Rub the whole chickens with a mixture of the olive oil, lemon juice and salt. Place in large roasting pan and bake at 375° for 30 minutes. Melt butter; add tomatoes, pepper, oregano and salt to taste. Cook at medium heat in saucepan for 5 minutes. Pour over chickens. Reduce oven temperature to 350° and bake chickens for additional 20 to 30 minutes. Baste frequently. Serve with rice. Makes 6 to 8 servings.

MRS. FRANK ANNUNZIO, Wife of Representative (Illinois)

CHINESE ROAST CHICKEN

1 3¼ pound fryer
1 cup soy sauce
1 tablespoon sherry
1 tablespoon honey

1 teaspoon salt
4 cloves garlic, crushed
1 tablespoon minced fresh ginger
¼ cup chopped green onions

Rub chicken inside and out with a mixture of all other ingredients and let stand in sauce for 1 hour. Remove chicken from sauce mixture and roast 55 minutes at 375°, basting about every 20 minutes with sauce. Cut chicken into pieces. Makes 4 servings.

MRS. WM. JENNINGS BRYAN DORN, Wife of former Representative (South Carolina)

ROAST CHICKEN

1 3 pound roasting chicken
salt and pepper
stuffing
3 tablespoons vegetable oil
1 cup dry white wine
1 cup chicken giblet broth
1 tablespoon wine vinegar
1 garlic clove, crushed
1 teaspoon brown seasoning sauce

1 teaspoon corn starch
water
vegetables (carrots, potatoes or peas)

Glaze:
2 tablespoons honey
¼ cup wine (or cider)
½ teaspoon brown seasoning sauce

Rub chicken with salt and pepper. Fill with any stuffing. Truss chicken, brown on all sides in oil in skillet and place in oven casserole. Pour off most of the oil from the skillet and add the wine, giblet broth, vinegar, garlic and seasoning sauce. Bring to a boil, lower heat and simmer until amount is slightly reduced. Add corn starch mixed with a little water. Pour sauce over chicken. Cover and roast 30 minutes at 350°. Add vegetables. Cover and return to oven. Continue cooking for 15 minutes or until chicken and vegetables are tender. Combine honey, wine and seasoning sauce for glaze and spoon over chicken. Raise oven temperature to 400° and cook uncovered for an additional 10 minutes. Makes 4 servings.

Mrs. Robert H. Mollohan

MRS. ROBERT H. MOLLOHAN, Wife of Representative (West Virginia)

QUICK AND EASY BAKED CHICKEN

1 3 pound whole chicken
Season All

¼ pound butter or margarine

Wash chicken and pat dry. Put 2 pieces of aluminum foil, running in opposite directions, in baking dish large enough to hold chicken. Place chicken on foil, breast side up, sprinkle heavily with Season All inside and out, dot with butter and wrap tightly in foil, first one way and then the other. Bake in preheated 450° oven for 1 hour. Reduce heat to 325° and bake at least 1 additional hour.

Mrs. Hubert H. Humphrey

MRS. HUBERT H. HUMPHREY, Wife of former Vice President of the United States, presently Senator (Minnesota)

QUICK CHICKEN BAKE

2 large fryers, cut up
1 pint dairy sour cream

1 16 ounce box cheddar cheese
crackers, crumbled
¼ pound butter

Spread chicken pieces with sour cream and roll in crumbs. In oven melt butter on large cookie sheet with sides. Lay chicken pieces, 1 at a time, in melted butter and immediately turn buttered side up. Bake in preheated 350° oven 1 to 1¼ hours or until tender. Makes 6 servings.

Mrs. Jerry L. Pettis

MRS. JERRY L. PETTIS, Representative (California)

DELICIOUS CHICKEN

6 chicken breasts
salt and pepper to taste
Nabisco sesame snack crackers,
crumbled
butter or margarine

1 cup chopped celery
½ cup chopped onions
1 can water chestnuts, sliced
¾ cup water (or sauterne)

Skin and bone chicken and season with salt and pepper. Cover chicken with cracker crumbs and brown on both sides in butter. Remove chicken and saute celery, onions and water chestnuts in the butter. Place chicken in baking pan and cover with sauteed ingredients. Pour water over all. Bake covered in a 350° oven for 25 minutes.

Mrs John C. Kunkel

MRS. JOHN C. KUNKEL, Wife of former Representative (Pennsylvania)

CHICKEN IN WINE

4 whole chicken breasts, split
¼ cup soy sauce
¾ cup red wine
¼ teaspoon ground oregano
1 clove garlic, sliced

¼ cup salad oil
4 tablespoons water
1 teaspoon ground ginger
1 tablespoon brown sugar
parsley flakes

Place chicken breasts, flat side down, in a shallow casserole dish. Combine remaining ingredients and pour over chicken. Bake, covered, at 350° for 1 hour. Makes 4 servings.

Mrs. Robert L. F. Sikes

MRS. ROBERT L. F. SIKES, Wife of Representative (Florida)

CHICKEN KIEV

3 large chicken breasts, skinned and boned
salt
pepper
¼ pound butter
1 tablespoon chopped chives
1 tablespoon lemon juice
½ teaspoon rosemary
flour
2 eggs, slightly beaten
2 tablespoons water
1 cup fine dry bread crumbs
cooking oil

Split each breast lengthwise. Season with salt and pepper. Pound meat between 2 pieces of wax paper until as thin as possible without breaking flesh. Cream butter and work in chives, lemon juice and rosemary; shape into 6 rolls and place on foil in freezer until firm. Center a roll of butter on each chicken portion, fold outer edges over butter and fold tightly crosswise. Dredge in flour. Dip in egg, whipped with water, then in crumbs. If heavier coating is desired, dip again in egg and crumbs. Chill 1 hour. Fry in deep fat at 350° for 10 minutes. May be frozen before frying. Makes 6 servings.

Mrs. Edward V. Long

MRS. EDWARD V. LONG, Wife of former Senator (Missouri)

CHICKEN BREASTS IN CREAM

6 whole breasts of chicken, boned
butter
salt
1½ cups dairy sour cream
½ cup canned sliced mushrooms
½ cup chicken stock
½ cup chopped chives

Wash chicken breasts and dry thoroughly in a clean towel. Slit each breast lengthwise and insert a pat of butter in each slit. Salt lightly. Roll up tightly and fasten with skewer or toothpick. Place in small glass baking dish. Heat sour cream, mushrooms, chicken stock and chives until warm. Pour over chicken breasts and bake in 350° oven for 1 hour or until done. May be frozen. Makes 6 servings.

Mrs. James E. Holshouser, Jr.

MRS. JAMES E. HOLSHOUSER, JR., Wife of Governor (North Carolina)

248

LEMON CHICKEN

2 pounds chicken breasts
2 tablespoons margarine
⅔ can cream of chicken soup

½ cup dry sherry
1½ tablespoons lemon juice
½ teaspoon paprika

Brown chicken in margarine. Mix and add remaining ingredients. Cook covered over low heat 45 minutes or until tender. Stir occasionally. Makes 4 servings.

Mrs. Henry O. Talle

MRS. HENRY O. TALLE, Wife of former Representative (Iowa)

CHICKEN BREASTS WITH ALMONDS

salt and pepper to taste
4 to 5 chicken breasts
4 tablespoons cooking oil
1 can cream of mushroom soup
½ cup cooking sherry

¼ cup grated cheddar cheese
3 tablespoons grated onion
2 tablespoons Worcestershire sauce
½ cup slivered almonds

Salt and pepper chicken, brown in oil and place in baking dish. Combine soup, wine, cheese, onion and Worcestershire sauce and pour over chicken. Place almonds on top and cover with aluminum foil. Bake at 350° for 45 minutes. May be frozen.

Mrs. Thomas P. Salmon

MRS. THOMAS P. SALMON, Wife of Governor (Vermont)

CHICKEN CASSEROLE

salt and pepper
6 to 8 chicken breasts (or 1 fryer cut in pieces)
⅔ stick margarine

1 can cream of mushroom soup
⅔ soup can of water
1 teaspoon dried onion flakes
cooked rice or biscuits

Salt and pepper chicken and brown slowly in margarine. Remove chicken to a casserole. Pour off excess margarine from pan and add soup and water. Heat slowly until the soup has mixed with the brown particles left in saucepan. Pour over chicken and sprinkle with onion flakes. Bake covered in 350° oven 1 hour and 20 minutes. Serve with rice or biscuits. May be frozen. Makes 6 servings.

Mrs. Phil Landrum

MRS. PHIL M. LANDRUM, Wife of Representative (Georgia)

BUTTERMILK CHICKEN

4 large chicken breasts (or thighs)
1½ cups buttermilk
¾ cup flour
1½ teaspoons salt

¼ teaspoon white pepper
¼ cup margarine
1 can cream of chicken soup

Dip chicken pieces in buttermilk and roll in flour seasoned with the salt and pepper. Melt margarine in baking dish, place chicken in it skin side down and bake at 425° for 30 minutes. Turn and bake an additional 15 minutes. Mix remaining buttermilk with soup until smooth. Pour over chicken and bake for at least another 15 minutes. Reduce oven heat to 350° if chicken appears dry. May be frozen. Makes 4 servings.

Mrs. Joe L. Evins

MRS. JOE L. EVINS, Wife of Representative (Tennessee)

BARBECUED CHICKEN

⅔ cup vinegar
½ pound margarine
3 tablespoons dry mustard
1 heaping tablespoon brown sugar

3 tablespoons Worcestershire sauce
2 tablespoons salt
½ teaspoon black pepper
12 chicken quarters

Heat vinegar to a boil. Add other sauce ingredients and cook until blended. Bake chicken, bony side down, in sauce for 2 hours in a 325° oven. Turn and cook with skin side down for ½ hour. Baste often with sauce. May be frozen.

Mrs. Laurie C. Battle

MRS. LAURIE C. BATTLE, Wife of former Representative (Alabama)

TARRAGON CHICKEN CASSEROLE

3 pound broiler fryer, disjointed
2 medium onions, chopped
1½ teaspoons tarragon
¼ teaspoon poultry seasoning
1¼ teaspoons salt

¼ teaspoon pepper
1 10½ ounce can cream of chicken
 soup
¼ cup milk
¼ cup sliced or slivered almonds

Arrange the pieces of chicken, skin side up, in a rectangular baking dish so that
they do not overlap. Layer the onions over the chicken and sprinkle with the
tarragon, poultry seasoning, salt and pepper. Mix soup with milk and spoon over
chicken. Bake in a 375° oven for 40 minutes. Sprinkle almonds over the top,
return to oven and continue to bake for another 10 minutes or until chicken is
tender. May be frozen. Makes 4 to 6 servings.

Mrs Frank A. Stubblefield

MRS. FRANK A. STUBBLEFIELD, Wife of former Representative (Kentucky)

CHICKEN CURRY

3 whole boned chicken breasts
flour
salt and pepper
cooking oil

1 can cream of chicken soup
1 teaspoon curry powder
½ cup dairy sour cream
½ cup toasted slivered almonds

Halve chicken breasts, dip in flour seasoned with salt and pepper and brown lightly
in oil. Remove to baking dish. Mix together the soup and curry powder and spread
over chicken. Cover dish and bake 40 minutes in a 350° oven. Remove from
oven, cover with sour cream and sprinkle with almonds. May be frozen. Makes
6 servings.

Mrs. Paul J. Kilday

MRS. PAUL KILDAY, Wife of former Representative (Texas)

251

CHICKEN TERIYAKI

⅔ cup soy sauce
½ cup dry sherry
2 tablespoons brown sugar
1 cup water
3 cloves garlic, minced
1 teaspoon ground ginger

1 frying chicken, cut into pieces
cooked rice
butter
parsley
slivered almonds

Combine first 6 ingredients for marinade and place in a large bowl. Add chicken parts and marinate for 1 day in refrigerator. To cook, place chicken in a flat baking dish and cover with marinade sauce. Bake at 325° for 1½ to 2 hours until very tender. Serve on a bed of rice to which you have added butter, parsley and almonds. Serve remaining marinade as a sauce accompaniment. Makes 4 servings.

Mrs. Thomas G. Morris

MRS. THOMAS G. MORRIS, Wife of former Representative (New Mexico)

CHICKEN CORDON ROUGE

4 large boned chicken breasts
¼ cup butter, melted
1 teaspoon mei yen seasoning
½ teaspoon thyme
¼ teaspoon hot mustard
⅛ teaspoon ground nutmeg

4 slices boiled ham
8 slices Swiss cheese
¼ cup white dinner wine
¼ cup water
1 tablespoon arrowroot

Flatten chicken breasts by pounding with a mallet or the edge of a saucer. Blend butter with mei yen, thyme, mustard and nutmeg. Brush chicken with seasoned butter. Place 1 slice of ham on each chicken breast and top with 1 slice of cheese. Roll chicken around the ham cheese filling, puling skin over opening, and skewer to close completely. Turn remaining seasoned butter into a heavy skillet, add chicken and saute until golden brown. Add wine, cover and simmer 30 minutes until chicken is tender. Remove chicken to a baking dish. Combine water and arrowroot until well blended. Stir into pan juices until mixture thickens and boils. Pour thickened sauce over chicken. Top each chicken breast with a slice of cheese. Place under broiler 5 inches from source of heat. Broil until cheese is melted and golden brown. Serve at once. Makes 4 servings.

Mrs. Howard W. Cannon

MRS. HOWARD W. CANNON, Wife of Senator (Nevada)

CHICKEN BREASTS WITH HAM

3 whole chicken breasts, halved,
   skinned and boned
⅓ cup plus 2 tablespoons flour
1½ teaspoons salt
¼ teaspoon freshly ground pepper
⅓ cup butter
6 slices baked country ham

½ pound mushrooms, sliced
1 teaspoon dried savory
¼ cup finely chopped celery leaves
½ cup boiling chicken broth
1 cup dairy sour cream
1 ripe avocado, sliced

Dredge chicken in ⅓ cup of flour, season with salt and pepper and brown in butter. Put ham slices in lightly buttered 9 x 13 inch baking dish. Place chicken on ham. Saute mushrooms 3 minutes in same skillet used for chicken, scatter over chicken and sprinkle with savory and celery leaves. Add broth to skillet and loosen bits of brown solids. Stir remaining flour into sour cream, add broth, heat and pour over chicken. Cover with aluminum foil and bake in a preheated 300° oven for 1¼ hours or until chicken is tender. Just before serving, place slices of avocado on each serving. Makes 6 servings.

Mrs. James M. Collins

MRS. JAMES M. COLLINS, Wife of Representative (Texas)

CHICKEN SALTIMBOCCA

3 large chicken breasts, skinned, boned
   and halved lengthwise
6 thin slices boiled ham
3 slices mozzarella cheese, halved
1 medium tomato, seeded and chopped
½ teaspoon dried sage, crushed

⅓ cup fine dry bread crumbs
2 tablespoons grated parmesan cheese
2 tablespoons snipped parsley
4 tablespoons butter or margarine,
   melted

Pound plastic wrapped pieces of chicken, under side up, lightly with a meat mallet into 5 inch squares. Remove plastic. Place a ham slice and a half slice of cheese on each cutlet, cutting to fit. Top with some tomato and dash of sage. Tuck in sides and roll up, jelly roll style, pressing to seal well. Combine bread crumbs, parmesan and parsley. Dip chicken in butter and roll in crumbs. Place in shallow baking pan. Bake in 350° oven 40 to 45 minutes. Makes 6 servings.

Mrs. John Kyl

MRS. JOHN KYL, Wife of former Representative (Iowa)

CHICKEN ROSEMARY

6 chicken breasts, split, boned, skinned
12 extra thin slices Smithfield ham (or Polish or Danish ham)
1 can pate de foie gras (or 1 14 ounce can Alsace Lorraine brand)
4 tablespoons butter
2 cups dry white wine (French chablis type)

cooked rice
fresh asparagus (or canned white asparagus)

Hollandaise sauce:
4 egg yolks
½ pound melted unsalted butter (or unsalted Chiffon margarine)
juice of 1 lemon

Lay each breast halve out flat and place 1 slice of ham on top of each. Spread ham thinly with pate de foie gras. Fold each breast halve back into shape. Melt butter in large frying pan and place folded breasts in pan and saute until done, about 10 to 15 minutes, turning once or twice. Add wine. Serve on top of or with rice and asparagus. Top all with the hollandaise sauce. Makes 6 servings.

Hollandaise sauce: Put egg yolks in blender and blend until color lightens. Add cooled, melted butter very slowly at first, blending after each addition. As yolks take in butter and color of mixture lightens, the procedure may be speeded up by adding butter in a thin stream, blending all the while at slow speed. Add the lemon juice. Heat very slowly over hot, but not boiling water, so sauce will not curdle.

Mrs. Frank Thompson, Jr

MRS. FRANK THOMPSON, JR., Wife of Representative (New Jersey)

CHICKEN AND BEEF

8 slices bacon
4 whole chicken breasts, halved and boned
¼ pound chipped beef

1 can condensed mushroom soup
½ cup dairy sour cream
paprika
cooked rice or noodles

Wrap bacon around each piece of chicken. Line an 8 x 8 inch shallow baking dish with chipped beef. Place bacon wrapped chicken on top of beef. Mix soup with sour cream and spread over chicken. Sprinkle top with paprika. Do not salt. Bake at 275° for 2 hours. Serve over rice or noodles.

Mrs. George M. O'Brien

MRS. GEORGE M. O'BRIEN, Wife of Representative (Illinois)

PARTY CHICKEN

4 chicken breasts, boned and split	1 can mushrooms, drained
3 tablespoons butter	2 tablespoons flour
salt and pepper	2 cups cream
2 cans small potatoes	½ cup white wine
1 cup cubed cooked ham	1 can white grapes, drained

Saute chicken breasts in butter. Season with salt and pepper. Transfer to a buttered casserole. Brown the potatoes in the skillet, add the ham and mushrooms. Place the potatoes, ham and mushrooms around the chicken breasts in the casserole.

Make a cream sauce using drippings in the skillet. Blend in the flour and slowly stir in cream and wine. Cook until smooth and thickened. Pour sauce over ingredients in the casserole. Cover and bake in a 350° oven for 1 hour. Add grapes to casserole for last 10 minutes of baking time. May be frozen. Makes 4 servings.

Mrs. William G. Milliken

Mrs. WILLIAM G. MILLIKEN, Wife of Governor (Michigan)

CHICKEN HAWAIIAN

1 2 pound chicken, cut in pieces	1 package Lipton's onion soup
1 bottle Kraft's French dressing	1 12 ounce can whole cranberries

Place chicken in a 2 inch deep baking pan. Combine other ingredients; pour over chicken. Bake 1½ hours at 400°, turning and basting chicken parts several times.

Rebecca Dial

REBECCA DIAL, Daughter of former Senator Nathaniel Barksdale Dial (South Carolina)

255

GLAZED CHICKEN AND PEARS

1 29 ounce can Bartlett pear halves
2 chicken fryers, cut up
oil
4 teaspoons corn starch
1 tablespoon soy sauce

½ teaspoon dry mustard
2 tablespoons lemon juice
½ teaspoon grated lemon peel
¼ cup chopped peanuts
parsley

Drain pears, reserve syrup. Brown fryer pieces in hot oil. Prepare glaze by combining pear juice with corn starch, soy sauce, mustard, lemon juice and peel. Bring to a boil, cook until thickened, stirring constantly, and keep warm. Place browned chicken in baking pan and cover with glaze. Bake at 350° for 30 minutes, basting frequently with glaze. Turn chicken pieces and add pear halves. Bake 20 minutes more or until chicken is tender, basting chicken and pears with glaze. Arrange on serving platter, sprinkle with chopped peanuts, garnish with parsley. Makes 6 to 8 servings.

Mrs. John Dellenback

MRS. JOHN DELLENBACK, Wife of former Representative (Oregon)

CHICKEN JUBILEE

1 chicken, quartered
melted butter
salt
pepper
garlic salt
2 onions, sliced
½ cup raisins

1 bottle chili sauce
½ cup brown sugar
1 tablespoon Worcestershire sauce
1 cup sherry
1 can bing cherries, drained
cooked brown rice

Brush chicken pieces with butter and seasonings. Broil until brown and transfer to a casserole. Combine next 5 ingredients and pour over the chicken. Cover and bake at 325° for 1 hour or until tender. Add the sherry and cherries. Bake an additional 15 minutes. Serve with brown rice. May be frozen. Makes 4 servings.

Mrs Hugh Scott

MRS. HUGH SCOTT, Wife of Senator (Pennsylvania)

KATIE'S CURRIED CHICKEN AND FRUIT

1 2½ to 3 pound chicken, cut up
1 tablespoon flour
1½ teaspoons curry powder
¾ teaspoon salt
⅛ teaspoon pepper
liberal dash of cinnamon and nutmeg

2 teaspoons margarine or butter
1 small can sliced peaches, drained
1 small can pears, sliced, drained
1 cup seedless white grapes (optional)
½ cup syrup from fruit
cooked rice

Preheat oven to 375° and then reduce it to 350°. Wash and dry chicken pieces and place in shallow, foil lined baking pan. Combine flour, 1 teaspoon curry powder, salt, pepper, cinnamon and nutmeg and sprinkle over chicken. Dot with butter. Bake uncovered 30 minutes. Place fruit around chicken, sprinkle with remaining curry powder and spoon fruit syrup over all. Return to oven and bake 25 to 30 minutes or until chicken is tender. Serve over rice. May be frozen. Makes 4 servings.

Mrs. William L. Hungate

Mrs. William L. Hungate, Wife of Representative (Missouri)

FARMER'S FARE THEE WELL

4 cups long grain and wild rice
1 frying chicken, cut up
salt and pepper to taste
⅓ cup vegetable oil
1 green pepper, coarsely chopped
1 onion, chopped
1 clove garlic, minced

3 teaspoons curry powder
2 teaspoons flour
½ cup cold water
1 large can stewed tomatoes
½ cup seedless raisins
¼ cup toasted almonds or cashews
chutney

Cook rice until slightly underdone and put in a 4 quart casserole. Season chicken with salt and pepper, brown in oil in skillet and place on rice. Pour off half the oil from skillet and cook pepper, onion and garlic in remaining oil. Mix curry powder, flour and water to a smooth paste and add it with the tomatoes, raisins and nuts to the browned vegetables. Stir well and heat to boiling. Cook a few minutes and pour over chicken and rice. Cover and bake at 350° for 1 hour. Serve with chutney. Makes 6 servings.

Mrs Caspar W Weinberger

Mrs. Caspar Weinberger, Wife of former Secretary of Health, Education and Welfare (California)

CHICKEN AND WILD RICE CASSEROLE

12 pieces chicken
3 tablespoons shortening
1 cup wild rice
4 cups water
2 teaspoons instant chicken bouillon
½ cup white rice
1 can mushroom soup

1 cup sour cream
¾ teaspoon curry powder
½ cup sherry
1 pound fresh mushrooms, sliced
salt
chopped parsley

Brown chicken pieces in shortening. Rinse wild rice and cook in the water with bouillon added for 25 minutes. Add white rice and cook an additional 20 minutes. Mix soup, sour cream, curry powder and sherry and add to the undrained rice. Saute the mushrooms and add to rice, reserving some for garnish. Place rice mixture over bottom of large flat casserole, press chicken pieces into rice, sprinkle with salt, cover and bake for 1 hour at 350°. Garnish with mushooms and parsley. May be frozen. Makes 8 to 10 servings.

Mrs. Albert H. Quie

MRS. ALBERT H. QUIE, Wife of Representative (Minnesota)

CHICKEN AND RICE WITH BLACK OLIVES

4 large chicken pieces
6 tablespoons butter, melted
4 green onions, sliced
½ pound fresh mushrooms, sliced

2½ cups chicken broth (or bouillon)
1 cup uncooked rice
salt and pepper to taste
1 cup pitted black olives, drained

Brown chicken lightly in butter. Remove chicken to a casserole. Put green onions and mushrooms in butter and cook briefly. Pour in chicken broth, rice, salt and pepper. Bring to a boil and stir in black olives. Spoon rice mixture over chicken. Cover and bake in 300° for 1 hour. May be frozen. Makes 4 servings.

Mrs. Hamilton Fish, Jr.

MRS. HAMILTON FISH, JR., Wife of Representative (New York)

258

BAKED CHICKEN SUPREME

1 7 ounce box quick cooking rice
1 can cream of celery soup
1 can cream of mushroom soup

1 soup can milk
1 3 pound chicken, cut up
1 envelope dry onion soup

Spread dry rice in bottom of shallow pan. Blend soups and milk and pour evenly over rice and stir lightly. Place chicken on rice, skin side up. Sprinkle dry soup mix evenly over all. Cover and bake in 300° oven 2 hours. Makes 6 servings.

Mrs. Tom Steed

MRS. TOM STEED, Wife of Representative (Oklahoma)

CHICKEN AND RICE DINNER

1 cup rice
2 cups chicken bouillon
8 raw chicken breasts
1 4 ounce can mushrooms with liquid

½ package dry onion soup mix
1 can cream of mushroom soup
1 2 ounce jar pimientos

Place rice and bouillon in pan, add chicken breasts and cover with remaining ingredients in order given. Bake in 350° oven 1 hour. Makes 6 to 8 servings.

Mrs. Richard P. Yates

MRS. RICHARD P. YATES, Daughter of Representative Wilbur D. Mills (Arkansas)

CHINESE ALMOND BAKE

4 large chicken breast halves
2 cups chopped celery
2 cups chopped onion
4 cans cream of celery soup

2 cups small almonds
1 cup Carnation milk
dash Worcestershire sauce
2 large cans chow mein noodles

Simmer chicken breasts until tender. When cool, bone and mix with the next 6 ingredients. About 1 hour before baking, spread 1 can of chow mein noodles over bottom of an ungreased 9 x 12 inch casserole. Cover with the chicken mixture and top with remaining noodles. Bake 35 to 45 minutes at 350°. Makes 8 to 10 servings.

Mrs. Al Ullman

MRS. AL ULLMAN, Wife of Representative (Oregon)

CHICKEN AND CRAB CASSEROLE

2 3 pound chickens, cut up
1 cup water
1 cup sherry
¾ teaspoon curry powder
1½ teaspoons salt
1 medium onion, quartered
2 stalks celery, sliced

2 packages long grain and wild rice
  with seasonings
1 pound fresh mushrooms
¼ cup butter
1 8 ounce can water chestnuts, sliced
1 14 ounce package frozen crabmeat
1 can cream of mushroom soup
1 cup dairy sour cream

Cook chicken in water and sherry seasoned with curry powder, salt, onion and celery. Simmer 1 hour or until tender. Remove chicken, strain broth and refrigerate both. When well chilled, cut chicken into bite size pieces. Skim fat from broth. Cook rice according to package directions using the reserved chicken broth instead of water. Saute mushrooms in butter. Combine chicken, rice and mushrooms with all remaining ingredients, pour into greased casserole and bake at 350° for 1 hour. This casserole may be prepared and refrigerated until it is to be baked. May be frozen. Makes 8 to 10 servings.

Mrs. John B. Conlan

Mrs. John B. Conlan, Wife of Representative (Arizona)

CHICKEN SPAGHETTI

1 stewing chicken, cut up
2 quarts water
2 stalks celery with leaves
1 onion, quartered
salt and pepper
1 16 ounce package spaghetti
½ cup chopped onion
½ cup chopped green pepper

1 4 ounce can chopped pimientos
1 stick margarine
1 can tomato soup
2 cans cream of mushroom soup
1 teaspoon Worcestershire sauce
¼ cup chopped black olives
½ pound Velvetta cheese, cubed

Boil chicken covered in water with celery, onion and seasonings until tender. Remove chicken and strain broth. Skin and bone cooled chicken and cut into bite size pieces. Return to boiling broth and slowly add spaghetti. Cook until most of the broth is absorbed. Saute onion, green pepper and pimientos in margarine. Add soups, Worcestershire sauce and olives. Bring soup mixture to a boil, add cheese and stir until cheese is melted. Combine with the spaghetti and chicken mixture in a casserole. May be frozen. Makes 10 to 12 servings.

Mrs. J. J. Pickle

Mrs. J. J. Pickle, Wife of Representative (Texas)

HAWAIIAN CHICKEN

3 pounds chicken pieces
1 onion, chopped
1 stalk celery, chopped
1 carrot, chopped
¼ teaspoon thyme
½ teaspoon salt
¼ teaspoon pepper
1 20 ounce can pineapple chunks,
   drain and reserve syrup

1 cup pineapple juice
3 tablespoons corn starch
3 tablespoon soy sauce
¼ cup vinegar
¼ cup brown sugar
1 green pepper, sliced
1 cup cashew nuts

Combine chicken with vegetables and seasonings, cover with water and simmer until tender. Remove from heat but let chicken cool in liquid. Skin and bone chicken, cut into bite size pieces and place in a 2 quart casserole. Combine the syrup from the pineapple with the pineapple juice, corn starch, soy sauce, vinegar and sugar and cook until clear. Add pepper slices, pineapple chunks and nuts and simmer 5 minutes. Pour sauce over chicken and bake in a preheated 325° oven for 30 minutes. Makes 6 servings.

Mrs. Spark Matsunaga

MRS. SPARK MATSUNAGA, Wife of Representative (Hawaii)

CREAM OF CHICKEN TACOS

3 large fryers, cut up
6 packages tortillas
cooking oil
4 medium onions, chopped
4 bell peppers, chopped
4 16 ounce cans tomatoes
4 cans tomato sauce
2 cans green chilies, chopped

2 cloves garlic, chopped
salt to taste
8 tablespoons flour
¼ pound butter
1½ quarts milk
1 pint chicken broth
1½ pounds sharp cheddar cheese,
   grated

Boil chicken until tender. Let cool in broth. Bone chicken and cut into bite size pieces. Cut tortillas in half, fry lightly in deep fat and drain. Skim off 1 cup chicken fat from broth and in it fry onions and bell peppers until tender. Add tomatoes, tomato sauce, green chilies and garlic. Cook 20 minutes. Salt to taste. Mix flour and butter to a paste, gradually add milk and chicken broth and cook until it is a thin white sauce. Let cool and add tomato mixture. Alternate layers of chicken, tortillas, grated cheese and sauce in a casserole until it is almost filled. Top with grated cheese and bake in a 350° oven for 1½ hours. Serve extra sauce with tacos. May be frozen. Makes 20 servings.

Mrs. Harold Runnels

MRS. HAROLD L. RUNNELS, Wife of Representative (New Mexico)

261

CREAMED CHICKEN AND ARTICHOKES

4 whole chicken breasts
6 tablespoons flour
12 tablespoons butter (or chicken fat or margarine)
3 cups chicken broth
2 cups heavy cream
½ cup sherry
salt and pepper to taste
2 packages frozen artichoke hearts, thawed
1 cup slivered almonds
½ cup buttered bread crumbs

Boil chicken in water until tender. Remove chicken, cool, bone and cut in pieces. Blend flour and butter. Add broth and cream. Cook over low heat until thick, stirring constantly. Add sherry, salt and pepper. In a rectangular baking dish, layer sauce, chicken, uncooked artichokes and almonds, in that order, until all ingredients are used, ending with the sauce. Top with crumbs. Bake uncovered at 350° until bubbly, approximately 30 minutes. Makes 10 servings.

Mrs. Henry J. Nowak

Mrs. Henry J. Nowak, Wife of Representative (New York)

CHICKEN CASSEROLE

1 2½ pound fryer (or 4 or 5 chicken breasts)
1 cup egg noodles
salt and pepper
3 hard cooked eggs, sliced
2 or 3 tablespoons diced pimiento
1 can cream of mushroom soup (or cream of celery soup)
1½ cups hot chicken broth
1 cup buttered bread crumbs (or Pepperidge Farm herb dressing crumbs)

Cook chicken until tender. Cool and reserve broth. Bone and cut meat into bite size pieces. Cook noodles according to package directions. Drain. In a buttered casserole, alternate layers of noodles and chicken. Season. Arrange egg slices and pimiento on top. Dilute soup with broth and pour over casserole. Top with crumbs. Heat thoroughly in a 350° oven. Makes 8 servings.

Mrs. G. Elliott Hagan

Mrs. G. Elliott Hagan, Wife of former Representative (Georgia)

SNAZZY CASSEROLE

2 3 pound whole broiler fryers
1 cup water
1 cup dry sherry
1½ teaspoons salt
½ teaspoon curry powder
1 medium onion, sliced
½ cup sliced celery

1 pound fresh mushrooms
¼ cup butter or margarine
2 6 ounce packages long grain and
wild rice with seasonings
1 cup dairy sour cream
1 can cream of mushroom soup

Place chicken in a deep kettle. Add water, sherry, salt, curry powder, onion and celery. Bring to a boil and cover tightly. Reduce heat and simmer for 1 hour. Remove from heat, strain and reserve broth. Refrigerate chicken and broth at once. When chicken is cool, bone, discard skin and cut into bite size pieces. Wash mushrooms, pat dry and saute in butter until golden brown. Measure broth and use as part of liquid for cooking rice, following package directions for firm rice. Combine chicken, rice and mushrooms in a 3½ quart casserole. Blend sour cream and mushroom soup and toss with chicken mixture. Cover and refrigerate. Bake in a 350° oven for 1 hour. May be frozen before baking. Makes 8 to 10 servings.

Mrs. Clarence J. Brown

MRS. CLARENCE J. BROWN, Wife of Representative (Ohio)

VIRGINIA BRUNSWICK STEW

1 large stewing chicken (or 2 fryers),
disjointed
2 quarts water
2 slices bacon, cut up
1 onion, sliced
3 teaspoons salt
3 large tomatoes
2 large potatoes, sliced

2 cups lima beans
1 teaspoon sugar
½ teaspoon black pepper
dash red pepper
corn cut from 3 large ears
2 tablespoons butter
2 tablespoons flour

Put chicken in a heavy pot, add water, bacon, onion and 1 teaspoon salt and stew for 2 hours. Remove chicken from bones and cut into large pieces. Return to stew liquid and add tomatoes, potatoes, beans, sugar, remaining salt, pepper and red pepper. Cook ½ hour. Add corn; cook ½ hour. Add butter and flour; simmer ½ hour. Be careful during the whole process to maintain low heat to prevent sticking to bottom of pan. May be frozen. Makes 8 to 10 servings.

Mrs. David Satterfield III

MRS. DAVID E. SATTERFIELD III, Wife of Representative (Virginia)

BRUNSWICK STEW

1 3 pound fryer
2 pounds potatoes
2 medium cans tomatoes
2 small cans butter beans
1 small can cream style corn
1 12 ounce can tomato juice

1 stick margarine
¼ cup sugar
salt and pepper to taste
Worcestershire sauce to taste
Texas Pete sauce to taste

Boil chicken until tender. If boiled the day before stew is to be prepared, allow chicken to remain in broth overnight. Remove chicken from broth and bone. Cook potatoes in broth, remove and mash. Heat other vegetables in broth, remove and mash. Place all ingredients in an 8 quart pot. Simmer for 1 hour, stirring often. May be frozen. Makes 7 to 8 quarts.

Mrs. Walter B. Jones

MRS. WALTER B. JONES, Wife of Representative (North Carolina)

CHICKEN LOAF

1 large hen, cut up
water
1 celery stalk
1 thyme leaf
1 carrot
2½ cups cracker crumbs
2½ cups chicken stock
3 hard cooked eggs, chopped
3 raw eggs
1 cup diced celery
¼ cup chopped pimiento
salt

pepper
garlic (optional)
cracker crumbs
butter

Giblet gravy:
flour
2½ cups chicken stock
2 hard cooked eggs, chopped
giblets, chopped
salt and pepper to taste

Cook chicken in water with celery stalk, thyme leaf and carrot until chicken is tender. Remove chicken from bone. Dice the white meat. Grind dark meat and a portion of the skin together. Add next 9 ingredients and mix well. Pour into a greased 9 x 13 inch pan; cover with more cracker crumbs and dot with butter. Bake at 350° until brown, about 30 minutes.

Make gravy in usual way by adding flour to a small amount of chicken stock and then gradually adding remaining stock, eggs and giblets. Add seasoning and simmer a few minutes. Cut chicken loaf in squares and serve with the gravy.

Mrs. Ray Roberts

MRS. RAY ROBERTS, Wife of Representative (Texas)

264

POLLO TETRAZZINI (CREAMED CHICKEN WITH NOODLES)

4 pound stewing chicken
1 teaspoon white salt
½ teaspoon white pepper
½ teaspoon dried rosemary
water
½ pound fettucine (or other egg
   noodles)

¼ cup butter
1 onion, minced
1 pepper, minced
1 can mushrooms, drained
½ cup heavy cream
1½ cups grated parmesan cheese
¼ cup minced parsley

Place chicken in a deep pot. Add salt, pepper, rosemary and enough water to cover. Bring to a gentle boil and simmer for 2½ hours. Drain the broth into a large saucepan. Add enough water to make 2 quarts. Bring to a rolling boil and add the noodles. Cook until tender and drain. Meanwhile, bone and skin the chicken and cut the chicken meat into bite size pieces. Melt the butter in a large skillet. Add onion and pepper and saute for 5 minutes, stirring constantly. Add mushrooms and cook for 5 minutes longer. Add cream, chicken meat, noodles, 1 cup of cheese and parsley. Mix and heat through. Serve with remaining cheese. Makes 4 to 6 servings.

Mrs. Jane J. Howard

MRS. JAMES J. HOWARD, Wife of Representative (New Jersey)

CHICKEN BROCCOLI CASSEROLE

3 quarts cold water
1 carrot, cut in chunks
1 stalk celery, with leaves
1 small onion, halved
salt
8 peppercorns
2 to 3 pounds chicken pieces (or 2
   turkey legs)

3 packages frozen prepared broccoli in
   cheese sauce
½ to 1 can condensed cheddar cheese
   soup (or cream of chicken or
   mushroom soup)
1 tablespoon dry vermouth
parsley flakes

Combine first 6 ingredients in a large kettle, heat to boiling and add chicken. Cover and simmer until tender. Remove chicken and let cool. Skin and bone the chicken and cut into bite size pieces. Place over bottom of a flat buttered casserole. Bake the broccoli following the package instructions but only until thawed, about half done. Pour off the cheese sauce into a bowl, add the soup and vermouth to it and mix well. Arrange broccoli over the chicken, spread the sauce over all and top with parsley flakes. Bake at 350° until hot and bubbly, about 20 to 30 minutes. May be frozen. Makes 4 to 6 servings.

Mrs. Neil Staebler

MRS. NEIL STAEBLER, Wife of former Representative (Michigan)

CHICKEN CHEESE CASSEROLE

2 pounds chicken thighs (or breasts)
2 packages frozen broccoli (or French style string beans)
1 tablespoon minced dried onions
⅛ teaspoon grated nutmeg
1 can cheddar cheese soup

Simmer chicken in water to cover until just done. Bone and cut in pieces. Cook broccoli as package directs and drain. In a casserole, place a layer of chicken and then a layer of broccoli. Sprinkle with half the minced onion and half the nutmeg. Cover with half the soup. Repeat layers with remaining ingredients, ending with soup. Bake in a 325° oven for 30 minutes. May be frozen. Makes 3 to 4 servings.

Mrs. William F. Norrell

MRS. WILLIAM F. NORRELL, former Representative (Arkansas)

CHICKEN BROCCOLI DELIGHT

4 whole chicken breasts
2 boxes frozen chopped broccoli
2 cans cream of chicken soup
1 cup mayonnaise
1 tablespoon curry powder
1 tablespoon lemon juice
bread crumbs
butter

Bake chicken breasts in 350° oven about an hour until tender. Cool and bone. Thaw frozen broccoli and drain. Mix together soup, mayonnaise, curry powder and lemon juice. In buttered casserole arrange layers of broccoli, chicken and sauce. Repeat layers. Sprinkle with bread crumbs and dot with butter. Bake in 350° oven 20 to 30 minutes. May be frozen. Makes 6 servings.

Mrs. Fred W. Drogula

MRS. FRED W. DROGULA, Daughter of former Representative Paul J. Kilday (Texas)

CHICKEN AND SAUSAGE

2 pounds sausage
1½ cups uncooked wild rice
1½ cups uncooked brown rice
2 pounds mushrooms, sliced

butter
6 large whole chicken breasts, cooked, boned and halved
4 cans cream of mushroom soup

Brown sausage, breaking up with fork so it is in pieces. Cook rice according to package directions. Saute mushrooms in a little butter. Combine sausage, mushrooms, cooked rice and chicken. Add soup and bake for 45 minutes at 375°. If it seems dry, add more liquid. May be frozen. Makes 12 servings.

MRS. JOHN J. RHODES, Wife of Representative (Arizona)

MOCK CHICKEN DIVAN

8 pieces chicken, cooked and boned
2 cups cream of chicken soup
1 cup mayonnaise
1 tablespoon Worcestershire sauce

2 packages broccoli spears
bread crumbs
1 cup grated cheddar cheese
cooked rice (optional)

Combine chicken, soup, mayonnaise, Worcestershire sauce and broccoli and put in greased casserole. Cover with crumbs and cheese. Bake in 350° oven for 45 minutes to 1 hour. Serve over rice if desired. Makes 8 servings.

MRS. JOHN J. DUNCAN, Wife of Representative (Tennessee)

SPANISH STYLE CHICKEN

5 pounds chicken, boiled
flour
salt, paprika
½ cup butter
1 large onion, grated
1 clove garlic, grated

1 green pepper, chopped
2 cups tomatoes, strained
1 pound mushrooms, sauteed
seasoning as desired
minced parsley
minced chives

Remove chicken meat from bones in large pieces. Dredge with flour mixed with salt and paprika. Brown in hot butter and remove to a casserole. Simmer onion, garlic, and green pepper in the same butter until tender. Mix with tomatoes and mushrooms. Season and pour over chicken. Cover and bake in a 350° oven 30 to 40 minutes. When ready to serve, sprinkle with parsley and chives. May be frozen. Makes 6 servings.

Mrs. Howard Baker Jr

Mrs. Howard H. Baker Jr., Wife of Senator (Tennessee) ,

CHICKEN AND BROCCOLI CASSEROLE

2 10 ounce packages frozen broccoli
spears
4 large chicken breasts, cooked, boned
and diced
1 cup mayonnaise

1 tablespoon lemon juice
2 cans cream of chicken soup
½ tablespoon curry
½ cup shredded sharp cheese

Cook broccoli as directed and place in bottom of baking dish. Add chicken. Combine the next 4 ingredients and pour over chicken. Bake 30 to 40 minutes at 350°. Top with cheese about 20 or 30 minutes after start of baking or at least 10 minutes before done. Makes 10 servings.

Mrs. Walter Moeller

Mrs. Walter Moeller, Wife of former Representative (Ohio)

268

CHICKEN ALMOND CASSEROLE

2½ cups cubed cooked chicken
1 can cream of chicken soup
1 cup uncooked Minute rice
1½ cups chicken broth
½ cup finely chopped celery

1 small onion, grated
6 tablespoons mayonnaise
1 small can chopped mushroom pieces
blanched almonds, chopped (or
    buttered Ritz cracker crumbs)

Mix chicken, chicken soup, rice and chicken broth. Add other ingredients except nuts. Put in lightly greased baking dish and top with almonds. Bake at 350° for 30 minutes. May be prepared and refrigerated until baking time. Makes 6 to 8 servings.

Mrs James Thomas Broyhill

MRS. JAMES T. BROYHILL, Wife of Representative (North Carolina)

MEXICAN CHICKEN CASSEROLE

1 4 pound chicken, cooked
1 can cream of mushroom soup
1 can cream of chicken soup
1 can RoTel tomatoes
½ cup chicken stock

2 teaspoons salt
1 teaspoon black pepper
1 small package corn chips
2 onions, finely chopped
3 cups grated sharp cheese

Cut chicken in bite size pieces. Combine soups, tomatoes, chicken stock, salt and pepper. In a 3 quart casserole, layer corn chips, chicken, tomato mixture, onions, and cheese in the order given. Bake in a 350° oven for 45 minutes. May be frozen. Makes 8 servings.

Mrs. Jack Brooks

MRS. JACK BROOKS, Wife of Representative (Texas)

CHICKEN GUMBO

¾ cup chopped green pepper
1 onion, chopped (about ¾ cup)
3 tablespoons butter (or chicken fat)
1 cup chicken broth
1 20 ounce can tomatoes
1 package frozen okra (or ¾ pound fresh okra, sliced)
2 cups diced, cooked chicken
1 small piece bay leaf

½ teaspoon salt
¼ teaspoon black pepper, freshly ground
1 teaspoon sugar
¼ teaspoon oregano
1 tablespoon minced parsley
1 tablespoon corn starch (optional)
¼ cup cold water (optional)
rice (or spoon bread)

Saute green pepper and onion in butter until soft. Add remaining ingredients and simmer until thick, about 15 minutes. If desired, mix the corn starch with cold water and add to sauce to thicken. Serve over rice or with spoon bread. This may be frozen. Makes 6 servings.

Mrs. Tom Bevill

MRS. TOM BEVILL, Wife of Representative (Alabama)

CAROLINA CHICKEN SOUFFLE

1½ cups diced cooked chicken
1 cup mushroom soup
1¼ cups milk
3 tablespoons butter, melted
3 tablespoons flour

¾ teaspoon salt
1 teaspoon pepper
4 egg yolks, slightly beaten
4 egg whites, stiffly beaten

Heat together the chicken, soup and ¼ cup milk. Put into a large casserole. Blend butter and flour and stir in remaining milk. Cook over low heat, stirring until thick. Season with salt and pepper. Stir hot sauce into egg yolks and blend. Fold in egg whites. Pour over chicken mixture. Set casserole in a pan in 1 inch of hot water and bake at 350° for 30 minutes. Makes 6 to 8 servings.

Mrs. Richardson Preyer

MRS. RICHARDSON PREYER, Wife of Representative (North Carolina)

SAVORY CRESCENT CHICKEN SQUARES

1 3 ounce package cream cheese
3 tablespoons margarine
2 cups cooked cubed chicken (turkey, pork or beef)
¼ teaspoon salt
⅛ teaspoon pepper
2 tablespoons milk
1 tablespoon chopped chives or onion
1 tablespoon chopped pimiento
1 8 ounce can refrigerated crescent rolls
¾ cup seasoned croutons, crushed

Preheat oven to 350°. Blend softened cream cheese and 2 tablespoons melted margarine until smooth. Add cooked chicken, salt, pepper, milk, chives and pimiento. Mix well. Separate dinner rolls into 4 rectangles. Seal perforations. Spoon ½ cup chicken mixture onto center of each rectangle; pull four corners of dough to center of mixture; seal. Brush tops with 1 tablespoon of melted margarine. Dip in crushed croutons. Bake 20 to 25 minutes until golden brown. Makes 4 servings.

Mrs. Tennyson Guyer

Mrs. Tennyson Guyer, Wife of Representative (Ohio)

CHICKEN STRATA

8 slices bread, cubed
2 cups diced cooked chicken
½ cup chopped celery
½ cup chopped onions
½ cup mayonnaise
½ cup chopped green pepper
½ cup grated sharp cheddar cheese
1 can mushroom soup
2 eggs
1½ cups milk
grated cheese

Mix first 7 ingredients together and put into 2 buttered casseroles. Refrigerate overnight. Just before baking, spread mushroom soup over top of each. Beat eggs, add milk and pour over casseroles. Sprinkle cheese on top and bake at 350° until silver knife inserted in center comes out clean, about 1 hour. May be frozen. Makes 4 to 5 servings.

Mrs. Otis R. Bowen

Mrs. Otis R. Bowen, Wife of Governor (Indiana)

TEXAS CHICKEN ENCHILADA

1 dozen frozen tortillas
1 can cream of chicken soup
2 cans boned chicken
1 can cream of mushroom soup
1 small can green chilies
1 pound grated cheese

Line greased casserole with 6 tortillas and over them spread cream of chicken soup and 1 can of chicken. Over this, layer the remaining tortillas and spread with cream of mushroom soup and the other can of chicken. Top with green chilies and grated cheese. Bake in 350° oven until bubbly. Flavor will improve if it is prepared and refrigerated 24 hours before it is baked. May be frozen but thaw completely before cooking. Makes 8 servings.

Mrs. John Dowdy

MRS. JOHN DOWDY, Wife of former Representative (Texas)

CHICKEN ENCHILADA

1 large onion, chopped
3 tablespoons butter
1 13 ounce can evaporated milk
2 cans cream of chicken soup
2 4 ounce cans green chilies, chopped
3 5 ounce cans boned chicken
12 corn tortillas
2 cups grated cheddar cheese

Saute onion in butter. Add evaporated milk and chicken soup. Stir until smooth. Add chilies and chicken. Stir all together. Grease a 9 x 14 inch glass cake dish. Line dish with 6 tortillas, pour half of chicken mixture over them and sprinkle with half the grated cheese. Repeat layers with remaining tortillas, chicken mixture and cheese. Cover dish loosely with aluminum foil. Bake 45 minutes at 350°. May be frozen. Makes 6 servings.

Mrs. James P. Johnson

MRS. JAMES P. JOHNSON, Wife of Representative (Colorado)

CHICKEN AND RICE CASSEROLE

6 cups cut up cooked chicken
3 cans cream of mushroom soup
4 cups chopped hard cooked eggs
2 cups Hellmann's mayonnaise
4 tablespoons grated onion
½ cup whole cashew nuts

½ cup chopped almonds
3 tablespoons lemon juice
6 cups cooked white rice
3 cups diced celery
2 cans sliced mushrooms
corn flake crumbs

Mix all ingredients except crumbs. Divide into 2 large baking dishes. Top with corn flake crumbs. Bake at 375° for 25 to 30 minutes. Serves 10 to 15 people.

Mrs. John C. Stennis

Mrs. John C. Stennis, Wife of Senator (Mississippi)

CHICKEN TETRAZZINI

3 quarts water
1 tablespoon salt
1 14 ounce package long spaghetti
3 slices bacon, shredded
1 large onion, chopped
1 4 ounce can pimientos, diced
1 large green pepper, finely chopped

1 pound cheese, grated
1 8 ounce can mushrooms
2 teaspoons salt
¼ teaspoon black pepper
4 cups diced cooked chicken
1 cup chicken broth

Bring water to a rapid boil and add salt. Add spaghetti gradually. Cook uncovered at rapid boil for 15 minutes or until tender. Drain but do not rinse. Cook the bacon in a large kettle. Add onion and brown slightly. Add pimiento, green pepper, cheese, mushrooms, salt and pepper. Add chicken and spaghetti. Heat thoroughly, using chicken broth to moisten as needed. May be frozen. Makes 8 to 12 servings.

Mrs. Walter B. Jones

Mrs. Walter B. Jones, Wife of Representative (North Carolina)

CHICKEN SPAGHETTI

½ pound butter
4 onions, chopped
4 to 6 cloves garlic, minced
2 to 3 bell peppers, chopped
1 large stalk celery, chopped
½ teaspoon chili powder
1 teaspoon Evangeline hot sauce
½ teaspoon red pepper
1 teaspoon paprika
2 tablespoons Worcestershire sauce
1 teaspoon comino seeds
½ teaspoon black pepper
1 5 pound cooked hen, cut up
1 quart chicken stock
3 small cans tomato paste
1½ pounds spaghetti
1 20 ounce can English peas
1 20 ounce can mushrooms
grated cheese

Melt butter and add next 4 ingredients, frying until brown and tender. Add all seasonings and fry until well mixed, stirring constantly. Cook chicken with chicken stock and tomato paste for 30 minutes. Add fried mixture and stir. Cook spaghetti according to package directions. Add spaghetti, peas and mushrooms. Simmer 20 to 30 minutes, stirring often. Sprinkle grated cheese over top. Makes 15 to 20 servings.

Mrs Wright Patman

MRS. WRIGHT PATMAN, Wife of Representative (Texas)

KATIE'S CHICKEN CREPES

5 tablespoons butter
¾ cup plus 5 tablespoons flour
⅝ teaspoon salt
⅛ teaspoon pepper
1 cup cream
1 cup chicken broth
½ teaspoon Worcestershire sauce
2 tablespoons chopped parsley
1 cup grated Swiss cheese
¾ cup sauterne
2 cups diced cooked chicken
½ cup chopped ripe olives
2 eggs, well beaten
¾ cup milk
paprika

Melt butter, blend in 5 tablespoons flour, ½ teaspoon salt and pepper. Add cream, chicken broth and Worcestershire. Cook, stirring constantly, until thickened. Stir in parsley, ¾ cup cheese and wine. Place 1 cup sauce in bowl; add chicken and olives. Put remaining sauce in double boiler and keep warm.

Mix eggs and milk; add remaining flour and remaining salt. Beat until smooth. Pour about 2 tablespoons batter into 7 inch skillet. Roll around in pan until very thin. Cook until brown underneath but do not turn.

Place 2 tablespoonfuls chicken mixture on each pancake and roll up. Place in shallow baking dish and pour remaining sauce over top. Sprinkle with remaining cheese and paprika. Bake at 375° for 15 minutes. Place under broiler until browned and bubbly. May be frozen. Makes 4 to 6 servings.

Mrs. Tim Lee Carter

MRS. TIM LEE CARTER, Wife of Representative (Kentucky)

EASY CHICKEN CASSEROLE

1 can cream of mushroom soup
1 can cream of chicken soup
2 whole cooked chicken breasts, boned and cubed

1 can evaporated milk
1 5½ ounce can chow mein noodles
sliced almonds

Mix together all ingredients except nuts and put in greased casserole. Cover with almonds. Bake in 350° oven for 30 to 40 minutes. May be frozen. Makes 8 servings.

Mrs. Clifford G. McIntire

MRS. CLIFFORD MCINTIRE, Wife of former Representative (Maine)

HOT TURKEY SALAD

2 cups cubed cooked turkey (or chicken)
2 cups sliced celery
1 cup mayonnaise
½ cup chopped toasted almonds
2 tablespoons lemon juice

2 teaspoons grated onion
½ teaspoon salt
½ cup grated cheese
1 cup crushed potato chips

Combine first 7 ingredients and toss lightly. Put in casserole dish or individual baking dishes. Sprinkle cheese and potato chips over top. Bake 10 minutes in 450° oven. Makes 6 servings.

Mrs. Garner E. Shriver

MRS. GARNER E. SHRIVER, Wife of Representative (Kansas)

GREAT TURKEY CASSEROLE

1 can mushroom soup
1 soup can liquid (milk and water)
1 cup instant uncooked rice
2 cups cut up, cooked turkey
1 can pineapple chunks, drained

1 cup chopped celery
3 tablespoons minced onion
3 tablespoons minced green pepper
black olives, sliced
toasted almonds

Mix soup and liquid. Mix with all other ingredients except almonds. Put in greased casserole and bake at 350° for 30 minutes. Cover with almonds and serve. Makes 6 servings.

Mrs. Don Bonker

MRS. DON BONKER, Wife of Representative (Washington)

TURKEY TETRAZZINI

4 cups cooked turkey in chunks
1 can mushroom soup
1 can cream of chicken soup
1 can cream of celery soup
2 tablespoons Lipton's chicken noodle soup mix
½ green pepper, chopped

1 tablespoon chopped onion
2 cups grated American cheese
1 teaspoon dried parsley flakes
4 slices bacon, chopped, fried and drained
1 8 ounce package spaghetti, cooked
1 3 ounce can Chinese noodles

Combine all ingredients except Chinese noodles in 3½ quart casserole and bake at 350° for 30 minutes. Sprinkle top with Chinese noodles and bake an additional 5 or 10 minutes. May be frozen. Makes 10 servings.

Mrs. Robert M. Lemke

MRS. ROBERT M. LEMKE, Daughter-in-law of former Representative William Lemke (North Dakota)

276

CHICKEN LIVERS IN MADEIRA

1 onion, finely chopped
¼ cup butter
1½ pounds chicken livers
1 tablespoon flour

1 cup chicken broth
½ cup Madeira wine
salt and pepper to taste
pilaff

Saute onion in butter until soft and golden. Dust chicken livers with the flour and saute them with the onion for 3 or 4 minutes or until they are brown on all sides Remove livers and onion to a plate and keep warm. Stir flour into pan drippings smoothly. Gradually add chicken broth and Madeira and cook sauce, stirring constantly, until smooth and thickened. Season with salt and pepper. Return liver mixture to the pan and cook over low heat for about 10 minutes or until cooked through. Serve the chicken livers and sauce on a bed of pilaff. Makes 8 servings.

Mrs. John Sparkman,

MRS. JOHN SPARKMAN, Wife of Senator (Alabama)

CHICKEN LIVERS FLAMBE (COOKED IN CHAFING DISH)

1 pound chicken livers, halved
1 tablespoon flour
¼ cup butter
1 jigger cognac
1 teaspoon tarragon

1 cup heavy cream, heated
2 egg yolks, beaten
salt to taste
cooked rice (optional)

Dust the chicken livers with flour and saute them lightly in butter in a chafing dish. When they are delicately colored on all sides, pour on the cognac and ignite it. When the flames subside, put the chafing dish over the hot water jacket and sprinkle with tarragon. Add the hot cream gradually to the egg yolks and pour over chicken livers. Add salt to taste and serve as soon as sauce thickens. Excellent with rice or on hot buttered toast. Makes 4 servings.

Mrs. Alfred D. Sieminski

MRS. ALFRED D. SIEMINSKI, Wife of former Representative (New Jersey)

STUFFED DUCK BORDELAISE

2 4½ to 5 pound ducks
salt and pepper
1 pound mushrooms, sliced
2 carrots, coarsely chopped
2 sticks celery, coarsely chopped
1 bay leaf
pinch of rosemary
2 cups chicken stock
1 cup dry white wine
2 tablespoons Madeira wine

Stuffing:
2 tablespoons butter
4 tablespoons shallots, finely chopped
duck livers, chopped
1 tablespoon parsley, chopped
8 green olives, chopped
sage
thyme
grated nutmeg
salt and pepper
4 slices bread, finely diced
2 eggs

Stuff ducks, tie with string and season with salt and pepper. Brown them on both sides in a roasting pan over medium heat. Add mushrooms, carrots, celery, bay leaf, rosemary, chicken stock and white wine. Cover and bake in a preheated 350° oven for 1 to 1½ hours. Remove ducks from roasting pan and strain the pan juices. Remove the fat from the juices. Boil juices until they are reduced to 2½ cups. Add Madeira wine and bring to a boil. Cut duck into pieces and arrange on large serving platter. Serve hot juices separately. If desired, surround duck with braised lettuce (page 113) and serve with celery root puree (page 54). Duck may be frozen. Makes 6 servings.

Stuffing: Melt butter in saucepan, add shallots and simmer for 2 minutes. Add livers and saute for 2 additional minutes. Add remaining ingredients except the bread and eggs. Remove from heat and add the bread, mixing well with a rubber spatula. Add eggs, 1 at a time, mixing well after each addition.

Mrs. Gerald R. Ford

MRS. GERALD R. FORD, Wife of President of the United States (Michigan)

278

DUCK A L'ORANGE

2 ducks, quartered
salt and pepper to taste
½ pint apricot brandy
½ pint sherry

1 12 ounce can frozen orange juice,
   diluted as directed
2 jars currant jelly
finely grated rind of 1 orange
1 teaspoon corn starch

Season ducks with salt and pepper. Mix brandy, sherry, orange juice and jelly. Heat until jelly dissolves. Remove ⅓ of this sauce and set aside. Bake ducks for approximately 1 hour in a preheated 350° oven, draining fat several times. Continue baking for about 1 additional hour, basting continually with sauce. Add grated rind to reserved sauce and cook for ½ hour over low heat, thickening with corn starch. Serve with the duck.

Mrs. Edward Levi

Mrs. Edward H. Levi, Wife of Attorney General (Illinois)

PHEASANT DELUXE

1 package wild rice mix
1 can cream of chicken soup
1 can cream of celery soup
1 soup can white wine

1 package dry onion soup
3 pheasants (or chickens), cut into
   serving pieces

Put rice in large casserole. Add soups, wine and dry soup mix and let stand for 2 hours. Bake at 325° for 30 minutes. Brown pheasant pieces in butter. Place on top of baked rice mixture, return to oven and bake covered for 2 hours at 325°. Makes 8 servings.

Mrs. Milton R. Young

Mrs. Milton R. Young, Wife of Senator (North Dakota)

279

BATTER FRIED PHEASANT

2 eggs
2 tablespoons milk
pheasant pieces
flour
fine bread crumbs

cooking oil
1 can mushroom soup or cream of
  chicken soup
½ soup can of water
water and milk, equal parts (optional)

Beat together the eggs and milk and chill 1 hour. Dip pheasant pieces into egg batter and roll in flour. Dip in egg batter again and roll in bread crumbs. Refrigerate about 2 hours. Heat cooking oil, at least ½ inch deep in fryer, to 375°. Put pheasant pieces in hot oil, browning well on both sides but turning only once. Put pieces in casserole. Dilute soup with water and pour over pheasant. Cover tightly and bake at 350° for 1 hour. If needed during baking, add a half water, half milk combination.

Mrs. J. Floyd Breeding

MRS. J. FLOYD BREEDING, Wife of former Representative (Kansas)

WILD GOOSE A LA SOUTH DAKOTA

1 5 to 8 pound goose
garlic salt
paprika
1½ stalks celery, chopped
1 carrot, chopped
1 onion, chopped
fat sufficient for browning

4 tablespoons flour
1 cup giblet stock
½ teaspoon rosemary
¼ teaspoon thyme
1¼ teaspoons salt
1 cup dairy sour cream
1 4 ounce can button mushrooms

Season goose inside and out with garlic salt and paprika. Place on rack in shallow pan. Roast uncovered in a 325° oven for 1 hour. Brown celery, carrot and onion in fat until soft. Stir in 2 tablespoons flour; then blend in the giblet stock to make a gravy. Season with rosemary, thyme and salt. Stir remaining flour into sour cream to keep it from curdling during roasting. Blend into gravy. Remove goose from shallow pan and place in roasting pan. Pour gravy and drained mushrooms over it. Cover and continue roasting another 2 hours or until tender. May be frozen. Makes 8 to 10 servings.

Mrs. Richard F. Kneip

MRS. RICHARD F. KNEIP, Wife of Governor (South Dakota)

280

BAKED DOVES

8 dove breasts
flour
salt and pepper
cooking oil

1 can consomme
water
1 teaspoon Worcestershire sauce
½ cup sherry

Roll dove breasts in flour seasoned with salt and pepper and brown in hot cooking oil in skillet. Remove breasts and place in a roaster. Pour off all but 4 tablespoons of hot oil in skillet and add 4 tablespoons of the seasoned flour, stirring until smooth and cooking until frothy. To consomme add enough water to make 2 cups. Add to mixture in skillet. Cook until it is a good gravy consistency, about 5 to 10 minutes. Stir in the Worcestershire sauce. Pour gravy over dove breasts. Add sherry and bake in a 325° oven about 1 hour. May be frozen. Makes 8 servings.

Mrs. Frank William Boykin

MRS. FRANK WILLIAM BOYKIN, Wife of former Representative (Alabama)

SAUSAGE STUFFING FOR TURKEY

2 pounds smoked pork sausage
1 large onion, finely minced
4 ribs celery, chopped
2 apples, pared, cored and chopped
2 8 ounce packages seasoned stuffing mix

3 beef bouillon cubes
3 cups water
1 cup chopped pecans
¼ cup finely chopped parsley
salt and pepper to taste
2 eggs, well beaten

Saute sausage in skillet until brown. Remove and place in large mixing bowl. Cook onion, celery and apple in skillet fat until tender; add to sausage in bowl. Combine seasoned stuffing mix with bouillon cubes dissolved in water, mixing well until moistened. Add to sausage mixture along with pecans, parsley and seasonings. Add beaten eggs and stir until blended. Add more water if a moister dressing is desired. Makes enough dressing for 1 large turkey.

Lindy (Mrs. Hale) Boggs

LINDY (MRS. HALE) BOGGS, Representative (Louisiana)

281

OYSTER DRESSING (FOR TURKEY)

1 package Pepperidge Farm corn bread
   stuffing
4 slices white bread, cut in small cubes
3 cups essence from cooked turkey
warm water as needed

3 eggs, beaten
salt and pepper
4 tablespoons butter
1 pint (or more) whole oysters

Let corn bread stuffing and cubed white bread soak in turkey essence until soft. Add a little warm water if necessary. Stir in eggs and add salt and pepper to taste. Melt butter in casserole in oven. Add dressing and bake at 350° for about 20 minutes. Remove from oven and add oysters. Return to oven and continue to bake at 350° about 40 minutes until brown. Increase heat to 450° and bake for another 10 minutes. May be frozen. Makes 8 servings.

Mrs. Mills Godwin

MRS. MILLS E. GODWIN, JR., Wife of Governor (Virginia)

CRANBERRY SAUCE

2 cups cranberries
1 cup sugar

½ cup brandy (or to taste)

Do not wash cranberries. Put cranberries in shallow baking dish and sprinkle with sugar. Cover and bake ½ hour at 350°. Remove cover and bake another half hour. Remove from oven and while still very hot, lace with brandy. Cool until jelled. Makes 6 to 8 servings.

Mrs. Bob Wilson

MRS. BOB WILSON, Wife of Representative (California)

MEAT, SAUCES & ACCOMPANIMENTS

Neck of Mutton called the Hasty Dish

Take a large silver or pewter dish, made like a deep soup-dish, with an edge about an inch deep in the inside, on which the lid fixes (with a handle on top) so fast, that you may lift it up by that handle without letting it fall; this dish is called a necromancer. Take a neck of mutton about six pounds, take off the skin, cut it into chops, but not too thick, cut a French roll and a large onion into thin slices, pare and dice three or four turneps, lay a row of mutton in the dish, on that a row of roll, then turneps, then onion, a little salt, then the meat, and so on till all is in, put in a bundle of sweet herbs and a blade or two of mace; have a tea kettle of boiling water, fill the dish, cover it close, and hang the dish on the back of two chairs by the rim; have ready three sheets of brown paper, tear each sheet into five pieces, draw them through your hand, light one piece and hold it under the bottom of your dish, moving the paper about as fast as it burns, proceed thus till all the paper is burnt, and your meat will be enough, (fifteen minutes just does it) and send it to table hot in the dish.

This dish was first contrived by the late Mr. Rich, and is now much admired by the nobility and gentry.

The New Art of Cookery
Richard Briggs, 1792

CHUCK ROAST WITH VEGETABLES

6 pound boneless chuck roast
salt and pepper
flour
2 tablespoons corn oil
2 cups beef bouillon

6 potatoes, peeled and halved
12 small onions, peeled
6 medium white turnips, peeled and halved
12 small carrots, peeled

Season meat with salt and pepper and roll in flour to coat all sides. Brown meat in corn oil in iron skillet. When well browned, transfer meat to a roasting pan, add bouillon and cover. Roast for 1½ hours in 350° oven, occasionally basting the meat with the bouillon. Surround meat with all the vegetables, salt them and spoon any remaining bouillon over them. Cover and roast for 1 additional hour or until tender. Remove meat to a platter and let rest for 15 minutes. Keep vegetables warm. Slice meat and arrange on a serving platter. Arrange vegetables around the meat. Bring meat juices to a boil and remove from heat. Remove fat from juices by placing a paper towel on top to absorb fat. Serve hot juices separately. May be frozen.

Mrs. Gerald R. Ford

MRS. GERALD R. FORD, Wife of President of the United States (Michigan)

BRANDYWINE BEEF

4 to 6 pounds boneless chuck
⅛ teaspoon cinnamon
freshly ground pepper
salt
2 tablespoons cooking oil

1 small onion, sliced
1 clove garlic (optional)
3 tablespoons brandy (or bourbon)
1 bay leaf
½ cup dry white wine

Sprinkle meat with cinnamon, pepper and salt. Heat oil in a large pot over a medium high heat until hot but not smoking. Add meat and brown well on all sides. Add onion slices and brown. Add garlic if desired. Reduce heat. Heat brandy, ignite and pour over meat, spooning the burning brandy over the meat until the flame dies. Add bay leaf and wine, cover tightly, reduce heat and cook about 1½ hours or until meat is fork tender but not too soft. After first hour of cooking, turn meat over and taste gravy to adjust seasonings. When meat is done, remove to a hot platter. Remove bay leaf, increase heat under liquid and boil rapidly until reduced by a third. To serve, cut meat into ½ inch slices and pour meat liquid over it. Makes 8 to 10 servings.

Mrs. Jim Wright

MRS. JIM WRIGHT, Wife of Representative (Texas)

BEEF BRISKET AND SAUCE

4 pound brisket
onion salt
garlic salt
liquid smoke
thin onion slices
thin lemon slices

Sauce:
1 cup catsup
1 teaspoon salt
1 cup Worcestershire sauce
2 cups water
dash of Tabasco

Season brisket by rubbing into it onion salt, garlic salt and a generous portion of liquid smoke. Wrap in foil and bake at 300° for 4½ hours or until tender. Remove meat to shallow pan and drain juice. Place onion and lemon slices on meat and broil 5 to 10 minutes until browned. Combine sauce ingredients and heat. Pour hot sauce over meat and put in 300° oven for 45 minutes, basting every 15 minutes. Pour off sauce and reserve. Wrap cooled meat in foil and chill. Slice thinly, rewrap in foil and heat 30 minutes to serve. Heat and serve sauce separately. May be frozen.

MRS. RAY ROBERTS, Wife of Representative (Texas)

CORNED BEEF BRISKET

2 to 3 pound corned beef brisket
1 small onion
1 stalk celery
1 carrot

2 tablespoons pickling spice
¼ cup water
horse radish sauce (optional)

Soak brisket for 30 minutes in enough water to cover. Remove from water and place on a shallow baking pan lined with aluminum foil. Place vegetables, spice and water in with the brisket and wrap all loosely in the foil. Bake at 300° for 3 to 4 hours. Slice and serve with horse radish sauce if desired. May be frozen. Makes 6 servings.

MRS. JOHN E. HENDERSON, Wife of former Representative (Ohio)

286

BEER ROAST

4 pound beef roast (round, rump or
  sirloin)
salt
pepper
½ cup sugar
1 small bottle catsup

2 cans beer
4 medium carrots, ¼ inch slices
2 medium onions, sliced
1 large green pepper, coarsely diced
2 large stalks celery, sliced
cooked rice or noodles

Place roast in an open pan, season with salt and pepper and bake at 350° for 1½ hours. Combine sugar, catsup and beer and add to meat with the vegetables. Reduce oven heat to 325°. Cook uncovered until tender. Refrigerate overnight in the juice. Slice the cold meat and arrange slices on an oven to table serving dish. Place vegetables on the meat and spoon the juice over all. Heat. Delicious served with rice or egg noodles. May be frozen. Makes 12 to 16 servings.

Mrs. William L. Hungate

MRS. WILLIAM L. HUNGATE, Wife of Representative (Missouri)

QUICK AND EASY ROAST

1 6 pound boneless top sirloin roast
  (or prime rib)

salt
1 clove garlic

Rub roast with garlic and sprinkle with salt. Place in preheated 500° oven and roast for 30 minutes for a rare roast or 35 minutes for one more well done. Turn heat off but do not open oven door for exactly 2 hours. Then remove roast.

Mrs. M. Blaine Peterson

MRS. M. BLAINE PETERSON, Wife of former Representative (Utah)

MARINATED EYE OF RIB ROAST

6 to 8 pound eye of rib roast
8 to 10 thick slices fresh ginger root
3 or 4 tablespoons peanut (or
  vegetable) oil

1½ cups soy sauce
2 or 3 cloves garlic, sliced

Place meat in a very large plastic bag. Mix ginger root, oil and soy sauce and add to bag. Squeeze out all air and tie securely. Place in pan in case the bag leaks. Marinate for at least 24 hours, turning often. Before roasting, remove meat from bag, make small gashes in meat and insert slices of garlic and ginger. Roast in preheated 500° oven for 35 to 40 minutes. Turn off heat and allow to stand 20 minutes. Remove from oven, place on platter and allow to stand for 10 additional minutes before carving. Makes 8 servings.

Mrs. James R. Mann

MRS. JAMES R. MANN, Wife of Representative (South Carolina)

EASY ROAST BEEF

5 or 6 pound eye of round roast
1 tablespoon Worcestershire sauce
salt

lemon pepper
½ cup chopped onions

Place roast on a large piece of heavy duty aluminum foil in a shallow baking pan. Place under broiler and broil until very brown. Put Worcestershire over the top of the roast and sprinkle with salt and lemon pepper on all sides. Add onions. Wrap the foil around the roast, sealing very tightly. Bake at 300° for 2½ hours. Makes 8 to 10 servings.

Mrs. David S. King

MRS. DAVID S. KING, Wife of former Representative (Utah)

BEEF MARINADE

3 to 4 pound eye of round beef
meat tenderizer
1 envelope McCormick's marinade mix
1 tablespoon water

2 tablespoons vinegar
¼ cup oil
1 teaspoon soy sauce

Sprinkle beef with meat tenderizer and stick with fork. Combine marinade mix, water, vinegar, oil and soy sauce. Pour over beef and marinate 4 to 4½ hours at room temperature, turning beef and basting several times. Bake uncovered for 15 minutes at 475°. Reduce temperature to 275° and continue to bake for 45 minutes. May be frozen.

Mrs. Dan Daniel

MRS. DAN DANIEL, Wife of Representative (Virginia)

BRAISED SHORT RIBS BURGUNDY

6 large beef short ribs
1 cup California burgundy (or red
dinner wine)
¼ cup red wine vinegar
1 medium size onion, sliced
2 cloves garlic, sliced
½ green pepper, sliced
2 tablespoons chopped parsley
3 small bay leaves, crushed

1 teaspoon dry mustard
¼ teaspoon powdered ginger
3 to 4 tablespoons oil
1 cup bouillon

Optional:
1 tablespoon corn starch
½ cup cold water
2 tablespoons tomato paste

Place short ribs in casserole and add all remaining ingredients except oil and bouillon. Cover and marinate several hours or overnight. Turn meat several times to distribute flavors. Remove meat and drain well. Strain and reserve marinade. Brown meat well over high heat in heated oil. Drain off all fat. Pour marinade and bouillon over meat. Cover and simmer until meat is tender, about 1½ to 2 hours. Remove meat and keep hot. Skim all fat from pan liquid. Thicken gravy, if desired, with corn starch mixed with water. To enrich gravy color, add tomato paste. May be frozen. Makes 6 servings.

Mrs. Evan Howell

MRS. EVAN HOWELL, Wife of former Representative (Illinois)

MEXICAN STEAK

4 pound boneless sirloin tip roast
coarsely ground black pepper
cooking oil
3 large onions, sliced
4 large tomatoes, sliced

4 fresh long green chili peppers, sliced
in rings (or 1 4 ounce can green
chilies, cut in strips)
salt to taste

Cut meat into slices about 4 x ½ inch thick. Sprinkle pepper generously over both sides of meat and press into meat with fingers. Sear each steak on both sides in small amount of cooking oil, no longer than a minute. In a heavy roasting pan, layer the onion, tomato slices, chili peppers and meat, in that order, until all meat is used up, but reserving a small amount of vegetables to use as garnish. Salt each layer lightly. Cover and simmer 30 minutes. Makes 8 servings.

Mrs. Jerry Apodaca

Mrs. Jerry Apodaca, Wife of Governor (New Mexico)

COUNTRY FRIED STEAK

8 minute steaks
salt and pepper
flour
margarine, melted
2 small cans sliced mushrooms, drained
1 large onion, chopped

garlic powder to taste
Worcestershire sauce
soy sauce
oregano
Tabasco
boiling water

Season each steak with salt and pepper. Place a generous amount of flour on a platter and roll the meat over and over in it, rubbing it well into both sides until completely coated. Brown each steak in margarine, adding more margarine as needed, and remove to another dish. Add more margarine to the skillet and cook the mushrooms and onion in it until onion is transparent and a little brown. While they are cooking, add garlic powder, Worcestershire, soy sauce, oregano, Tabasco and any flour left from the coating of the meat. Mix and cook until done. Leaving onion on the bottom, return steaks to skillet, layer by layer. Pour boiling water slowly into skillet until steak pieces are just covered. Stir gently but thoroughly mix the liquid, onion and seasoning. Lower heat, cover tightly and cook at least 2 hours until steak is very tender and gravy is thick. Stir occasionally, moving the meat pieces to prevent them from burning.

Mrs. James B. Allen

Mrs. James B. Allen, Wife of Senator (Alabama)

BRAISED STEAKS

1 large onion, sliced
2 to 4 tablespoons corn oil
¼ teaspoon thyme
6 8 ounce beef round steaks
seasoned salt
flour

1 cup V8 cocktail juice
1 cup beef broth
1½ cups mixed julienne strips of
    carrots, leeks and celery
2 tablespoons chopped parsley

In a large ovenproof skillet, saute onion in 1 tablespoon of the oil until golden. Remove from heat and add thyme. Set aside. Dust steaks on both sides with seasoned salt and flour. Heat remaining oil in an iron skillet and brown steaks on both sides. Transfer to pan with onions. Pour vegetable juice and broth over steaks. Cover and bake very slowly in the oven or simmer on top of the stove for 1 hour. Turn steaks, add the vegetables julienne and continue to cook for 30 minutes longer. To serve, spoon sauce and vegetables over steaks and sprinkle with parsley. Makes 6 servings.

MRS. RICHARD NIXON, Wife of former President of the United States (California)

ROUND STEAK

round steak
½ package dry onion soup mix

1 can cream of mushroom soup

Place round steak, cut in serving pieces, in a buttered casserole. Sprinkle dry onion soup mix over the meat. Spread mushroom soup over all. Cover and bake at 300° for 3 hours. Makes 4 servings.

Note: Do not add salt as the soups contain enough salt.

MRS. ARTHUR A. LINK, Wife of Governor (North Dakota)

ROUND STEAK WITH MUSHROOM STUFFING

1 medium onion, finely chopped	¼ teaspoon sage
1 9 ounce can sliced mushrooms, drained	1½ pounds round steak
	salt and pepper to taste
2 tablespoons melted butter or margarine	flour
	cooking oil
1 cup bread crumbs	¼ cup water
¼ teaspoon thyme	

Saute onion and mushrooms in butter; add bread crumbs, thyme and sage, stirring well. Season steak with salt and pepper and spread with crumb mixture. Roll up steak, fasten with skewers and dredge in flour. Brown in hot oil. Add water. Cover and bake at 325° for 45 minutes or until meat is tender. Makes 6 servings.

Mrs. Bill Hefner

Mrs. BILL HEFNER, Wife of Representative (North Carolina)

BEEF OLIVES

½ pound sausage meat	2 tablespoons corn oil
1 onion, finely chopped	1½ cups beef bouillon
3 tablespoons bread crumbs	1 teaspoon tomato paste
1 lemon rind, grated	1 tablespoon butter, softened
1 teaspoon salt	1½ tablespoons flour
¼ teaspoon black pepper	cooking wine (optional)
1 egg, lightly beaten	2 tablespoons parsley, chopped
1½ pounds round beef, tenderized	

Cook sausage. Add onion, bread crumbs, lemon rind, salt, pepper and egg. Spread on the beef and roll lengthwise. Tie with string in 4 places. Brown beef lightly in hot oil and place in glass baking dish. Combine bouillon and tomato paste and pour over meat. Cover with foil and bake at 350° for 1½ hours. Combine butter and flour and stir into beef broth to thicken. For a gourmet treat, English style, add a little wine during cooking and slice crosswise as with a filet. Garnish with parsley. May be frozen. Makes 6 servings.

Mrs. Helen D. Dingell

Mrs. HELEN H. DINGELL, Member of Congressional Club (Michigan)

GRILLED FLANK STEAK

flank steak
soy sauce
salt
freshly ground pepper
1 teaspoon dried thyme, crumbled

Sauce:

1¼ cups chopped shallots
1¼ cups red wine
1 stick butter
salt to taste
2 tablespoons chopped parsley

Brush flank steak with soy sauce and sprinkle well with salt, pepper and thyme. Let stand 1 hour. Combine shallots and wine and bring to a boil. Add butter, salt and parsley. Simmer. Brush steak again with soy sauce. Grill over brisk fire 5 to 6 minutes on each side for rare. Slice steak very thin on a diagonal and serve with wine sauce.

Mrs. Edward Hutchinson

MRS. EDWARD HUTCHINSON, Wife of Representative (Michigan)

BEEF KABOBS

⅔ cup chopped onion
¼ cup wine vinegar
½ cup salad oil
1 teaspoon salt
1 teaspoon pepper
1 tablespoon lemon juice

¼ cup Worcestershire sauce
1 pound steak, 1 inch thick, cubed
1 cup whole mushrooms
2 green peppers, sliced
3 tomatoes, quartered
Italian salad dressing

Combine onion, vinegar, oil, salt, pepper, lemon juice and Worcestershire sauce and mix well. Add meat and refrigerate overnight or let stand at room temperature for 2 to 3 hours. Before grilling or broiling, skewer meat alternately with mushrooms, peppers and tomatoes brushed with Italian dressing. Cook 2 to 3 minutes per side for rare meat or 5 to 6 minutes for well done meat. Makes 4 servings.

Mrs. Kevin E. VanderSchel

MRS. KEVIN VANDERSCHEL, Daughter of Representative Neal Smith (Iowa)

293

5 HOUR STEW

2 pounds chuck, cubed
4 to 6 carrots, sliced
1 cup sliced celery
2 onions, sliced

1 16 ounce can tomatoes
1½ tablespoons Minute tapioca
4 ounces white chestnuts, sliced
½ cup red wine

Put all ingredients together in large pot. Cover. Bake in 225° oven for 5 hours.
Makes 8 servings.

Mrs. John Sparkman

MRS. JOHN SPARKMAN, Wife of Senator (Alabama)

BEER BEEF STEW

1 to 2 pounds stewing beef, cubed
1 can mushroom soup
1 package dry onion soup mix
1 soup can beer (or wine)

1 package frozen soup vegetables
 (or fresh vegetables)
water as needed

Combine beef, soup, soup mix and beer in casserole and bake, covered, in a preheated
300° oven for 3 hours. Add vegetables and cook 1 additional hour. Increase cooking
time a little if fresh vegetables are used. Check occasionally and add a little water
if stew is not moist enough. May be frozen. Makes 6 servings.

Mrs. Joseph L. Carrigg

MRS. JOSEPH L. CARRIGG, Wife of former Representative (Pennsylvania)

DRUNKARD STEW

2 pounds stew beef, cut in 1 inch cubes
¾ cup dry vermouth
2 cans golden mushroom soup

½ package onion soup mix
cooked rice

Combine and mix all ingredients except rice and place in a greased baking dish.
Cover tightly and bake at 325° for at least 3 hours. Serve over rice. Makes 6
servings.

Mrs. Fred J. DeMeritte

MRS. FRED J. DeMERITTE, Daughter-in-law of former Associate Justice Hugo L. Black, Supreme Court

BLACK WALNUT STEW

6 pounds chuck rib, cut up
1 can beef broth
water
salt and pepper
1 large onion, halved

1 pound twice ground round
3 jars black pickled walnuts
¼ pound butter
5 or 6 tablespoons flour
cooked rice (or noodles)

Cover chuck with beef broth and water. Add seasonings and onion and cook slowly 4 hours or until tender. Skim off fat. Form ground round into small meat balls and add to boiling broth. Mash 1 jar of walnuts and add them with the juice to the broth. Continue cooking 1 hour. In a small pan cook and stir butter and flour until browned, add a little of the hot liquid, then stir mixture gradually into hot stew and cook until thickened. Add 2 jars of walnuts. Serve with rice or noodles. Makes 8 servings.

Mrs. Barry Goldwater

MRS. BARRY M. GOLDWATER, Wife of Senator (Arizona)

BURGUNDY STEW

2 pounds round steak, cut in 1 inch
   strips
2 cups sliced carrots
1 cup sliced celery
2 medium onions, sliced
1 5 ounce can water chestnuts, drained
   and sliced

1 6 ounce can mushrooms, drained
3 tablespoons flour
1 tablespoon sugar
1 tablespoon salt
1 1 pound can tomatoes
1 cup burgundy wine

Combine meat, carrots, celery, onions, water chestnuts and mushrooms in a Dutch oven. Mix together flour, sugar, and salt and stir into meat and vegetables. Stir in tomatoes and wine. Cover and cook 4 hours in a preheated 325° oven. Makes 6 servings.

Mrs. George Arthur Weaver

MRS. GEORGE ARTHUR WEAVER, Daughter of former Representative M. G. Burnside (West Virginia)

295

BEEF WITH WINE

2 cans condensed mushroom soup
1 envelope dry onion soup mix
¾ cup sherry

3 pounds sirloin chunks (or similar stew meat)
noodles or rice

Combine soup, soup mix and wine. Mix with meat and put into casserole. Cook covered at 325° for 3 hours. It will be the consistency of thin gravy. Serve over noodles or rice. Makes 6 servings.

Mrs James A. Rhodes

MRS. JAMES A. RHODES, Wife of Governor (Ohio)

BOEUF BOURGUIGNONNE

½ pound salt pork, cut in 1 inch squares
24 small white onions
4 pounds chuck beef, cut in 2 inch cubes
2½ tablespoons flour
freshly ground pepper
1 or 2 garlic cloves, crushed
½ teaspoon dried orange peel

2 small bay leaves
1 sprig thyme
1 sliver nutmeg (or mace)
½ teaspoon marjoram (or oregano)
dry red table wine, heated
1 cup tiny button mushrooms
butter
4 sprigs parsley, finely chopped

Fry salt pork in heavy pan or Dutch oven until crisp and brown. Remove pork and keep warm. Saute onions in pork fat until brown. Remove onions and set aside. Brown beef cubes in remaining fat. Return salt pork to pan and sprinkle with flour. Add pepper, garlic, orange peel and all spices, mixing thoroughly. Add sufficient wine to cover meat completely. Cover tightly and cook over very low heat or in a 250° oven about 3 hours. If mixture becomes dry, add more hot wine. About 15 minutes before serving, brown mushrooms in butter. Add with browned onions to the meat mixture. Sprinkle generously with parsley. Makes 8 to 10 servings.

Mrs. Robert A. Grant

MRS. ROBERT A. GRANT, Wife of former Representative (Indiana)

296

SHERRIED BEEF

3 pounds sirloin (or round steak), cut
in ½ inch pieces
2 cans cream of mushroom soup

½ pound fresh mushrooms (or 6 ounce
can)
¾ cup sherry
½ package Lipton onion soup mix

Combine all ingredients, place in casserole and bake at 325° for 3 hours or at
300° for 4 hours. May be frozen. Makes 6 servings.

Mrs. Henry J. Nowak

MRS. HENRY J. NOWAK, Wife of Representative (New York)

HUNGARIAN GOULASH

3 pounds beef chuck, cubed
¼ cup salad oil
1 pound onions, peeled and sliced
1 tablespoon paprika
1½ teaspoons salt

⅛ teaspoon pepper
1 can beef bouillon
3 tablespoons flour
1 cup dairy sour cream

Brown meat in oil until browned on all sides. Remove meat from Dutch oven
and add onions. Saute onions until golden brown. Return meat to the pan and
add paprika, salt and pepper, stirring until well blended. Stir in ¾ cup bouillon
and bring to a boil. Reduce heat and simmer for 2 hours. Combine flour and
remaining bouillon, stirring until smooth. Add to beef mixture, stirring as it is added.
Cook an additional 15 minutes. Before serving, remove ½ cup of hot gravy from
the pan, blend with the sour cream and then return it to beef mixture, blending
well.

Mrs. Wm. J. Randall

MRS. WILLIAM J. RANDALL, Wife of Representative (Missouri)

BEEF STROGANOFF

1½ pounds lean round steak, cubed
1 cup flour
1 tablespoon fines herbs
cooking oil
½ cup diced sweet onion
2 cubes beef bouillon
1¼ cups boiling water
½ cup diced dill pickles

1 6 ounce can tomato paste
1 cup sherry
1 teaspoon dry mustard
1 tablespoon Worcestershire sauce
1 4 ounce can mushrooms
½ cup sour cream
1 pound package broad noodles

Shake steak cubes with flour and herbs in brown paper bag. Brown cubes in oil about 5 minutes. Saute onions until tender. Dissolve bouillon cubes in boiling water and mix with steak, onions, pickle, tomato paste, sherry, mustard, Worcestershire and mushrooms and simmer at 200° in an electric skillet for 2 hours. Add sour cream and simmer 15 minutes longer. Serve over broad noodles cooked according to package directions. May be frozen. Makes 6 servings.

Mrs. Richard P. Yates

MRS. RICHARD P. YATES, Daughter of Representative Wilbur D. Mills (Arkansas)

EASY BEEF STROGANOFF

5 pounds sirloin steak
4 tablespoons butter
1 pound fresh mushrooms, sliced
1 50 ounce can LeGout Sauce
   Stroganoff
paprika

pinch of nutmeg
2 tablespoons sherry
1 6 ounce box Uncle Ben's long grain
   wild rice
1⅓ cups Minute rice

Cut beef into slices ½ inch thick x 1 inch wide. Saute in butter, 1 pound at a time, until brown. Remove meat and saute mushrooms in same skillet. Return meat to pan and add stroganoff sauce with paprika and nutmeg. Add sherry just before serving. Serve with rice cooked according to package directions and mixed together. May be frozen. Makes 10 servings.

Mrs. J. Kenneth Robinson

MRS. J. KENNETH ROBINSON, Wife of Representative (Virginia)

298

WESTERN BEEF STROGANOFF

1½ cups chopped onion
2 garlic cloves, chopped
shortening (or bacon grease)
flour
3 pounds sirloin tip, sliced ⅓ inch
  thick
1 can tomato soup
1 can beef bouillon

2 tablespoons Worcestershire sauce
dash of Tabasco
1 teaspoon salt
¼ teaspoon pepper
½ pound fresh mushrooms
2 tablespoons butter (or margarine)
1½ cups dairy sour cream
cooked rice

Saute onions and garlic in fat in a Dutch oven until tender. Remove from pan. Flour meat slices and brown in the same skillet in additional shortening. Remove from pan. Bring soup and bouillon to a boil and add Worcestershire, Tabasco, salt and pepper. Return meat, onions and garlic to the soup mixture, cover and cook in 275° oven for 2 hours or until meat is tender. Saute mushrooms in butter and mix with meat. Stir in sour cream and keep warm below boiling point. Serve over rice. Makes 8 servings.

Mrs. John F. Baldwin

Mrs. John F. Baldwin, Wife of former Representative (California)

BEEF STROGANOFF

1½ pounds tenderloin of beef, cut into
  shoestring strips
salt and pepper to taste
1 tablespoon flour
2 tablespoons butter
2 cups beef bouillon

1 tablespoon tomato paste
½ pound mushrooms, sliced
butter
1 tablespoon chopped onion
2 tablespoons dairy sour cream
cooked noodles

Season the meat with the salt and pepper and let stand for 1 hour. Brown flour in the butter, making a smooth paste. Stir in bouillon gradually, stirring until ingredients come to a boil. Stir in tomato paste and mushrooms. Sear meat in butter with the chopped onion until brown. When meat is browned, add sauce and simmer 5 minutes. Add sour cream and heat through. Serve with noodles. Makes 6 servings.

Mrs. Phillip Burton

Mrs. Phillip Burton, Wife of Representative (California)

ROUND STEAK GOULASH

2 pounds round steak, cut in strips
1/4 cup flour
1/2 cup chopped onions
6 tablespoons butter
1 1/2 teaspoons salt
1/2 teaspoon pepper

1/2 cup water
1 4 ounce can mushrooms, undrained
1 cup cream of mushroom soup
1 cup dairy sour cream
rice or noodles

Dust steak with flour and brown with onions in butter. Add seasoning, water, mushrooms and soup and cook gently until beef is tender, 45 minutes to 1 hour. Turn off heat and add sour cream. Serve over rice or noodles. Makes 8 servings.

Mrs. John J. Duncan

MRS. JOHN J. DUNCAN, Wife of Representative (Tennessee)

BEEF TERIYAKI

2 pounds sirloin tip, sliced
2/3 cup soy sauce
1/3 cup sugar
1 teaspoon monosodium glutamate
2 tablespoons chopped green onion

1 teaspoon grated fresh ginger root
5 cloves garlic, minced
1 tablespoon sesame oil (optional)
1 tablespoon sesame seeds, roasted and crushed (optional)

Combine all ingredients except beef. Additional sugar may be added to sweeten. Marinate beef in sauce a half hour before grilling. May be frozen. Makes 4 to 5 servings.

Mrs. George Ariyoshi

MRS. GEORGE R. ARIYOSHI, Wife of Governor (Hawaii)

BEEF COOKED WITH PEEL OF MANDARIN ORANGE

1⅓ pounds beef tenderloin slices, ⅛ inch thick
½ cup Chinese rice wine
½ ounce soy sauce
6 ounces corn oil
12 ounces chicken broth
4 dried aniseed buds
4 scallions, chopped
½ ounce fresh ginger, minced

peel of 3 mandarin oranges, thinly sliced
4 shakes powdered cloves
¼ pound sugar
¼ cup vinegar
5 dried hot red peppers
1 tablespoon salt
½ tablespoon spice powder

Coat beef with rice wine and soy sauce. Cook in hot oil in a heavy frying pan until all water evaporates from beef. Add chicken broth, aniseed buds, ½ of the scallions, ½ of the ginger, orange peel, powdered cloves, sugar, vinegar and red peppers. Cover and simmer ½ hour. Just before serving add salt, spice powder, and remaining scallions and ginger. Red peppers may be removed. Serve hot or cold. May be frozen. Makes 4 to 6 servings.

Mrs. George Bush.

Mrs. George Bush, Wife of former Representative (Texas), presently Director of the Central Intelligence Agency

BEEF AND PEPPER RICE SKILLET

1½ pounds round steak, cut in thin strips
2 tablespoons cooking oil
1 cup sliced onion
1 cup Uncle Ben's converted rice

1 10½ ounce can beef broth
1 soup can water
3 tablespoons soy sauce
2 green peppers, coarsely chopped

Brown beef in oil in 10 inch skillet. Stir in onion, rice, beef broth, water and soy sauce. Bring to a boil. Reduce heat, cover and cook over low heat until liquid is absorbed, about 25 minutes. Stir in green pepper and heat through. Makes 4 to 6 servings.

Mrs. Jerry Litton

Mrs. Jerry Litton, Wife of Representative (Missouri)

CROWN MEAT LOAF

2 pounds ground beef
1 cup warm water
1 teaspoon Accent
2 eggs
1 package onion soup mix
1½ cups bread crumbs

Topping:
3 egg whites
½ teaspoon cream of tartar
½ cup mayonnaise

Mix beef with next 5 ingredients and form into a loaf. Bake in 350° oven for 1½ hours. Remove from oven and spread topping over it. Return to oven for 20 minutes or until it is lightly browned. Makes 6 servings.

Topping: Beat egg whites with cream of tartar until soft peaks form when beater is raised. Fold in mayonnaise.

Mrs. Bill Hefner

MRS. BILL HEFNER, Wife of Representative (North Carolina)

NOVEL MEAT LOAF

2 pounds ground beef
2 teaspoons salt
2 tablespoons chopped onion
⅛ teaspoon pepper

1½ cups condensed milk
3 cups hot mashed potatoes
1 teaspoon salt
dash of pepper

Combine first 4 ingredients with ¾ cup condensed milk. When well mixed, put on a sheet of wax paper and pat out to a rectangle about 8 x 12 x ⅓ inch thick. Combine remaining ingredients and beat together until light and fluffy. Form into a roll about 4 inches in diameter and 12 inches long. Place lengthwise in center of meat rectangle. With the aid of the wax paper, wrap meat around potatoes. Remove paper and put roll in greased baking pan. Bake in 400° oven 45 minutes or until brown. Makes 6 servings.

Mrs. Russell V. Mack

MRS. RUSSELL V. MACK, Wife of former Representative (Washington)

TOMATO MEAT LOAF

2½ cups condensed tomato soup
1 pound hamburger
½ cup cracker crumbs
1 small onion

1 tablespoon Worcestershire sauce
1 teaspoon salt
¼ teaspoon pepper

Mix ½ cup soup with other ingredients and bake at 350° for 1 hour. Use remaining soup as a topping to the meat loaf the last 15 minutes of baking time. May be frozen. Makes 8 servings.

Mrs. Jerry Litton

MRS. JERRY LITTON, Wife of Representative (Missouri)

MEAT LOAF DE LUXE

2 pounds lean ground beef
1 cup oats
1 8 ounce can tomato sauce
2 eggs
1 tablespoon Worcestershire sauce

1 teaspoon thyme
salt and pepper

Optional:
hollandaise or bearnaise sauce
cooked green vegetable

Mix together first 7 ingredients. Place in lightly greased tube pan. Bake 45 minutes in a preheated 350° oven. Place on a round platter and pour over it any favorite sauce such as hollandaise or bearnaise. Fill the center with a green vegetable. Makes 8 servings.

Mrs. Alfred D. Sieminski

MRS. ALFRED D. SIEMINSKI, Wife of former Representative (New Jersey)

TASTY MEAT LOAF

1 pound each ground beef, veal and
   pork
1 medium onion, finely chopped
3 tablespoons minced parsley
2 eggs
2 tablespoons flour
2 tablespoons bread crumbs

1½ teaspoons salt
1 teaspoon ground pepper
¼ teaspoon paprika
¼ teaspoon oregano
¼ teaspoon thyme
1 6 ounce can V8 juice
3 strips bacon

Combine all ingredients except bacon and mix well to make certain everything
is blended together. Put in an ungreased meat loaf pan, pressing mixture down
so there are no air pockets. Place the bacon strips on top. Put in preheated 350°
oven for 1½ hours. May be frozen. Makes 8 servings.

Mrs. George M. O'Brien

MRS. GEORGE M. O'BRIEN, Wife of Representative (Illinois)

SWISS MEAT LOAF

2 pounds ground beef
1½ cups diced Swiss cheese
2 eggs, beaten
½ cup chopped onion
½ cup chopped green pepper (optional)
1½ teaspoons salt

½ teaspoon pepper
1 teaspoon celery salt
½ teaspoon paprika
2½ cups milk
1 cup dry bread crumbs
⅓ cup cooking sherry

Mix all ingredients, except sherry, in the order listed. Press into greased loaf pan.
Bake, uncovered, at 350° for 1 hour. Add sherry and bake another half hour.
May be frozen. Makes 6 to 8 servings.

Mrs. James E. Van Zandt

MRS. JAMES E. VAN ZANDT, Wife of former Representative (Pennsylvania)

MEAT LOAF

1 pound ground chuck
½ pound lean ground pork
¾ cup quick cooking rolled oats
2 eggs, beaten
¼ cup chopped onion
  (or 2 teaspoons onion salt)
1 teaspoon salt

¼ teaspoon pepper
1 teaspoon celery salt
½ teaspoon thyme
½ teaspoon sage
2 teaspoons Worcestershire sauce
1 cup tomato juice
3 slices salt pork

Combine meat, oats, eggs, onion, seasonings and tomato juice thoroughly and pack into a loaf pan. Cover with salt pork. Bake for 1 hour at 400°. Let stand for 5 minutes before slicing. May be frozen. Makes 6 servings.

Mrs Lionel Van Deerlin

Mrs. Lionel Van Deerlin, Wife of Representative (California)

ECONOMY MEAT LOAF

1 pound ground beef
½ cup uncooked rolled oats
¼ teaspoon celery salt
1 teaspoon salt
¼ teaspoon pepper

1 egg
⅔ cup milk
¼ cup catsup
2 tablespoons minced onion

Combine all ingredients and mix thoroughly. Pack into lightly buttered small loaf pan. Bake in 350° oven 1 hour. Let stand 5 minutes before slicing. May be frozen. Makes 6 servings.

Amy Gronna Cowing

Mrs. Amy Gronna Cowing, Daughter of former Senator A. J. Gronna (North Dakota)

BARBECUED MEAT LOAF

1½ pounds ground beef
1 cup fresh bread crumbs
1 onion, chopped
1 egg, slightly beaten
1½ teaspoons salt
¼ teaspoon pepper
½ 8 ounce can tomato sauce

Barbecue Sauce:
1½ 8 ounce cans tomato sauce
½ cup water
3 tablespoons vinegar
3 tablespoons brown sugar
2 tablespoons prepared mustard
2 teaspoons Worcestershire sauce

Combine ground beef, crumbs, onion, egg, salt, pepper and tomato sauce and mix well. Press into a loaf pan. Blend sauce ingredients, mix well and pour over meat loaf. Bake in a 350° oven for 1¼ hours. May be frozen. Makes 6 servings.

Mrs. Armistead I. Selden

MRS. ARMISTEAD I. SELDEN, Wife of former Representative (Alabama), presently Ambassador to New Zealand

RICE AND BEEF DRESSING CASSEROLE

2 pounds lean ground beef
1 cup chopped white onions
1 cup chopped celery
1 cup chopped sweet green peppers

dry mustard, salt, pepper and cayenne
   pepper to taste
water as needed
1 cup short grain rice
2 cups water

Saute beef in large, heavy saucepan (preferably black cast iron), until well browned. Add half the chopped vegetables and seasonings. Continue to cook over low heat for about 1 hour, keeping moist by adding small amounts of water as needed.

After meat mixture has simmered 1 hour, add remaining chopped vegetables and correct seasoning. Continue to cook approximately 45 additional minutes, adding small amounts of water as needed. In the meantime, cook rice in water. When ready to serve, combine rice with meat mixture and serve at once. Makes 10 to 12 servings.

Mrs. Edwin W. Edwards

MRS. EDWIN W. EDWARDS, Wife of Governor (Louisiana)

306

WILD RICE CASSEROLE

½ pound ground beef
1 cup wild rice
1 can cream of mushroom soup
1 can chicken with rice soup
2 soup cans water

½ pound smoked sausage, cut in small pieces
1 teaspoon soy sauce
½ cup diced onions

Brown ground beef and drain fat. Mix remaining ingredients with beef. Put in greased casserole. Bake uncovered at 350° for 1½ to 2 hours. May be frozen. Makes 8 servings.

Mrs. Earl L. Butz

MRS. EARL LAUER BUTZ, Wife of Secretary of Agriculture (Indiana)

AFTER SKI HAMBURGER CHEESE BAKE

1 pound ground beef
½ cup chopped onion
2 8 ounce cans tomato sauce
1 teaspoon sugar
¾ teaspoon salt
¼ teaspoon garlic salt
¼ teaspoon pepper

4 cups uncooked medium noodles
1 cup cream style cottage cheese
1 8 ounce package cream cheese, softened
¼ cup dairy sour cream
⅓ cup sliced green onion
¼ cup chopped green pepper
¼ cup shredded parmesan cheese

In large skillet, cook meat and onion until meat is lightly browned and onion is tender. Stir in tomato sauce, sugar, salt, garlic salt and pepper. Remove from heat. Meanwhile, cook noodles according to package directions. Drain. In a separate bowl, combine cottage cheese, cream cheese, sour cream, green onion and green pepper. Spread ½ the noodles in an 11 x 7 x 1½ inch baking dish and top with a little of the meat sauce. Cover with the cheese mixture. Add remaining noodles and meat sauce. Sprinkle with parmesan cheese. Bake at 350° for 30 minutes. This may be prepared early in the day and refrigerated until baking time. Makes 8 to 10 servings.

Mrs. Frank Church

MRS. FRANK CHURCH, Wife of Senator (Idaho)

BOEUF A LA CREME

1 large package cream cheese
1 pint sour cream
2½ pounds ground chuck
1 onion, diced
1 teaspoon salt

½ teaspoon pepper
½ teaspoon garlic salt
2 10 ounce cans tomato sauce
1 8 ounce package noodles
½ pound sharp cheddar cheese, grated

Blend cream cheese and sour cream. Brown meat in its own juices, add onion, salt, pepper, garlic salt and tomato sauce and let simmer for 20 minutes. Cook noodles, drain and line a 9 x 13 inch glass baking dish with them. Add cream cheese mixture to the meat and pour over noodles. Sprinkle grated cheese on top of casserole. Bake at 325° for 40 minutes. Makes 6 to 8 servings.

Miss Susan H. Boren

MISS SUSAN HOPE BOREN, Daughter of former Representative Lyle H. Boren (Oklahoma)

MACARONI DELIGHT

1 8 ounce package shell macaroni
2 pounds beef chuck, ground
3 medium onions, chopped
1 green pepper, chopped
3 cloves garlic, chopped
¼ pound butter
4 8 ounce cans tomato sauce
1 can whole kernel corn, drained
1 3 ounce can mushrooms, undrained

1 cup grated sharp cheddar cheese
1 tablespoon brown sugar
1 tablespoon Worcestershire sauce
½ cup sherry
1 teaspoon salt
¼ teaspoon pepper
1 tablespoon chili powder (optional)

Cook macaroni according to directions. Drain. Saute small amounts of meat, onions, green pepper and garlic in butter. With a slotted spoon transfer the browned meat and vegetables to a large mixing bowl. When all meat is cooked, stir in all remaining ingredients, except macaroni, and mix thoroughly. Finally, add the macaroni and toss carefully. Refrigerate overnight. This is very important. Bake covered in a 350° oven for 1 hour 55 minutes. Makes 10 to 12 servings.

Mrs. Melvin Price

MRS. MELVIN PRICE, Wife of Representative (Illinois)

308

BISCUITBURGER CASSEROLE

1 pound ground beef
½ cup chopped onion
¼ cup diced green pepper
1 8 ounce can tomato sauce
½ teaspoon garlic salt
2 teaspoons chili powder

½ cup shredded pizza cheese
½ cup dairy sour cream
1 egg, slightly beaten
1 8 ounce can biscuits
4 slices American cheese

Brown ground beef, onion and green pepper. Drain. Stir in tomato sauce, garlic salt and chili powder and simmer. Combine pizza cheese, sour cream and egg and mix well. Remove meat mixture from heat and stir in sour cream mixture. Separate biscuits into halves. Put 10 halves into bottom of a 9 x 9 inch pan. Spoon meat sauce over biscuits. Arrange other biscuits on top of meat and cover with slices of American cheese. Bake at 375° for 25 to 30 minutes until golden brown. Makes 4 servings.

Mrs. David Jack Dixon

Mrs. DAVID JACK DIXON, Daughter of Representative Wilbur D. Mills (Arkansas)

TACO PIE

1½ pounds ground chuck
1 large yellow onion, chopped
2 garlic cloves, minced
1 10 ounce can Las Palmas red chili sauce
1 8 ounce can tomato sauce
1 small can Oretega green chili salsa
½ cup water

1 small can olives, chopped
2 hard cooked eggs, chopped
½ teaspoon salt
1 small can whole kernel corn
8 tortillas
¾ pound jack cheese, grated
grated parmesan cheese

Brown meat with onion and garlic. Combine red chili sauce, tomato sauce, ½ can green chili salsa and water in pan and heat. Add ½ cup of this sauce to meat along with the remaining green chili salsa, olives, eggs, salt and corn. Mix well. Using half the tortillas, dip each one in the remaining sauce and place in bottom of casserole dish. Layer over them, in the order given, the meat mixture, jack cheese and parmesan cheese. Repeat these layers. Top with more tortillas and sprinkle with parmesan. Pour remaining sauce over all. Bake, covered, in 350° oven for 35 to 40 minutes. Makes 10 to 12 servings.

Mrs. Harold T. Johnson

Mrs. HAROLD T. JOHNSON, Wife of Representative (California)

NAN'S CHILI CON CARNE

4 slices bacon
2 large onions, chopped
1½ pounds ground beef
2 21 ounce cans dark red kidney beans

1 20 ounce can tomatoes
salt and pepper to taste
1 teaspoon Gebhardt's chili powder

Brown bacon slowly in frying pan. Add chopped onions, saute in fat until golden and drain. Add ground meat and brown. Add beans, tomatoes, salt, pepper and chili powder. Pour into large casserole and bake in 325° oven at least 1 hour. May be prepared, refrigerated overnight and reheated at serving time. Makes 4 to 6 servings.

Mrs Charles A. Vanik

MRS. CHARLES A. VANIK, Wife of Representative (Ohio)

TOMATO CHOW MEIN CASSEROLE

2 pounds ground beef
butter or margarine
1 medium onion, chopped
1 can bean sprouts
1 can water chestnuts, sliced
1 8 ounce can tomato sauce
1 cup chopped celery

1 8 ounce can sliced mushrooms with juice
1 package frozen peas
1 can chow mein noodles
½ cup chopped cashews (or slivered almonds)

Brown beef in butter with onion. Mix with remaining ingredients, except noodles and nuts, and pour into greased casserole. Bake about 30 minutes or until hot and bubbly. Top with noodles and nuts and return to oven until noodles are hot. May be frozen. Makes 8 servings.

Mrs. James E. Van Zandt

MRS. JAMES E. VAN ZANDT, Wife of former Representative (Pennsylvania)

310

ORIENTAL MEAL-IN-ONE

Meat balls:
- 1½ pounds ground beef
- 2 cups ready to eat high protein cereal
- ½ cup finely chopped onion
- ⅔ cup milk
- 1 egg
- 2 tablespoons chopped parsley
- 1 tablespoon soy sauce
- 1 teaspoon salt
- ⅛ teaspoon garlic powder
- cooking oil

Other Ingredients:
- 1 can chicken broth
- 1 6 ounce package frozen Chinese pea pods, defrosted
- 1 tablespoon corn starch
- 1 tablespoon soy sauce
- 1 can water chestnuts, drained and sliced
- 1 medium tomato, cut in thin wedges

Combine all meat ball ingredients except oil. Shape into 32 balls using a rounded tablespoon. In a large skillet brown balls in cooking oil over moderate heat. Drain off excess fat. Add ½ cup chicken broth to meat balls; cover. Cook slowly until meat balls are done, about 30 minutes. Add pea pods, cover and heat through. Blend together the remaining chicken broth, corn starch and soy sauce. Add this mixture to meat balls. Cook until sauce is clear and thickened. Add water chestnuts and tomato wedges. Heat well. Serve with additional soy sauce if desired. Makes 8 servings.

Mrs. Fred E. Busbey

MRS. FRED E. BUSBEY, Wife of former Representative (Illinois)

HAZEL'S HOT DISH

- 2 pounds ground beef
- 1 small onion, chopped
- 1 can mixed vegetables
- 1 can mushroom soup
- 1 box Potato Buds

Saute meat and onion. Add vegetables and soup. Top with Potato Buds fixed according to package directions. Bake 30 minutes in a 350° oven.

Mrs. Odin Langen

MRS. ODIN LANGEN, Wife of former Representative (Minnesota)

GROUND MEAT AND EGGPLANT CASSEROLE

1 medium size eggplant
4 teaspoons salt
3 tablespoons butter or margarine
3 medium sized onions, chopped
3 cups diced fresh tomatoes
1 teaspoon paprika
¼ teaspoon pepper

1 teaspoon ground nutmeg
1 pound ground beef
½ pound ground pork
1 cup soft bread crumbs
2 tablespoons melted butter
½ cup shredded cheddar cheese

Wash eggplant and cut crosswise into ½ inch slices. Peel slices, sprinkle with 1 teaspoon salt and set aside. Heat butter in a skillet and saute onions and tomatoes. Add remaining salt, paprika, pepper, nutmeg, beef and pork. Mix well. Cook five minutes or until lightly browned. Rinse eggplant slices in cold water. Place alternate layers of meat mixture and eggplant in a 13 x 9 x 2 inch baking dish, beginning and ending with meat. Cover with foil and bake in a preheated 350° oven for 40 minutes. Remove foil, sprinkle with soft bread crumbs mixed with melted butter and cheese. Bake 10 minutes or until brown. Makes 8 servings.

Mrs. Garner E. Shriver

MRS. GARNER E. SHRIVER, Wife of Representative (Kansas)

ARMENIAN MOUSSAKA (EGGPLANT WITH GROUND BEEF)

1 large eggplant
corn oil to coat eggplant
1 tablespoon corn oil
1 pound lean ground beef
½ cup chopped onion
1 small clove garlic, finely chopped

3 tablespoons chopped parsley
salt to taste
paprika to taste
3 large tomatoes, sliced ¼ inch thick
3 to 4 tablespoons boiling water

Wash and dry eggplant. Peel skin in alternate strips so that skin remains on every other row. Slice lengthwise approximately ¼ inch thick and coat very lightly with corn oil. Place eggplant under heated broiler until light brown on both sides. Place tablespoon of corn oil into frypan, add ground meat. Heat, separate meat particles and stir constantly with large fork until cooked. Add onion and cook uncovered 7 to 8 minutes. Add garlic, parsley, salt and paprika. In another large frypan, alternate layers of eggplant, cooked meat and tomatoes. Add boiling water, cover, cook at high heat on top of stove to boiling point. Then lower heat to about the simmering stage and continue cooking for about 20 to 25 minutes. Makes 3 to 4 servings.

Mrs. George, E. Danielson

MRS. GEORGE E. DANIELSON, Wife of Representative (California)

NON CHILI CHILI

½ stick butter
2 onions, chopped
1 pound ground round steak
salt and pepper to taste
1 large can Redeye kidney beans
Tabasco to taste

Worcestershire sauce to taste
1 large can tomato juice

Garnish:
shredded lettuce (or shredded cheese,
    chopped onion, fritos or saltines)

Melt butter in a large skillet and saute onions until clear and yellow. Crumble the ground round and add to onion, cooking and stirring until meat is no longer red. Season with salt and pepper. Add kidney beans, Tabasco and Worcestershire, mixing well. Add enough tomato juice to fill skillet and simmer for at least 6 hours, stirring occasionally and adding more tomato juice as needed. Garnish with shredded lettuce.

Mrs. Bill Brock

MRS. BILL BROCK, Wife of Senator (Tennessee)

ITALIAN SHELLS

1 package jumbo pasta shells
cooking oil
4 cups spaghetti sauce
1 pound ground beef (or Italian
    sausage)
1 clove garlic, chopped

1 pound ricotta cheese
1 egg
1 teaspoon sweet basil
salt and pepper
mozzarella cheese

Partially cook shells in boiling salted water with a little oil. Spread a little spaghetti sauce over the bottom of a greased 11 x 13 inch baking dish. Brown beef with garlic, add remaining spaghetti sauce and simmer until cooked. Combine ricotta cheese, egg, sweet basil, salt and pepper and fill each shell with the mixture. Layer the filled shells over the sauce in the baking dish and cover with the sauce and meat mixture. Top with mozzarella cheese. Bake at 350° for 20 minutes or until bubbly. Makes 6 to 8 servings.

Mrs. Howard Robison

MRS. HOWARD ROBISON, Wife of former Representative (New York)

LASAGNE

1 pound ground beef
½ pound pork sausage
1 clove garlic, minced
1½ tablespoons parsley flakes
1 tablespoon basil
1½ teaspoons salt
1 1 pound can tomatoes
2 6 ounce cans tomato paste

3 cups cream style cottage cheese
2 tablespoons parsley flakes
2 beaten eggs
2 tablespoons salt
½ teaspoon pepper
¾ cup freshly grated parmesan cheese
10 ounces lasagne noodles
1 pound mozzarella cheese, thinly sliced

Brown meat slowly, spooning off excess fat. Add next 6 ingredients. Simmer uncovered 30 minutes to blend flavors, stirring occasionally. Combine cottage cheese with parsley, eggs, seasonings and parmesan cheese. Cook noodles in boiling salted water until tender; drain, rinse in cold water. Place half the noodles in a 13 x 9 x 2 inch baking dish, spread half the cottage cheese mixture over them, then half the mozzarella cheese and half the meat sauce. Repeat layers. Bake at 375° for 30 minutes. Let stand for 15 minutes before cutting into squares. May be frozen. Makes 12 servings.

Mrs. William E. Simon

MRS. WILLIAM E. SIMON, Wife of the Secretary of the Treasury (Virginia)

AMERICAN LASAGNE

6 lasagne noodles
1½ pounds ground beef
2 cloves garlic, chopped
1 onion, chopped
1½ teaspoons salt
¼ teaspoon pepper

2 tablespoons olive oil
23 ounces tomato sauce
American cheese slices
cottage cheese
grated parmesan cheese

Cook noodles in boiling salted water 15 minutes. Drain and rinse in cold water. Brown beef, garlic and onion with salt and pepper in oil. Add tomato sauce and cook 30 minutes. In buttered 12 inch baking dish, arrange layers of 2 noodles, American cheese slices, cottage cheese and ⅓ of meat mixture. Repeat these 4 layers twice. Top with parmesan cheese and bake at 350° for 1 hour. May be frozen before baking. Makes 8 servings.

Mrs. Edward V. Long

MRS. EDWARD V. LONG, Wife of former Senator (Missouri)

LAGO LASAGNE

8 tablespoons butter
1 cup olive oil
4 whole green onions, chopped
1 pound lean ground beef
½ cup chopped parsley
3 celery stalks with tops, chopped
3 carrots, grated
1 cup cooked spinach, drained
2 6 ounce cans tomato sauce
1 cup Half and Half cream
2 garlic cloves, crushed
2 teaspoons oregano

1 tablespoon salt
¼ teaspoon pepper
1 tablespoon olive oil
salt
boiling water
1 pound lasagne noodles
1 pound mozzarella cheese, in
  shoestring slices
1 8 ounce carton ricotta cheese
¼ pound brick parmesan cheese,
  grated

Combine butter and olive oil in a large deep saucepan. Add onions and meat and cook ½ hour over medium heat. Add parsley, celery, carrots, spinach and tomato sauce and cook ½ hour over low heat. Add cream, garlic, oregano, salt and pepper. Put 1 tablespoon olive oil and salt in large pan of boiling water, add noodles, cook uncovered 15 minutes. Spread 1 cup of sauce over bottom of greased 8 x 12 x 2 inch baking dish. Add a layer of noodles, mozzarella and ricotta. Repeat layers ending with sauce. Sprinkle with parmesan. Bake uncovered at 250° for 45 minutes. May be frozen. Makes 8 servings.

Mrs. Robert Lagomarsino

Mrs. Robert J. Lagomarsino, Wife of Representative (California)

EASY LASAGNE

8 ounces lasagne noodles
1 pound hamburger
dash of oregano
dash of garlic salt

1 29 ounce can tomato sauce
1 16 ounce carton cottage cheese
1 8 ounce package mozzarella cheese
1 8 ounce package parmesan cheese

Boil lasagne 20 minutes. Drain. Fry hamburger until lightly browned. Drain off fat and add oregano, garlic salt and tomato sauce to the meat. Layer noodles, cottage cheese and meat mixture in greased 9 x 12 inch baking dish. Top with mozzarella and parmesan cheese. Bake at 375° for 20 minutes. May be frozen before baking. Makes 8 servings.

Mrs. Frank E. Moss

Mrs. Frank E. Moss, Wife of Senator (Utah)

BAKED LASAGNE WITH ITALIAN SAUCE

Sauce:
1 pound lean ground beef
1 medium onion, minced
4 6 ounce cans tomato paste
9 tomato paste cans water
1 4 ounce can mushrooms, chopped
½ teaspoon minced garlic
½ teaspoon red pepper
1 teaspoon sweet basil
⅓ teaspoon sugar
salt to taste

Other Ingredients:
1 pound lasagne noodles
2 tablespoons salt
1 tablespoon oil
6 quarts boiling water
½ cup grated romano cheese
12 meat balls (optional)

To make sauce, brown ground beef and onions, add tomato paste and water and mix well. Add all other sauce ingredients and cook to a full boil. Reduce heat and simmer at least 3 hours, stirring occasionally.

Cook lasagne noodles as directed on package, adding salt and oil to the boiling water. Spread some meat sauce lightly over bottom of greased casserole. Cover with a layer of noodles, spread a thin covering of sauce over them and sprinkle with cheese. Repeat layers in the order given until all noodles and sauce are used, ending with the cheese. If desired, place meat balls evenly spaced on top of noodles. Cover with heavy aluminum foil and bake at 250° for 40 minutes. Cut into 4 inch squares and spoon sauce over top of each. May be frozen and then baked for 1 hour at 200° plus 40 minutes at 250°. Makes 8 servings.

MRS. ROMANO L. MAZZOLI, Wife of Representative (Kentucky)

BAKED MANICOTTI WITH CHEESE FILLING

Sauce:
⅓ cup olive oil
1½ cups finely chopped onion
1 clove garlic, crushed
1 35 ounce can Italian tomatoes, undrained
1 6 ounce can tomato paste
2 tablespoons chopped parsley
1 tablespoon salt
1 tablespoon sugar
1 teaspoon dried oregano leaves
1 teaspoon dried basil leaves
¼ teaspoon pepper
1½ pounds ground beef
1½ cups water

Manicotti:
6 eggs, at room temperature
1½ cups flour
¼ teaspoon salt
1½ cups water

Filling:
2 pounds ricotta cheese
1 8 ounce package mozzarella cheese, diced
½ cup grated parmesan cheese
2 eggs
1 teaspoon salt
¼ teaspoon pepper
1 tablespoon chopped parsley

Sauce: In hot oil in a 5 quart Dutch oven, saute onion and garlic 5 minutes. Mix in remaining sauce ingredients, mashing tomatoes with a fork. Bring to a boil and reduce heat. Simmer mixture, covered, stirring occasionally, for 1 hour.

Manicotti: Combine eggs, flour, salt and water and beat with an electric mixer just until smooth. Let stand at least ½ hour. Slowly heat an 8 inch skillet, pour in 3 tablespoons batter and rotate skillet quickly to spread batter evenly over bottom of skillet. Cook over medium heat until top is dry but bottom is not brown. Continue cooking until all batter is used. Cool on a wire rack. These shells may be frozen.

Filling: Combine ricotta, mozzarella, parmesan, eggs, salt, pepper and parsley. Beat with a wooden spoon. Spread about ¼ cup of filling on each manicotti, fold top over, place in baking dish and cover with sauce. Bake at 350° for ½ hour until bubbly.

Mrs. Patrick H. Mathews

Mrs. Patrick Mathews, Daughter of former Representative C. A. Fuller (Arkansas)

COLLEGE EDUCATED HAMBURGERS

1 pound boneless chuck beef, ground
3 tablespoons chili sauce
1 teaspoon Worcestershire sauce
1 tablespoon minced onion
1 teaspoon prepared mustard
1 teaspoon horse radish

¼ teaspoon mace
½ cup fine bread crumbs
salt and pepper to taste
tiny clove garlic, minced
   (or dash of garlic powder)
¼ cup consomme (or bouillon)

Combine all ingredients, mixing well. Shape gently into loose patties and broil.
May be frozen.

Mrs. RALPH S. REGULA, Wife of Representative (Ohio)

MOCK CHICKEN FRIED STEAK

1 egg
1 cup cracker crumbs (coarsely
   crumbled)
¼ cup milk
2 tablespoons chopped onion

¼ teaspoon salt
1 teaspoon chili powder
1 teaspoon Worcestershire sauce
1 pound lean ground beef
2 tablespoons cooking oil

Combine egg, ½ cup crumbs, milk, onion, salt, chili powder and Worcestershire.
Add ground beef and mix well. Shape into 6 patties ½ inch thick. Coat with
remaining cracker crumbs. Cook in hot oil over medium heat about 3 minutes
on each side.

Mrs. J. FLOYD BREEDING, Wife of former Representative (Kansas)

DILL BURGER

1 thick slice Bermuda onion
1 thick slice tomato
salt and pepper
1 teaspoon chopped dill

1 tablespoon chili sauce
¼ pound lean ground beef patty
1 slice provolone cheese

In a 2 x 4½ inch individual casserole dish place onion, tomato, salt, pepper, dill, chili
sauce, ground beef patty and cheese, in that order. Bake in 350° oven for 20
minutes. Makes 1 serving.

Mrs. GOODLOE BYRON, Wife of Representative (Maryland)

318

NORWEGIAN MEAT BALLS AND GRAVY

2 pounds hamburger
2 eggs, slightly beaten
¾ cup flour
1 cup milk
1 teaspoon salt
¼ teaspoon pepper
1 teaspoon nutmeg

¼ cup cooking oil
1 cup chopped onions
2 cans beef consomme
2 cans water
1 cup milk
¼ cup flour
2 tablespoons Heinz 57 sauce

Mix hamburger, eggs, flour, milk, salt, pepper and nutmeg. Form into balls 1¼ inches in diameter. Brown well on all sides in cooking oil. Set aside. Saute onions in same skillet in which meat balls were browned. Combine onions with the consomme and water. Bring to a boil and add meat balls. Simmer for 20 minutes. Remove meat balls from broth. Strain broth and thicken with the milk and flour. Season with the 57 sauce. Pour gravy over meat balls. Makes 8 servings.

Mrs. Wendell R. Anderson

Mrs. WENDELL R. ANDERSON, Wife of Governor (Minnesota)

SWEDISH MEAT BALLS

1 cup bread crumbs
½ cup milk
1 pound hamburger
¾ cup grated American cheese
¼ cup chopped green pepper

1 egg
flour
cooking oil
1 can mushroom soup
1 soup can milk

Soften bread crumbs in ½ cup milk and then add next 4 ingredients. Shape into balls; flour and brown slightly in cooking oil. Meat balls may be frozen at this stage of preparation. Place in baking dish. Cover with a mixture of soup and milk. Bake at 325° for 30 minutes. Makes 6 servings.

Mrs. Jerry Litton

Mrs. JERRY LITTON, Wife of Representative (Missouri)

SWEET AND SOUR MEAT BALLS

1½ pounds ground beef
2 eggs
4 tablespoons corn starch
1 onion, minced
¼ teaspoon pepper
¼ teaspoon nutmeg
1 teaspoon salt
¼ teaspoon garlic powder
2 tablespoons salad oil

1¼ cups pineapple juice
1 tablespoon soy sauce
3 tablespoons wine vinegar
⅓ cup water
½ cup brown sugar
1 16 ounce can pineapple chunks
2 green peppers, diced
½ cup chopped toasted almonds
cooked rice

Blend together beef, eggs, 1 teaspoon corn starch, onion, pepper, nutmeg, salt and garlic powder. Shape into 1 inch balls and brown on all sides in heated oil. Combine remaining corn starch and pineapple juice, add soy sauce, vinegar, water and brown sugar and cook until thickened, stirring constantly. Add meat balls, pineapple and green peppers and cook about 5 minutes or until fruit is well heated. Sprinkle with almonds and serve with hot fluffy rice. May be frozen before the pineapple and green peppers are added to the meat balls. Makes 6 to 8 servings.

Mrs. Armistead I. Selden

MRS. ARMISTEAD I. SELDEN, Wife of former Representative (Alabama), presently Ambassador to New Zealand

MEAT BALLS

¼ loaf Italian bread
water
2 pounds ground beef
½ cup grated Italian romano cheese
2 cloves of garlic, pressed

1 tablespoon salt
½ teaspoon black pepper
3 eggs
3 tablespoons chopped parsley
cooking oil

Tear bread into pieces and soak in water. Drain in colander and squeeze out any excess liquid. Combine with other ingredients except cooking oil and blend together. Cook in oil over moderate heat.

Mrs. Frank Annunzio

MRS. FRANK ANNUNZIO, Wife of Representative (Illinois)

GLADYS' MEAT BALLS

1½ pounds ground round (or chuck)	*Gravy:*
5 saltines, rolled into crumbs	2 tablespoons flour
2 eggs, beaten until fluffy	1 cup consomme
¼ cup milk	½ cup water
1 teaspoon Worcestershire sauce	salt to taste
½ onion, finely chopped (optional)	pepper to taste
salt and pepper	1 4 ounce can mushrooms, drained
flour	(optional)
oil	

Mix all ingredients for meat balls except flour and oil. Form into balls the size of a large walnut. Roll in flour and brown in the oil. Put meat balls in 1½ quart casserole. To make gravy discard all but 2 tablespoons of fat from skillet. Brown flour in the fat. Gradually add consomme, water and seasonings. Cook and stir until slightly thickened. Add mushrooms and pour over meatballs. Cover and bake at 350° for 30 minutes. May be frozen. Makes 6 to 8 servings.

Mrs. Thomas S. Kleppe

MRS. THOMAS S. KLEPPE, Wife of former Representative (North Dakota), presently Secretary of the Interior

GROUND MEAT AND TOMATO SAUCE

1 pound ground round	½ green pepper, chopped
½ teaspoon salt	¼ teaspoon oregano
1 small onion	1 large can tomato sauce
1 tablespoon Worcestershire sauce	spaghetti or rice

Brown meat, add other ingredients and simmer for about 20 minutes. May be used over spaghetti or rice. May be frozen. Makes 4 servings.

Mrs. Spiro T. Agnew

MRS. SPIRO T. AGNEW, Wife of former Vice President (Maryland)

SPAGHETTI SAUCE WITH HAMBURGER

2 pounds hamburger
4 12 ounce cans spaghetti sauce
2 teaspoons marjoram
2 teaspoons garlic salt
1 teaspoon salt

1 teaspoon pepper
½ cup chopped green peppers
½ cup chopped onions
4 4 ounce cans mushrooms
spaghetti

Brown hamburger and drain off fat. Add remaining ingredients except spaghetti and simmer 10 minutes. Serve over cooked spaghetti.

Mrs. Tolise G. Norwood

MRS. TOLISE G. NORWOOD, Daughter of former Representative E. C. Gathings (Arkansas)

VEAL CHOPS IN CASSEROLE

¾ stick butter
6 veal loin chops, 1 inch thick
1½ teaspoons salt
½ teaspoon black pepper
1 cup dry bread crumbs
2 cloves
6 small white onions

½ pound mushrooms, sliced
1 large clove garlic, minced
1 cup dry white wine
3 cups beef broth
1 bay leaf
¼ teaspoon thyme
3 tablespoons parsley, minced

Melt the butter in a large flameproof casserole or Dutch oven. Dust the chops with the salt and pepper and brown on both sides in the hot butter over medium heat. When well browned, remove the chops to a hot dish and keep warm. Stir bread crumbs into the butter remaining in the casserole and saute until browned. Return the chops to the casserole. Stick the cloves into 2 of the onions. Add all the onions to the casserole. Add the mushrooms, garlic, wine, beef broth, bay leaf and thyme. Cover the casserole and bake in 375° oven for about 1 hour. Remove the cover for the last 15 minutes to allow the sauce to thicken a little. Sprinkle with the parsley. This may be served directly from the casserole or the chops may be arranged on a deep platter with the sauce and vegetables spooned over them. Makes 6 servings.

Mrs. Brendan T. Byrne

MRS. BRENDAN T. BYRNE, Wife of Governor (New Jersey)

322

JERRY'S VEAL PARMESAN

1½ pounds veal scaloppine
2 eggs, beaten
seasoned bread crumbs
olive oil
1 8 ounce package sliced mozzarella
    cheese
¼ cup parmesan cheese

Sauce:
½ cup chopped onion
1 clove garlic, minced
2 tablespoons olive oil
1 can Italian tomatoes
2 teaspoons sugar
1 teaspoon salt
½ teaspoon oregano
¼ teaspoon basil
¼ teaspoon pepper

Dip veal in eggs, then crumbs and brown in oil. Place in large baking dish, cover with mozzarella cheese and parmesan cheese. Cover with foil and bake at 350° 30 to 45 minutes. Serve with sauce. May be frozen. Makes 6 servings.

Sauce: Saute the onion and garlic in hot oil until soft but not brown. Add remaining ingredients. Simmer while preparing meat.

Mrs. William H. Harsha

Mrs. WILLIAM H. HARSHA, Wife of Representative (Ohio)

VEAL AND WILD RICE CASSEROLE

1 tablespoon shortening
1 pound veal, cut in 1 inch cubes
1 teaspoon salt
1 package Wilderness precooked wild
    rice
1 can cream of mushroom soup

¼ cup chopped onion
½ cup chopped celery
½ teaspoon Worcestershire sauce
2 tablespoons sherry
¼ cup grated cheese

Melt shortening and brown veal. Add all remaining ingredients except cheese. Mix well. Pour into greased 1½ quart casserole. Sprinkle cheese over top. Bake at 350° about 50 minutes. Makes 4 servings.

Mrs. Harrison A. Williams Jr.

Mrs. HARRISON A. WILLIAMS JR., Wife of Senator (New Jersey)

HUNGARIAN VEAL BALLS

1 pound ground veal
1 clove garlic, minced
2 tablespoons chopped parsley
1 teaspoon salt
few grains pepper
¼ cup milk
1 egg, beaten
½ cup fine, dry bread crumbs

¼ cup cooking fat
1 teaspoon Kitchen Bouquet
2 tablespoons flour
1 3 ounce can sliced mushrooms
1½ cups dairy sour cream
1 6 ounce package wide noodles
2 tablespoons poppy seeds (optional)

Combine veal, garlic, parsley, seasonings, milk, egg and crumbs. Mix thoroughly. Shape into small balls. Brown meat balls in mixture of melted fat and Kitchen Bouquet. Remove meat balls and stir in flour; add mushrooms and sour cream. Cook until thickened, stirring constantly. Add meat balls to the gravy and cook, covered, over low heat about 20 minutes. Cook noodles in boiling, salted water and drain. Sprinkle with poppy seed. Serve in a ring around meat balls and gravy. Makes 6 servings.

Mrs. CLARENCE MILLER, Wife of Representative (Ohio)

JELLIED VEAL RING

2 pounds veal from shin
knuckle and shin bone of veal, cracked
3 quarts boiling, salted water
2 onions, sliced
2 stalks celery, diced
pinch of thyme
¼ cup vinegar
¼ teaspoon white pepper

salt to taste
small bunch of parsley
sliced tomatoes
sliced hard cooked eggs
sliced cucumbers
lettuce
cherry tomatoes
dill

Cook veal and bones in salted water with next 7 ingredients about 2 hours or until tender. Remove the veal, cut in cubes and scrape any meat from bones. Return the bones to stock and simmer until reduced to 1 quart. Strain and cool. Skim off any grease. When stock begins to thicken, stir in the veal. Turn all into a ring mold. Add sliced tomatoes, eggs and cucumbers around sides of mold and chill in refrigerator. Unmold and serve on bed of lettuce. Put cherry tomatoes sprinkled with dill in the center when serving.

Mrs. HUGH SCOTT, Wife of Senator (Pennsylvania)

324

ROAST LOIN OF PORK

1 cup dried prunes
1 onion, chopped
1 4 to 6 pound pork loin, boned and tied
3 cloves garlic, chopped
¼ cup sugar
1 teaspoon sesame oil

2 tablespoons Hoi Sin sauce
½ cup soy sauce
1½ teaspoons salt
3 tablespoons oyster sauce
1 teaspoon Worcestershire sauce
½ cup dry sherry
fresh parsley

Combine prunes and onion and stuff into center of roast, using handle of a long wooden spoon. Combine all other ingredients except parsley and use to marinate the meat overnight, turning at least twice. Reserve marinade. Bake pork at 325° for 3 hours or until brown and well done. To serve, slice on a warm platter and pour heated marinade over the meat. Garnish with fresh parsley. May be frozen. Makes 8 to 10 servings.

MRS. MARK O. HATFIELD, Wife of Senator (Oregon)

RICE AND PORK CASSEROLE

1 package wild rice mix
3 to 5 pound pork tenderloin (or 6 to 8 boned chicken breasts)

1 can mushroom soup
3 cups water
1 package dry onion soup mix

Grease long, flat glass baking dish. Spread rice evenly in bottom of dish. Lay tenderloin over rice. Combine mushroom soup and water and pour over meat. Sprinkle onion soup mix over the top. Bake at 350° for 1½ hours. May be frozen. Makes 6 to 8 servings.

MRS. BILL BURLISON, Wife of Representative (Missouri)

SUPER PORK CHOPS

8 butterfly pork chops
8 onion slices, ¼ inch thick
8 green pepper rings, 1 inch thick

2 cups cooked rice, seasoned to taste
2 cans tomato soup, undiluted

Put 1 onion slice and 1 green pepper ring on each chop. Fill pepper rings with rice. Pour soup over each chop. Preheat oven to 325° and bake, uncovered, for at least 1 hour. Makes 8 servings.

MRS. ROBERT D. RAY, Wife of Governor (Iowa)

325

STUFFED PORK CHOPS

2 tablespoons chopped onion
2 tablespoons chopped parsley
2 tablespoons butter
2 cups white bread crumbs
2 eggs, beaten
¼ cup cream (or evaporated milk)

1 teaspoon poultry seasoning
1 cup chopped fresh apples
8 pork chops, cut with pocket
1 teaspoon salt
1 teaspoon pepper
1 cup stock (or water)

Saute onion and parsley in butter; add crumbs, eggs, cream, poultry seasoning and apples. Mix well. Stuff pork chops; salt and pepper. Brown on both sides in heavy skillet. Pour the stock over the chops and bake at 350° for 1½ hours. Add more liquid if needed. Makes 8 servings.

Mrs. George Corley Wallace

MRS. GEORGE CORLEY WALLACE, Wife of Governor (Alabama)

PORK CHOPS IN GRAVY

4 large pork chops
salt
pepper
garlic salt

vegetable oil
1 can cream of mushroom soup
½ can beer

Season the chops with salt, pepper and garlic salt. Pan fry in the vegetable oil. When brown and thoroughly cooked, remove from pan and turn temperature to medium low. Blend mushroom soup and beer in heated pan until smooth. Return chops to the pan with the soup and beer gravy, cover and simmer for about 15 minutes. Turn the chops occasionally to prevent sticking. Serve with the extra gravy left in the pan. Makes 2 servings.

Mrs. Marvin Esch

MRS. MARVIN L. ESCH, Wife of Representative (Michigan)

PORK CHOPS AND SAUERKRAUT CASSEROLE

2 large cans sauerkraut, rinsed and
   drained
1 large onion, sliced
4 tart apples, peeled and sliced
8 thick pork chops, well trimmed
salt and pepper to taste

2 stalks celery, sliced
1 cup beer (or light wine or flat 7 Up)
fennel
cinnamon
cloves

Spread ½ of the sauerkraut in a greased casserole large enough to hold pork chops in a single layer. Cover with ½ of the onions and ½ of the apples. Add pork chops, seasoning, celery, remaining sauerkraut, onions and apples. Pour on preferred liquid, season lightly with fennel, cinnamon and cloves. Cover and bake 40 minutes at 400°. Remove cover and bake an additional half hour. Add liquid if casserole appears dry. May be frozen. Makes 8 servings.

Mrs. Frank E. Evans

MRS. FRANK E. EVANS, Wife of Representative (Colorado)

PORK CHOP AND POTATO CASSEROLE

6 pork chops
½ cup flour
2 tablespoons peanut oil
3 or 4 potatoes, peeled and sliced
1 large onion, sliced and ringed
½ cup water

2 beef bouillon cubes
1 can cream of mushroom soup
salt to taste
¼ teaspoon rosemary
½ teaspoon parsley

Dust pork chops in flour and brown in oil. In oblong casserole, place layer of potatoes, a layer of onion rings and top with browned chops. Add water, bouillon cubes and soup to skillet drippings. Stir until cubes are dissolved and pour mixture over pork chops. Sprinkle seasonings over top and bake 1½ hours at 350°.

Mrs. Henry Bellmon

MRS. HENRY BELLMON, Wife of Senator (Oklahoma)

PORK CHOPS AND POTATO SCALLOP

4 pork chops
1 can condensed mushroom soup
½ cup dairy sour cream
¼ cup water

2 tablespoons chopped parsley
4 cups thinly sliced Idaho potatoes
salt and pepper to taste

Brown pork chops. Blend soup, cream, water and parsley. In 2 quart casserole alternate layers of potatoes, salt, pepper and soup mixture. Top with chops. Cover and bake at 375° for 1¼ hours or until chops and potatoes are tender. May be frozen.

Mrs. George Hansen

MRS. GEORGE HANSEN, Wife of Representative (Idaho)

JESSICA'S CHILE VERDE (GREEN CHILI)

1 pound pork, cut in small pieces
1 tablespoon flour
1 small onion, chopped
2 tablespoons lard
4 to 6 green chilies, chopped

1 clove garlic, finely chopped
2 cups boiling water
1 teaspoon salt
1 small can tomatoes (optional)

Sprinkle pork with flour and brown with onions in hot lard. Add chilies, garlic, water and seasoning. Simmer about 50 minutes. If necessary, add more boiling water. Tomatoes may be added. May be frozen. Makes 2 to 3 servings.

Mrs. Richard D. Lamm

MRS. RICHARD D. LAMM, Wife of Governor (Colorado)

328

MANDARIN PORK

2 pounds boneless pork loin, cut into
   ½ inch cubes
flour
¼ cup salad oil
4 green peppers, quartered
1 large onion, cut in thick slices

1 15 ounce can pineapple chunks
½ cup soy sauce
½ cup cooking sherry
2 tablespoons vinegar
1 tablespoon sugar
1 16 ounce can sliced carrots, drained

Dredge meat in flour, saute in oil 5 minutes or until golden brown on all sides. Remove meat with slotted spoon; set aside. Add green pepper and onion to remaining oil; cook 2 minutes. Return pork to skillet. Drain pineapple, reserving juice. Combine pineapple juice, soy sauce, sherry, vinegar and sugar; add to pork. Simmer 5 minutes. Add pineapple chunks and carrots; cook 2 minutes. May be frozen. Makes 6 to 8 servings.

MRS. RICHARD H. ICHORD, Wife of Representative (Missouri)

JAKE'S SWEET AND SOUR PORK

3 pound pork roast
1 bunch green onions, chopped
1 green pepper, cut in strips
1 cup sliced celery
butter (or margarine)
1 medium can pineapple chunks,
   drained, reserve liquid

Sauce:
1½ teaspoons corn starch
2 teaspoons water
¼ cup vinegar
1 teaspoon soy sauce
½ cup brown sugar
1 cup catsup
juice from pineapple

cooked rice

Roast pork, cool and dice meat into bite size pieces. Saute onions, green pepper and celery in butter 2 or 3 minutes. Add pork, pineapple and sauce, made by combining all sauce ingredients in a jar and shaking vigorously until thoroughly blended. Cover and simmer a few more minutes. Vegetables should be crisp. Serve over hot rice. Makes 6 to 8 servings.

MRS. JAKE GARN, Wife of Senator (Utah)

CHINESE BARBECUED SPARERIBS

2 pounds tender young pork ribs   1 package barbecue sauce mix

Place ribs in low pan on a rack. Prepare sauce mix according to package directions. Rub ½ of sauce on both sides of ribs. Let stand in refrigerator at least 1 hour. Remove and let stand at room temperature for 1 hour before barbecuing or baking. Just before cooking, pour remaining sparerib sauce over the ribs and rub thoroughly. Place ribs on a rack in a clean, low pan. Place in the lowest part of the oven and bake for 30 minutes at 350°. Turn ribs over and bake for another 30 minutes. May be frozen. Makes 4 servings.

Mrs Hiram L. Fong

MRS. HIRAM L. FONG, Wife of Senator (Hawaii)

HAWAIIAN SPARERIBS

3 to 4 pounds pork spareribs
salt and pepper
1 20 ounce can pineapple chunks,
  drained
1 onion, minced
1 green pepper, diced
2 tablespoons butter

2 tablespoons corn starch
2 tablespoons brown sugar
¼ cup vinegar
¾ cup pineapple juice
3½ ounces soy sauce
½ cup sherry (or port)

Season ribs with salt and pepper and bake at 350° about 45 minutes. Remove from oven and drain off fat. Cover with pineapple chunks. Saute onion and green pepper in butter. Add next 5 ingredients. Cook together until fairly thickened. Add sherry. Pour over ribs and pineapple. Cover and bake at 325° for 1 to 1½ hours. May be frozen. Makes 6 to 8 servings.

Elizabeth P. Farrington

ELIZABETH P. FARRINGTON, former Representative (Hawaii)

BARBECUED SPARERIBS

6 pounds lean spareribs, cut
1 12 ounce bottle chili sauce
2½ cups water
½ teaspoon allspice

2 teaspoons Worcestershire sauce
2 tablespoons brown sugar
1 teaspoon salt
1 medium onion, chopped

Place spareribs in shallow pan, lean side up, and cook in 400° oven for 30 minutes. Drain off fat. Make a sauce with remaining ingredients and pour over the spareribs. Return to oven and bake at 350° for 1 hour, basting frequently. Makes 12 servings.

Mrs. Wallace F. Bennett

MRS. WALLACE F. BENNETT, Wife of former Senator (Utah)

MINNESOTA WILD RICE CASSEROLE

½ pound pork sausage
1 medium onion, chopped
1 small can sliced mushrooms, drained
1 cup wild rice, washed
⅛ cup flour
¼ cup heavy cream
1½ cups condensed chicken broth

pinch of thyme
pinch of oregano
pinch of marjoram
½ teaspoon monosodium glutamate
½ teaspoon salt
pepper to taste
slivered blanched almonds (optional)

Saute sausage and, as it browns, break into small pieces. Remove meat from pan, drain and put in large bowl. Saute onion in sausage fat. Add onion and mushrooms to sausage meat. Meanwhile, cook wild rice in boiling, salted water until tender, drain and rinse thoroughly under hot running water. Drain well. Mix flour and cream until smooth. Add chicken broth and cook until thick and smooth. Add seasonings. Combine ingredients, mixing well, and put in casserole. If desired, sprinkle with almonds. Bake at 350° for 1 hour or until done. May be frozen. Makes 6 to 8 servings

Mrs. Wendell R. Anderson

MRS. WENDELL R. ANDERSON, Wife of Governor (Minnesota)

331

BAKED ZITI

1 pound sweet Italian sausage, skinned
2 onions, minced
3 cans mushrooms
6 cups drained canned tomatoes
1/2 cup minced peppers
1/2 teaspoon dried sage leaves
1 teaspoon dried basil
1 teaspoon salt
1/4 teaspoon black pepper
1 cup water
1 pound ziti pasta
1/2 pound mozzarella cheese, diced
1 cup grated parmesan cheese

Combine sausage, onions and mushrooms in a large heavy saucepan and cook over medium heat, stirring constantly to break up sausage. Continue cooking until all the fat has cooked out of the sausage. Pour off excess fat. Add the remaining ingredients, except the pasta, mozzarella and the parmesan. Simmer, uncovered, over very low heat for 2 hours, stirring occasionally to prevent sticking. Parboil ziti and drain. Put in a deep casserole dish, cover with hot sauce, add the mozzarella cheese and mix well. Sprinkle parmesan over the top, cover and bake in a preheated 350° oven for 15 minutes. Remove cover and continue baking for 10 minutes. May be frozen. Makes 6 to 8 servings.

Mrs. James J. Howard

MRS. JAMES J. HOWARD, Wife of Representative (New Jersey)

SAUSAGE STROGANOFF

1 clove garlic
2 pounds mild sausage
3 tablespoons flour
2 cups milk
2 small onions, minced
1 large can mushrooms
1/2 stick butter
2 tablespoons Worcestershire sauce
2 teaspoons soy sauce
salt and pepper to taste
1 pint dairy sour cream, room
  temperature
cooked rice or noodles

Rub skillet with garlic. Cook sausage until lightly browned. Drain off grease and dredge sausage with flour. Add milk and cook until thickened, stirring constantly. Set aside. Saute onions and mushrooms in butter. Add to sausage along with Worcestershire, soy sauce, salt and pepper. When mixture bubbles, add sour cream and mix well. Serve over rice or noodles. Makes 6 to 8 servings.

Mrs. Durward G. Hall

MRS. DURWARD G. HALL, Wife of former Representative (Missouri)

SAUSAGE CASSEROLE

1½ pounds lean sausage
1 cup uncooked rice
2 2 ounce packages dehydrated noodle
  soup
½ cup finely chopped onion

1 cup sliced celery
2½ cups water
1 tablespoon soy sauce
½ cup slivered blanched almonds

Brown sausage in ungreased skillet, breaking it up with a fork and pouring off excess fat as it accumulates. Mix sausage with remaining ingredients and place in a 2 quart casserole. Cover and bake at 350° for 1 hour. May be frozen. Makes 6 servings.

Mrs. William H. Harsha

MRS. WILLIAM H. HARSHA, Wife of Representative (Ohio)

SAUSAGE LOAF FOR BRUNCH

1½ pounds bulk pork sausage
2 eggs, slightly beaten
¼ pound shredded American cheese

¾ cup fine cracker crumbs
⅓ cup milk
¼ cup chopped onions

Mix together all ingredients. Shape into loaf, place in shallow pan and bake at 350° for 1¼ hours. Pour off fat halfway through baking time. May be frozen. Makes 4 to 6 servings.

Mrs. Alvin E. O'Konski

MRS. ALVIN E. O'KONSKI, Wife of former Representative (Wisconsin)

SAUSAGE RING

2 pounds bulk sausage
1½ cups cracker crumbs
2 eggs, slightly beaten
2 cups milk

¼ cup minced onion
1 cup finely chopped apple
parsley
1 can peaches (or apricots), drained

Mix thoroughly first 6 ingredients. Press into 9 inch ring mold. Bake for 1 hour at 350°. Invert onto platter and decorate with parsley. Fill center with peaches. Makes 8 to 10 servings.

Mrs. Henry P. Smith

MRS. HENRY P. SMITH III, Wife of former Representative (New York)

SAUSAGE BRUNCH CASSEROLE

8 slices bread, cubed
2 cups grated cheddar cheese
2 pounds sausage, crumbled
4 eggs

2¾ cups milk
¾ teaspoon dry mustard
1 can mushroom soup

Place bread evenly in bottom of greased 8 x 12 inch pan. Top with cheese. Brown sausage, drain, crumble and spread over cheese. Beat eggs with 2¼ cups milk and add mustard. Pour over sausage. Cover and refrigerate overnight. When ready to bake, dilute soup with remaining milk. Pour over top of mixture and bake at 300° for 1½ hours until set. Makes 9 to 12 servings.

Mrs. Wm. L. Armstrong

MRS. WILLIAM L. ARMSTRONG, Wife of Representative (Colorado)

CHOUCROTE

¼ pound bacon, diced
3 medium onions, finely chopped
2 tablespoons bacon fat
1 27 ounce can sauerkraut
8 large frankfurters
4 German sausages

1 can stewed tomatoes
1 can Rotel tomatoes with green chilies
1 teaspoon sugar
1 pound Irish new potatoes
1 teaspoon crushed caraway (optional)

In deep skillet brown bacon. Drain. Saute the onions in 2 tablespoons of bacon fat. Add sauerkraut. Cover and cook 30 minutes. Add meat which has been cut into 1 inch lengths. Add stewed tomatoes, Rotel tomatoes with chilies and sugar. Simmer for 30 minutes. Cut potatoes in large chunks and cook in boiling water until just tender. Add to sauerkraut mixture. Caraway may be added if desired. Serve hot. Makes 8 servings.

Mrs Ralph W. Yarborough

MRS. RALPH W. YARBOROUGH, Wife of former Senator (Texas)

COUNTRY HAM

12 to 16 pound country ham
½ pound brown sugar
1 cup vinegar
1 cup molasses
½ cup flour

½ cup brown sugar
1 teaspoon ground cloves
1 tablespoon dry mustard
vinegar to make paste

Remove hock end of ham and soak ham overnight in cold water. In the morning scrub and wash ham in fresh cold water. Place on rack in large boiler and cover with cold water. Add ½ pound brown sugar, vinegar and molasses. Bring to a boil and simmer 4 hours. Leave in water in boiler overnight. The following morning remove skin and excess fat. Cover with paste of flour, ½ cup brown sugar, cloves, mustard and vinegar. Bake at 300° for an hour.

For cold sliced ham it is not necessary to perform the baking process. After ham has been boiled and allowed to stand overnight, bone and then chill well before slicing. Makes 30 servings.

Mrs. John Currie Mackie

MRS. JOHN CURRIE MACKIE, Wife of former Representative (Michigan)

KENTUCKY COUNTRY HAM FLAMBE

2 ham steaks
2 tablespoons brown sugar

2 jiggers bourbon

Brown steaks in a heavy skillet. Pour off all but about 2 tablespoons of fat from the pan. Mix sugar and bourbon in a bowl until sugar is dissolved. Add mixture to steaks and ignite.

Mrs. Julian M. Carroll

MRS. JULIAN CARROLL, Wife of Governor (Kentucky)

335

HAM LOAF WITH SAUCE

2½ pounds ham
2½ pounds lean pork
2½ cups bread crumbs (no crusts)
2 eggs
pepper

milk
½ cup vinegar
¾ cup light brown sugar
1 teaspoon dry mustard
½ teaspoon cloves

Grind ham and pork together and mix with bread crumbs, eggs, pepper and enough milk to make mixture more moist than an ordinary loaf. Shape into individual loaves or 1 or 2 large ones. Mix remaining ingredients into a sauce and pour over loaves before placing in oven. Bake 1 hour at 350°, basting occasionally. Makes 10 servings.

Mrs. Arch A. Moore, Jr.

Mrs. ARCH A. MOORE, JR., Wife of Governor (West Virginia)

HAM LOAF SUPERB

¾ pound ham
½ pound veal
¼ pound pork
2 eggs, beaten
¾ cup soft bread crumbs
¾ cup milk
dash of pepper
2 teaspoons prepared mustard

¼ cup brown sugar
⅓ cup pineapple juice (or pickled peach juice)

Easy Horse Radish Sauce:
3 tablespoons horse radish, drained
½ teaspoon salt
½ cup whipping cream, whipped

Grind together ham, veal and pork. Mix in eggs, bread crumbs, milk and pepper. Pat mixture into a 9 x 5 x 3 inch loaf pan. Spread mixture of mustard and brown sugar on top of loaf. Pour juice over loaf. Bake 1½ hours at 350°. Baste loaf several times during baking. Serve with horse radish sauce made by folding horse radish and salt into whipped cream. May be frozen. Makes 5 to 6 servings.

Mrs. Donald J. Mitchell

Mrs. DONALD J. MITCHELL, Wife of Representative (New York)

336

TASTY HAM LOAF

1 pound ground ham	2 eggs
2 pounds ground pork	⅛ cup whole cloves
1 cup Zwieback crumbs	1 cup tomato juice
1 cup milk	

Mix first 5 ingredients. Shape into loaf and put in baking pan. Bake ½ hour at 350° and then drain off excess fat. Stud with whole cloves and pour tomato juice over loaf. Bake 1½ hours longer at same oven temperature. May be frozen. Makes 8 servings.

Mrs. Maurice G. Burnside

MRS. MAURICE G. BURNSIDE, Wife of former Representative (West Virginia)

HAM LOAF AND SAUCE

1 pound ground cured ham	1 teaspoon dry mustard
2 pounds ground lean shoulder pork	½ teaspoon pepper
2 eggs	juice of 1 small lemon
1 cup bread (or cracker) crumbs	currant jelly
1 cup milk	prepared mustard

Mix all ingredients except the last 2. Put into a loaf pan, set in a pan of water and bake at 300° for 3 hours. Combine equal amounts of jelly and mustard and cook together until melted. Serve sauce over sliced ham loaf. May be frozen. Makes 10 servings.

Mrs. Jack F. Kemp

MRS. JACK F. KEMP, Wife of Representative (New York)

HAM LOAF

3 pounds smoked ham, ground	2 cans tomato soup
2 pounds fresh pork, ground	2 eggs, beaten
2 cups bread crumbs	cream sauce
1 teaspoon paprika	

Combine all ingredients except sauce, mix thoroughly and mold into loaves. Bake at 350° for 1½ hours. Serve hot with cream sauce. May be frozen. Makes 14 servings.

Mrs. George Hansen

MRS. GEORGE HANSEN, Wife of Representative (Idaho)

SAUERKRAUT BALLS

¼ pound ham
¼ pound pork
¼ pound corned beef
2 tablespoons chopped onion
1 tablespoon chopped parsley
1 cup flour
1 cup milk

½ teaspoon dry mustard
½ teaspoon salt
1 pound sauerkraut
flour
beaten egg
bread crumbs

Put meat and onion and parsley through food chopper and pan fry until brown. Blend in flour; add milk slowly; stir in seasoning. Cook until light and fluffy. When cooked, add the sauerkraut, force the entire mixture through the food chopper and mix thoroughly. Shape into balls the size of a walnut. Roll each ball in flour, in beaten egg and lastly in bread crumbs. Fry in deep fat until golden brown. Serve hot. Makes 4 servings.

MRS. CHARLES A. VANIK, Wife of Representative (Ohio)

HAM AND BROCCOLI CASSEROLE

8 ounces macaroni
1½ pounds frozen broccoli spears
2 tablespoons margarine
½ cup flour
1 quart milk
¾ teaspoon grated onion
¼ teaspoon dry mustard

⅛ teaspoon vinegar
1/16 teaspoon white pepper
½ teaspoon salt
½ pound grated cheddar cheese
1 pound cooked ham, cubed
2 tablespoons parmesan cheese

Cook macaroni as directed on package. Drain and rinse. Boil broccoli until nearly tender and cut into 1 inch pieces. Combine margarine, flour, milk, onion, mustard, vinegar and seasonings to make sauce. Add grated cheese; cook until cheese is melted. Lightly combine macaroni, ham and broccoli with sauce. Pour mixture into greased pan or individual casseroles and sprinkle with parmesan cheese. Bake at 375° until cheese is melted and sauce is bubbly. May be frozen. Makes 10 servings.

MRS. J. JAMES EXON, Wife of Governor (Nebraska)

338

HAM JAMBALAYA

5 slices bacon
1½ cups regular long grain rice
1 medium onion, minced
1 medium green pepper, diced
1 garlic clove, crushed
1 16 ounce can tomatoes
1 13¾ ounce can chicken broth

1 bay leaf
½ teaspoon salt
½ teaspoon thyme leaves
1 pound cooked ham, cubed
½ pound shrimp, shelled and deveined
3 or 4 drops hot pepper sauce

In large skillet over medium heat, fry bacon until crisp; drain on paper towels; crumble and set aside. In same skillet over medium heat, in remaining bacon drippings, cook rice, onion, green pepper and garlic until rice is lightly browned. Stir in tomatoes and their liquid, chicken broth, bay leaf, salt and thyme leaves. Cover and simmer 15 minutes. Stir in ham, shrimp and hot pepper sauce. Cook, covered, 15 to 20 minutes until rice is tender, stirring occasionally. Spoon onto platter; sprinkle with bacon. May be frozen. Makes 6 servings.

Mrs. George Dekle Busbee

MRS. GEORGE BUSBEE, Wife of Governor (Georgia)

CREPES AUX CHAMPIGNONS

1 8 ounce can mushroom stems and
    pieces, drained
¼ cup minced cooked ham
2 tablespoons heavy cream

salt
crepes
6 tablespoons melted butter
½ cup grated Swiss cheese

Dry mushrooms and puree in blender. Mix with ham, cream and salt. Spread on crepes, roll each one and place side by side in buttered au gratin dish. Drizzle with butter and sprinkle with cheese. Bake at 325° for 20 minutes. Makes 4 servings.

Mrs. John H. Ware

MRS. JOHN H. WARE, Wife of former Representative (Pennsylvania)

ROAST LEG OF LAMB

1 5 to 6 pound leg of lamb
2 tablespoons ginger
juice of ½ lemon

salt
pepper

Remove lamb from refrigerator ½ hour before cooking. Mix ginger and lemon juice to a paste and brush meat lightly with ½ of mixture. Salt and pepper to taste. Place meat fat side up on a rack in an uncovered pan. Put in a preheated 450° oven and immediately reduce heat to 325°. Cook for 2 hours for medium rare, ½ hour longer for well done. About 15 minutes before meat is done, brush with remaining lemon juice and ginger mixture. Makes 6 to 8 servings.

Mrs. Calvin L. Rampton

Mrs. Calvin L. Rampton, Wife of Governor (Utah)

BROILED BUTTERFLIED LEG OF LAMB

5 to 6 pound leg of lamb
⅓ cup white wine
1 onion, chopped
2 tablespoons lemon juice

1 teaspoon salt
freshly ground pepper to taste
2 garlic cloves, minced
1 cup olive oil

Have butcher bone, butterfly and flatten leg of lamb. With wire whisk, blend together wine, onion, lemon juice and seasonings and gradually add oil. Pour over lamb in a shallow glass dish and marinate at least 2 hours, turning 2 or 3 times. Drain the meat and dry with paper towels. Grill over charcoal, turning frequently and basting with marinade, for 25 to 30 minutes or until lamb is slightly pink inside. Cut across grain in thin slices. Makes 8 to 10 servings.

Mrs. Herman T. Schneebeli

Mrs. Herman T. Schneebeli, Wife of Representative (Pennsylvania)

BRAISED LEG OF LAMB (GIGOT BRAYAUDE)

1 leg of lamb, trimmed
2 cloves garlic, chopped
1 stick butter
5 carrots, peeled and sliced
1 cup minced onions

1 sprig thyme (or
  ½ teaspoon dried thyme)
1 bay leaf
½ pound bacon rind
1 cup dry white wine
1 quart stock (or bouillon)

Make slits in various places of the leg of lamb and insert garlic pieces. Melt butter in a Dutch oven and brown lamb on all sides. Remove lamb and set aside. Brown the carrots, onions, thyme, bay leaf and bacon rind in the same pan for a few minutes. Replace meat and add wine. Bring to a boil and continue boiling, uncovered, until all the liquid has evaporated. Add stock. Cover and bake in 350° oven for 40 minutes per pound. Makes 8 servings.

Mrs Howard Baker jr

MRS. HOWARD H. BAKER JR., Wife of Senator (Tennessee)

LAMB SHANKS ARMENIAN

4 lamb shanks
1 cup well seasoned salad dressing
2 green peppers, sliced

2 onions, sliced
2 tomatoes, sliced
1 package rice pilaf

Arrange lamb shanks in baking dish and pour salad dressing over them. Marinate in refrigerator for at least 4 hours, turning from time to time. Remove from refrigerator 1 hour before cooking. Toss peppers, onion and tomatoes with shanks. Bake, covered, at 350° for about 1½ hours. Cook rice pilaf for about 5 minutes according to package directions. Remove all excess fat and skin from shanks. Pour rice and liquid over meat. Cover and continue cooking for another 30 minutes or until meat is tender and all moisture is absorbed by rice. Serve from baking dish. Makes 4 servings.

Mrs Frank Annunzio

MRS. FRANK ANNUNZIO, Wife of Representative (Illinois)

SHISHKABOB

3½ pounds leg of lamb, cut in 1½
    inch cubes
fresh mushrooms

bacon slices, cut in 5 pieces
onions, quartered
salt and pepper to taste

Put ingredients on wooden skewers in the order as follows: meat, mushroom, bacon and onion. Repeat until the skewer is filled, ending with meat. Season with salt and pepper. Place the shishkabobs in the broiler pan itself instead of on its rack so that the juices will run together and make the meat and vegetables juicier and more delicious. Place under the broiler, as far from the heat as possible. As the meat looks well roasted, turn the skewers and broil on the other sides. Makes 6 to 8 servings.

Mary Hamilton O'Neal

MARY HAMILTON O'NEAL, Daughter of former Representative Emmet O'Neal (Kentucky)

LAMB STUFFED RED PEPPERS

6 large sweet scarlet bell peppers
1 large stalk celery
2 small onions
1 carrot
1½ cups cooked lamb, ground
1 cup small bread crumbs (or cooked
    white rice)

parsley flakes
salt
pepper
gravy or meat stock
sour cream

Cut tops off peppers, remove seeds and tough white membranes. Parboil 10 minutes. Drain and cool. Grind celery, onions and carrot, reserving juice. Mix ground vegetables thoroughly with lamb and bread crumbs. Add parsley flakes, salt and pepper to taste. Add juice from vegetables and enough gravy to make a firm, moist mixture. Fill peppers, set in baking dish and bake at 350° for about ½ hour. Peppers are done when tops are lightly browned. Serve with topping of sour cream. Makes 6 servings.

Mrs. Clarence D. Long

MRS. CLARENCE D. LONG, Wife of Representative (Maryland)

342

SWEETBREADS CHAUMIERE

2 pairs sweetbreads
½ pound dried beef, chopped
½ stick butter
1½ cups light cream
2 tablespoons flour

1½ pounds fresh mushrooms, peeled
  and sliced
salt and pepper to taste
buttered crumbs

Parboil and prepare sweetbreads, breaking them into pieces. Saute the dried beef in half the butter until it curls. Add cream and flour. Saute mushrooms in remaining butter until brown and moisten with a little cream. Add to dried beef and sweetbreads. Season to taste. Place mixture in casserole, cover with buttered crumbs and place in a 350° oven just until the top has browned slightly.

Frances P. Bolton

FRANCES P. BOLTON, former Representative (Ohio)

WINE MARINADE

1½ cups peanut (or Wesson) oil
¾ cup soy sauce
2 tablespoons Worcestershire sauce
2 tablespoons salt

1 tablespoon freshly ground pepper
1 cup dry red wine
2 teaspoons dried parsley flakes
⅓ cup fresh lemon juice

Combine all ingredients in a quart jar and shake vigorously. Use to add flavor to or tenderize meat. Marinade may be reused. May be frozen.

Mrs. Rufus C. Holman

MRS. RUFUS C. HOLMAN, Wife of former Senator (Oregon)

MINT SAUCE FOR LEG OF LAMB

1 bunch fresh mint
5 heaping tablespoons sugar

apple cider vinegar

In the morning remove leaves from mint which has been cleaned thoroughly. Chop up leaves and put in a small deep bowl. Add sugar. Cover this completely with the vinegar and stir well. Cover and let stand all day, stirring every hour.

Mrs. Bill Brock

MRS. BILL BROCK, Wife of Senator (Tennessee)

BAR-B-QUE SAUCE

1 cup water
½ cup sugar
1 clove garlic, crushed
½ cup lemon juice
½ cup vinegar

1 cup chili sauce
1 3 ounce bottle horse radish
1½ teaspoons salt
1 tablespoon prepared mustard
1 teaspoon celery salt
1½ cups oil

Boil first 3 ingredients together for 5 minutes. Cool and add remaining ingredients. Shake in a jar or whisk until thoroughly blended. Will keep for weeks in refrigerator. This may also be used as a French dressing. Makes 1¼ quarts.

Mrs. Bob Wilson

MRS. BOB WILSON, Wife of Representative (California)

SAUCE BEARNAISE

2 shallots (or 3 small green onions), finely chopped
½ cup wine vinegar
1 teaspoon dried tarragon (or 1 tablespoon chopped fresh)

3 egg yolks
1 tablespoon warm water
¼ pound butter, softened
salt to taste
heavy cream (optional)

Bring shallots, vinegar and tarragon to a boil. Cook down slowly until it is merely a glaze. Whisk egg yolks and water in a bowl over hot, not boiling, water. Slowly add butter, 1 tablespoon at a time, whisking constantly. Cook over very low heat so water under the bowl never boils. When sauce thickens, add glaze and salt. If sauce is too thick, thin with a little cream. Makes 2 to 4 servings. Serve with steak.

Mrs. Walter E. Powell

MRS. WALTER E. POWELL, Wife of former Representative (Ohio)

344

MUSTARD SAUCE

1 cup dry Colman's mustard
1 cup white wine vinegar

1 cup sugar
2 egg yolks

Beat together mustard and vinegar and let stand 2 hours. Beat in sugar and egg yolks, using an egg beater. Cook in double boiler 30 minutes to an hour. Sauce becomes hotter the longer it is cooked. Will keep indefinitely in the refrigerator. Makes about 2½ cups.

Mrs. Bob Wilson

MRS. BOB WILSON, Wife of Representative (California)

JEZEBEL'S SAUCE

1 small jar pineapple preserves
1 small jar prepared mustard

1 small jar apple jelly
1 bottle horse radish

Mix all ingredients well. Use electric mixer if possible. Store in glass jar in refrigerator indefinitely. This is particularly good with country ham. May be frozen. Makes 3 cups.

Mrs. Ed Jones

MRS. ED JONES, Wife of Representative (Tennessee)

RAISIN SAUCE FOR HAM

1½ cups boiling water
½ cup raisins
2 cups dairy sour cream

½ teaspoon salt
1 tablespoon horse radish
2 tablespoons lemon juice

Pour boiling water over raisins and let stand 10 minutes. Drain and combine with sour cream, salt, horse radish and lemon juice. Chill. Makes 2½ cups.

Mrs. Bill Nichols

MRS. BILL NICHOLS, Wife of Representative (Alabama)

RED AND GREEN PEPPER JELLY (FOR MEAT)

6½ cups sugar
1½ cups white vinegar
¾ cup chopped hot green peppers

¾ cup chopped red bell pepper
1 bottle Certo

Mix sugar and vinegar together and bring to a boil. Add peppers and boil for 10 minutes. Remove from heat and add Certo. Let stand and cool, stirring occasionally until it begins to thicken. Pour into jelly glasses and cover with paraffin.

Mrs. Don Brotzman

MRS. DONALD G. BROTZMAN, Wife of former Representative (Colorado)

YORKSHIRE PUDDING

1 cup sifted flour
1 teaspoon salt
1 cup milk

2 eggs, beaten
3 tablespoons beef drippings (optional)

Sift flour and salt. Add milk gradually to form a smooth paste. Add eggs to mixture. If pudding is baked separately from beef roast, add beef drippings to pan, add batter and bake at 400° for 40 minutes. If it is baked with the roast, remove all but 3 tablespoons of drippings from the roasting pan, add batter and bake at 400° during the last 40 minutes of the roast's baking time. Makes 6 servings.

Mrs. Henry O. Talle

MRS. HENRY O. TALLE, Wife of former Representative (Iowa)

APPLES, ILLINOIS

8 firm apples
4 cups sugar
2 cups water
6 blades mace

juice and shredded peel of 2 small
   lemons
1 peppercorn
few small bits of cinnamon stick
whole cloves

Pare apples and drop in cold water to stand while the syrup is made. Combine sugar and water and bring to a boil. Add mace, lemon peel, peppercorn and cinnamon. Stick 4 cloves in each apple and drop them into the boiling syrup with the strained lemon juice. Boil fruit rapidly 5 minutes, turn it over and let it simmer until tender and transparent. Skim apples out with perforated skimmer, draining away all syrup. Arrange apples in a deep glass dish. Boil the syrup until it jellies when dropped on a cold plate. Dip it by spoonfuls over the apples. Set in a cool place and allow to harden. This is good served with ham or poultry.

Mrs. Daniel Walker

MRS. DANIEL WALKER, Wife of Governor (Illinois)

BAKED APRICOTS

2 30 ounce cans apricots, drained and
   pitted
2 cups light brown sugar, firmly packed

1 12 ounce box Ritz crackers,
   crumbled
1½ to 2 sticks butter

Layer half the apricots in a lightly greased baking dish. Over them layer half of the brown sugar and half of the cracker crumbs. Dot generously with half the butter. Repeat layers in this order. Bake in a 300° oven for 1 hour. This is an excellent dish to serve with meat and vegetables. Makes 8 to 10 servings.

Mrs. Armistead I. Selden

MRS. ARMISTEAD I. SELDEN, Wife of former Representative (Alabama), presently Ambassador to New Zealand

CURRIED FRUIT WITH MEAT

1 16 ounce can pear halves
1 15 ounce can sliced pineapple
1 16 ounce can peach halves
1 17 ounce can apricot halves

1 4 ounce jar maraschino cherries
⅓ cup butter, melted
¾ cup brown sugar, tightly packed
4 teaspoons hot curry powder

Drain fruit well, cut into small pieces and turn into a 2 quart casserole dish. To butter, add brown sugar and curry powder and blend well over low heat. Pour over fruit. Bake at 275° for 15 minutes. Baste and bake 15 minutes longer. Serve as an accompaniment to a meat course. May be frozen. Makes 6 to 8 servings.

Mrs. Jim Wright

MRS. JIM WRIGHT, Wife of Representative (Texas)

PINEAPPLE CASSEROLE

½ cup butter
¾ cup sugar
4 eggs

1 20 ounce can crushed pineapple
5 slices white bread, crusts removed,
   cubed

Cream butter and sugar. Add eggs and beat well. Add pineapple. Stir bread into egg mixture. Bake in a greased 1½ quart casserole 45 minutes at 350° or until brown and bubbly. Serve with baked ham. Makes 6 servings.

Mrs. Richard Schultz Schweiker

MRS. RICHARD SCHULTZ SCHWEIKER, Wife of Senator (Pennsylvania)

TIME TABLE FOR ROASTING
MEAT AND POULTRY

Standing Roasts	Temperature Fahrenheit	Minutes per pound
Beef		
Rare	325°	20 to 22
Medium	325°	24 to 27
Well Done	325°	30 to 32
Veal	325°	35 to 40
Lamb	325°	30 to 35
Fresh Pork		
Loin	325°	35 to 40
Crown	325°	50 to 55
Ham		
Fully cooked	325°	12 to 15
Uncooked ··················	325°	18 to 20
Rolled roasts ················	allow 10 minutes more per pound	

		Total Time
Poultry		
Chicken, 3½ to 4½ pounds ·······	325°	3 to 3½ hours
Turkey, 8 to 12 pounds ·········	325°	4 to 4½ hours

RECOMMENDED STORAGE PERIODS
FROZEN MEATS AND FISH HELD AT 0° FAHRENHEIT

Product	Storage period (months)	Product	Storage period (months)
Beef:		Pork, cured:	
Ground	3 to 4	Bacon	1 or less
Roasts	6 to 12	Ham	1 to 2
Steaks	6 to 12	Pork, fresh:	
Stew	3 to 4	Chops	3 to 4
Fish	6 to 9	Roasts	4 to 8
Lamb:		Sausage	1 to 2
Chops	6 to 9	Veal:	
Ground	3 to 4	Cutlets, chops	6 to 9
Roasts	6 to 9	Ground	3 to 4
Stew	3 to 4	Roasts	6 to 9

NOTES

BREADS

English Bread the London Way

Take a bushel of good flour, ground about five or six weeks, put it in one end of your trough, and make a hole in the middle of it; take nine quarts of warm water (which the bakers call liquor) and mix it with one quart of good yeast, put it into the flour, and stir it well with your hands till it is weak and tough, let it lie till it rises as high as it will go, which will be in about one hour and twenty minutes; mind and watch it when it is at the height, and do not let it fall; then make up your dough with eight quarts more of warm liquor, and one pound of salt, work it well up with your hands; then cover it over with a coarse cloth, or a sack; then put your fire into the oven, and heat it well, and by the time your oven is hot the dough will be ready; then make your dough into loaves of about five pounds each; then sweep out your oven clean, put in your loaves, shut it up close, and two hours and a half will bake them; then open your oven and draw them out.

N.B. In summer let your liquor be just blood warm, and in winter a little warmer, and in hard frosty weather as hot as you can bear your hand in it, but not so hot that it will scald the yeast, for if the yeast is scalded it will spoil the whole batch of bread.

The English Art of Cookery
Richard Briggs, 1798

IRISH OATMEAL BREAD

4 cups whole wheat flour
¾ cup all purpose flour
⅔ cup quick cooking oats
1 tablespoon baking soda

1½ teaspoons salt
2½ to 3 cups buttermilk
 (approximately)
corn meal

Mix both flours, oats, soda and salt. Add enough buttermilk to make a dough. Dough will be sticky. Wet hands to shape into 2 round or oval loaves. Place on cookie sheet sprinkled with corn meal. Bake in 375° oven for 50 minutes. Cool. May be frozen.

Mrs. Glenn Davis

MRS. GLENN DAVIS, Wife of former Representative (Wisconsin)

GOLDEN ONION BREAD

2 cups biscuit mix
½ teaspoon dry mustard
1 egg, slightly beaten
1 tablespoon instant minced onion

1 tablespoon chopped parsley
⅔ cup milk
⅓ cup melted butter or margarine
½ cup grated American cheese

Combine biscuit mix and mustard. Combine egg, onion, parsley, milk and butter. Stir into dry mixture. Turn into a greased 8 inch round pan. Sprinkle cheese over top. Bake in 400° oven for 15 minutes until bread is done and cheese is melted and browned.

Mrs. Don Bonker

MRS. DON BONKER, Wife of Representative (Washington)

QUICK WHOLE WHEAT BREAD

2½ cups whole wheat flour
½ teaspoon cinnamon
¼ teaspoon salt
1 teaspoon baking soda
1 egg, beaten

½ cup molasses
¼ cup brown sugar
¼ cup oil
1 teaspoon grated lemon rind
⅔ cup plain yogurt

Sift together the dry ingredients. Combine the egg, molasses, sugar, oil and rind and add to dry ingredients alternately with the yogurt. Pour into a buttered 9 x 5 inch loaf pan. Bake for 50 minutes in a 375° oven. May be frozen.

Ella Grasso

ELLA GRASSO, Governor (Connecticut)

SPICED APPLESAUCE BREAD

1½ cups applesauce
1 cup granulated sugar
3 tablespoons milk
½ cup salad oil
2 eggs
2 cups flour
1 teaspoon baking soda

½ teaspoon baking powder
¼ teaspoon each of nutmeg, salt and allspice
1 teaspoon cinnamon
1 cup chopped nuts
¾ cup raisins
¼ cup brown sugar

Thoroughly combine applesauce, sugar, milk, salad oil and eggs. Sift together flour, baking soda, baking powder, nutmeg, salt and allspice. Add ½ teaspoon cinnamon. Add to applesauce mixture. Fold in ¾ cup nuts and raisins. Pour into greased loaf pan. Combine and sprinkle over top of batter the remaining nuts, brown sugar and remaining cinnamon. Bake for at least 1 hour at 350°. Cool on rack and remove from pan. May be frozen.

Elizabeth C. Rhodes

ELIZABETH C. RHODES, Daughter of Representative John J. Rhodes (Arizona)

MOTHER'S BANANA BREAD

1 cup sugar
½ teaspoon salt
½ cup shortening
3 ripe bananas, mashed

2 eggs, well beaten
2 cups sifted flour
1 teaspoon baking soda
⅓ cup nutmeats (optional)

Cream together sugar, salt and shortening. Add bananas and eggs. Sift together the flour and baking soda. Add and mix well. Add nuts. Bake in buttered 4 x 8 inch loaf pan in 350° oven for approximately 30 minutes. Cool before slicing. May be frozen. Makes 12 to 16 servings.

Mrs. James R. Schlesinger

MRS. JAMES R. SCHLESINGER, Wife of former Secretary of Defense (Virginia)

KATHY'S BANANA WHOLE WHEAT BREAD

1¼ cups all purpose flour
½ cup whole wheat flour
1 cup sugar
1 teaspoon baking soda
1 teaspoon salt
1 egg

⅓ cup raisins
1½ cups mashed bananas
¼ cup butter or margarine, softened
2 tablespoons orange juice
¼ teaspoon lemon juice (optional)

Blend all ingredients together and beat at medium speed in an electric mixer for 3 minutes. Pour batter into a greased and floured 9 x 5 inch loaf pan. Bake in a preheated 325° oven for 60 to 70 minutes or until toothpick inserted comes out clean. Remove from pan and cool on rack. May be frozen.

Mrs. John R. Foley

MRS. JOHN R. FOLEY, Wife of former Representative (Maryland)

BANANA NUT BREAD

1 cup shortening
2 cups sugar
4 eggs
2½ cups flour
1 teaspoon salt

2 teaspoons baking soda
5 medium bananas, mashed
3 teaspoons buttermilk (or milk)
1 teaspoon vanilla
1 cup chopped walnuts

Mix shortening and sugar until creamy. Add eggs, 2 at a time, mixing well. Sift flour, salt and baking soda together. Combine creamed mixture, dry ingredients, bananas and buttermilk, using ⅓ of each at a time. Add vanilla and nuts. Mix well. Bake in 2 greased 9 x 5 inch loaf pans at 325° for approximately 1 to 1¼ hours. May be frozen.

Mrs. Barry M. Goldwater Jr.

MRS. BARRY M. GOLDWATER JR., Wife of Representative (California)

CINNAMON BREAD

1/4 cup margarine
1 1/3 cups sugar
1 egg
1 teaspoon baking soda

1 cup buttermilk
1/2 teaspoon salt
2 cups flour
1 teaspoon cinnamon

Combine margarine, 1 cup sugar, egg, baking soda, buttermilk and salt and beat until fluffy. Add flour. Mix remaining sugar with the cinnamon in another bowl. Pour half of batter into a greased pan and sprinkle half of sugar cinnamon mixture over it. Then add remaining batter and sprinkle with remaining sugar cinnamon mixture. Swirl mixture through batter with a knife. Bake at 350° for 40 to 45 minutes. May be frozen.

Mrs. Bert Bandstra

MRS. BERT BANDSTRA, Wife of former Representative (Iowa)

DATE NUT BREAD

2 cups boiling water
2 cups chopped dates
2 cups sugar
2 tablespoons melted butter
4 cups flour
2 teaspoons baking soda

2 teaspoons baking powder
1/2 teaspoon salt
2 eggs
1 cup chopped nuts
2 teaspoons vanilla

Pour water over dates, sugar and butter. Let stand while preparing other ingredients. Sift dry ingredients and add to date mixture. Add eggs, nuts and vanilla. Beat well. Pour into greased and floured loaf pans, 2 large or 4 small ones. Bake large loaves 1 hour or small ones 50 minutes at 375°. May be frozen.

Mrs. Wallace F. Bennett

MRS. WALLACE F. BENNETT, Wife of former Senator (Utah)

HOBO BREAD

1½ cups raisins
1½ teaspoons salt
grated rind of 1 orange
1 cup boiling water
1 cup sugar

2 tablespoons shortening
1 egg
1 teaspoon vanilla
2 cups flour
1 teaspoon baking powder

Wash and drain raisins, add 1 teaspoon salt and grated orange rind and cover with boiling water. Set aside to cool. Cream sugar, shortening, egg and vanilla. Add flour, remaining salt and baking powder to creamed mixture. Add cooled raisins and beat well. Put into 4 well greased 1 pound soup cans, filling each half full. Bake at 350° for 1 hour and 10 minutes. May be frozen.

Mrs. Fred J. DeMeritte

MRS. FRED J. DeMERITTE, Daughter-in-law of former Associate Justice Hugo L. Black, Supreme Court

LICKITY QUICK LEMONADE BREAD

½ cup shortening
1 cup sugar
2 eggs
1½ cups flour

2 teaspoons baking powder
½ cup milk
⅓ cup plus 1 tablespoon frozen
lemonade, thawed

Combine all ingredients except lemonade in large mixer bowl and blend well. Beat 3 minutes at medium speed. Bake in greased 5 x 9 inch pan for 50 to 60 minutes in 350° oven. Loosen bread from edges. Pour lemonade over bread and let cool.

Mrs. Odin Langen

MRS. ODIN LANGEN, Wife of former Representative (Minnesota)

ORANGE PECAN BREAD

1 cup sugar
1 egg
2 tablespoons soft butter or margarine
2 tablespoons grated orange rind
¾ cup orange juice
2 cups flour

1 teaspoon baking powder
½ teaspoon baking soda
1 teaspoon salt
½ cup dates, halved
½ cup chopped pecans
cream cheese, whipped

Mix together quickly all ingredients except dates, nuts and cheese. Batter will be slightly lumpy. Fold in dates and nuts and pour into greased 9 x 5 x 3 inch loaf pan. Bake at 350° for 50 minutes. Cool thoroughly. Refrigerate overnight before slicing. Spread with cream cheese. May be frozen. Makes 8 to 10 servings.

Mrs. William H. Ayres

MRS. WILLIAM H. AYRES, Wife of former Representative (Ohio)

PLUM NUT BREAD

3 cups flour
4 teaspoons baking powder
1 teaspoon salt
1 cup sugar
1 cup coarsely chopped walnuts or pecans
1⅓ cups coarsely cut, pitted, fresh prune plums (cut with scissors)

¾ cup milk
½ cup orange juice
1 tablespoon grated orange rind
3 tablespoons vegetable oil (or shortening), melted and cooled
1 egg, well beaten

Mix first 4 ingredients and add nuts and plums. Add remaining ingredients and stir just to blend. Put in greased 9 x 5 x 3 inch loaf pan and let stand 20 minutes. Cover with same size pan, lightly greased, or with double thickness of foil, rounded over top. Bake in 350° oven 20 minutes. Remove top pan or foil and bake 50 minutes longer. Turn out on rack and cool thoroughly before slicing. May be frozen.

Mrs. Benjamin F. James

MRS. BENJAMIN F. JAMES, Wife of former Representative (Pennsylvania)

PUMPKIN BREAD

3 cups sugar
1 cup salad oil
4 eggs, beaten
1 1 pound can pumpkin
3½ cups flour
2 teaspoons baking soda
2 teaspoons salt

1 teaspoon baking powder
1 teaspoon nutmeg
1 teaspoon allspice
1 teaspoon cinnamon
½ teaspoon ground cloves
⅔ cup water

Cream sugar and oil. Add eggs and pumpkin and mix well. Sift together all the dry ingredients. Add alternately with water to pumpkin mixture. Pour into 2 well greased and floured 9 x 5 inch loaf pans. Bake at 350° for 1½ hours or until it tests done. Cool 10 minutes before removing from pans. May be frozen.

Mrs. James B. Longley

MRS. JAMES B. LONGLEY, Wife of Governor (Maine)

FRESH ZUCCHINI BREAD

2 cups sugar
3 eggs
1 cup oil
2 cups grated zucchini
3 cups flour
1 teaspoon cinnamon

1 teaspoon baking soda
1 teaspoon baking powder
1 teaspoon salt
½ cup milk
1 teaspoon vanilla
⅔ cup chopped nuts (optional)

Blend together sugar, eggs, oil and zucchini. Add flour, cinnamon, baking soda, baking powder, salt, milk and vanilla and blend thoroughly. Stir in nuts and pour mixture into 2 greased and floured regular size loaf pans and bake at 325° for about 1 hour. May be frozen.

Mrs. Kevin E. VanderSchel

MRS. KEVIN VANDERSCHEL, Daughter of Representative Neal Smith (Iowa)

ZUCCHINI BREAD

3 eggs
1 cup vegetable oil
2 cups sugar
2 cups peeled, grated zucchini
2 teaspoons vanilla
3 cups flour

1 teaspoon baking soda
¼ teaspoon baking powder
1 teaspoon salt
3 tablespoons cinnamon
½ cup nuts

Beat eggs until light and foamy. Add next 4 ingredients, mixing lightly but well. Combine dry ingredients and blend with egg mixture. Add nuts. Divide batter into 2 greased loaf pans and bake at 325° for 1 hour or until done. Test with toothpick. Remove from pan at once and cool on rack. May be frozen.

Mrs. Al Ullman

MRS. AL ULLMAN, Wife of Representative (Oregon)

MOTHER'S ZUCCHINI BREAD

½ box Jiffy corn muffin mix
1 medium onion, shredded
⅛ teaspoon garlic powder
¼ stick margarine, melted

2 cups shredded, unpeeled zucchini
½ cup milk
2 eggs
¼ cup parmesan cheese

Mix above ingredients together. Bake at 350° about 40 minutes or until brown. Will be consistency of spoon bread. Makes 6 servings.

Mrs. David N. Henderson

MRS. DAVID N. HENDERSON, Wife of Representative (North Carolina)

HARD CRUST CORN BREAD

1½ cups white corn meal
1 teaspoon salt
2 tablespoons lard (or shortening)
pinch of baking soda

½ cup buttermilk
¼ cup boiling water
2 tablespoons bacon drippings

Mix meal and salt; cut in lard with hand or fork. Add soda to buttermilk and stir into meal mixture. Add boiling water. Mixture should be thick and just moist enough to hold together well. Heat bacon drippings in iron skillet at 475°. Shape meal mixture into 6 pones; place side by side in skillet; spoon hot bacon drippings on top of pones. Bake at 475° about 25 minutes. After bottoms get brown, brown tops of pones under boiler. Makes 6 servings.

Mary A. Evins

MARY ADELAIDE EVINS, Daughter of Representative Joe L. Evins (Tennessee)

CORN MEAL DELIGHT

1 cup water
1 cup milk
1 teaspoon salt
1 teaspoon sugar

1 cup corn meal
1 cup cubed brick cheese (or ½ pint creamed cottage cheese)
sour cream

Bring water, milk, salt and sugar to a boil. Add corn meal, slowly stirring all the time. Cook for 15 minutes and then add the cheese. Mix and continue cooking until cheese is melted, about 15 minutes. Serve hot with sour cream on top. Makes 4 to 6 servings.

Mrs Joe Skubitz

MRS. JOE SKUBITZ, Wife of Representative (Kansas)

SPOON BREAD

2¼ cups milk
2 tablespoons butter or margarine
1 teaspoon salt

⅔ cup corn meal
3 eggs, separated
butter

Heat milk to scalding; add butter and salt and slowly stir in corn meal. Cook for 1 minute, stirring constantly. Remove from heat, cool a few minutes and then stir into well beaten egg yolks. Fold in stiffly beaten eggs whites and pour into greased 1 quart casserole. Bake in 375° oven for 35 to 40 minutes. Serve from baking dish with butter. Makes 5 servings.

Mrs. James H. Quillen

MRS. JAMES H. QUILLEN, Wife of Representative (Tennessee)

CHEDDAR SPOON BREAD

3 cups milk
1 cup yellow corn meal
1 cup shredded sharp cheddar cheese
1 teaspoon salt

1 teaspoon baking powder
3 egg yolks, well beaten
3 egg whites, stiffly beaten

Heat 2 cups milk in 3 quart saucepan. Add corn meal gradually, stirring about 5 minutes or until thickened. Remove from heat and stir in cheese. Mix until cheese melts. Add remaining milk, salt, baking powder and egg yolks. Mix well. Fold in egg whites. Pour into lightly greased 2 quart casserole. Bake 1 hour in preheated 325° oven or until set. Makes 8 servings.

Mrs. Richard Kelly

MRS. RICHARD KELLY, Wife of Representative (Florida)

CHEESE SPOON BREAD

2 cups milk
⅓ cup corn meal
1 tablespoon butter
3 or more tablespoons grated cheese

1 teaspoon salt
¼ teaspoon paprika
3 egg yolks, beaten
3 egg whites, stiffly beaten

Scald milk and stir in other ingredients except eggs. Stir and cook to consistency of mush. Add egg yolks and cook for 1 minute. Cool slightly. Add egg whites, folding gently. Pour into a greased casserole and bake at 350° for 45 minutes. Makes 6 servings.

Mrs. Berkley Bedell

MRS. BERKLEY BEDELL, Wife of Representative (Iowa)

362

JIFFY SPOON BREAD

1 can condensed cheddar cheese soup
¾ cup milk
¼ cup margarine
½ cup yellow corn meal
cold water

¼ teaspoon cayenne (optional)
3 eggs, separated
½ teaspoon salt
¼ teaspoon baking powder

Mix soup and milk in saucepan until smooth. Heat to boiling; add margarine. Remove from heat and gradually stir in corn meal which has been dampened with cold water. Add cayenne if desired. Beat egg yolks until thick and blend into soup mixture. Sprinkle salt and baking powder over egg whites and beat until stiff but not dry. Fold into soup mixture. Bake in well greased 1½ quart casserole at 350° until puffed and brown, about 1 hour. Makes 8 servings.

Mrs. Ralph W. Yarborough

MRS. RALPH W. YARBOROUGH, Wife of former Senator (Texas)

KENTUCKY SPOON BREAD

¾ cup self rising corn meal (or ¾ cup regular meal and 3 teaspoons baking powder)
3 cups milk
3 eggs, well beaten

1 teaspoon sugar
1 teaspoon salt (optional)
2 tablespoons melted butter or margarine

Stir corn meal into 2 cups of milk, bring to a boil and cook until thick, about 5 minutes. Add remaining milk and the eggs. Stir in the sugar, salt and butter. Turn into a greased 2 quart baking dish and bake at 350° for 30 minutes or until firm and brown. Serve immediately. Makes 6 servings.

Mrs. Frank A. Stubblefield

MRS. FRANK A. STUBBLEFIELD, Wife of former Representative (Kentucky)

EASY MEXICAN SPOON BREAD

2 packages corn muffin mix
1 can whole kernel corn, drained

1 4 ounce can green chilies, drained
and chopped
1½ cups shredded cheddar cheese

Prepare 1 package corn muffin mix according to directions on box. Spread on bottom of greased 9 x 13 x 2 inch casserole. Sprinkle with corn, chilies and cheese. Prepare remaining package of muffin mix and spread over top. Bake at 400° for 45 minutes. Cool 10 minutes before cutting into serving pieces. Makes 16 to 20 servings.

MRS. JOHN J. RHODES, Wife of Representative (Arizona)

MEXICAN SPOON BREAD

1 teaspoon salt
1 teaspoon baking powder
½ teaspoon baking soda
¾ cup white corn meal (water ground preferably)
2 eggs, slightly beaten

1 20 ounce can cream style corn
⅓ cup Wesson oil
¾ cup buttermilk
1 4 ounce can green chili peppers, drained
1½ cups grated sharp cheese

Mix together salt, baking powder, baking soda and corn meal and gradually add to eggs. Stir in corn and gradually add oil and buttermilk. Pour half of mixture into an 8 x 8 x 2 inch casserole. Over this layer half the peppers, either whole or chopped, and half the cheese. Pour remaining corn meal mixture on top and add remaining peppers. Top with remaining cheese. Bake at 425° for about 35 minutes or until golden brown. May be frozen. Makes 8 servings.

MRS. HUGO L. BLACK, Wife of former Associate Justice, Supreme Court (Alabama)

364

HUSH PUPPIES

¾ cup white corn meal
¾ cup flour
1 teaspoon salt
3 teaspoons baking powder
1 onion, chopped

1 small tomato, chopped (optional)
1 cup milk
1 egg, beaten
cooking oil

Sift dry ingredients together and add onion and tomato. Beat milk into egg, add to dry ingredients and stir to moisten thoroughly. Drop by iced tea spoonfuls into hot deep fat. Fry 2 to 3 minutes, turning once. Drain on paper towels and serve piping hot. These are light like fritters. Makes 6 to 8 servings.

Mrs. Andrew G. Pattillo, Jr.

MRS. ANDREW G. PATTILLO, JR., Daughter of former Representative A. Sydney Herlong, Jr. (Florida)

OLD FASHIONED HUSH PUPPIES

2 cups yellow corn meal
2 tablespoons butter
1 teaspoon salt

finely chopped green onions with tops
(optional)
boiling water
cooking oil

Mix first 4 ingredients together; add enough boiling water to make a medium stiff batter. Drop by rounded teaspoonful into deep hot fat and cook until brown. Makes 8 servings.

Mrs. John S. Cross

MRS. JOHN S. CROSS, Daughter of former Representative Claude A. Fuller (Arkansas)

POPOVER

1 tablespoon butter
1 cup flour
½ teaspoon salt

1 cup milk
3 eggs

Place butter in heavy 10 inch skillet and heat in oven. Meanwhile, beat remaining ingredients with rotary beater just until smooth. Pour into heated skillet. Bake 30 minutes at 425°. Serve hot in pie shaped wedges. Makes 6 servings.

Mrs. Edward H. Jenison

MRS. EDWARD H. JENISON, Wife of former Representative (Illinois)

NEVER FAIL, NO BEAT POPOVERS

2 eggs
1 cup milk

1 cup flour
½ teaspoon salt

To the eggs add milk, flour and salt. Mix well with a spoon, disregarding lumps. Fill well greased Pyrex custard cups ¾ full. Place in a cold oven. Turn oven on to 450° and bake for 30 minutes. Makes 8 popovers.

Mrs. James D. Weaver

MRS. JAMES D. WEAVER, Wife of former Representative (Pennsylvania)

BEER ROLLS

4 cups Bisquick
12 ounces beer

4 tablespoons sugar

Mix ingredients together and put in greased muffin tins. Bake at 400° for 20 minutes if they are to be served immediately. Bake only 10 minutes if they are to be frozen and finish baking when they are to be served. Makes 16 to 20 rolls.

Mrs. Robert Thomas Ashmore

MRS. ROBERT THOMAS ASHMORE, Wife of former Representative (South Carolina)

RUBY'S BISCUITS

2 cups flour
2 scant teaspoons baking powder
1 teaspoon salt

⅔ cup Crisco
½ cup milk (approximately)

Sift dry ingredients together. Add half the Crisco and, using a fork, chop in very finely as for a pie crust in order to make the biscuits flaky. Add remaining Crisco and chop in coarsely to make the biscuits light. While tossing flour mixture with a fork, sprinkle on the milk, but just until dough sticks together. Roll on a floured surface to a ½ to ¾ inch thickness and cut with a biscuit cutter. Place on cookie sheet, prick each biscuit with a fork twice and bake at 425° for 10 to 12 minutes. Recipe may be tripled without endangering quality of biscuits. May be frozen unbaked on cookie sheet and then stored in a plastic bag in freezer for weeks. Makes 20 to 22 biscuits.

Mrs. Andrew G. Pattillo, Jr.

MRS. ANDREW G. PATTILLO, JR., Daughter of former Representative A. Sydney Herlong, Jr. (Florida)

GOLD BRICKS

1 loaf unsliced French bread
1 stick butter

2 cups grated sharp cheese

Remove crusts from bread. Cut in chunks about 2 x 3 inches. Butter on all sides. Shake in a bag of grated cheese. Place on cookie sheet and bake at 325° about 7 to 10 minutes, turning once.

Mrs. James Harvey

MRS. JAMES HARVEY, Wife of former Representative (Michigan)

APPLESAUCE MUFFINS

½ pound soft margarine
2 cups sugar
2 eggs
1 teaspoon vanilla
4 cups flour
3 teaspoons cinnamon

1 teaspoon ground cloves
2 teaspoons allspice
2 teaspoons baking soda
1 1 pound can applesauce
1 cup chopped nuts

Cream margarine, sugar, eggs and vanilla. Sift flour and spices and add to creamed mixture. Stir soda into applesauce, add nuts and fold into batter. Mix well. Pour into greased muffin tins and bake at 400° for 20 minutes. This batter may be refrigerated, covered, for 2 or 3 weeks and used as needed.

Mrs. B. Everett Jordan

MRS. B. EVERETT JORDAN, Wife of former Senator (North Carolina)

PINEAPPLE SOUR CREAM MUFFINS

1 cup dairy sour cream
1 egg, well beaten
2 tablespoons sugar
1 tablespoon soft butter
1½ cups sifted flour

1 teaspoon baking powder
½ teaspoon baking soda
¾ teaspoon salt
1 9 ounce can pineapple tidbits, well drained

Blend sour cream, egg, sugar and butter together, mixing well. Resift flour with baking powder, soda and salt. Add to first mixture, stirring just until blended. Stir in pineapple. Spoon into greased medium size muffin pans. Bake in 400° oven about 25 minutes. May be frozen. Makes 1 dozen muffins.

Mrs. Howard W. Cannon

MRS. HOWARD W. CANNON, Wife of Senator (Nevada)

BRAN MUFFINS

1 cup bran
¾ to 1 cup raisins
1 cup boiling water
1 cup sugar
½ cup plus 1 tablespoon Crisco

2 eggs, beaten
2 cups buttermilk
2½ cups flour
2½ teaspoons baking soda
2 cups bran beads

Put bran, raisins and boiling water into bowl. Set aside. Cream sugar and Crisco. Add eggs, buttermilk, flour, soda and bran beads. Beat together with bran and raisin mixture, pour into greased muffin tins and bake 18 to 20 minutes at 400°. Unbaked dough will keep in refrigerator for 6 weeks. Makes 3 dozen.

Mrs. William S. Broomfield

MRS. WILLIAM S. BROOMFIELD, Wife of Representative (Michigan)

TEA MUFFINS

1¾ cups flour
½ teaspoon salt
2 teaspoons baking powder
¼ cup sugar

¾ cup milk
1 egg
¼ cup melted shortening

Sift flour with salt, baking powder and sugar. Mix milk, egg and shortening. Add at once to dry ingredients. Mix until they are moistened. Pour into greased muffin pans ⅔ full. Bake in 400° oven about 25 minutes. Makes 1 dozen.

Mrs. Joseph A. Herbert, Jr.

MRS. JOSEPH A. HERBERT, JR., Daughter of former Senator A. J. Gronna (North Dakota)

RUM BUNS

¼ cup sugar
2 cups flour
½ tablespoon salt
1 cup warm water
2 tablespoons melted margarine
1 yeast cake (or 1 envelope dry yeast)
1 egg, beaten

1½ cups flour
rum flavoring
brown sugar
margarine
honey
currants
frosting

Combine first 7 ingredients and stir. Knead in 1½ cups flour. Knead and put to rise until doubled in bulk. Brush top with melted margarine. Roll dough, half at a time, into a thin rectangle. Brush on rum flavoring. Sprinkle with brown sugar, dot with margarine, drizzle with honey and sprinkle with currants. Roll up like a jelly roll, slice and flatten slightly on cookie sheet. Brush slices with melted margarine; let rise about 1 hour. Bake at 350° for 15 to 20 minutes until a light brown. May be frozen. Before serving, frost with confectioners sugar frosting flavored with rum flavoring. Makes 2 dozen buns.

Mrs. William Henry Harrison

MRS. WILLIAM HENRY HARRISON, Wife of former Representative (Wyoming)

LYDIA'S FATAYA (FILLED SWEET ROLLS)

1 package refrigerator Hungry Jack
flaky biscuits

Filling:
1 tablespoon cinnamon
2 tablespoons sugar
3 tablespoons finely chopped black
walnuts (or pecans)

Filling variation:
1 small package cream cheese

Glaze:
1 cup sugar
¼ cup water
1 teaspoon lemon juice

Split each unbaked biscuit in half crosswise, making 2 rounds. Combine cinnamon, sugar and nuts and place ½ teaspoon of mixture on each biscuit round. Fold biscuit over making a half circle. Carefully press around sides to seal edge. The same procedure is followed if a cream cheese filling is desired. Bake at 400° for 9 to 11 minutes. Remove from oven and immediately dip in hot glaze. Makes 20 pastries.

Glaze: Bring sugar and water to a boil and add lemon juice.

Maureen Ellen Foley

MAUREEN ELLEN FOLEY, Daughter of former Representative John R. Foley (Maryland)

PAULINE'S CINNAMON FLUFF

½ cup shortening
⅔ cup sugar
2 eggs, beaten
1½ cups sifted flour
2 tablespoons cinnamon
1 teaspoon baking powder
1 teaspoon baking soda

½ teaspoon salt
1 cup sour milk (or buttermilk)

Topping:
½ cup sugar
1 tablespoon butter
1 tablespoon cinnamon

Cream shortening and sugar. Add eggs and beat well. Sift together dry ingredients and add to creamed mixture alternately with milk, beating after each addition. Pour into greased 9 x 13 inch pan. To make topping, mix sugar, butter and cinnamon to make coarse crumbs. Sprinkle topping over batter and bake in 325° oven 40 to 45 minutes. May be frozen. Makes 8 to 10 servings.

Mrs. John Myers

MRS. JOHN MYERS, Wife of Representative (Indiana)

370

COFFEE CAKE

½ pound margarine
2 cups sugar
2 eggs
1 cup dairy sour cream
2 cups sifted flour
1 teaspoon baking powder
¼ teaspoon salt

½ teaspoon vanilla

Topping:
½ cup chopped nuts
½ teaspoon cinnamon
2 tablespoons brown sugar
confectioners sugar

Cream margarine and sugar until fluffy. Beat in the eggs and fold in sour cream. Add sifted dry ingredients and vanilla. Pour half the batter in greased and floured bundt pan. Combine nuts, cinnamon and brown sugar and sprinkle half of mixture over batter. Pour on remaining batter and cover with remaining topping. Bake in 350° oven 55 to 60 minutes. Remove from pan and sprinkle top with confectioners sugar.

Mrs Fred Schwengel

MRS. FRED SCHWENGEL, Wife of former Representative (Iowa)

GLADYS' HEAVENLY COFFEE CAKE

5 eggs
½ cup sugar
1 cup dairy sour cream
¾ cup vegetable oil
1 package lemon cake mix

Topping:
¾ cup chopped pecans
3 tablespoons brown sugar
2 tablespoons cinnamon

Beat eggs and sugar together. Add sour cream and oil. Beat in cake mix. Combine topping ingredients. Pour half of batter in baking pan and sprinkle with half of topping mix. Pour remaining batter over nut mixture and sprinkle with remaining topping. Bake for 1 hour at 350°. May be frozen. Makes 12 servings.

Mrs. James Lee Fisk

MRS. JAMES L. FISK, Daughter of former Representative Jed Johnson, Sr. (Oklahoma)

FRENCH BUTTER COFFEE CAKE

¾ cup shortening
2 cups sugar
1 teaspoon vanilla
2 eggs, well beaten
2 cups flour

1 cup milk
¼ pound butter
1 teaspoon cinnamon
2 cups Bisquick
confectioners sugar

Cream shortening with 1 cup sugar. Add vanilla and eggs and mix well. Add flour alternately with milk. Spread onto large cookie sheet. Mix together butter, remaining sugar, cinnamon and Bisquick. Spread evenly over batter on cookie sheet. Bake at 375° for 25 minutes. While cake is still warm, sprinkle with confectioners sugar. May be frozen.

Mrs. Albert L. Vreeland

Mrs. Albert L. Vreeland, Wife of former Representative (New Jersey)

ROSEMARY'S OLD FASHIONED COFFEE CAKE

¼ pound margarine
¾ cup sugar
2 eggs, beaten
1⅓ cups milk
3 cups flour, sifted
¾ teaspoon salt
4 teaspoons baking powder
1 teaspoon vanilla
1 teaspoon grated lemon rind

Topping:
½ stick margarine
½ cup sugar
¼ cup flour
1 cup brown sugar
2 teaspoons cinnamon
chopped pecans to taste

Cream together margarine and sugar. Add the eggs and milk. Sift in flour with salt and baking powder. Add vanilla and lemon rind. Pour batter into a 9 x 13 inch pan. Bake at 375° for 25 minutes. Combine topping ingredients, mixing by hand. Spread over coffee cake. May be frozen.

Mrs. Clarence J. Brown

Mrs. Clarence J. Brown, Wife of Representative (Ohio)

SOUR CREAM COFFEE CAKE

½ pound butter
2 cups plus 4 teaspoons sugar
2 eggs
1 cup sour cream
½ teaspoon vanilla

2 cups flour
1 teaspoon baking powder
¼ teaspoon salt
1 cup chopped pecans
1 teaspoon cinnamon

Cream butter and add 2 cups sugar gradually, beating until very light and fluffy. Beat in eggs, 1 at a time, beating very well. Fold in cream and vanilla. Fold in flour sifted with baking powder and salt. Combine remaining sugar, pecans and cinnamon. Place ½ of batter in a well greased and floured 9 inch tube pan. Sprinkle with ¾ of pecan mixture. Add rest of batter and sprinkle with remaining pecan mix. Bake 60 minutes in a preheated 350° oven. May be frozen. Makes 10 servings.

Mrs. Eugene Siler

MRS. EUGENE SILER, Wife of former Representative (Kentucky)

BUTTERMILK BREAD

1 cup buttermilk
¼ cup sugar
2½ teaspoons salt
⅓ cup butter

1 package dry yeast
1 cup warm water
½ teaspoon baking soda
6 cups flour (approximately)

Heat buttermilk until hot enough to melt the butter. Stir in sugar, salt and butter. Cool. Dissolve yeast in warm water and add to cooled milk mixture. Combine soda and half the flour. Add to yeast mixture and beat until smooth. Add rest of flour gradually, turn out and knead until very smooth and elastic. Place in greased bowl and let rise until doubled. Punch down, turn out and shape into 2 loaves. Place in greased loaf pans. Brush tops with melted butter and let rise. Bake in 400° oven about 50 minutes. This bread is very fined grained and excellent for toast and sandwiches. May be frozen.

Mrs. Glenn Davis

MRS. GLENN DAVIS, Wife of former Representative (Wisconsin)

CASSEROLE BREAD

1 package dry yeast (or 1 cake)
1/4 cup warm water
1 cup creamed cottage cheese
2 tablespoons sugar
1 tablespoon instant minced onion
1 tablespoon butter
2 teaspoons dillseed

1 teaspoon salt
1/4 teaspoon baking soda
1 egg, unbeaten
2 1/2 cups flour (approximately)
soft butter
salt

Soften yeast in warm water. Heat cottage cheese to lukewarm and combine it with sugar, onion, butter, dillseed, salt, baking soda and egg. Add softened yeast. Gradually add enough flour to form a stiff dough, beating well after each addition. Put dough in greased bowl; cover with wax paper and towel. Let rise in warm place until double in size. Punch down and knead well. Make into a round loaf and put in greased pan. Let rise 30 to 40 minutes. Bake at 350° for 40 to 50 minutes. Brush with soft butter and sprinkle with salt.

MRS. BURT L. TALCOTT, Wife of Representative (California)

COFFEE CAN BREAD

4 cups unsifted flour
1 package dry yeast
1/2 cup water
1/2 cup milk

1/4 pound butter or margarine
1/4 cup sugar
1 teaspoon salt
2 eggs, beaten

Mix 2 cups flour with yeast. Put water, milk, butter, sugar and salt in small saucepan over low heat. Stir occasionally until butter melts. Cool 5 minutes. Add liquids to flour and yeast. Add eggs alternately with remaining flour. Mix well. Knead by hand until stiff. Divide dough in half and put each half in a 1 pound coffee can and allow to rise until 1 inch from the top. Bake in a 375° oven for about 35 minutes. May be frozen.

MRS. RAY ROBERTS, Wife of Representative (Texas)

COFFEE CAN WHEAT BREAD

1 package active dry yeast
½ cup warm water
⅛ teaspoon ground ginger
3 tablespoons honey
1 13 ounce can evaporated milk

1 teaspoon salt
2 tablespoons vegetable oil
1½ cups whole wheat flour
3 cups white flour
butter or margarine

Dissolve yeast in water in large mixer bowl, blend in ginger and 1 tablespoon honey. Let stand in warm place until mixture is bubbly, about 15 minutes. Stir in remaining honey, milk, salt and oil. With mixer on low speed, beat in flour, 1 cup at a time, beating very well after each addition. Beat in last cup of flour with a heavy spoon, adding flour until dough is very heavy and stiff but too sticky to knead. Place dough in a well greased 2 pound coffee can or two 1 pound cans. Cover with well greased plastic can lids. Dough may be frozen at this time.

Let covered cans stand in warm place until dough rises and pops off lids, 45 to 60 minutes for small cans or 1 to 1½ hours for a large can. If dough has been frozen, it will take 4 to 5 hours for small cans or 6 to 8 hours for a large one. Bake uncovered in a 350° oven 45 minutes for small loaves and 1 hour for a large one. Crust will be very brown. Brush top lightly with butter. Let cool for 5 to 10 minutes on cooling rack and then loosen crust around edge of can with a thin knife. Slide bread from can and cool in an upright position on rack. Baked bread may be frozen.

Mrs. Clarence J. Brown

MRS. CLARENCE J. BROWN, Wife of Representative (Ohio)

HONEY WHOLE WHEAT BREAD

4 cups whole wheat flour
½ cup non fat dry milk
1 tablespoon salt
2 packages active dry yeast
3 cups water

½ cup honey
2 tablespoons cooking oil
4 to 4½ cups all purpose flour
(or whole wheat flour)

Combine 3 cups whole wheat flour, milk, salt and dry yeast. Mix the water, honey and oil in saucepan, place over low heat until warm and pour over flour mixture. Blend at low speed in electric mixer for 1 minute and at medium speed for 2 minutes. By hand, stir in remaining whole wheat flour and the all purpose flour. Knead on floured surface for about 5 minutes. Place dough in greased bowl, cover and let rise for 45 to 60 minutes until light and doubled in bulk. Punch down dough and divide in half. Shape each half into a loaf by rolling the dough out to a 14 x 7 inch rectangle. Starting with the shorter side, roll up jelly roll fashion. Place each loaf in a greased 9 x 5 inch pan. Cover and let rise for 30 to 45 minutes until light and doubled. Bake in a preheated 375° oven for 40 to 45 minutes or until loaf sounds hollow when lightly tapped. Remove from pan and cool on wire rack.

Mrs. David S. King

MRS. DAVID S. KING, Wife of former Representative (Utah)

HEALTH BREAD

1 quart milk, scalded
2 packages yeast
3 cups warm water
½ cup plus 1 teaspoon sugar
5 teaspoons salt
6 cups white flour (or half white and half whole wheat flour)

½ cup potato flour
½ cup gluten flour
2 tablespoons peanut oil
4 tablespoons wheat germ
2 tablespoons sesame seeds

Mix together the milk, yeast, warm water, sugar and salt. Sift the flour and add the potato and gluten flour. Sift this mixture into the liquid and beat until dough is shiny. Add the peanut oil, wheat germ and sesame seeds and beat very well. Add a little additional flour if necessary in order to knead the dough on a board. Knead the dough, place in a greased bowl, cover and let rise until the dough falls in the center. Remove from bowl, divide into 5 equal parts and make into round loaves. Let rise for 25 minutes. Using the side of the hand, pound out the air in each loaf. Start to roll it into a loaf shape, continuing to pound it. Place the molded loaves in greased loaf pans leaving a little space at each end. Let rise again. Bake at 375° for 45 minutes. May be frozen. Makes 5 loaves.

Mrs Anita W. Ullman

MRS. ANITA ULLMAN, Member of Congressional Club (Oregon)

376

OATMEAL BREAD

⅔ cup powdered milk
2 cups quick rolled oats
¼ cup brown sugar
1 tablespoon salt
2 tablespoons shortening

2 cups hot water
1 package dry yeast
½ cup warm water
5 cups sifted flour (approximately)

Place milk powder, oats, sugar, salt and shortening in large bowl. Add hot water and cool to lukewarm. Sprinkle yeast on warm water and allow to dissolve. Combine oat and yeast mixtures with about 2 cups of flour and beat well. Add remaining flour, a little at a time, to make a soft dough that leaves the sides of the bowl. Turn out and knead 8 to 10 minutes. Place in greased bowl, turn, cover and allow to rise until doubled, about 1 to 1½ hours. Punch down and allow to rise 30 minutes. Divide in half, shape and place in 2 greased bread pans. Allow to rise until about double. Bake in 375° oven about 40 minutes. May be frozen.

Mrs. Glenn Davis

Mrs. Glenn Davis, Wife of former Representative (Wisconsin)

OATMEAL DATE BREAD

3½ cups unbleached flour
1½ cups oatmeal
¼ cup raw sugar
1½ teaspoons salt
2 tablespoons dry yeast
¼ cup bottled water

¾ cup milk
¼ cup butter
2 eggs
1 cup finely chopped dates (or nuts)
water
oatmeal for topping

Mix flour and oatmeal. Combine 1½ cups flour mixture with sugar, salt and undissolved yeast in large bowl. Combine water, milk and butter in pan and place over low heat until warm. Gradually add liquid mixture to dry ingredients. Beat at medium speed for 2 minutes, scraping bowl now and then. Add eggs, dates and 1½ cups of flour mixture or enough to make a thick batter and beat at high speed 2 minutes. Stir in enough of the remaining flour mixture to make a soft dough. Turn out on lightly floured board and knead until smooth and elastic. Place in a greased bowl, turning so as to grease all sides. Cover and let rise in warm place until double in bulk. Punch down and let rest for 10 minutes. Shape into a round loaf and place in a greased pan or on a cookie sheet. Brush top with a little water and sprinkle oatmeal on top. Cover with a plastic bag and let rise until double in bulk. Discard plastic bag and bake bread at 350° about 50 minutes. Cool on a rack.

Mrs. Reinhold Puetz

Mrs. Reinhold Puetz, Daughter of former Representative Courtland C. Gillen (Indiana)

NEVER FAIL WHITE BREAD

1 package dry yeast
2 cups warm water
½ cup honey
1 tablespoon salt

6 to 6¼ cups sifted flour
½ cup powdered milk
4 tablespoons butter (margarine or shortening), melted

Put yeast into mixing bowl. Add water, honey and salt and stir to dissolve completely. Add ½ of the flour and powdered milk and beat until smooth and elastic. Beat in butter. Add remaining flour and work it in well with hands. Turn onto a greased board and let it rest 10 minutes. Knead until smooth and elastic. Cover and let rise until double in bulk. Punch down and let rise again until almost double in bulk. Shape into 2 loaves and place in greased loaf pans. Let rise until double in bulk. Bake in 375° oven 45 to 60 minutes or until golden brown. May be frozen.

Mrs. John B. Conlan

MRS. JOHN B. CONLAN, Wife of Representative (Arizona)

BATTER BREAD

1 cake yeast (or package)
¼ cup lukewarm water
¼ cup plus 1 teaspoon sugar
½ cup milk, scalded
¾ teaspoon salt
3 tablespoons butter
1 egg, beaten
2 cups flour

Topping:
¼ cup brown sugar
1 tablespoon butter
¼ cup chopped nuts

Combine the yeast with lukewarm water and 1 teaspoon of sugar. To the milk add remaining sugar, salt and butter. When yeast is dissolved and milk mixture is lukewarm, combine them. Add egg and flour, stirring until flour takes up the moisture. Pour batter into a well greased 8 inch square pan. Blend topping ingredients with a fork or the fingers and sprinkle over top of the batter. Let rise until doubled in bulk, about 50 minutes. Bake at 400° for 25 to 30 minutes. Score into 9 pieces and serve while still warm. Makes 4 servings.

Mrs. Lee Metcalf

MRS. LEE METCALF, Wife of Senator (Montana)

SUSAN'S CARDAMOM BRAID BREAD

1 package hot roll mix
2 tablespoons butter or margarine, melted
1½ teapoons ground cardamom

½ cup golden seedless raisins
milk
sugar

Prepare hot roll mix according to package directions; add butter, cardamom and raisins. Mix well. Cover. Let rise in warm place until double in size, about 1 hour. On lightly floured surface, knead dough about 1 minute; divide in thirds. Roll each third under hands to form a strand 10 inches long, tapering ends. Place strands 1 inch apart on greased baking sheet. Beginning in middle, braid strands loosely, working toward either end. Pinch ends together. Cover and let rise until almost double, about 40 minutes. Brush braid with milk and sprinkle with sugar. Bake in 375° oven for 25 minutes or until done. May be frozen.

Mrs. William H. Bates

MRS. WILLIAM H. BATES, Wife of former Representative (Massachusetts)

ICEBOX ROLLS

1 quart milk
1 cup shortening
¾ cup sugar
1 cake yeast
8 cups flour

2 teaspoons baking powder
2 teaspoons salt
1 teaspoon baking soda
melted shortening

Scald the milk with shortening and sugar and cool to lukewarm. Add yeast and stir to dissolve. Add 4 cups flour and let rise 2 hours. Add remaining flour, baking powder, salt and baking soda. Mix well. Cut out rolls with small cutter, dip each one in melted shortening and fold over to make a half circle. Place in greased pan and keep in refrigerator until they are to be baked. Bake in a 350° oven until rolls are a golden brown. Makes 2 dozen small rolls.

Mrs. Glenn English

MRS. GLENN ENGLISH, Wife of Representative (Oklahoma)

379

REFRIGERATOR ROLLS

½ cup boiling water
¼ pound butter
½ cup sugar
1 teaspoon salt
2 eggs, beaten

2 packages yeast
½ cup warm water
2 teaspoons sugar
4 cups flour

Pour boiling water over butter, sugar and salt. Blend and cool. Add eggs. Let yeast stand in warm water with the 2 teaspoons of sugar about 10 to 15 minutes. Add yeast to first mixture and stir. Mix in flour. Dough will be sticky. Cover and place in refrigerator overnight. Remove from bowl and cut in half. Flour board and roll each half into a circle. Cut into pie shaped pieces and roll up starting at wide end. Let rise, covered, on a greased sheet until doubled in bulk. Bake at 350° for 12 minutes. May be frozen. Makes 16 rolls.

Mrs. Douglas R. Smith

Mrs. Douglas R. Smith, Daughter-in-law of Representative Neal E. Smith (Iowa)

BRAN ROLLS

1 cup all bran cereal
1 cup shortening
1 cup boiling water
⅔ cup sugar
¾ teaspoon salt

2 packages dry yeast
1 cup warm water
2 eggs, beaten
7 cups flour

Cover bran cereal and shortening with boiling water, blending well. Add sugar and salt. Set aside to cool. Dissolve yeast in warm water and add eggs. Combine both mixtures and add flour gradually. Cover and let stand at room temperature until double in bulk. Press down, cover tightly and refrigerate at least 4 or 5 hours. Bake rolls as needed. May be frozen but remove from freezer about 3 hours before baking time. For making rolls, remove desired amount of dough, shape, let rise to double its bulk and bake at 375° until lightly browned. Makes 6 dozen rolls.

Mrs. Harold Runnels

Mrs. Harold L. Runnels, Wife of Representative (New Mexico)

GRANDMA'S SCONES

1 package dry yeast
4 cups warm milk
¼ cup sugar
1 teaspoon salt

2 teaspoons oil
6 cups flour
butter, honey or jam

Dissolve yeast in milk. Beat in sugar, salt, oil and flour. Knead and let rise about 1½ hours or until double in bulk. Punch down on floured board and cut into rectangles about 5 x 2 inches. Fry in deep fat until golden brown. Serve with butter, honey or jam. Makes about 3 dozen.

Mrs. Jake Garn

MRS. JAKE GARN, Wife of Senator (Utah)

ORANGE BOWKNOTS

1 package yeast
½ cup lukewarm water
1 cup scalded milk
½ cup shortening
⅓ cup sugar
1 teaspoon salt
5 to 5½ cups sifted flour
2 eggs, beaten

2 tablespoons grated orange peel
¼ cup orange juice

Icing:
1 teaspoon orange peel
2 tablespoons orange juice
1 cup sifted confectioners sugar

Soften yeast in water. Combine milk, shortening, sugar and salt and cool until lukewarm. Stir in about 2 cups of flour and beat well. And eggs and mix. Stir in softened yeast. Add peel, juice and remaining flour. Cover and let stand for 10 minutes. Knead dough 8 to 10 minutes. Place in greased bowl. Cover and let rise until double, about 2 hours. Punch down, cover and let stand 10 minutes. Roll dough into an 18 x 10 inch rectangle, ½ inch thick. Cut strips 10 inches long and ¾ inch wide. Roll each strip and tie in a knot. Arrange on a greased sheet, cover and let rise about 45 minutes. Bake in a 400° oven for 12 to 15 minutes. Combine icing ingredients and, when bowknots are cool, brush on with a pastry brush. Makes 2 dozen.

Mrs Anita W. Ullman

MRS. ANITA W. ULLMAN, Member of Congressional Club (Oregon)

BENYA

1 package yeast
1 cup hot water
sugar
10 very soft bananas
3 tablespoons cinnamon (or cinnamon berries)

2 tablespoons nutmeg
2½ pounds flour
1½ pounds sugar
grated rind of medium size orange
¼ teaspoon salt

Add yeast to hot water and sprinkle in a little sugar. Cover and let stand to start rising process. Mash bananas thoroughly in large mixing bowl with yeast. Add cinnamon, nutmeg, flour, sugar, grated orange rind and salt. Mix thoroughly and let stand overnight. Mixture will rise and triple amount. Drop by spoonful in deep hot fat; fry until brown. Serve either hot or cold. May be frozen. Makes 36 pastries.

Mrs. Cyril E. King

MRS. CYRIL E. KING, Wife of Governor (Virgin Islands)

BANANA FRITTERS

1 egg
1 cup water
¼ cup vegetable oil
½ cup flour
½ cup corn starch

1 teaspoon baking powder
cooking oil
bananas, firm and ripe
    (Brazilian or Cavendish variety)

Mix egg, water and oil. Add to dry ingredients. Beat with electric beater until smooth. Peel bananas and cut in half lengthwise. Dip bananas into batter, letting excess drip off. Deep fry until golden in 1 inch of oil heated to 375°.

Mrs. Hiram L. Fong

MRS. HIRAM L. FONG, Wife of Senator (Hawaii)

FRENCH TOAST

2 eggs, well beaten
1 tablespoon sugar
1 cup milk
2 teaspoons vanilla

¼ pound margarine
6 slices bread
confectioners sugar (or maple syrup)

To eggs, gradually add sugar, milk and vanilla. Place margarine in an electric skillet and heat to 350°. Place each slice of bread in egg mixture, letting it remain until amount desired is absorbed. Brown on both sides in heated skillet. To serve, sprinkle with confectioners sugar or serve with maple syrup.

Mrs. George M. Grant

Mrs. George M. Grant, Wife of former Representative (Alabama)

BERNICE'S BUTTERMILK PANCAKES

2 cups sifted flour
2 teaspoons baking powder
½ teaspoon salt
2½ cups buttermilk

2 eggs
1 teaspoon baking soda
¼ cup oil

Sift together flour, baking powder and salt. Stir in the buttermilk and eggs. Batter will be somewhat lumpy. Mix soda with a small amount of batter and pour back into batter, mixing well. Fold in oil. Bake on seasoned griddle. Makes 16 pancakes.

Mrs. John F. Baldwin

Mrs. John F. Baldwin, Wife of former Representative (California)

COTTAGE CHEESE PANCAKES

1 cup cottage cheese, sieved
4 eggs, well beaten
6 tablespoons flour

6 tablespoons butter, melted
pinch of salt
jelly, confectioners sugar or syrup

Combine first 5 ingredients and mix well. Bake on hot buttered griddle. Serve with jelly, confectioners sugar or syrup.

Mrs. John E. Henderson

Mrs. John E. Henderson, Wife of former Representative (Ohio)

383

FRENCH OR JELLY PANCAKES

3 eggs, separated
1 teaspoon sugar
½ teaspoon salt
1 cup milk

½ cup sifted flour
1 tablespoon melted shortening
tart fruit jelly
confectioners sugar (optional)

Beat egg yolks and add sugar, salt and ½ cup milk. Add flour and shortening and mix until smooth. Add remaining milk. Fold in stiffly beaten egg whites. Bake on 400° griddle, making the cakes extra large and very thin. Spread with jelly and roll up while hot. Serve with the overlapping edges of cakes on bottom to keep them from unrolling. Sprinkle with confectioners sugar if desired. Makes 12 servings.

Mrs. Russell V. Mack

Mrs. Russell V. Mack, Wife of former Representative (Washington)

LUCERNE PANCAKES

3 eggs, separated
¾ cup cottage cheese
¼ cup milk

¼ teaspoon salt
¼ cup flour
red raspberry jam (optional)

Beat egg yolks and cheese until smooth. At low speed, beat in milk, salt and flour. Whip egg whites until stiff. Fold into yolk and cheese mixture. Bake carefully on a very hot, heavy griddle, preferably of cast iron. A drop of water will vaporize instantly when the griddle temperature is right. When pancakes puff, they should be turned. They will deflate slightly when done. This low calorie, low carbohydrate pancake is good served with red raspberry jam. Makes 12 to 14 small pancakes.

Mrs. James R. Schlesinger

Mrs. James R. Schlesinger, Wife of former Secretary of Defense (Virginia)

SUNDAY MORNING SPECIAL PANCAKES

2 tablespoons oil
1 egg, beaten
1 cup plus 2 tablespoons milk
1 cup flour

½ teaspoon salt
2 tablespoons sugar
2 teaspoons baking powder

Mix oil, egg and 1 cup milk. Sift dry ingredients together and add to first mixture. Add remaining milk. Fry on hot griddle. Makes 4 servings.

Mrs. Ralph Harvey

Mrs. Ralph Harvey, Wife of former Representative (Indiana)

384

WALLY'S FLANNEL CAKES

1 cup cake flour
½ teaspoon salt
½ teaspoon baking soda
1 cup buttermilk
1 egg, lightly beaten

2 tablespoons butter, melted
2 tablespoons water
butter
maple or fruit syrup

Sift flour, salt and baking soda together. Add buttermilk and then the egg and butter. Mix well and thin with water. Cook on lightly greased hot griddle. Serve with butter and syrup. Makes 10 medium cakes.

Mrs. Lyle H. Boren

MRS. LYLE H. BOREN, Wife of former Representative (Oklahoma)

GRAN'S APFELPFANNKUCHEN

1 cup flour
¼ teaspoon salt
4 eggs
2 tablespoons cooking oil
1 cup milk
6 tart apples, peeled and sliced

3 tablespoons butter
cinnamon and sugar (or 3 tablespoons
    peach or apricot preserves)
confectioners sugar
syrup

Combine flour and salt in a bowl. Make a well in center and add eggs, oil and ½ cup of milk. Mix well; set aside to rest for 20 to 30 minutes. Batter will be lumpy at this stage. Saute apples in butter until golden and transparent. Add cinnamon and sugar to taste and keep warm over low heat. Add the remaining milk to batter and whisk until smooth. Add a little more milk if necessary to make a thin batter. Wipe heated iron skillet with very lightly greased paper. Pour batter in center of skillet and rotate until batter reaches edges. Turn pancake before browned. Flip onto plate, add a tablespoon of apple mixture and roll up. Keep warm in low oven. To serve, sprinkle with confectioners sugar or serve syrup at the table. May be frozen. Makes 4 servings.

Mrs. Frank E. Evans

MRS. FRANK E. EVANS, Wife of Representative (Colorado)

KENTUCKY CORN CAKES

1 teaspoon baking soda
1 pint buttermilk
white corn meal

1 egg
salt
butter

Add baking soda to buttermilk. Add enough corn meal to make a thin batter. Add egg and salt. Mix thoroughly. Drop from a spoon onto a hot, well greased griddle. Brown on both sides and serve with butter. Makes 6 to 8 servings.

MRS. EMMET O'NEAL, Wife of former Representative (Kentucky)

OLD FASHIONED BUCKWHEAT CAKES

½ ounce compressed yeast
warm water for dissolving yeast
1 cup natural flour
3½ cups buckwheat flour
1 quart lukewarm water

1 teaspoon salt
2 tablespoons molasses
1 tablespoon butter, melted
maple syrup

Dissolve yeast in a little warm water. Mix with natural flour, buckwheat flour, water and salt to a thin batter. Let rise overnight. In the morning add the molasses and melted butter. Cook on hot griddle. Serve with maple syrup.

FRANCES P. BOLTON, former Representative (Ohio)

WAFFLES

1¾ cups sifted cake flour
2 teaspoons double acting baking
  powder
½ teaspoon salt
1 tablespoon sugar

3 egg yolks, well beaten
5 tablespoons melted butter
1½ cups milk
3 egg whites

Sift cake flour before measuring. Resift with baking powder, salt and sugar. Add egg yolks to the butter and milk. Make a hole in center of sifted ingredients. Pour in liquid ingredients and combine with a few quick strokes. Do not beat; batter need not be smooth. Beat egg whites stiff but not dry. Fold lightly into batter until just blended. To cook, follow waffle iron instructions. Never try to remove waffle while still steaming. May be frozen. Makes 6 servings.

MRS. LEE METCALF, Wife of Senator (Montana)

PASTRIES

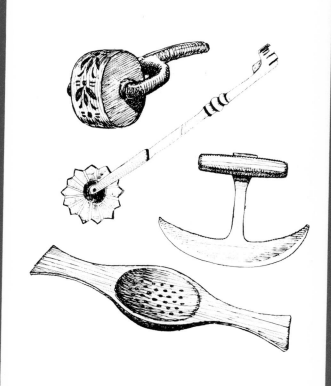

Morella Cherry Pie

Lay a thin paste round the rim of your dish, put a little sugar at the bottom, pick the stalks off the cherries, lay them in, with sugar over them, put a little water in the dish, put on a thin puff-paste lid, and bake it; when it is cold send it to table.

All sorts of plumbs, damsons, and cranberry pies, are made the same way. You may ice all these fruit pies in the following manner: beat up the white of an egg to a froth, then with a paste brush rub it over the crown of the pie, and sift fine powder sugar over it, and just before you put it into the oven sprinkle a little water over it, or it will catch and burn them. You may leave the icing alone, according as the company likes it.

The English Art of Cookery
Richard Briggs, 1798

APPLE PIE (SOUR CREAM PASTRY SHELL)

2½ cups flour
1 teaspoon salt
¾ cup shortening
5 generous tablespoons sour cream

Filling:

5 to 7 tart apples
¾ to 1 cup sugar
2 tablespoons flour
dash of salt
1 teaspoon cinnamon
¼ teaspoon nutmeg
2 tablespoons butter
milk or cream
sugar

Mix flour and salt. Blend in shortening with pastry blender until particles are very small. Mix in sour cream. Mixture will form into a smooth ball. Divide dough in half. Roll on towel sprinkled generously with flour and sugar. Roll to size and place in 9 or 10 inch pie pan. Repeat with top crust.

Pare apples; slice very thin. Mix sugar, flour, salt, cinnamon and nutmeg. Toss with sliced apples, coating them thoroughly. Fill pie shell. Dot with butter. Cover with top crust. Brush this crust with milk or cream and sprinkle with sugar. Bake in 400° oven about 50 minutes. May be frozen.

Mrs. Philip W. Noel

MRS. PHILIP W. NOEL, Wife of Governor (Rhode Island)

DUTCH APPLE PIE

6 medium apples, peeled and sliced
1 unbaked pie shell
½ cup sugar
2 tablespoons flour
½ teaspoon nutmeg
2 tablespoons lemon juice

Topping:

½ cup sugar
½ cup flour
¼ pound butter or margarine

Place apple slices in pastry shell. Combine sugar, flour and nutmeg and pour over apples. Sprinkle lemon juice over all. Mix topping ingredients together and crumble over top of pie. Place in a brown paper bag and bake in a 425° oven for 1 hour.

Mrs. Carroll Hubbard

MRS. CARROLL HUBBARD, Wife of Representative (Kentucky)

NEW YORK STATE FLAT APPLE PIE

½ cup butter
½ cup margarine
2 cups flour
3 to 4 tablespoons ice water

Filling:
11 or 12 medium New York State
   apples, peeled and cored
1 cup sugar
1 tablespoon cinnamon
juice of ½ lemon
½ cup New York State maple syrup
New York State sharp cheese, sliced

Cut butter and margarine into flour with knife or pastry blender until like corn meal. Add ice water gradually and work in just enough to have dough hold together. Roll out on a lightly floured board or marble slab until it is 1 inch thick. Place in refrigerator for 20 minutes. Remove and roll again, this time to a ⅛ inch thickness. Use a flat 15 x 10 inch pan or baking sheet and cover with the prepared crust.

Cut each apple into 6 sections and arrange in 1 layer on the crust. Mix sugar and cinnamon and sprinkle over the apples. Then sprinkle with lemon juice. Bake in a preheated 450° oven for 20 minutes, reduce the heat to 350° and bake for an additional 30 minutes. Remove from oven, sprinkle with maple syrup and serve warm with a generous slice of cheese. Makes 6 to 8 servings.

Mrs. Nelson Rockefeller

MRS. NELSON A. ROCKEFELLER, Wife of Vice President of the United States (New York)

ALABAMA BLACKBERRY PIE

pastry for 2 crust pie
4 cups fresh blackberries
1 cup sugar

2 tablespoons flour
½ stick butter, cut into pieces

Line a deep pie plate with pastry. Toss washed, drained berries with sugar and flour; put into pastry shell. Dot with butter. Cover with top crust, sealing edges well. Prick with a fork. Bake in 450° oven 10 minutes. Reduce heat to 350° and bake 30 minutes longer or until juices begin to run. May be frozen. Makes 6 servings.

MRS. TOM BEVILL, Wife of Representative (Alabama)

BLACKBERRY COBBLER PIE

3 cups blackberries (or other fruit)
water
1 cup plus 2 teaspoons sugar

1½ tablespoons butter
pastry for 2 crust pie
2 teaspoons flour

Cover blackberries with water, add 1 cup sugar and 1 tablespoon butter and boil 10 minutes. Add more sugar if needed. Roll out pastry and place in deep dish pie pan. Pour berries into pie shell and sprinkle them with the flour. Fold top crust over berries, dot crust with remaining butter and sprinkle with remaining sugar. Bake at 415° until brown, about 20 minutes. May be frozen. Makes 6 servings.

MARY ADELAIDE EVINS, Daughter of Representative Joe L. Evins (Tennessee)

BLUEBERRY PIE

¾ cup sugar
3 tablespoons corn starch
¼ teaspoon salt
¾ cup water
4 cups fresh blueberries

2 tablespoons butter
1½ tablespoons lemon juice
1 9 inch baked pie shell
whipped cream

Combine sugar, corn starch and salt. Add water and 1 cup blueberries. Bring to a boil and cook until clear and thick. Stir in butter and lemon juice. Cool. Fold in remaining blueberries and pour into baked pie shell. Chill and top with whipped cream.

Mrs. William Broomfield

MRS. WILLIAM S. BROOMFIELD, Wife of Representative (Michigan)

CHEF LARRY'S PAPAYA PIE

2 pounds half ripe papaya, shredded
1½ pounds brown sugar
20 ounce can crushed, unsweetened
   pineapple
2 tablespoons butter

1 pint papaya nectar
6 tablespoons corn starch
pastry for 2 double crust pies
1 egg, beaten

Mix together first 5 ingredients and boil about 20 minutes or until papaya is soft. Dissolve corn starch in 1 pint of papaya mixture, return to the hot mixture and mix thoroughly. Cool and pour into pie shells. Cover with top crusts and brush with egg. Bake at 400° for 25 to 30 minutes. Chill. May be frozen.

Mrs. Ricardo J. Bordallo

MRS. RICARDO J. BORDALLO, Wife of Governor (Guam)

PEACH CREAM PIE

6 fresh peaches
1 9 inch unbaked pie shell
1 cup granulated sugar
2 tablespoons corn starch

1 cup heavy cream
1 teaspoon vanilla
dash of salt

Peel, halve and stone peaches and arrange cut side up in pie shell. Combine sugar and corn starch. Add cream, vanilla and salt. Stir well. Pour over peaches. Bake at 450° for 15 minutes. Reduce the heat to 325° and continue to bake for 30 minutes or until peaches are tender.

Mrs. Richard P. Yates

MRS. RICHARD YATES, Daughter of Representative Wilbur D. Mills (Arkansas)

LATTICE TOP FRESH PEACH PIE

5 cups peeled, sliced, ripe, sweet
  peaches
¾ cup sugar
2 tablespoons corn starch

¼ teaspoon salt
1 teaspoon vanilla
pastry for 2 crust 9 inch pie
2 tablespoons butter or margarine

Combine peaches, sugar, corn starch, salt and vanilla. Place in pie plate lined with pastry rolled ⅛ inch thick. Dot with butter. Roll remaining pastry into a rectangle 5 by 10 inches. Cut into 10 strips ½ inch wide and arrange over pie, lattice fashion. Bake at 425° for 15 minutes. Lower heat to 375° and bake 30 minutes longer or until crust is brown and peaches are tender. May be frozen.

Mrs. William H. Ayres

MRS. WILLIAM H. AYRES, Wife of former Representative (Ohio)

PISTACHIO PINEAPPLE PIE

1 3 ounce package lemon Jello
1 cup hot water
½ cup pineapple juice
1 pint pistachio ice cream
1 cup crushed pineapple, drained

1 9 inch baked pie shell
1 cup whipping cream, whipped
  (or 1 envelope Dream Whip)
grated chocolate (optional)

Dissolve Jello in hot water. Add pineapple juice. Stir ice cream into warm Jello mixture. Chill until mixture begins to set. Fold in pineapple. Pour into pie shell and place in refrigerator. Just before serving, cover with whipped cream. Grated chocolate may be sprinkled over topping. Makes 5 to 6 servings.

Mrs. Joe L. Evins

MRS. JOE L. EVINS, Wife of Representative (Tennessee)

FRESH FRUIT PIE

3 tablespoons corn starch
1 small can crushed pineapple
1 small package strawberry Jello
1 cup fresh strawberries

1 cup sugar
4 ripe bananas, diced
1 cup chopped pecans
1 large baked pie shell

Mix corn starch with pineapple and heat to a boil. Add Jello, strawberries, sugar, bananas and pecans. Stir well and set aside to cool. Pour into your favorite pie crust, graham cracker or regular baked crust. Omit the sugar if you use frozen strawberries.

Mrs. John Dowdy

MRS. JOHN DOWDY, Wife of former Representative (Texas)

MOTHER'S FRESH RHUBARB PIE

3 cups fresh rhubarb
1½ cups sugar
⅛ teaspoon salt
2 eggs

1 tablespoon butter
pastry for 2 crust 9 inch pie
cinnamon (or nutmeg)

Mix the first 5 ingredients together and let stand while preparing pastry. Put rhubarb mixture in pastry shell and sprinkle with cinnamon. Cover with a lattice of pastry. Bake at 400° for 1 hour. May be frozen but then increase baking time approximately 10 minutes. Makes 6 servings.

Mrs. Neal Smith

MRS. NEAL SMITH, Wife of Representative (Iowa)

394

FRENCH STRAWBERRY GLACE PIE

4 cups strawberries
1 cup water
1 cup sugar
3 tablespoons corn starch

1 3 ounce package cream cheese, softened
1 9 inch baked pie shell
whipped cream (or ice cream)

Wash, drain and hull strawberries. Simmer 1 cup strawberries and ⅔ cup water about 3 minutes. Blend sugar, corn starch and remaining water and add to boiling mixture. Boil 1 minute, stirring constantly. Cool. Spread cream cheese over bottom of cooled pie shell. Reserve ½ cup choice berries. Put remaining berries in pie shell. Cover with cooked mixture and garnish with the reserved berries. Refrigerate until firm, about 2 hours. Serve with sweetened whipped cream or ice cream.

Mrs. Donald J. Mitchell

MRS. DONALD J. MITCHELL, Wife of Representative (New York)

STRAWBERRY PIE

1 cup sugar
3 tablespoons corn starch
1 cup cold water
3 tablespoons strawberry Jello

2 cups fresh strawberries
1 baked pastry shell
whipped cream

Mix sugar and corn starch and add cold water. Cook until it thickens. Add Jello, stir until dissolved and set aside to cool. Put strawberries in baked crust and pour cooked mixture over them. Chill until firm. Top with whipped cream.

Mrs. John J. Flynt, Jr.

MRS. JOHN J. FLYNT, JR., Wife of Representative (Georgia)

OLD FASHIONED CARAMEL PIE

4 tablespoons corn starch
1/4 teaspoon salt
1 rounded cup sugar
2 cups milk
3 tablespoons melted butter
3 egg yolks
1 teaspoon vanilla
1 10 inch baked pie shell

Meringue:
3 egg whites
1/4 teaspoon cream of tartar
6 tablespoons sugar

Mix corn starch, salt and ¾ cup sugar and set aside. Scald milk, cover and keep warm. Put 1 tablespoon butter in heavy iron skillet and add remaining sugar. Caramelize sugar over medium heat, stirring frequently. Remove from heat after sugar starts to brown but before it deepens to a golden brown. Continue stirring sugar and add to warm milk. Mix until sugar is dissolved. Add corn starch mixture and mix well. Beat yolks in top of large double boiler. Stir a small amount of milk mixture into eggs and mix well. Add remaining milk mixture. Cook in double boiler until thick enough for pie filling. Remove from heat, stir in remaining butter and add vanilla. Pour, while still hot, into pie shell.

Meringue: Beat egg whites until foamy, add cream of tartar and beat until almost stiff. Add sugar and beat until stiff. Spread on top of pie, covering inside rim of crust to allow for shrinkage. Bake in 300° oven about 20 minutes. Check after 15 minutes to make sure meringue does not burn. Makes 8 servings.

Mrs. John Sanders

MRS. JOHN SANDERS, Daughter of former Representative John E. Rankin (Mississippi)

AUNT MARY'S CREAM PIE

⅓ cup flour
⅔ cup sugar
¼ teaspoon salt
2 cups milk
2 tablespoons butter

2 egg yolks, slightly beaten
½ teaspoon vanilla
1 9 inch baked pastry shell
meringue (or whipped cream)

Mix thoroughly the flour, sugar and salt. Scald milk in top of double boiler. Add the dry ingredients slowly, stirring constantly. Cook over hot water until thickened, about 15 minutes. Add butter and egg yolks and cook 2 more minutes. Stir in vanilla. Pour into pastry shell and cool. Cover with meringue or whipped cream. Refrigerate. Makes 8 servings.

Variations:

Chocolate: Increase sugar to 1 cup. Add 4 squares unsweetened chocolate to scalded milk and stir until melted. Continue with basic recipe.

Fruit: Add 2 or 3 sliced bananas, an equal amount of strawberries or ¼ cup drained pineapple to basic recipe.

Butterscotch: Substitute 1 cup brown sugar for granulated sugar.

Chocolate chip: Add 1 ounce grated sweet chocolate to basic recipe.

Caramel: Caramelize ¼ cup sugar until smooth and golden. Add scalded milk gradually, stir until well blended and proceed with basic recipe.

Mrs. J. Kenneth Robinson

MRS. J. KENNETH ROBINSON, Wife of Representative (Virginia)

CHOCOLATE ALMOND PIE

4 large Hershey chocolate almond bars
20 large marshmallows
⅔ cup milk

½ pint whipping cream, whipped
8 or 9 inch baked pie shell
whipped cream for garnish

Melt chocolate bars and marshmallows in milk in top of double boiler, mixing well. Chill thoroughly in the refrigerator. Fold whipped cream into chocolate mixture, pour into pie shell and chill until set. Garnish with whipped cream.

Mrs. Henry Bellmon

MRS. HENRY BELLMON, Wife of Senator (Oklahoma)

QUICK CHOCOLATE PIE

1 9 ounce carton Cool Whip
1 8 ounce plain Hershey milk
   chocolate bar
1 teaspoon almond flavoring

pinch of salt
1 9 inch baked pie shell
slivered almonds (optional)

Thaw Cool Whip to room temperature. Melt Hershey bar over hot water in double boiler. Blend Cool Whip and chocolate. Add flavoring and salt. Pour into pie shell. Top with slivered almonds if desired. May be frozen. Makes 6 servings.

Mrs. Hugo L. Black

MRS. HUGO L. BLACK, Wife of former Associate Justice, Supreme Court (Alabama)

CHOCOLATE FUDGE PIE

¼ pound butter
2½ ounces unsweetened baking
    chocolate
4 eggs
3 tablespoons white Karo syrup
1½ cups sugar
¼ teaspoon salt

1 teaspoon vanilla
1 unbaked 9 inch pastry shell

Optional:
ice cream
chopped nuts

In top of double boiler melt butter and chocolate. Beat eggs in mixing bowl until light. Blend in Karo, sugar, salt and vanilla. Add slightly cooled chocolate mixture. Mix thoroughly. Pour into pastry shell. Bake at 350° for 25 or 30 minutes or until top is crusty and filling set but somewhat soft. May be served topped with ice cream or a sprinkling of chopped nuts.

Mrs. James O. Eastland

MRS. JAMES O. EASTLAND, Wife of Senator (Mississippi)

398

PECAN FUDGE PIE

½ cup butter
3 squares unsweetened chocolate
4 eggs
3 tablespoons white corn syrup
1½ cups sugar

¼ teaspoon salt
1 teaspoon vanilla
1 cup chopped pecans
1 9 inch unbaked pastry shell
ice cream or whipped cream (optional)

Melt butter and chocolate in top of double boiler. Beat eggs in mixing bowl until light. Beat syrup, sugar, salt and vanilla into the eggs. Add the nuts and then the slightly cooled chocolate mixture. Mix thoroughly and pour into pastry shell. Bake at 350° for 25 to 35 minutes or until top is crusty and filling is set but soft inside. Do not overbake. Pie should shake like custard so it will not be too stiff when cooled. May be served plain or with ice cream or whipped cream. Makes 8 to 10 servings.

Mrs. George Dekle Busbee

MRS. GEORGE BUSBEE, Wife of Governor (Georgia)

CHOCOLATE WHIP ICEBOX DELIGHT PIE

1 6 ounce chocolate bar with almonds
1 9 ounce container Cool Whip
2 tablespoons bourbon

2 tablespoons rum
1 9 inch baked pie shell

Melt chocolate bar in top of double boiler. Fold in Cool Whip, reserving some for topping. Stir in bourbon and rum and pour into pie shell. Cool in refrigerator. Decorate with reserved Cool Whip.

Mrs. Daniel J. Flood

MRS. DANIEL J. FLOOD, Wife of Representative (Pennsylvania)

COCOA CHESS PIE

1½ cups sugar
2 tablespoons flour
2 tablespoons cocoa
½ teaspoon vanilla

2 eggs, unbeaten
1 cup milk
2 tablespoons melted butter
1 unbaked pie shell

Mix dry ingredients. Add eggs, milk and butter, stirring to thoroughly blend. Pour into pie shell and bake at 350° for 35 to 40 minutes. This makes a large pie, so use a deep shell. Makes 6 servings.

Mrs. Robert E. Jones

Mrs. ROBERT E. JONES, Wife of Representative (Alabama)

CHOCOLATE CHESS PIE

¼ pound butter or margarine
1 square chocolate
1 cup sugar
2 eggs, beaten

1 teaspoon vanilla
1 9 inch unbaked pie shell
vanilla ice cream (or whipped cream)

Melt butter and chocolate. Add sugar, eggs and vanilla. Stir together thoroughly and pour into unbaked pie shell. Bake at 350° for 25 to 30 minutes. Top baked pie with ice cream or whipped cream. May be served warm or cold. May be frozen. Makes 6 to 8 servings.

Mrs. George Arthur Weaver

Mrs. GEORGE ARTHUR WEAVER, Daughter of former Representative M. G. Burnside (West Virginia)

CHOCOLATE PIE

1 cup chocolate chips
2 tablespoons sugar
3 tablespoons milk
4 egg yolks

1 teaspoon vanilla
4 egg whites, stiffly beaten
1 9 inch baked pie shell
whipping cream, whipped

Melt chocolate chips, add sugar and milk. Add egg yolks, 1 at a time, and stir over low heat until mixed well. Add vanilla. Cool. Fold in egg whites. Pour into baked pie shell and chill. Serve with whipped cream. Makes 6 servings.

Mrs. William H. Harsha

Mrs. WILLIAM H. HARSHA, Wife of Representative (Ohio)

KENTUCKY PIE

1 cup sugar
½ cup flour
¼ pound butter, melted
2 eggs, slightly beaten

1 6 ounce package chocolate chips
1 cup chopped pecans
1 teaspoon vanilla
1 9 inch unbaked pie shell

Mix together sugar and flour. Add melted butter and blend well. Stir in eggs, chips, nuts and vanilla. Pour mixture into pie shell. Bake in preheated 325° oven 1 hour or until golden brown. May be frozen. Makes 6 to 8 servings.

Mrs. Wendell Ford

MRS. WENDELL H. FORD, Wife of Senator (Kentucky)

COCONUT CREAM PIE

1 package Flako pie crust mix
1 package Jello vanilla pudding
1 cup milk
1 cup cream

1 teaspoon vanilla
1 large container Cool Whip
1 package Baker's Angel Flake coconut

Make pie crust according to package directions. Combine pudding mix with milk and cream and cook according to directions on package. After pudding has cooled, fold in vanilla and Cool Whip. Pour into baked pie crust and top heavily with coconut. Refrigerate for at least 1 hour before serving.

Mrs. John C. Kunkel

MRS. JOHN C. KUNKEL, Wife of former Representative (Pennsylvania)

401

PEANUT BUTTER CREAM PIE

1 cup sifted flour
½ teaspoon salt
⅓ cup shortening
3 or 4 tablespoons cold water

¼ cup corn starch
½ teaspoon salt
2½ cups milk
3 egg yolks, lightly beaten
1 teaspoon vanilla

Filling:
¾ cup confectioners sugar
½ cup creamy peanut butter
½ cup granulated sugar

Meringue:
3 egg whites
6 tablespoons sugar

Combine flour and salt in mixing bowl and cut in shortening with pastry blender until crumbs are size of small peas. Sprinkle with water and stir with a fork until dough is moist enough to hold together. Form into ball and roll in circle 1½ inches larger than inverted 9 inch pie pan. Fit loosely into pan, fold edge to form a standing rim and flute. Prick with fork and bake at 450° for 10 or 12 minutes until slightly browned. Cool.

Filling: Mix confectioners sugar and peanut butter together until crumbs form. Cover bottom of baked pastry shell with crumbs, reserving 3 tablespoons for topping. Mix together granulated sugar, corn starch and salt in saucepan. Add milk to egg yolks and stir into corn starch mixture until well blended. Cook over medium heat, stirring constantly, and boil 1 minute. Remove from heat and stir in vanilla. Cool to room temperature and spoon into pastry shell.

Meringue: Make meringue by beating egg whites until foamy. Add sugar, 1 tablespoon at a time, beating well after each addition, until stiff peaks form. Spread meringue over filling to edge of crust and top with reserved peanut butter crumbs. Bake at 425° about 5 minutes or until meringue is lightly browned.

Mrs. Richard M. Simpson

Mrs. Richard M. Simpson, Wife of former Representative (Pennsylvania)

WALNUT MAPLE PIE

2¼ cups sifted flour
¾ teaspoon salt
¾ cup shortening
5 tablespoons ice water

Filling:
½ cup butter
1 cup sugar

¼ teaspoon salt
¾ cup maple syrup
3 large eggs, beaten
1 cup chopped walnuts
2 tablespoons flour
1 teaspoon black walnut flavoring
whipped cream (optional)

Sift flour and salt together. Cut in shortening. Add water, a few drops at a time. Roll out and fit into two 9 inch pie tins. Refrigerate 1 shell while preparing filling and freeze the extra shell for later use.

Combine butter, sugar, salt and maple syrup in top of double boiler over boiling water and stir until thoroughly dissolved. Remove from heat and pour mixture very slowly over eggs, stirring constantly. Add the walnuts mixed with the flour. Add the flavoring. Pour into pastry shell and bake 40 to 45 minutes at 375°. Serve with whipped cream. Makes 7 servings.

Mrs. Hugh Q. Alexander

MRS. HUGH Q. ALEXANDER, Wife of former Representative (North Carolina)

CHESS PIE

1½ cups sugar
⅔ stick butter or margarine, melted
4 eggs, beaten
1 teaspoon flour

juice of ½ lemon
1 teaspoon vanilla
1 teaspoon corn meal
1 8 inch unbaked pie shell

Add sugar to hot butter and cool slightly. Add other filling ingredients to eggs and then add them to the butter and sugar. Pour into pie shell and bake in a 300° oven for 45 minutes. Makes 6 servings.

Mrs. Frank William Boykin

MRS. FRANK WILLIAM BOYKIN, Wife of former Representative (Alabama)

JEFF DAVIS PIE

1½ cups flour
1 teaspoon salt
½ cup Mazola corn oil
¼ cup water
¼ pound butter

2 cups sugar
2 heaping tablespoons flour
5 eggs
1¼ cups milk
1½ teaspoons vanilla

Sift flour and salt together in bowl. Add oil and water and stir until well blended. Roll out between sheets of wax paper until large enough to fit an 11 inch pie pan. Cream butter, sugar and flour. Add eggs and milk and beat well. Add vanilla. Pour into unbaked crust and bake at 325° until brown and center is still shaky, approximately 45 minutes. May be frozen. Makes 8 servings.

Mrs. William Lowe Waller

MRS. WILLIAM LOWE WALLER, Wife of Governor (Mississippi)

PENNSYLVANIA DUTCH FUNNY CAKE

Chocolate Sauce:
1 cup warm water
1 cup sugar
½ cup cocoa
¾ teaspoon vanilla

2 9 inch unbaked pie shells

Cake Batter:
½ cup butter
2 cups sugar
2 eggs
2 cups plus 2 tablespoons flour
2 teaspoons baking powder
1 cup milk
½ teaspoon vanilla

Combine all ingredients for chocolate sauce, mix thoroughly and set aside. To make batter, cream butter, add sugar and mix well. Add eggs and beat. Stir in flour and baking powder. Add milk and vanilla. Pour chocolate sauce into the pie shells. Spoon cake batter over sauce. Bake at 375° for 45 minutes.

Mrs. Richard Schultz Schweiker

MRS. RICHARD SCHULTZ SCHWEIKER, Wife of Senator (Pennsylvania)

404

SHOOFLY PIE

Crumb topping:
1 cup unsifted flour
½ cup light brown sugar
¼ cup vegetable shortening

Liquid bottom:
1 teaspoon baking soda
1 cup boiling water
1 cup golden table molasses
¼ teaspoon salt

9 inch unbaked pie shell
whipped cream or ice cream

Combine flour, brown sugar and shortening in a bowl and cut with a pastry blender or rub with your fingers until it forms fine crumbs. Set side.

Dissolve soda in boiling water. Add molasses and salt and stir to blend well. Pour liquid mixture into pie shell and sprinkle the crumb topping evenly over it. Bake in a 375° oven for 10 minutes. Reduce temperature to 350° and bake for 30 minutes longer or until set. When pie is given a gentle shake, the top should remain firm. Serve warm with whipped cream or ice cream.

Mrs. Edwin D. Eshleman

MRS. EDWIN D. ESHLEMAN, Wife of Representative (Pennsylvania)

TOMMY'S BUTTERMILK PIE

1⅓ cups sugar
2 teaspoons corn meal
1 teaspoon flour
⅔ stick margarine or butter, melted

2 large eggs
½ cup buttermilk
1 teaspoon vanilla
1 unbaked pie shell

Mix ingredients together in order given, adding 1 egg at a time and beating well after each addition. Pour into pie shell. Bake at 350° until top is brown, about 10 minutes. Reduce heat to 250° and continue baking until filling is firm when gently shaken. May be frozen. Makes 6 servings.

Mary A. Evins

MARY ADELAIDE EVINS, Daughter of Representative Joe L. Evins (Tennessee)

LEMON PIE

2 lemons, sliced paper thin
2 cups sugar

pastry for 2 crust 8 inch pie
4 eggs, well beaten

Place lemon slices in bowl and cover with sugar. Mix well and let stand overnight. Next day arrange lemon slices in unbaked pie shell. Pour eggs over lemons. Cover with top crust, making small vents to allow steam to escape. Bake at 450° for 15 minutes, reduce heat to 400° and bake until tip of silver knife inserted into custard comes out clean. Serve warm. Makes 6 servings.

Mrs. Omar Burleson

MRS. OMAR BURLESON, Wife of Representative (Texas)

LEMON CAKE PIE

1 cup sugar
4 tablespoons corn starch
pinch of salt
3 tablespoons butter

3 eggs, separated
1 lemon, juice and grated rind
1½ cups milk
1 8 inch unbaked pie shell

Mix and sift sugar, corn starch and salt. Add butter and mix well. Add beaten egg yolks, lemon juice and rind. Then add milk and stiffly beaten egg whites. Put in pie shell and bake at 325° for 45 minutes or until firm. Makes 5 servings.

Mrs. Carl T. Curtis

MRS. CARL T. CURTIS, Wife of Senator (Nebraska)

LEMON CHESS PIE

2 cups sugar
2 tablespoons corn meal
2 tablespoons flour
3 eggs, slightly beaten

½ stick margarine, melted
¼ cup milk
2 lemons, juice and grated rind
1 unbaked pie shell

Mix sugar, corn meal and flour together. Add eggs and mix. Add margarine, milk, lemon juice and grated rind. Blend well. Pour in pie shell. Bake 30 minutes or longer at 350°.

Mrs. L. H. Fountain

MRS. L. H. FOUNTAIN, Wife of Representative (North Carolina)

LEMON MERINGUE PIE

1 cup sugar
¼ cup flour
1¼ cups milk
3 egg yolks, beaten
¼ cup lemon juice
grated rind of 1 lemon
1 9 inch baked pie shell

Meringue:
3 egg whites
⅛ teaspoon salt
¼ teaspoon cream of tartar
½ cup sugar

Cook sugar, flour and milk over low heat until thickened. Add egg yolks and cook 5 minutes longer, stirring constantly. Add lemon juice. Strain, then stir in lemon rind and chill. When filling is cold, pour into pie shell and top with meringue. To make meringue, whip egg whites with salt and cream of tartar and beat until stiff. Add sugar gradually, beating after each addition until stiff peaks form. Spread over pie filling, sprinkle with additional sugar and bake at 350° about 20 minutes or until lightly browned.

Mrs. Edward V. Long

Mrs. Edward V. Long, Wife of former Senator (Missouri)

LIME CHIFFON PIE

1 tablespoon gelatin
¼ cup cold water
½ cup fresh lime juice
1 cup sugar
½ teaspoon salt
4 egg yolks, beaten

1 teaspoon grated lime rind
few drops green food coloring
4 egg whites
1 cup heavy cream, whipped
1 baked deep pie shell

Soak gelatin in cold water. Set aside. Combine, cook and stir in a double boiler the lime juice, ½ cup sugar, salt and egg yolks until the mixture is the consistency of custard. Stir in softened gelatin and grated lime rind. Tint custard a light green, if desired. Cool. When custard begins to set, whip egg whites until stiff, very slowly adding the remaining sugar. Whisk the custard mixture and add the whipped egg whites and whipped cream, folding all together carefully. Pile into the cooled pie shell and allow to set for at least 2 hours in refrigerator. Makes 8 servings.

Mrs. William H. Rehnquist

Mrs. William H. Rehnquist, Wife of Associate Justice, Supreme Court (Arizona)

RASPBERRY RIBBON PIE

1 3 ounce package raspberry Jello
¼ cup granulated sugar
1 10 ounce package frozen raspberries
1½ cups boiling water
1 3 ounce package cream cheese
⅓ cup confectioners sugar

1 teaspoon vanilla
pinch of salt
1 tablespoon lemon juice
1 cup heavy cream, whipped
1 9 inch baked pie shell
whipped cream for topping

Combine and mix Jello, granulated sugar and raspberries in water. Chill until partially set. Blend cheese, confectioners sugar, vanilla, salt and lemon juice until creamy. Fold in whipped cream in small amounts. Spread half of cheese mixture on bottom of crust. Cover with half of Jello mixture. Repeat layers and chill overnight. Serve with whipped cream.

MRS. HENRY J. NOWAK, Wife of Representative (New York)

PECAN PIE

1 cup sugar
½ stick butter, melted
⅔ cup dark corn syrup
1 tablespoon flour (or ½ tablespoon corn starch)

¼ teaspoon salt
3 eggs, slightly beaten
1 teaspoon vanilla
1 cup chopped pecans
1 9 inch unbaked pie shell

Combine sugar, butter and syrup and mix very well. Stir in flour, salt and eggs. Add vanilla and pecans. Pour into pie shell and bake in preheated 450° oven for 10 minutes. Reduce heat to 375° and bake another 25 to 30 minutes or until filling is almost firm in center. Cool on a rack. May be frozen. Makes 8 servings.

MRS. RAY BLANTON, Wife of Governor (Tennessee)

DELICIOUS PECAN PIE

1 cup pecans
1 9 inch unbaked pie shell
3 eggs, slightly beaten
¾ cup sugar

¾ cup light Karo syrup
¼ cup molasses
¼ teaspoon salt

Spread pecans over pie shell. Mix together next 5 ingredients and pour over pecans. Bake about 40 minutes at 350°. May be frozen.

MRS. J. J. PICKLE, Wife of Representative (Texas)

BROWN SUGAR PECAN PIE

3 eggs
1 cup brown sugar
1 cup dark corn syrup
1 cup broken pecans

1 teaspoon vanilla
½ teaspoon salt
1 9 inch unbaked pie shell

Beat eggs and sugar together until thick. Add corn syrup, pecans, vanilla and salt. Mix well. Pour into pie shell and bake at 300° for 1 hour or until firm.

MRS. RICHARD C. WHITE, Wife of Representative (Texas)

SOUTHERN PECAN PIE

1 cup dark Karo syrup
3 tablespoons melted butter
  (or margarine)
½ cup sugar
3 eggs, beaten

¼ teaspoon salt
1 teaspoon vanilla
1 cup chopped pecans
1 9 inch pie shell, partially baked

Combine syrup, butter and sugar. Add eggs and mix thoroughly. Add salt and vanilla. Beat well. Add pecans, stirring until nuts are well coated. Pour into pie shell. Bake at 325° for 45 minutes to 1 hour.

MRS. J. GLENN BEALL, JR., Wife of Senator (Maryland)

MISSISSIPPI PECAN PIE

1 cup sugar
3 tablespoons margarine or butter
3 large eggs, beaten
1 cup white Karo syrup
⅛ teaspoon salt

1 cup sugar
1 teaspoon vanilla
1 cup pecan halves
1 10 inch pie shell, slightly baked

Cream sugar and margarine thoroughly. Add eggs to creamed mixture. Add Karo, salt, sugar and vanilla. Mix well. Add pecans. Pour into pie shell. Bake at 350° for 15 minutes and then at 300° for 45 minutes. Pie is done when cake tester comes out clean. If crust rim browns before filling cooks, cover rim with aluminum foil strips to slow browning. Makes 8 servings.

Mrs. John Sanders

MRS. JOHN SANDERS, Daughter of former Representative John E. Rankin (Mississippi)

MOOSE MEAT MINCEMEAT

1 pound moose meat
½ pound beef suet
boiling water
4 apples, finely chopped
1 quince, finely chopped
¾ pound sugar
½ cup molasses
1 pint cider
1 pound seeded raisins
¾ pound currants

1 tablespoon finely cut citron
1½ cups meat stock
½ pint cooking brandy
1 teaspoon cinnamon
1 teaspoon mace
1 teaspoon nutmeg
¼ teaspoon pepper
salt to taste
1 teaspoon cloves

Cover meat and suet with boiling water and cook until tender. Leave in water to cool. When cool, remove layer of fat. Finely chop the meat and suet. Add the apples, quince, sugar, molasses, cider, raisins, currants and citron. These ingredients should be equal to twice the amount of meat and suet. Add the meat stock to the fruit and meat mixture. Heat gradually, stirring occasionally. Cook slowly 2 hours. Add brandy and spices.

This may be put in jars while boiling hot and sealed for future use. Use as for any mincemeat pie. This recipe makes 7 to 8 pints.

Mrs. Jay S. Hammond

MRS. JAY S. HAMMOND, Wife of Governor (Alaska)

410

SOUR CREAM PUMPKIN PIE

1 cup sugar
2 tablespoons pumpkin pie spice
1 tablespoon flour
½ teaspoon salt
3 eggs
1½ cups mashed cooked pumpkin

1 cup dairy sour cream
½ cup seedless raisins (optional)
1 9 inch unbaked pie shell (or
   graham cracker crust)
whipped cream

Combine sugar, spice, flour and salt; set aside. Beat eggs slightly; blend in pumpkin, sour cream and raisins. Stir sugar mixture into pumpkin. Pour into pie shell. Bake at 400° for 50 minutes. Garnish with whipped cream.

Mrs. Robert N. Giaimo

MRS. ROBERT N. GIAIMO, Wife of Representative (Connecticut)

BUTTERNUT SQUASH PIE

1 cup cooked squash
1 teaspoon flour
1 teaspoon lemon juice
⅛ teaspoon salt
2 egg yolks
¼ teaspoon cinnamon
¼ teaspoon allspice

¼ teaspoon nutmeg
¾ cup sugar (or ½ cup granulated
   sugar and ¼ cup light brown sugar)
1 cup evaporated milk
2 egg whites, beaten
1 9 inch unbaked pie shell

Mix all filling ingredients together, folding in egg whites last. Pour into pie shell and bake in a 400° oven for 30 to 45 minutes. Makes 6 to 8 servings.

Mrs. James G. Polk

MRS. JAMES G. POLK, Wife of former Representative (Ohio)

HAPPY TIME TARTS

1 9 ounce package condensed
    mincemeat
1 6 ounce can frozen orange juice,
    thawed and undiluted

¾ cup water
12 to 15 unbaked tart shells

Put mincemeat into saucepan and break into small pieces; add orange juice and water. Cook over medium heat, stirring constantly, until free from lumps. Boil 1 minute. Cool. Fill tart shells and bake at 400° for 20 to 25 minutes or until crust is brown. May be frozen.

Mrs. Richard H. Ichord

MRS. RICHARD H. ICHORD, Wife of Representative (Missouri)

EASY PIE CRUST MIX

2 cups flour
½ teaspoon salt

½ cup milk
½ cup Wesson oil

Sift flour and salt. Add milk and oil. Stir until blended. Roll between wax paper on smooth, flat surface. Mold to bottom and sides of pie pans. Bake at 350° to 400° until brown. May be frozen. Makes two 8 inch crusts.

Mrs. Walter Moeller

MRS. WALTER MOELLER, Wife of former Representative (Ohio)

EASY MAYONNAISE PIE CRUST

2 cups sifted unbleached flour
¼ teaspoon salt

½ cup mayonnaise
¼ cup cold water

Mix flour and salt. Stir in mayonnaise with a fork until consistency of coarse salt. Sprinkle with cold water and stir until a ball is formed. Place half of dough between pieces of plastic wrap and roll out 1 inch larger than an inverted pie pan. Put in pie pan, mold to bottom and sides and shape rim of crust with thumb and forefinger for a fluted edge. Prick center with fork gently and bake in 450° to 475° oven about 10 minutes. May be frozen. Makes 2 single pie crusts.

Mrs. Joe L. Evins

MRS. JOE L. EVINS, Wife of Representative (Tennessee)

412

PIE CRUST MIX

4 cups sifted flour
1 tablespoon sugar
2 teaspoons salt
1½ cups lard

1 tablespoon vinegar
1 egg
½ cup water

Sift together flour, sugar and salt. Cut in the lard with a pastry blender until crumbly. With a fork beat together the vinegar, egg and water and stir into the flour mixture until moistened. Dough will be sticky. With hands, mold dough into a ball and divide into 5 parts. Chill at least 15 minutes before rolling into shape. The dough may be stored in refrigerator up to 3 days or frozen indefinitely. Makes five 9 inch pie crusts.

Mrs. John F. Baldwin

MRS. JOHN F. BALDWIN, Wife of former Representative (California)

NOTES

CAKES

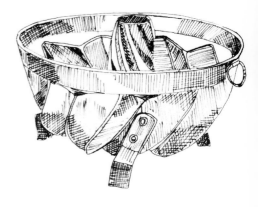

A rich CAKE

Take six pounds of the best fresh butter, work it to a cream with your hands; then throw in by degrees three pounds of double refined sugar, well beat and sifted; mix them well together, then work in three pounds of blanched almonds; and having beat four pounds of eggs, and strained them through a sieve, put them in; beat them all together till they are thick and look white. Then add half a pint of French brandy, half a pint of sack, a small quantity of ginger, and about two ounces each of mace, cloves, and cinnamon, with three large nutmegs, all beaten in a mortar as fine as possible. Then shake in gradually four pounds of well dried and sifted flour. When the oven is well prepared, and a tin hoop to bake it in, stir into this mixture (as you put it into the hoop) seven pounds of currants well washed and rubbed, and such a quantity of candid orange, lemon, and citron, in equal proportions, as shall be thought convenient. The oven must be quick, and the cake will at least take four hours to bake it.

The Frugal Housewife or Complete Cook
Susannah Carter, 1795

ITALIAN CREAM CAKE

2 cups sugar
1 stick margarine
½ cup Crisco
5 eggs, separated
2 cups flour
1 cup buttermilk
1 teaspoon baking soda
1 teaspoon vanilla
1 can coconut

Frosting:
1 8 ounce package cream cheese
1 stick margarine
1 pound confectioners sugar
1 teaspoon vanilla
1½ cups toasted, chopped pecans

Cream sugar with margarine and Crisco. Beat in egg yolks, 1 at a time. Add flour alternately with buttermilk to which the baking soda has been added. Add vanilla. Fold in the stiffly beaten egg whites. Fold in coconut. Put in three 9 inch cake pans and bake in 350° oven for 25 minutes. Combine frosting ingredients and mix well. When cake is cool, frost between layers and over top and sides. May be frozen.

Mrs. Glenn English

Mrs. Glenn English, Wife of Representative (Oklahoma)

STEVE'S FAVORITE CARAMEL CAKE

½ pound butter, softened
½ cup shortening
3 cups sugar
6 eggs, room temperature
3 cups cake flour, sifted
1 cup evaporated milk
½ teaspoon baking powder
1 teaspoon vanilla

Frosting:
½ pound butter
2 cups light brown sugar, packed
½ cup evaporated milk
1½ teaspoons vanilla
4 cups confectioners sugar, sifted

Combine butter and shortening. Add sugar, a cup at a time, and beat until fluffy. Add eggs, an egg at a time, with mixer at low speed. Add flour and milk alternately, a little at a time, beginning and ending with flour. When batter is thoroughly mixed, add baking powder and vanilla. Pour into 3 greased and floured 9 inch cake pans and bake at 325° for 30 to 35 minutes.

For frosting, melt butter in saucepan and add brown sugar and milk. Cook on medium high for 2 minutes, stirring constantly. Remove from heat, add vanilla and pour over confectioners sugar. Beat until smooth. Let cool before frosting cake.

Mrs. Stephen L. Neal

Mrs. Stephen L. Neal, Wife of Representative (North Carolina)

CALIFORNIA SUNSHINE CAKE

1½ cups sifted cake flour
½ cup sugar
¼ teaspoon salt
2 teaspoons baking powder
2 eggs, separated
½ stick butter, softened
½ cup strained orange juice
2 teaspoons Cointreau

Filling:
½ cup flour
¾ cup sugar

1 teaspoon grated orange peel
2 egg yolks, beaten
1 cup orange juice
1½ cups water

Frosting:
4 tablespoons butter, softened
2 cups sifted confectioners sugar
2 teaspoons Cointreau
2 tablespoons orange juice
freshly grated coconut

Sift flour, sugar, salt and baking powder into large mixer bowl. Add egg yolks, butter, orange juice and Cointreau and blend at low speed. Scrape bowl often until all is well mixed. Increase to medium speed and beat 4 minutes. Scrape sides of bowl and beat an additional 2 minutes on high speed. Fold in stiffly beaten egg whites. Pour into two 9 inch round layer cake pans. Bake 20 to 25 minutes at 375°. Cool completely. May be frozen at this point.

For filling, add flour, sugar and orange peel to egg yolks and then mix in juice and water. Cook in top of double boiler, stirring until thick and smooth. Cool to lukewarm and spread between cake layers.

For frosting, combine butter, sugar, Cointreau and orange juice, blend and then beat at high speed until smooth and creamy. Cover top of cake with frosting and sprinkle well with coconut.

Mrs C W Weinberger

MRS. CASPAR WEINBERGER, Wife of former Secretary of Health, Education and Welfare (California)

CHOCOLATE FUDGE CAKE

4 squares bitter chocolate
½ pound butter
2 cups sugar
4 eggs

1½ cups sifted flour
1 cup chopped pecans
1 teaspoon vanilla
pinch of salt

Melt chocolate and butter in top of double boiler. When melted, remove from heat and add sugar. Then add the eggs alternately with the flour. Lastly, stir in pecans, vanilla and salt. Pour into a greased 9 x 13 inch pan lined with brown paper and bake at 250° for 15 minutes. Increase the oven temperature to 350° and bake another 15 minutes. The completed cake depends on this baking procedure. Remove from oven as soon as the cake begins to look firm on top even though it may not look done. This will keep the center soft and a little chewy but with a nice crust on top.

Mrs. Richardson Preyer

MRS. RICHARDSON PREYER, Wife of Representative (North Carolina)

SOUR CREAM FUDGE CAKE

2 squares unsweetened chocolate
2 cups sifted cake flour
1½ cups sugar
1¼ teaspoons baking soda
1 teaspoon salt

½ cup shortening
1 cup dairy sour cream
2 large eggs
1 teaspoon vanilla extract
¼ cup hot water

Melt chocolate over hot, not boiling, water. Let cool. Into large bowl sift flour with sugar, soda and salt. Add shortening and sour cream. Beat 2 minutes at medium speed. Add eggs, vanilla, chocolate and hot water. Beat 2 minutes. Pour batter into 2 greased and floured 8 inch round cake pans. Bake in a preheated 350° oven for 30 to 35 minutes or until top springs back when pressed. Cool in pans 10 minutes. Remove and finish cooling on racks. Frost with your favorite frosting. Makes 10 servings.

Mrs. Wm. L. Armstrong

MRS. WILLIAM L. ARMSTRONG, Wife of Representative (Colorado)

CHOCOLATE ANGEL FOOD CAKE

¾ cup cake flour
4 tablespoons cocoa
1⅓ cups egg whites
¼ teaspoon salt
1⅓ teaspoons cream of tartar

1½ cups sifted sugar
1 teaspoon vanilla
1 pint whipping cream, whipped
coconut

Sift flour once, measure, add cocoa and sift again. Beat egg whites and salt in mixer until foamy and add cream of tartar. Continue beating until eggs are stiff enough to hold peaks but not dry. Fold in sugar carefully, 2 tablespoons at a time. Fold in vanilla. Fold in flour and cocoa mixture, 2 tablespoons at a time. Pour batter into ungreased angel food pan and bake at 325° for 1 hour. Invert pan for 1 hour or until cold. To serve, top each slice with whipped cream and garnish with 1 teaspoon coconut. Makes 10 to 12 servings.

Mrs. William S. Broomfield

MRS. WILLIAM S. BROOMFIELD, Wife of Representative (Michigan)

CHOCOLATE CAKE

2 cups sugar
¼ pound margarine
2 eggs
3 rounded tablespoons cocoa
2 teaspoons baking soda

1 cup boiling water
1 cup sour milk
2 cups flour
2 teaspoons vanilla

Beat first 4 ingredients together until smooth. Add the baking soda to the boiling water and add to first mixture along with the other remaining ingredients. Stir until well mixed. Pour into a greased 9 x 13 inch pan and bake at 325° for 25 to 30 minutes. May be frozen. Makes 12 servings.

Mrs. Neal Smith

MRS. NEAL SMITH, Wife of Representative (Iowa)

CHIPMUNK CAKE

1 cup boiling water
1 cup finely chopped dates
1 ¾ cups flour
¼ cup cocoa
1 teaspoon baking soda
½ teaspoon salt

1 cup shortening
1 cup sugar
2 eggs, beaten
1 teaspoon vanilla
½ cup chopped nuts
1 cup semi-sweet chocolate bits

Combine water and dates and let cool. Sift the flour, cocoa, soda and salt. Cream shortening and sugar until fluffy and add eggs and vanilla. Beat well with mixer. Add flour alternately with date mixture, mixing well after each addition. Spoon batter into a well greased and floured 9 x 13 inch pan. Sprinkle nuts and chocolate bits on top, pressing lightly into batter. Bake in 350° oven for 45 minutes. Cut into squares. May be frozen. Makes 12 servings.

MRS. J. EDGAR CHENOWETH, Wife of former Representative (Colorado)

HONOLULU CAKE

1 cup brown sugar
½ cup ground sweet chocolate
½ cup milk
1 egg yolk
¼ teaspoon baking soda
½ cup shortening
1 cup white sugar

3 egg yolks
2½ cups flour
3 teaspoons baking powder
½ teaspoon salt
¾ cup milk
1 teaspoon vanilla
4 egg whites, stiffly beaten

Boil first 4 ingredients together for 3 minutes, cool and add baking soda. Cream shortening, add sugar and cream again. Add yolks and beat. Mix flour, baking powder and salt together and add to creamed mixture alternately with milk and vanilla. Fold in boiled chocolate mixture. Fold in egg whites. Bake in 3 greased, lightly floured 9 inch round cake pans for 20 minutes at 375°.

MRS. DEL M. CLAWSON, Wife of Representative (California)

421

FAMILY FAVORITE CHOCOLATE CAKE

¼ pound margarine	1½ teaspoons baking soda
1½ cups sugar	1 teaspoon salt
2 eggs, unbeaten	1½ cups sour milk
2 cups sifted flour	1 teaspoon vanilla
½ cup cocoa	chocolate frosting

Cream margarine with sugar. Add eggs, 1 at a time, and beat well after each is added. Sift dry ingredients together and add to creamed mixture alternately with sour milk, blending well after each addition. Beat for 1 minute. Add vanilla. Pour into 2 greased 9 inch layer cake pans. Bake in a 350° oven for approximately 30 minutes. When cool, spread with chocolate frosting. May be frozen.

Mrs. John R. Foley

MRS. JOHN R. FOLEY, Wife of former Representative (Maryland)

POTATO CAKE

½ cup shortening	2 eggs
2 cups sugar	1⅔ cups flour
1 cup mashed potatoes	½ teaspoon salt
1 cup milk	2 teaspoons baking powder
2 squares chocolate, melted	1 teaspoon vanilla

Cream together shortening and sugar. Mix together potatoes, milk, chocolate and eggs. Sift together flour, salt and baking powder. Alternate flour mixture and chocolate mixture into shortening and sugar mixture. Add vanilla. Pour batter into regular size bundt pan. Bake for 60 minutes in 325° oven. May be frozen.

Mrs. Garner E. Shriver

MRS. GARNER E. SHRIVER, Wife of Representative (Kansas)

422

HAZELNUT TORTE

6 eggs, separated
1 whole egg
¾ cup sugar
1 cup ground hazelnuts
⅓ cup bread crumbs
1 teaspoon flour

Topping:
1½ cups heavy cream
1 tablespoon sugar
1 teaspoon vanilla
⅓ cup ground hazelnuts

Beat egg yolks and whole egg until thick and a light yellow. Beat in ½ cup sugar gradually; beat in nuts and bread crumbs until it is a thick, moist mass. Beat egg whites until foamy and gradually add ¼ cup sugar, beating until stiff. Mix ¼ of egg whites into yellow mixture to lighten it. Sprinkle flour over top of yellow mixture, add remaining egg whites and fold gently without overfolding. Pour into a buttered and floured 10 inch spring form pan, bake for 45 to 50 minutes in a preheated 275° oven. Remove the outside of pan and let cool. Split cake crosswise making 2 layers. For topping, whip the cream, adding sugar and vanilla. Spread topping between layers and over top and sides. Sprinkle nuts on top and sides. Refrigerate. Makes 12 servings.

Mrs. Alfred D. Sieminski

MRS. ALFRED D. SIEMINSKI, Wife of former Representative (New Jersey)

SACHER TORTE

1 package yellow cake mix
1 medium jar apricot preserves

1 package chocolate frosting mix

Prepare yellow cake mix following package directions. Put into 2 round cake pans. Bake as directed. Remove from oven, cool and slice each layer horizontally. Cover top of first 3 layers with apricot preserves. Stack layers on serving dish. Cover top and sides with chocolate frosting prepared according to directions on package.

Mrs. E. Ross Adair

MRS. E. ROSS ADAIR, Wife of former Representative (Indiana)

SPECIAL EGGNOG CAKE

2 cups sifted cake flour
2 teaspoons baking powder
½ teaspoon ground nutmeg
¼ teaspoon baking soda
¼ teaspoon salt
¼ pound butter
1 cup sugar
2 eggs, separated
½ cup orange juice
½ cup light rum
½ teaspoon grated orange peel
1 teaspoon vanilla

Filling:
1¼ cups milk
5 tablespoons flour
½ pound butter
¾ cup sugar
2 teaspoons rum
¼ teaspoon ground nutmeg

Frosting:
4 squares unsweetened chocolate, melted
1¼ cups sifted confectioners sugar
¾ teaspoon cinnamon
⅛ teaspoon ground nutmeg
2 tablespoons hot water
2 eggs
6 tablespoons butter

Sift flour with baking powder, nutmeg, baking soda and salt; set aside. Cream butter with ¾ cup of sugar until fluffy. Add egg yolks; beat well. Blend orange juice with ¼ cup of rum, orange peel and vanilla. Add alternately with flour to butter mixture. Beat egg whites until soft peaks form; gradually add remaining ¼ cup sugar, beating until stiff but not dry. Fold into batter. Pour into 2 buttered 8 or 9 inch round cake pans lined with wax paper. Bake at 350° 25 minutes or until cake tester inserted in center comes out clean. Cool in pan 5 minutes before inverting on wire rack to cool thoroughly. Split each layer crosswise and sprinkle each with remaining rum. Spread filling between layers and cover top and sides with frosting. Makes 10 to 14 servings.

Filling: Combine milk and flour and cook, stirring constantly, until mixture thickens. Cool. Cream butter and sugar until light and fluffy. Stir in rum and nutmeg. Add cooled flour mixture by the spoonful, beating until light and fluffy.

Frosting: Combine chocolate with sugar, cinnamon and nutmeg. Beat well. Gradually add hot water, blending until smooth. Beat in eggs 1 at a time. Add butter and blend until smooth.

Mrs Clarence Miller

Mrs. Clarence Miller, Wife of Representative (Ohio)

424

CHERRY PIE CREAM CAKE

3 eggs
1 cup sugar
1 tablespoon lemon juice
1 cup sifted cake flour
1 teaspoon baking powder
¼ teaspoon salt
1 tablespoon butter
½ cup hot milk

Cream filling:
½ cup sugar
3 tablespoons corn starch
½ teaspoon salt
1½ cups milk
2 egg yolks, slightly beaten
2 tablespoons butter
1 teaspoon lemon extract

Cherry topping:
1 can cherry pie filling
1 large package Cool Whip (or 1 cup whipping cream with 1 tablespoon confectioners sugar)

Beat eggs until thick, gradually add sugar and beat until light and fluffy. Add lemon juice. Sift together flour, baking powder and salt and fold into egg mixture only until blended. Melt butter in hot milk and quickly stir into batter. Pour into a greased 8 inch square pan lined with wax paper. Bake in a preheated 350° oven for 30 minutes or until done. Let stand 10 minutes, remove from pan and invert on wire rack.

For filling, combine sugar, corn starch and salt and gradually add milk. Cook over medium heat, stirring constantly until thickened. Cook 2 additional minutes. Blend a small amount of hot mixture into egg yolks and then return all to pan. Cook 1 minute but do not boil. Stir in butter and lemon extract. Press a circle of wax paper over surface of filling to prevent drying as it cools. Chill.

When cake is completely cooled, cut crosswise into 2 layers. Spread filling between layers. Just before serving, spoon cherry pie filling over top of cake and frost sides of cake with Cool Whip. Cake may be frozen before filling is spread between layers. Makes 9 servings.

MRS. EVAN HOWELL, Wife of former Representative (Illinois)

SALLIE CAKE

3 cups cake flour
½ teaspoon baking powder
1 cup chopped black walnuts (or 1 cup chopped pecans plus 2 teaspoons black walnut flavoring)
½ cup Crisco
½ pound margarine
3 cups sugar
5 eggs
1 cup milk

Sift flour with baking powder. Add chopped nuts and mix well. Cream Crisco, margarine and sugar. Add eggs, 1 at a time, beating constantly. Beat mixture well. Add flour mixture and milk alternately, mixing slowly. Spoon this thick batter into teflon cake pan, lined with greased brown paper. Place in cold oven, set at 325° and bake for 1½ hours. May be frozen. Makes 12 to 16 servings.

Mrs. Earl L. Butz.

MRS. EARL LAUER BUTZ, Wife of Secretary of Agriculture (Indiana)

CITRUS POUND CAKE

1 package lemon cake mix
1 cup water
¼ cup Wesson oil
1 3 ounce package lemon Jello
4 eggs
yellow food coloring (optional)

Glaze: (optional)
confectioners sugar
lemon juice
lemon rind

Combine all cake ingredients except eggs and beat until well mixed. Add eggs 1 at a time, beating well after each addition. A little food coloring may be added. Pour into a 10 inch tube pan, well greased and dusted with flour. Bake at 350° for 45 to 50 minutes or until a toothpick inserted comes out clean. Let cool on rack.

If glaze is desired, combine the ingredients, keeping it thin enough to pour easily. Make holes in top of cake with a 2 prong fork and pour glaze over it. Let it harden before cutting cake. This cake keeps well in the refrigerator.

Mrs. Burt L. Talcott

MRS. BURT L. TALCOTT, Wife of Representative (California)

LEMON POUND CAKE

½ pound butter, softened
3 cups sugar
6 large eggs
1 teaspoon vanilla

1 teaspoon lemon extract
3 cups cake flour
½ pint heavy cream

Blend butter with sugar and beat in eggs, 1 at a time. Add vanilla, lemon extract, flour and cream. Mix well. Pour into a buttered tube pan and bake at 325° for 1 hour. Cool ½ hour before removing from pan. May be frozen. Makes 12 servings.

MRS. JOHN H. TERRY, Wife of former Representative (New York)

SOUTHERN POUND CAKE

3 sticks butter
2½ cups sugar
8 eggs, medium size

3 cups flour, sifted
1½ teaspoons vanilla

Cream butter and sugar well in electric mixer. Add eggs, 1 at a time, while beating at low speed and then increase speed to high until light and fluffy. Change to low speed and add flour, ½ cup at a time. Beat in vanilla flavoring. Cut brown paper to fit bottom of a 9 inch tube cake pan. Grease pan and paper well. Pour in batter and bake at 350° for about 1½ hours or until cake pulls away from sides of pan. May be frozen. Makes 20 servings.

MRS. JAMES O. EASTLAND, Wife of Senator (Mississippi)

COCONUT POUND CAKE

3 cups sugar
1 cup Crisco (or margarine)
3 cups flour
1 teaspoon baking powder
½ teaspoon salt

1 cup milk
3 teaspoons lemon juice
5 eggs
1 cup Angel Flake coconut

Combine sugar, Crisco, flour, baking powder, salt, milk and lemon juice and mix well. Then add the eggs, 1 at a time, and beat well after each is added. Fold in coconut. Bake in an oiled, floured tube or bundt pan at 300° for 1¾ hours. Let set in pan on wire rack for 15 minutes before turning out on rack to cool. May be frozen. Makes 24 servings.

Mrs. Lionel Van Deerlin

MRS. LIONEL VAN DEERLIN, Wife of Representative (California)

LEMON SUPREME YELLOW CAKE

4 eggs, beaten
¾ cup Wesson oil
¾ cup peach nectar
2 teaspoons lemon extract
1 package yellow cake mix, sifted

1 cup chopped pecans (optional)

Icing:
½ cup combined lemon and orange
   juice
1½ cups confectioners sugar

Combine cake ingredients, mix well and pour into greased and floured tube pan. Bake 55 minutes at 325°. Remove from pan. Mix ingredients for icing and pour over hot cake. Makes 12 to 14 servings.

Mrs. James Thomas Broyhill

MRS. JAMES THOMAS BROYHILL, Wife of Representative (North Carolina)

428

LEMON BUNDT CAKE

1 box white cake mix
1 3 ounce box lemon Jello
¾ cup water
¾ cup oil
4 eggs
1 tablespoon lemon extract

Glaze:
grated rind of 1 lemon
juice of 1 lemon
1½ cups confectioners sugar

Beat together cake mix, Jello, water and oil. Add eggs, 1 at a time, beating after each addition. Add lemon extract. Pour into greased and floured bundt pan. Bake in 300° oven 1 hour and 5 minutes. Remove from pan immediately. Beat glaze ingredients together until smooth. Brush on warm cake with pastry brush. May be frozen. Makes 12 servings.

Mrs. Edward V. Long

MRS. EDWARD V. LONG, Wife of former Senator (Missouri)

PINEAPPLE UPSIDE DOWN CAKE

1½ cups brown sugar
2 tablespoons butter
1 20 ounce can sliced pineapple
1½ cups sugar
3 eggs, well beaten

1½ cups flour
1½ teaspoons baking powder
1 teaspoon salt
½ cup water
1 teaspoon vanilla

In bottom of a large iron skillet or a 9 x 13 inch loaf cake pan, spread brown sugar and dot with butter. Place pineapple slices on top of sugar. Cream the sugar and eggs. Sift flour, baking powder and salt together and add alternately with water to creamed mixture. Add vanilla. Pour over pineapple. Bake in 350° oven for 1 hour. Invert immediately on cake plate. May be frozen. Makes 12 servings.

Mrs. Laurie C. Battle

MRS. LAURIE C. BATTLE, Wife of former Representative (Alabama)

FRUIT CAKE

1 can fruit pie filling
2 cups flour
1 cup sugar
1½ teaspoons baking soda
1 teaspoon salt
2 eggs, beaten
1 teaspoon vanilla
¾ cup oil

Topping:
1 cup sugar
½ cup dairy sour cream
½ teaspoon baking soda

Topping variation:
juice of 2 lemons
2 cups confectioners sugar
¾ cup chopped nuts (optional)

Spread pie filling on bottom of a 9 x 13 inch pan. Combine flour, sugar, baking soda and salt and sprinkle over pie filling. In bowl combine remaining cake ingredients and mix well. Pour over ingredients in pan. Gently stir into dry ingredients only and only until blended. Smooth batter evenly in pan. Bake at 350° for 40 to 50 minutes. Prick cake while still warm and pour topping over. it. Sprinkle with nuts. Makes 8 servings.

Topping: Combine ingredients and cook until they come to a boil, stirring constantly. For the topping variation, just combine lemon juice and sugar and mix thoroughly.

Mrs. Harold T. Johnson

MRS. HAROLD T. JOHNSON, Wife of Representative (California)

TEA CAKE WITH RAISINS AND MADEIRA

1 cup Sultana raisins
Madeira wine
¾ cup all purpose flour
½ cup cake flour
1 teaspoon baking powder
1¼ sticks sweet butter

grated rind of 1 orange
2 eggs
2 egg yolks
¾ cup sugar
⅛ teaspoon salt

Soak raisins overnight in enough wine to cover. Drain raisins, reserving wine, and gently dry them. Sift both kinds of flour together. Combine 1 tablespoon of the sifted flour with the baking powder and sprinkle it over the raisins, coating them well. In a small bowl cream together the butter and orange rind. Beat together the eggs, egg yolks, sugar, ¼ cup of reserved wine and salt for 8 to 10 minutes. Quickly and lightly fold in the flour and then the creamed butter, being careful not to overmix. Fold in raisins. Turn the batter into a buttered 5 cup loaf pan and smooth the top gently. Bake in a preheated 350° oven for 1 hour. Let stand for 10 minutes to cool and then unmold on a rack. May be frozen. Makes 10 servings.

Alicia Grant

ALICIA GRANT, Daughter of former Representative George M. Grant (Alabama)

MADISON CAKE

½ pound butter
1 3 ounce package cream cheese
1½ cups sugar
4 eggs
1½ teaspoons vanilla

2½ cups flour
1½ teaspoons baking powder
¾ cup chopped apricots
½ cup chopped walnuts

Cream together thoroughly butter, cream cheese and sugar. Add eggs 1 at a time, beating after each addition. Add vanilla. Sift flour and baking powder together and add to creamed mixture. Fold in apricots and walnuts. Bake at 325° in greased 10 inch tube pan for 1 hour and 20 minutes. May be frozen. Makes 12 servings.

Mrs. Emilio Q. Daddario

MRS. EMILIO Q. DADDARIO, Wife of former Representative (Connecticut)

STRAWBERRY LOAF CAKE

1 package strawberry Jello
½ cup warm water
1 package white cake mix
1 package frozen strawberries, thawed

½ cup salad oil
4 eggs
¼ pound butter, melted
1 pound confectioners sugar

Dissolve Jello in warm water. Add cake mix, ½ cup strawberries and salad oil. Beat eggs 2 minutes and add to first mixture. Pour into a 9 x 13 inch cake pan and bake for 50 minutes at 300°. Combine butter, sugar and remaining strawberries. Blend together until smooth. Spread over cake. Makes 12 servings.

Mrs. Jerry Litton

MRS. JERRY LITTON, Wife of Representative (Missouri)

STRAWBERRY TUBE CAKE

1 package strawberry Jello
1 box white cake mix
2/3 cup Wesson oil
1/3 cup strawberry juice
4 eggs
1 cup frozen sliced strawberries,
    thawed and drained

Frosting:
2 cups confectioners sugar
3/4 stick butter
pinch of salt
strawberry juice

Add Jello to dry cake mix. Add Wesson oil and juice, mixing well. Add eggs, 1 at a time, blending well after each addition. Fold in strawberries. Put in tube pan and bake at 325° for 35 minutes. For frosting, cream sugar and butter and add salt. Add enough juice to make the frosting a good spreading consistency. Frost the cooled cake. May be frozen.

Mrs. Eugene Siler

MRS. EUGENE SILER, Wife of former Representative (Kentucky)

APRICOT NUT LOAF CAKE

1 12 ounce can apricot nectar
3/4 cup chopped dried apricots
1/2 cup white raisins
2 cups sifted flour
3 teaspoons baking powder
1 cup sugar

1/2 teaspoon salt
1/3 cup milk
2 tablespoons cooking oil
1 egg, beaten
1/2 cup chopped almonds

In a heavy saucepan mix together 1 cup of apricot nectar, apricots and raisins. Heat to boiling. Remove from heat and cool. Sift together flour, baking powder, sugar and salt. Combine milk and oil and add egg and remaining nectar. Add to flour mixture, beating until smooth. Fold in fruit mixture and almonds. Turn into a greased and floured 9 x 5 x 3 inch loaf pan. Bake in preheated 350° oven for 1 hour. Cool in pan 10 minutes before removing to rack. May be frozen.

Mrs John J. Williams

MRS. JOHN J. WILLIAMS, Wife of former Senator (Delaware)

432

BANANA NUT CAKE

¼ pound margarine
1½ cups sugar
3 eggs, separated
3 small bananas, mashed
¼ cup sour milk
1½ cups flour

½ teaspoon salt
1 teaspoon baking powder
1 teaspoon baking soda
1 cup chopped nuts
coffee icing

Cream margarine and sugar. Add egg yolks, bananas and sour milk. Sift in dry ingredients. Beat egg whites until stiff and fold into cake mixture. Add nuts. Bake in a 350° oven about 23 minutes. Frost with any coffee icing.

Mrs. Jack F. Kemp

MRS. JACK F. KEMP, Wife of Representative (New York)

FRENCH ORANGE CAKE

¼ cup hot water
1 teaspoon baking soda
½ cup chopped dates
¼ pound butter
1½ cups sugar
1 egg

2 cups sifted flour
1 teaspoon baking powder
1 cup milk
½ cup finely chopped pecans
1 orange, juice and grated rind
whipped cream

Combine hot water and baking soda and pour over dates. Let stand for 5 or 6 minutes. Cream butter and 1 cup sugar together; then add unbeaten egg. Sift flour and baking powder together and add to creamed mixture, alternating with milk, a little at a time, mixing thoroughly with each addition. Add nuts, orange rind and dates last. Pour in greased pan 9 to 10 inches square. Batter should be about 1½ inches thick in pan. Bake in 350° oven 20 to 25 minutes. Mix orange juice with remaining sugar and pour over the cake as soon as it is removed from the oven. When cool, cut in squares and serve with whipped cream. Makes 10 to 12 servings.

Mrs. Ralph Harvey

MRS. RALPH HARVEY, Wife of former Representative (Indiana)

ORANGE DATE CAKE

3½ cups sifted flour
3 cups sugar
1 cup shortening
4 egg yolks
1 cup sour milk
½ teaspoon salt
4 tablespoons grated orange peel

½ cup boiling water
1 teaspoon baking soda
1 8 ounce package dates, chopped
1 cup chopped pecans
4 egg whites, stiffly beaten
1 cup orange juice

Mix flour, 2 cups sugar, shortening, egg yolks, sour milk, salt and 2 tablespoons orange peel. Beat until creamy. Pour water over soda and dates. Add date mixture and pecans to batter and mix well. Fold egg whites into mixture. Bake in greased and floured tube pan at 325° for 1 hour. Combine remaining sugar and orange peel with orange juice and pour slowly over cake while it is still in the pan. Leave cake in pan several hours. May be frozen. Makes 18 servings.

Mrs. LaMar Baker

MRS. LAMAR BAKER, Wife of former Representative (Tennessee)

YETIVE'S DATE NUT CAKE

1 cup boiling water
1 cup chopped dates
1 teaspoon baking soda
1 cup sugar
1 cup mayonnaise

2 cups flour
1 teaspoon vanilla
1 cup chopped walnuts or pecans
1 small bottle maraschino cherries

Pour hot water over dates, add soda and cool. Add remaining ingredients. Bake in flat cake pan for approximately 1 hour at 350°.

Mrs. Delwin M. Clawson

MRS. DEL M. CLAWSON, Wife of Representative (California)

ALMOND CAKE

3 eggs, separated
pinch of cream of tartar
⅓ cup chocolate chips
1 teaspoon instant Sanka (optional)
¾ cup sugar
¼ pound margarine, softened

pinch of salt
¼ teaspoon almond extract
¾ cup flour
⅓ cup pulverized blanched almonds
whipped cream (optional)

Beat egg whites with cream of tartar until stiff but not dry. Set aside. Melt chocolate chips over hot water, adding Sanka if desired. Beat egg yolks; add sugar, margarine, salt, almond extract, flour and almonds. Add melted chocolate. Fold in egg whites. Pour into a greased and lightly floured 8 inch round cake pan and bake in a 350° oven for 25 minutes. May be served with whipped cream. May be frozen. Makes 6 to 8 servings.

Mrs. David S. King

MRS. DAVID S. KING, Wife of former Representative (Utah)

WHITE FRUIT CAKE

½ pound butter
2 cups sugar
1 cup milk
3½ cups cake flour
1 teaspoon baking powder
¼ teaspoon salt

1 teaspoon vanilla
1 cup white raisins
2 cups moist coconut
½ cup chopped almonds
½ pound citron, thinly sliced
5 egg whites, stiffly beaten

Cream butter and sugar until smooth and fluffy. Alternate the milk with the flour which has been sifted with the baking powder and salt. Add vanilla and beat thoroughly. Add raisins, coconut, almonds and citron which have been dusted with a little of the flour. Mix thoroughly; then fold in egg whites. Place in a tube pan lined with wax paper and bake in a 325° to 350° oven for about 1 to 1½ hours. Makes 12 servings.

Mrs. Raúl H. Castro

MRS. RAÚL H. CASTRO, Wife of Governor (Arizona)

FRUIT CAKE WITH BROWN SUGAR

5 eggs, separated
2 tablespoons white sugar
½ pound butter
1½ cups light brown sugar
1 tablespoon vanilla
1 teaspoon lemon extract
2 cups cake flour

½ teaspoon baking powder
¼ teaspoon salt
¾ pound crystallized cherries, sliced
1 pound crystallized pineapple, diced
4 cups pecans, lightly toasted without salt or fat

Beat egg whites until stiff and gradually fold in white sugar. Cream butter and brown sugar, add egg yolks, 1 at a time, and beat well. Fold egg whites and flavorings into the batter. Sift flour, baking powder and salt twice, add to fruit and nuts mixing well. Fold into cake batter. Bake in tube pan lined with one layer of brown paper and one layer of wax paper well greased. Bake in 250° oven for 2 hours, and at 275° for an additional 30 minutes.

Mrs. Phil Landrum

Mrs. Phil M. Landrum, Wife of Representative (Georgia)

NO SPICE FRUIT CAKE

1½ pounds pitted dates
1 pound candied red cherries
1 pound candied green cherries
½ pound candied orange peel
2 pounds shelled walnuts
2 cups sifted flour
2 teaspoons baking powder

½ teaspoon salt
4 eggs, beaten
½ cup dark corn syrup
¼ cup firmly packed brown sugar
¼ cup corn oil
¼ cup brandy

Grease 10 x 4 inch tube cake pan and line with greased paper. Mix fruits and nuts. Sift dry ingredients. Mix eggs, corn syrup, sugar and oil. Gradually beat in dry ingredients. Pour over fruit mixture and mix. Pack firmly into pan. Bake in 275° oven about 2¼ hours or until top appears dry. Cool in pan. Remove from pan and pour brandy over the top. Flavor is improved if cake is tightly wrapped and stored in air tight container for about a month before slicing.

Mrs Harlan Hagen

Mrs. Harlan Hagen, Wife of former Representative (California)

FAMILY CHRISTMAS FRUITCAKE

1 pound butter
2 cups sugar
6 eggs, beaten
4 cups flour
1 teaspoon baking powder
¼ teaspoon salt

3 teaspoons vanilla
1 teaspoon lemon extract
½ pound candied cherries, chopped
½ pound candied pineapple, chopped
1 quart chopped pecans

Cream butter and sugar. Add beaten eggs. Combine 3 cups of flour, baking powder and salt. Add to butter mixture gradually. After flour is mixed well with butter mixture, add vanilla and lemon flavoring and mix well. Coat nuts and fruit with remaining cup of flour and stir into cake batter. Pour into greased and floured 10 x 4¼ inch round pan and bake 3 hours at 250°. May be frozen.

Mrs. Dawson Mathis

MRS. DAWSON MATHIS, Wife of Representative (Georgia)

SOUTHERN CHRISTMAS CAKE

1½ sticks butter
2 cups sugar
6 eggs
4 cups sifted cake flour
1 teaspoon baking soda
2 teaspoons ground cloves
2 teaspoons cinnamon
½ teaspoon salt
1 cup buttermilk
2 cups blackberry jam
2 cups peach preserves
1 cup nuts

Filling:
1 cup chopped candy orange slices
1 cup cut up marshmallows
1½ cups white raisins
1½ cups coconut
1½ cups sugar
1½ cups chopped nuts
1¾ cups milk
1½ teaspoons flour

Cream butter, add sugar gradually and cream until fluffy. Add eggs, 1 at a time, beating after each addition. Combine dry ingredients and add, alternating with milk. Mix well; add preserves and nuts. Bake in 4 greased 9 inch layer cake pans at 350° about 30 minutes. Combine filling ingredients and cook until thick. Spread between layers. Makes two 2 layer cakes.

Mrs. James H. Quillen

MRS. JAMES H. QUILLEN, Wife of Representative (Tennessee)

FRESH APPLE CAKE WITH CARAMEL TOPPING

Caramel topping:
½ cup brown sugar
½ stick margarine or butter
½ cup water
1 tablespoon corn starch (or
   2 tablespoons flour)

Cake:
2 cups sugar
½ cup Wesson oil
2 eggs, well beaten
2 cups sifted flour
1½ teaspoons baking soda
½ teaspoon salt
1½ teaspoons cinnamon
2 cups diced, unpeeled apples
1 cup chopped nuts

Before starting cake, combine topping ingredients and bring to a boil or cook until mixture thickens. Set aside to cool.

Combine all cake ingredients except apples and nuts. Batter will be very thick. Mix well. Add apples and nuts, a few at a time, and mix well. Pour into well greased and floured bundt pan or 9 x 13 inch loaf pan. Pour cooled topping over batter and bake at 350° for 1¼ hours.

Mrs. Wm J. Randall

MRS. WILLIAM J. RANDALL, Wife of Representative (Missouri)

CONNIE'S APPLE DAFFLE CAKE

3 cups flour
1 teaspoon salt
1 teaspoon baking soda
2 cups sugar
3 eggs
1¼ cups cooking oil
1 teaspoon vanilla
1 teaspoon rum flavoring
1 teaspoon almond flavoring

3 cups freshly chopped peeled apples
1 cup raisins
1 cup chopped pecans

Topping (optional):
1 cup dark brown sugar
¼ pound butter
¼ cup milk

Sift flour, salt and baking soda together. Cream together the sugar, eggs and oil and blend with dry ingredients. Add flavorings and mix well. Fold in fruit and nuts. Pour into a greased tube pan and bake in a 350° oven for 1 hour and 20 minutes. Set on rack for 5 minutes before removing from pan. Combine topping ingredients and boil without stirring for 2 minutes. Pour over top and sides of cake while both topping and cake are hot. May be frozen without topping. Makes 12 servings.

Mrs. John R. Foley

MRS. JOHN R. FOLEY, Wife of former Representative (Maryland)

FRESH APPLE CAKE

2 cups sugar
1¼ cups Wesson oil
3 eggs
2 teaspoons vanilla
2½ cups sifted flour
1 teaspoon baking soda

½ teaspoon salt
1 teaspoon cinnamon
3 cups chopped apples
1 cup chopped dates
1 cup chopped pecans

Mix sugar, oil, eggs and vanilla. Sift together flour, soda, salt and cinnamon. Blend dry ingredients with sugar mixture and add apples, dates and pecans. Bake 1½ hours in greased, floured bundt pan at 300°. Cool 15 minutes before removing from pan. Needs no icing. May be frozen. Makes 10 servings.

Mrs. Wendell Ford

MRS. WENDELL H. FORD, Wife of Senator (Kentucky)

CINNAMON APPLE CAKE

5 to 6 peeled apples, chopped
2 teaspoons cinnamon
5 teaspoons sugar
3 cups flour
2 cups sugar
3 teaspoons baking powder
1 teaspoon salt
1 cup oil

4 eggs
2½ teaspoons vanilla
¼ cup orange juice

Topping:
¼ cup sugar
1 teaspoon cinnamon

Sprinkle apples with cinnamon and sugar. Set aside. Beat together flour, sugar, baking powder, salt, oil, eggs, vanilla and orange juice. Pour half the batter into a greased 10 inch tube pan and arrange half the apple mixture on top. Repeat with remaining half of batter and remaining apples. Mix the sugar and cinnamon for topping and sprinkle over top. Bake at 350° for 1½ hours until golden brown.

Mrs. Arthur L. Miller

MRS. ARTHUR L. MILLER, Wife of former Representative (Nebraska)

439

PRALINE APPLESAUCE CAKE

2¾ cups sifted cake flour
1⅓ cups sugar
1½ teaspoons baking soda
¼ teaspoon baking powder
1½ teaspoons ground cinnamon
½ teaspoon ground cloves
½ teaspoon salt
½ cup shortening
1¾ cups applesauce

2 eggs
1½ cups seedless raisins

Praline topping:
¼ pound butter or margarine
¾ cup brown sugar, firmly packed
¼ cup cream
1½ cups chopped pecans
⅔ cup flaked coconut

Sift together flour, sugar, baking soda, baking powder, cinnamon, cloves and salt. Add shortening and applesauce and beat 2 minutes at medium speed with an electric beater. Add eggs. Beat 2 minutes longer or until blended. Fold in raisins. Pour into a greased and lightly floured 13 x 9 x 2 inch cake pan. Bake at 350° for 35 minutes or until center springs back when lightly pressed. Remove from oven and cool in pan on wire rack for 15 minutes. Spread praline topping evenly over warm cake. Put under broiler, 6 inches from heat, for 3 to 4 minutes or until topping bubbles up and turns golden. Cool on a wire rack. Cut into squares. Makes 24 servings.

Praline topping: Cream butter with brown sugar until light and fluffy. Add cream and beat until smooth. Stir in pecans and coconut.

Mrs. Richard Kelly

MRS. RICHARD KELLY, Wife of Representative (Florida)

CHIP'S FAVORITE APPLESAUCE CAKE

3½ cups flour
2 teaspoons cinnamon
½ teaspoon ground cloves
½ teaspoon nutmeg
½ teaspoon ginger
4 cups raisins
2 cups chopped dates
2 cups chopped walnuts

3 eggs
1½ cups sugar
½ pound butter or margarine
½ teaspoon salt
4 teaspoons baking soda
2 teaspoons vanilla (or 2 inch vanilla bean)
2 cups applesauce

Mix first 8 ingredients and set aside. Mix eggs, sugar, butter, salt, baking soda and vanilla. Blend and then add applesauce and mix well. Add flour mixture, mixing thoroughly. Pour into a tube pan and bake at 325° for 1¾ hours. If a bundt pan is used, bake for 1½ hours. May be frozen. Makes 24 servings.

Mrs. Lionel Van Deerlin

MRS. LIONEL VAN DEERLIN, Wife of Representative (California)

440

PAT'S APPLESAUCE CAKE

¼ pound butter or margarine
1 cup white sugar
1 egg, unbeaten
1¾ cups cake flour
½ teaspoon salt
1 teaspoon baking soda

1 teaspoon cinnamon
½ teaspoon ground cloves
1 cup raisins
1 cup lightly sweetened applesauce
½ cup chopped nuts (optional)

Cream butter until soft, add sugar and cream well. Add egg. Add flour sifted with dry ingredients and then raisins. Mix in applesauce and nuts. Bake in loaf pan in 350° oven for 50 to 60 minutes but no longer. Needs no icing. May be frozen. Makes 10 servings.

Mrs. Clifford G. McIntire

MRS. CLIFFORD MCINTIRE, Wife of former Representative (Maine)

GRANDMOTHER'S STACK CAKE

1½ cups brown sugar
2 eggs
1 cup molasses
1 cup shortening
1 teaspoon baking soda
2 teaspoons baking powder
1 teaspoon ginger
2 tablespoons cinnamon
1 cup buttermilk

Filling:
country style apple butter
cinnamon

Topping:
molasses
confectioners sugar

Mix all cake ingredients together into a soft dough. Knead well. Separate into 7 or 8 sections and roll each one thin. Use a plate as a pattern to make them uniform in size. Mix apple butter with some cinnamon and spread it thickly between layers. Bake at 375° until brown. Remove from the oven and spread top layer with a very thin coating of molasses sprinkled with confectioners sugar.

Mrs. James H. Quillen

MRS. JAMES H. QUILLEN, Wife of Representative (Tennessee)

APPLE BUTTER CAKE

½ pound butter
2 cups sugar
3 eggs
2 teaspoons soda
¼ teaspoon allspice
¼ teaspoon ground cloves

3 cups flour
½ cup buttermilk
2 cups apple butter
1 teaspoon vanilla
1½ cups chopped English walnuts
1½ cups floured raisins

Cream butter and sugar; add eggs and beat until creamy. Add soda, allspice and cloves to flour and sift together. Add to creamed mixture, alternating with buttermilk and apple butter. Add vanilla, walnuts and raisins. Bake in tube pan at 350° until a broom straw inserted in center comes out clean.

Mrs Fred Bradley

MRS. FRED BRADLEY, Wife of former Representative (Michigan)

APRICOT SPICE CAKE

1 box butter golden cake mix
2 jars baby food strained apricots
1 cup oil
3 eggs
1 teaspoon cinnamon
1 teaspoon nutmeg
1 cup chopped pecans (optional)

Glaze (optional):
juice of 1 lemon
1 cup confectioners sugar

Combine all cake ingredients except pecans and mix for 4 minutes. Fold in pecans. Pour into a greased bundt or tube pan and bake in a 325° oven for 50 minutes. Mix lemon juice and sugar together and pour over cake while it is still warm. May be frozen.

Mrs. Jack Brooks

MRS. JACK BROOKS, Wife of Representative (Texas)

BANANA CAKE

½ cup butter
½ cup Wesson oil
2 cups sugar
4 eggs, well beaten
3 cups flour
1½ teaspoons ground cloves (or allspice)

2 teaspoons cinnamon
1½ teaspoons baking soda
½ teaspoon salt
5 or 6 ripe bananas, well mashed
2 cups chopped pecans
2 cups candied cherries, halved

Cream butter, oil and sugar. Add eggs. Sift flour and other dry ingredients together 3 times. Add alternately with bananas to the above mixture. Fold in nuts and cherries. Bake in greased tube pan 1½ hours at 300°. May be frozen.

Mrs. John C. Stennis

MRS. JOHN C. STENNIS, Wife of Senator (Mississippi)

EASY PLUM CAKE

2 cups sugar
1 teaspoon ground cinnamon
1 teaspoon ground cloves
1 cup corn oil

3 eggs
2 small jars baby food strained plums
2 cups self rising flour
1 cup chopped pecans (optional)

Put all ingredients in large mixing bowl, blending in flour and nuts last. Bake in greased and floured bundt pan at 325° for about 1 hour or until a broom straw inserted in center comes out clean. May be frozen.

Mrs. Horace R. Kornegay

MRS. HORACE R. KORNEGAY, Wife of former Representative (North Carolina)

RICH PRUNE CAKE

3 eggs
1 cup buttermilk
1 cup vegetable oil
2 cups whole wheat flour
1½ cups sugar
1 teaspoon baking soda
1 teaspoon cinnamon
1 teaspoon nutmeg
1 teaspoon allspice
1 teaspoon salt
2 teaspoons vanilla

2 cups chopped prunes
2 cups chopped nuts
⅓ cup wheat germ

Buttermilk Icing:
1 cup sugar
½ cup buttermilk
½ teaspoon baking soda
1 tablespoon white corn syrup
¼ pound butter
1 teaspoon vanilla

Mix together eggs, buttermilk and vegetable oil. Sift together flour, sugar, soda, cinnamon, nutmeg, allspice and salt. Combine liquid mixture with dry ingredients. Mix thoroughly. Add vanilla, prunes, nuts and wheat germ. Mix well. Pour into greased and floured 13 x 9 x 2 inch cake pan and bake at 300° for 45 minutes or until done.

Prepare buttermilk icing by combining sugar, buttermilk, soda, corn syrup, butter and vanilla in a saucepan and heat for about 2 minutes until it comes to a hard boil. Remove from heat and beat until foam disappears. While cake is still warm, pour icing over it, letting it soak into the top and sides of the cake. Keep in refrigerator. Cut into squares to serve. May be frozen. Makes 12 servings.

Mary A. Evins

MARY ADELAIDE EVINS, Daughter of Representative Joe L. Evins (Tennessee)

CRUMB CAKE

2 cups flour
1 cup sugar
¼ pound butter
1 cup sour milk
1 teaspoon baking soda

1 teaspoon cinnamon
pinch of salt
1 egg
1 cup raisins
1 cup currants

Work flour, sugar and butter together until crumbly. Reserve 1 cup of crumbs and mix remainder with remaining ingredients. Put into a 6 x 8 inch loaf pan, sprinkle reserved crumbs on top and bake in 350° oven for 45 minutes. May be frozen. Makes 12 servings.

Mrs. Carl T. Curtis

MRS. CARL T. CURTIS, Wife of Senator (Nebraska)

STRUDEL CAKE

1 box yellow cake mix
1 box instant French vanilla pudding
1¼ cups water
¾ cup Crisco oil

4 eggs
¼ to ½ cup brown sugar
2 teaspoons cinnamon

Place cake mix, pudding, water, oil and eggs in bowl and mix. In separate bowl mix brown sugar and cinnamon. Place wax paper on bottom of greased and floured tube pan. Pour ½ of cake mixture into pan and gently stir in ½ cinnamon mixture to produce marble effect. Pour in remaining cake mixture and bake in 350° oven for 50 minutes. Sprinkle remaining cinnamon mixture over top of cake and continue to bake for another 5 minutes. Cool and cut. May be frozen.

Mrs. John J. Duncan

MRS. JOHN J. DUNCAN, Wife of Representative (Tennessee)

SPICE CAKE

1½ cups sugar
3 eggs
1 cup Wesson oil
2 cups flour
1 teaspoon salt
1 teaspoon nutmeg
1 teaspoon allspice
1 teaspoon cinnamon
½ cup buttermilk
1 teaspoon baking soda

1 teaspoon vanilla
1 cup chopped nuts
1 cup cooked, mashed prunes

Glaze:
¼ pound margarine
1¼ cups sugar
½ cup buttermilk
1 teaspoon baking soda
¼ teaspoon cinnamon

Combine all cake ingredients and mix thoroughly. Pour into a tube pan and bake in a 350° oven for 45 minutes to 1 hour. Remove from pan. Mix ingredients for the glaze, bring to a boil and cook for 1 or 2 minutes. Pour over warm cake. May be frozen.

Mrs. Jack Edwards

MRS. JACK EDWARDS, Wife of Representative (Alabama)

OATMEAL CAKE

1 cup quick cooking oats
1½ cups hot water
¼ pound margarine
1 cup dark brown sugar
1 cup white sugar
2 eggs
1⅓ cups sifted flour
½ teaspoon salt
1 teaspoon baking soda

1 teaspoon vanilla
1 teaspoon cinnamon
½ teaspoon nutmeg
1 cup chopped nuts

Topping:
6 tablespoons butter
¾ cup dark brown sugar
4 tablespoons canned milk

Combine oats and hot water and set aside for 20 minutes. Cream margarine, brown sugar and white sugar and beat for 5 minutes. Add eggs and beat again. Add dry ingredients, vanilla, spices and nuts, mixing well. Add oatmeal mixture, stir and pour into an oblong baking pan. Bake at 350° for 35 to 40 minutes. Mix topping ingredients together, spread on baked cake and set in broiler about 3 inches from the heat, broiling until brown and bubbly. May be frozen.

Mrs. Patrick Mathews

Mrs. PATRICK H. MATHEWS, Daughter of former Representative C. A. Fuller (Arkansas)

EGGLESS, BUTTERLESS, MILKLESS CAKE

1 cup sugar
1 cup water
⅓ cup shortening
1 cup raisins
½ teaspoon salt
⅓ teaspoon ground cloves

⅓ teaspoon cinnamon
¼ teaspoon nutmeg
1 teaspoon baking soda
½ teaspoon baking powder
2 cups flour
½ teaspoon vanilla

Combine the first 8 ingredients. Boil for 3 minutes; cool. Combine remaining dry ingredients and add to cooked mixture. Add vanilla. Put in a greased 9 x 13 inch pan and bake in a 350° oven for 30 minutes or until a toothpick comes out dry. May be frozen. Makes 15 servings.

Mrs Berkley Bedell

Mrs. BERKLEY BEDELL, Wife of Representative (Iowa)

446

COUNTRY FAIR CARROT CAKE

3 cups grated carrots
4 eggs
1¼ cups vegetable oil
2 cups sugar
2 cups self rising flour
1 cup chopped black walnuts
1 teaspoon vanilla
¼ teaspoon black walnut extract
1 teaspoon cinnamon

Buttermilk glaze:
½ cup buttermilk
1 cup sugar
½ teaspoon baking soda
1 tablespoon white corn syrup

Place all cake ingredients in a bowl and blend well. Pour into a 10 inch greased tube pan. Bake 1½ hours in a 350° oven. Combine glaze ingredients and blend well. Remove cake from oven and pour glaze over top of hot cake. Let cake cool before removing from pan. May be frozen.

Ella Grasso

ELLA GRASSO, Governor (Connecticut)

CARROT CAKE WITH CREAM CHEESE FROSTING

2 cups flour
2 cups sugar
2 teaspoons baking powder
2 teaspoons cinnamon
1 teaspoon salt
4 eggs
3 cups finely grated raw carrots
1½ cups Wesson oil

Frosting:
1 8 ounce package cream cheese
¼ pound butter
1 box confectioners sugar
1 cup chopped nuts
1 teaspoon vanilla

Mix together flour, sugar, baking powder, cinnamon and salt. Beat in the eggs, 1 at a time. Blend together and add carrots and oil. Pour into greased tube pan and bake at 325° for 45 to 55 minutes. Cream frosting ingredients together and spread on cooled cake. Refrigerate. May be frozen.

Mrs. James D. Weaver

MRS. JAMES D. WEAVER, Wife of former Representative (Pennsylvania)

CARROT CAKE

1 pound carrots
lemon juice
1 cup oil
2½ cups sugar
2½ cups flour
2 teaspoons baking powder
1 teaspoon baking soda
1 teaspoon nutmeg
1 teaspoon cinnamon

1 teaspoon ginger
1 teaspoon ground cloves
1 teaspoon allspice
6 eggs
2 tablespoons vanilla
grated lemon rind
1 cup chopped walnuts
1 cup raisins

Pare carrots and soak in some water with a little lemon juice before grating. Mix carrots, oil and sugar together in mixing bowl. Add other dry ingredients and mix thoroughly. Beat eggs, vanilla and grated lemon rind until light and fluffy and add to mixture. Add walnuts and raisins. Mix all ingredients thoroughly and pour into regular cake or loaf pan. Bake in 450° oven for 20 to 30 minutes, reduce heat to 350° and continue baking an additional 30 minutes or until done. No frosting is needed. May be frozen. Makes 14 servings.

Mrs. Cyril E. King

MRS. CYRIL E. KING, Wife of Governor (Virgin Islands)

CARROT PINEAPPLE CAKE

2 cups flour
2 cups sugar
2 teaspoons cinnamon
1½ teaspoons baking soda
½ teaspoon salt
1½ cups cooking oil
4 eggs, beaten
2 cups grated raw carrots
1 15 ounce can crushed pineapple, drained
1 cup chopped nuts

Frosting:
1 8 ounce package cream cheese, softened
½ box confectioners sugar
½ cup butter (or margarine), softened
½ teaspoon vanilla
milk

Sift together first 5 ingredients. Add oil, eggs, carrots, pineapple and nuts. Mix well. Pour into 9 x 13 inch pan and bake at 350° for 35 to 45 minutes. Cool before frosting. For frosting, combine cheese, sugar, butter and vanilla in small bowl and blend thoroughly. Add small amount of milk if necessary to make frosting the proper consistency to spread on cake. May be frozen. Makes 12 servings.

Mrs. Richard M. Simpson

MRS. RICHARD M. SIMPSON, Wife of former Representative (Pennsylvania)

448

MY GRANDMOTHER'S GINGER CAKE

½ cup vegetable shortening
½ cup sugar
2½ cups sifted flour
1 cup sorghum
2 teaspoons baking soda
½ teaspoon salt

2 eggs
1 cup boiling water
2 teaspoons ground ginger
1 teaspoon ground cinnamon
½ teaspoon ground cloves
½ teaspoon allspice

Combine all ingredients and mix thoroughly. Pour into a greased, shallow 10 x 13 inch baking pan and bake at 350° about 1 hour.

Mrs. John J. Flynt, Jr.

MRS. JOHN J. FLYNT, JR., Wife of Representative (Georgia)

AUNT LOU'S GINGERBREAD

¼ cup Crisco
½ cup sugar
2 teaspoons ginger
1 teaspoon cinnamon
½ teaspoon ground cloves
½ teaspoon baking soda

1 teaspoon salt
1⅓ cups sifted flour
½ cup buttermilk
½ cup molasses
1 egg, lightly beaten

Cream Crisco and sugar until light and fluffy. Sift together remaining dry ingredients and add to creamed mixture alternately with buttermilk and molasses. Mix until well blended. Add egg and mix well. Batter should be light and fluffy. Pour into a greased 8 x 10 inch baking pan and bake at 325° for 30 minutes. May be frozen. Makes 6 servings.

Mrs. Lyle H. Boren

MRS. LYLE H. BOREN, Wife of former Representative (Oklahoma)

449

HOT GINGERBREAD

¼ pound butter
½ cup brown sugar
1 cup dark molasses
2 eggs
2½ cups sifted flour
¼ cup cocoa
2 teaspoons baking powder
½ teaspoon baking soda

½ teaspoon salt
1 teaspoon ginger
1 teaspoon cinnamon
½ teaspoon nutmeg
½ teaspoon ground cloves
¾ cup strong, hot coffee
whipped cream or buttered sugar icing

Cream butter and sugar. When blended, add molasses and the eggs 1 at a time, beating vigorously. Mix and sift flour, cocoa, baking powder, soda, salt and spices. Return to sifter and sift into batter, adding alternately with hot coffee, to the first mixture. Beat until smooth. The batter will be thin. Pour into a 9 x 9 inch buttered pan. Bake in 350° oven 30 minutes. Serve hot with whipped cream or buttered sugar icing. May be frozen. Makes 8 servings.

Mrs. Dolph Briscoe

MRS. DOLPH BRISCOE, Wife of Governor (Texas)

OLD FASHIONED GINGERBREAD

2½ cups sifted flour
1½ teaspoons baking soda
½ teaspoon salt
1 teaspoon cinnamon
½ teaspoon cloves
1 teaspoon ginger

¼ pound butter
½ cup sugar
1 egg, well beaten
1 cup molasses (or cane syrup)
1 cup boiling water

Sift the flour with soda, salt and spices. Cream butter until light and fluffy. Add sugar gradually, beating after each addition. Add egg and molasses and beat until smooth. Add sifted dry ingredients; mix thoroughly. Add hot water and stir until smooth. Turn into well greased and floured 13½ x 9½ x 1½ inch pan. Bake at 350° for 35 to 40 minutes. May be frozen. Makes 16 servings.

Mrs. G. Elliott Hagan

MRS. G. ELLIOTT HAGAN, Wife of former Representative (Georgia)

RUM CAKE

½ cup chopped nuts
1 package yellow cake mix
1 small package vanilla pudding
½ cup light rum
½ cup water
½ cup cooking oil
4 eggs

Glaze:
1 cup sugar
¼ pound butter or margarine
¼ cup light rum
¼ cup water

Cover bottom of a greased and floured bundt pan with nuts. Mix cake ingredients in order named and pour over nuts in pan. Bake in 350° oven 1 hour. Combine ingredients for glaze and boil about 5 minutes. Pour over cake immediately after removing from oven. Allow to cool in pan. May be frozen.

Mrs. Tom Steed

MRS. TOM STEED, Wife of Representative (Oklahoma)

APRICOT RUM CAKE

1 package yellow cake mix
4 large eggs
¾ cup salad oil
¾ cup apricot nectar

Glaze:
1 stick butter or margarine
⅔ cup sugar
⅓ cup Myer's rum

Combine cake mix, eggs, oil and apricot nectar and beat with mixer 10 minutes. Pour into lightly greased and floured tube pan and bake for 50 minutes at 325°. Combine butter, sugar and rum in saucepan and bring to a boil. Prick cake with a long pronged fork; slowly pour glaze over top and sides. May be frozen.

Mrs. Dan Daniel

MRS. DAN DANIEL, Wife of Representative (Virginia)

451

SCOTT'S GALLIANO CAKE

1 package Duncan Hines yellow cake mix
1 package Jello vanilla pudding
4 eggs
½ cup cooking oil
¾ cup orange juice
¼ cup Galliano liqueur
¼ cup vodka
¼ cup chopped nuts (optional)

Glaze:
1 cup sifted confectioners sugar
1 tablespoon vodka
1 tablespoon Galliano liqueur

Mix ingredients in order given and beat 4 minutes. Pour into well greased and lightly floured bundt pan. Bake 45 to 50 minutes at 350°. Combine glaze ingredients and pour over cake while still warm. May be frozen. Makes 12 servings.

Mrs. William H. Bates

Mrs. WILLIAM H. BATES, Wife of former Representative (Massachusetts)

WINE CAKE

1 package yellow cake mix
1 package instant vanilla pudding
2 teaspoons grated nutmeg
¾ cup oil
¾ cup cream sherry
4 eggs
confectioners sugar

Combine cake mix, pudding mix and nutmeg. Add oil, sherry and eggs. Beat all with mixer 4 minutes. Pour into well greased tube pan and bake 50 minutes in 350° oven. Remove from oven and sprinkle with confectioners sugar. Let cool in pan 20 minutes. Remove from pan onto tray sprinkled with confectioners sugar. Sprinkle additional sugar on sides of cake. Serves 10.

Mrs. George Arthur Weaver

Mrs. GEORGE ARTHUR WEAVER, Daughter of former Representative M. G. Burnside (West Virginia)

452

WHIPPED CREAM CAKE

1 cup whipping cream
3 egg whites
½ cup cold water
1 teaspoon vanilla

1 cup sugar
3 teaspoons baking powder
2 cups cake flour
pinch of salt

Whip cream until stiff. Beat egg whites until stiff. Fold cream into egg whites. Gradually fold in other ingredients. Pour into layer pans, either 2 deep or 3 regular ones, and bake in 350° oven for 25 to 30 minutes. May be frozen.

Mrs. Ed Herschler

MRS. ED HERSCHLER, Wife of Governor (Wyoming)

COCA COLA CAKE

2 cups flour
2 cups sugar
½ pound butter
2 tablespoons cocoa
1 cup Coca Cola
½ cup buttermilk
1 teaspoon baking soda
¼ teaspoon salt
2 eggs
1 teaspoon vanilla
1½ cups miniature marshmallows

Icing:
¼ pound butter
2 tablespoons cocoa
6 tablespoons Coca Cola
1 pound confectioners sugar
1 cup chopped nuts
1 teaspoon vanilla

Sift together flour and sugar. Bring butter, cocoa and coke to a boil and stir into flour and sugar. Add buttermilk, soda, salt, eggs and vanilla and mix well. Add marshmallows. Batter will be thin and marshmallows will float to top. Do not use a beater. Pour into greased and floured oblong cake pan and bake at 350° for 30 to 35 minutes. Cool 10 minutes before icing.

Icing: Heat butter, cocoa and coke to boiling point. Stir into sugar and add nuts and vanilla. Pour hot icing over warm cake.

Mrs. John M. Ashbrook

MRS. JOHN M. ASHBROOK, Wife of Representative (Ohio)

DUMP CAKE

1 can cherry pie mix
1 large can crushed pineapple
1 package yellow cake mix

½ pound margarine, melted
1 cup coconut
1 cup chopped pecans

Dump ingredients in the order given into a 9 x 13 inch cake pan. Spread evenly, layer upon layer. Bake in a 325° oven for 1 hour or until topping is brown and cake is firm. May be served warm or cold. Makes 20 servings.

MRS. JAMES G. POLK, Wife of former Representative (Ohio)

FUDGE CUPCAKES

4 squares semi-sweet chocolate
½ pound butter or margarine
3 cups broken pecans
1¾ cups sugar

1 cup unsifted flour
4 large eggs, unbeaten
1 teaspoon vanilla

Melt chocolate and butter in saucepan. Add pecans and stir until well coated. In mixing bowl, combine sugar, flour and eggs. Mix until well blended. Do not beat. Stir in chocolate and pecan mixture. Do not beat. Stir in vanilla. Place paper baking cups in muffin tins and completely fill with batter. Bake at 325° for 35 minutes. Cool 8 to 10 minutes before removing from tins. May be frozen. Makes 14 to 16 average size cupcakes.

MRS. LON M. BUZICK, Member of Congressional Club (Kansas)

454

ORANGE DATE CUP CAKES

¼ pound butter
1 cup sugar
2 cups sifted flour
½ teaspoon baking soda
1 teaspoon baking powder
2 eggs, beaten
⅔ cup buttermilk

1 cup chopped dates
1 cup chopped pecans

Glaze:
1 cup sugar
juice of 2 oranges
grated rind of 1 orange

Cream butter and sugar until fluffy. Add flour sifted with soda and baking powder. Add eggs and buttermilk and mix thoroughly. Fold in dates and pecans. Bake in small muffin tins at 370° until light brown. For the glaze, make a clear syrup by boiling sugar, orange juice and rind about 5 minutes. While cup cakes are still warm, pour a teaspoon of hot glaze over each. Cool before removing cakes from muffin tins.

Mrs. Charles G. Rose, III

MRS. CHARLES G. ROSE, III, Wife of Representative (North Carolina)

SURPRISE CUPCAKES

4 eggs, separated
¼ pound butter or margarine
1 cup brown sugar
1 cup white sugar
2 cups flour

½ teaspoon baking powder
¼ cup maraschino cherry juice
chopped pecans
maraschino cherries
confectioners sugar

Beat egg whites until stiff. Set aside. Cream butter; add sugar and egg yolks. Sift flour and baking powder together and add alternately with cherry juice to creamed mixture. Fold in egg whites. In paper cup lined muffin tins sprinkle pecans, add 1 teaspoon dough, pop in a cherry, add another teaspoon of dough and sprinkle with more pecans. Bake 15 to 20 minutes at 375°. Dust with confectioners sugar. May be frozen. Makes 4 dozen.

Mrs. Laurie C. Battle

MRS. LAURIE C. BATTLE, Wife of former Representative (Alabama)

FEATHER LIGHT CUPCAKES

2 cups sifted cake flour
2½ teaspoons baking powder
¼ teaspoon salt
½ stick butter or margarine

¾ cup sugar
1 egg, unbeaten
⅔ cup milk
1 teaspoon vanilla

Sift first 3 ingredients together 3 times. Cream butter and sugar well. Add egg, blending thoroughly. Add dry ingredients alternately with milk and vanilla and beat well. Fill greased muffin pans about ⅓ full. Bake in 375° oven 18 to 20 minutes or until lightly browned. May be frozen. Makes 18 to 24 cupcakes.

Amy Gronna Cowing

MRS. AMY GRONNA COWING, Daughter of former Senator A. J. Gronna (North Dakota)

WHITE FROSTING

2 tablespoons water
4½ tablespoons granulated sugar
2⅓ cups sifted confectioners sugar

1 egg
⅔ cup vegetable shortening
1 teaspoon vanilla

Boil water and granulated sugar for 1 minute and set aside to cool. Mix confectioners sugar and egg together and blend with syrup. Add remaining ingredients and beat until creamy. Will frost a 9 x 13 inch loaf cake.

Mrs. Neal Smith

MRS. NEAL SMITH, Wife of Representative (Iowa)

456

TUPELO CARAMEL ICING

3½ cups sugar
1 stick margarine
½ stick butter

1½ cups milk
1 teaspoon vanilla
hot water (optional)

Combine 3 cups sugar, margarine and 3 tablespoons butter in a saucepan. Add milk and bring to a very rapid boil over high heat, stirring constantly with a wooden spoon, for about 10 minutes. When mixture runs in a thread from the spoon and then drips, remove from heat. Melt remaining butter in a heavy skillet, add remaining sugar and brown over medium heat, stirring constantly with a rubber spatula. When this becomes a golden brown, remove from heat and add immediately to mixture in saucepan. Return mixture to high heat, stirring constantly with a wooden spoon until mixture forms a soft ball, about 4 or 5 minutes. Pour into a bowl and let cool, without stirring, until only slightly warm. Stir in vanilla and, if too thick, add a little hot water. Beat with mixer until creamy, about 4 or 5 minutes. Frost cake immediately. Makes enough frosting for a 3 layer cake.

Mrs. John Sanders

MRS. JOHN SANDERS, Daughter of former Representative John E. Rankin (Mississippi)

NOTES

COOKIES

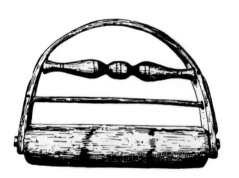

Another Christmas Cookey

To three pound flour, sprinkle a tea cup of fine powdered coriander seed, rub in one pound butter, and one and half pound sugar, dissolve three tea spoonfuls of pearl ash in a tea cup of milk, kneed all together well, roll three quarters of an inch thick, and cut or stamp into shape and size you please, bake slowly fifteen or twenty minutes; tho' hard and dry at first, if put into an earthern pot, and dry cellar, or damp room, they will be finer, softer and better when six months old.

The American Cookery
Amelia Simmons, 1796

SWISS CHOCOLATE SQUARES

1 cup water
¼ pound margarine
1½ squares unsweetened chocolate
2 cups flour
2 cups sugar
2 eggs
½ cup dairy sour cream
1 teaspoon baking soda
½ teaspoon salt

Milk Chocolate Frosting:
¼ pound margarine
6 tablespoons milk
1½ squares unsweetened chocolate
1 pound confectioners sugar, sifted
1 teaspoon vanilla

Combine water, margarine and chocolate, bring to a boil, remove from heat and stir until smooth. Mix flour and sugar together and stir into chocolate. Add eggs, sour cream, baking soda and salt and mix well. Pour into a greased 15½ x 18½ inch jelly roll pan and bake at 375° for 20 to 25 minutes. For frosting combine margarine, milk and chocolate, heat to a boil and boil for 1 minute. Remove from heat, add sugar and beat until smooth. Stir in vanilla. Frost cooled cake and cut to desired size.

Mrs. James A. Burke

Mrs. James A. Burke, Wife of Representative (Massachusetts)

20 MINUTE CHOCOLATE SQUARES

2 cups flour
2 cups sugar
¼ pound margarine
1 cup boiling water
¼ cup cocoa
2 eggs, well beaten
½ cup buttermilk
1 teaspoon baking soda
1 teaspoon vanilla

Frosting:
¼ cup cocoa
⅓ cup milk
¼ pound margarine
1 pound confectioners sugar, sifted
1 cup coarsely chopped nuts
1 teaspoon vanilla

Combine flour and sugar. In a saucepan mix the margarine, water and cocoa, bring to a boil and pour over dry ingredients, stirring until smooth. Combine eggs, buttermilk, baking soda and vanilla, add to the first mixture and mix well. Pour into a greased jelly roll pan and bake in a 400° oven for 20 minutes. During the last 5 minutes of baking time, make the frosting by combining the cocoa, milk and margarine and bringing it to a boil. Remove mixture from heat when cake is removed from oven and quickly stir in sugar, nuts and vanilla, mixing it well. Frost cake immediately with the hot frosting. Cool in pan on rack. Makes 24 servings.

Mrs. Anita W. Ullman

Mrs. Anita W. Ullman, Member of Congressional Club (Oregon)

SCHOKOLADE SCHNITTEN (BROWNIES)

¼ pound butter
2 tablespoons cocoa
1 cup sugar
2 eggs, beaten
¾ cup flour
¼ teaspoon salt
1 teaspoon vanilla
1 cup chopped nuts

Frosting:
½ stick butter
½ cup heavy cream
½ cup cocoa
1½ cups confectioners sugar
1 teaspoon vanilla

Melt butter and blend in cocoa. Gradually beat sugar into eggs. Stir eggs into cocoa mixture. Add flour and salt, mix well. Add vanilla and nuts. Pour into greased and floured 8 inch square pan. Bake in 350° oven for 30 minutes. Combine all frosting ingredients. Blend well. Beat until smooth and fluffy. Spread on cooled cake. May be frozen.

Mrs. Douglas R. Smith

MRS. DOUGLAS R. SMITH, Daughter-in-law of Representative Neal E. Smith (Iowa)

SUZY'S BLUE RIBBON BROWNIES

½ pound butter or margarine
4 squares unsweetened chocolate
2 cups sugar
4 eggs, well beaten

1 cup cake flour
dash of salt
chopped nuts
vanilla

Melt together the butter and chocolate. Set aside. Add sugar to the eggs. Add butter and chocolate mixture and mix well. Add flour, salt, nuts and vanilla. Bake in 9 x 13 inch cake pan for 10 minutes at 300°, 10 minutes at 325° and 10 minutes at 350°. Test center with toothpick before removing from oven. Cut into squares. May be frozen. Makes 10 to 12 servings.

Elizabeth C. Rhodes

ELIZABETH C. RHODES, Daughter of Representative John J. Rhodes (Arizona)

462

SUPER SQUARES

1/4 pound butter, softened
6 tablespoons white sugar
6 tablespoons brown sugar
1/2 teaspoon vanilla
1/4 teaspoon water

1 egg
1 cup plus 2 tablespoons sifted flour
1/2 teaspoon salt
1/2 cup chopped nuts
1 6 ounce package chocolate bits

Beat until creamy butter, white sugar, brown sugar, vanilla and water. Beat in egg. Add flour and salt, mixing well. Add nuts. Spread in a greased 13 x 9 x 2 inch pan. Sprinkle with chocolate bits. Put in 375° oven. After baking 1 minute, run knife through batter, marbleizing it. Continue baking for 12 to 14 minutes longer. May be frozen. Makes 24 squares.

Mrs. M. Blaine Peterson

MRS. M. BLAINE PETERSON, Wife of former Representative (Utah)

APPLE ORANGE BROWNIES

6 tablespoons butter or margarine
1 cup brown sugar
1/2 cup applesauce
2 teaspoons grated orange peel
1 egg, beaten
1 teaspoon vanilla
1 1/4 cups sifted flour
1 teaspoon baking powder
1/2 teaspoon salt

1/4 teaspoon baking soda
1/2 cup chopped walnuts

Orange Glaze:
1 1/2 cups sifted confectioners sugar
1/2 teaspoon vanilla
dash of salt
2 tablespoons orange juice

Combine butter and sugar in saucepan and cook and stir until melted. Remove from heat, beat in applesauce, orange peel, egg and vanilla. Sift together flour, baking powder, salt and soda and fold into applesauce mixture. Stir in walnuts. Spread in greased and floured 15½ x 10½ x 1 inch pan. Bake at 350° for 15 minutes. Combine all glaze ingredients and beat until smooth. Pour immediately over warm cake. Makes 36 squares.

Mrs. John B. Conlan

MRS. JOHN B. CONLAN, Wife of Representative (Arizona)

BANANA SQUARES

¼ pound butter
1½ cups sugar
1 egg plus 1 yolk
2 cups sifted flour
1 teaspoon baking powder
1 teaspoon salt
1 teaspoon baking soda
¾ cup buttermilk (or sour milk)

1 cup sieved bananas
1 teaspoon vanilla

Frosting:
2 cups confectioners sugar
1 teaspoon vanilla
cream
chopped nuts

Cream butter and sugar. Add egg and egg yolk. Sift flour, baking powder and salt. Dissolve soda in buttermilk. Add dry ingredients alternately with buttermilk to creamed mixture. Add bananas and vanilla. Mix well. Bake at 350° for 25 minutes on greased cookie sheet. Mix confectioners sugar with vanilla and enough cream to make a good spreading consistency. Frost cookies and sprinkle with nuts. May be frozen.

Mrs Fred Schwengel

MRS. FRED SCHWENGEL, Wife of former Representative (Iowa)

YUMMIE DATE COOKIES

1½ sticks butter
1 cup dark brown sugar
1 8 ounce package dates, chopped
1 teaspoon vanilla

pinch of salt
1 cup chopped nuts
3 cups Rice Krispies
confectioners sugar

Melt butter over low heat and add brown sugar and dates, stirring with a wooden spoon. Cook gently as it scorches easily. Stir constantly until mixture is thickened, about 5 minutes. Remove from heat and stir in vanilla, salt, nuts and Rice Krispies. Turn into a buttered 8 x 12 inch pan and sprinkle with confectioners sugar. Cut into squares when cool. May be frozen. Makes 4 dozen.

Mrs Evan Howell

MRS. EVAN HOWELL, Wife of former Representative (Illinois)

464

EASY CHEESY LEMON BARS

1 package lemon cake mix
¼ pound butter, melted
3 eggs

1 package lemon frosting mix
1 8 ounce package cream cheese

Combine cake mix, butter and 1 slightly beaten egg. Mix with fork until moist. Pat into 9 x 13 inch pan, greased on bottom only. Blend frosting mix with cream cheese. Reserve ½ cup of cheese and frosting mixture. Add 2 eggs to remaining frosting mixture. Beat 3 to 5 minutes. Spread over cake mixture in the pan. Bake at 350° for 30 to 40 minutes. Cool. Spread with reserved frosting mixture. May be frozen. Makes 20 squares.

Mrs. Tom S. Gettys

MRS. TOM S. GETTYS, Wife of former Representative (South Carolina)

LEMON PECAN GLAZE SQUARES

First layer:
1½ cups sifted flour
½ cup sifted self rising flour
½ cup brown sugar
½ pound butter

½ teaspoon baking powder
½ teaspoon salt
1 teaspoon vanilla
1 3½ ounce can coconut
1 cup chopped pecans

Second layer:
1 cup brown sugar
2 eggs, beaten
2 tablespoons flour

Glaze:
2 cups confectioners sugar
juice of 2 lemons

Blend first layer ingredients and press into greased, floured 9 x 12 inch pan. Bake 12 minutes at 350°. Mix second layer ingredients and spread over top of cooked layer. Bake 25 minutes at 350°. Let cool in pan. Cover with glaze of sugar dissolved in lemon juice.

Mrs. Wm. Jennings Bryan Dorn

MRS. WM. JENNINGS BRYAN DORN, Wife of former Representative (South Carolina)

CHEESE CAKE COOKIES

⅓ cup butter
⅓ cup brown sugar, firmly packed
1 cup flour
½ cup finely chopped walnuts
¼ cup sugar

8 ounce package cream cheese
1 egg
2 tablespoons milk
1 tablespoon lemon juice
½ teaspoon vanilla

Cream butter with brown sugar. Add flour and walnuts; mix to make a crumb mixture. Reserve 1 cup for topping. Press remainder into bottom of 8 inch square pan. Bake at 350° for 12 to 15 minutes until lightly browned. Blend sugar with cream cheese until smooth. Add egg, milk, lemon juice and vanilla; beat well. Spread over baked crust. Sprinkle with reserved crumb mixture. Bake at 350° for 25 minutes. Cool and cut into squares. Makes 16 squares.

Mrs. Al Ullman

MRS. AL ULLMAN, Wife of Representative (Oregon)

MAGIC COOKIE BARS

¼ pound butter or margarine, melted
1½ cups graham cracker crumbs
1 cup chopped nut meats
1 6 ounce package semi-sweet
chocolate bits

1 3½ ounce can flaked coconut
1 can sweetened condensed milk

Pour melted butter over bottom of a 13 x 9 x 2 inch pan. Sprinkle crumbs evenly over the butter. Sprinkle the nuts over the crumbs and scatter the chocolate bits over the nuts. Spread the coconut evenly over the chocolate. Pour milk over the top of all. Bake in a 350° oven for 25 minutes or until lightly browned on top. Cool in pan 15 minutes and then cut into 1½ by 3 inch bars. Makes 2 dozen.

Jaynie K. Miller

JAYNIE K. MILLER, Daughter of former Senator Jack R. Miller (Iowa)

RICE KRISPIES COOKIES

1 6 ounce package butterscotch chips   3½ cups Rice Krispies
½ cup smooth peanut butter

Melt butterscotch chips in top of double boiler. Stir in peanut butter, mix thoroughly and cook 10 minutes. Gradually stir in Rice Krispies and beat until well blended. Spread evenly into buttered 8 inch square pan. Cut into squares. Store in air tight container.

Mrs. John L. McMillan, Jr.

MRS. JOHN L. McMILLAN, Wife of former Representative (South Carolina)

QUICK AND EASY BARS

32 single graham crackers, finely   1 can sweetened condensed milk
    crushed   1 teaspoon vanilla
1 6 ounce package chocolate bits

Place cracker crumbs, chocolate bits and milk into a large mixing bowl and mix thoroughly. Add vanilla. Pour into a well greased 9 x 9 inch baking pan and bake at 325° for 25 minutes. Remove from oven and cut into squares.

Mrs. Melvin Price

MRS. MELVIN PRICE, Wife of Representative (Illinois)

APRICOT BARS

⅔ cup dried apricots
¼ pound butter, softened
¼ cup granulated sugar
1 cup sifted flour
1 cup brown sugar, packed
2 eggs, well beaten

⅓ cup flour
½ teaspoon baking powder
¼ teaspoon salt
½ teaspoon vanilla
confectioners sugar

Rinse apricots, cover with water, boil 10 minutes, drain and chop. Combine butter, granulated sugar and flour and pack into a greased 8 x 8 x 2 inch pan. Bake at 350° until lightly browned, checking after 20 minutes. Combine brown sugar, eggs, flour, baking powder, salt and vanilla; add apricots and spread over the baked layer. Bake in a 350° oven for about 30 minutes. Cool in pan, cut into bars and roll in confectioners sugar directly before serving. Makes 12 bars.

Mrs. Charles Thone

MRS. CHARLES THONE, Wife of Representative (Nebraska)

CHERRY CHEWS

1 cup sifted flour
¾ pound butter
3 tablespoons confectioners sugar
2 eggs, beaten
1 cup sugar
¼ cup flour

½ teaspoon baking powder
¼ teaspoon salt
1 teaspoon vanilla
¾ cup chopped walnuts
½ cup coconut
½ cup diced maraschino cherries

Mix flour, butter and sugar. Spread in an 8 x 8 inch pan. Bake 25 minutes at 350°. Combine remaining ingredients. Spread over baked portion. Bake an additional 25 minutes at 350°. Cut in bars. May be frozen.

Mrs Walt Horan

MRS. WALT HORAN, Wife of former Representative (Washington)

FRUIT STRIPS

1½ cups sugar
1½ cups flour
½ pound dates
½ teaspoon salt
1 cup chopped English walnuts

2 level teaspoons baking powder
3 eggs, well beaten
4 tablespoons milk
1 teaspoon vanilla (or ¾ teaspoon almond extract)
confectioners sugar

Mix first 6 ingredients and add eggs, milk and flavoring. Pour into cake pan and bake in a 325° oven for 25 to 35 minutes. Cut in bars and roll in confectioners sugar. May be frozen.

Mrs Bert Bandstra

MRS. BERT BANDSTRA, Wife of former Representative (Iowa)

LEMON PIE BARS

1½ sticks butter
½ cup confectioners sugar
1½ cups flour
3 eggs

1½ cups granulated sugar
3 tablespoons flour
juice of 1 lemon
confectioners sugar for top

Combine first 3 ingredients and crumble into a 9 x 12 inch pan and bake at 350° for 20 minutes. Mix next 4 ingredients and beat slightly. Pour over hot crust. Bake at 350° for 20 minutes longer. Sprinkle with confectioners sugar while warm. May be frozen. Makes 24 bars.

Mrs Barry M. Goldwater, Jr.

MRS. BARRY M. GOLDWATER, JR., Wife of Representative (California)

RASPBERRY BARS

1 cup flour
1 teaspoon baking powder
¼ pound butter
1 egg, beaten
raspberry jam

Topping:
⅓ cup butter
¾ cup sugar
1 egg, well beaten
1 teaspoon vanilla
1 cup coconut

Mix flour, baking powder, butter and egg as for pastry and spread on bottom of well greased 10 x 15 inch cake pan. Over this spread a thin covering of raspberry jam. For topping, cream butter and sugar; add egg, vanilla and coconut. Spread this mixture over top of jam and bake in 350° oven for 45 minutes. May be frozen. Makes 12 bars.

Mrs. Carl T. Curtis

MRS. CARL T. CURTIS, Wife of Senator (Nebraska)

PUMPKIN BARS

¾ cup sifted flour
¾ teaspoon salt
½ teaspoon baking soda
½ teaspoon nutmeg
½ teaspoon ginger
½ teaspoon cinnamon
1 cup brown sugar
2 eggs, beaten
¼ cup salad oil

½ cup minced dates
½ cup chopped nuts
⅔ cup canned pumpkin

Frosting:
1½ cups sifted confectioners sugar
1½ tablespoons melted butter
1½ tablespoons milk
1½ teaspoons vanilla

Sift flour, salt, soda and spices. Add sugar gradually to eggs and beat well. Add oil, dates and nuts and mix well. Add sifted ingredients alternately with pumpkin to egg mixture, mixing enough to keep batter smooth. Bake in greased 9 x 9 x 2 inch pan in a 350° oven for 30 minutes. Cool 5 minutes, cut into bars, remove from pan and cool on rack. Combine frosting ingredients and beat vigorously to a spreading consistency. Frost cooled bars. Makes 32 bars.

Mrs. Jackson E. Betts

MRS. JACKSON E. BETTS, Wife of former Representative (Ohio)

CHEWY COOKIE BARS

11 tablespoons butter
2 cups brown sugar
1 cup broken nut meats
1 cup flour

¼ teaspoon baking powder
2 eggs
confectioners sugar

Mix all the ingredients except confectioners sugar. Spoon into buttered and floured 8 inch square pan. Bake in 275° oven for 65 minutes. Cut in finger length strips and roll in confectioners sugar.

Mrs. Paul L Rogers

MRS. PAUL G. ROGERS, Wife of Representative (Florida)

DREAM BARS

1 cup Spry
3 cups dark brown sugar
2 cups sifted flour
1 teaspoon salt
2 teaspoons vanilla

4 eggs
4 tablespoons flour
1 teaspoon baking powder
3 cups coconut
2 cups broken nuts

Cream Spry with 1 cup of sugar. Add 2 cups flour and salt and mix well. Spread in greased 10½ x 15½ inch pan and bake at 350° for 15 minutes. Cool. Mix remaining sugar, vanilla and eggs and beat thoroughly. Add 4 tablespoons flour, baking powder, coconut and nuts. Pour this mixture on top of first baked mixture and bake at 350° for 25 minutes. Makes 48 bars.

Mrs. Robert A. Grant

MRS. ROBERT A. GRANT, Wife of former Representative (Indiana)

CRUNCHY CHOCOLATE BALLS

3½ cups Rice Krispies
1 pound confectioners sugar
1½ cups chunky peanut butter

¼ pound margarine, melted
½ cake paraffin
1 large package milk chocolate chips

Mix Rice Krispies, sugar, peanut butter and margarine. Roll into balls about the size of a walnut. In a double boiler melt paraffin, add chocolate chips and thoroughly mix. Drop balls into chocolate coating mixture, coating well, and put on wax paper to harden. Makes 3 to 4 dozen.

Mrs. Larry Winn, Jr.

MRS. LARRY WINN, JR., Wife of Representative (Kansas)

DATE BALLS

1 cup sugar
1 egg, beaten
1 cup chopped dates
4 tablespoons butter

1 teaspoon vanilla
2½ cups Rice Krispies
½ cup chopped nuts
1 can coconut

Combine the sugar, egg, dates and butter in a saucepan and cook on medium heat for about 10 minutes. Remove from heat and stir in vanilla. Combine Rice Krispies and nuts in a large bowl; stir in date mixture. With buttered hands, roll into small balls and then roll each one in coconut. May be frozen. Makes 2 dozen.

MRS. JAMES HARVEY, Wife of former Representative (Michigan)

GRANDMA'S GINGER SNAPS

¾ cup shortening
1 cup granulated sugar (or half white, half brown)
⅓ cup molasses
2 eggs, beaten
2 cups sifted flour

¼ teaspoon salt
2 teaspoons baking soda
1 teaspoon ginger
1 teaspoon cinnamon
1 teaspoon ground cloves
sugar for coating

Cream shortening and sugar and beat in molasses and eggs. Fold in dry ingredients which have been sifted together. Form into small balls, roll in sugar and place on greased cookie sheet 3 inches apart. Bake at 350° for 15 minutes. Remove from cookie sheet while hot. May be frozen. Makes 4 dozen.

MRS. THOMAS S. KLEPPE, Wife of former Representative (North Dakota), presently Secretary of the Interior

POWDER PUFF COOKIES

2 cups sifted flour
1 teaspoon cream of tartar
½ teaspoon baking soda
1 cup confectioners sugar

½ pound margarine
1 egg
1 teaspoon vanilla
granulated sugar

Sift together flour, cream of tartar and baking soda. Beat together the sugar, margarine, egg and vanilla. Add dry ingredients and mix until smooth. Chill. Form into small balls, place on cookie sheet and flatten them by pressing crosswise with moist fork dipped in granulated sugar. Bake at 350° for 8 minutes. May be frozen. Makes 4 dozen cookies.

Mrs Ralph W. Yarborough

MRS. RALPH W. YARBOROUGH, Wife of former Senator (Texas)

BUTTER CHRISTMAS COOKIES

½ pound butter
4 tablespoons sugar
1½ teaspoons vanilla

2 cups cake flour
2 cups crushed pecans
confectioners sugar

Combine first 5 ingredients; mix well. Roll into balls the size of a large marble and place on an ungreased cookie sheet. Bake in a 290° oven for 45 minutes. Remove from oven and roll in confectioners sugar while still hot. Makes 2 dozen.

Mrs. Kevin E. VanderSchel

Mrs. Kevin VanderSchel, Daughter of Representative Neal Smith (Iowa)

POWDERED SUGAR COOKIES

¼ pound butter
1½ cups confectioners sugar
1 egg, well beaten
2½ cups flour
½ teaspoon salt

1 teaspoon baking soda
1 teaspoon cream of tartar
1 teaspoon vanilla
¼ teaspoon almond extract
1 small jar candied cherries, halved

Cream butter and sugar until fluffy. Add egg. Sift dry ingredients and add to mixture. Add vanilla and almond extract and mix well. Shape into small balls and place 2 inches apart on ungreased cookie sheet. Press candied cherry half into top and bake at 375° until a very, very light brown, about 10 or 12 minutes. Cool before storing. Makes 5 dozen.

Mrs. Craig Hosmer

MRS. CRAIG HOSMER, Wife of former Representative (California)

472

SWEDISH JAM COOKIES

¼ pound butter
½ cup brown sugar
1 egg, separated

1 cup flour
chopped nuts
jam

Cream butter and add sugar gradually. Add egg yolk and then flour. Roll in small balls and dip first in slightly beaten egg white and then in nuts. Place on cookie sheet and make a deep thumb impression in center of each ball and bake 5 minutes at 425°. Again press down center and bake 15 minutes longer. Fill small hollows with jam as soon as they come from oven. May be frozen.

Mrs. Carl T. Curtis

MRS. CARL T. CURTIS, Wife of Senator (Nebraska)

NO COOK COOKIES

2½ cups vanilla wafers, crushed
2 tablespoons cocoa
1 cup confectioners sugar
1 cup chopped walnuts

3 tablespoons corn syrup (or honey)
¼ cup bourbon (brandy or rum)
½ cup granulated sugar

Mix thoroughly first 6 ingredients. Form into balls. Roll in sugar. Store in tin box with tight lid. Will keep for several weeks. Makes 25 cookies.

Mrs. Henry P. Smith

MRS. HENRY P. SMITH III, Wife of former Representative (New York)

SWEDISH NUT COOKIES

½ pound butter or margarine
½ cup sugar
1¾ cups flour

1 cup ground nuts
1 teaspoon vanilla

Cream butter and sugar; add flour, nuts and vanilla. Mix well. Chill for 1 hour. Roll into balls. Press flat with a fork. Bake on ungreased cookie sheets at 350° for 12 minutes. Makes 4 dozen.

Mrs. Robert N. Giaimo

MRS. ROBERT N. GIAIMO, Wife of Representative (Connecticut)

BULA'S GERMAN COOKIES

½ pound butter
4 tablespoons confectioners sugar
1 tablespoon vanilla

2 cups sifted flour
1 cup ground walnuts
confectioners sugar

Cream butter and sugar until light; add vanilla. Stir in flour and walnuts. Make into small balls and flatten on greased cookie sheet. Bake in 350° oven about 12 minutes until lightly browned. When cool, dip in confectioners sugar. Makes about 5 dozen.

Mrs. Walter Norblad

MRS. WALTER NORBLAD, Wife of former Representative (Oregon)

PEANUT COOKIES

¼ pound butter or margarine
1 cup white sugar
1 cup brown sugar
2 eggs, unbeaten
1 teaspoon vanilla
¼ teaspoon salt

2 cups sifted flour
1 teaspoon baking soda
1 teaspoon baking powder
1 cup salted peanuts
1 cup crushed corn flakes
1 cup quick rolled oats
granulated sugar

Cream shortening, white sugar and brown sugar. Add eggs, vanilla and salt. Sift flour with soda and baking powder. Add to creamed mixture. Add peanuts, corn flakes and oats. Roll dough into walnut size balls, dip in granulated sugar. Put on lightly oiled baking sheet but do not press balls down. Bake 10 minutes in 375° oven. May be frozen. Makes about 3 dozen.

Mrs. John Kyl

MRS. JOHN KYL, Wife of former Representative (Iowa)

474

BROWN SUGAR OATMEAL COOKIES

1 cup shortening
1 cup dark brown sugar
1 cup white sugar
1 teaspoon vanilla
2 eggs, beaten

1½ cups sifted flour
1 teaspoon salt
1 teaspoon baking soda
3 cups quick cooking oats
1 cup chopped nuts

Cream shortening, both sugars and vanilla. Add eggs, flour, salt, soda, oats and nuts. Roll in wax paper and store in refrigerator overnight. Slice and bake on ungreased cookie sheet at 350° for 10 minutes. May be frozen. Makes 6 dozen.

Mrs. LaMar Baker

Mrs. LaMar Baker, Wife of former Representative (Tennessee)

SESAME SEED COOKIES

4 cups sifted flour
1 cup sugar
1 tablespoon baking powder
¼ teaspoon salt

½ pound butter
2 eggs, slightly beaten
½ cup milk
¾ cup sesame seeds

Sift together the dry ingredients. With 2 kitchen knives, a pastry blender or your fingers, cut in the butter until mixture resembles coarse meal. Stir in eggs and milk gradually to make a soft dough. Form into rolls about 2 inches long and ½ inch in diameter. Roll in sesame seeds and place at least ¾ inch apart on a greased baking sheet. Bake in a preheated 375° oven 12 to 15 minutes or until delicately browned. May be frozen. Makes 5 dozen cookies.

Mrs. Otis G. Pike

Mrs. Otis G. Pike, Wife of Representative (New York)

PECAN CRESCENT COOKIES

¼ pound butter	¼ teaspoon almond extract
¼ cup unsifted confectioners sugar, firmly packed	1¼ cups sifted cake flour
¼ teaspoon vanilla	¾ cup coarsely chopped pecans
	confectioners sugar

Cream butter until soft and smooth, add sugar and flavorings and blend until smooth. Stir in flour gradually; finally stir in nuts. Using about 1 teaspoon of dough for each, mold into small crescent shaped rolls. Place on ungreased baking sheet and bake in a 350° oven for about 20 minutes. While still warm, roll in more sugar. May be frozen. Makes about 3½ dozen.

Mrs. Sam M. Gibbons, Wife of Representative (Florida)

COCOONS

½ pound butter or margarine	1 cup chopped pecans
½ cup sugar	1 teaspoon cinnamon
2 cups flour	confectioners sugar
1 teaspoon vanilla	

Beat butter in electric mixer until lemon colored. Add sugar, flour and vanilla gradually, mixing well. Add nuts. Roll into cocoon shapes and place on ungreased cookie sheet. Bake in 350° oven for 25 or 30 minutes. Mix cinnamon with confectioners sugar. While cookies are still hot, roll in sugar mixture. Makes 3 dozen.

Mrs. Jamie L. Whitten, Wife of Representative (Mississippi)

476

OLD FASHIONED CHOCOLATE COOKIES

½ pound butter or margarine
1½ cups sugar
2 eggs, slightly beaten
4 ounces Hershey's baking chocolate, melted
2 teaspoons vanilla

3⅓ cups flour
1 cup Hershey's Instant
1½ teaspoons baking soda
1 teaspoon salt
⅔ cup buttermilk

Cream butter and sugar until light and fluffy. Add eggs and beat well. Add baking chocolate and vanilla and blend well. Combine flour, Instant, soda and salt and add alternately with buttermilk to creamed mixture. Drop by rounded tablespoon onto ungreased cookie sheet. Bake at 375° for 12 to 14 minutes or until no imprint remains when touched lightly. Makes about 3 dozen 3 inch cookies.

Mrs. Herman T. Schneebeli

MRS. HERMAN T. SCHNEEBELI, Wife of Representative (Pennsylvania)

LITTLE CAKES (COOKIES)

½ cup shortening
¾ cup sugar
1 egg
2 squares chocolate, melted
1¾ cups flour

½ teaspoon salt
½ teaspoon baking soda
½ cup cold coffee
½ teaspoon vanilla
frosting

Blend the first 4 ingredients. Mix flour, salt and soda and add to chocolate mixture alternately with cold coffee and vanilla. Drop from spoon on greased sheet. Bake 8 minutes in 375° oven. Frost when cool. May be frozen. Makes 5 dozen cookies.

Mrs. Edward Hutchinson

MRS. EDWARD HUTCHINSON, Wife of Representative (Michigan)

CHOCOLATE MOLASSES DROP COOKIES

⅓ cup butter
⅓ cup sugar
½ cup molasses
2 squares unsweetened chocolate, melted

1 egg, beaten
1 cup flour
½ teaspoon baking powder
¾ cup chopped nuts (optional)

Cream butter and add other ingredients in the order given. Drop from a teaspoon onto buttered cookie sheet. Bake in a 350° oven for 10 minutes. Makes 3 dozen.

Mrs. John W. Byrnes

MRS. JOHN W. BYRNES, Wife of former Representative (Wisconsin)

PETE'S TOLL HOUSE COOKIES

½ cup Crisco
¼ cup white sugar
½ cup brown sugar
½ teaspoon vanilla
1 egg

1 cup plus 2 tablespoons flour
½ teaspoon baking soda
salt
1 cup black walnuts, chopped
16 ounce package chocolate bits

Cream Crisco, sugars and vanilla. Add egg and beat. Add flour, soda and salt. Add nuts and chocolate bits. Drop by teaspoonful on cookie sheet and bake at 325° for 12 minutes. Makes 3 dozen cookies.

Mrs. Harrison A. Williams Jr.

MRS. HARRISON A. WILLIAMS, JR., Wife of Senator (New Jersey)

478

OLD FASHIONED BROWN EDGE COOKIES

½ pound butter
1 cup sugar
2 egg whites, unbeaten

1½ cups flour
1 teaspoon vanilla
cinnamon and sugar

Cream butter and add sugar gradually. Mix well. Blend in egg whites. Add flour gradually and vanilla. Beat well. Drop small teaspoon of batter on greased cookie sheet. Bake in preheated 350° oven until edges are brown, about 15 minutes. Sprinkle with cinnamon and sugar while hot. Makes 4 dozen.

Mrs. Jack Edwards

MRS. JACK EDWARDS, Wife of Representative (Alabama)

BUTTER COOKIES

1 pound butter
1½ cups sugar
1 egg

1 teaspoon vanilla
4 cups sifted flour
pecan halves

Cream butter and sugar. Add egg and mix well. Add vanilla. Add flour gradually. Drop by heaping teaspoonful onto ungreased cookie sheet, press with a fork and add pecan to top of each one. Bake at 375° for 15 minutes. May be frozen. Makes about 7 dozen cookies.

Mrs. John S. Cross

MRS. JOHN S. CROSS, Daughter of former Representative Claude A. Fuller (Arkansas)

SOFT DROP SUGAR COOKIES

1 cup vegetable shortening
2 cups sugar
2 eggs
1½ cups buttermilk
2 teaspoons vanilla

4 cups sifted flour
1 teaspoon baking soda
1 teaspoon baking powder
1 teaspoon salt

Cream shortening, sugar and eggs until light and fluffy. Beat in buttermilk and vanilla. Sift together flour, baking soda, baking powder and salt. Stir into batter. Drop by rounded teaspoonful onto greased cookie sheets. Bake at 375° for 10 to 12 minutes. Cookies should brown around the edge but not in the center. Makes 6 dozen cookies.

Mrs. Mike McCormack

MRS. MIKE McCORMACK, Wife of Representative (Washington)

COFFEE DROPS

½ cup butter or margarine
¾ cup brown sugar, firmly packed
1 egg
½ teaspoon vanilla
1¼ cups sifted flour

1 tablespoon instant coffee
½ teaspoon baking soda
½ teaspoon salt
1 cup butterscotch or caramel bits

Cream butter and sugar and beat in egg and vanilla. Sift in flour, coffee, soda and salt, beating well. Fold in candy bits. Drop from teaspoon onto ungreased cookie sheet. Bake at 375° for 10 to 12 minutes or until firm. Cool on rack. Makes 5 dozen.

Mrs. Melvin Price

MRS. MELVIN PRICE, Wife of Representative (Illinois)

LACE COOKIES

½ cup flour
½ cup coconut
¼ cup Karo syrup

¼ cup brown sugar, firmly packed
4 tablespoons margarine
½ teaspoon vanilla

Mix flour with coconut. Combine syrup, sugar and margarine and cook over medium heat, stirring constantly until well blended. Remove from heat and stir in vanilla. Gradually blend in flour mixture. Drop by teaspoonful 3 to 4 inches apart on ungreased cookie sheet. Bake at 325°.

Mrs. Lyndon B. Johnson

MRS. LYNDON B. JOHNSON, Wife of former President of the United States (Texas)

CORN FLAKE MACAROONS

4 egg whites
2 cups sugar
2 cups shredded coconut
4 cups slightly crushed corn flakes

1 teaspoon almond extract
1 teaspoon vanilla
pinch salt

Beat egg whites, gradually adding sugar. Fold in coconut, corn flakes, flavorings and salt. Drop from tip of spoon onto greased cookie sheet and bake in 350° oven for 20 minutes. Makes 6 dozen cookies.

Mrs. James D. Weaver

MRS. JAMES D. WEAVER, Wife of former Representative (Pennsylvania)

CORN FLAKE AND NUT MERINGUES

1 egg white
½ cup sugar
½ teaspoon vanilla

½ cup chopped walnuts
1 cup corn flakes

Beat egg white in large bowl. Beat in sugar gradually; beat in the vanilla. Fold in walnuts and corn flakes. Take a heaping teaspoonful of the mixture and, using another teaspoon, push off onto a well greased, preferably oiled, baking sheet. Let bake in a preheated 300° oven for 20 minutes or until outer surface appears dry. Do not brown. Remove from baking sheet with a spatula while warm. Makes 2 dozen meringues.

Mrs. Walter Moeller

MRS. WALTER MOELLER, Wife of former Representative (Ohio)

KISSES

1 egg white
3 tablespoons sugar

¾ teaspoon vanilla
¾ cup chopped nuts

Beat egg white well. Add sugar slowly while beating. Continue beating for several minutes. Add vanilla and chopped nuts. Place in small mounds on a cookie sheet. Cookies puff as they cook. Bake in 275° oven for an hour.

Mrs. John Sparkman

MRS. JOHN SPARKMAN, Wife of Senator (Alabama)

FORGOTTEN COOKIES

2 egg whites
⅔ cup sugar

1 small package chocolate chips
½ cup chopped nuts (optional)

Preheat oven to 350°. Have egg whites at room temperature and beat until stiff. Mix in sugar and add chocolate chips and nuts. Drop by spoonful on ungreased cookie sheet. Turn off oven. Put cookies in oven and leave until oven cools. Makes 2 to 3 dozen.

Mrs. Larry Winn Jr.

MRS. LARRY WINN, JR., Wife of Representative (Kansas)

481

AUSTRIAN PECAN COOKIES

2½ tablespoons butter	½ cup sifted cake flour
2 cups brown sugar	1 teaspoon baking powder
2 eggs	½ teaspoon salt
1 teaspoon vanilla	1½ cups chopped pecans

Cream butter and sugar. Add well beaten eggs and vanilla. Stir in sifted dry ingredients. Add pecans. Batter will be very thin. Drop by teaspoonful, 2 or more inches apart, on greased and floured cookie sheet. Bake in 375° oven until browned on edges, about 8 minutes. Remove cookies at once, handling very carefully. If they should stick to sheet before you can remove them all, return to oven for half a minute or more to warm.

Mrs. Sidney R. Yates

Mrs. SIDNEY R. YATES, Wife of Representative (Illinois)

BROWN SUGAR NUT ROUNDS

1 cup margarine	½ teaspoon baking soda
2½ cups packed brown sugar	¼ teaspoon salt
2 eggs	1 cup chopped pecans (or walnuts)
2½ cups sifted flour	

Mix margarine, sugar and eggs and beat well. Stir in remaining ingredients. Drop by teaspoonful 2 inches apart on ungreased cookie sheet. Bake in preheated 350° oven for 12 to 15 minutes. May be frozen. Makes 6 dozen.

Mrs. V. Ayres Mount

Mrs. VIRGINIA AYRES MOUNT, Daughter of former Representative William H. Ayres (Ohio)

CRISP OATMEAL COOKIES

1 cup margarine
1 cup brown sugar
1 cup white sugar
2 eggs
1 teaspoon vanilla
1¼ cups sifted flour

1 teaspoon baking soda
½ teaspoon salt
½ teaspoon cinnamon
3 cups old fashioned oats (or part quick oats)

Cream margarine with sugars. Add eggs and vanilla. Sift flour with baking soda, salt and cinnamon and add to above mixture. Stir in oats. Drop by small teaspoonful onto greased cookie sheet, leaving plenty of space between each one. Bake 12 to 15 minutes until golden brown. Cool only 2 minutes and remove immediately. May be frozen. Makes 5 dozen cookies.

Mrs. William L. Hungate

MRS. WILLIAM L. HUNGATE, Wife of Representative (Missouri)

PEANUT BUTTER CRISPIES

1 cup Karo syrup
1 cup sugar
½ cup brown sugar

1½ cups chunky peanut butter
5 cups Special K cereal

Place Karo, sugar and brown sugar in heavy pan. Bring this to a rolling boil. Remove from heat at once and add peanut butter. Mix well and pour over the cereal. Mix and drop by teaspoonful on wax paper. Do not bake. May be frozen. Makes 50 cookies.

Mrs. Earl L. Butz

MRS. EARL LAUER BUTZ, Wife of Secretary of Agriculture (Indiana)

PEANUT BUTTER COOKIES

1 cup shortening
1 cup brown sugar
1 cup white sugar
2 eggs

1 cup peanut butter
1 teaspoon vanilla
2 teaspoons baking soda
3 cups flour

Cream shortening and sugars; add eggs and peanut butter. Beat until smooth. Add remaining ingredients and drop by teaspoonful onto greased cookie sheet and press down with fork. Bake in 350° oven until brown. May be frozen. Makes 3 dozen.

Mrs. George Hansen

MRS. GEORGE HANSEN, Wife of Representative (Idaho)

POTATO CHIP COOKIES

¼ pound plus 2 tablespoons butter
⅓ cup sugar
1 teaspoon vanilla

¾ cup flour
¾ cup coarsely crushed potato chips
food coloring (optional)

Cream butter, sugar and vanilla thoroughly. Gradually stir in flour and fold in potato chips. Tint with food coloring if desired. Drop by teaspoonful on ungreased cookie sheet. Bake at 350° about 10 minutes. Cool before removing from pan. May be frozen. Makes 3 dozen.

Mrs Robert H. Askren

MRS. ROBERT H. ASKREN, Daughter of former Representative Karl Stefan (Nebraska)

AUNT NANCY'S TEA COOKIES

½ cup butter
1 cup sugar
1 egg, beaten
2 teaspoons baking powder

2½ cups flour
¼ cup milk
2 teaspoons vanilla

Cream butter. Gradually add sugar. Add egg. Sift together dry ingredients and add alternately with milk, a little at a time, to other ingredients. Add vanilla. Thoroughly chill. Using a floured board and a very small amount of dough at a time, roll to a ¼ inch thickness and cut with a cookie cutter. Bake on greased pan in 400° oven for 10 or 15 minutes. Makes 4 dozen.

Mrs. George M. Grant

MRS. GEORGE M. GRANT, Wife of former Representative (Alabama)

ANNIE'S SUGAR COOKIES

1 cup butter or margarine
1 cup sugar
1 egg
1 teaspoon vinegar

2 teaspoons vanilla
½ teaspoon baking soda
1 teaspoon salt
2½ cups flour

Cream butter and sugar. Add egg, vinegar and vanilla. Combine dry ingredients. Add to creamed mixture and blend. Chill. Roll out dough, cut in desired shapes and bake at 350° for 10 to 12 minutes. May be frozen. Makes 2 dozen.

Mrs. Frank H. Miller

MRS. FRANK H. MILLER, Daughter of former Senator Edward V. Long (Missouri)

CHILDREN'S SUGAR COOKIES

2 cups sugar
1 cup shortening
2 eggs
1 teaspoon vanilla
1 teaspoon baking soda

¾ cup sour milk
5 cups flour (or enough to make a
  stiff batter)
2 teaspoons baking powder
frosting (optional)

Cream sugar, shortening and eggs; add vanilla. Stir baking soda into milk and add to mixture. Sift flour and baking powder together. Stir enough flour into creamed mixture to make a very stiff batter. Using a floured dough board, knead cookie dough in small portions. Roll and cut into desired shapes and place on cookie sheets about ¼ inch apart. Bake in preheated 350° oven about 10 minutes. Decorate with frosting if desired. May be frozen. Makes 3 dozen cookies.

Mrs. George Hansen

MRS. GEORGE HANSEN, Wife of Representative (Idaho)

BISCOCHITOS (MEXICAN HOLIDAY COOKIES)

2 cups lard
1⅓ cups sugar
1 cup orange juice (or wine)
4 cups flour

½ teaspoon salt
1 teaspoon baking powder
2 teaspoons ground anise seed
1 teaspoon cinnamon

Cream lard, add ⅓ cup sugar and cream some more. Add liquid and let it stand. Combine dry ingredients except cinnamon and sift into creamed mixture. Knead more flour into dough until it forms a ball and is not sticky. Roll out on wax paper to ⅛ to ¼ inch. Cut into diamond shapes, using knife or pastry wheel. Bake at 400° 12 minutes or until light brown. Dip, while still hot, in a mixture of remaining sugar and cinnamon. May be frozen.

Mrs. Jerry Apodaca

MRS. JERRY APODACA, Wife of Governor (New Mexico)

KHVOROST (RUSSIAN FRIED PASTRY COOKIES)

6 ounces flour
½ teaspoon salt
2 eggs
¼ cup water

2 tablespoons rum
cooking oil
confectioners sugar
cinnamon

Sift flour and salt together. Add eggs, water and rum. Beat well to make a stiff dough. If necessary, add more flour. Knead well until the dough becomes elastic. Roll out carefully to paper thinness. Cut in strips, about 6 inches long and 1½ inches wide. Make a slit in the center of each and twist 1 end through. Fry in moderately hot oil until golden brown, about 2 or 3 minutes. Drain well on paper towel. Dust with a mixture of sugar and cinnamon.

Mrs. Carlton R. Sickles

MRS. CARLTON R. SICKLES, Wife of former Representative (Maryland)

GINGER COOKIES

½ cup shortening
½ cup sugar
½ cup light molasses
½ tablespoon vinegar
1 egg, beaten

3 cups flour
¼ teaspoon salt
½ teaspoon baking soda
½ teaspoon cinnamon
½ teaspoon ginger

Combine and bring shortening, sugar, molasses and vinegar to a boil. Cool and add egg. Add sifted dry ingredients and mix well. Chill. Roll out on lightly floured surface. Cut into any desired shape. Bake on greased cookie sheet in 375° oven for 12 to 15 minutes. Makes about 2½ dozen cookies.

Mrs. Joseph A. Herbert, Jr.

MRS. JOSEPH A. HERBERT, JR., Daughter of former Senator A. J. Gronna (North Dakota)

NOTES

DESSERTS

Ice Cream

Take a dozen ripe apricots, pare them very thin and stone them, scald and put them into a mortar and beat them fine; put to them six ounces of double-refined sugar, a pint of scalded cream, and rub it through a sieve with the back of a spoon; then put it into a tin with a close cover, and set it in a tub of ice broken small, with four handfuls of salt mixed among the ice; when you see your cream get thick round the edges of your tin, stir it well, and put it in again till it becomes quite thick; when the cream is all froze up, take it out of the tin, and put it into the mould you intend to turn it out of; mind that you put a piece of paper on each end, between the lids and the ice-cream, put on the top lid, and have another tub of ice ready, as before, put the mould in the middle, with the ice under and over it; let it stand four hours, and do not turn it out before you want it; then dip the mould into cold spring-water, take off the lids and paper, and turn it into a plate. You may do any sort of fruit the same way.

The New Art of Cookery
Richard Briggs, 1792

AMBROSIA

1 20 ounce can apricots
1 20 ounce can peaches
1 20 ounce can blue plums
3 to 4 thin orange slices
½ cup orange juice

lemon peel
¼ cup brown sugar
½ cup coconut
melted butter

Drain canned fruit well and arrange with orange slices in shallow dish. Mix juice, peel and sugar. Pour over fruit. Sprinkle with coconut and drizzle melted butter over top of fruit. Bake 15 minutes at 425° or until hot. Makes 10 to 12 servings.

Mrs Edward Jenison

MRS. EDWARD H. JENISON, Wife of former Representative (Illinois)

ORANGE COMPOTE

4 cups peeled, seeded orange
   segments
⅛ cup sugar

½ cup Cointreau
¼ cup slivered almonds
½ cup canned shredded coconut

Cut oranges in bite size pieces, mix with sugar and Cointreau and refrigerate overnight. Spread almonds in shallow pan and toast in a 350° oven about 5 minutes or until they start to turn color. To serve, spoon orange mixture into glass serving bowl, mix in the coconut and sprinkle with the almonds. Makes 6 servings.

Mrs Craig Hosmer

MRS. CRAIG HOSMER, Wife of former Representative (California)

CURRIED FRUIT

1 large can apricot halves
1 large can peach halves
1 large can pear halves
1 large can pineapple slices

1 jar maraschino cherries
⅓ cup butter
¾ cup brown sugar
2 teaspoons curry powder

Let fruit drain overnight. Melt butter, brown sugar with curry in oblong baking dish. Add fruit and turn each piece until well coated with butter mixture. Bake, uncovered, at 350° for 1 hour. Serve hot. Makes 8 to 10 servings.

Mrs. Omar Burleson

MRS. OMAR BURLESON, Wife of Representative (Texas)

COOKED FRUIT SALAD DESSERT

¼ pound butter, melted	1 11 ounce can apricots, drained
½ cup light brown sugar	1 11 ounce can pineapple chunks, drained
1 tablespoon curry powder	
½ cup frozen orange juice	1 bottle maraschino cherries, drained
1 11 ounce can pears, drained	

To the butter add sugar, curry and orange juice. Add fruit. Bake, uncovered, at 350° for 1 hour. Makes 4 to 5 servings.

Mrs. Charles A. Vanik

MRS. CHARLES A. VANIK, Wife of Representative (Ohio)

BICENTENNIAL BAKED APPLES

6 large baking apples	honey
pecan halves	1 cup water
cinnamon	

Wash apples, remove cores and place in baking dish. Fill centers with pecan halves and sprinkle with cinnamon. Lace apples with honey. Add water. Cover and bake in 375° oven approximately 45 minutes or until tender. Serve hot or cold.

Mrs. George E. Danielson

MRS. GEORGE E. DANIELSON, Wife of Representative (California)

CARAMEL PEACHES

8 fresh firm medium peaches	4 tablespoons butter or margarine
8 tablespoons brown sugar	ice cream (optional)

Peel peaches; halve and pit. Place hollow side up in frying pan. Place 1 tablespoon of sugar and ¼ tablespoon butter in each hollow. Cook over low heat, turning once, until juices become syrupy, about 10 or 15 minutes. Add more sugar for thicker syrup if desired. Serve hot or cold with ice cream for topping, if desired.

Mrs. George M. O'Brien

MRS. GEORGE M. O'BRIEN, Wife of Representative (Illinois)

492

COCONUT PEACH ISLAND

3 tablespoons corn starch
2 cups coconut milk
2 envelopes unflavored gelatin

¾ cup sugar
1 cup fresh milk
yellow cling peach halves

Mix corn starch with ¼ cup coconut milk. Mix gelatin, sugar, milk and balance of coconut milk together thoroughly. Place over heat, stirring constantly, until gelatin is dissolved. Bring mixture to a boil. Turn to low heat. Pour in corn starch mixture slowly. Stir constantly until mixture comes to a boil again. Remove from heat.

Place peaches, cutside down, in individual serving dishes and pour warm coconut pudding over peach which will float in dish.

MRS. HIRAM L. FONG, Wife of Senator (Hawaii)

CANTALOUPE A LA MODE WITH BLUEBERRY SAUCE

½ cup sugar
1 tablespoon corn starch
3 thin slices lemon
¾ cup grape juice

1½ cups fresh blueberries
vanilla ice cream
cantaloupe rings

In a small saucepan combine first 4 ingredients. Simmer about 5 minutes or until clear. Remove lemon slices and add blueberries. Chill. To serve, place ice cream on cantaloupe ring and top with blueberry sauce. Makes 8 servings.

MRS. JACK F. KEMP, Wife of Representative (New York)

PEACH MELBA

fresh peaches
blanched almonds
raspberry juice

currant jelly, melted
vanilla ice cream
brandy

Select fairly large perfect peaches. Peel but do not remove stones. Set in glass dish and stick (porcupine like) with almonds. Over all pour juice and melted jelly. Chill in refrigerator. Serve with a sauce made by beating vanilla ice cream, flavored with brandy.

MRS. SIDNEY R. YATES, Wife of Representative (Illinois)

493

STRAWBERRY FLUFF

1 pouch frozen strawberries   **2 to 3 ounces Cool Whip**

Thaw strawberries as directed on package. Lift the berries out of the juice and place in a small bowl. Fold the berries into the Cool Whip. Pile into serving dishes and chill. Just before serving, pour the strawberry juice over the fluff. Makes 2 servings.

Mrs. Neil Staebler

MRS. NEIL STAEBLER, Wife of former Representative (Michigan)

STRAWBERRIES AND CUSTARD SAUCE

2 quarts strawberries   *Custard sauce:*
2 cups strawberry jam   **2 cups heavy cream**
¼ cup Kirsch   **2 tablespoons sugar**
                                    4 egg whites
                                    1 teaspoon vanilla

Wash, hull and drain strawberries. Chill several hours. Pour off any water and spread strawberry jam thinned with Kirsch over berries. Serve with custard sauce.

Custard sauce: Scald 1 cup of cream in top of double boiler and stir in sugar. Beat egg whites with remaining cream and warm this mixture with a little of the hot cream. Stir well and gradually add to hot cream. Continue to cook over boiling water until thick, stirring constantly. Stir in vanilla. Pour into glass jar, cover and chill. This custard sauce will keep weeks in the refrigerator and may be used over other types of berries. Makes 6 servings.

Mrs. Pierre S. du Pont, IV

MRS. PIERRE S. du PONT, IV, Wife of Representative (Delaware)

494

GEORGIA MOUNTAIN APPLE CRISP

6 or 7 apples (Stayman or Winesap)
¾ cup sugar
3 teaspoons cinnamon
½ cup brown sugar

1 cup sifted flour
¼ pound margarine or butter
½ cup broken pecans
vanilla ice cream

Peel and slice apples into a large bowl. Add sugar and 1 teaspoon cinnamon and let set a few minutes. Mix sugar, flour and remaining cinnamon and cut in margarine until small lumps form. Add pecans. Place apples in a greased baking pan and top with flour and nut mixture. Bake in 350° oven 1 hour. Serve hot or cold with vanilla ice cream. Makes 6 to 8 servings.

Mrs. Phil Landrum

MRS. PHIL M. LANDRUM, Wife of Representative (Georgia)

APPLE BETTY

1 dozen medium apples, peeled and
   quartered
1 cup sugar
1 cup flour

1 stick margarine
cinnamon
whipped cream

Cook apples in small amount of water until soft but not mushy. Drain and place in a greased casserole. Combine sugar and flour, blend in margarine and put over top of apples. Sprinkle with cinnamon. Bake in 325° oven for 45 minutes until crust on top is brown and bubbly. Serve warm and top with whipped cream. May be frozen. Makes 6 servings.

Mrs. Romano L. Mazzoli

MRS. ROMANO L. MAZZOLI, Wife of Representative (Kentucky)

APPLE CRISP

1½ cups flour
½ cup sugar
¼ teaspoon baking soda
¼ teaspoon salt

¼ pound margarine, melted
1 25 ounce can chunky apple sauce
whipped cream (optional)

Mix flour with sugar, baking soda and salt; add margarine and stir with a fork until mixture becomes crumbly. Put ¾ of this crumbly mixture in a baking dish and pat down. Over this spread apple sauce and then sprinkle remaining crumbly mixture on top. Bake in a 375° oven for 45 minutes. Serve with whipped cream. Makes 9 servings.

MRS. JOSEPH L. CARRIGG, Wife of former Representative (Pennsylvania)

CHERRY THING

2 sticks butter or margarine
1 cup sugar
1 teaspoon vanilla
2 eggs

2 cups flour
1 cup chopped nuts
1 can cherry pie filling
confectioners sugar

Cream butter until soft. Add sugar and vanilla and beat until creamy. Beat in eggs, 1 at a time. Stir in flour. Add nuts last. Spread ¾ of batter in greased 13 x 9 inch pan. Cover with cherry pie filling. Drop remaining batter by spoonful over top. Bake at 350° for 45 minutes. Cool and sprinkle with confectioners sugar.

MRS. HENRY J. NOWAK, Wife of Representative (New York)

496

RHUBARB CRUNCH

1 cup flour
¾ cup rolled oats
1 cup brown sugar
¼ pound butter, melted
1 teaspoon cinnamon
4 cups chopped rhubarb

1 cup white sugar
1 cup water
2 tablespoons corn starch
1 teaspoon vanilla
vanilla ice cream

Mix flour, oats, brown sugar, butter and cinnamon until crumbly. Pat ½ of mixture into a 9 inch square pan. Top with rhubarb. Mix white sugar, water, corn starch and vanilla. Bring to a boil and cook, stirring, until clear. Pour sauce over rhubarb and top with remaining crumbs. Bake at 350° 1 hour. Serve with vanilla ice cream.

Mrs. Jack F. Kemp

MRS. JACK F. KEMP, Wife of Representative (New York)

APPLE COBBLER

¾ cup sugar
2 tablespoons flour
½ teaspoon cinnamon
¼ teaspoon salt
5 cups sliced apples
¼ cup water
1 tablespoon butter

Batter:
1 cup flour
1 tablespoon sugar
1½ teaspoons baking powder
½ teaspoon salt
3 tablespoons shortening
½ cup milk

Combine the sugar, flour, cinnamon and salt. Mix with apples and put in baking dish. Sprinkle with water, dot with butter, cover with aluminum foil and bake in a preheated 400° oven for 15 minutes. For batter, sift dry ingredients together, cut in shortening and stir in milk. Drop by spoonful on hot apples. Bake, uncovered, at 400° for 25 to 35 minutes. Makes 6 servings.

Mrs. Robert L. F. Sikes

MRS. ROBERT L. F. SIKES, Wife of Representative (Florida)

QUICK APPLE DESSERT

1 cup flour
2 tablespoons sugar
1 teaspoon baking powder
½ teaspoon salt
¾ cup water
⅔ cup vegetable shortening

1 egg
1 21 ounce can apple pie filling
1 tablespoon lemon juice
½ teaspoon apple pie spice (or cinnamon)

In small mixer bowl, combine first 7 ingredients, blend well with an electric mixer at low speed and then beat 2 minutes at medium speed. Spread batter in a 10 inch deep dish pie pan. Combine remaining ingredients in mixing bowl. Carefully spoon filling into center of batter and do not stir. Bake at 425° for 40 to 45 minutes until crust is golden brown. Makes 6 servings.

Mrs. Kevin E. VanderSchel

Mrs. Kevin VanderSchel, Daughter of Representative Neal Smith (Iowa)

BLUEBERRY PEACH COBBLER

1 package Duncan Hines wild blueberry muffin mix
1 cup sugar
2 teaspoons cinnamon
¾ stick butter or margarine

¾ cup chopped pecans
2 21 ounce cans peach pie filling
1 teaspoon almond extract
¼ cup Cointreau (optional)
ice cream (optional)

Wash and drain blueberries from box of mix. Set aside. Combine dry muffin mix, ½ cup sugar and 1 teaspoon cinnamon. Cut in butter to make crumb mixture. Stir in nuts. Combine peaches, remaining sugar, remaining cinnamon, almond extract and blueberries in a 13 x 9 inch baking dish. Sprinkle Cointreau on top. Spoon crumb topping over the fruit mixture. Bake in a preheated 350° oven for 35 to 40 minutes or until topping is golden brown. Serve with ice cream if desired. May be frozen. Makes 12 servings.

Mrs. Hugo L. Black

Mrs. Hugo L. Black, Wife of former Associate Justice, Supreme Court (Alabama)

CREME AU CHOCOLAT

3 squares Baker's bitter chocolate
water
½ cup sugar

3 cups light cream
5 egg yolks, beaten
1 teaspoon vanilla

Melt chocolate in double boiler with a few drops of water. In another pot, mix sugar and cream and then heat. Add melted chocolate and stir thoroughly. Slowly add egg yolks to chocolate mixture. Add vanilla and strain into small custard cups. Place cups in a pan of warm water and bake in a 350° oven until mixture is set. Refrigerate when cool. Serve cold. Makes 4 servings.

MRS. PHILLIP BURTON, Wife of Representative (California)

PINEAPPLE BAVARIAN

2 tablespoons unflavored gelatin
½ teaspoon cold water
1½ cups scalded pineapple juice
⅔ cup sugar

2 teaspoons lemon juice
1 cup drained crushed pineapple
2 cups whipped cream

Soften gelatin in cold water, add pineapple juice and sugar and stir until dissolved. When cool, add lemon juice. When the mixture congeals, fold in the pineapple and whipped cream. Turn into mold and chill. Makes 6 servings.

MRS. HENRY O. TALLE, Wife of former Representative (Iowa)

LEMON CREAM

1 envelope gelatin
¼ cup cold water
zest of 1 large lemon
½ cup boiling water
4 egg yolks

1 cup sugar
juice of 2 large lemons, strained
pinch of salt
2 cups heavy cream, whipped

Soften gelatin in cold water. Grate the zest from lemon and soak it in boiling water for 10 minutes. Beat yolks with sugar until mixture is creamy, add lemon juice and blend well. Stir in lemon zest and water in which it soaked. Add salt. Cook over hot but not boiling water, stirring constantly, until it is thick enough to coat the spoon. Add softened gelatin and stir until it is dissolved. Strain custard and cool. Whip cream until it holds a definite point and fold into cooled lemon mixture gently but thoroughly. Pour lemon cream into a mold and chill until it is firm. Unmold to serve.

Mrs. James Day Hodgson

MRS. JAMES DAY HODGSON, Wife of former Secretary of Labor, presently Ambassador to Japan (California)

COLD LEMON SOUFFLE

1 tablespoon gelatin
¼ cup cold water
3 eggs, separated
1 cup sugar
⅓ cup lemon juice

grated rind of 2 lemons
pinch of salt
2 cups whipping cream
2 packages frozen raspberries
(optional)

Soften gelatin in cold water. Dissolve over simmering water. Beat egg yolks and sugar until very light and thick. Beat in the juice and rind of lemons. Fold gelatin into lemon mixture. Beat egg whites with salt until stiff but not dry. Whip 1½ cups of the cream. Fold egg whites and whipped cream into lemon mixture. Mix again with electric mixer for 20 seconds. Put in souffle dish or individual dishes. Place in refrigerator until firm and cold. Garnish with remaining whipping cream, whipped. For an alternate topping, puree frozen raspberries in an electric blender and strain through a sieve. Makes 8 to 10 servings.

Mrs. Daniel J Evans

MRS. DANIEL J. EVANS, Wife of Governor (Washington)

500

COLD LEMON SOUFFLE WITH FRUIT PUREE

4 eggs
3 egg yolks
6 tablespoons sugar
2 packages unflavored gelatin
3 tablespoons lemon juice
3 tablespoons water
grated rind of lemon
4 tablespoons frozen lemonade,
  thawed
3 egg whites
3 tablespoons sugar
2 cups whipping cream, whipped

Strawberry Raspberry Puree:
2 teaspoons corn starch
1 tablespoon water
1 package frozen strawberries
1 package frozen raspberries
1 teaspoon lemon juice
⅓ cup currant jelly
1 tablespoon Kirsch
1 teaspoon Cointreau or Curacao
red food coloring (optional)
fresh strawberries (optional)

Beat eggs, egg yolks and sugar until mixture is smooth and thick. Put gelatin in a small pan with lemon juice and water and stir over a low fire until gelatin is dissolved. Carefully stir this mixture into egg yolk mixture. Add lemon rind and lemonade. Beat egg whites until stiff, gradually adding sugar. Fold into lemon mixture. Fold in whipped cream. Put a band of lightly oiled wax paper around an 8 inch souffle dish and pour in souffle mixture. Chill overnight or at least 6 hours.

For puree, dissolve corn starch in water. Puree berries in blender, strain and add corn starch. Cook over low heat until mixture begins to thicken. Add lemon juice, and currant jelly. Stir until jelly dissolves. Remove from heat, cool and add liqueurs. Food coloring may be added. Add fresh strawberries if desired. Chill and serve over lemon souffle.

Mrs. Christopher Bond

MRS. CHRISTOPHER S. BOND, Wife of Governor (Missouri)

CHOCOLATE SOUFFLE (UNCOOKED)

1 envelope gelatin
¾ cup hot water
3 squares chocolate
5 eggs, separated
1 teacupful confectioners sugar

1 teaspoon vanilla
½ pint whipping cream, whipped
grated chocolate
maraschino cherries

Dissolve gelatin in water, beat and let cool. Melt chocolate in double boiler. Beat egg yolks and sugar until light. Add melted chocolate, gelatin and vanilla. Beat egg whites to a stiff froth. Add to chocolate mixture and pour into glass dish or sherbet glasses. When set, decorate with whipped cream, grated chocolate and maraschino cherries. Makes 6 to 8 servings.

Mrs. Edwin Fuller Parham

MRS. EDWIN FULLER PARHAM, Daughter of former Representative Edward William Pou (North Carolina)

COFFEE SOUFFLE

1½ cups coffee
1 tablespoon gelatin
⅔ cup sugar
½ cup milk

3 eggs, separated
¼ teaspoon salt
½ teaspoon vanilla
whipped cream

Mix coffee, gelatin, ⅓ cup sugar and milk. Heat in double boiler. Add slightly beaten egg yolks. Mix in the remaining sugar and salt. Cook until thickened. Cool. Add stiffly beaten egg whites and vanilla. Pour into mold. Chill and serve with whipped cream. Makes 6 servings.

Mrs Henry Amiss Hornthal

MRS. HENRY AMISS HORNTHAL, Daughter of former Representative Thomas Hall (North Dakota)

SOUFFLE AU GRAND MARNIER

2 tablespoons butter
¾ cup sugar
5 egg yolks
¼ cup Grand Marnier

4 tablespoons freshly grated orange peel
7 egg whites
¼ teaspoon cream of tartar
confectioners sugar

Preheat oven to 425°. Grease a 2 quart souffle dish with the butter, coat with ¼ cup sugar and set aside. Beat the egg yolks with the remaining sugar in a double boiler over hot water until the mixture makes a ribbon when spoon is held up. Add the Grand Marnier and 3 tablespoons orange peel. Transfer mixture to a bowl. Mix carefully, cover and place in the refrigerator to cool. Beat egg whites until firm but not dry and add cream of tartar. Fold whites into yolk mixture, blend thoroughly and pour into prepared souffle dish. Bake 25 minutes, turning oven temperature down to 400° after 2 minutes. Sprinkle top of souffle with confectioners sugar and remaining orange peel. Makes 4 to 5 servings.

Mrs. James Day Hodgson

MRS. JAMES DAY HODGSON, Wife of former Secretary of Labor, presently Ambassador to Japan (California)

LEMON SOUFFLE

1 cup sugar
1 large lemon, grated rind and juice

4 large eggs, separated

To the sugar add the grated rind and juice of the lemon and mix well. Beat egg yolks until thick and lemon colored. Add to lemon mixture and blend well. Gently fold in stiffly beaten egg whites. Put in a baking dish, set in a pan of hot water and bake at 325° for 40 minutes. Makes 4 servings.

Mary Hamilton O'Neal

MARY HAMILTON O'NEAL, Daughter of former Representative Emmet O'Neal (Kentucky)

APRICOT MOUSSE

¾ cup dried apricots
1 cup water
1 cup sugar
1 teaspoon vanilla
water as needed
8 egg yolks

4 egg whites
1 cup whipping cream, whipped

Garnish:
dried apricots
green maraschino cherries, drained

Cook apricots with 1 cup water for 10 minutes over medium heat. Stir in ½ cup sugar and vanilla. Blend in blender at medium speed until smooth; add enough water to make 2 cups. Beat egg yolks at high speed until thick and lemon colored. Gradually beat in apricot mixture. Cook over low heat, stirring constantly until mixture is very thick, about 15 minutes. Refrigerate, stirring occasionally, until cooled. Beat egg whites at high speed until soft peaks form. Gradually add remaining sugar, beating well after each addition until mixture is glossy and stiff peaks form. Fold apricot mixture into egg whites; fold in whipped cream. Pour into 10 cup mold, cover and freeze. Unmold 2 hours before serving, garnish with flowers formed from apricots and cherries. Makes 12 servings.

Mrs. John Dellenback

MRS. JOHN DELLENBACK, Wife of former Representative (Oregon)

503

LEMON MOUSSE

2 cups boiling water
1 6 ounce package lemon gelatin
2 7 ounce bottles lemon lime
    carbonated drink (or 7 Up)

1 lemon, grated rind and juice
2 cups heavy cream, whipped
fresh berries
sugar

Pour boiling water over gelatin and stir until dissolved. Add lemon lime drink, grated rind and lemon juice. Chill until slightly thick. Beat until foamy. Fold into the whipped cream and turn into a 2 quart souffle dish. Serve with fresh berries, lightly sugared. Makes 8 servings.

Mrs. Paul Simon

MRS. PAUL SIMON, Wife of Representative (Illinois)

FRUIT MOUSSE

2 cartons fruit yogurt
1 pint fruit, sweetened (same flavor
    as yogurt)

Kirsch or other liqueur
1 large container Cool Whip
strawberries

Fold yogurt into fruit, add liqueur and let stand for 30 minutes. Add Cool Whip. Rinse individual molds or 1 large mold with cold water. Pour in mousse and freeze overnight. Remove from freezer 1 hour before serving, unmold and garnish with strawberries. Makes 6 to 8 servings.

Mrs. Wm. J. Randall

MRS. WILLIAM J. RANDALL, Wife of Representative (Missouri)

504

CHOCOLATE MOUSSE

2 envelopes unflavored gelatin
½ cup water
⅔ cup creme de cacao
1¼ cups brown sugar
1 12 ounce package semi-sweet
  chocolate bits
8 eggs, separated

½ teaspoon salt
2 cups whipping cream, whipped

Garnish (optional):
whipped cream
shaved chocolate

Mix gelatin, water, creme de cacao and ½ cup sugar over low heat until melted. Add chocolate bits. Stir until melted and remove from heat. Beat egg yolks, 1 at a time, into chocolate mixture. Cool. Add salt to egg whites and beat until stiff. Beat in remaining brown sugar. Fold egg whites into chocolate mixture and then fold in whipped cream. Refrigerate. May be served topped with whipped cream and shaved chocolate. May be frozen. Makes 12 to 14 servings.

MRS. JOHN H. TERRY, Wife of former Representative (New York)

MOUSSE AU CHOCOLAT

1 6 ounce package chocolate bits
5 tablespoons boiling water
4 egg yolks

2 tablespoons dark rum
4 egg whites, stiffly beaten

Put chocolate bits into blender and run on high speed for 6 seconds. Scrape chocolate from sides of container, add hot water and blend on high speed for 10 seconds. Add egg yolks and rum and blend for 3 seconds or until smooth. Fold chocolate mixture into egg whites, spoon dessert into serving dishes and chill for 1 hour before serving. Makes 8 servings.

MRS. JAMES DAY HODGSON, Wife of former Secretary of Labor, presently Ambassador to Japan (California)

MEREGON

Caramel:
1 cup sugar
1 teaspoon water

Meringue:
12 egg whites
24 tablespoons sugar
2 teaspoons vanilla

Chantilly sauce:
2 cups milk
1/8 teaspoon salt
lemon rind
10 egg yolks
1 cup sugar
1 teaspoon vanilla

Make caramel by boiling sugar with water over low heat until it reaches caramel color. Pour caramel into a round tube cake pan. Turn pan so that sides and bottom are covered with caramel. Let cool. Then butter the cake pan right over the caramel.

Meringue: Whip egg whites to peak consistency. Add sugar slowly while continuing to whip. Add 1 teaspoon vanilla. Pour into prepared cake pan. Place pan in a larger container partially filled with water and bake in a 350° oven, not preheated, for 25 to 30 minutes. Remove from oven and immediately turn upside down and remove from pan. Pour remaining vanilla over cake. Place in refrigerator at once.

Sauce: Boil milk, salt and lemon rind. Cool. Whip egg yolks with sugar and continue whipping while milk and vanilla are added. Strain. Using a different saucepan, cook over low heat, stirring constantly, until it thickens a bit.

To serve, fill the center of meringue with part of the sauce and use the remainder over the meringue.

MRS. LILA M. DE HERNÁNDEZ-COLON, Wife of Governor (Puerto Rico)

LEMON ANGEL PIE

Meringue:
1 teaspoon vanilla
1 teaspoon vinegar
4 egg whites
1 cup sugar

Filling:
4 egg yolks, beaten
½ cup plus 2 teaspoons sugar

2 large lemons, juice and grated rind
1 cup whipping cream, whipped
1 teaspoon vanilla

Topping:
unsweetened whipped cream

Add vanilla and vinegar to egg whites and beat until stiff. Add sugar slowly, beating until glossy. Put in a greased 10 inch pie plate and bake at 275° for 1 hour.

For filling, cook egg yolks, ½ cup sugar, juice and rind in top of double boiler until thick. Cool. Add whipped cream, vanilla and remaining sugar. Place in meringue shell and refrigerate. When ready to serve, top with unsweetened whipped cream. Makes 8 servings.

MRS. CHALMERS P. WYLIE, Wife of Representative (Ohio)

ANGEL PIE

4 egg whites
¼ teaspoon cream of tartar
1 cup sugar

Filling:
4 egg yolks plus 2 whole eggs,
  well beaten

¾ cup sugar
2½ tablespoons lemon juice
2 tablespoons orange juice
3 teaspoons grated orange rind
1 pint whipping cream, whipped

Beat egg whites with cream of tartar until stiff. Continue beating, adding sugar gradually. When well beaten, put into buttered pie plate and bake 1 hour at 250°.

Mix together all filling ingredients except cream and cook in top of double boiler until thick. Place a layer of whipped cream in cooled crust and spread the filling over it. Top with a layer of the remaining whipped cream. Chill 24 hours before serving. Makes 6 servings.

MRS. JOHN S. CROSS, Daughter of former Representative Claude A. Fuller (Arkansas)

LEMON MERINGUE DESSERT

4 eggs, separated
¼ teaspoon cream of tartar
1½ cups sugar

3 tablespoons lemon juice
2 tablespoons lemon rind
1 cup whipping cream, whipped

Beat egg whites with cream of tartar until stiff. Add 1 cup sugar and beat until glossy. Place in 8 x 12 inch greased baking dish and bake 1 hour at 275°.

Beat egg yolks until thick and lemon colored. Add remaining sugar, lemon juice and rind. Cook until thick. Cool. Cover cooled meringue with half of the whipped cream. Spread lemon mixture over this and top with remaining whipped cream. Refrigerate 24 hours. Makes 8 to 10 servings.

MARGARET CHASE SMITH, former Senator (Maine)

FORGOTTEN DESSERT

5 egg whites
½ teaspoon salt
½ teaspoon cream of tartar
1½ cups sugar
1 teaspoon vanilla (or almond
flavoring)

½ pint whipping cream, whipped (or
large package Dream Whip)
strawberries (or other fresh fruit)

Combine egg whites, salt, cream of tartar and beat until stiff. Add sugar 1 tablespoon at a time and then vanilla. Beat 15 minutes with electric mixer. Spread on a 10 × 18 inch greased pan. Put in preheated 450° oven and turn off heat. Leave overnight. Do not open oven door for 8 hours. At end of that time, spread whipped cream over dessert and refrigerate. Serve with berries. May be frozen with whipped cream on top. Recipe cannot be doubled. Makes 12 to 15 servings.

MRS. CHARLES A. MOSHER, Wife of Representative (Ohio)

KISSES

3 egg whites
1 drop vanilla
1 cup sugar

strawberries
whipped cream

Beat egg whites with vanilla. Add sugar slowly, beating until stiff. Drop tablespoons of mixture on cookie sheet and make slight impression in the middle. Bake at 250° for 1 hour. When cool and ready to serve, fill impression with strawberries and a dab of whipped cream.

Mrs. Fred W. Drogula

MRS. FRED W. DROGULA, Daughter of former Representative Paul J. Kilday (Texas)

PECAN CRUNCH PIE

3 egg whites
½ teaspoon baking powder
1 cup sugar
11 graham crackers, crushed

1 cup pecans, chopped
1 teaspoon vanilla
1 cup whipping cream, whipped

Beat egg whites with baking powder; add sugar slowly. Beat until very stiff. Combine graham cracker crumbs and nuts. Fold into egg white mixture. Add vanilla. Spread in a well buttered 10 inch pie pan. Bake at 350° for 25 to 30 minutes. Chill for 5 hours. Top with whipped cream. Serves 8.

Mrs. Thos. A. Wadden

MRS. THOMAS A. WADDEN, Daughter of former Representative Edward W. Pou (North Carolina)

KUGLER TORTE

7 egg yolks
⅝ cup sugar
5 ounces semi-sweet chocolate, melted
½ teaspoon almond flavoring
7 egg whites
pinch of salt
5 ounces almonds, ground

Chocolate Cream Frosting:
¼ pound butter
1 egg yolk
½ teaspoon vanilla
4 ounces sweet unsalted chocolate, melted
1 to 2 tablespoons superfine sugar (optional)

Cream yolks and sugar until light and fluffy. Add cooled chocolate and blend with whisk. Add almond flavoring. Whip egg whites with salt until they are stiff but not dry. Add ⅓ of the whipped egg whites alternately with the ground almonds to the yolk and sugar mixture. Gently fold in remaining egg whites so that air bubbles of egg whites stay in batter. Pour batter into a buttered and floured 9 inch round cake pan and bake in preheated 325° oven for 35 to 45 minutes until a cake tester comes out clean. Cool in cake pan for 5 minutes. Remove from pan and place upright on cake rack. Cool completely before frosting.

For frosting, cream butter until very smooth. Add the yolk, vanilla and cooled chocolate. Taste and add sugar if necessary. Continue to cream the frosting until it is a good spreading consistency. Ice top and sides of cake. Chill in refrigerator. Remove ½ hour before serving. May be frozen. Makes 12 servings.

Mrs. Robert McClory

MRS. ROBERT MCCLORY, Wife of Representative (Illinois)

UNUSUAL BAKED CHOCOLATE PUDDING

1 cup flour
¾ teaspoon salt
2 teaspoons baking powder
8 tablespoons cocoa
3 tablespoons lard
1¼ cups white sugar
½ cup milk

1 teaspoon vanilla
½ cup chopped nuts
dates, chopped (optional)
½ cup brown sugar
1 cup hot water
cream (or ice cream)

Sift together flour, salt, baking powder and 2 tablespoons cocoa. Cream lard and ¾ cup white sugar. Combine milk and vanilla and add alternately with dry ingredients to the creamed mixture. Mix thoroughly. Pour into a well greased baking dish. Cover top with nuts and dates. Combine remaining white sugar and cocoa with brown sugar and sprinkle over nuts. Pour hot water over this and bake at 350° for 40 minutes. Serve with cream or ice cream. This makes a cake with its own syrup. Makes 6 servings.

Mrs. Roy A. Taylor

MRS. ROY A. TAYLOR, Wife of Representative (North Carolina)

FRENCH CHOCOLATE PUDDING

2 cups milk
¼ cup sugar
3 ounces sweet chocolate, grated
4 egg yolks, beaten
¾ cup heavy cream
1 teaspoon vanilla
2 tablespoons brandy

Optional:
whipped cream
slivered pistachio nuts
maraschino cherries, well drained
green citron leaves

Stir and scald milk over low heat, slowly adding sugar and chocolate. Add the hot chocolate mixture, a spoonful at a time, to egg yolks and beat until smooth. Return sauce to low heat, stirring constantly until it thickens. Strain. Cool by placing pan in cold water. Whip cream until stiff, adding vanilla and brandy. Fold cold custard into whipped cream mixture until well blended. Fill custard cups with pudding and chill thoroughly. If desired, before serving pipe a large scroll of whipped cream on top of each one and sprinkle with pistachio nuts or garnish with a maraschino cherry and green citron leaves. Makes 6 servings.

MRS. EDWARD J. DERWINSKI, Wife of Representative (Illinois)

DATE PUDDING

2 eggs
1 cup sugar
1 teaspoon baking powder
4 tablespoons flour
½ teaspoon salt

¾ cup milk
1 cup dates, chopped
1 cup nuts, chopped
whipped cream

Mix the first 8 ingredients in the order given. Spoon into greased 8 x 8 inch cake pan and bake at 350° about 1 hour. Serve with whipped cream. May be frozen. Makes 16 servings.

MRS. JOHN J. RHODES, Wife of Representative (Arizona)

CHEWY DATE PUDDING

2 eggs, well beaten
½ cup sugar
1 tablespoon flour (more if needed)
1 cup chopped dates

1 cup chopped nuts
1 teaspoon baking powder
pinch of salt
whipped cream

Mix all ingredients together. Pour into 9 x 9 inch well greased, floured cake pan. Bake in preheated 350° oven until toothpick inserted into center comes out clean. Top with whipped cream. This is not a soft pudding, but a very chewy pudding. Makes 9 servings.

Mrs. Tennyson Guyer

MRS. TENNYSON GUYER, Wife of Representative (Ohio)

SCHAUM PUDDING

4 tablespoons corn starch
1½ cups sugar
1 cup orange juice
grated rind and juice of 1 lemon
1 cup water

3 egg whites
1½ cups milk
3 egg yolks
1 teaspoon vanilla

Blend corn starch and 1 cup sugar in saucepan, add orange and lemon juice, grated rind and water. Cook over medium heat until it comes to a boil and is thick and transparent looking, stirring frequently. Cool. Beat egg whites until stiff and add to first mixture. Refrigerate. In another saucepan combine milk, remaining sugar and egg yolks. Cook and stir constantly until custard coats spoon. Cool; add vanilla. Refrigerate. To serve, spoon custard over pudding in individual dishes. Makes 6 to 8 servings.

Mrs. Albert H. Quie

MRS. ALBERT H. QUIE, Wife of Representative (Minnesota)

512

TOP HAT PUDDING

3 egg whites
3 tablespoons granulated sugar
2 tablespoons orange marmalade
1/4 teaspoon orange extract
3 egg yolks

3/4 cup confectioners sugar
1/2 teaspoon vanilla
pinch of salt
1 cup heavy cream, whipped
1/2 cup chopped toasted almonds

Whip egg whites very stiffly. Gradually add sugar and continue beating until mixture forms peaks. Add marmalade and extract. Pour into greased top of double boiler. Cover; cook 45 minutes. Beat egg yolks with confectioners sugar, vanilla and salt. Fold in whipped cream. Chill. Serve the hot pudding with the chilled sauce. Sprinkle "top hat" with almonds.

Mrs. Sidney R. Yates

MRS. SIDNEY R. YATES, Wife of Representative (Illinois)

MARJORIE'S LEMON DELICACY

2 tablespoons butter
3/4 cup sugar
2 eggs, separated
2 tablespoons flour

juice of 1 lemon
grated rind of 1/2 lemon
1 cup milk

Cream butter, add sugar gradually and cream well together. Add well beaten egg yolks, flour, lemon juice and rind. Mix thoroughly. Add milk and fold in stiffly beaten egg whites. Pour into a greased baking dish. Set in a pan of hot water and bake in a 350° oven about 45 minutes. A delicate crust will form on top and the pudding will supply its own sauce. Makes 6 servings.

Mrs. Roy A. Taylor

MRS. ROY A. TAYLOR, Wife of Representative (North Carolina)

INDIAN PUDDING

1 quart milk
2 teaspoons butter
3 rounded tablespoons yellow corn
   meal
3 tablespoons quick cooking tapioca

½ cup maple syrup
½ teaspoon salt
½ cup evaporated milk (or cream)
whipped cream (or ice cream)

Scald milk and butter in top of a double boiler. Mix together the corn meal and tapioca in a bowl. Add gradually to the milk and stir until tapioca is transparent, about 5 minutes. Add syrup and salt. Pour into greased casserole and let stand at least 10 minutes. Pour evaporated milk over the top. Cover and bake 1 hour at 300°. Remove cover the last 10 minutes of baking time to brown top. Serve warm with whipped cream or ice cream. Makes 6 to 8 servings.

Mrs. Charles A. Mosher

MRS. CHARLES A. MOSHER, Wife of Representative (Ohio)

BREAD PUDDING

bread to fill a 9 x 13 inch cake pan
3 eggs
1½ cups sugar

2 teaspoons vanilla
cinnamon
milk

Break up bread in pan and let dry. Mix the eggs, sugar, vanilla, cinnamon and milk. Pour over bread and smash down. Bread should be completely covered. Sprinkle with cinnamon. Stir once or twice after 20 minutes. Bake at 350° for 1 hour. May be frozen. Makes 18 servings.

Mrs. Richard F. Kneip

MRS. RICHARD F. KNEIP, Wife of Governor (South Dakota)

NANCY'S TOP OF THE STOVE BREAD PUDDING

1 cup brown sugar	3 eggs
3 slices white bread	2 cups milk
2 tablespoons butter	⅛ teaspoon salt
1 cup raisins	1 teaspoon vanilla

Put sugar in top of double boiler. Spread bread with butter and cut in cubes. Put on top of sugar. Add raisins. Beat eggs with the milk. Add salt and vanilla, then pour over bread and raisins. Do not stir. Cook 1 hour, uncovered, over boiling water. Chill. Unmold when cold. Makes 4 servings.

Mrs. Carroll D. Kearns

MRS. CARROLL D. KEARNS, Wife of former Representative (Pennsylvania)

PINEAPPLE NOODLE KUGEL

½ pound creamed cottage cheese	1 1 pound can crushed pineapple, drained
½ pint dairy sour cream	¼ pound butter (or margarine), melted
½ cup pineapple yogurt	
1 jar chunk applesauce	
1 pound broad egg noodles, cooked and drained	*Topping:*
8 eggs, beaten	4 tablespoons butter (or margarine)
¼ cup confectioners sugar	½ cup crushed corn flakes
¼ cup brown sugar	½ teaspoon cinnamon
	1 tablespoon sugar

Cottage cheese may be whipped in blender for a few seconds first if desired. Combine all the Kugel ingredients, mix gently and spoon into shallow pan. Combine all the topping ingredients and sprinkle on top of pudding. Bake in a 350° oven about 1 hour until top is browned. May be frozen before baking. Serve warm or chilled. Makes 12 servings.

Mrs. Elford A. Cederberg

MRS. ELFORD A. CEDERBERG, Wife of Representative (Michigan)

GRANDMA'S CHRISTMAS PUDDING

2¾ cups flour
1 teaspoon baking soda
1 teaspoon salt
1 teaspoon cinnamon
1 teaspoon nutmeg
¼ teaspoon allspice
¼ teaspoon ground cloves
½ cup sugar
1 cup coarsely ground suet
   (tender leaf part)
1 cup finely chopped nuts
1 cup coarsely ground raisins
½ cup molasses
½ cup dark Karo syrup
1 cup hot water

Sauce:
2 cups water
2 tablespoons butter
¼ teaspoon salt
1 cup sugar
½ scant cup flour
nutmeg
vanilla

Topping:
whipped cream

Sift dry ingredients together and sprinkle some over the suet, nuts and raisins. Mix, coating them to prevent them from sticking together. Mix remaining dry ingredients with the liquids. Stir in suet mixture. Pour into a greased and sugared 8 cup pudding mold. Set the tightly covered mold on a trivet in an inch of boiling water in a heavy kettle. Cover kettle closely and turn the heat on high. As steam begins to escape, lower the heat. Steam for 3 hours, adding more boiling water to the kettle as needed. When it is done, remove lid and let stand a while before unmolding. Serve with a hot sauce and top with whipped cream. Makes 18 servings.

Sauce: Boil together the water, butter and salt. Mix sugar and flour and add to boiled mixture. Add nutmeg and vanilla. Stir until thickened.

Mrs. James A. McClure

Mrs. James A. McClure, Wife of Senator (Idaho)

ENGLISH PLUM PUDDING

⅓ pound citron
⅓ pound currants
⅔ pound seeded raisins, chopped
1 teaspoon baking soda
½ teaspoon cinnamon
½ teaspoon mace
½ teaspoon nutmeg
½ teaspoon cloves

½ pound brown sugar
½ pound fresh beef suet, ground
½ pound bread crumbs
6 eggs, beaten
⅙ cup wine
⅙ cup brandy
hard butter sauce with sherry or
    brandy to taste

Dredge fruit with a mixture of baking soda, cinnamon, mace, nutmeg and cloves. Add sugar, suet and crumbs to eggs. Mix in other ingredients, adding wine and brandy last. Put in a 3 pound can or 2 or 3 small cans and cover with several thicknesses of aluminum foil. Put on a rack in a covered container, letting boiling water come half way up can. Steam for 3 hours. Serve hot with hard butter sauce seasoned with sherry or brandy. Will keep indefinitely in refrigerator. Makes 16 servings.

Mrs. Robert G. Stephens, Jr.

Mrs. Robert G. Stephens, Jr., Wife of Representative (Georgia)

SUET PUDDING

1 cup chopped suet
1 cup milk
1 cup molasses
3 cups flour
1 teaspoon baking soda
1½ teaspoons salt

1 teaspoon cinnamon
½ teaspoon ginger
½ teaspoon cloves
½ teaspoon nutmeg
1 cup currants
hard sauce

Mix first 3 ingredients together. Sift the dry ingredients together and add to first mixture. Mix well. Add currants. Steam in steamer for 3 hours. Serve hot with hard sauce. Makes 10 servings.

Mrs. Edward Hutchinson

Mrs. Edward Hutchinson, Wife of Representative (Michigan)

GRANDMA'S CARROT PUDDING

1 cup butter	2 teaspoons baking powder
1 cup brown sugar	¼ teaspoon baking soda
2 eggs, beaten	½ teaspoon salt
1 cup grated carrots	1 teaspoon cinnamon
1 cup raisins	1 teaspoon nutmeg
1 cup peeled, diced apples	½ teaspoon cloves
2 cups bread crumbs	sweetened heavy cream, heated
1 cup flour	

Cream butter and sugar. Add eggs and beat, then add carrots, raisins and apples. Stir in bread crumbs and dry ingredients. Fill greased molds ⅔ full and simmer 3 hours in steamer or large kettle. Serve hot with warm cream. Makes 12 servings.

Mrs. Jake Garn

MRS. JAKE GARN, Wife of Senator (Utah)

CUSTARD

4 eggs, slightly beaten	3 cups hot milk
⅓ cup sugar	1 teaspoon vanilla
¼ teaspoon salt	

Combine eggs, sugar and salt. Stir in the milk gradually. Add vanilla. Pour into a casserole and set in a pan of hot water. Bake at 325° for 1¼ hours or until the tip of a knife inserted in the center comes out clean. Makes 4 to 6 servings.

Mrs Harlan Hagen

MRS. HARLAN HAGEN, Wife of former Representative (California)

518

ZABAGLIONE (EGG CUSTARD)

8 egg yolks   1 cup sweet sherry
2/3 cup sugar

Have all ingredients at room temperature. Combine egg yolks and sugar in the top of a double boiler. Beat with wire whisk until thick. Place pan over hot, but not boiling, water and gradually mix in sherry, beating constantly until smooth, thick and frothy. Makes 6 to 8 servings.

Mrs. James J. Howard

MRS. JAMES J. HOWARD, Wife of Representative (New Jersey)

CUSTARD WITH BLACK CHERRIES

1 cup sugar   1 teaspoon vanilla
6 cups milk   pinch of nutmeg
6 eggs   1 16 ounce can black cherries, drained

Mix first 5 ingredients and beat gently for 1 minute. Pour into buttered pan, set in a pan of water and bake in a 350° oven for 1 hour. Spoon cherries over custard when ready to serve. Makes 6 servings.

Mrs Homer Ferguson

MRS. HOMER FERGUSON, Wife of former Senator (Michigan)

LEMON CURD

3 eggs
6 tablespoons butter
1 cup sugar

grated rind and juice of 2 lemons
pastry cups (optional)

Whisk eggs in top of double boiler. Add butter, sugar, lemon rind and juice. Cook over boiling water, stirring constantly until mixture is thick and smooth. May be served as a cold custard or used as filling for pastry cups. Makes 4 servings.

Mrs. Henry O. Talle

MRS. HENRY O. TALLE, Wife of former Representative (Iowa)

CHEESE CAKE ELEGANTE

Crust:
1½ cups graham cracker crumbs
¼ cup confectioners sugar
1 teaspoon allspice
⅓ cup melted butter

Filling:
2 8 ounce packages cream cheese, softened
2 eggs, beaten slightly
⅔ cup sugar
2 teaspoons pure vanilla

Topping:
1½ cups dairy sour cream
4 tablespoons pure vanilla

Make crust by combining graham cracker crumbs, sugar, allspice and butter. Spread in bottom of a 9 inch spring form pan, pressing some up the sides to form a rim about ½ to ¾ inch high.

For filling, stir cheese until soft and creamy. Add eggs, sugar and vanilla. Beat until thoroughly creamed and smooth. Pour into crust. Bake in a 350° oven for 25 minutes. Remove from oven and top with sour cream to which the vanilla has been added. Return to oven, increase oven temperature to 450° and bake 7 minutes. Cool and then chill. This is very rich so serve small slices.

Mrs. Howard W. Cannon

MRS. HOWARD W. CANNON, Wife of Senator (Nevada)

GREAT CHEESE CAKE

Crust:
1½ cups flour
¼ cup brown sugar, firmly packed
¼ pound butter or margarine
½ cup chopped pecans

Filling:
2 8 ounce packages cream cheese,
   softened

3 egg yolks
¾ cup sugar
1 teaspoon vanilla
3 egg whites

Topping:
1 cup dairy sour cream
2 tablespoons sugar
1 teaspoon vanilla

Combine flour and brown sugar; cut in butter until particles are fine. Stir in pecans. Press firmly onto bottom of greased 9 inch square pan. Bake at 350° for 10 to 12 minutes until lightly browned. Beat cream cheese until smooth. Add egg yolks and beat well. Gradually add sugar and vanilla; mix thoroughly. Beat egg whites until stiff, but not dry. Fold into cream cheese mixture. Spread over baked crust. Bake at 325° for 45 minutes or until set. Combine topping ingredients and blend well. Spread over baked cake and bake an additional 5 minutes. Cool completely and then chill. May be frozen. Makes 12 to 16 servings.

Mrs. Tennyson Guyer

MRS. TENNYSON GUYER, Wife of Representative (Ohio)

THE BIG CHEESE CAKE

1½ cups graham cracker crumbs
1⅓ cups sugar
1 teaspoon cinnamon
¼ pound butter or margarine, melted
2 envelopes unflavored gelatin
¼ cup cold water
2 egg yolks, slightly beaten
½ cup milk
1 teaspoon salt
1 tablespoon grated lemon peel

2 cups small curd, creamed
   cottage cheese
½ cup lemon juice
2 teaspoons vanilla
1 cup heavy cream, whipped
2 egg whites, stiffly beaten

Garnish:
whipped cream
tart jelly

Combine the graham cracker crumbs, ⅓ cup sugar and cinnamon. Blend in butter. Press ½ of crumb mixture onto bottom of 9 inch spring form pan, reserving rest of mixture for topping. Soften gelatin in cold water. In double boiler combine yolks, milk, remaining sugar and salt. Cook over hot, not boiling, water, stirring constantly until mixture coats metal spoon. Remove from heat. Dissolve softened gelatin in hot mixture and add lemon peel. Cool; beat well. Mix cheese, lemon juice and vanilla; add to gelatin mixture. Fold in whipped cream, then egg whites. Pour into crumb lined pan. Sprinkle top with reserved crumbs. Chill overnight. Garnish with whipped cream and tart jelly. Makes 12 servings.

Mrs Ralph S. Regula

MRS. RALPH S. REGULA, Wife of Representative (Ohio)

CHEESE CAKE DELUXE

30 graham crackers, crushed
¼ pound margarine, melted
1 tablespoon confectioners sugar
1 3 ounce package lemon Jello
1 cup boiling water

2 small packages cream cheese
1 cup granulated sugar
2 tablespoons vanilla
1 12 ounce can Carnation milk
fruit for topping (optional)

Combine cracker crumbs with margarine and sugar. Line pan with half the crumbs. Dissolve Jello in boiling water, cool and let thicken slightly. Cream the cheese with the granulated sugar and vanilla. Beat milk until thick. Add Jello and mix. Add cheese mixture and mix. Pour over graham cracker crust and top with remaining crumbs or fruit topping. Refrigerate until ready to serve. Makes 12 servings.

Mrs. Harold C. Hagen

MRS. HAROLD C. HAGEN, Wife of former Representative (Minnesota)

PENNSYLVANIA CHEESE CAKE

Crust:
1/4 pound butter, melted
18 to 20 graham crackers, crushed

pinch of salt
1/2 teaspoon vanilla
2 scant teaspoons lemon extract

Filling:
2 large packages Philadelphia cream
  cheese
2 eggs
1/2 cup sugar

Topping:
1 cup dairy sour cream
2 tablespoons sugar
pinch of salt
1/2 teaspoon vanilla

Mix butter with graham cracker crumbs. Line pie plate and bake 10 minutes at 350°. Beat cheese, eggs and sugar in electric mixer until thoroughly mixed. Add salt, vanilla and lemon extract and beat gently. Pour into crust and bake 20 minutes in 350° oven. Remove from oven and let cool for 5 minutes. Mix topping ingredients gently in electric mixer. Spread on top of pie and bake at 350° for 5 minutes. Let cool and refrigerate. May be frozen. Makes 8 servings.

Mrs. Milton J. Shapp

Mrs. Milton J. Shapp, Wife of Governor (Pennsylvania)

CHEESE CAKE

1 1/2 cups graham cracker crumbs
1/4 pound butter or margarine, melted
12 ounces cream cheese
1/2 cup sugar
1 tablespoon flour

3 whole eggs
3/4 cup dairy sour cream
1 teaspoon vanilla
fruit (optional)

Line pie plate with graham cracker crumbs mixed with melted butter and bake in 350° oven about 5 minutes. Set aside. Soften cream cheese and beat with sugar and flour until smooth. Add eggs and beat well. Finally add sour cream and vanilla and beat until very smooth. Pour this mixture into the graham cracker crust and bake in 350° oven until the center has just set, about 25 minutes. Do not overcook. This is good served with any canned, frozen or fresh fruit. May be frozen. Makes 6 servings.

Mrs. Ed Jones

Mrs. Ed Jones, Wife of Representative (Tennessee)

NEVER FAIL CHEESE CAKE

12 graham crackers, crumbled
2 tablespoons brown sugar
pinch of cinnamon
1/4 pound butter, melted

Topping:
2 tablespoons sugar
1 teaspoon vanilla
1 pint dairy sour cream

Filling:
1 pound cream cheese
1 cup sugar
2 tablespoons water
3 eggs

Glaze:
1 can pitted cherries, drained and
   halved, reserve juice
1 heaping tablespoon corn starch

Mix graham cracker crumbs, brown sugar, cinnamon and butter and pat into bottom of a spring form pan. Cream the cheese. Dissolve the sugar in the water, blend into cheese and beat for 10 minutes. Add eggs, 1 at a time, mixing well after each addition. Pour into prepared crust and cook in a preheated 350° oven for 20 to 25 minutes.

For topping, fold sugar and vanilla into sour cream. Gently spread over filling and bake at 350° for 12 to 15 minutes. Cool. Mix juice into corn starch, bring to a boil and boil until thickened, stirring constantly. Remove from heat, add fruit and cool. Spoon over top of cheese cake and refrigerate for 8 hours. To serve, run a knife around edge, unlatch the spring and ease over to serving dish. Makes 10 to 12 servings.

Fleur M. Feighan

FLEUR M. FEIGHAN, Daughter of former Representative Michael A. Feighan (Ohio)

CHERRY CREAM CHEESE PIE

1/3 cup margarine or butter, melted
1/4 cup sugar
1 cup corn flake crumbs
1 8 ounce package cream cheese,
   softened

1 can sweetened condensed milk
1/2 cup Realemon
1 teaspoon vanilla
1 21 ounce can cherry pie filling,
   chilled

Cook margarine and sugar over low heat, stirring constantly, until mixture boils. Remove from heat. Mix in corn flake crumbs. Press evenly and firmly into 9 inch pie pan to form crust. Chill. Beat cream cheese until smooth. Gradually mix in sweetened condensed milk. Stir in Realemon and vanilla. Spread in crust. Refrigerate 3 to 4 hours or until firm. Top with chilled cherry pie filling. To remove pie pieces easily, place hot, wet towel around sides and bottom of pan before cutting. Makes 8 servings.

Mrs. Sterling Cole

MRS. STERLING COLE, Wife of former Representative (New York)

CALIFORNIA CHEESE CAKE

32 single graham crackers, crumbled
¼ pound butter, melted
6 tablespoons sugar

Filling:
4 eggs, slightly beaten
12 ounces cream cheese
½ cup sugar

½ teaspoon vanilla
¼ pint dairy sour cream

Topping:
¾ pint dairy sour cream
3 tablespoons sugar
1 teaspoon vanilla

Combine graham cracker crumbs with butter and sugar and press into two 9 inch pie plates. Bake 5 minutes in a 350° oven. Mix together filling ingredients, blending well. Pour into shells and bake at 350° for 20 minutes. Cool for 1 hour. Blend topping ingredients together and spread on cooled pie filling. Bake 5 minutes in a 350° oven.

Mrs. Clair W. Burgener

MRS. CLAIR W. BURGENER, Wife of Representative (California)

SLICED BANANA CAKE

3 sticks margarine
2 cups graham cracker crumbs
2 eggs
1 pound confectioners sugar
6 bananas, sliced lengthwise
1 small can crushed pineapple, drained

1 9 ounce carton Cool Whip
2 tablespoons sugar
½ teaspoon almond flavoring
½ teaspoon vanilla
1 small jar maraschino cherries, chopped
1 cup chopped English walnuts

Blend 1 stick margarine with graham cracker crumbs and press into 9 inch cake pan. Cream remaining margarine and beat in eggs and confectioners sugar for 15 minutes. Set aside. Arrange banana slices over crust, cover with pineapple and spread egg and sugar mixture over all. Cover with Cool Whip mixed with sugar, almond flavoring and vanilla. Sprinkle cherries and walnuts over top. Makes 8 to 12 servings.

Mrs. Bill Nichols

MRS. BILL NICHOLS, Wife of Representative (Alabama)

CAROL'S CHERRY CREAM PIE

1 cup crumbled corn flakes
2 tablespoons sugar
⅓ cup butter or margarine, melted
1 8 ounce package cream cheese,
    softened

1 15 ounce can sweetened condensed
    milk
⅓ cup lemon juice
1 teaspoon vanilla
1 21 ounce can prepared cherry pie
    filling

Combine crumbs, sugar and butter and mix well. Press evenly and firmly on bottom and sides of a 9 inch pie tin and chill. Beat cream cheese until fluffy and gradually add condensed milk. Stir until well mixed. Stir in lemon juice and vanilla until well blended. Turn into prepared crust. Chill 2 to 3 hours but do not freeze. At serving time, garnish with cherry pie filling. Makes 6 to 8 servings.

Mrs. Walter B Jones

MRS. WALTER B. JONES, Wife of Representative (North Carolina)

LEMON PIE

14 to 16 graham cracker squares,
    crushed
4 tablespoons margarine, melted
1 can sweetened condensed milk
3 egg yolks
2 lemons, juice and rind
dash of salt

Meringue:
3 egg whites
⅛ teaspoon cream of tartar
dash of salt
3 tablespoons sugar, superfine
    granulated

Mix graham cracker crumbs with margarine. Press into a 9 inch pie pan. Combine milk, egg yolks and juice and rind of lemons in that order. Add salt. Put the lemon filling in the crust and set aside. It needs no baking.

Beat egg whites partially; slowly add cream of tartar, salt and sugar. Continue beating until stiff. Spread over top of pie. Brown lightly under broiler. Makes 8 servings.

Mrs. Richard D. Lamm

MRS. RICHARD D. LAMM, Wife of Governor (Colorado)

KEY LIME PIE

1⅓ cups graham cracker crumbs
½ stick butter, melted
3 eggs, separated
1 can sweetened condensed milk

¾ cup fresh Key lime juice
6 tablespoons sugar
1 teaspoon vanilla

Mix crumbs and butter and press onto sides and bottom of a 9 inch pie plate. Beat yolks until light. Beat in condensed milk and lime juice, beating until mixture is thick. Pour into pie shell. Beat the egg whites until they hold stiff peaks. Beat in sugar, 1 tablespoon at a time, until mixture is stiff and glossy. Beat in vanilla. Spread meringue on top of pie, sealing edges to the crust. Bake at 425° for 5 to 7 minutes. Chill before serving. Makes 6 servings.

Mrs Jack R. Miller

MRS. JACK R. MILLER, Wife of former Senator (Iowa)

ORANGE CHIFFON PIE

3 egg yolks, slightly beaten
1 cup water
½ cup sugar
1 3 ounce package orange gelatin
1½ teaspoons grated orange rind
⅔ cup liquid, juice of 1 orange plus
water
3 egg whites
dash of salt

Chocolate Coconut Crust:
2 tablespoons butter
2 squares unsweetened chocolate
⅔ cup sifted confectioners sugar
2 tablespoons hot milk (or water)
2 cups flaked coconut

Garnish (optional):
orange slices
chocolate shavings

Combine egg yolks and water in top of double boiler, add ¼ cup sugar and mix well. Cook over boiling water, stirring constantly, until mixture coats the spoon. Remove from heat, add gelatin and stir until dissolved. Blend in orange rind and juice. Chill until it is the consistency of an egg white. Beat egg whites with salt until foamy. Add remaining sugar gradually, beating thoroughly after each addition. Continue beating until mixture forms soft rounded peaks. Beat gelatin mixture slightly, fold into egg whites and beat very slightly. Pour into chocolate coconut crust and chill until firm, at least 4 hours. Garnish with orange slices and shaved chocolate. Makes 8 servings.

Chocolate Coconut Crust: Melt butter and chocolate in top of double boiler, stirring until blended. Combine sugar and milk and add to chocolate mixture, stirring well. Add coconut and mix well. Spread on bottom and sides of a greased 9 inch pie pan. Refrigerate until firm.

Mrs. Frank M. Karsten

MRS. FRANK M. KARSTEN, Wife of former Representative (Missouri)

PINEAPPLE DESSERT

60 Ritz crackers, crushed
⅔ cup margarine
7 egg yolks, beaten
1 20 ounce can crushed pineapple

1¼ cups sugar
1 3 ounce box cherry Jello
7 egg whites
⅔ cup chopped nuts

Combine the cracker crumbs and margarine. Pat ⅔ of this mixture into the bottom of a 13 x 9 inch baking pan. Mix beaten egg yolks, pineapple and ½ cup sugar. Bring to a boil and cook until slightly thickened, stirring constantly. Stir in Jello; cool. Beat egg whites until stiff. Gradually add remaining sugar. Fold into egg yolk mixture and pour over crust. Combine remainder of cracker mix with nuts and sprinkle over top. Refrigerate. Flavor improves if it stands overnight. Makes 12 servings.

Mrs Tennyson Guyer

MRS. TENNYSON GUYER, Wife of Representative (Ohio)

PEGGY'S RASPBERRY DESSERT

½ stick butter, melted
1¼ cups graham cracker crumbs
¼ cup chopped nuts (optional)
2 10 ounce packages frozen red
  raspberries in syrup
1 cup water
½ cup sugar

2 teaspoons lemon juice
4 tablespoons corn starch
¼ cup cold water
50 large marshmallows
1 cup milk
2 cups heavy cream, whipped

Mix butter with graham cracker crumbs and nuts and press firmly into bottom of 13 x 9 inch pan. Heat raspberries with 1 cup of water, sugar and lemon juice. Dissolve corn starch in cold water. Stir into raspberry mixture and cook and stir until thickened and clear. Cool. Melt marshmallows in milk in top of double boiler over boiling water. Cool thoroughly. Then fold whipped cream into marshmallow mixture and spread over crumb crust. Spread raspberry mixture over top. Refrigerate until firm. Makes 15 to 18 servings.

Mrs. Richard Schultz Schweiker

MRS. RICHARD SCHULTZ SCHWEIKER, Wife of Senator (Pennsylvania)

528

RASPBERRY DESSERT

40 vanilla wafers, crushed
1½ sticks butter
2 cups confectioners sugar
2 eggs
chopped walnuts

1 package raspberry Jello
1 cup boiling water
2 packages frozen raspberries
1½ cups whipping cream
3 tablespoons sugar

Line the bottom of a large cake pan with wafer crumbs; reserving some for the top. Press down. Mix butter with the confectioners sugar. Beat eggs until thick and lemon colored. Add butter mixture to egg mixture and beat well. Spread carefully over crumb layer. Spread on a layer of chopped walnuts. Dissolve Jello in boiling water. Add frozen raspberries. Chill until quite thick. Spread over nuts. Whip the cream and sweeten with the sugar. Spread over Jello. Top with a few vanilla wafer crumbs. Refrigerate overnight. Makes 15 servings.

Mrs. Arthur A. Link

MRS. ARTHUR A. LINK, Wife of Governor (North Dakota)

FRESH STRAWBERRY PIE

1 3 ounce package strawberry gelatin
1⅔ cups boiling water
1 4½ ounce container non-dairy whipped topping, thawed

2 tablespoons sugar
1 9 inch baked crumb crust
1½ cups strawberry halves (or slices)

Dissolve gelatin in boiling water and chill. When it is slightly thickened, measure ½ cup of it and blend it into whipped topping. Blend in sugar. If necessary, chill mixture until firm enough to mound. Spread over the bottom and sides of crumb crust. Stir strawberries into remaining thickened gelatin and gently spoon onto top of mixture. Chill 3 hours. Makes 6 to 8 servings.

Margaret Mackie Sanders MD

MARGARET MACKIE SANDERS M.D., Daughter of former Representative John C. Mackie (Michigan)

RUM CREAM PIE

1 cup sugar
6 egg yolks, beaten
1 envelope unflavored gelatin
½ cup cold water

¼ cup rum
½ pint heavy cream, whipped
1 vanilla wafer crumb pie shell
German chocolate shavings

Add sugar to egg yolks and beat well. Soak gelatin in cold water, put over low flame and bring to a boil. Pour over egg mixture and stir briskly. Fold rum into whipped cream and add to egg mixture. Cool mixture in refrigerator until it begins to set. Stir gently, pour into pie shell and refrigerate. Sprinkle with chocolate shavings before serving. Makes 6 servings.

MRS. CHARLES THONE, Wife of Representative (Nebraska)

MINT MARSHMALLOW DESSERT

Crust:
½ cup melted butter
¼ cup sugar
2 cups graham cracker crumbs

Filling:
4 cups small colored marshmallows
1 cup colored mints
1 pint whipping cream, whipped

Combine ingredients for crust. Press down ¾ of crumbs into 9 x 12 inch pan. Add marshmallows and mints to whipped cream. Spread over crust. Sprinkle top with remaining crumbs. Refrigerate at least overnight. Makes 24 servings.

MRS. ODIN LANGEN, Wife of former Representative (Minnesota)

PUMPKIN FLUFF PIE

¾ cup brown sugar
1 envelope unflavored gelatin
½ teaspoon salt
1 teaspoon cinnamon
½ teaspoon nutmeg
¼ teaspoon ginger

3 egg yolks, slightly beaten
¾ cup milk
1¼ cups canned pumpkin
3 egg whites
⅓ cup granulated sugar
1 9 inch corn flake pie crust

In saucepan, combine brown sugar, gelatin, salt and spices. Combine egg yolks and milk; stir into brown sugar mixture. Cook and stir until mixture is boiling. Remove from heat and stir in pumpkin. Chill until mixture mounds slightly when spooned. Test every now and then and do not let it get too stiff. Beat egg whites until soft peaks form. Gradually add granulated sugar, beating to stiff peaks. Fold pumpkin mixture thoroughly into egg whites. Turn into cooled corn flake crust. Chill until firm.

Mrs. Bill Hefner

MRS. W. G. (BILL) HEFNER, Wife of Representative (North Carolina)

HOLIDAY MINCEMEAT PIE

1 package graham cracker pie crust
   mix
1 9 ounce package mincemeat

1½ cups hot water
1 to 3 tablespoons sugar
½ cup heavy cream, whipped

Prepare graham cracker crust according to package directions. Press into an 8 inch Pyrex cake dish. Break mincemeat into small pieces and add water and sugar. Place over heat and stir until lumps are thoroughly broken. Boil gently 10 minutes. Cool slightly. Pour into crust and chill. Top with whipped cream. Makes 6 servings.

Mrs Hubert H. Humphrey

MRS. HUBERT H. HUMPHREY, Wife of former Vice President of the United States, presently Senator (Minnesota)

531

FRENCH PUDDING

¼ pound butter
1½ cups confectioners sugar
2 eggs, beaten
1 cup crushed pineapple, drained

½ pound vanilla wafers, crushed
½ pint whipping cream, whipped
1 cup chopped nuts

Cream butter and sugar. Stir in eggs. Fold pineapple into creamed mixture. Place ½ of wafer crumbs in buttered 2 quart casserole. Cover with the pineapple mixture, then the whipped cream and top with remaining wafer crumbs. Sprinkle with nuts. Chill before serving. May be frozen. Makes 8 servings.

Mrs. Julian M. Carroll

MRS. JULIAN CARROLL, Wife of Governor (Kentucky)

LEMON SUPREME CHIFFON

24 graham crackers, crushed
¼ cup melted butter
¼ cup sugar

juice of 2 lemons
6 eggs, separated
⅔ cup sugar

1 large package lemon Jello
2 cups boiling water

1 cup whipping cream
3 tablespoons sugar

Mix graham cracker crumbs with the butter and ¼ cup sugar. Spread half of this mixture on the bottom of a 9 x 13 inch loaf pan.

Mix the Jello, water and lemon juice. Chill until partially set. Beat egg whites stiffly and add the ⅔ cup sugar. Set aside. Beat egg yolk and add to Jello mixture, mixing thoroughly. Fold in beaten egg whites. Pour over crumb mixture in pan.

Whip the cream, adding 3 tablespoons sugar gradually. Spread over Jello mixture. Top with remaining crumb mixture. Refrigerate several hours before serving. Makes 12 to 15 servings.

Mrs. James A. McClure

MRS. JAMES A. McCLURE, Wife of Senator (Idaho)

STRAWBERRY ICEBOX CAKE

1 pound Nabisco pink wafers, ground	3 eggs
½ pound butter	2 pints fresh strawberries
1 pound confectioners sugar	1 pint whipping cream, whipped

Grease a 13 x 8 inch pan and line with wafer crumbs, reserving some for the top. Cream the butter and sugar. Beat in eggs, 1 at a time. Continue to beat 10 or 15 minutes. Spread over crumbs in pan. On top of this place strawberries in rows and cover with whipped cream. Sprinkle reserved crumbs on top. Chill for at least 5 hours. Cut in squares. May be frozen. Makes 15 servings.

Mrs. John C. Brophy

MRS. JOHN C. BROPHY, Wife of former Representative (Wisconsin)

TIPSY PIE

1 package ladyfingers	½ pound miniature marshmallows
½ cup cocktail sherry	½ pint whipping cream, whipped

Slice ladyfingers in half and line pie plate with them, cut side up. Cut ⅓ off each ladyfinger to line sides of pie plate. Heat wine and marshmallows in double boiler and stir until dissolved. Add whipped cream to wine marshmallow mixture after it has cooled for about 5 minutes. Pour entire mixture over ladyfingers. Refrigerate for several hours. Makes 6 servings.

Mrs. Robert Thomas Ashmore

MRS. ROBERT THOMAS ASHMORE, Wife of former Representative (South Carolina)

MACADAMIA NUT ICEBOX CAKE

1 envelope unflavored gelatin
¼ cup cold water
½ cup plus 2 tablespoons sugar
pinch of salt
4 egg yolks, beaten
2 cups milk, scalded

½ teaspoon vanilla
1 13½ ounce jar macadamia nuts,
 finely chopped
1½ cups heavy cream
14 lady fingers, split

Soften gelatin in cold water, set in pan of simmering water and stir until dissolved. Remove from heat but leave in pan of hot water to keep it warm. Add ¼ cup of sugar and salt to egg yolks. Gradually stir in milk and cook over low heat, stirring constantly, until mixture coats spoon. Add vanilla and gelatin. Cool to room temperature, stirring occasionally to prevent setting. Add all but 2 tablespoons of chopped nuts. Beat 1 cup of cream, gradually adding ¼ cup sugar and fold into custard mixture. Line a 10 inch spring form pan, sides and bottom, with lady fingers. Pour in mixture and chill. Just before serving, whip remaining cream, adding remaining sugar. Spread over custard and decorate with reserved nuts. Makes 8 servings.

Mrs. Spark Matsunaga

MRS. SPARK MATSUNAGA, Wife of Representative (Hawaii)

FRENCH CHOCOLATE CREME CAKE

1 bar dot sweet chocolate (or 1½ bars
 German sweet chocolate)
3 tablespoons sugar
3 tablespoons boiling water
5 egg yolks, beaten
5 egg whites, stiffly beaten

2 dozen lady fingers
1 tablespoon confectioners sugar
2 teaspoons water
whipped cream
shaved chocolate

Melt chocolate in top of double boiler over hot water. Add sugar and boiling water and mix well. Blend in egg yolks. Cool. Fold in egg whites. In a wax paper lined 9 inch layer cake pan, line bottom and sides with lady fingers. To make it easier to stand the lady fingers against the sides, first dip each one in a little paste made with the confectioners sugar and water. Pour in half the chocolate mixture and cover with a layer of lady fingers. Pour in remaining chocolate and cover with more lady fingers. Refrigerate overnight. It should be firm before it is removed from the pan. Cover with whipped cream and sprinkle with the shaved chocolate. Makes 8 to 10 servings.

Mrs. Howard Robison

MRS. HOWARD ROBISON, Wife of former Representative (New York)

STRAWBERRY CHARLOTTE

2 envelopes unflavored gelatin	2 teaspoons lemon juice
½ cup water	1 teaspoon vanilla
1 quart firm, ripe strawberries, washed and hulled	4 drops red food coloring
1 cup sugar	1 3 ounce package ladyfingers, split
	2 cups heavy cream, whipped

Soften gelatin in water 5 minutes. Slice enough strawberries to make 4 cups and set aside. Puree the remaining berries in electric blender or food mill. Puree should measure about 1¾ cups. Combine softened gelatin, strawberry puree and sugar in a medium size saucepan. Cook over low heat, stirring occasionally, until sugar and gelatin dissolve. Remove from heat. Stir in lemon juice, vanilla and food coloring. Chill until mixture thickens and mounds when spooned.

Line sides of 8 inch spring form pan with ladyfingers, rounded sides out. Fold whipped cream into gelatin mixture and pour about half of it into lined pan. Over this quickly spread half the reserved, sliced strawberries. Top with remaining gelatin mixture. Refrigerate 2 to 3 hours or until filling is firm. Remove sides of pan and arrange remaining sliced strawberries over top in sunburst design. Makes 10 servings.

Mrs. Douglas R. Smith

MRS. DOUGLAS R. SMITH, Daughter-in-law of Representative Neal Smith (Iowa)

PINEAPPLE ANGEL FOOD CAKE

1 envelope unflavored gelatin	1 cup crushed pineapple, drained
½ cup cold water	1 cup chopped nuts
3 eggs, separated	2 cups whipping cream, whipped
1 cup sugar	1 small angel food cake
2 cups milk	

Dissolve gelatin in water. Combine beaten egg yolks, sugar and milk and cook in double boiler until mixture coats spoon. While mixture is hot, add gelatin. When cool, add pineapple and nuts. Fold in whipped cream and beaten egg whites.

Tear angel food cake into walnut sized pieces. Put half of these pieces into bottom of greased tube pan and pour half of pineapple mixture over them. Add remaining cake pieces and cover with remaining pineapple mixture. Refrigerate. Unmold before serving. Makes 12 servings.

Mrs. Charles H. Leavy

MRS. CHARLES H. LEAVY, Wife of former Representative (Washington)

MARTIN'S ENGLISH TRIFLE

2 packages instant vanilla pudding mix
4½ teaspoons vanilla
8 slices pound cake, cut ½ inch thick
⅓ cup red raspberry jam

4 tablespoons Cointreau
1 package frozen red raspberries, thawed
1 cup heavy cream

Prepare pudding mix as directed. Stir in 2 teaspoons of vanilla. Set aside. Spread 1 side of 4 slices of cake with raspberry jam. Arrange, preserve side up, in a 2 quart glass serving bowl. Sprinkle with 2 tablespoons of the Cointreau. Pour half of the pudding over this. Arrange remaining 4 cake slices on pudding; sprinkle with remaining Cointreau. Reserve a few whole raspberries for garnish. Gently stir 1 teaspoon vanilla into remaining raspberries; spoon over cake. Pour remaining pudding over berries. Refrigerate until thoroughly chilled.

In chilled bowl, combine whipping cream with remaining vanilla and whip until stiff. Spread half over pudding and use other half to decorate the top, garnishing with reserved berries. May be refrigerated or frozen but do not add whipped cream until just before serving. Makes 10 to 12 servings.

Mrs. William H. Bates

MRS. WILLIAM H. BATES, Wife of former Representative (Massachusetts)

TRIFLE

½ pound plain pound cake
½ cup strawberry or raspberry jam
   (or cooked fruit or berries)
½ cup sherry (or sherry flavoring)
½ cup sugar
3 egg yolks

1 teaspoon corn starch
2 cups milk, heated
½ teaspoon almond extract
1 cup heavy cream, whipped
¼ cup slivered, toasted almonds
angelica (optional)

Cut cake into 1 inch thick slices and coat with jam. Place cake slices, jam side up, in bottom of glass serving bowl. If cooked fruit is used, place cake in bottom of bowl and cover with fruit. Sprinkle sherry over all. Allow to stand at least 30 minutes.

Combine sugar, egg yolks, corn starch, milk and almond extract in top of double boiler and cook over boiling water, stirring constantly, until thickened. Pour the cooled custard over the soaked cake and chill. Just before serving, spread whipped cream over cake and custard mixture. Sprinkle almonds all over the surface and finish off with slivers of angelica. Makes 4 to 6 servings.

Mrs. James R. Mann

MRS. JAMES R. MANN, Wife of Representative (South Carolina)

536

E Z TIPSY CAKE

1 package vanilla pudding
¼ cup bourbon
1 small sponge cake, crumbled
1 small can slivered almonds

1 pint whipping cream, whipped
   (or Cool Whip)
maraschino cherries

Cook pudding according to package directions. Cool and add bourbon. Layer cake pieces, almonds, pudding and whipped cream in a bowl in the order given. Repeat until bowl is filled, ending with whipped cream. Refrigerate. To serve, spoon into individual compotes and top each with a cherry. Makes 10 to 12 servings.

Mrs. Walter B Jones

MRS. WALTER B. JONES, Wife of Representative (North Carolina)

LIME ICE CREAM PIE

Filling:
2 eggs
½ cup sugar
½ cup cream
⅓ cup fresh lime juice
few drops of green food coloring

Crust:
1½ cups graham cracker crumbs
¼ cup melted butter
⅓ cup sugar

1 quart vanilla ice cream

Beat filling ingredients together and freeze until firm. Beat again. Mix crust ingredients well, reserving ¼ cup for top. Press into a greased 9 inch pie pan. Soften the vanilla ice cream slightly and spread over crust. Spread the lime filling over the ice cream. Sprinkle reserved crumbs over top. Freeze. Keeps well in freezer. Makes 7 servings.

Mrs. Harry S. Truman

MRS. HARRY S. TRUMAN, Wife of former President of the United States (Missouri)

CRUNCHY NUT CRUST

1½ cups finely chopped pecans or
   walnuts
3 tablespoons sugar

2 tablespoons soft butter
ice cream
chocolate sauce, warmed

Combine nuts, sugar and butter and stir until nuts are thoroughly coated. Press mixture firmly and evenly against bottom and sides of buttered 9 inch pie pan. Bake in a preheated 450° oven for 6 to 8 minutes. Cool. Fill pie shell with a favorite ice cream. Keep in freezer. Serve with a chocolate sauce.

Mrs Paul G. Rogers

Mrs. Paul G. Rogers, Wife of Representative (Florida)

FROZEN LEMON DESSERT

1 can Eagle Brand condensed milk
1 6 ounce can frozen lemonade or
   limeade, thawed

1 pint whipping cream, whipped
vanilla wafers, crushed (or graham
   cracker crumbs)

Mix condensed milk and juice together until well blended. Then fold mixture into whipped cream. Spread a layer of crumbs on bottom of 9 x 9 inch pan. Cover with whipped cream mixture. Sprinkle crumbs on top. Freeze in covered container. Remove from freezing unit ½ hour before serving. Makes 12 servings.

Mrs. Milton R. Young

Mrs. Milton R. Young, Wife of Senator (North Dakota)

FROZEN LIME PIE

1 can Eagle Brand milk
½ cup lime juice
3 eggs, separated
⅛ teaspoon green food coloring
1 9 inch graham cracker crust
   (or baked pie shell)

½ cup whipping cream
1 tablespoon sugar
1 teaspoon vanilla

Combine milk, lime juice and egg yolks. Fold in stiffly beaten egg whites and green food coloring. Put into prepared crust and bake at 300° for 15 minutes. Cool. Whip cream, adding sugar and vanilla. Spread over pie. Freeze. Remove from freezer 1 hour before serving. May be refrozen. Makes 8 servings.

Mrs. Robert M. Lemke

Mrs. Robert M. Lemke, Daughter-in-law of former Representative William Lemke (North Dakota)

MINT FROZEN CAKE

¼ cup margarine, melted
24 creme filled chocolate cookies, crushed
2 jars marshmallow creme

½ cup creme de menthe
2 pints heavy cream, whipped
shaved chocolate

Combine margarine and crushed cookies; press into bottom of 9 inch spring form pan. Mix marshmallow creme and creme de menthe; fold in whipped cream; pour into pan. Decorate top with chocolate and freeze.

Mrs. Carlton R. Sickles, Wife of former Representative (Maryland)

HERSHEY BAR PIE

8 small chocolate almond Hershey bars
½ cup milk
16 large marshmallows

1 cup whipping cream, stiffly whipped
9 inch graham cracker crust

Place chocolate bars, milk and marshmallows in top of double boiler, melt and mix thoroughly. Remove and cool thoroughly. Fold whipped cream into mixture. Pour into graham cracker crust. Chill. May be frozen and served frozen or thawed.

Mrs. Clarence J. Brown, Wife of Representative (Ohio)

KENTUCKY BOURBON PIE

¼ to ⅓ cup melted butter
20 Nabisco thin chocolate wafers, finely crumbled
½ package gelatin
2½ tablespoons cold water
½ cup sugar

2 tablespoons bourbon
½ square bitter chocolate, grated
½ cup broken pecans
1 teaspoon vanilla
½ pint whipping cream, whipped
grated chocolate for garnish

Combine butter and chocolate wafer crumbs. Pat into a 9 inch pie pan and chill in refrigerator or bake in a warm oven 10 to 15 minutes. Soften gelatin in cold water. Combine sugar, gelatin, bourbon, chocolate, nuts and vanilla. Fold in whipped cream. Pour into pie shell. Freeze and serve with whipped cream and a touch of grated chocolate. Makes 8 servings.

Mrs. Tim Lee Carter, Wife of Representative (Kentucky)

539

BUTTERSCOTCH CRUNCH SQUARES

1 cup sifted flour
¼ cup quick cooking oats
¼ cup brown sugar
¼ pound butter

½ cup chopped nuts
1 12 ounce jar butterscotch ice cream
  topping (or caramel)
1 quart chocolate or vanilla ice cream

Combine flour, oats and sugar; cut in butter until mixture resembles coarse crumbs. Stir in nuts. Pat mixture into a 13 x 9 x 2 inch baking pan. Bake in 400° oven for 15 minutes. Stir, while still warm, until it is all crumbled. Cool. Spread half the crumbs in 9 x 9 x 2 inch baking pan and drizzle half the ice cream topping over them. Stir ice cream to soften; spoon carefully into pan. Drizzle with remaining topping and sprinkle with remaining crumbs. Freeze. Makes 8 servings.

Mrs Anita W. Ullman

MRS. ANITA W. ULLMAN, Member of Congressional Club (Oregon)

FRENCH MINT DESSERT

1 cup butter
2 cups confectioners sugar
4 squares Baker's chocolate, melted
4 eggs

1 teaspoon peppermint flavoring
2 teaspoons vanilla
½ cup chopped nuts
1½ cups vanilla wafer crumbs

Cream butter with sugar and add cooled chocolate. Beat very well. Add eggs and beat again. Add peppermint flavoring and vanilla and continue to beat. Add nuts. Put half the vanilla wafer crumbs in the bottom of 20 paper lined muffin tins, fill with chocolate mixture and top with remaining crumbs. May be frozen or refrigerated.

Mrs. Charles H. Leavy

MRS. CHARLES H. LEAVY, Wife of former Representative (Washington)

CHOCOLATE FRANGES

½ pound butter
2 cups sifted confectioners sugar
4 squares bitter chocolate, melted
2 teaspoons vanilla

1 teaspoon peppermint flavoring (optional)
4 eggs
vanilla wafers, crushed

Cream butter and sugar. Add chocolate, vanilla, peppermint flavoring and eggs. Beat well. Cover bottoms of small cups or little glasses with vanilla wafer crumbs, fill with chocolate and sprinkle additional crumbs on top. Freeze. Makes 12 to 15 servings.

Mrs. Charles Thone

MRS. CHARLES THONE, Wife of Representative (Nebraska)

ITALIAN BISCUIT TORTONI

1 egg white
1 cup whipping cream
6 tablespoons confectioners sugar

4 tablespoons Bicardi rum (or vanilla)
5 tablespoons chopped almonds
lady fingers

Whip egg white until very stiff. Whip cream until foamy, add sugar gradually and beat until stiff. Add rum and beat again. Fold in egg white. Pour into 6 chilled molds or fluted paper cups. Sprinkle almonds on top. Place in freezer until firm. Serve with lady fingers. This may be made in the morning if it is to be served at dinner time.

Mary Park Clements

MARY PARK CLEMENTS, Daughter of former Representative Judson C. Clements (Georgia)

FROZEN RUM PUDDING

1 tablespoon gelatin
¼ cup cold water
1 cup warm milk
1 tablespoon vanilla
⅓ cup sugar
3 egg yolks

2 ripe bananas, crushed
2 tablespoons rum
3 egg whites
whipped cream
butterscotch sauce

Dissolve gelatin in cold water in top of double boiler. Add milk, vanilla, sugar and egg yolks. Cook over boiling water, stirring until liquid coats the spoon. Cool off over ice and add crushed bananas and rum. Fold in the egg whites, stiffly beaten but not dry. Pour into a mold and freeze overnight. Remove from mold and decorate with whipped cream. Serve with a butterscotch sauce.

Mrs. Jack R. Miller

MRS. JACK R. MILLER, Wife of former Senator (Iowa)

THE GOVERNOR'S FAVORITE ICE CREAM

1 quart buttermilk
1 pint whipping cream

2 cups sugar
1 tablespoon vanilla

Mix all ingredients and pour into ice cream churn and freeze.

Mrs James Burrows Edwards

MRS. JAMES BURROWS EDWARDS, Wife of Governor (South Carolina)

STRAWBERRY ICE CREAM

2 cups fresh or frozen strawberries
  (or any fruit)
1½ quarts Half and Half
3 cups sugar

dash of salt
1 13 ounce can evaporated milk
6 tablespoons fresh lemon juice

Combine all ingredients in ice cream freezer and follow manufacturers directions for freezing it. Makes 2 quarts.

Mrs Richard G Scott

MRS. RICHARD G. SCOTT, Daughter of former Senator Arthur Vivian Watkins (Utah)

542

ELEGANT QUICKIE

1 scoop coffee ice cream
1 tablespoon Cointreau

½ maraschino cherry
1 nutmeat (almond, walnut or pecan)

Place ice cream into serving dish or long stemmed glass. Spoon Cointreau over ice cream and garnish with cherry and nutmeat. Serve immediately. Makes 1 serving.

Mrs. Warren G. Magnuson

MRS. WARREN G. MAGNUSON, Wife of Senator (Washington)

CREME DE MENTHE FRAPPE

1 quart rich vanilla ice cream
1 cup creme de menthe

¼ cup brandy

Soften ice cream. Gently beat all 3 ingredients in mixer just until well mixed. Freeze. The mixture will not get extremely hard because of the alcohol. Serve in champagne glasses. It is thick but easy to drink. Makes 6 servings.

Mrs. Thomas G. Abernethy

MRS. THOMAS G. ABERNETHY, Wife of former Representative (Mississippi)

FROZEN DAIQUIRI MOUSSE

2 large egg yolks
¼ cup sugar
1 teaspoon grated lime rind
2 tablespoons lime juice
1 drop green food coloring

1½ tablespoons rum
1 egg white
⅓ cup heavy cream, whipped
lime slice twists, wafer thin

Beat yolks until fluffy. Gradually add sugar and beat until mixture is thick and pale. In top of a double boiler combine yolk and sugar mixture with juice and rind and cook over barely simmering water (not boiling), stirring constantly, until thick enough to coat spoon, 3 or more minutes. Cool and stir in green food coloring and rum. Beat egg white until it holds stiff peaks. In another bowl whip cream until it holds soft peaks. Fold cream into yolk mixture, then fold in egg white. Spoon into ramekins and freeze several hours or overnight. Remove from freezer about 15 minutes before serving. Garnish with lime slice twists. Makes 6 servings.

Mrs. David C. Treen

MRS. DAVID C. TREEN, Wife of Representative (Louisiana)

MAPLE MOUSSE

4 eggs, separated
1 cup maple syrup

2 cups heavy cream, whipped

Beat egg yolks, mix with syrup and bring slowly to a boil, stirring constantly. Cool and fold in stiffly beaten egg whites and whipped cream. Freeze. Makes 8 servings.

Mrs. James A. Burke

MRS. JAMES A. BURKE, Wife of Representative (Massachusetts)

FRUIT SHERBET

1 cup sugar
2 cups hot water
juice of 2 lemons
1 can frozen orange juice

2 bananas, coarsely crushed
1 16 ounce can crushed pineapple
1 small bottle maraschino cherries, chopped

Dissolve sugar in hot water. Mix all ingredients and place in refrigerator trays. Freeze. Stir several times while it is freezing. Remove from freezer ½ hour before serving to make it easier to spoon into sherbet dishes. Makes 6 servings.

Mrs Otis R. Bowen

MRS. OTIS R. BOWEN, Wife of Governor (Indiana)

RHUBARB SHERBET

1 quart unpeeled, diced rhubarb
1½ cups water
1¾ cups sugar
juice 1 lemon

1½ teaspoons unflavored gelatin
2 tablespoons cold water
2 egg whites

Boil the rhubarb, water and 1½ cups of sugar for 15 minutes, then put through a sieve. There should be 2½ cups of rhubarb syrup. Add lemon juice. Soften gelatin in cold water and stir into hot syrup. Pour mixture into freezing tray and freeze until almost firm. Beat egg whites until stiff but not dry. Add the remaining sugar slowly, beating well. Pour sherbet into cold bowl and beat. Fold in meringue, put back into freezing tray and return to refrigerator. Freeze until firm. Strawberry rhubarb makes the most attractive color. Makes 8 servings.

Mrs. Meldrim Thomson, Jr.

MRS. MELDRIM THOMSON, JR., Wife of Governor (New Hampshire)

BLUEBERRY ICE

½ cup granulated sugar
2 cups water

1½ cups blueberry juice
2 tablespoons lemon juice, unstrained

Cook sugar and water to boiling point and boil 5 minutes. Add juices. Freeze in ice cream freezer or refrigerator tray. Makes 4 servings.

Mrs. Howard Baker Jr.

MRS. HOWARD H. BAKER JR., Wife of Senator (Tennessee)

PAPAYA SHERBET

1½ cups ripe papaya pulp, strained
½ cup orange juice
3 tablespoons lemon juice

1 cup sugar
1½ cups milk

Mix papaya pulp and fruit juices well. Dissolve sugar in milk and add fruit mixture gradually. Pour into freezing pan and freeze quickly, stirring after 30 minutes. Makes 8 servings.

Mrs. Spark Matsunaga

MRS. SPARK MATSUNAGA, Wife of Representative (Hawaii)

LEMON CHESS PASTRIES

Crust:
1 3 ounce package Philadelphia
   cream cheese
¼ pound butter
1 cup flour

Filling:
3 eggs, well beaten
1½ cups sugar
juice of 1½ lemons
grated rind of 1 lemon
3 tablespoons melted butter
dash of salt

Mix cheese, butter and flour until smooth. Chill. Place a small amount in little muffin tins. Press evenly around sides and bottom of each. To make filling, combine eggs and sugar, add other ingredients and mix well. Place 1 to 2 teaspoons of filling in each pastry shell. Bake at 350° for 25 minutes. May be frozen. Makes 12 pastries.

Mrs James Thomas Broyhill

MRS. JAMES THOMAS BROYHILL, Wife of Representative (North Carolina)

PUMPKIN PIE SQUARES

Crust:
1 cup sifted flour
½ cup quick cooking oats
½ cup brown sugar
¼ pound butter

Filling:
1 1 pound can pumpkin
1 cup evaporated milk
2 eggs
¾ cup sugar

½ teaspoon salt
1 teaspoon cinnamon
½ teaspoon ginger (or pumpkin pie spice)
¼ teaspoon ground cloves

Topping:
½ cup finely chopped pecans
½ cup brown sugar
2 tablespoons butter

Combine flour, oats, sugar and butter. Mix until crumbly. Press into ungreased 9 x 13 inch pan. Bake at 350° for 15 minutes. For filling, combine pumpkin, milk, eggs, sugar, salt and spices. Beat well. Pour into crust. Bake at 350° for 20 minutes. For topping, combine pecans, brown sugar and butter. Sprinkle over pumpkin. Bake at 350° 15 to 20 minutes longer. Cool. Cut into squares when ready to serve. May be frozen. Makes 15 servings.

Mrs. Wm. L. Armstrong

MRS. WILLIAM L. ARMSTRONG, Wife of Representative (Colorado)

OLD FASHIONED STRAWBERRY SHORTCAKE

2 cups sifted flour
3 tablespoons sugar
½ teaspoon salt
few grains freshly grated nutmeg (optional)
4 teaspoons baking powder
¼ pound butter

1 egg, lightly beaten
⅓ cup milk (approximately)
4 cups crushed or sliced strawberries
superfine sugar to taste
½ pint heavy cream, whipped
whole strawberries for garnish

Sift dry ingredients together. Cut in butter until mixture is mealy. With a fork, stir in egg and enough milk to make dough easy to handle. It does not have to be smooth. Shape dough, patting it into one large round layer, ½ inch thick, and place in a buttered 8 inch round cake pan. Bake in preheated 450° oven for 15 to 20 minutes. If preferred, dough may be cut into 2 or 3 inch round pieces and arranged 1 inch apart on a buttered baking sheet. Shorten baking time to 12 to 15 minutes. When baked, split cake through center, crosswise into 2 layers. Butter lower layer generously, spoon sugared fruit over it, add top layer and top with whipped cream. Decorate with whole berries. Makes 6 to 8 servings.

Mrs. George Marvin Wallhauser

MRS. GEORGE M. WALLHAUSER, Wife of former Representative (New Jersey)

FUDGE PIE

¼ pound butter	¼ cup flour
2 squares Baker's chocolate	2 eggs
1 cup sugar	

Melt butter and chocolate, remove from heat and add sugar, flour and eggs. Stir well. Pour in well greased 8 inch pie plate. This pie makes its own crust. Preheat oven to 450°. Reduce temperature to 300° when pie is put in the oven. Bake 20 minutes. Center should remain springy to touch. Makes 6 servings.

Mrs. Edward Hutchinson

MRS. EDWARD HUTCHINSON, Wife of Representative (Michigan)

SNOW SQUARES

1 envelope unflavored gelatin	*Butter sauce:*
4 tablespoons cold water	5 egg yolks
1 cup boiling water	⅓ cup melted butter
⅔ cup sugar	1 tablespoon grated lemon rind
3 egg whites, unbeaten	2 tablespoons lemon juice
¼ teaspoon salt	⅓ cup whipping cream, whipped
1 teaspoon vanilla	
16 graham crackers, finely crushed	

Sprinkle gelatin over cold water and let soak 5 minutes. Add boiling water and stir until dissolved. Add sugar and stir again. Let cool slightly. Add egg whites, salt and vanilla. Beat with rotary egg beater at high speed until it resembles thick cream. Turn into a flat 10 x 8 inch pan and chill in refrigerator. Cut in 1 inch squares and roll in graham cracker crumbs.

For sauce, beat egg yolks until lemon colored. Add butter, lemon rind and juice. Blend well. Fold in cream and chill. Serve over squares. Makes 10 servings.

Mrs. Russell V. Mack

MRS. RUSSELL V. MACK, Wife of former Representative (Washington)

DIET CHINESE ALMOND FLOAT

1 envelope unflavored gelatin
1¼ cups cold water
sweetener equal to 4 tablespoons sugar
1 tablespoon almond extract

¾ cup skim evaporated milk
1 small can unsweetened pineapple
   chunks (or mandarin oranges)

Sprinkle gelatin on cold water, let soften and then heat to dissolve, stirring constantly. Add sweetener, extract and milk. Pour into flat pan. Chill. When set, cut in ½ inch squares or diamonds. Place in serving dishes and add pineapple chunks with juice. Makes 4 to 6 servings.

Mrs. Glenn Davis

MRS. GLENN DAVIS, Wife of former Representative (Wisconsin)

CRANBERRY RUM SAUCE

2 cups fresh cranberries
½ cup pineapple juice
¾ cup sugar
1 teaspoon grated orange peel
¼ teaspoon grated lemon peel

¼ cup rum
2 tablespoons butter
dash of salt
rice pudding, vanilla ice cream or
   waffles

In saucepan combine first 5 ingredients. Bring to a boil and simmer 10 minutes or until cranberries are tender. Remove from heat and stir in rum, butter and salt. Serve over rice pudding, ice cream or waffles. Makes 2 cups.

Mrs. Al Ullman

MRS. AL ULLMAN, Wife of Representative (Oregon)

LEMON BUTTER SAUCE

⅓ cup butter
1 cup sugar
3 egg yolks
⅓ cup boiling water

3 tablespoons lemon juice
grated rind of lemon
angel food or pound cake

Cream butter and sugar. Add egg yolks and boiling water. Add lemon juice and rind last. Cook over hot water until thick. Serve over angel food or pound cake. This may be prepared and kept warm over hot water until serving time. If it gets too thick, add a few drops of hot water. Makes 2 cups.

Mrs. Bill Burlison

MRS. BILL BURLISON, Wife of Representative (Missouri)

548

HOT CHOCOLATE SAUCE

6 squares bitter chocolate
2 cups sugar
1 stick butter

dash of salt
1 large can evaporated milk
1 teaspoon vanilla

Melt chocolate. Add sugar, butter and salt and cook over medium heat, boiling for a few minutes. Add milk. Bring to a boil and add vanilla. Serve hot over ice cream. This may be kept in a tightly closed jar in refrigerator for weeks and reheated in a double boiler before serving. Makes 1 quart.

Mrs. Horace R. Kornegay

MRS. HORACE R. KORNEGAY, Wife of former Representative (North Carolina)

NOTES

CANDIES &
SNACKS

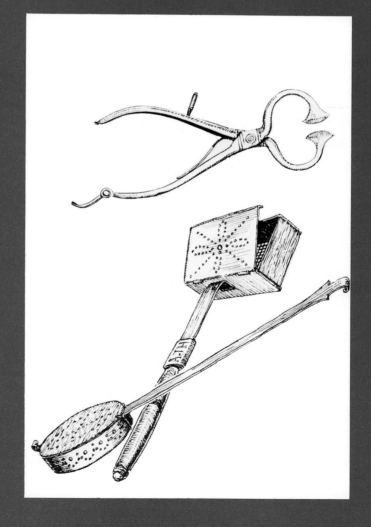

Apricot Chips

Take your apricots, pare them, and cut them very thin into chips;
take three quarters of their weight in sugar finely searced, then
put the sugar and apricots into a pewter dish, set them upon coals,
and when the sugar is dissolved turn them upon the edge of a
dish out of the syrup, and set them by till the next day; then
warm them again in the syrup, but do not let them boil, and
keep them turning till they have drank up all the syrup; then
lay them on a plate, and dry them in a stove.

The New Art of Cookery
Richard Briggs, 1792

GREAT CHOCOLATE FUDGE

1 envelope unflavored gelatin
3 cups sugar
¼ pound butter
3 squares chocolate

½ cup white Karo
1 cup milk
2 teaspoons vanilla
1 cup broken pecans (or black walnuts)

Sprinkle gelatin on sugar, combine with butter and chocolate and stir constantly over very low heat until butter and chocolate are melted. Add Karo and milk and cook slowly until a few drops in cold water form a firm ball. Cool 15 minutes. Beat until thick and creamy, fold in vanilla and nuts and pour on buttered platter.

Mrs. Charles G. Rose, III

MRS. CHARLES G. ROSE, III, Wife of Representative (North Carolina)

CHOCOLATE FUDGE

3 squares Baker's unsweetened
   chocolate
1 cup milk
3 cups sugar

dash of salt
2 tablespoons butter
1 teaspoon vanilla

Add chocolate to milk and cook until mixture is blended, stirring constantly. Add sugar and salt and stir until mixture boils. Continue boiling, without stirring, until a small amount of mixture forms a very soft ball in cold water. Add butter and vanilla. Cool to lukewarm and beat until mixture thickens and loses its gloss. Turn at once into greased 8 x 4 inch pan. When cold, cut into squares. Makes 18 large pieces.

Mrs. John S. Cross

MRS. JOHN S. CROSS, Daughter of former Representative Claude A. Fuller (Arkansas)

MOTHER'S NEVER FAIL FUDGE

4 cups sugar
1 large can condensed milk
1 stick butter
2 packages chocolate chips

1 cup chopped walnuts
1 teaspoon vanilla
20 marshmallows, cut up

Mix sugar, milk and butter and boil, stirring constantly, over medium heat to the soft ball stage. Remove from heat and add chocolate, nuts, vanilla and marshmallows. Stir until chocolate and marshmallows are melted. Pour into an 11 x 7 inch pan and refrigerate until ready to serve.

Mrs. Jim Santini

MRS. JIM SANTINI, Wife of Representative (Nevada)

NUT FUDGE

4½ cups sugar
1 large can evaporated milk
3 5 ounce plain chocolate bars,
   broken into pieces
2 6 ounce packages semi-sweet
   chocolate, chopped

1 8 ounce jar marshmallow whip
1½ teaspoons salt
1 cup chopped nuts
1 teaspoon vanilla

Combine sugar and milk and heat to the boiling point. Cook over medium heat exactly 4½ minutes, stirring occasionally. Mix the chocolates, marshmallow whip and salt in a large bowl. Over this pour half the hot mixture, mixing thoroughly. Repeat with the remaining hot mixture. Add nuts and vanilla. Pour into an 8 x 12 inch buttered pan. Pat it down evenly, using your hands. Cool in refrigerator. Cut in squares. Keeps beautifully in air tight container. Makes about 60 pieces.

Mrs. Kenneth Allison Roberts

MRS. KENNETH ALLISON ROBERTS, Wife of former Representative (Alabama)

PEANUT BUTTER FUDGE

2 cups sugar
¾ cup milk
½ teaspoon salt
1 tablespoon cocoa

1 tablespoon butter
¾ cup peanut butter
1 teaspoon vanilla

Mix sugar and milk in a heavy saucepan. Stir until sugar is dissolved. Add salt and cocoa. Cook over slow heat, stirring occasionally to prevent scorching, to a soft ball stage. Remove from heat and add butter and peanut butter. When the mixture is cool, add vanilla. Beat until creamy. When fudge thickens, pour on greased platter. Cut in squares.

Mrs. John Sparkman

MRS. JOHN SPARKMAN, Wife of Senator (Alabama)

CARAMELS

2 cups sugar
½ pound butter
1½ cups white Karo syrup

2 cups cream
2 teaspoons vanilla

Combine first 3 ingredients and 1 cup cream and bring to a hard boil. Add remaining cream and continue boiling slowly, stirring occasionally, until a firm ball is formed in cold water, approximately 1 hour. Do not scrape the cooking pan in order to avoid sugaring the caramels. Remove from heat and add vanilla. Pour into a well buttered 9 x 13 inch pan and cool several hours. When cool, cut into squares and wrap individually in wax paper.

Mrs. Mark Andrews

MRS. MARK ANDREWS, Wife of Representative (North Dakota)

BUTTERMILK CARAMELS

2 cups sugar
1 cup buttermilk
1 teaspoon baking soda

1 tablespoon white Karo
2 tablespoons butter
1 cup chopped nuts

Combine all ingredients except nuts and cook in large kettle to a soft ball stage. Beat until it begins to cream and then add nuts. Pour into buttered dish. When cool, cut into squares.

Mrs. Robert J. Huber

Mrs. Robert J. Huber, Wife of former Representative (Michigan)

PLANTATION PRALINES

2 cups granulated sugar
1 teaspoon baking soda
1 cup buttermilk
pinch of salt

2 tablespoons butter
2⅓ cups pecan pieces
⅔ cup perfect pecan halves

In large, heavy saucepan, combine first 4 ingredients. Cook over high heat for 5 minutes or to 210° on candy thermometer, being sure to stir frequently and to scrape bottom and sides of pan while stirring. Add butter and pecan pieces. Continue to cook, stirring frequently and scraping bottom and sides of pan, until a little mixture forms a very soft ball in cold water, about 5 minutes or 230°. Remove from heat. Let mixture cool a minute or two. Then beat with a spoon until thick and creamy. Immediately drop by tablespoonful onto wax paper, aluminum foil or lightly greased cookie sheet. Top each one with a perfect pecan half. Makes 14 large or 18 small pralines.

Mrs. Edwin W. Edwards

Mrs. Edwin W. Edwards, Wife of Governor (Louisiana)

556

COCONUT PECAN CANDY

2 pounds confectioners sugar
2 7 ounce cans Angel Flake coconut
3 cups chopped pecans
1 can Eagle Brand condensed milk

1 teaspoon vanilla
1¼ sticks margarine, melted
12 ounces semi-sweet chocolate chips
¾ cake paraffin

Mix sugar, coconut, nuts, milk and vanilla. Add margarine and mix thoroughly. Roll into balls about 1 inch in diameter. Insert a toothpick in each ball and place on cookie sheet in freezer for 15 to 20 minutes or in refrigerator about 1 hour. Slowly· melt the chocolate and the paraffin together in top of double boiler. Dip each ball in chocolate and place on wax paper. Carefully remove toothpick and drip a drop of chocolate on ball to cover small hole made by pick. Makes 100 pieces.

Mrs. Walter E. Powell

MRS. WALTER E. POWELL, Wife of former Representative (Ohio)

DIVINITY CANDY

2½ cups sugar
½ cup white Karo syrup
⅔ cup water

2 egg whites
¼ teaspoon salt
24 pecan halves

Combine sugar, syrup and water and place over heat. Stir just until sugar is dissolved. Boil until mixture will form light, feathery threads when dropped from spoon or until a small amount dropped into cold water forms a firm ball. Beat egg whites with salt until stiff. Gradually add hot mixture. Continue beating until thick and mixture loses its shine. Drop by spoonful on oiled paper or well greased plate. Top each piece with a pecan half. Makes 24 pieces.

Note: This may be used as an icing for a 3 layer cake. If it is too thick to spread, add a few drops of hot water and beat again.

Mrs. George M. Grant

MRS. GEORGE M. GRANT, Wife of former Representative (Alabama)

BARKLEY LOAF

4 cups sugar
1 pint cream
1 cup dark Karo syrup
pinch of salt

1 teaspoon vanilla
1 cup chopped brazil nuts
bitter chocolate, melted

Combine all ingredients except chocolate and boil until a few drops in cold water form a soft ball. Beat well. When cool enough to handle, butter hands and work mixture until stiff enough to mold. Form into rolls on wax paper and chill. Brush chocolate over tops of rolls, coating heavily. Keep in refrigerator. Cut in slices to serve. Makes 3 rolls.

Mrs. Charles Thone

MRS. CHARLES THONE, Wife of Representative (Nebraska)

CHRISTMAS STRAWBERRIES

1 8 ounce package pitted dates,
   chopped
½ cup flaked coconut
½ cup sugar
½ stick butter
1 egg, slightly beaten

dash of salt
1½ cups Rice Krispies
½ cup chopped walnuts
1 teaspoon vanilla
red sugar
frosting for trim

Combine first 6 ingredients in skillet and cook over low heat until mixture thickens. Boil for 5 to 10 minutes. Remove from heat. Mix Rice Krispies, nuts and vanilla together and stir into first mixture. Cool for 10 minutes. Mold into berry shapes. Roll in red sugar and trim with frosting. Makes 2 dozen.

Mrs. Albert L. Vreeland

MRS. ALBERT L. VREELAND, Wife of former Representative (New Jersey)

STRAWBERRY CANDY (MARZIPAN)

1 14 ounce package coconut
3½ ounces pecans
2 6 ounce packages strawberry Jello
1 can sweetened condensed milk

1 package almonds, cut in little stick shapes
1 small container red sugar crystals
green cake coloring

Pulverize coconut in blender, a very little at a time, pushing the coconut down from sides of blender with a spatula, until about the consistency of confectioners sugar. Chop pecans very fine in blender. Mix Jello, coconut, pecans, and condensed milk. Roll into small balls and then form into strawberry shape. Roll in red crystals. Use almond sticks which have been dipped in green coloring for stems of the strawberries. Store in air tight cans. May be frozen. Makes 100 strawberries.

Mrs. Charles Raper Jonas

MRS. CHARLES RAPER JONAS, Wife of former Representative (North Carolina)

CANDY PUDDING FONDANT

1 quart sugar
pinch of salt
pinch of baking powder
1 quart boiling water
chopped pecans
vanilla
strawberry flavoring

pink food coloring
raisins
lemon flavoring
coconut
bitter chocolate, melted
pecan halves
maraschino cherries (optional)

Mix sugar with salt and baking powder. Pour half of boiling water over sugar and stir. Add remaining water to dissolve sugar thoroughly. Boil without stirring until a few drops in cold water will form a soft ball. Wash off sugar adhering to sides of kettle with a pastry brush dipped in cold water. Pour mixture slowly onto slightly oiled marble slab and let stand a few minutes to cool. Scrape fondant to the end of the slab with a knife. Work with a wooden spatula until white and creamy. It will start to lump, so knead with the hands until smooth.

Divide fondant into 3 parts. To the first part, add pecans and vanilla and shape into a long oval. Add strawberry flavoring, pink coloring and raisins to the second part, shape it and put on top of first layer. Repeat with the third part, this time adding lemon flavoring and coconut. Ice the stacked layers with the melted chocolate and garnish with pecans and cherries if desired.

Mary Hamilton O'Neal

MARY HAMILTON O'NEAL, Daughter of former Representative Emmet O'Neal (Kentucky)

CANDIED GRAPEFRUIT PEEL

peel of 3 large grapefruit
2½ quarts cold water

Syrup:
3 cups sugar
1½ cups water

sugar for coating

Cut peel in strips, cover with cold water and bring to a boil. Change water several times and boil until peel is tender and not too bitter. Make syrup of sugar and water and cook until syrup reaches 242° on candy thermometer or to thread stage. Add peel and cook over low heat, stirring occasionally, until syrup is absorbed. Roll each strip in sugar and let cool.

Mrs. Robert G. Stephens, Jr.

MRS. ROBERT G. STEPHENS, JR., Wife of Representative (Georgia)

FROSTBITTEN SUGARED CRANBERRIES

1 package fresh cranberries
1 egg white

1 pound confectioners sugar, sifted

Freeze cranberries in package for 24 hours. Thaw overnight. Freeze again. Thaw when ready to use. Wash and dry well. Whisk a small amount of egg white in a dinner plate with a fork. Roll 1 handful of cranberries in egg white and then in sugar until well coated. Repeat with remaining egg white, cranberries and sugar. Spread on wax paper covered tray in 1 layer to dry. When dry, cranberries may be kept in a covered plastic container for 5 to 7 days. May be used as a dessert garnish.

Mrs Lon M. Buzick

MRS. LON M. BUZICK, Member of Congressional Club (Kansas)

POPCORN BALLS

2 cups sugar	1 teaspoon vinegar
1½ cups water	1 teaspoon vanilla
⅓ teaspoon salt	food coloring
½ cup light corn syrup	5 quarts popped corn

Mix the sugar, water, salt and syrup in a saucepan and boil until mixture reaches 256°, about 10 minutes. Add vinegar, vanilla and food coloring and boil until it reaches 270°. This happens quickly. Pour hot syrup over popped corn. Wear buttered rubber gloves to form balls. Form balls lightly and do not squeeze or they will be too heavy. Makes 24 balls.

Mrs. Mike McCormack

MRS. MIKE McCORMACK, Wife of Representative (Washington)

POPCORN BALLS

3 quarts popped corn

	⅓ cup water
	½ stick butter
Syrup:	¾ teaspoon vanilla
1 cup sugar	¾ teaspoon salt
⅓ cup white Karo	

Boil syrup ingredients together to crack stage. Pour over the popcorn and coat it evenly. Form balls as soon as cool enough to handle. Makes 9 balls.

Mrs. Mark Andrews

MRS. MARK ANDREWS, Wife of Representative (North Dakota)

561

FRUIT LEATHER

10 cups peeled, sliced, fresh, fully ripe peaches (or apples)   **1 cup sugar**

Combine fruit with sugar. Heat to boiling point, stirring until sugar is dissolved. Put in blender and puree it. Cool mixture to lukewarm. Cover 2 cookie sheets with clear plastic wrap and pour fruit puree onto them, spreading it to a ¼ inch thickness. Place pans in full outdoor sunlight. To keep surface clean, secure a piece of cheesecloth on sticks placed at each end of pans. Stretch cheesecloth over but not on surface. Drying may take 20 to 24 hours. Bring puree inside at end of day and finish drying second day. Drying may be finished indoors by setting pans in a gas oven with a very warm pilot light, shutting the door and leaving it for 1 to 2 days until the leather pulls clean from the plastic wrap. Roll up the fruit leather with the plastic wrap and seal tightly. To eat, unroll and tear off strips or pieces of it. May be frozen. Makes 2 rolls.

Mrs. William Henry Harrison, Jr.

MRS. WILLIAM HENRY HARRISON, JR., Daughter-in-law of former Representative William Henry Harrison (Wyoming)

CHILDREN'S DELIGHT (SNACKS)

4 cups sugar coated cereal
2 pounds chocolate bits (or chocolate covered peanuts)
2 cups raisins
2 pounds salted peanuts
3 cups caramel covered popcorn

Mix all ingredients together. Store in canister or cookie jar.

Mrs. M. Blaine Peterson

MRS. M. BLAINE PETERSON, Wife of former Representative (Utah)

GRANOLA

6 to 7 cups rolled oats
2 cups sesame seeds
2 cups wheat germ
2 to 3 cups shredded unsweetened coconut
2 cups chopped nuts
¾ cup oil
¾ cups honey
1½ teaspoons vanilla
raisins (optional)

Combine all ingredients except raisins and roast at 325° for 15 minutes or at 250° for 1 hour. Add raisins if desired.

Mrs. Thomas Paul Salmon

MRS. THOMAS P. SALMON, Wife of Governor (Vermont)

562

CRUNCHY GRANOLA

3 cups quick cooking oats
1 cup wheat germ
1 cup sunflower seeds, shelled
1 cup sesame seeds and (or) nuts
1 cup raisins

1 cup dark brown sugar
1 cup coconut
1 cup vegetable oil
1 cup honey

Mix all ingredients together and bake on cookie sheet for 1 hour at 200°, turning frequently. Makes 20 servings.

Maureen Ellen Foley

MAUREEN ELLEN FOLEY, Daughter of former Representative John R. Foley (Maryland)

TOASTY NUTTY GRANOLA

6 cups uncooked oats
½ cup brown sugar
¾ cup wheat germ
½ cup lecethin
⅓ cup sesame seeds

1 cup chopped almonds (or walnuts)
½ cup safflower vegetable oil
⅓ cup honey
1½ teaspoons vanilla
raisins (optional)

Bake oats for 10 minutes at 350°. Combine all ingredients, mix, place in two 9 x 13 inch pans and bake at 350° for 20 minutes. Stir every 5 minutes. Cool. Add raisins if desired. Store in covered container in refrigerator. May be frozen. Makes 8 cups.

Mrs. Charles A. Mosher

MRS. CHARLES A. MOSHER, Wife of Representative (Ohio)

NOTES

PRESERVES, PICKLES, RELISHES

Fresh Ruby Beets

Onions

Take your onions when they are dry enough to lay up for winter, (the smaller they are the better they look) put them into a pot, and cover them with spring water with a handful of white salt, and let them boil up; then strain them off, take three coats off, lay them on a cloth, and let two people take hold of it, one at each end, and rub them backward and forward till they are very dry; then put them in your bottles, with some blades of mace and cloves, a nutmeg cut in pieces, with some double-distilled white wine vinegar; boil it up with a little salt, let it stand till it is cold and put it over the onions; cork them close, and tie a bladder and leather over them.

The New Art of Cookery
Richard Briggs, 1792

APRICOT MARMALADE

1 pound dried apricots, ground
1 20 ounce can crushed pineapple
5 cups sugar

Optional:
candied cherries
nuts

Combine the apricots, pineapple and the sugar. Cook over low heat until slightly thickened. Candied cherries and nuts may be added for extra goodness. Put into 6 sterilized pint jars. May be used over ice cream.

Mrs. Ray Roberts, Wife of Representative (Texas)

PETE'S PEACH CONSERVE

½ peck fresh peaches, peeled
4 oranges
8 pounds sugar

juice of 1 lemon
½ pound English walnuts, coarsely
chopped

Put peaches and oranges, rind and all, through coarse blade of food chopper. Add sugar and lemon juice. Bring mixture to a boil and simmer for 1 hour. Then skim foam off and continue to simmer until it reaches the consistency of jelly, approximately 2 hours. Skim foam off again and add walnuts. Pour into 8 ounce jars and seal. Makes 12 jars.

Mrs. Harrison A. Williams, Jr., Wife of Senator (New Jersey)

LBJ RANCH PEACH PRESERVES

1 bushel peaches

10 pounds sugar

Peel and slice peaches into a large roasting pan. Build up layers of peaches with sugar in between and on top. Let mixture set overnight. The next morning bring peaches to a boil. As peaches cook, a film will form that should be skimmed off the top. Continue removing this film until syrup is clear. Simmer for 3 to 3½ hours. Cook longer for thicker and darker preserves. Pour into sterilized jars and seal.

Mrs. Lyndon B. Johnson, Wife of former President of the United States (Texas)

PEACH PRESERVES

7 firm peaches
boiling water
grated rind of ½ orange

juice of 2 lemons
6 cups sugar

Drop peaches in boiling water a few seconds to facilitate peeling. Cut peaches in small pieces and pack firmly to measure 1½ quarts. Mix all ingredients and cook slowly, stirring frequently, 35 to 40 minutes or until syrup is thick. Pour in sterilized jars and seal while hot. Makes 3½ pints.

Mrs. J. J. Pickle

Mrs. J. J. PICKLE, Wife of Representative (Texas)

PEACH AND TOMATO PRESERVES

1 pound fresh tomatoes, peeled and diced
2 pounds fresh peaches, peeled and diced

1 tablespoon grated orange rind
1 stick cinnamon
5 cups sugar
1 box powdered fruit pectin

Bring tomatoes to a boil. Drain off and discard ½ of juice. Add peaches, orange rind, cinnamon, sugar and pectin. Stirring constantly, bring to a full rolling boil and boil for 2 minutes. Remove from heat and skim off foam. Pour into hot, sterilized 6 ounce jars. Makes 8 jars.

Mrs David S. King

Mrs. DAVID S. KING, Wife of former Representative (Utah)

568

AUNT MARY'S BREAD AND BUTTER PICKLES

1 gallon medium large cucumbers
8 small white onions
ice cubes
½ cup salt
5 cups sugar
1½ teaspoons tumeric

1½ teaspoons ground cloves (or
    2 tablespoons whole cloves)
2 tablespoons white mustard seed
2 teaspoons celery seed
5 cups vinegar

Slice washed, unpeeled cucumbers to ⅛ to ¼ inch thick. Prepare onions and slice to same thickness. Spread into large baking pan and cover with ice cubes. Pour salt over the cubes, let stand 3 hours and then drain. Make a syrup by combining dry ingredients and then adding vinegar. Heat syrup to a boil but do not boil. Add drained cucumbers and onions to syrup. Heat again to a boil but do not boil. Place in sterilized jars and seal. Makes 8 pints.

Mrs. William L. Hungate

MRS. WILLIAM L. HUNGATE, Wife of Representative (Missouri)

MOTHER'S 7 DAY PICKLES

9 pounds cucumbers, 3 to 4 inches
    long
salt water
4 pints vinegar

2 tablespoons alum
3 pounds sugar
1 ounce cinnamon bark
½ ounce whole allspice

Soak cucumbers in salt water to cover for 3 days. Water should be so salty that an egg, in the shell, will float in it. Then soak cucumbers in clear water for 3 days, changing water each day. On 7th day, split cucumbers, cover with water, add 1 pint of vinegar and the alum and simmer for 2 hours. Drain and, when cool, put in jars. Combine remaining vinegar with sugar, cinnamon bark and allspice, bring to a boil and pour over cucumbers in the jars and seal.

Mrs. Neal Smith

MRS. NEAL SMITH, Wife of Representative (Iowa)

5 DAY SWEET CHUNK PICKLES

1 gallon sliced cucumbers
1½ quarts water
1 cup pickling salt
½ gallon boiling water
liquid, ½ vinegar and ½ water
alum powder

Syrup:
1 quart vinegar
2½ cups sugar
2 tablespoons pickling spices
grape leaves

Cucumbers should be no more than 1½ to 2 inches in diameter. Cut into 1½ inch slices and place in stone crock or enameled kettle. Mix the water and pickling salt and pour over cucumbers, pressing them down. Cover with a weighted plate and let stand 24 hours in a cool place.

The second day, drain off the brine but do not rinse. Add the boiling water. Let stand overnight.

The third day, drain the cucumbers again. Combine vinegar and water in sufficient equal quantities so as to cover cucumbers again. Sprinkle with alum powder. Let stand overnight.

The fourth day, drain off the liquid again. Make a syrup of vinegar, 1½ cups sugar and pickling spices. Pour over pickles and let cool before covering. Let stand overnight.

The fifth day, drain off the syrup and add the remaining sugar to it. Boil the syrup. Pack pickles in grape leaf lined jars. Pour the hot syrup over them and seal.

Mrs. Odin Langen

MRS. ODIN LANGEN, Wife of former Representative (Minnesota)

CARROT PICKLES

4 cups ¾ inch sliced carrots
boiling salted water
1 cup cider vinegar
¾ cup water

¾ cup sugar
10 whole cloves
2 sticks cinnamon, broken into pieces
1½ teaspoons salt

Place carrot slices in saucepan and add just enough boiling salted water to come about half way up the carrots. Cover and cook until crisp tender, about 5 minutes. Drain. Combine remaining ingredients in saucepan and bring to a boil. Boil 3 minutes. Pack carrots in hot sterilized jars and pour boiling syrup over them. Cover and refrigerate for 1 to 2 days. Will keep 1 to 2 weeks. Makes 2 pints.

Mrs. Arthur L. Miller

MRS. ARTHUR L. MILLER, Wife of former Representative (Nebraska)

CARROT RELISH

2 pounds carrots, thinly sliced
1 green pepper, chopped
1 6 ounce jar pickled cocktail onions, drained
1 can tomato soup

¾ cup sugar
½ cup tarragon vinegar
¼ cup salad oil
1 teaspoon dry mustard

Cook carrots until just tender, about 5 minutes. Drain. Combine remaining ingredients in pan; bring to boil. Pour over drained carrots. Refrigerate. Keeps six weeks.

Mrs Glenard P. Lipscomb

MRS. GLENARD P. LIPSCOMB, Wife of former Representative (California)

CAROLINA CHOW CHOW

1 peck green tomatoes
18 onions
24 green peppers
2 medium heads cabbage
salt
1 gallon vinegar
½ gallon water

2 tabespoons black pepper
¼ ounce celery seed
2 tablespoons ground cinnamon
1 box tumeric
3 pounds brown sugar
¼ pound ground white mustard seed

Put tomatoes, onions, peppers and cabbage through coarse grinder or meat chopper. Pack in salt overnight. In the morning drain off the brine. Combine ½ gallon vinegar with the water, pour it over the ground vegetables and let soak for 2 days. Drain. Sift in pepper and spices. Boil remaining vinegar and brown sugar together and while it is still hot, pour it over the vegetable mixture. Each morning for the next 3 days, drain off the liquid, reheat it and pour it over the vegetables again. On the third morning also mix in the mustard seed. Do not cook the vegetables. Pour into glass jars and seal while hot. Makes 24 pints.

Mrs. Richardson Preyer

MRS. RICHARDSON PREYER, Wife of Representative (North Carolina)

CHILI SAUCE

12 tomatoes, chopped
2 onions, chopped
2 peppers, chopped
2 tablespoons salt
1 cup sugar

2 cups vinegar
½ teaspoon cinnamon
½ teaspoon ground cloves
½ teaspoon ginger
½ teaspoon nutmeg

Combine all ingredients and mix well. Simmer uncovered on top of stove for 4 hours, stirring occasionally. Makes 3 pints.

Mrs. R. Walter Riehlman

MRS. R. WALTER RIEHLMAN, Wife of former Representative (New York)

BEAN RELISH

1 can water chestnuts, thinly sliced
1 can La Choy fancy mixed Chinese vegetables
1 can French style string beans
1 can tiny English peas

1 small can pimientos, chopped
1 small sweet onion, thinly sliced
¾ cup vinegar
1 cup sugar

Drain all canned products. Mix first 6 ingredients together. Bring vinegar and sugar to a boil. While still hot, pour over mixed vegetables. Cover and put in refrigerator.

Mrs. S. H. Fountain

MRS. L. H. FOUNTAIN, Wife of Representative (North Carolina)

HENNIE'S ZUCCHINI RELISH

10 cups coarsley ground zucchini
4 cups coarsely ground onions
2 green peppers
2 red peppers
⅓ cup salt
1 teaspoon turmeric

1 teaspoon curry powder
1 teaspoon celery seed
½ teaspoon black pepper
1 tablespoon corn starch
2½ cups vinegar
4½ cups sugar

Grind zucchini, onions and peppers together. Mix with salt, cover and refrigerate 24 hours. Rinse well with cold water. Drain in colander. Add remaining ingredients. Cook for 30 minutes. Pour into sterilized pint jars and seal. Makes 8 pints.

Mrs. Hamer H. Budge

MRS. HAMER H. BUDGE, Wife of former Representative (Idaho)

MEN ONLY

To Roast Beef:

The general rules are, to have a brisk hot fire, to hang down rather than to spit, to baste with salt and water, and one quarter of an hour to every pound of beef, tho' tender beef will require less, while old tough beef will require more roasting; pricking with a fork will determine you whether done or not; rare done is the healthiest and the taste of this age.

The American Cookery
Amelia Simmons, 1796

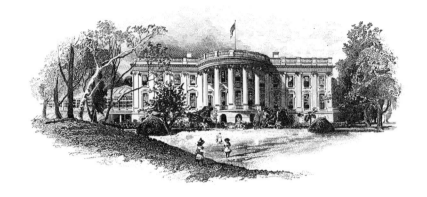

LIVER DELUXE

1 lb. liver, sliced thin
2 cups brown gravy
sprinkle of parsley
dash of salt, pepper

1 large onion, sliced thin
8 pcs. bacon, fried crisp
1/2 cup flour
2 Tbsp. butter

Melt butter in skillet and saute onion. Dredge slices of liver in flour and brown each side. Pour gravy on liver and season with parsley, salt and pepper to taste. Simmer for 2 minutes and arrange on a serving platter. Place bacon on top of liver. Serves 4.

Gerald R. Ford

LINGUINE WITH CLAM SAUCE

1 clove garlic, chopped
1 tablespoon cooking oil
1 can tomato paste
1 cup water
1 can minced clams
½ teaspoon salt
½ teaspoon pepper
1 teaspoon oregano
1 teaspoon parsley flakes
1 pound linguine (or spaghetti)
parmesan cheese

Brown garlic in oil and then add tomato paste. Stir well for 5 minutes. Add water and simmer an additional 10 minutes. Combine clams, salt, pepper, oregano and parsley. Cook linguine as directed on package and drain in colander. Add clam mixture to linguine in a bowl. Sprinkle with parmesan, add sauce, mix well and serve. Makes 4 servings.

FRANK ANNUNZIO, Representative (Illinois)

GREEN CHILI ENCHILADAS

4 tablespoons butter
6 tablespoons flour
5 cups milk
2 teaspoons salt
1 cup grated American cheese
½ to 1 cup chopped green chilies
½ clove garlic, minced
12 corn tortillas
hot cooking oil
grated cheese
shredded lettuce
ripe olives
tomato wedges

Melt butter in a saucepan. Blend in flour and stir in milk. Cook and stir over direct heat until mixture thickens. Add salt, American cheese and the chilies. Add the garlic and mix well. Cover and let stand while frying tortillas. Fry each tortilla in small amount of hot oil, turning once for about 5 seconds on each side. Do not allow tortillas to become crisp. Drain on absorbent paper. Roll and arrange in shallow casserole. Pour sauce over enchiladas. Top each with grated cheese and bake at 350° for 8 to 10 minutes. Garnish with shredded lettuce, ripe olives and tomato wedges. May be frozen. Makes 6 servings.

JERRY APODACA, Governor (New Mexico)

GREEN CHILI STEW

2½ pounds lean beef, cubed
2 tablespoons lard
2 cloves garlic
3 tablespoons flour
3 cups bouillon
2 large onions, chopped
8 large green chilies, finely chopped

3 half ripe, peeled tomatoes
1 tablespoon chili powder
salt to taste
½ teaspoon oregano
dash of monosodium glutamate
4 potatoes, cubed

Brown meat in lard, add garlic and cook until it is brown. Remove meat and stir in flour. Cook over high heat, stirring vigorously for a few minutes. Reduce heat, return meat to pan and add all other ingredients except potatoes. Simmer until meat is tender. Add potatoes near the end of cooking time. Makes 4 servings.

JERRY APODACA, Governor (New Mexico)

GUAVA CHIFFON CAKE

2 cups plus 2 tablespoons cake flour,
  sifted
1½ cups sugar
1 tablespoon baking powder
1 teaspoon salt
½ cup salad oil
8 egg yolks
¾ cup concentrated guava juice
½ teaspoon red coloring

8 egg whites
½ teaspoon cream of tartar

Icing:
½ cup shortening
3½ cups sifted confectioners sugar
4 to 5 tablespoons concentrated
  guava juice

Sift together first 4 ingredients. Add, in order, oil, egg yolks, guava juice and red coloring. Mix well. Beat egg whites and cream of tartar in a large bowl until very stiff peaks form. Fold egg yolk batter into egg whites until well blended. Pour into ungreased 10 inch tube pan. Bake for 55 to 60 minutes. Invert and cool completely before removing from pan. For icing, blend together shortening and sugar. Add guava juice until mixture is of spreading consistency. Frost cake. May be frozen. Makes 8 to 10 servings.

GEORGE R. ARIYOSHI, Governor (Hawaii)

577

ROULADEN

1 slice round steak, ¼ inch thick (ask butcher to pound it)
mustard
bacon
chopped onion
flour
salt
pepper
shortening
water

Trim out the bone and trim off all fat. Fry fat in skillet. Cut meat along veins. A few pieces of meat will be large but cut these in half. Spread each piece with mustard and cover with a strip of bacon and some onion. Roll into bundles and secure with 2 round toothpicks. Dredge in flour seasoned with salt and pepper and brown in fat already prepared. Usually it will be necessary to add some shortening. A good brown crust adds to the flavor of this dish, so do not hurry this process. When all bundles are browned, add water and cover the pan. Simmer for 1½ to 2 hours, adding water as necessary.

Otis R. Bowen, M.D., Governor (Indiana)

CARAMEL POPCORN

2 sticks margarine
2 cups brown sugar
½ cup white sugar
1 teaspoon baking soda
1 teaspoon salt
6 quarts popped popcorn

Bring margarine, brown sugar and white sugar to a boil and cook 6 minutes. Remove from heat and add soda and salt. Pour over popcorn. Mix well and place in a 200° oven for 1 hour, stirring occasionally.

J. Floyd Breeding, former Representative (Kansas)

QUAIL

quail	milk (optional)
salt	cooking oil (or half margarine)
pepper (optional)	water
flour	cream (or Half and Half)

Split quail down the back as it is dressed. Season well with salt and pepper. Do not use other spices as it will ruin the flavor. Roll quail in flour. If desired, dip quail in milk before rolling in flour. Brown in hot cooking oil. Brown both sides. For added flavor, use half margarine in cooking. Reduce heat, cover and simmer in water until quail is ready to fall from bones and most of the liquid has cooked away. To make the gravy, pour cream over the quail and let it cook until thickened. Serve the quail with the gravy.

J. F. Loyd Breeding

J. FLOYD BREEDING, former Representative (Kansas)

BLENDER HOLLANDAISE

2 tablespoons lemon juice	pinch cayenne
4 egg yolks	½ pound butter
¼ teaspoon salt	

Warm lemon juice and place in blender with yolks, salt and cayenne. Blend briefly. Heat butter to bubbling and immediately add it in a slow steady stream while blending at slow speed.

Bill Brock

BILL BROCK, Senator (Tennessee)

CHILDREN'S FAVORITE

salt and pepper
2 fryers, cut up
cooking oil
1½ cups uncooked rice
1 medium onion, chopped

1 large can mushroom pieces, undrained
4 chicken bouillon cubes
3½ cups hot water
1 stick butter

Salt and pepper chicken pieces and brown in skillet with bottom well covered in oil. In casserole put rice, onion and mushrooms with liquid. Pile browned chicken on top. Dissolve bouillon cubes in water, pour over chicken and dot with pieces of butter. Cover and bake at 350° for 1 hour or longer. Holds very well. May be frozen. Makes 8 servings.

BILL BROCK, Senator (Tennessee)

NEW ENGLAND INDIAN PUDDING

5 tablespoons corn meal
1 quart scalded milk
2 tablespoons butter
1 cup molasses
1 teaspoon salt

1 teaspoon cinnamon
2 eggs, beaten
1 cup cold milk
vanilla ice cream (or whipped cream)

Add meal gradually to scalded milk, stirring constantly, and cook in top of double boiler over hot water 20 minutes. Add butter, molasses, seasonings and eggs. Turn into buttered pudding dish and pour cold milk over mixture. Bake 1 hour in 350° oven. Serve with a generous topping of vanilla ice cream or whipped cream.

JAMES A. BURKE, Representative (Massachusetts)

580

VALLEY OF THE SUN SOUP

1¼ pounds lean ground beef
2 tablespoons chopped onion
½ teaspoon chili powder
1 can vegetable beef soup

1 can tomato soup
1½ soup cans water
½ cup cooked small twist macaroni
corn curls

Brown beef and cook with onion and chili powder until onion is tender but not brown. Stir to separate the meat particles. Add soups and water. Simmer 5 minutes to blend flavors. Stir often. Add macaroni and reheat. Pour into tureen and garnish with corn curls. Makes 4 servings.

HOWARD W. CANNON, Senator (Nevada)

JULIAN'S CHILI

2 pounds ground beef
1 medium onion, chopped
1 package spaghetti
3 quarts salted water
2 cans chili beans
¾ cup sugar

2 cans tomato paste
1 quart home canned tomato juice
4 to 6 tablespoons chili powder
salt and garlic to taste
½ cup red wine

Brown beef and onion together. Cook spaghetti in salted water. Drain and retain water for part of liquid if chili needs thinning. Add other ingredients. Simmer for 1½ hours, adding wine for the last 30 minutes.

JULIAN M. CARROLL, Governor (Kentucky)

581

HAMBURG CHILI BAKE

1 pound ground beef
1 medium onion, chopped
1 can cream of chicken soup
1 large can evaporated milk

1 small can green chilies, chopped (optional)
12 corn tortillas, cut in fourths
½ pound cheddar cheese, shredded

Crumble beef into heated skillet and add onion. Cook over moderate heat until meat loses red color. Combine beef, soup, milk and chilies. Cover bottom of greased pan with half of tortilla quarters. Spoon half of meat mixture over tortillas. Arrange remaining tortillas on top and cover with remaining meat mixture. Sprinkle top with shredded cheese. Bake, uncovered, in 350° oven about 30 minutes. May be frozen. Makes 8 servings.

J. EDGAR CHENOWETH, former Representative (Colorado)

PINEAPPLE FREEZE

1 8 ounce can pineapple, finely diced
1 cup nuts
½ cup sugar

½ pound marshmallows
1 pint whipping cream, whipped

Mix together and freeze.

FRANK CHURCH, Senator (Idaho)

YES WE HAVE NO BANANAS

1 cup sugar
1 teaspoon vanilla
1 quart heavy cream, whipped

1 cup pecans (or walnuts)
½ package marshmallows
1½ cups sliced bananas

Mix sugar and vanilla into whipped cream. Add other ingredients and freeze.

FRANK CHURCH, Senator (Idaho)

582

ASOPAO DE POLLO (CHICKEN WITH RICE)

4 cups rice
water
¾ cup cooking ham, minced
¾ cup salt pork, minced
2 tablespoons corn oil
¾ cup minced green peppers
¾ cup tomato chunks
¾ cup chopped onions
3 chili peppers
3 cloves garlic
½ teaspoon wild marjoram
pinch of salt
⅛ teaspoon pepper

2 tablespoons salt
3 to 4 pounds chicken, cut in pieces
1 8 ounce can tomato sauce
3 tablespoons Spanish olives
   (small, with seeds)
2 tablespoons capers
1 tablespoon juice from olives
1 tablespoon juice from capers
3½ quarts water
1 can small peas
1 can red pimientos
1 can asparagus tips

Soak the rice in water to cover for about 4 hours. In a 6 quart earthenware kettle, cook ham and salt pork with the corn oil until both are crisp. Add green peppers, tomatoes, onions and chili peppers and saute. Grind garlic with marjoram and pinch of salt and add to mixture. Add pepper and salt. Add chicken pieces and saute. Add tomato sauce, olives, capers and olive and caper juice. Add water. Cover and cook mixture until chicken is done, approximately 1 hour. Drain rice and add to mixture. Stir occasionally. After rice is cooked, about 15 minutes, add peas and decorate with pimientos and asparagus tips. Serve in earthenware kettle. When cooking is completed, rice will be slightly soupy. Makes 10 servings.

GEORGE E. DANIELSON, Representative (California)

DANIELSON MEAT LOAF

1 slice bread, finely crumbled
sea salt
paprika
1 egg
1 pound lean ground beef

1 small onion, finely chopped
2 tablespoons minced parsley
1 teaspoon minced mint (optional)
small pinch dry mustard (optional)

Add crumbled bread, salt and paprika to egg and mix together. Add to ground beef along with onion, parsley, mint and mustard. Mix together well, by hand or fork. Shape into meat loaf. Bake in 350° oven 1 hour. May be frozen. Makes 2 to 3 servings.

GEORGE E. DANIELSON, Representative (California)

POLISH HOT POT

6 large potatoes
½ pound Polish sausage (or bologna)
6 onions, thickly sliced
1 1 pound can tomatoes

1½ teaspoons paprika
1 teaspoon salt
½ cup dairy sour cream

Pare potatoes and cut into ½ inch slices. Arrange in bottom of large greased casserole. Cut sausage into 1 or 2 inch cubes and place over potatoes. Top with onion slices. Mix together tomatoes, paprika and salt and add to casserole. Bake at 350° for 45 minutes. Stir in sour cream and bake 15 minutes longer. Makes 6 servings.

EDWARD J. DERWINSKI, Representative (Illinois)

MAUREEN'S FUDGE

3½ cups sugar
1 cup evaporated milk
1½ tablespoons Karo light syrup
½ teaspoon salt

1 teaspoon vanilla
2 teaspoons butter
4 ounces chocolate, melted

In a very heavy saucepan, mix sugar and milk. Place over low heat, stir constantly to dissolve sugar and add syrup and salt. Turn heat up until boiling starts. Cook at a slow boil until soft ball stage is reached. Add vanilla, butter and chocolate. Cool 10 minutes. Stir fudge until it loses its gloss. Pour into a buttered 8 x 8 inch pan. When firm, cut into pieces. Makes 20 pieces.

JOHN R. FOLEY, former Representative (Maryland)

BYRDDIE BYRD'S CHEESE SOUFFLE

3 tablespoons butter
1 cup milk
3 tablespoons flour
¾ cup grated cheese

3 eggs, separated
¼ teaspoon salt
⅛ teaspoon paprika
dash of cayenne

Mix butter, milk and flour over medium heat. Reduce heat and stir in cheese. When melted, add beaten egg yolks, salt, paprika and cayenne. Cook and stir ingredients for 1 minute longer to permit yolks to thicken. Cool slightly. Whip egg whites until stiff. Fold lightly into cheese mixture. Bake in an ungreased 7 inch dish at 325° for 40 minutes or until firm. Makes 4 servings.

MILLS E. GODWN, JR., Governor (Virginia)

PRALINES

1½ cups dark brown sugar
1½ cups light brown sugar
1 cup milk
3 tablespoons maple syrup

1 tablespoon butter or margarine
1 tablespoon vanilla
1 cup pecan halves

Cook sugars and milk together, stirring constantly. When it begins to boil, add syrup and cook to soft ball stage. Add butter and vanilla. Remove from heat; let stand a few minutes. Beat until creamy. Add nuts. Drop by spoonfuls onto oiled paper. Makes 25 pralines.

GEORGE M. GRANT, former Representative (Alabama)

MEXICAN WEDDING CAKES

¼ pound butter or margarine
1½ cups flour
3 tablespoons sugar

1 teaspoon vanilla
1 cup crushed nuts
confectioners sugar

Preheat oven to 350°. Combine all ingredients, except confectioners sugar, and mix thoroughly. Take approximately 1 teaspoon of mixture and roll into a round ball. Place on greased cookie sheet. Cakes can be placed close together as they do not spread when baked. Bake approximately 35 minutes. While still warm, roll cakes in the confectioners sugar.

TENNYSON GUYER, Representative (Ohio)

APPLE DAPPLE

2 cups sugar
1½ cups butter flavored oil
3 eggs, beaten
3 cups flour
1 teaspoon cinnamon
1 teaspoon baking soda
1 teaspoon salt
1 cup flaked coconut

3 cups diced raw apples
1 cup nuts, chopped
2 teaspoons vanilla

Frosting:
1 cup brown sugar
¼ cup milk
¼ pound butter

Add sugar and oil to eggs and beat well. Sift together flour, cinnamon, soda and salt. Add to egg mixture. Fold in coconut, apples, nuts and vanilla. Pour into greased 9 x 13 x 2 inch pan, and bake at 350° for 45 to 60 minutes. For frosting, mix together all ingredients and boil 4 minutes. Pour over warm cake when it comes from the oven. Makes 12 servings.

Durward G. Hall

DURWARD G. HALL, former Representative (Missouri)

PORK CHOPS WITH VEGETABLE SAUCE

4 pork chops
¼ teaspoon salt
dash pepper
4 onion slices

1 cup V 8 juice
1 tablespoon brown sugar
2 tablespoons water
1 tablespoon flour

Brown chops on thermostatically controlled burner set at 320°. Pour off fat. Season with salt and pepper. Place onion slice on each chop. Add V 8 juice and sugar. Cover, turn burner to 200° and cook 45 minutes or until tender. Stir now and then. Gradually blend water into flour; slowly stir into sauce. Cook, stirring until thickened. Makes 4 servings.

W. G. Bill Hefner

W. G. (BILL) HEFNER, Representative (North Carolina)

586

STUFFED PORK CHOPS

8 pork chops
1½ tablespoons salt
6 to 8 cloves garlic, minced
1 tablespoon vinegar
2 teaspoons oil

2 cups soft fresh bread crumbs
1 cup milk
½ pound onions, chopped
2 tablespoons butter or margarine
1½ tablespoons flour

Each pork chop should be slit laterally on the side opposite the bone in order to form a pocket for the filling. Brown pork chops for several minutes on each side. This is done so that both sides acquire a rich golden brown color and lose some of their natural fat.

Prepare a marinade with salt, garlic, vinegar and oil. This marinade should have a texture like paste. The oil makes it easier to spread. Spread marinade on the pork chops both outside and inside the pockets.

Mix bread crumbs with milk. Brown onions in butter. Remove onions and set aside. Add flour to butter and mix well. Add bread crumb mixture and onions. Mix well. Each pork chop should be stuffed with this filling and then placed in shallow baking pan to be placed in oven at 325° for 30 minutes. Makes 8 servings.

RAFAEL HERNÁNDEZ-COLÓN, Governor (Puerto Rico)

BROWN ELK IN BEER

1 pound elk meat (or beef chuck)
7 Up
1 tablespoon butter or margarine
1 12 ounce can beer
½ teaspoon basil

½ teaspoon salt
⅛ teaspoon pepper
1 package mushroom gravy mix
rice

Marinate elk meat in 7 Up overnight to tenderize. Cut elk meat in 2 x 2½ inch julienne strips; brown in butter in a heavy sauce pan. Add beer, basil, salt and pepper. Simmer covered for 30 to 45 minutes or until meat is very tender. Stir in gravy mix. Cook for 5 to 7 minutes longer. Serve with rice. May be frozen. Makes 4 servings.

ED HERSCHLER, Governor (Wyoming)

BROWN SUGAR PIE

2 eggs
2 cups brown sugar
½ cup canned milk
¼ pound butter or margarine

3 heaping tablespoons flour
1 unbaked pastry shell
whipped cream or ice cream
pecan halves (optional)

Beat eggs slightly with hand beater and add next 4 ingredients. Mix with hand beater and pour into pastry shell. Bake at 400° until firm. Cool before serving. Serve in small slices with whipped cream or ice cream. For pecan pie, arrange whole pecan halves over top of pie before baking. May be frozen. Makes 8 servings.

JAMES E. HOLSHOUSER, JR., Governor (North Carolina)

588

PAMPERED BEEF FILETS

6 large fresh mushroom crowns
2 tablespoons butter or margarine
6 beef filets, 1 inch thick
½ cup chopped fresh mushroom
   stems and pieces
¼ cup chopped green onion
4 teaspoons corn starch

1 cup burgundy
½ cup water
2 tablespoons snipped parsley
1 teaspoon salt
dash of pepper
garlic salt (optional)

Cut mushroom crowns off the stems. For a fluted effect, cut around the tops in a zig zag fashion. Set aside. Heat butter in heavy skillet until golden brown and bubbling. Quickly brown steaks on both sides over high heat, about 1 minute per side. Place each filet on a square of heavy aluminum foil on a baking sheet. Allow to cool slightly.

Add chopped mushrooms and onion to skillet drippings and cook until tender but not brown. Blend in corn starch. Add remaining ingredients and cook and stir until thick and bubbly. Continue to cook for 1 minute. Spoon a generous 3 tablespoons of sauce over each filet and top with mushroom crown. Bring corners of each foil square up over steak, twist gently and seal. Refrigerate packets. Before baking filets, open top of packet slightly. Bake in a 500° oven for 14 to 15 minutes for rare or 16 to 18 minutes for medium. Makes 6 servings.

Frank M. Karsten

FRANK M. KARSTEN, former Representative (Missouri)

ROAST PHEASANT

1 pheasant, prepared for baking
¼ cup Madeira wine
1 tangerine, peeled
1 wedge unpeeled apple
3 strips bacon
salt
1 onion

Gravy:
2 tablespoons butter
2 tablespoons flour
1 cup chicken broth

Wash out pheasant with wine. Place tangerine and apple in cavity and tie legs and wings. Crisscross bacon over breast and thighs. Salt. Put in pan greased with bacon, add onion and cover tightly with foil. Bake in 350° oven about 50 minutes. Uncover and roast until brown. Remove to platter, cover and place in warm oven. To make gravy, add butter and flour to pan drippings, heat and gradually add chicken broth. Boil until thickened. Makes 2 servings.

Carroll D. Kearns

CARROLL D. KEARNS, former Representative (Pennsylvania)

CORN DODGERS

1 cup southern enriched corn meal
1 teaspoon salt
1 heaping tablespoon bacon grease
  (or butter)

¾ cup boiling water
butter

Mix corn meal, salt and bacon grease in mixing bowl and then add boiling water. Beat until well blended. Drop batter from spoon onto a well greased baking sheet. Bake for 20 minutes in a 400° oven. These may be cooked on top of stove on a well greased cast iron skillet or griddle. Butter them on top and eat while hot. Makes 4 servings.

HORACE R. KORNEGAY, former Representative (North Carolina)

ROAST PHEASANT WITH BRANDY AND CREAM

8 shallots, thinly sliced
½ stick butter
3 pheasants
½ cup brandy
2 cups chicken bouillon
1 teaspoon salt

pepper
6 slices bacon
2 cups heavy cream
¼ cup horse radish
wild rice

Saute shallots in butter in roasting pan for 5 minutes. Add pheasants and saute over high heat for 15 minutes or until brown on all sides. Pour some brandy into ladle and rest over pheasants. Warm ladle over match, light brandy and flame pheasant. When flames die, add bouillon, salt and pepper. Put bacon over pheasant breast and roast uncovered in 375° oven for 45 minutes, basting frequently. Stir cream and horse radish into pan juices and continue roasting for 15 minutes, basting frequently. Serve pheasants and sauce with wild rice.

Note: While you serve cocktails, your guests may enjoy watching the flaming of the pheasant.

ROBERT J. LAGOMARSINO, Representative (California)

HOME BAKED BEANS

2 cups dried pea beans
¾ pound lean salt pork
5 tablespoons dark brown sugar
2 tablespoons molasses

2 cups boiling water
1 teaspoon dried English mustard
1 teaspoon cold water
boiling water

Pick over beans and throw out any dark gray or black ones. Put in strainer and wash under cold running water. Put in bowl and cover with cold water. Soak overnight. Drain. Cover with fresh water and heat slowly, keeping water below boiling point. Cook until skins burst open if a few beans are held on the end of a spoon and blown upon.

Scald pork by frying it briefly on all 6 sides. Cut through rind of pork every half inch with 1 inch deep cuts. Put pork in pot with drained beans and cover. Dissolve sugar and molasses in boiling water. Add mustard to cold water and stir into a paste. Add paste to molasses mixture and stir. Add to beans and pork. Add enough extra boiling water to cover beans. Cover bean pot and bake at 250° for about 8 hours. Check every 2 hours to make sure beans are covered with water. Makes 8 to 10 servings.

CLARENCE D. LONG, Representative (Maryland)

BARBEQUE (BEEF)

7 to 9 pound beef filet (or ½ or
　whole New York strip)
garlic

salt
pepper

Trim off ¾ of fat and score beef with sharp knife. Using a garlic press, press enough garlic juice for both sides of meat. Rub it in well. Cover meat with a heavy coating of salt, rubbing it in well. Repeat with pepper, again actually covering meat. Cook about 16 inches above a good bed of coals. For well done, cook 1 hour 15 minutes, for medium, 45 minutes and for rare, 25 to 30 minutes, turning every 10 minutes. Slice and serve. Makes at least 10 servings.

P. H. MATHEWS, Son-in-law of former Representative C. A. Fuller (Arkansas)

TERIYAKI SAUCE

1 cup soy sauce
½ cup sugar
1 clove garlic, grated

½ teaspoon ginger, grated
1 tablespoon sesame oil
1 tablespoon wine

Bring soy sauce and sugar to a boil. Set aside to cool. Add garlic, ginger, sesame oil and wine, stirring well. Sauce should be used to marinate steak for 30 minutes before broiling in oven or over charcoals; to brush on fish prior to broiling; or to put over chicken before baking at 350° for 1 hour. Leftover sauce may be refrigerated for later use.

SPARK M. MATSUNAGA, Representative (Hawaii)

SOUR MILK (OR BUTTERMILK) PANCAKES

2 cups flour
2 teaspoons baking powder
½ teaspoon baking soda
4 tablespoons granulated sugar
1 teaspoon salt

2 eggs, well beaten
1 tablespoon cooking oil (or melted butter)
2 cups sour milk (or thinned buttermilk)

Sift flour and other dry ingredients; add eggs and cooking oil. Stir in sour milk until batter reaches desired consistency. The thinner the batter is, the thinner the pancakes will be. Cook pancakes on medium heat using a teflon frying pan if possible. Serves 10 adults on a diet or a family of 4, including 2 hungry teenage boys.

ROBERT MCCLORY, Representative (Illinois)

592

FRESH APPLE CAKE

4 cups peeled, diced apples (Golden
  Delicious)
1 cup chopped pecans
2 cups sugar
3 cups flour
½ teaspoon nutmeg

½ teaspoon cinnamon
½ teaspoon salt
2 teaspoons baking soda
1 cup vegetable oil
1 teaspoon vanilla
2 eggs, beaten

Mix apples, pecans and sugar and let stand 1 hour. Stir often so mixture makes its own juice. Add dry ingredients to apples, stirring by hand. Then add oil, vanilla and eggs. Pour into a large well greased tube pan. Bake 1½ hours at 325°. May be frozen.

MIKE MCCORMACK, Representative (Washington)

MOM'S CHRISTMAS COOKIES

1 cup shortening
1 pound brown sugar
2 eggs
12 cups flour
1 tablespoon cinnamon
1 teaspoon cloves
1 tablespoon salt
2 heaping teaspoons baking soda

½ cup shredded citron
2 cups shredded nuts
1 pint honey
½ cup cherry juice (or any fruit
  juice)
½ cup sweet cream
frosting (optional)

This full batch of cookies must be mixed in a large kettle. Cream shortening and sugar. Add eggs and beat well. Mix dry ingredients, citron and nuts and add alternately with honey, juice and cream. Dough may be used for drop cookies or rolled and cut in fancy shapes. Bake in a 350° oven about 12 minutes. The batter will keep well in refrigerator for several weeks. When baked, they store well. Baked cookies may be frozen.

MIKE MCCORMACK, Representative (Washington)

593

BUL GO GI (KOREAN)

2 pounds beef tenderloin, thinly sliced
2 large green onions, thinly sliced
1 clove garlic, minced
1 tablespoon brown sugar
4 ounces soy sauce
1 tablespoon sesame seed

3 tablespoons salad oil
½ teaspoon salt
¼ teaspoon black pepper
½ teaspoon Accent
½ teaspoon crushed red pepper
rice

Mix together all ingredients except rice and marinate for approximately 2 hours. Arrange meat on broiler rack and cook meat to desired taste. Pour meat drippings from broiler pan over cooked meat and serve with rice. May be frozen. Makes 6 servings.

JACK R. MILLER, former Senator (Iowa)

SANGRIA

1 bottle red or white wine
1 ounce triple sec
1 ounce brandy

sliced oranges and lemons
sugar to taste
1 small bottle club soda

Mix all ingredients except soda. Chill in refrigerator. Just before serving, uncap club soda and shake bottle before adding to other ingredients. Add plenty of ice and serve. Makes 4 servings.

JACK R. MILLER, former Senator (Iowa)

SPOON BREAD

1½ cups water
1 teaspoon salt
1 cup white corn meal

2 tablespoons butter
1 cup milk
2 eggs, separated

Bring water and salt to boiling point. Gradually stir in corn meal. When smooth, add butter, milk and well beaten egg yolks. Mix well and fold in stiffly beaten egg whites. Pour into greased baking dish and bake in 350° oven about 30 minutes or until firm.

G. V. "SONNY" MONTGOMERY, Representative (Mississippi)

594

TUNA SHRIMP CASSEROLE

2 7 ounce cans tunafish
1 can cream of mushroom soup
1 medium onion, chopped
1 8 ounce bag potato chips, crushed
1 3 ounce jar chopped mushrooms
water

1 pound small shrimp
½ can beer
½ cup vinegar
water
¼ pound butter

Mix together first 5 ingredients. Add just enough water to moisten all ingredients. Bake in casserole for 35 to 45 minutes at 350°. Boil shrimp in beer, vinegar and enough water to cover until shrimp turn pink. Shell, devein and saute in butter 5 minutes. Place shrimp on top of hot tuna casserole. Makes 5 or 6 servings.

CLAUDE PEPPER, Representative (Florida)

PEAR RELISH

8 large or 12 small hard pears
  (Kiefer preferred)
3 medium onions
5 red bell peppers
3 green bell peppers
3 cups white vinegar

3 cups sugar
1 teaspoon celery seed
1 teaspoon white mustard seed
2 teaspoons salt
1 tablespoon corn starch

Pare and core pears and grind together with onions and peppers in food grinder. Drain off most of the juice. Mix vinegar, sugar, celery seed, mustard seed and salt together, pour over pear mixture and boil 20 minutes. Add corn starch mixed with a little water and boil 15 more minutes. Pour in sterilized jars and seal. Makes 6 pints.

Note: My wife and I make this together. I peel and grind. She measures and cooks.

J. J. PICKLE, Representative (Texas)

CHUCK WAGON PEPPER STEAK

1 3 pound round bone arm chuck roast (or boneless round roast), cut about 2 inches thick
2 teaspoons unseasoned meat tenderizer
2 tablespoons instant minced onion
2 teaspoons thyme
1 teaspoon marjoram
1 bay leaf, crushed
1 cup vinegar
½ cup olive oil (or salad oil)
3 tablespoons lemon juice
¼ cup peppercorns, coarsely crushed (or 2 tablespoons bottled cracked pepper)

Sprinkle meat evenly on both sides with meat tenderizer, pierce deeply all over with a fork and place in a shallow baking pan. Mix onion, thyme, marjoram, bay leaf, vinegar, olive oil and lemon juice in a small bowl and pour over and around meat. Marinate at room temperature 2 to 3 hours, turning meat every half hour. When ready to grill, remove meat from marinade; pound half the crushed peppercorns into each side, using a wooden mallet. Grill to a rich brown on rack set about 6 inches above hot coals. Turn and grill until meat is as done as you like it. It should average at least 15 minutes on each side for rare. To serve, place on carving board and cut meat diagonally into ½ inch thick slices. Makes 6 servings.

MELVIN PRICE, Representative (Illinois)

STRAMMER MOX

2 slices pumpernickel bread
butter
Westphalian ham slices
1 fried egg, sunny side up

Place slices of bread side by side. Cover with butter and ham. Top with the fried egg. Makes 1 serving.

REINHOLD PUETZ, Son-in-law of former Representative Courtland C. Gillen (Indiana)

HAWAIIAN TOAST

2 slices white bread, toasted
2 pineapple rings
2 slices ham
2 cocktail cherries
Swiss cheese

Place toast side by side. Cover with ham, pineapple rings, cherries and top with cheese. Put in 400° oven until cheese melts. Makes 1 serving.

REINHOLD PUETZ, Son-in-law of former Representative Courtland C. Gillen (Indiana)

NUTTY FUDGE PIE

¾ cup pecans
2 tablespoons cooking oil
salt to taste
1 cup chocolate chips
1 cup miniature marshmallows

1 cup evaporated milk
dash of salt
vanilla wafers
vanilla ice cream

Roast pecans in oil in a 350° oven for 15 to 30 minutes. Stir occasionally. Drain on paper towel. Salt. Combine the chocolate, marshmallows, milk and salt to make a fudge sauce. Cook over medium heat until thick. Stir to prevent sticking. Cool. Line bottom and sides of pie tin with vanilla wafers. Fill the tin half full with ice cream. Pour ½ the fudge sauce over the ice cream. Finish filling the tin with ice cream, pressing it into the pan. Cover with remaining fudge sauce. Sprinkle top with pecans. Freeze. Makes 8 servings.

ROBERT D. RAY, Governor (Iowa)

REGULA ANGEL PIE

1⅓ cups graham cracker crumbs
¼ pound melted butter (or fortified
   margarine)
4 egg whites
¼ teaspoon salt
1 teaspoon vinegar

1 cup sugar
1½ cups heavy cream, whipped
1 cup shredded coconut
2 tablespoons sugar
1 teaspoon vanilla

Combine graham cracker crumbs and butter; pat firmly into a 9 inch pie pan. Beat egg whites until frothy, add salt and vinegar and beat until stiff. Gradually add the 1 cup sugar, 2 tablespoons at a time, beating thoroughly after each addition. Spread in prepared crust and bake in a 275° oven for 1¼ hours. Cool. Into whipped cream fold ½ cup coconut, remaining sugar and vanilla. Spread whipped cream over top of pie. Toast remaining coconut and sprinkle over whipped cream. Makes 6 servings.

RALPH S. REGULA, Representative (Ohio)

PINEAPPLE SQUARES

1½ cups sugar
2 cups flour
1½ teaspoons baking soda
1½ teaspoons salt
1 20 ounce can crushed pineapple
2 eggs, beaten

Icing:
1½ cups sugar
1 stick margarine
1 6 ounce can evaporated milk
1 cup chopped pecans
1 7 ounce can coconut
1 teaspoon vanilla

Mix ingredients, in order given, with a spoon and pour into a greased and floured 9 x 13 inch pan. Bake in a 350° oven for about 30 minutes. Pour hot icing over pineapple squares as soon as they are taken from the oven.

Icing: Boil sugar, margarine and evaporated milk for 4 minutes, stirring constantly. Remove from heat, add the pecans, coconut and vanilla and mix well.

RAY ROBERTS, Representative (Texas)

CORN CAKES

1¼ cups stone ground yellow corn meal
1 egg
1 teaspoon baking powder
1 tablespoon corn oil

1 cup milk
1 teaspoon salt
⅛ teaspoon sugar

Combine all ingredients. Drop by tablespoon on well greased 400° griddle. Makes 4 servings.

J. KENNETH ROBINSON, Representative (Virginia)

ESCALLOPED OYSTERS

1 quart select oysters, drain, reserve
   liquor
milk

1½ sticks butter, melted
salt and pepper
oyster crackers

Add milk to oyster liquor to make 1 cup. Heat with butter, salt and pepper. Alternate layers of crackers and oysters in buttered casserole ending with crackers. Add hot liquid. Bake at 350° for 20 to 25 minutes or until lightly browned.

CHARLES G. ROSE, III, Representative (North Carolina)

598

SHERRY ALMOND MACAROON PARFAIT

¾ cup sherry
12 almond macaroons

½ gallon vanilla ice cream (or ice milk)
whipped cream

Pour sherry over macaroons and let stand until macaroons are saturated. Mix thoroughly with fork and add to softened vanilla ice cream. Mix quickly and scoop mixture into parfait glasses. Freeze several hours. Top with whipped cream when ready to serve. Makes 7 or 8 servings.

CHARLES G. ROSE, III, Representative (North Carolina)

RARE ROAST BEEF

2 to 4 rib roast, weighing 4½ to
12 pounds

flour
salt and pepper

Remove roast from refrigerator 2½ to 4 hours before cooking. Preheat oven to 500°. Place roast in shallow roasting pan, fat side up. Sprinkle with flour and rub lightly into fat. Season generously with salt and pepper. Roast according to chart below.

Ribs	Weight	Roasting time at 500°
2	4½ to 5 pounds	25 to 30 minutes
3	8 to 9 pounds	40 to 45 minutes
4	11 to 12 pounds	55 to 60 minutes

When cooking time is finished, turn off heat. Keep roast in oven until oven is lukewarm, about 2 hours. Do not open the door at any time. Roast will be crunchy brown outside and very rare inside. This method should be used only in a well insulated oven.

HERMAN T. SCHNEEBELI, Representative (Pennsylvania)

599

PICKLED SHRIMP

3 pounds fresh shrimp in shells
¾ cup chopped celery tops
½ cup mixed pickling spices
1 tablespoon salt
2½ cups sliced onion
10 bay leaves

Marinade:
2 cups salad oil
1 cup white vinegar
4 tablespoons capers with juice
3 teaspoons celery seed
2 teaspoons salt
few drops Tabasco

Cover shrimp with boiling water, add celery tops, spices and salt. Cover and simmer 5 minutes. Drain, peel and devein shrimp under cold water. Alternate cleaned shrimp, onions and bay leaves in shallow baking dish. Combine marinade ingredients, mix well, pour over shrimp and cover. Chill at least 24 hours, spooning marinade over shrimp occasionally. Keeps about a week in refrigerator. Serve as hors d'oeuvres. May be frozen.

ADMIRAL TAZEWELL SHEPARD, Son-in-law of Senator John Sparkman (Alabama)

SHRIMP GOURMET

6 tablespoons butter
3 tablespoons flour
2 cups clam juice
1 cup chopped fresh tomatoes
3 tablespoons chopped onion
1 tablespoon chopped green pepper
1 tablespoon chopped celery

1 bay leaf
¼ teaspoon thyme
½ cup sliced mushrooms
2 pounds raw shrimp, peeled and
   deveined
½ cup dry white wine
wild rice

Make a roux using 3 tablespoons butter and 3 tablespoons flour. Slowly add clam juice followed by tomatoes. Saute onion and green pepper in remaining butter. Add to clam juice mixture. Add celery, bay leaf, thyme, mushrooms and shrimp. Simmer 20 minutes until shrimp are done. Add wine and let set a few minutes after heat has been turned off. Serve over wild rice.

ROBERT L. F. SIKES, Representative (Florida)

600

VENISON CHILI

3 pounds coarsely ground venison
1 cup diced onions
1 cup chili powder
1 tablespoon paprika
1 tablespoon cayenne
1 clove garlic, minced

2 bay leaves
1 20 ounce can tomatoe puree
1 quart water
2 tablespoons corn starch
salt and pepper to taste
kidney beans (optional)

Sear venison. When browned, add next 8 ingredients. Cook 45 or 50 minutes. Thicken with corn starch. Season with salt and pepper. Add kidney beans if desired. Makes 15 servings.

ROBERT L. F. SIKES, Representative (Florida)

PICKLED SHRIMP

2½ quarts water
3 tablespoons salt
15 to 20 whole allspice
6 to 8 peppercorns
⅛ teaspoon black pepper
juice and rind of 1 lemon
15 to 20 cloves
6 garlic cloves, sliced
3 small onions, diced
3 large stalks celery, crushed
  or broken
2 large bay leaves
2 pinches dried thyme (or 1 sprig
  fresh thyme)
several sprigs parsley
few bits dried red pepper

1 tablespoon Worcestershire sauce
2 to 2½ pounds raw shrimp, peeled
  and deveined
4 medium onions, thinly sliced
1 box bay leaves

Sauce:
1¼ cups salad oil
¾ cup warm white vinegar
½ teaspoon salt
2½ teaspoons celery salt
2½ tablespoons capers with juice
dash of hot sauce
¼ cup Worcestershire sauce
1 tablespoon yellow mustard

Season water with salt and add all other ingredients except the shrimp, sliced onions and box of bay leaves. Bring to a boil and allow to simmer 20 minutes. Add shrimp and bring to a boil again. Simmer 8 to 10 minutes. Drain and cool. Combine sauce ingredients. In a large bowl arrange shrimp in layers with onion slices and bay leaves, pouring sauce over each layer. Cover bowl and refrigerate at least 24 hours. When serving, arrange entire mixture on large platter. Will keep 1 week in refrigerator.

ROBERT L. F. SIKES, Representative (Florida)

601

POPCORN BALLS

2½ cups sorghum
½ cup water
½ teaspoon salt

½ teaspoon vinegar
1 teaspoon vanilla
5 quarts popped popcorn

Mix sorghum, water, salt and vinegar and bring to a hard ball, 250°. Add vanilla, pour over popcorn and mix evenly. Let cool until sticky. Butter hands and form popcorn mixture into balls. Wrap in plastic to keep fresh.

Neal Smith

NEAL SMITH, Representative (Iowa)

PULLED TAFFEE

2 cups sugar
¾ cup white Karo syrup
1 tablespoon butter

1 teaspoon vinegar
½ teaspoon vanilla

Boil first 4 ingredients together until a few drops of it in cold water will form a hard ball. Add vanilla, pour into buttered pie tins and cool until the mixture can be handled. Butter hands and pull, pull, pull! When candy holds shape and is creamy in color, twist to about the size of one's little finger; then cut with scissors into bite size portions and drop onto wax paper.

Neal Smith

NEAL SMITH, Representative (Iowa)

DEVILED CRAB

1 pound crabmeat
2 hard cooked eggs, minced
2 tablespoons lemon juice
4 tablespoons butter or margarine
3 tablespoons flour
1 tablespoon dry mustard

1 tablespoon salt
¼ tablespoon pepper
1 tablespoon Accent (optional)
1 cup milk
1 cup buttered bread crumbs
paprika

Remove any bits of shell from crabmeat. Add eggs and lemon juice. Set aside. Melt butter and add flour, mustard, salt, pepper and Accent. Add milk and heat, stirring constantly, until it just begins to thicken. Mix this sauce with crab mixture. Put in greased casserole or individual shells. Top with buttered bread crumbs. Sprinkle with paprika. Heat in 400° oven until it bubbles and crumbs are brown. Serve at once. May be frozen. Makes 8 servings.

John Sparkman

JOHN SPARKMAN, Senator (Alabama)

602

LEMON CAKE

1 3 ounce package lemon Jello
1 cup boiling water
¾ cup Wesson oil
1 package yellow cake mix
4 eggs

Glaze:
¾ cup sugar
juice of 2 lemons
grated lemon rind (optional)

Dissolve Jello in boiling water and cool. Add oil. Mix this with cake mix, beat thoroughly, adding eggs 1 at a time while beating. Pour into greased tube pan. Bake in 350° oven 50 to 60 minutes. Remove from pan and cover with glaze made by dissolving sugar in lemon juice. Grated lemon rind may be added to glaze.

John C. Stennis

JOHN C. STENNIS, Senator (Mississippi)

SOUTHERN PECAN PIE

3 eggs, beaten
1 cup sugar
1 cup light or dark corn syrup
½ teaspoon salt

1 teaspoon vanilla
1 cup pecan halves
1 unbaked 9 inch pie shell

Beat eggs and sugar until thick. Add corn syrup, salt, vanilla and pecan halves. Pour into pie shell and bake in preheated 300° oven 50 to 60 minutes or until filling is set. Makes 6 servings.

John C. Stennis

JOHN C. STENNIS, Senator (Mississippi)

MOM'S CHICKEN STEW

2 fryers
2 or 3 cups tomatoes, fresh or canned
water
1 clove garlic
2 bay leaves
½ cup barley, brown rice or noodles

8 or 10 carrots, trimmed and chopped
6 medium leeks, trimmed and split
in half
½ cup mushroom halves
butter
poached eggs (optional)

Simmer chicken until tender in tomatoes and water with garlic and bay leaves. Lift chicken to a platter. Remove all the meat and return the bones to the broth. Simmer for 20 more minutes and remove bones. Add barley and simmer for 15 minutes. Add carrots and continue to simmer. Saute leeks with mushrooms in butter for 3 or 4 minutes. Add these to the broth 10 minutes before serving. Add chicken pieces for the last 5 minutes of cooking. Makes 6 servings.

For an extra touch, at the last minute poach an egg for each person and serve on top of soup in individual bowls.

BOB STRAUB, Governor (Oregon)

TACO SALAD

1 pound ground beef
1 15 ounce can kidney beans, drained
½ teaspoon salt
2 tablespoons dry minced onions
½ cup tomato paste
1 head iceberg lettuce (or mixed
greens)
2 to 4 tomatoes, cut in wedges

4 to 8 ounces grated cheddar cheese
8 ounces cheese, cheese garlic or
Italian dressing
hot sauce to taste
small bag tortillas chips, plain or
taco flavored, crumbled
1 avocado, sliced

Brown ground beef; add beans, salt, onions, and tomato paste. Simmer 10 to 15 minutes. Cool. Chop lettuce and add tomatoes. Toss with cheese, dressing and meat mixture. Add hot sauce. Cover with crumbled chips and top with avocado. Makes 6 servings.

STEVEN D. SYMMS, Representative (Idaho)

ARTICHOKE NIBBLES

2 6 ounce jars marinated artichoke
   hearts
3 green onions, chopped
4 eggs
½ cup fine bread crumbs

¼ teaspoon salt
⅛ teaspoon hot pepper seasoning
½ pound Monterey jack cheese, grated
2 tablespoons minced parsley

Drain marinade from 1 jar of artichoke hearts into frying pan. Drain other jar and chop artichoke hearts from both jars and set aside. Saute onions in marinade 5 minutes. Combine eggs, crumbs and seasonings. Beat vigorously. Stir in cheese, parsley, artichokes and onions. Place in greased baking dish and bake 30 minutes in 325° oven. Cut in 1 inch squares and serve hot or cold. Makes 6 dozen appetizers.

Burt L. Talcott

BURT L. TALCOTT, Representative (California)

CHICKEN ARTICHOKE SOUP

1 tablespoon butter
2 tablespoons oil
1 onion, finely chopped
1 clove garlic, pressed
2 cups diced, cooked artichoke bottoms
1 tablespoon curry powder
salt and pepper to taste

2 tablespoons flour
2 cups clear chicken broth
¾ cup whipping cream (or Half
   and Half)
½ cup finely shredded, cooked
   chicken

Heat butter and oil, add onion and garlic and cook slowly for 3 minutes. Add artichoke bottoms, curry powder, salt and pepper. Continue cooking very slowly until thoroughly warmed. Remove from fire and add flour and chicken broth. Return to fire and stir constantly until it boils. Remove from heat and put through blender. Return to pan. Add cream and chicken. Taste for seasonings. Reheat and serve. May be served cold. Makes 4 to 5 servings.

Burt L. Talcott

BURT L. TALCOTT, Representative (California)

CRANBERRY CRUNCH

1 cup quick cooking oats
½ cup flour
½ teaspoon salt
1 cup brown sugar, firmly packed

¼ pound butter or margarine
1 can whole cranberry sauce
ice cream or whipped cream

Mix oats, flour, salt and brown sugar together. Cut in butter until mixture is crumbly. Pack ½ of mixture in bottom of 1½ quart greased baking dish. Cover with cranberry sauce. Top with remaining crumb mixture. Wrap in foil and freeze. If frozen, bake at 350° for 40 minutes. If thawed, bake until brown. Serve warm with ice cream or whipped cream. Makes 6 to 8 servings.

Roy A. Taylor, Representative (North Carolina)

ESCALLOPED EGG PLANT

1 medium egg plant
salt to taste
3 tablespoons grated onion
1 can mushroom soup

1 cup grated sharp cheese
¾ cup buttered bread crumbs
butter

Peel and cube egg plant. Cook until tender in boiling salted water. Drain well. Place egg plant in baking dish and sprinkle grated onion over it. Cover with the mushroom soup and over that sprinkle ½ of the grated cheese. Top with buttered bread crumbs. Dot with butter and sprinkle with remaining cheese. Bake at 350° about 45 minutes until nicely browned. Makes 4 servings.

Roy A. Taylor, Representative (North Carolina)

606

CHOCOLATE CAKE

½ cup cocoa
½ cup boiling water
1 stick butter, softened
1½ cups sugar
2 eggs
½ cup buttermilk
1 teaspoon baking soda
2 cups sifted flour
pinch of salt
1 teaspoon vanilla

Frosting:
1 stick butter, softened
7 tablespoons cocoa
1 box confectioners sugar
4 tablespoons cream (or a little more)
pinch of salt
1 teaspoon vanilla

Mix cocoa with boiling water. Set aside. In large mixing bowl, cream butter and sugar. Add eggs and mix well. Blend in cocoa, then buttermilk and baking soda. Mix in flour, salt and vanilla. Pour into 2 buttered and floured cake pans. Bake at 350° for 20 to 25 minutes. When cooled, spread with frosting. May be frozen. Makes 12 servings.

Frosting: Cream butter. Add cocoa and sugar a little at a time. Add cream. If too thick, add a little additional cream. Add salt and vanilla and mix well.

DAVID C. TREEN, Representative (Louisiana)

SCRUMPTIOUS BREAD

1 cup whole wheat flour
½ cup corn meal
½ cup sugar
1 teaspoon salt
1 teaspoon baking powder

1 teaspoon baking soda
3 cups 100% bran
1 egg
2 cups buttermilk (or sour milk)
1 cup raisins

Sift together flour, corn meal, sugar, salt, baking powder and baking soda. Add bran, egg and milk. Mix well. Add raisins. Put into loaf pan and bake slowly at 325° for 1½ hours. May be frozen. Makes 12 servings.

LIONEL VAN DEERLIN, Representative (California)

TAMALE CASSEROLE

1½ cups yellow corn meal
2 tablespoons chili powder
1 tablespoon salt
1 cup salad oil

1 20 ounce can chopped tomatoes
1 11 ounce can cream style corn
1 11 ounce can pitted black olives
2 cups (or more) cubed beef, chicken
or pork

Mix corn meal, chili powder, salt and oil. Add to this mixture the tomatoes, corn, olives and cubed meat. Cook over low heat until mixture thickens. Place in a casserole and bake covered, at 350° for 45 minutes. May be frozen. Makes 8 servings.

LIONEL VAN DEERLIN, Representative (California)

HOQUIAM CLAM CHOWDER

8 strips bacon
2 medium whole dry onions, chopped
2 stalks celery, chopped
2 7 ounce cans clams, ground (or 2
cups minced fresh clams with
water to cover)
4 medium potatoes, diced

2 small carrots, diced
2 tablespoons minced parsley
1 tablespoon minced dry onion
water as needed
cream (optional)
salt and pepper to taste

Brown bacon in pan with chopped onions and celery. Place clams with liquid in kettle and add potatoes and carrots. Also add parsley and minced onion. When ingredients in pan are sauteed, add to those in kettle. Add water to cover completely and cook ½ hour. Add cream if desired. Season to taste.

CHARLES A. VANIK, Representative (Ohio)

SPINACH CASSEROLE

2 packages frozen chopped spinach
4 tablespoons butter
2 tablespoons flour
2 tablespoons chopped onion
½ cup evaporated milk
½ teaspoon black pepper
¾ teaspoon celery salt

¾ teaspoon garlic salt
½ teaspoon salt
1 teaspoon Worcestershire sauce
6 ounce roll jalapena cheese, diced
red pepper to taste
bread crumbs (optional)

Cook spinach according to directions on package. Drain and reserve ½ cup spinach liquid. Melt butter in saucepan and add flour, stirring until blended. Add onion and cook until soft. Add liquid slowly and cook until smooth and thick. Add seasonings and cheese and stir until melted. Combine with cooked spinach. May be served immediately or poured into buttered casserole, topped with bread crumbs and heated at 350° until bubbly. Suitable for freezing. Makes 8 servings.

WILLIAM LOWE WALLER, Governor (Mississippi)

DEVILED EGGS

4 hard cooked eggs
3 ounces cream cheese
1 tablespoon mayonnaise
1 tablespoon prepared mustard
¼ teaspoon salt

1 teaspoon vinegar
1 dash cayenne
⅛ teaspoon dry mustard
paprika

Cut eggs in half lengthwise. Remove yolks and put through strainer. Add remaining ingredients. Blend until smooth. Fill hollow egg whites. Decorate with paprika.

JAMES D. WEAVER M.D., former Representative (Pennsylvania)

BRUNSWICK STEW

2 pounds lean beef, cut into small
  pieces
2 cans tomatoes
1 can mixed vegetables
1 can whole kernel corn
4 medium potatoes, diced

4 medium onions, diced
3 teaspoons Worcestershire sauce
garlic salt to taste
black pepper to taste
bouillon cubes (optional)
hot water (optional)

Simmer meat in water to cover until very tender. Add vegetables and seasoning to meat and stock. Simmer on top of stove 4 to 6 hours, stirring frequently. If more liquid is needed, add bouillon cubes dissolved in hot water. Makes 8 servings.

Jamie L. Whitten

JAMIE L. WHITTEN, Representative (Mississippi)

MYSTERY PUDDING

1½ cups flour
½ teaspoon salt
1 cup sugar
1 teaspoon baking soda
1 egg, beaten

1 20 ounce can fruit salad, drain and
  reserve juice
1 cup brown sugar
½ cup chopped nuts

Sift flour, salt, sugar and baking soda together. Add egg to dry ingredients. Add reserved fruit juice and mix well. Fold in fruit. Pour into greased pan and top with brown sugar and nuts. Bake 1 hour at 325°. May be frozen. Makes 6 servings.

Bob Wilson

BOB WILSON, Representative (California)

BUTTERMILK LEMON PIE

1⅓ cups sugar
¼ cup corn starch
2 tablespoons flour
⅛ teaspoon salt
2 cups buttermilk
4 egg yolks, slightly beaten

⅓ cup lemon juice
1 teaspoon grated lemon rind
2 tablespoons butter
1 baked 9 inch pie shell
4 egg whites, stiffly beaten (or whipped cream)

Combine sugar, corn starch, flour and salt. Gradually stir in buttermilk. Cook over low heat, stirring constantly until thickened. Beat a little of the hot mixture into the egg yolks, then beat yolks into hot mixture and cook 2 additional minutes. Blend in lemon juice, rind and butter. Pour into pie shell. Top with meringue and brown in a 300° oven for 10 to 15 minutes. Whipped cream may be used instead of a meringue. Makes 6 to 8 servings.

BOB WILSON, Representative (California)

ARTICHOKE CHICKEN ELEGANTE

3 artichokes
lemon juice
4 small chicken breasts
4 tablespoons butter or margarine
¾ cup julienne carrots
1 cup sliced mushrooms
½ cup sliced green onions

½ cup water chestnuts, drained and sliced
½ teaspoon salt
⅛ teaspoon pepper
⅛ teaspoon dried thyme, crushed
1½ cups chicken broth
½ cup dry white wine
2 tablespoons corn starch

Remove and discard 2 or 3 layers of outer artichoke leaves. Cut off and discard stem and top ⅔ of each artichoke. Cut in quarters and rub cut surfaces with lemon juice. Cook in boiling salted water 15 minutes or until tender. Drain; remove chokes, the fuzzy portion.

In large skillet, brown chicken on both sides in butter. Arrange chicken in an 11¾ x 7½ x 1¾ inch baking dish with the artichokes. Add carrots to skillet and cook, covered, 5 minutes over low heat. Add mushrooms, onions, water chestnuts, salt, pepper and thyme and cook, covered, 1 minute more. Stir together chicken broth, wine and corn starch. Add to vegetables in skillet; cook and stir until mixture thickens and bubbles. Pour sauce over all in baking dish. Bake, covered, in 375° oven for 40 minutes or until chicken is tender, basting occasionally with chicken broth and wine sauce. Makes 4 servings.

CHALMERS P. WYLIE, Representative (Ohio)

NOTES

EMBASSY

AFGHANISTAN

AUSHAK (RAVIOLI) WITH LEEKS FILLING

Aush Dough:
3 cups sifted white flour
1 teaspoon salt
1 cup water

Filling:
2 to 3 cups chopped leeks
1 teaspoon salt
½ teaspoon red pepper
1 tablespoon vegetable oil

Yogurt and Meat Sauce:
1 quart yogurt
3 cloves fresh garlic, ground
1 teaspoon salt
½ cup vegetable oil
1 medium onion, chopped
1 pound ground beef, crumbled
½ teaspoon salt
1 teaspoon black pepper
½ cup tomato juice
2½ quarts water
1 tablespoon dry mint

Aush Dough: Place flour and salt in a bowl and mix well. Add water. Stir to form a very stiff dough, as for noodles. Divide dough into 3 balls, cover and set aside.

Leek Filling: Wash leeks, cut in ¼ inch pieces and wash again. Squeeze with hands to remove water. Place in a bowl the chopped leeks, salt and red pepper. Mix and squeeze to remove more water. Add vegetable oil and set aside.

Yogurt and Meat Sauce: Drain yogurt to yield 2 cups chaka. Place in a bowl and mix with garlic and salt. Set aside. Heat oil in saucepan and brown onion in it. Add beef, salt and pepper. Brown meat and add tomato juice and 2 cups of water. Boil until liquid evaporates and sauce is oily.

Roll out a ball of dough on a floured board until it is very thin. Cut with a round cutter 1½ inches in diameter or in squares the same size. Put a few of the drained leeks on half the dough, moisten edges and seal shut tightly so they will not open during boiling. Place on a tray and cover until all are prepared, repeating this process with the remaining dough and leeks. Heat remaining water in a kettle and drop several aushaks in at a time, adding a little cold water as needed to keep it from boiling over. Boil for 10 minutes.

Place half of chaka (yogurt) on a platter. Lift cooked aushaks with a slotted spoon and arrange on chaka. Cover with remaining chaka. Sprinkle with mint and top with meat sauce. Serve at once. Makes 6 to 8 servings.

A. Malikyar

MRS. ABDULLAH MALIKYAR, Wife of Ambassador (Afghanistan)

AFGHANISTAN

AFGHAN PALAW

2 tablespoons dry onion flakes
2 tablespoons fat (Crisco)
1½ cups water
1 chicken (cut as for frying)
1 box long grain rice
water for cooking rice

Masalla:
1 teaspoon ground cardamon
2 teaspoons ground cumin seed
½ teaspoon black pepper

Brown onion in fat; add 1 cup of water and cook until water evaporates. Add chicken to browned onions. Add remaining water, cover and cook until chicken is tender, adding more water if necessary. Remove chicken from sauce.

In another pot cook the rice submerged in water with 1 inch of water above rice level. Boil about 5 minutes. Thoroughly drain rice in a colander.

Put rice on the sauce and cook until the sauce is absorbed by the rice. Put chicken on rice and sprinkle masalla on entire mixture. Bake in oven at 400° for 20 minutes.

Note: A lamb shank may be substituted for the chicken.

A. Malikyar

Mrs. Abdullah Malikyar, Wife of Ambassador (Afghanistan)

ARGENTINA

SOLE MARIA LAURA

3 pounds filet of sole
salt
freshly ground pepper
1 small onion, finely chopped
¼ pound unsalted butter
2 cups beef bouillon
2 tablespoons flour

½ pint light cream
4 egg yolks
3 28 ounce cans whole mushrooms, drained
3 pounds shrimp, shelled and cleaned
1 lemon, pressed
1 glass sherry

Preheat oven to 320°. Pat filet dry and see that it is fresh and has no bones. Season with salt, freshly ground pepper and the onion. In large baking dish, melt half the butter and place the filets in it. Add bouillon, cover with aluminum foil and bake 20 minutes. Melt remaining butter in a pan over low heat, stirring with a wooden spoon. Add flour, salt, pepper, cream, egg yolks, mushrooms, shrimp, lemon and sherry, stirring until warm. Open the oven and remove aluminum foil from dish. Cover filets with sauce, leave in the oven for 8 more minutes and serve. Makes 8 servings.

Mrs. Hector Subiza

Mrs. Hector Subiza, Wife of Minister (Argentina)

AUSTRALIA

SHERRY ALMOND CREAM

Cream:
1 teaspoon gelatin
1¼ cups boiling water
1 cup sugar
6 egg whites
½ teaspoon almond essence
⅓ cup sherry
1 cup chopped almonds

Sauce:
1 pint milk
6 egg yolks
¼ cup sugar
pinch of salt
½ teaspoon vanilla
½ pint whipping cream, whipped
3 tablespoons sherry

Start by dissolving the gelatin in the boiling water. Stir well, add sugar and stir until dissolved. Chill mixture until it begins to set and then beat until frothy. Beat egg whites very stiffly and mix with gelatin. Continue beating until mixture is completely blended. Add almond essence and sherry. Pour into mould, alternating layers of the mixture with a sprinkling of chopped nuts. Put in refrigerator for 2 hours. Serve accompanied by a custard sauce. To make sauce, scald milk in a double boiler. Beat egg yolks slightly and add sugar and salt. Pour scalded milk slowly into egg mixture and return to double boiler. Cook until custard coats the spoon, then let cool. When cold, add vanilla, whipped cream and sherry. Makes 8 to 10 servings.

NUT BREAD

4 cups flour
4 flat teaspoons cream of tartar
4 flat teaspoons bicarbonate of soda
1 teaspoon salt
1 cup sugar

¾ cup chopped dates and (or) raisins
1½ cups milk
1 egg
1 cup chopped walnuts

Sift flour with cream of tartar, soda and salt 3 times. Add sugar and fruits. Mix well with the milk, in which egg has been beaten. Add nuts. Bake in a greased loaf tin at 375° for 1 hour. For serving, slice thin and butter like bread. May be frozen. Makes 20 to 25 slices.

C. Le. Shaw —

Lady Shaw, Wife of former Ambassador (Australia)

AUSTRIA

SCHINKENFLECKERL (VIENNESE HAM AND NOODLE SOUFFLE)

¾ to 1 pound smoked ham (small boneless smoked pork butt)
1 pound egg noodles (homemade or ready purchased wide noodles)
¼ pound butter, softened
3 egg yolks

1 whole egg
salt to taste
½ pint sour cream
3 egg whites
fine white bread crumbs

Finely chop or grind the boiled ham after boiling it per package instructions. Boil noodles per package instructions. (If using homemade noodles, boil about 10 minutes or "al dente".) Do not overcook. Strain through colander and run cold water through strained noodles. Beat softened butter until fluffy and beat in the egg yolks, the whole egg and salt. Adjust salt according to saltiness of ham. Fold in the ham, sour cream, noodles and finally the stiffly beaten egg whites. Souffle dish or casserole should be well buttered and a layer of bread crumbs dusted over the butter. Fill in the souffle mixture and bake approximately 45 minutes in a 325° oven until nicely browned. Serve at once. Makes 6 to 8 servings.

Note: If you wish to restrict use of eggs, 2 egg yolks and 2 egg whites may be used. If smoked pork butt is not available or time is a factor, ready boiled ham may be used. A further short cut method is to add the beaten eggs without separating the yolks from the whites and to use a little bechamel sauce (white sauce) instead of the beaten egg whites; top the dish with a little butter and bread crumbs and simply place under broiler to brown the top. This method will produce a "quick Schinkenfleckerl" but it will not have the souffle consistency.

Mrs. Arno Halusa

Mrs. Arno Halusa, Wife of Ambassador (Austria)

AUSTRIA

SACHER TORTE

4 ounces semi-sweet chocolate
1 tablespoon water
3 ounces unsalted butter
½ cup fine granulated sugar
4 eggs, separated
1 egg white (optional)

1 cup cake flour, sifted 3 times (or
  1 cup less 1½ tablespoons all
  purpose flour)
¼ cup apricot jam
chocolate icing
whipped cream (optional)

Melt chocolate with water in double boiler. Cream butter and sugar together, beating well until fluffy. Add egg yolks, 1 at a time, beating well after each addition until batter is very light and fluffy. Then add the slightly cooled chocolate and water mixture, again beating very well as you pour this mixture in gradually. Then, fold in the stiffly beaten egg whites (using the extra egg white if your preference is a slightly moister torte) and lastly fold in carefully the sifted flour.

Pour into a well buttered and floured (shake out excess flour) torte pan with removable bottom. Bake in a 325° to 350° oven. Cool in pan about 5 minutes, then set over cake cooling rack and let stand until the next day before icing it.

Make an apricot glaze by heating the jam in a small, heavy saucepan until thick, stirring constantly to avoid scorching. While the glaze is still hot, spread it over cake and place in refrigerator until glaze is set. Then cover top and sides with a dark chocolate icing and let set in cool place. Serve with whipped cream. May be frozen. Makes 8 to 10 servings.

Note: If preferred, torte may be cut in half horizontally and the glaze spread between the layers.

Mrs. Arno Halusa

MRS. ARNO HALUSA, Wife of Ambassador (Austria)

THE BAHAMAS

BAHAMIAN CONCH CHOWDER

2 pounds conch
3 carrots
3 green peppers
3 green onions
6 stalks celery
1 pound butter (or drippings from bacon or salt pork)
2 16 ounce tins tomatoes

1 8 ounce tin tomato paste
water or fish stock
thyme leaves
salt and pepper to taste
Worcestershire sauce
corn starch
½ pint cooking sherry

Grind conch and vegetables separately in a food grinder. Saute conch in butter or drippings for 15 minutes. Add vegetables and saute for 25 minutes. Add tomatoes and tomato paste. Be careful not to let the mixture scorch. Simmer for about 10 minutes. Add the desired amount of water or fish stock and seasonings. Cook slowly until conch is tender, about 60 minutes. Thicken to your liking with corn starch. Add sherry wine before serving. If properly cooked and cooled, can be placed in refrigerator and kept for days. Makes 12 to 18 servings.

BAKED GROUPER

1 5 to 6 pound grouper (before cleaning)
1 medium onion, sliced
¼ sweet green pepper, thinly sliced
¼ cup cooking oil
4 cups stewed tomatoes

¼ teaspoon dried marjoram (or 1 tablespoon of fresh)
¼ teaspoon dried thyme (or 1 tablespoon of fresh)
1 teaspoon salt
1 bay leaf

Preheat oven to 350° heat. Clean grouper thoroughly leaving head and tail (for appearance when serving). It is easier to serve if fish is boned when cleaning but it is not necessary. Place cleaned fish in flat casserole dish and set aside. In large skillet saute onion and green pepper in cooking oil until lightly brown. Then add stewed tomatoes and spices and bring to a boil. Spoon some of sauce inside fish and pour the rest over it. Bake for 30 minutes or until fish appears flaky when tested with fork. Delicious served with plain cooked rice. Makes 8 servings.

Mrs. Livingston B. Johnson,

MRS. LIVINGSTON BASIL JOHNSON, Wife of Ambassador (The Bahamas)

BANGLADESH

MATAR PULAU (PILAF WITH PEAS)

2 medium onions	6 cardamons
2 cups long grain rice	1 teaspoon salt
½ stick butter (or oil)	1 teaspoon sugar
6 cloves	1 cup freshly shelled peas
2 small pieces cinnamon stick	3 cups hot water

Peel onions and cut in thin slices. Wash and soak the rice for 45 to 60 minutes. Heat the butter in a heavy aluminum pan and put in the cloves, the pieces of cinnamon and cardamon. Keep the heat very low, stir slowly and fry these only for a minute. Add onion slices and fry until they get brownish. Then add the drained rice, salt, sugar and peas. Mix and fry gently for 5 minutes. Add water and bring to a boil quickly. After 5 minutes put the pan in preheated 350° oven. Cook for 6 to 7 minutes. When the water dries up, it is ready for serving. Makes 4 servings.

PHIRNI (RICE PUDDING)

½ cup long grain rice	2 dozen pistachio nuts (or almonds), shredded
1 pint Half and Half	12 to 15 raisins
½ cup sugar	crushed seeds of 5 cardamons

Wash the rice in cold water. Cover with water and soak for 30 minutes. Drain. Put Half and Half in a large heavy aluminum pan and bring to a boil. Continue boiling on medium heat for 15 minutes stirring frequently. Add rice and keep boiling for another 25 minutes. Then add sugar along with all other ingredients (which are also to be soaked in water beforehand for about 30 minutes). After boiling it for another 5 minutes, pour it into the serving dish. The mixture should be fairly thick. May be frozen. Makes 4 servings.

FW Begum

Mrs. M. Hossain Ali, Wife of Ambassador (Bangladesh)

BELGIUM

GAUFRES CHANTILLY

1 cup cold milk	1 pinch salt
4 egg yolks	1 teaspoon sugar
1 teaspoon dried or fresh yeast	7 teaspoons softened butter
2 tablespoons warm water	4 egg whites
⅔ cup flour	whipped cream

Beat the cold milk with the egg yolks. Dissolve the yeast in warm water. Sift flour into a bowl with the salt and sugar and gradually beat in the egg yolks and milk mixture with the yeast and the softened butter. Leave the batter to rise until it is double in bulk.

Beat the egg whites until stiff and fold them into the batter. Spoon a little into a hot waffle iron, close it immediately and turn it over to be sure the batter is evenly spread. Continue to heat the iron gently on each side until the waffles are done. When they are cold, serve them with whipped cream.

WATERZOOI DE POULET A LA GANTOISE
(CHICKEN STEW, GHENT STYLE)

2 stalks celery	grated nutmeg to taste
2 medium onions	1 bay leaf
1 carrot	1 3 pound stewing chicken
1 leek	2 tablespoons flour
3 tablespoons butter	2 egg yolks
1½ quarts water	½ cup light cream
2 sprigs parsley	1 teaspoon chopped parsley
salt and pepper to taste	boiled potatoes

Chop celery, onions, carrot and the white portion of the leek. Simmer for 15 minutes in covered stewpan with 1 tablespoon butter. Add water, bring to a boil and then add the parsley, salt, pepper, nutmeg and bay leaf. Then add the chicken, cut into serving pieces. Cook over low heat for about 1 hour. Strain stock; reserve vegetables and chicken. Keep warm.

Melt remaining butter, add flour and 2½ cups of the chicken stock. Stir until thick but do not boil. Mix eggs yolks into cream and add carefully to sauce. Correct seasoning. Return chicken and vegetables to sauce. Serve in deep plates, sprinkled with parsley and accompanied by boiled potatoes. Makes 4 servings.

Mrs. W. van Cauwenberg.

MRS. WILLY VAN CAUWENBERG, Wife of Ambassador (Belgium)

REPUBLIC OF CHINA

DEEP FRIED WALNUTS

A. (Sweet):
- 1 pound walnuts
- ⅓ pound white sugar
- 5 cups peanut oil

B. (Spicy):
- 1 cup walnuts
- 1 teaspoon Chinese pepper salt
- ½ teaspoon five spices powder

A. Boil the walnuts in boiling water for 2 to 3 minutes. Put the walnuts in a big bowl; add white sugar. Soak the walnuts in the sugar for about 6 hours. Fry the walnuts in deep oil (medium heat). Stir constantly. When slightly brown (about 3 minutes), take all the walnuts out at once and spread over absorbent paper. Let cool and serve.

B. Boil the walnuts in boiling water for 2 to 3 minutes. Put the walnuts in a big bowl; add Chinese pepper salt mixed with five spices powder. Soak the walnuts in the salt for about 6 hours. Fry the walnuts in deep oil (medium heat). Stir constantly. When slightly brown (about 3 minutes), take all the walnuts out at once and spread over absorbent paper. Let cool and serve.

SPICY FISH SLICES

- 1 pound fish meat (with fish skin)
- 2 green onions
- 3 slices ginger
- 4 tablespoons soy sauce
- ½ teaspoon salt
- 1 tablespoon cooking wine
- 5 cups peanut oil
- 4 tablespoons sugar
- 1 teaspoon five spices powder (or curry powder)
- 1 cup boiling water

Slice the fish meat into pieces 2 inches long by 1 inch wide. Crush green onions and ginger. Put in a bowl with soy sauce, salt and wine. Marinate the fish slices with this mixture for about 3 to 4 hours. Heat oil very hot in frying pan; fry the fish about 3 to 4 minutes. While frying the fish, at the same time, mix sugar and five spices powder with boiling water in a bowl. Remove the fish from the frying pan and put in sugar mixture immediately. Soak about 3 minutes and take out the fish. Cook the leftover soy sauce over low heat. Dip the fish in the soy sauce for a second. Remove the fish and lay on platter. Let it cool before serving. The spicy fish may be preserved for a few days. May be frozen.

Mrs. James Shen

MRS. JAMES C. H. SHEN, Wife of Ambassador (Republic of China)

CZECHOSLOVAKIA

VEAL WITH PAPRIKA GRAVY

1 onion
3 tablespoons butter
½ cup cubed bacon, browned
2 pounds veal round steak
salt and pepper

water
1 cup sour cream
2 tablespoons flour
paprika

Saute onion in butter. Add browned cubed bacon. Cut veal into serving pieces and season with salt and pepper. To the onions and bacon add veal pieces and enough water to stew the veal until done. Then add sour cream, thickened with flour, and as much paprika as you desire. Simmer for a few minutes. Chicken may also be prepared this way. May be frozen. Makes 4 servings.

DUMPLINGS

2 eggs
1 cup milk
1 teaspoon salt
1 heaping teaspoon baking powder
  (or yeast)

flour (Wondra)
3 slices white bread
butter

Beat eggs and add milk, salt, baking powder and enough flour to make a thick dough which can be thoroughly beaten with a spoon. Beat until dough is smooth. Set the dough aside. Cube the bread and brown it in butter in the oven. Let cool. Work into dough. Make dumplings size of a small apple. Boil in salted water for 10 minutes. Remove from water and split each dumpling, using 2 forks. May be frozen. Makes 4 servings.

Růžena Spáčil

MRS. DUŠAN SPÁČIL, Wife of Ambassador (Czechoslovakia)

ECUADOR

CEBICHE

1 pound cooked prawns or shrimp
juice of 7 lemons
juice of ¼ orange
½ teaspoon sugar
¾ teaspoon salt

1 16 ounce can stewed strained tomatoes
3 tablespoons catsup
1 medium red onion
2 cups boiling water

In a pretty bowl mix all the ingredients except the juice of 1 lemon, ¼ teaspoon salt, the onion and the boiling water. Put the prawn or shrimp preparation in the refrigerator for at least 3 hours.

In a separate bowl cut into fine slices the red onion, sprinkle with ¼ teaspoon salt and cover with the juice of 1 lemon and the boiling water. Let this marinate until the onion is red, about 20 minutes. Later pour out the liquid and place the onions on top of the prawn or shrimp preparation. Return to the refrigerator for about ½ hour or until ready to serve.

At the side you can serve popcorn and slices of French bread. This recipe may be served before lunch as an appetizer or as an entrance course. Makes 4 servings.

Mrs. José C. Cardenas, Wife of Ambassador (Ecuador)

FEDERAL REPUBLIC OF GERMANY

HASELNUSSKRÄNZCHEN

¼ pound butter
½ cup sugar
1 egg
2 cups flour

vanilla
¾ cup ground almonds
¾ cup ground hazelnuts
egg yolk
additional ground hazelnuts for topping

Mix butter and sugar; add the egg, flour, vanilla and the ground almonds and nuts. Stir well. Roll out, in thickness of small finger. Cut out with 2 glasses of different size, forming rings and rounds. Brush with egg yolk. Sprinkle ground hazelnuts on top. Bake fast in 370° oven. May be frozen. Makes about 20 pieces.

Mrs. Berndt von Staden, Wife of Ambassador (Federal Republic of Germany)

FEDERAL REPUBLIC OF GERMANY

MAULTASCHEN

Dough:
½ pound flour
2 eggs
4 teaspoons water
pinch of salt

Filling:
10 ounces cooked meat, minced
10 ounces sieved spinach
finely chopped onions
butter

1 egg
white roll, soaked in water
salt
nutmeg
milk
chopped parsley

egg white
butter
browned onions

Dough: Mix flour, eggs, water and salt well and knead into a stiff dough. Let rest 1 hour. Roll out thinly and cut into sections about 4 inches square.

Filling: Mix meat, spinach, onions browned in butter, egg, white roll, salt and spice. Add milk and parsley and work into an even consistency. Spread filling into the middle of dough squares, fold latter diagonally, brush the edges with white of egg, press together firmly and boil in salted water for about 10 minutes. Drain and toss in a pan with butter. Garnish with additional browned onions. It is best served with fresh salad. May be frozen. Makes 4 servings.

Wendelgard v. Staden

Mrs. Berndt von Staden, Wife of Ambassador (Federal Republic of Germany)

625

GREAT BRITAIN

PERSIAN LAMB WITH RICE

boiling water
1 pound dried apricots
2 boned shoulders of lamb
2 ounces cooking butter
4 onions, chopped
salt

freshly ground black pepper
2 teaspoons ground coriander
1 teaspoon ground cinnamon
2 teaspoons ground cumin
water to cover meat

Pour boiling water on apricots to cover and soak for 2 hours. Trim fat off the meat and cut into cubes. Melt butter in a flameproof casserole and fry the chopped onions in it for 2 to 3 minutes. Add the apricots with the water in which they have been soaked and the salt and pepper. Add the meat and spices. If the quantity of meat is reduced, do not reduce quantity of spices. Add enough water to cover the meat and cook in the oven for 2 hours at about 200° to 250°. Makes 12 servings.

PERSIAN RICE

boiling water
2 pounds long grain rice
cold water

1 tablespoon salt
2 ounces butter, melted

Put rice in a sieve and pour boiling water over it. Separate the grains and soak for 3 to 4 hours in cold water. Put in a large pan with cold water and a tablespoon of salt and boil for 8 minutes. Drain and wash under cold tap; put drained rice in iron casserole with half the butter. Put remaining butter on top. Place in low 200° to 250° oven with the lamb, covering the rice with a clean cloth and then the lid of the casserole. Leave for about 20 minutes. This will produce marvelous rice. Makes 12 servings.

Lady Ramsbotham.

LADY RAMSBOTHAM, Wife of Ambassador (Great Britain)

GREECE

MOUSSAKA

1 pound 9 ounces finely ground veal (or beef)	salt and pepper
1 medium onion, thinly sliced	9 to 10 medium eggplants
1 to 2 tablespoons butter or margarine	oil for frying
4 ounces white wine	7 to 8 teaspoons bread crumbs
4 ounces water	2 eggs, separated
4 tomatoes (or tomato puree)	bechamel sauce
3 teaspoons chopped parsley	a handful grated parmesan cheese
	melted shortening

Saute the meat and onions in the butter. Add wine, water, tomatoes, parsley, salt and pepper. Mix well and simmer, covered, for 1 hour. In the meantime, cut the eggplant in long, thin slices and saute in oil until golden brown. When the meat is cooked (with very little sauce remaining), mix in 3 to 4 teaspoons bread crumbs and egg whites. Sprinkle ovenproof dish with a few bread crumbs and put in a layer of eggplant, half the meat, a second layer of eggplant, the rest of the meat, and finish with a layer of eggplant. Cover with a bechamel sauce, enriched with the beaten egg yolks and some grated parmesan. Sprinkle top with remaining cheese and bread crumbs and dot with melted shortening. Bake in a slow 215° oven for ½ hour until lightly browned. May be frozen. Makes 4 to 6 servings.

MRS. MENELAS D. ALEXANDRAKIS, Wife of Ambassador (Greece)

GUATEMALA

ALMOND TART

½ pound peeled almonds	2 eggs
8 ounces water	4 egg yolks
1 pound sugar	

In a blender thoroughly blend almonds in water until very fine. Pour into large mixing bowl (preferably copper or steel) and add sugar. Cook, stirring constantly with wooden spoon until thick. The mixture will separate from bowl. Remove from fire and continue stirring until cool. Lightly beat the 2 eggs and 4 yolks and add to mixture until well blended. Turn into a greased flat Pyrex dish or other ovenware and bake at 300° for 20 minutes. When golden in color, remove and let cool at room temperature. Makes 8 servings.

MRS. JULIO ASENSIO-WUNDERLICH, Wife of Ambassador (Guatemala)

COCONUT FINGERS

1 coconut	speck of salt
some milk	1 tablespoon vanilla
3 cups sugar	

Open coconut and remove water. Put water in pan and add enough milk to complete 1½ cups of liquid. Add sugar and salt. Bring to boiling point and cook until a drop of liquid in cold water forms a ball. Cool. Add vanilla and beat until thick. Add well ground and thoroughly drained coconut meat. Beat and smooth with hands until well blended. Form long thin rolls. Place on greased flat surface and let cool. When cold, cut into small pieces and serve.

Mena Ade Asensio

MRS. JULIO ASENSIO-WUNDERLICH, Wife of Ambassador (Guatemala)

GUYANA

COCONUT MOUSSE

1 large coconut	½ ounce powdered gelatin
½ pint water	2 cups hot water
1 tin evaporated milk	food coloring (optional)
3 tablespoons sugar	chopped fruit or nuts

Remove skin from coconut and grate coconut meat. Add water to grated coconut and squeeze dry to extract the milk. Add undiluted evaporated milk and the sugar. Dissolve gelatin thoroughly in hot water and stir into the coconut milk mixture. Add coloring if desired and stir well. Pour into 1 large dish or small individual glasses. Place in refrigerator and allow to set. Decorate with chopped fruit or nuts. Makes 6 servings.

CARROT RICE

½ stick margarine	2 tablespoons soy sauce
1 large onion, finely chopped	3 cups cooked rice
2 cups diced carrots	3 tablespoons chopped spring onions
½ cup diced green peppers	sprigs of parsley
1 cube beef bouillon	

In a large pot, melt margarine and cook onions until tender. Add carrots and green peppers, and cook for 5 minutes. Add bouillon and soy sauce. Cook for 3 minutes longer on low heat. Add rice and mix in spring onions. Before serving, garnish with sprigs of parsley. Makes 8 servings.

SRTalbot

MRS. FREDERICK H. TALBOT, Wife of Ambassador (Guyana)

628

INDONESIA

SOTO AYAM MADURA

½ chicken (about 1½ pounds)
6 cups water
1 piece lemon grass (optional)
2 slices fresh ginger
salt to taste
3 cloves garlic
3 macadamia nuts
¾ teaspoon turmeric powder
½ teaspoon ground pepper
2 tablespoons vegetable oil

Garnishes:
⅓ cup cooked and drained Chinese
   vermicelli, cut in short pieces
¼ cup chopped celery
¼ cup chopped spring onion
2 hard cooked eggs, sliced
2 tablespoons fried onion flakes

Topping:
4 lemon slices (or ½ lemon)
1 cup potato chips

Place chicken with water in a pan with the lemon grass and ginger. Salt lightly. Bring to the boil and cook until the chicken is tender. Remove the chicken, drain and keep it aside. Pound the garlic and nuts to a smooth paste. Add the turmeric and pepper. Heat the oil in a saucepan and fry the garlic, nut, turmeric and pepper paste until it is light brown. Add this to the chicken stock. Add salt to taste and allow to simmer gently about 30 minutes. Cut the chicken meat into nice little cubes. Put chicken meat and all the garnishes in a deep serving bowl. Pour the hot soup on top of these. Squeeze lemon juice over all and sprinkle potato chips on top. Serve hot. Makes 4 servings.

PEANUT CRACKERS

1 cup rice flour
2 teaspoons ground coriander
garlic powder and salt to taste
1 egg

1 cup cold water
1 pound peanuts, shelled and cut
   in small pieces
vegetable oil

Sift rice flour and dry ingredients into a bowl. Make a well in center of flour, add egg and mix with water to a smooth batter. Add peanuts to the batter mixture. Drop by spoonful into medium heated vegetable oil and fry until brown. Makes 40 to 50 pieces.

Mrs. Roesmin Nurjadin, Wife of Ambassador (Indonesia)

IRAN

MEAT AND STRING BEAN PILO

3 cups long grain rice
2 medium onions, diced
¼ cup Mazola oil
1 pound frying steak, cubed
salt and pepper to taste

1 6 ounce can tomato sauce
2 cups water
1 pound string beans, cleaned and
   cut into ½ inch lengths
½ stick butter

Soak rice in 8 cups of salted tepid water for at least 3 hours. Fry the onions in oil until golden. Add cubed steak and fry together. Add salt, pepper, tomato sauce and water. Leave to simmer until half cooked. Add beans and continue cooking until water is absorbed and meat is tender.

In a big pot boil 8 cups of water. Add previously drained rice and boil until half cooked. Drain and rinse with water. Mix rice and meat mixture together. Butter a deep ovenproof dish and place rice mixture in it. Place remaining butter on top. Cover and bake in 350° oven for 1 hour. Turn back into a serving dish and serve with salad. Makes 6 to 8 servings.

PERSIAN PUDDING

1 cup wheat starch
3 to 3½ cups cold water
2 cups sugar
½ cup rose water

1½ sticks sweet butter
½ cup almond pieces
pistachios or walnuts

Mix starch with cold water until soft. Place over low heat and stir constantly until mixture thickens. Add the sugar, rose water, butter and almonds and continue cooking until mixture resembles thick cream. Remove from heat. Place mixture in individual serving dishes and cool in refrigerator. Decorate with crushed pistachios or walnuts. Makes 6 to 8 servings.

MRS. NASSER MAJD, Wife of Minister Counselor (Iran)

630

ISRAEL

STUFFED AVOCADO WITH WHITE FISH

1 pound cooked white fish
2 cups water
dash of salt
1 tablespoon lemon juice
16 cut black olives
1 heaping tablespoon mayonnaise
1 heaping tablespoon sour cream
1 grated fresh onion
¼ teaspoon salt

dash pepper
1 tablespoon chopped parsley
1 tablespoon each of thinly cubed
   pimiento, capers, diced pickled
   cucumbers, diced green pepper
4 avocados
8 lettuce leaves
8 orange segments

Cook the white fish for 15 minutes in the water to which has been added a dash of salt and the lemon juice. Cool. Cut fish into pieces, mix with all ingredients except the avocados, lettuce leaves and orange segments. Wash the avocados, cut into half lengthwise, remove pit. Fill avocado halves with firsh mixture. Line 8 plates with lettuce leaves. Place stuffed avocado on each and decorate with orange segment. Makes 8 servings.

Mrs. Simcha Dinitz

MRS. SIMCHA DINITZ, Wife of Ambassador (Israel)

ITALY

RICE "ALLA MILANESE"

½ pound butter
2 small onions, minced
3 cups rice
9 cups chicken broth

1 teaspoon saffron in 4 tablespoons
   of broth
8 tablespoons grated parmesan cheese

Melt half the butter in saucepan, add onion and brown. When brown, add rice and stir well until all the butter is absorbed. Add broth a little at a time. Do not let rice become too dry. Cook 40 to 45 minutes over low flame. Stir frequently. When done, add remaining butter and saffron and mix well. Sprinkle with parmesan cheese and serve. Makes 4 servings.

Giulia Ortona

MRS. EGIDIO ORTONA, Wife of former Ambassador (Italy)

631

JAPAN

CHAWAN-MUSHI (EGG CUSTARD)

4 eggs
3 cups cooled chicken broth
½ teaspoon soy sauce
salt to taste
12 thin slices boned white chicken meat (about ½ inch)

6 small cooked shrimp, shelled
3 medium mushrooms, sliced
3 water chestnuts (canned), sliced
¼ pound spinach, boiled

Put eggs in a bowl and beat well. Add cooled chicken broth, soy sauce and salt and mix well. In 6 Japanese Chawan-mushi cups arrange chicken, shrimp, sliced mushrooms, sliced water chestnuts and spinach attractively. These cups are a little larger than pudding cups. Pour the mixture of egg, chicken broth, soy sauce and salt in the cups. Place cups in a baking pan and cover each cup with aluminum foil. Pour hot water in the baking pan so that ⅓ of each cup is covered. Bake in a 425° oven for about 25 to 30 minutes. Serve hot. If a proper Chawan-mushi cup is used, serve covered with its lid. Makes 6 servings.

Note: If you use dried Japanese mushrooms, soak in water for 24 hours and remove stems. The Chawan-mushi cups may be available at some of the Japanese groceries or at Chinese gift shops.

YAKITORI (BARBECUED CHICKEN)

20 pieces boneless chicken, cut in 1 inch cubes
20 pieces spring onion, cut in 1 inch pieces

Yakitori Sauce:
½ cup soy sauce
⅓ cup sake (Japanese wine)
4 teaspoons sugar
2 teaspoons corn starch
cayenne pepper

Spit chicken and onion alternately on 5 inch metal skewers. Boil mixture of soy sauce, sake and sugar in a pot. Add corn starch, dissolved in water, to the mixture and boil once in order to give the sauce some thickness. Put oil on the surface of baking pan and place skewered chicken on it. Pour half of the sauce over the chicken and place the pan in the oven. Bake at 425° for about 13 to 15 minutes. Take the pan out of the oven and pour the rest of the sauce over the chicken. Sprinkle cayenne pepper over the chicken. Serve hot. Makes 5 servings.

Sueko Yasukawa

Mrs. Takeshi Yasukawa, Wife of Ambassador (Japan)

632

JORDAN

EGGPLANT DIP

2 large eggplants
½ cup tahini (sesame oil)
⅔ cup lemon juice
2 cloves garlic, crushed
1¼ teaspoons salt
cold water as needed
salt and pepper to taste

Optional:
olive oil
1 tablespoon chopped parsley
radishes
green onions

Make a few slits in the eggplants to allow the steam to escape. Bake or broil them until the skin becomes crisp and begins to crack. Scoop out the pulp and mash it thoroughly. Blend in the tahini, lemon juice, garlic and salt and continue beating. Stir in a little cold water if the mixture is too thick. Cold water, when added to tahini, will give it a whiter colour. More lemon juice or salt and pepper may be added if desired.

Serve this creamy dip in a deep bowl. If it is being served as a side dish to meat or fish, serve it in a shallow platter topped with olive oil and garnished with chopped parsley, radishes and green onions.

STUFFED VINE LEAVES

½ pound fresh vine leaves (or 1
   small jar preserved)
¾ cup uncooked rice
1 pound lamb, coarsely chopped and
   not too lean
1 teaspoon salt

½ teaspoon allspice
1 pound lamb cutlets
2 tablespoons butter
1 small can tomato sauce
water as needed
2 tablespoons lemon juice

Wash the vine leaves and soak them in cold water for 2 hours. Wash and drain the rice. Prepare the stuffing by combining the rice, chopped meat, salt and allspice. Line a cooking pot with the lamb cutlets. Place the vine leaves one at a time on a wooden board, coarse side up. Place a small portion of the filling lengthwise on the inner edge of the leaf. Roll half way. Fold in the 2 ends and continue rolling into a finger shaped roll. Place the rolls in layers in the cooking pot and press them down lightly with a plate to prevent them from loosening while cooking. Dot with butter and pour the tomato sauce mixed with water over the layers of vine leaves, enough to cover. Bring to a boil on high heat. Reduce the heat and simmer for 1½ to 2 hours or until the sauce is absorbed. Half an hour before the vine leaves are done, add the lemon juice. Unmold on a round platter and serve hot. May be frozen. Makes 4 to 6 servings.

Fadwa Salah

MRS. ABDULLAH SALAH, Wife of Ambassador (Jordan)

KOREA

BUL-KOGI (KOREAN BARBECUE)

1½ pounds tender beef
2½ tablespoons sugar
4 tablespoons soy sauce
4 teaspoons chopped garlic

4 tablespoons minced green onion
2 tablespoons ground sesame seed
2 tablespoons sesame seed oil
1 teaspoon black pepper

Cut beef in very thin slices, ⅛ inch x 3 inches. Mix with sugar and set in refrigerator. Mix rest of seasoning: soy sauce, garlic, onion, sesame seed, sesame seed oil and black pepper. Mix this with beef and broil over charcoal fire or fry in pan. Makes 4 servings.

Note: When meat of any kind is marinated for a long time in soy sauce, the meat hardens, so it is best to start cooking the meat as soon as it has been mixed with soy sauce.

Mrs. Pyong Choon Hahm

MRS. PYONG-CHOON HAHM, Wife of Ambassador (Korea)

LATVIA

HONEY LOAF (MEDUS KARASA)

2½ pounds flour
2 cakes compressed yeast
2 cups milk, warmed
¼ pound butter
¼ cup sugar
½ teaspoon salt

Topping:
½ pound honey
½ pound butter
½ pound nuts, chopped
2 eggs, whipped

Combine ¾ of flour with diluted yeast and warm milk combination. Mix well and allow to rise. Add butter, sugar and salt. Work dough well until it no longer sticks to hands or sides of saucepan. Form dough into round loaves, ½ inch thick. Let rise, using remainder of flour to cover dough.

Combine honey and butter in saucepan. Bring to boil and allow to cool. Add chopped nuts and whipped eggs. Mix well and spread over tops of the loaves. Bake at 350° to 375° for 25 to 30 minutes. May be frozen. Makes 2 dozen.

Latvians are very hospitable people and they find events such as marriages, christenings, confirmations, birthdays and even funerals, occasions for relatives and friends to gather from near and far. Name-days are also marked and friends do not need an invitation to join in the celebration. On these occasions, among other things, the Honey Loaf may be served.

Mrs. Anatol Dinbergs

MRS. ANATOL DINBERGS, Wife of Charge d'Affaires (Latvia)

LATVIA

ST. JOHN'S CHEESE (JANU SIERS)

3 quarts milk
3 pounds dry cottage cheese
½ quart buttermilk
½ stick butter, melted

1½ teaspoons salt
3 egg yolks, whipped
caraway seeds

Heat milk in large saucepan until it reaches boiling point, stirring continuously. Add cottage cheese (after it has been put through meat grinder), continuing to stir. When the mixture has coagulated and juices have separated, add buttermilk and cease stirring. Allow milk clot to settle at the bottom of saucepan. Drain off all excess juices by pouring cottage cheese mass through a sieve. Work quickly so that cottage cheese mass remains hot.

Place cottage cheese mass into a saucepan which contains melted butter. Keep mixing slowly. Add salt, whipped egg yolks and caraway seeds. Heat until cottage cheese mass is mixed evenly with the ingredients. Pour mass into damp cheesecloth which has been placed in large bowl. Gather ends of cheesecloth, forming a ball with the cottage cheese mass. Tie a string around the cheesecloth, forming a round cheese mold. Place a heavy object on top of the cheesecloth/cottage cheese mold. Serve in slices with butter or honey as topping.

St. John's Cheese is served during Janu Vakars (St. John's Eve), the midsummer festival, when work in the fields has been completed and the farmers are looking forward to a good harvest. This celebration goes back to Latvia's pre-Christian past, when St. John's Eve was Ligo Day, the festival of the fairy of flowers. Young and old gather at nightfall, their heads adorned with wreaths and carrying country flowers and other decorative greenery. They sit by bonfires, singing virtually endless Ligo songs and, of course, include eating and drinking in the merry-making.

Mrs. Anatol Dinbergs

Mrs. Anatol Dinbergs, Wife of Charge d'Affaires (Latvia)

LEBANON

CHICKEN AND RICE

1 chicken
1 cup coarsely ground lamb meat
⅓ cup pine nuts, lightly toasted
1 cup rice, washed and drained
salt
pepper

allspice
cinnamon
1 ounce butter, melted
2 cups hot chicken broth
½ cup roasted, slivered almonds

Boil chicken in water until tender. Remove chicken and reserve broth. Bone and cut up chicken and set aside, keeping it warm. Combine in a saucepan lightly browned meat, pine nuts, rice, salt and spices to taste; add melted butter and hot broth; cover and simmer for 20 minutes or until rice is tender. Add more broth if needed. To serve, mound rice on large platter, cover rice with pieces of boneless chicken meat and sprinkle with toasted almonds. Makes 4 servings.

TABOOLEH

1 cup fine burghul
2 large bunches of parsley
1 large onion (or 2 medium)
2 medium tomatoes
½ bunch mint (or 1 tablespoon crushed mint leaves)

juice of 2 lemons
½ cup olive oil
salt and pepper to taste
lettuce

Soak burghul until soft, about ½ hour. Chop parsley, onion, tomatoes and mint leaves very fine. Add well drained burghul. Add lemon juice and olive oil, season to taste and mix well. Serve surrounded with fresh lettuce leaves. Makes 6 servings.

Note: Burghul is crushed wheat and is available at Lebanese or Greek delicatessen stores.

Mrs. Najati Kabbani

MRS. NAJATI KABBANI, Wife of Ambassador (Lebanon)

636

MOROCCO

POULET "MQUALLI" AUX CITRONS CONFITS
(CHICKEN "MQUALLI" WITH PICKLED LEMONS)

2 chickens, approximately 3 pounds
    each
salt
¾ cup peanut oil
1 tablespoon olive oil
50 grams butter (about ½ stick)
1 very full teaspoon ginger
1 small whole onion

crushed garlic
½ teaspoon saffron
2 cups water
10 black olives (Greek Kalamata olives)
1 whole rind of pickled lemon, cut
    in quarters
chicken liver

Place the chickens, whole or cut, in a deep pan with the necks, wing tips and so forth. Add salt, oil, butter, ginger, onion, crushed garlic, saffron and water. Place on stove and bring to a boil. When it boils, stir to mix the spices and then reduce the heat and simmer. Check often for the amount of liquid in the pan, adding a bit of water if necessary. Turn the chickens over from time to time. Remove the onion as soon as it is cooked but keep it aside. When the chickens are tender, that is, if the meat can be picked off the bones between two fingers, add the olives and the lemon rind cut in pieces. Keep on simmering. Check the seasoning.

Take a chicken liver and the onion that has been set aside and puree together, either in a mixer or in a vegetable grinder. Mix this paste to the juice in the pan as soon as the chicken is removed. Bring to a boil and remove from the heat as soon as the sauce thickens. Serve the chicken pieces in a round dish covered with the lemon bits and olives. Pour the sauce over the chicken. Serve hot. Makes 6 to 8 servings.

نزيـهـة بوطـالـب

MRS. ABDELHADI BOUTALEB (TOURIA), Wife of Ambassador (Morocco)

NETHERLANDS

SAINT NICHOLAS CAKE

9 ounces butter
30 tablespoons confectioners sugar
12 eggs, separated
20 tablespoons enriched bleached
all purpose flour

2 teaspoons baking powder
10 teaspoons ground cinnamon
4 teaspoons ground nutmeg
5 teaspoons ground cloves
1 teaspoon ground cardamom

Beat together butter, sugar and egg yolks. Add flour and spices and then the beaten egg whites. Pour into mold and bake at 350° for 40 minutes.

Mrs. Age R. Tammenoms Bakker.

Madame A. R. Tammenoms Bakker, Wife of Ambassador (Netherlands)

NEW ZEALAND

PAVLOVA CAKE

4 egg whites
1 pinch salt
1 teaspoon corn starch
1 teaspoon vanilla essence

1 teaspoon white vinegar
1 cup fine sugar
whipped cream
fresh fruit

Beat egg whites and salt very stiffly with an electric beater. Add corn starch; beat a little. Then add vanilla essence, white vinegar and beat some more. Lastly, add sugar slowly and beat all gently until mixture is smooth. Do not beat too long.

Place a piece of buttered wax paper on a cold cookie sheet and spoon mixture onto the paper into a round shape like a cake. Preheat an electric oven to 350° but use a lower temperature for gas. Place pavlova in oven and leave the heat on for 5 minutes only. Then turn heat off completely but leave pavlova in oven for at least 2 hours.

Just before serving top the cake with fresh whipped cream, then fresh fruit such as peach slices, kiwi fruit or strawberries. Makes 8 servings.

Mrs. Lloyd White

MRS. LLOYD WHITE, Wife of Ambassador (New Zealand)

PAKISTAN

BORANI

2 pounds eggplant
vegetable oil
½ teaspoon paprika
½ teaspoon cummin powder

½ teaspoon garlic paste
1 teaspoon salt
1 pound yogurt

Slice eggplant into rounds ¼ inch thick. Fry eggplant golden brown. Remove from pan and place on absorbent paper. Mix all spices and salt and add to yogurt. Whisk lightly. Add eggplant to spiced yogurt and mix. Prepare at least 1 hour before serving. Makes 4 to 6 servings.

TANDOORI CHICKEN

1 medium size chicken
½ teaspoon ginger paste
½ teaspoon garlic paste
½ teaspoon paprika
½ cup yogurt
¼ teaspoon pepper

¼ teaspoon cinnamon powder
¼ teaspoon clove powder
1 teaspoon salt
1 teaspoon lemon juice
1 tablespoon vegetable oil

Remove skin and neck of chicken. Cut into 4 or 6 serving pieces. Mix all other ingredients. Make 2 slashes across each piece of chicken. Rub spices well into chicken and leave to marinate at least 4 hours. Broil chicken pieces under medium heat until cooked and golden brown. Best results are obtained by barbecuing on charcoal brazier. Serve immediately. May be frozen. Makes 4 servings.

Begum Yaqub-Khan

BEGUM YAQUB-KHAN, Wife of Ambassador (Pakistan)

PHILIPPINES

CHICKEN AND PORK ADOBO

2 chickens, cut into pieces
6 pork chops
1 cup vinegar
2 cups water
2 bay leaves
12 peppercorns

¼ cup soy sauce
3 cloves garlic
1 cup oil for frying
2 tablespoons flour
1 tablespoon salt

Clean the chicken and the pork chops and place in a 5 quart pan. Add vinegar, water, bay leaves, peppercorns, soy sauce and 1 clove garlic. Let stand for ½ hour. Boil this mixture for about ½ hour or until chicken and pork are tender. Remove chicken and pork from pan and fry in oil until golden brown. In a saucepan, fry the remaining garlic until brown. Add the flour and fry until brown. Place this mixture in the stock in which the chicken and pork were cooked so as to form a sauce. Add the golden brown chicken and pork chops. Boil for 5 minutes and add seasoning. Serve hot. May be frozen. Makes 6 servings.

FLOATING ISLAND

2 cups sugar
6 egg whites
½ cup chopped walnuts
1 teaspoon vanilla

Sauce:
1 cup milk
4 egg yolks
⅓ cup sugar
1 teaspoon vanilla

Caramelize 1 cup sugar. Pour into a round or rectangular mold. Move the caramelized sugar around so as to cover the whole area of the mold. Set aside. Beat the egg whites until stiff. Add the remaining sugar gradually. Continue beating for 3 minutes. Fold in the chopped walnuts, then add the vanilla. Pour this mixture into the caramelized mold. Place the mold in a 3 inch deep pan half filled with hot water and bake for 30 minutes at 250°. Unmold into a deep platter and pour the sauce around it. May be frozen. Makes 8 servings.

Sauce: Scald the milk. Mix the egg yolks and the sugar. Pour the scalded milk into the mixture of egg yolks and sugar. Keep stirring until well mixed. Cook over low flame for about 10 minutes or until thick. Finally add vanilla.

Mrs. Eduardo Z. Romualdez

Mrs. Eduardo Z. Romualdez, Wife of Ambassador (Philippines)

POLAND

HARE POLISH STYLE

1 saddle and thighs of hare
4 ounces bacon
salt
3 ounces shortening
2 tablespoons water
2 tablespoons flour
1 cup sour cream
caramel

Marinade:
4 ounces onion, sliced
1 bay leaf
peppercorns
juniper berries
2 cups cold water
1 cup vinegar

To prepare marinade, place onion, bay leaf, peppercorns and juniper berries in a pan with cold water. Boil for 2 to 5 minutes. Cool and add vinegar. Rinse the hare, place it in an enamel, glass or stoneware bowl. Pour the marinade over the hare. Cover the bowl and place it in a refrigerator for 2 to 3 days, turning daily. Rinse the hare again, trim and thread strips of bacon through the meat (hare is usually lean). Sprinkle with salt. In a roasting pan melt the shortening, place the hare in it, pour the melted shortening over, add water and place in hot oven, about 375°. Roast for about 2 hours until it is tender, basting often. From time to time add water as water evaporates easily in the oven. Remove from the oven, take the hare out, cut into large pieces and place them on a hot serving platter. Stir flour into the drippings, bring to a boil, stirring constantly. Add sour cream and caramel and stir. Pour the gravy over the slices of hare. Makes 6 to 8 servings.

Mrs. Witold Trampczyński

Mrs. Witold Trąmpczyński, Wife of Ambassador (Poland)

SHRIMP IN DILL SAUCE

2 carrots, pared
1 parsnip
2 celery sticks
1 bay leaf
5 whole allspice
5 peppercorns
½ gallon salted water
2 ounces cognac
1 pound medium raw shrimp

3 sticks butter or margarine
2 onions, very well chopped
3 cloves garlic, minced
3 tablespoons Worcestershire sauce
2 tablespoons soy sauce
1 teaspoon Tabasco
½ cup minced fresh dill
½ cup dairy sour cream

Cook carrots, parsnip, celery sticks, bay leaf, allspice and peppercorns covered in salted water in a large saucepan for 20 minutes. Add cognac. Put in washed and peeled shrimp, bring to a boil and cook for 3 minutes. Cool them a few minutes and drain.

Combine in a large frying pan 2 sticks of butter, onions and garlic. Heat slowly, stirring constantly and simmer about 1 hour. Add Worcestershire sauce, soy sauce and Tabasco and simmer another 5 minutes. Stir in remaining butter, minced fresh dill and cooked shrimp. Simmer 15 minutes longer. Add sour cream and warm it for another minute but do not let it boil. Makes 4 servings.

Mrs. Witold Trampczyński

MRS. WITOLD TRĄMPCZYŃSKI, Wife of Ambassador (Poland)

PORTUGAL

CHICKEN NOT IN A PUCARA

3 tomatoes, peeled, seeded and
  chopped
6 ounces smoked lean ham, thinly
  sliced and cut into about ½ inch
  squares
8 small boiling onions
1 tablespoon Dijon style mustard
1 large clove garlic, minced or mashed

6 tablespoons dry white wine
6 tablespoons light colored port
1 2½ pound frying chicken cut
  into serving pieces
salt and black pepper
4 tablespoons butter
6 tablespoons brandy

Combine tomatoes, ham, onions, mustard, garlic, white wine, and port in a shallow baking pan or casserole. Season chicken with salt and pepper and arrange in a single layer on top of tomato mixture. Dot with butter. Bake in a moderate 350° oven for 1 hour or until chicken is browned and tender. Sprinkle with brandy. Serve chicken with sauce spooned over it. Makes 4 servings.

Lydia Hall Themido

MRS. JOÃO HALL THEMIDO, Wife of Ambassador (Portugal)

GOLDEN COD

½ pound soaked, dried cod
water
1 large onion, very finely chopped
⅓ cup olive oil
1⅓ cups shoestring potatoes

6 eggs
½ teaspoon freshly ground
  black pepper
chopped fresh parsley

To prepare cod, soak in cold water for 24 to 48 hours until it is very moist throughout; change water 2 or 3 times; drain. Simmer cod, covered, in water just to cover for 15 minutes or until tender. Drain, remove skin and bones and coarsely flake. In a large frying pan, saute onion in olive oil until golden. Stir in cod and potatoes. Beat eggs with pepper, pour into cod and stir with a fork and cook over low heat just until ingredients are moistened and eggs are barely set. Eggs should still be soft and shiny. Sprinkle with parsley and serve immediately. Makes 4 servings.

Shoestring potatoes: Peel and slice about 2 potatoes into thin, matchlike pieces and fry in hot fat (375°) until crisp and golden brown.

MRS. JOÃO HALL THEMIDO, Wife of Ambassador (Portugal)

SWEDEN

STROMMING

smelts
salt and pepper
butter
parsley, minced

1 egg
bread crumbs
lemon

We use Baltic herring in Sweden but smelts could be used with almost the same result. Remove head and backbone and flatten the fish out. Sprinkle with salt and pepper. Put 2 boned smelts together with the skin out. Stuff each pair with butter and minced parsley. Dip the fish in beaten egg and bread crumbs and fry in butter until golden crisp. Garnish with lemon. Serve with cut potatoes either boiled in milk, deep fried or parslied and a tomato and mayonnaise salad.

COUNTESS WILHELM WACHTMEISTER, Wife of Ambassador (Sweden)

SEVEN CHEESE

7 kinds of cheese	cayenne
butter	black pepper
heavy cream	garlic powder
paprika	cognac

Take all the different kinds of cheese you have at home and get some more if necessary. I suggest Suisse cheese, edam, Chantilly, camembert, cheddar, roquefort and Philadelphia. Grate them and mix them in the blender with the butter, cream and seasoning. Add garlic powder and cognac. Mixture should be rather thick. Put the mixture in refrigerator trays and freeze. Arrange the cheese beautifully on a big plate with water cress, radish roses, pyramid of small butter balls, crackers and pumpernickel.

COUNTESS WILHELM WACHTMEISTER, Wife of Ambassador (Sweden)

SWITZERLAND

VEAL EMINCE

1 pound veal, without bone	chicken or beef broth (optional)
4 tablespoons butter	salt and pepper
1 small onion, finely chopped	heavy cream (optional)
1 to 2 tablespoons flour	sliced mushrooms (optional)
2/3 cup white wine	

Remove any skin or membrane from meat. With a sharp knife cut meat in fine slivers, approximately 1 inch in size. Heat the butter and add the meat and the onion. Turn until the meat begins to look white. Dust the flour over it and turn until flour is absorbed. Add the wine (which can be mixed with chicken or beef broth) and cook just 5 minutes. Season with salt and pepper. If desirable, some heavy cream can be added, bring to a quick boil and serve at once on a hot platter. Veal emince is cooked very fast and served promptly, otherwise the veal becomes tough. This veal can be "stretched" by adding fine sliced mushrooms to the meat.

MRS. FELIX SCHNYDER, Wife of former Ambassador (Switzerland)

CHRÄBELI

2 eggs
2 cups sugar
2 cups flour
2 tablespoons aniseeds

½ teaspoon baking powder (or, following the recipe exactly, salt of hartshorn)

Beat eggs and sugar together until frothy, mix in other ingredients and form into strips about 1 inch in thickness. Cut into 3 inch pieces, make 3 small cuts on one side and place them, slightly curved, on a floured baking sheet. Leave them in a warm room overnight. The next day bake them for about 25 minutes in a very moderate oven.

Mrs Felix Schnyder.

MRS. FELIX SCHNYDER, Wife of former Ambassador (Switzerland)

TURKEY

YAYLA CORBASI (ANATOLIAN HIGHLANDS SOUP)

½ cup raw rice
4 cups broth (beef or chicken)
1 egg
2 tablespoons flour
1 pint unflavored yogurt

6 tablespoons butter
salt and pepper to taste
3 tablespoons finely crushed, dried (or finely chopped fresh) mint leaves

Cook rice in 2 cups of the broth. Add the rest of the broth and keep at boiling temperature. In a mixing bowl mix and stir to a smooth consistency: the egg, flour and yogurt. To this mixture gradually add, 1 tablespoonful at a time, the butter, stirring constantly to prevent curdling. Add this mixture to the boiling rice and broth and cook over medium heat for about 2 minutes, still stirring constantly. Remove from heat, add salt and pepper to taste, garnish top with the mint leaves and serve immediately. This is a creamy soup with an unusual sourish flavor. Makes 6 servings.

Mrs. Melih Esenbel

MRS. MELIH ESENBEL, Wife of Ambassador (Turkey)

MEASURES

3 teaspoons = 1 tablespoon = ½ ounce

4 tablespoons = ¼ cup = 2 ounces

2 cups = 1 pint = 16 ounces

2 pints = 1 quart = 32 ounces

EQUIVALENTS

Butter

1 ounce = 2 tablespoons

¼ pound = 1 stick = ½ cup

2½ cups = 2 cups melted

Crumbs

1 slice fresh bread = ¾ cup soft crumbs

3 to 4 slices oven dried bread = 1 cup fine crumbs

15 graham crackers = 1 cup fine crumbs

20 saltines = 1 cup fine crumbs

Flour and Sugar

1 pound all purpose flour = 4 cups sifted

1 pound whole wheat flour = 3½ cups

1 pound brown sugar = 2¼ cups, packed

1 pound confectioners sugar = 3½ cups sifted

Fruits and Vegetables

1 lemon = 2 to 3 tablespoons juice, 1½ teaspoons grated rind

1 orange = 6 to 7 tablespoons juice, 2 teaspoons grated rind

1 pound fresh mushrooms = 6 to 8 ounces canned, 3 ounces dried

1 medium onion = ½ cup chopped

Milk, Cheese and Eggs

1 cup heavy cream = 2 cups whipped

1 pound cheddar cheese, grated = 4 cups

1 pound cottage cheese = 2 cups

½ pound cream cheese = 1 cup

8 to 10 egg whites = 1 cup

Pastas and Rice

1 cup macaroni uncooked = 2 cups cooked

1 cup noodles uncooked = 1¾ cups cooked

1 cup spaghetti uncooked = 2 cups cooked

1 cup rice uncooked = 3 to 3½ cups cooked

1 cup precooked rice = 2 cups cooked

SUBSTITUTIONS

1 teaspoon baking powder = ¼ teaspoon baking soda plus ½ teaspoon cream of tartar

1 ounce baking chocolate = 3 tablespoons cocoa plus 1 tablespoon shortening

1 tablespoon corn starch = 2 tablespoons flour

1 cup sifted cake flour = ⅞ cup sifted all purpose flour

1 tablespoon flour for thickening = ½ to ⅔ tablespoon corn starch, potato starch or arrowroot

1 small clove garlic = ⅛ teaspoon garlic powder

1 tablespoon finely cut fresh herbs = 1 teaspoon dried herbs

1 cup sour milk = 1 tablespoon lemon juice or vinegar plus sweet milk to make 1 cup

1 teaspoon dry mustard = 1 tablespoon prepared mustard

METRIC GUIDE

WEIGHT

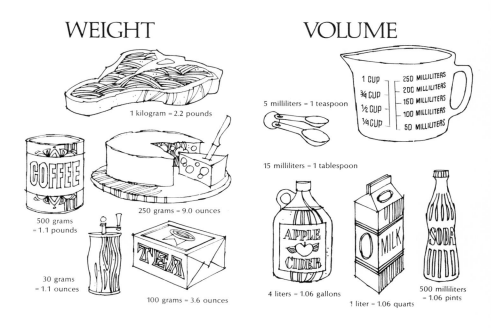

1 kilogram = 2.2 pounds

500 grams
= 1.1 pounds

250 grams = 9.0 ounces

30 grams
= 1.1 ounces

100 grams = 3.6 ounces

VOLUME

5 milliliters = 1 teaspoon

1 CUP — 250 MILLILITERS
¾ CUP — 200 MILLILITERS
½ CUP — 150 MILLILITERS
¼ CUP — 100 MILLILITERS
— 50 MILLILITERS

15 milliliters = 1 tablespoon

4 liters = 1.06 gallons

1 liter = 1.06 quarts

500 milliliters
= 1.06 pints

TEMPERATURE

Celsius		*Fahrenheit*
0°	Freezing point of water	32°
10°	A warm winter day	50°
20°	A mild spring day	60°
30°	Quite warm—almost hot	86°
37°	Normal body temperature	98.6°
40°	Heat wave conditions	104°
100°	Boiling point of water	212°

Greetings

from the

FORMER MEMBERS OF CONGRESS AUXILIARY

Our Objectives

PROMOTE GOOD GOVERNMENT

PRESERVE FRIENDSHIPS MADE DURING SERVICE IN THE UNITED STATES CONGRESS

SUPPORT THE FORMER MEMBERS OF CONGRESS IN RESEARCH AND EDUCATIONAL ACTIVITIES TO STRENGTHEN AND IMPROVE THE UNITED STATES CONGRESS AS AN INSTITUTION

We Invite

WIVES OF MEMBERS

of the

FORMER MEMBERS OF CONGRESS

and

WIDOWS

of

SENATORS AND REPRESENTATIVES TO JOIN WITH THE AUXILIARY IN THESE ENDEAVORS

ADVERTISEMENTS

649

What America's second-largest, world-wide airline can do for you:

Convertible 747C

If you travel, flying a charter on World Airways can let you vacation overseas for what it might cost you to vacation around the corner. Leave and arrive at your local jetport. Travel on roomy stretch DC-8's or 747C's.

Convertible stretch DC-8

If you're in the money, you can draw your own conclusions about a 28 year old international airline that's not only solvent but has $88 million in liquid assets out of total assets of $185 million.** We're listed on both the New York and Pacific Stock Exchanges. Write for our annual report.

If you ship, take advantage of World's expertise in getting the ordinary or the unusual to destinations around the world. If it's too much for a boxcar, and the boat's too slow, you may find that a full-plane charter on World is the most inexpensive way to get it there. All our planes are fully convertible from passenger to cargo. We can divide the cabin and fly equipment and passengers on the same plane.

Portable loader makes World's 747C independent of airport cargo facilities.

World Airways $14 million Maintenance and Engineering Center, Oakland, California.

If you're a competitor, we doubt if you'll find better service anywhere than you get at the $14 million World Airways Maintenance and Engineering Center. Fast turnaround. 24-hour quotes. 24-hour service. The capability to handle everything from paintjobs to retrofits and major overhauls. Whether you fly Convairs or 747's.

If you're looking ahead, count on World to find better ways to fly people and goods for less money. We had the first all-jet charter fleet. We pioneered the convertible 747. And, if the C.A.B. approves our request, we may be the first airline to jet you coast-to-coast for only $89.*

*Plus tax and nominal security surcharge. Request filed April 3, 1975.
**Assets as of June 30, 1975.

World Airways/Showing the way.

A U.S. Certificated Supplemental Carrier. Member National Air Carrier Association.
World Airways Sales Offices: Atlanta (404) 233-6705, Boston (617) 357-9080, Chicago (312) 467-6244, Denver (303) 573-6402, Detroit (313) 557-4400, Houston (713) 621-8292, Los Angeles (213) 990-5720, New York (212) 757-4207, Oakland/San Francisco (415) 562-8000, Philadelphia (215) 563-8397, Seattle (206) 682-3520, Toronto (416) 364-5131, Washington, D.C. (202) 298-7155.

652

*This engaging Giant Panda with its favorite meal, bamboo, was
inspired by the journey of Mrs. Edward Marshall Boehm and her colleagues
to the People's Republic of China in December 1974.
Limited to an issue of 100, 13½" H x 9½" W x 9" D.*

*For list of appointed agents and color brochures,
write Edward Marshall Boehm, Inc., P.O. Box 5051, Trenton, NJ 08638*

Find Washington in this picture

On a clear night, eastern United States looks like this from 450 miles up.

The image was taken from a weather satellite with Westinghouse sensor and display equipment. Bright spots are lights from metropolitan areas.

Without electricity, this picture wouldn't be possible . . . and neither

would much of anything else in factories, offices, homes, schools and hospitals.

 **Westinghouse**

Sunkist®

FOR THE BEST CITRUS

BRISTOL-MYERS COMPANY
Leaders in health, nutrition and personal care products.

Frank Bite Appetizers

⅓ cup cornstarch
¼ cup brown sugar
½ teaspoon salt
1½ cups (13 ¼ oz. can) pineapple chunks
1½ cups (12 oz.) 7UP, The Uncola
½ cup cider vinegar
1 tablespoon prepared mustard
1 package (1 lb.) frankfurters

Combine cornstarch, brown sugar and salt in large saucepan. Drain pineapple. Stir pineapple liquid, 7UP, vinegar and mustard gradually into cornstarch mixture. Cook and stir over medium heat until boiling and thickened. Cut frankfurters into bite-size pieces and add with pineapple to sauce. Cook 10 minutes longer. Stir occasionally. Serve hot. 12-15 servings.

7UP The Uncola

People all over the world talk the same language about the DC-10: "I like it."

Frankfurt...
"Ein phantastisches
Flugzeug."

Copenhagen...
"Den er skøn."

Dakar...
"J'adore."

New York...
"I like it."

Tokyo...
好きですね

If you've already enjoyed flying on a DC-10, you've shared a pleasant experience with millions of other people. Each day, more than 95,000 travelers fly a DC-10 to more than 140 cities in 67 countries. In many languages, they say they like the spacious, quiet comfort of the DC-10. So, ask your favorite airline or travel agent to book you aboard the DC-10.

DC-10: the choice of 34 airlines

MCDONNELL DOUGLAS

THE WORLD NEEDS TO TALK THINGS OVER.

OUR COMMUNICATIONS SATELLITES
ARE BRINGING THE PEOPLES OF
THE WORLD CLOSER TOGETHER.

HUGHES
HUGHES AIRCRAFT COMPANY

A touch of embossed.

Why can't today's women resist the "touch-me" appeal of USS embossed steel?

Maybe because they know rich texture is always high fashion. To them, embossed is chic. Classic. Expensive-looking.

Or maybe it's because embossed looks like fun. Its warm informality helps give kitchens a family-room feeling.

Or maybe it's simply that embossed steel is the first really new appliance surface in years.

The non-glare surface resists perceptible marring. It hides fingermarks, too, and it's a breeze to clean.

Look for embossed steel in your next refrigerator or other major appliance.

 United States Steel

TRADEMARK

660

GE TAKES THE GUESSWORK OUT OF MICROWAVE COOKING

MODEL JET 90

NEW Automatic Chef Cooking Control!

Now you get delicious cooking at microwave speed automatically

- **NO POT WATCHING . . . NO OVERCOOKING . . . NO GUESSWORK**

  The JET 90 has a temperature sensor that measures the internal temperature of foods . . . no need to turn the dish or the food. Automatic temperature cooking is completely carefree. When the food reaches the desired serving temperature, the oven automatically turns off and signals that the food is ready.

- **3 POWER LEVELS FOR BETTER COOKING**

- **BIG CAPACITY 1.3 CUBIC FT.**

- **60 MIN. DIGITAL TIMER**

- **ROLLING DRUM RECIPE GUIDE**

GENERAL  ELECTRIC

661

... to every man his chance,
to every man,
regardless of his birth,
his shining golden opportunity —
to every man the right to live, to work,
to be himself,
and to become whatever thing
his manhood and his vision
can combine to make him —
this seeker,
is this promise
of America.

THOMAS WOLFE

Published as a Bicentennial tribute by
GROCERY MANUFACTURERS OF AMERICA, INC.

GIANT

THE QUALITY FOOD PEOPLE

a bicentennial message

Our Bicentennial year comes in a time of troubles. And recalling the American Revolution, we are likely to reflect, "there were heroes in those days!"

Yet ponder these words :

"We have not men fit for the times. We are deficient in genius ... in fortune, in everything. I feel inutterable anxiety. God grant us wisdom and fortitude."

John Adams wrote these words one year before he signed the Declaration of Independence.

There is a message to learn from the Revolution: The future is now and belongs to those who believe passionately in principle and are willing to act for it.

In our democracy, this is both the right and the obligation of every citizen. It is the only road to a happy, free and secure tommorow. This we dare not forget.

(To 23,000,000 people we're the telephone company)
We get people talking.

(Sylvania color TV and stereo)
We entertain them.

(Sylvania lighting for home, industry and photography)
We brighten their lives a bit.

We're GTE.....
(a growing concern for your growing needs)

●General Telephone & Electronics, One Stamford Forum, Stamford, Conn. 06904

Bacardi rum cake.
Simply delicious.
And deliciously simple.

BACARDI® rum cake

Bake a cake that's been getting raves in homes all over America.

Cake:
  1 cup chopped pecans or walnuts
  1 18½-oz. pkg. yellow cake mix
  1 3¾-oz. pkg. instant vanilla pudding mix
  4 eggs
  ½ cup cold water
  ½ cup Wesson® oil
  ½ cup Bacardi dark rum

Glaze:
  ¼ lb. butter
  ¼ cup water
  1 cup granulated sugar
  ½ cup Bacardi dark rum

Preheat oven to 325°F. Grease and flour 10-inch tube or 12-cup Bundt® pan. Sprinkle nuts over bottom of pan. Mix all cake ingredients together.

Pour batter over nuts in pan. Bake one hour. Set on rack to cool. Invert on serving plate. Prick top. Drizzle and brush glaze evenly over top and sides.

For glaze, melt butter in saucepan. Stir in water and sugar. Boil 5 minutes, stirring constantly. Stir in rum.

Optional: Decorate with whole maraschino cherries and border of sugar frosting or whipped cream. Serve with seedless green grapes dusted with powdered sugar.

For a free Bacardi party booklet of recipes for entrées, hors d'oeuvres, snacks, drinks and punches, write to: Bacardi Imports, Inc., Dept. C, Bacardi Bldg., Miami, FL. 33137.

BACARDI® rum.The mixable one.

© 1975 BACARDI IMPORTS, INC., MIAMI, FL. RUM 80 PROOF.
"BACARDI" AND THE BAT DEVICE ARE REGISTERED TRADEMARKS OF BACARDI & COMPANY LIMITED.
WESSON IS A REGISTERED TRADEMARK OF HUNT-WESSON FOODS, INC.

We Put It All Together!

667

668

No deposit.
Many returns.

Some people believe one-way beverage containers play a major role in our nation's problems of solid waste disposal, energy shortages and litter. Make everyone use returnable bottles and cans, they say, and these problems will be minimized.

We believe in returnable packaging too. But not via the old-fashioned deposit system. We think there's a better way—resource recovery.

Either system—the one using returnable (deposit) containers or the one using no deposit containers returnable through resource recovery—will cost hundreds of millions of dollars and will take several years to implement. The real question is which system will do the best job.

Through resource recovery, we can reclaim from the refuse of our cities vast quantities of reusable materials—steel, aluminum, paper, glass, even a fuel. At the same time, we can solve some of the problems a deposit system *can't* solve.

● *Solid waste disposal*. Not just cans and bottles, but *all* packaging represents less than one-third of municipal solid waste. Banning one-way bottles and cans would have little effect on the overall problem. Resource recovery, on the other hand, would re-use almost *all* municipal solid waste—even the two-thirds that *isn't* packaging.

● *Energy shortages*. Proponents of deposit legislation say their laws will conserve the energy that would otherwise go into making new cans and bottles. But resource recovery would, too. A beer can made from recovered steel requires 75% less energy than one made from virgin raw materials. And resource recovery helps *produce* energy by creating a new fuel source for power plants.

● *Litter*. Thoughtless people cause litter, and resource recovery won't change their behavior. But a deposit system probably won't either.

American Can has a practical resource recovery system called Americology. We're building an Americology plant right now in Milwaukee. It will process *all* of Milwaukee's municipal refuse, recover valuable materials and produce a low-sulfur fuel for local power companies. If you'd like to know more, write: Americology, American Can Company, American Lane, Greenwich, CT 06830.

AMERICAN
CAN COMPANY

AEROJET - GENERAL CORPORATION

1120 CONNECTICUT AVENUE   WASHINGTON, D.C. 20036

HERSHEY'S ®

The great American chocolate bar.
Plain or with almonds.

Hershey Foods Corporation
® Hershey Chocolate & Confectionery Division
Hershey, Pa. 17033, U.S.A.

HERSHEY ESTATES

Cocoa Butter Soap

The world's finest cocoa butter soap, made from all
vegetable oil. Mixture contains 75% pure cocoa butter.
Delicately scented with Fougere perfume, this gentle
soap gives rich, velvety lather in any type of water.
Normalizes both dry and oily skin.

For additional information and/or orders contact:

Hershey Estates Soap Division
Hershey, Pa. 17033
Phone 717-534-3480

671

At the 1909 Syracuse County Fair, Mr. Willard Hadlock (A) became so incensed when the blueberry pie baked by his wife (B) did not win first prize that he hurled the pie at Judge Klugman (C) who ducked, thereby causing the pie to hit Mrs. Emma Eberhart (D) who was sneaking a cigarette at the time, putting out said cigarette, and thus proving to all the men that justice prevails.

You've come a long way, baby.

VIRGINIA SLIMS

Slimmer than the fat cigarettes men smoke.

17 mg.''tar,'' 1.0 mg. nicotine
av. per cigarette, FTC Report Nov.'75

672

WHAT CAN CHANGE A FIGHT FOR LIFE INTO A LIFE SAVING FLIGHT?

Becky Sharp has had a serious accident. And only one thing can save her life. An emergency operation in a hospital on the other side of the frozen mountains.

Alpine Air Charter's Flight for Life jet ambulance can get her to help in time. Because of an exclusive anti-icing fuel additive that prevents fuel lines from freezing–PFA 55MB·E.

This anti-icer works so well

Phillips' exclusive PFA 55MB·E additive prevents icing and microbial growth in this jet's fuel system.

that the FAA requires today's lighter weight jets to use it – eliminating bulky fuel system heaters that add weight and make longer runways necessary.

And who first developed this invaluable anti-icer?

The same company that makes fine products for your car. The Phillips Petroleum Company. Surprised?

The Performance Company

Rockwell International

...where science gets down to business

Santa Fe

107 year partnership
in the nation's
200 years of progress

Super C—the world's fastest freight
train salutes the nation's Bicentennial
with special diesel paint designs, speeding
freight by piggy-back and container,
Chicago—Southern California in just 40 hours.

The Atchison, Topeka and  Santa Fe
RAILWAY COMPANY

A Santa Fe Industries Company

65 SALES OFFICES COAST-TO-COAST, HAWAII, MEXICO AND TOKYO

674

The magic word is...

COMMUNICATION

The 26 basic editions of Reader's Digest are published in 13 languages and appear in more than 170 countries. They have a total circulation of 30 million copies monthly and are read by more than 100 million people around the world. The Digest deals with every aspect of life. It informs, it entertains, it teaches. It also "crusades" for the improvement of man's environment, for the uplift of his spirit, and for the preservation of his mental and physical health.

Cornucopia à la Truck

Ingredients

A generous handful of America's 11,000,000 trucks: large, small,
refrigerated, livestock, produce, and many more.

All the foods from the four corners of the globe,
from caviar to carrots, from canned peas to fresh eggs.

Mix Well

to form the most efficient food distribution network the world
has ever known. Then, amid the abundance of
your corner supermarket, try to choose what your family
might like best for today's lunch.

American Trucking Associations
1616 P Street, N.W., Washington, D.C. 20036

Better service. That's what trucks are driving for.

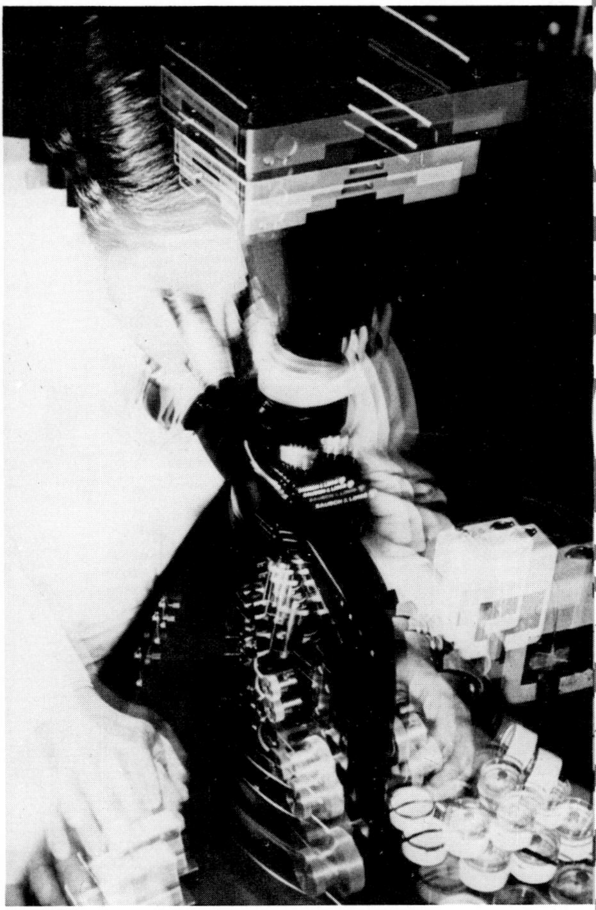

JOHNS-MANVILLE

RESEARCH WILL SHAPE THE NEXT 100 YEARS

First comes an idea . . . a spark of the imagination. Then the slow, hard process of fact-finding, testing, analyzing.

Research . . . where the future begins . . . where products which will serve man as tools to piece together the future are created and developed.

At Johns-Manville, the research function is at the root of our success. We've just constructed a new Research and Development Center in Colorado that offers us the technological advantages to get ready for tomorrow.

JM

Johns-Manville

JOHNS-MANVILLE IS IN YOUR FUTURE MAKING TODAY'S IDEAS WORK FOR YOUR TOMORROW

Only one U.S. airline can take you to all these places.

Europe
Asia
Africa
Australia
South America
North America

It doesn't look like much of a list. But where else can you go?

So choosing an airline for your trip abroad should be a very simple task.

Because not only can we take you to any of 96 cities in 65 countries on 6 continents, we can probably take you when it's most convenient.

(Just about every two minutes, somewhere in the world, a Pan Am jet is either taking off or landing.)

So next time you're plan-

See your Travel Agent.

ning to get out into the world, ask your travel agent to put you on Pan Am.

The only U.S. airline that flies to all of it.

680

R.J.Reynolds Industries, Inc.

This year R. J. Reynolds Industries, Inc. is celebrating the 100th anniversary of the business founded by Richard Joshua Reynolds in 1875.

From its beginnings as a single-product tobacco firm, the company has grown into a remarkably diverse, worldwide corporation with more than 32,000 employees and 1974 sales and revenues of $4.5 billion. One-third of the corporation's employees live outside the United States, and one-third of its revenue is generated abroad.

RJR's tobacco subsidiary is the nation's largest domestic manufacturer of cigarettes and other tobacco products, and its famous cigarette brands are sold internationally in more than 140 countries.

Many of these countries are also served by RJR's containerized freight transportation company, whose fleet of modern ships and special containers provide the fastest service of its kind in the world.

The corporation's international petroleum company produces and refines oil for sale to other oil companies, and is actively exploring for new oil and natural gas sources in the United States and overseas.

Supermarkets across the nation and in Canada carry convenience food products and beverages produced by RJR's food subsidiary.

And another RJR company makes a wide variety of aluminum products, packaging materials, gift wrap, bows and ribbons, and protective film wrap.

Reynolds Industries' worldwide operations are directed from its Winston-Salem, North Carolina, headquarters, just a few blocks from the spot where the company's founder started his tobacco business a century ago.

R. J. Reynolds Tobacco Company
Sea-Land Service, Inc.
American Independent Oil Company (Aminoil)
RJR Foods, Inc.
RJR Archer, Inc.

INDEX TO CONTRIBUTORS

Bradley, Mrs. Fred, Wife of former Representative (Michigan) 106, 128, 229, 442

Breeding, Mrs. J. Floyd, Wife of former Representative (Kansas) 112, 280, 318

Briscoe, Mrs. Dolph, Wife of Governor (Texas) 450

Brock, Mrs. Bill, Wife of Senator (Tennessee) 313, 343

Brooks, Mrs. Jack, Wife of Representative (Texas) 127, 160, 269, 442

Broomfield, Mrs. William S., Wife of Representative (Michigan) 163, 367, 392, 420

Brophy, Mrs. John C., Wife of former Representative (Wisconsin) 38, 533

Brotzman, Mrs. Donald G., Wife of former Representative (Colorado) 28, 346

Brown, Mrs. Clarence J., Wife of Representative (Ohio) 263, 372, 375, 539

Broyhill, Mrs. James Thomas, Wife of Representative (North Carolina) 269, 428, 545

Budge, Mrs. Hamer H., Wife of former Representative (Idaho) 125, 140, 572

Burgener, Mrs. Clair W., Wife of Representative (California) 137, 141, 525

Burke, Mrs. James A., Wife of Representative (Massachusetts) 39, 224, 461, 544

Burleson, Mrs. Omar, Wife of Representative (Texas) 78, 117, 406, 491

Burlison, Mrs. Bill, Wife of Representative (Missouri) 72, 325, 548

Burnside, Mrs. Maurice G., Wife of former Representative (West Virginia) 132, 186, 337

Burton, Mrs. Phillip, Wife of Representative (California) 299, 499

Busbee, Mrs. George, Wife of Governor (Georgia) 339, 399

Busbey, Mrs. Fred E., Wife of former Representative (Illinois) 8, 138, 218, 311

Bush, Mrs. George, Wife of former Representative (Texas), presently Director, Central Intelligence Agency, 301

Butz, Mrs. Earl Lauer, Wife of Secretary of Agriculture (Indiana) 107, 307, 426, 483

Buzick, Mrs. Lon M., Member of Congressional Club (Kansas) 198, 233, 454, 560

Byrne, Mrs. Brendan T., Wife of Governor (New Jersey) 224, 322

Byrnes, Mrs. John W., Wife of former Representative (Wisconsin) 15, 48, 115, 478

Byron, Mrs. Goodloe, Wife of Representative (Maryland) 29, 51, 170, 318

C

Cannon, Mrs. Howard W., Wife of Senator (Nevada) 158, 252, 368, 520

Carrigg, Mrs. Joseph L., Wife of former Representative (Pennsylvania) 97, 294, 496

Carroll, Mrs. Julian, Wife of Governor (Kentucky) 335, 532

Carter, Mrs. Tim Lee, Wife of Representative (Kentucky) 74, 110, 274, 539

Casey, Mrs. Bob, Wife of Representative (Texas) 99, 143, 230, 236

Castro, Mrs. Raul H., Wife of Governor (Arizona) 11, 435

Cederberg, Mrs. Elford A., Wife of Representative (Michigan) 22, 235, 515

Chenoweth, Mrs. J. Edgar, Wife of former Representative (Colorado) 100, 172, 421

Church, Mrs. Frank, Wife of Senator (Idaho) 215, 307

Clawson, Mrs. Del M., Wife of Representative (California) 421, 434

Clements, Mary Park, Daughter of former Representative Judson C. Clements (Georgia) 541

Cochran, Jill Teague, Daughter of Representative Olin E. Teague (Texas) 176

Cole, Mrs. Sterling, Wife of former Representative (New York) 114, 524

Cole, Mrs. Thomas E., Daughter-in-law of former Representative Sterling Cole (New York) 64, 130, 202

Collins, Mrs. James M., Wife of Representative (Texas) 59, 253

Conlan, Mrs. John B., Wife of Representative (Arizona) 62, 260, 378, 463

Cowing, Mrs. Amy Gronna, Daughter of former Senator A. J. Gronna (North Dakota) 196, 198, 305, 456

Cross, Mrs. John S., Daughter of former Representative Claude A. Fuller (Arkansas) 365, 479, 507, 553

Curtin, Mrs. Willard S., Wife of former Representative (Pennsylvania) 7, 135, 156

Curtis, Mrs. Carl T., Wife of Senator (Nebraska) 406, 444, 469, 473

G

Garn, Mrs. Jake, Wife of Senator (Utah) 329, 381, 518

Gathings, Mrs. E. C., Wife of former Representative (Arkansas) 88, 111, 180, 201

Gettys, Mrs. Tom S., Wife of former Representative (South Carolina) 80, 90, 465

Giaimo, Mrs. Robert N., Wife of Representative (Connecticut) 58, 64, 411, 473

Gibbons, Mrs. Sam M., Wife of Representative (Florida) 98, 476

Godwin, Mrs. Mills E., Jr., Wife of Governor (Virginia) 181, 282

Goldwater, Mrs. Barry M., Wife of Senator (Arizona) 96, 295

Goldwater, Mrs. Barry M., Jr., Wife of Representative (California) 355, 468

Grant, Alicia, Daughter of former Representative George M. Grant (Alabama) 53, 56, 93, 430

Grant, Mrs. George M., Wife of former Representative (Alabama) 41, 383, 484, 557

Grant, Mrs. George, Jr., Daughter-in-law of former Representative George M. Grant (Alabama) 11

Grant, Mrs. Robert A., Wife of former Representative (Indiana) 69, 200, 296, 470

Grasso, Ella, Governor (Connecticut) 353, 447

Guyer, Mrs. Tennyson, Wife of Representative (Ohio) 271, 512, 521, 528

H

Hagan, Mrs. G. Elliott, Wife of former Representative (Georgia) 134, 262, 450

Hagan, Mrs. Harold C., Wife of former Representative (Minnesota) 8, 239, 522

Hagen, Mrs. Harlan, Wife of former Representative (California) 436, 518

Hall, Mrs. Durward G., Wife of former Representative (Missouri) 50, 202, 332

Hammond, Mrs. Jay S., Wife of Governor (Alaska) 214, 410

Hansen, Mrs. George, Wife of Representative (Idaho) 328, 337, 484, 485

Harrison, Mrs. William Henry, Wife of former Representative (Wyoming) 14, 32, 369

Harrison, Mrs. William Henry, Jr., Daughter-in-law of former Representative William Henry Harrison (Wyoming) 562

Harsha, Mrs. William H., Wife of Representative (Ohio) 323, 333, 400

Harvey, Mrs. James, Wife of former Representative (Michigan) 129, 367, 471

Harvey, Mrs. Ralph, Wife of former Representative (Indiana) 31, 384, 433

Hatfield, Mrs. Mark O., Wife of Senator (Oregon) 6, 325

Hefner, Mrs. W. G. (Bill), Wife of Representative (North Carolina) 292, 302, 531

Henderson, Mrs. David N., Wife of Representative (North Carolina) 65, 182, 360

Henderson, Mrs. John E., Wife of former Representative (Ohio) 66, 286, 383

Herbert, Mrs. Joseph A., Jr., Daughter of former Senator A. J. Gronna (North Dakota) 368, 487

Herlong, Mrs. A. Sydney, Jr., Wife of former Representative (Florida) 113, 127, 185

Hernandez-Colon, Mrs. Lila M. de, Wife of Governor (Puerto Rico) 506

Herschler, Mrs. Ed, Wife of Governor (Wyoming) 453

Hodgson, Mrs. James Day, Wife of former Secretary of Labor, presently Ambassador to Japan (California) 212, 500, 502, 505

Holman, Mrs. Rufus C., Wife of former Senator (Oregon) 51, 192, 343

Holshouser, Mrs. James E., Jr., Wife of Governor (North Carolina) 194, 248

Horan, Mrs. Walt, Wife of former Representative (Washington) 76, 468

Hornthal, Mrs. Henry Amiss, Daughter of former Representative R. Thomas Hall (North Dakota) 89, 155, 502

Hosmer, Mrs. Craig, Wife of former Representative (California) 102, 199, 472, 491

Howard, Mrs. James J., Wife of Representative (New Jersey) 106, 265, 332, 519

Howell, Mrs. Evan, Wife of former Representative (Illinois) 108, 289, 425, 464

Hubbard, Mrs. Carroll, Wife of Representative (Kentucky) 109, 185, 390

Huber, Mrs. Robert J., Wife of former Representative (Michigan) 12, 34, 556

Huddleston, Mrs. Walter D., Wife of Senator (Kentucky) 103, 122, 180

Humphrey, Mrs. Hubert H., Wife of former Vice President of the United States, presently Senator (Minnesota) 37, 246, 531

Hungate, Mrs. William L., Wife of Representative (Missouri) 257, 287, 483, 569

Hutchinson, Mrs. Edward, Wife of Representative (Michigan) 293, 477, 517, 547

I

Ichord, Mrs. Richard H., Wife of Representative (Missouri) 99, 215, 329, 412

J

James, Mrs. Benjamin F., Wife of former Representative (Pennsylvania) 18, 175, 358

Jenison, Mrs. Edward H., Wife of former Representative (Illinois) 91, 235, 365, 491

Johnson, Mrs. Harold T., Wife of Representative (California) 159, 190, 309, 430

Johnson, Mrs. James P., Wife of Representative (Colorado) 145, 272

Johnson, Mrs. Lyndon B., Wife of former President of the United States (Texas) 3, 234, 480, 567

Jonas, Mrs. Charles Raper, Wife of former Representative (North Carolina) 21, 86, 173, 559

Jones, Mrs. Ed, Wife of Representative (Tennessee) 345, 523

Jones, Mrs. Robert E., Wife of Representative (Alabama) 29, 142, 194, 400

Jones, Mrs. Walter B., Wife of Representative (North Carolina) 264, 273, 526, 537

Jordan, Mrs. B. Everett, Wife of former Senator (North Carolina) 36, 367

Judge, Mrs. Thomas L., Wife of Governor (Montana) 12, 23

K

Karsten, Mrs. Frank M., Wife of former Representative (Missouri) 225, 527

Kearns, Mrs. Carroll D., Wife of former Representative (Pennsylvania) 57, 168, 190, 515

Kelly, Mrs. Richard, Wife of Representative (Florida) 141, 188, 362, 440

Kemp, Mrs. Jack F., Wife of Representative (New York) 337, 433, 493, 497

Kilday, Mrs. Paul, Wife of former Representative (Texas) 19, 76, 195, 251

King, Mrs. Cyril E., Wife of Governor (Virgin Islands) 382, 448

King, Mrs. David S., Wife of former Representative (Utah) 288, 376, 435, 568

Kleppe, Mrs. Thomas S., Wife of former Representative (North Dakota), presently Secretary of the Interior, 17, 176, 321, 471

Kneip, Mrs. Richard F., Wife of Governor (South Dakota) 280, 514

Kornegay, Mrs. Horace R., Wife of former Representative (North Carolina) 129, 134, 443, 549

Kunkel, Mrs. John C., Wife of former Representative (Pennsylvania) 99, 247, 401

Kyl, Mrs. John, Wife of former Representative (Iowa) 144, 173, 253, 474

L

Lagomarsino, Mrs. Robert J., Wife of Representative (California) 80, 111, 161, 315

Laird, Mrs. Melvin, Wife of former Representative (Wisconsin) 22

Lamm, Mrs. Richard D., Wife of Governor (Colorado) 328, 526

Landrum, Mrs. Phil M. Wife of Representative (Georgia) 152, 249, 436, 495

Langen, Mrs. Odin, Wife of former Representative (Minnesota) 311, 357, 530, 570

Leavy, Mrs. Charles H., Wife of former Representative (Washington) 40, 105, 535, 540

Lemke, Mrs. Robert M., Daughter-in-law of former Representative Wiliam Lemke (North Dakota) 11, 166, 276, 538

Levi, Mrs. Edward, Wife of Attorney General (Illinois) 279

Link, Mrs. Arthur A., Wife of Governor (North Dakota) 291, 529

Lipscomb, Mrs. Glenard P., Wife of former Representative (California) 25, 170, 571

Litton, Mrs. Jerry, Wife of Representative (Missouri) 301, 303, 319, 431

Long, Mrs. Clarence D., Wife of Representative (Maryland) 8, 66, 207, 342

Long, Mrs. Edward V., Wife of former Senator (Missouri) 248, 314, 407, 429

Long, Mrs. Russell B., Wife of Senator (Louisiana) 226, 231

Longley, Mrs. James B., Wife of Governor (Maine) 223, 359

M

Mack, Mrs. Russell V., Wife of former Representative (Washington) 151, 302, 384, 547

Mackie, Mrs. John Currie, Wife of former Representative (Michigan) 35, 79, 335

Magnuson, Mrs. Warren G., Wife of Senator (Washington) 96, 119, 207, 543

Mandel, Mrs. Marvin, Wife of Governor (Maryland) 52

Mann, Mrs. James R., Wife of Representative (South Carolina) 73, 187, 288, 536

Marshall, Mrs. Thurgood, Wife of Associate Justice, Supreme Court (Virginia) 147

Mathews, Mrs. Patrick H., Daughter of former Representative C. A. Fuller (Arkansas) 195, 317, 446

Mathis, Mrs. Dawson, Wife of Representative (Georgia) 437

Matsunaga, Mrs. Spark, Wife of Representative (Hawaii) 91, 261, 534, 545

Matthews, Mrs. D. R., Wife of former Representative (Florida) 38, 190, 201

Mayne, Mrs. Wiley, Wife of former Representative (Iowa) 63, 87, 100, 183

Mazzoli, Mrs. Romano L., Wife of Representative (Kentucky) 316, 495

McClory, Mrs. Robert, Wife of Representative (Illinois) 35, 61, 510

McClure, Mrs. James A., Wife of Senator (Idaho) 196, 203, 516, 532

McCollister, Mrs. John Y., Wife of Representative (Nebraska) 36, 40, 87, 146

McCormack, Mrs. Mike, Wife of Representative (Washington) 48, 160, 479, 561

McIntire, Mrs. Clifford, Wife of former Representative (Maine) 130, 275, 441

McMillan, Mrs. John L., Wife of former Representative (South Carolina) 74, 220, 467

McMillan, Mrs. John L., Jr., Daughter-in-law of former Representative John L. McMillan (South Carolina) 124, 188

Metcalf, Mrs. Lee, Wife of Senator (Montana) 227, 240, 378, 386

Michel, Mrs. Robert H., Wife of Representative (Illinois) 122

Miller, Mrs. Arthur L., Wife of former Representative (Nebraska) 3, 161, 439, 570

Miller, Mrs. Clarence, Wife of Representative (Ohio) 178, 324, 424

Miller, Mrs. Frank H., Daughter of former Senator Edward V. Long (Missouri) 26, 33, 485

Miller, Mrs. Jack R., Wife of former Senator (Iowa) 65, 527, 542

Miller, Jaynie K., Daughter of former Senator Jack R. Miller (Iowa) 39, 52, 466

Milliken, Mrs. William G., Wife of Governor (Michigan) 161, 255

Mitchell, Mrs. Donald J., Wife of Representative (New York) 49, 228, 336, 395

Moeller, Mrs. Walter, Wife of former Representative (Ohio) 187, 268, 412, 481

Mollohan, Mrs. Robert H., Wife of Representative (West Virginia) 46, 64, 165, 246

Moore, Mrs. Arch A., Jr., Wife of Governor (West Virginia) 175, 336

Morris, Mrs. Thomas G., Wife of former Representative (New Mexico) 10, 102, 157, 252

Mosher, Mrs. Charles A., Wife of Representative (Ohio) 135, 508, 514, 563

Moss, Mrs. Frank E., Wife of Senator (Utah) 315

Mount, Mrs. Virginia Ayres, Daughter of former Representative William H. Ayres (Ohio) 24, 482

Myers, Mrs. John, Wife of Representative (Indiana) 34, 241, 370

N

Neal, Mrs. Stephen L., Wife of Representative (North Carolina) 31, 144, 165, 417

Nedzi, Mrs. Lucien N., Wife of Representative (Michigan) 17, 92, 171

Nichols, Mrs. Bill, Wife of Representative (Alabama) 179, 345, 525

Nixon, Mrs. Richard, Wife of former President of the United States (California) 291

Noel, Mrs. Philip W., Wife of Governor (Rhode Island) 390

Norblad, Mrs. Walter, Wife of former Representative (Oregon) 19, 162, 474

Norrell, Mrs. William, former Representative (Arkansas) 16, 120, 162, 266

Norwood, Mrs. Tolise G., Daughter of former Representative E. C. Gathings (Arkansas) 94, 185, 322

Nowak, Mrs. Henry J., Wife of Representative (New York) 262, 297, 408, 496

O

O'Brien, Mrs George M., Wife of Representative (Illinois) 63, 254, 304, 492
O'Konski, Mrs. Alvin E., Wife of former Representative (Wisconsin) 70, 191, 333
O'Neal, Mrs. Emmet, Wife of former Representative (Kentucky) 386
O'Neal, Mary Hamilton, Daughter of former Representative Emmet O'Neal (Kentucky) 342, 503, 559

P

Parham, Mrs. Edwin Fuller, Daughter of former Representative Edward William Pou (North Carolina) 58, 71, 236, 501
Patman, Mrs. Wright, Wife of Representative (Texas) 219, 274
Pattillo, Mrs. Andrew G., Jr., Daughter of former Representative A. Sydney Herlong, Jr., (Florida) 90, 365, 366
Pepper, Mrs. Claude, Wife of Representative (Florida) 159
Peterson, Mrs. M. Blaine, Wife of former Representative (Utah) 287, 463, 562
Pettis, Mrs. Jerry L., Representative (California) 124, 247
Pickle, Mrs. J. J., Wife of Representative (Texas) 260, 409, 568
Pike, Mrs. Otis G., Wife of Representative (New York) 18, 108, 135, 475
Polk, Mrs. James G., Wife of former Representative (Ohio) 411, 454
Powell, Mrs. Walter E., Wife of former Representative (Ohio) 27, 32, 344, 557
Preyer, Mrs. Richardson, Wife of Representative (North Carolina) 177, 270, 419, 571
Price, Mrs. Melvin, Wife of Representative (Illinois) 121, 308, 467, 480
Prouty, Mrs. Winston L., Wife of former Senator (Vermont) 129, 167, 234, 240
Puetz, Mrs. Reinhold, Daughter of former Representative Courtland C. Gillen (Indiana) 169, 377

Q

Quie, Mrs. Albert H., Wife of Representative (Minnesota) 12, 55, 258, 512

Quillen, Mrs. James H., Wife of Representative (Tennessee) 115, 361, 437, 441

R

Rampton, Mrs. Calvin L., Wife of Governor (Utah) 211, 340
Randall, Mrs. William J., Wife of Representative (Missouri) 131, 297, 438, 504
Ray, Mrs. Robert D., Wife of Governor (Iowa) 152, 325
Regula, Mrs. Ralph, Wife of Representative (Ohio) 71, 85, 318, 522
Rehnquist, Mrs. William H., Wife of Associate Justice, Supreme Court (Arizona) 186, 407
Rhodes, Elizabeth C., Daughter of Representative John J. Rhodes (Arizona) 80, 118, 354, 462
Rhodes, Mrs. James A., Wife of Governor (Ohio) 184, 296
Rhodes, Mrs. John J., Wife of Representative (Arizona) 142, 267, 364, 511
Riehlman, Mrs. R. Walter, Wife of former Representative (New York) 184, 572
Roberts, Mrs. Kenneth Allison, Wife of former Representative (Alabama) 9, 132, 143, 554
Roberts, Mrs. Ray, Wife of Representative (Texas) 264, 286, 374, 567
Robinson, Mrs. J. Kenneth, Wife of Representative (Virginia) 23, 27, 298, 397
Robison, Mrs. Howard, Wife of former Representative (New York) 313, 534
Rockefeller, Mrs. Nelson A., Wife of Vice President of the United States (New York) 389
Rogers, Mrs. Paul G., Wife of Representative (Florida) 470, 538
Rose, Mrs. Charles G., III, Wife of Representative (North Carolina) 5, 47, 455, 553
Runnels, Mrs. Harold L., Wife of Representative (New Mexico) 95, 261, 380

S

Salmon, Mrs. Thomas P., Wife of Governor (Vermont) 249, 562
Sanders, Mrs. John, Daughter of former Representative John E. Rankin (Mississippi) 110, 396, 410, 457

689

Sanders, Margaret Mackie, M.D., Daughter of former Representative John C. Mackie (Michigan) 123, 529

Santini, Mrs. Jim, Wife of Representative (Nevada) 14, 554

Satterfield, Mrs. David E., III, Wife of Representative (Virginia) 51, 57, 78, 263

Schlesinger, Mrs. James B., Wife of former Secretary of Defense (Virginia) 354, 384

Schneebeli, Mrs. Herman T., Wife of Representative (Pennsylvania) 62, 201, 340, 477

Schweiker, Mrs. Richard Schultz, Wife of Senator (Pennsylvania) 116, 348, 404, 528

Schwengel, Mrs. Fred, Wife of former Representative (Iowa) 96, 178, 371, 464

Scott, Mrs. Hugh, Wife of Senator (Pennsylvania) 256, 324

Scott, Mrs. Richard G., Daughter of former Senator Arthur Vivian Watkins (Utah) 195, 542

Selden, Mrs. Armistead I., Wife of former Representative (Alabama), presently Ambassador to New Zealand, 145, 306, 320, 347

Shapp, Mrs. Milton J., Wife of Governor (Pennsylvania) 147, 523

Shepard, Mrs. Tazewell, Jr., Daughter of Senator John Sparkman (Alabama) 59, 139, 199

Shriver, Mrs. Garner E., Wife of Representative (Kansas) 88, 275, 312, 422

Sickles, Mrs. Carlton R., Wife of former Representative (Maryland) 486, 539

Sieminski, Mrs. Alfred D., Wife of former Representative (New Jersey) 140, 277, 303, 423

Sikes, Mrs. Robert L. F., Wife of Representative (Florida) 210, 227, 247, 497

Siler, Mrs. Eugene, Wife of former Representative (Kentucky) 189, 373, 432

Simon, Mrs. Paul, Wife of Representative (Illinois) 504

Simon, Mrs. William E., Wife of Secretary of the Treasury (Virginia) 58, 314

Simpson, Mrs. Richard M., Wife of former Representative (Pennsylvania) 216, 402, 448

Skubitz, Mrs. Joe, Wife of Representative (Kansas) 81, 361

Smith, Mrs. Douglas R., Daughter-in-law of Representative Neal Smith (Iowa) 118, 380, 462, 535

Smith, Mrs. Henry P., III, Wife of former Representative (New York) 59, 164, 333, 473

Smith, Margaret Chase, former Senator (Maine) 95, 214, 217, 508

Smith, Mrs. Neal, Wife of Representative (Iowa) 394, 420, 456, 569

Sparkman, Mrs. John, Wife of Senator (Alabama) 277, 294, 481, 555

Staebler, Mrs. Neil, Wife of former Representative (Michigan) 265, 494

Stafford, Mrs. Robert T., Wife of Senator (Vermont) 6, 133, 210, 238

Steed, Mrs. Tom, Wife of Representative (Oklahoma) 126, 178, 259, 451

Stennis, Mrs. John C., Wife of Senator (Mississippi) 4, 73, 273, 443

Stephens, Mrs. Robert G., Jr., Wife of Representative (Georgia) 37, 239, 517, 560

Straub, Mrs. Robert W., Wife of Governor (Oregon) 136

Stubblefield, Mrs. Frank A., Wife of former Representative (Kentucky) 104, 131, 251, 363

Symms, Mrs. Steven D., Wife of Representative (Idaho) 23, 37, 155, 216

T

Talcott, Mrs. Burt L., Wife of Representative (California) 126, 163, 374, 426

Talle, Mrs. Henry O., Wife of former Representative (Iowa) 249, 346, 499, 520

Taylor, Mrs. Dean P., Wife of former Representative (New York) 35, 60, 107, 166

Taylor, Mrs. Roy A., Wife of Representative (North Carolina) 79, 197, 510, 513

Teague, Mrs. Olin E., Wife of Representative (Texas) 105, 154, 186

Terry, Mrs. John H., Wife of former Representative (New York) 103, 117, 427, 505

Thompson, Mrs. Frank, Jr., Wife of Representative (New Jersey) 254

Thomson, Mrs. Meldrim, Jr., Wife of Governor (New Hampshire) 181, 544

Thone, Mrs. Charles, Wife of Representative (Nebraska) 467, 530, 541, 558

Treen, Mrs. David C., Wife of Representative (Louisiana) 50, 181, 231, 543

MEN ONLY

692

EMBASSY

Afghanistan

Mrs. Abdullah Malikyar, Wife of Ambassador 614, 615

Argentina

Mrs. Hector Subiza, Wife of Minister 615

Australia

Lady Shaw, Wife of former Ambassador 616

Austria

Mrs. Arno Halusa, Wife of Ambassador 617, 618

The Bahamas

Mrs. Livingston Basil Johnson, Wife of Ambassador 619

Bangladesh

Mrs. M. Hossain Ali, Wife of Ambassador 620

Belgium

Mrs. Willy van Cauwenberg, Wife of Ambassador 621

Republic of China

Mrs. James C. H. Shen, Wife of Ambassador 622

Czechoslovakia

Mrs. Dusan Spacil, Wife of Ambassador 623

Ecuador

Mrs. Jose C. Cardenas, Wife of Ambassador 624

Federal Republic of Germany

Mrs. Berndt von Staden, Wife of Ambassador 624, 625

Great Britain

Lady Ramsbotham, Wife of Ambassador 626

Greece

Mrs. Menelas D. Alexandrakis, Wife of Ambassador 627

Guatemala

Mrs. Julio Asensio-Wunderlich, Wife of Ambassador 627, 628

Guyana

Mrs. Frederick H. Talbot, Wife of Ambassador 628

Indonesia

Mrs. Roesmin Nurjadin, Wife of Ambassador 629

Iran

Mrs. Nasser Majd, Wife of Minister Counselor 630

Israel

Mrs. Simcha Dinitz, Wife of Ambassador 631

Italy

Mrs. Egidio Ortona, Wife of former Ambassador 631

Japan

Mrs. Takeshi Yasukawa, Wife of Ambassador 632

Jordan

Mrs. Abdullah Salah, Wife of Ambassador 633

Korea

Mrs. Pyong-choon Hahm, Wife of Ambassador 634

694

Lativa

Mrs. Anatol Dinbergs, Wife of Charge d'Affaires 634, 635

Lebanon

Mrs. Najati Kabbani, Wife of Ambassador 636

Morocco

Mrs. Abdelhadi Boutaleb (Touria), Wife of Ambassador 637

Netherlands

Madame A. R. Tammenoms Bakker, Wife of Ambassador 638

New Zealand

Mrs. Lloyd White, Wife of Ambassador 638

Pakistan

Begum Yaqub-Khan, Wife of Ambassador 639

Philippines

Mrs. Eduardo Z. Romualdez, Wife of Ambassador 640

Poland

Mrs. Witold Trampczynski, Wife of Ambassador 641, 642

Portugal

Mrs. Joao Hall Themido, Wife of Ambassador 642, 643

Sweden

Countess Wilhelm Wachtmeister, Wife of Ambassador 643, 644

Switzerland

Mrs. Felix Schnyder, Wife of former Ambassador 644, 645

Turkey

Mrs. Melih Esenbel, Wife of Ambassador, 645

INDEX TO RECIPES

701

711

East Front of United States Capitol 1826